Commentaries on the Laws of England

William Blackstone

A Facsimile of the First Edition
of 1765–1769

VOLUME II
Of the
Rights of Things
(1766)

With an Introduction by A. W. Brian Simpson

The University of Chicago Press
Chicago & London

Commentaries on the Laws of England, by
William Blackstone, is available in a clothbound
set and separate paperback volumes from the
University of Chicago Press.

Vol. 1 *Of the Rights of Persons*
Vol. 2 *Of the Rights of Things*
Vol. 3 *Of Private Wrongs*
Vol. 4 *Of Public Wrongs*

The University of Chicago Press, Chicago 60637
The University of Chicago Press, Ltd., London

86 85 84 83 82 81 80 79   5 4 3 2 1

ISBN: clothbound set
        0–226–05536–1

        paperback edition
        0–226–05538–8 (volume 1)
        0–226–05541–8 (volume 2)
        0–226–05543–4 (volume 3)
        0–226–05545–0 (volume 4)

LCN: 79–11753

INTRODUCTION TO BOOK II

BLACKSTONE, following a scheme devised nearly a century earlier by Sir Matthew Hale,[1] the great seventeenth-century jurist, devotes the second book of the *Commentaries* to what are curiously called the rights of things, *jura rerum*. By this expression are meant "those rights which a man may acquire in and to such external things as are unconnected with his person."[2] The subject matter therefore is property law, so considered as to embrace all rights which do not attach to individuals simply as such, whether naturally or as members of civil society. It would be hard to overemphasize the contemporary significance, both to professional lawyers and to Blackstone's lay readership, of property law, particularly real property law, as a branch of legal learning. His lectures at Oxford, out of which grew the *Commentaries*, were specifically directed to "gentlemen of independent estates and fortune, the most useful as well as considerable body of men in the nation . . . . It is their landed property, with it's long and voluminous train of descents and conveyances, settlements, entails and incumbrances, that forms the most intricate and most extensive object of legal knowledge."[3] For the propertied classes, land, the permanent endowment of the governors, represented power, status, and security; for the lawyer, whose activities were very largely parasitic on the propertied classes, property law was where the money was to be got. At a theoretical level its importance was again undisputed. In the legal and political thought of the time, an extraordinary significance was attributed to the protection of property; for some indeed this was both the principal function of municipal law and the very reason for the establishment of civil societies. Freedom of property, classed by Blackstone as the third absolute right, inherent in every Englishman, the notion of which was classically expressed in John Locke's *Two Treatises of Government* (1689),[4] was of leading importance in the tradition of liberal thought associated with the French and American revolutions; not until the nineteenth century did freedom of contract come to achieve a similar status. Blackstone's second volume therefore seeks to set out, explain, and justify the way in which the common law of England discharges one of its three principal obligations to its subjects.

The Theory of Property Rights

It is understandable, given the acknowledged primacy of the subject, that Blackstone begins with an incursion into the theory of property, "Of Property in General."[5] Today theories of property appear to excite neither the popular nor the specialist interest they once did. They rarely feature in legal study; much of the writing on the subject belongs to the tradition of natural law, and today few read the writings of authors in this tradition.[6] Such theories are concerned first with historical inquiry of a kind nowadays the preserve of anthropologists rather than historians: how did the institution of property come about? This question Blackstone tackles in a speculative manner, supposing a state of primitive simplicity, as in Genesis, in which all was in common. His views as to how and why private property in moveables, and eventually in immoveables, first emerged are derived from earlier writers, particularly the Swedish jurist Baron Pufendorf, whose *Of the Laws of Nature and Nations*[7] was available in an English edition published by the Oxford University Press in 1710 and widely read.

Theories of property are also concerned with the ethical justification of private property. Here Blackstone, who was primarily interested in property in land, took the orthodox view of the time: the individual's right derived from "occupancy."[8] But this left open the intriguing question of why the act of taking should confer an exclusive right to possession. Why, we might put it, should finding be keeping? Here there was a controversy. One school of thought claimed that the right depended upon some form of implied or tacit social contract, and that property rights therefore derived from the obligation to keep agreements; this was the view, for example, of Sir Robert Filmer,[9] Grotius,[10] and Pufendorf. In opposition was the view, primarily associated with John Locke, that there existed independently of contract, and thus independently of civil society, a *natural* right of property, derived from the individual's expenditure of labor in occupying; a form of this theory is now adopted by Marxists. Blackstone, never at his most lucid in high theory, belittles the controversy but, a theorist in spite of himself, he principally follows Locke, conceiving of property as essentially an institution of natural law, whose extension beyond its natural bounds was due to developments in human, civil law. For example, no form of inheritance seemed to him to be "natural."[11] Blackstone's theoretical views are to be found scattered about Book II, and not simply in the first chapter;[12] they cannot easily be isolated from his general views on the nature of law itself. Opinions may differ as to whether his treatment of the subject is sophisticated in its complexity or merely confused.

Blackstone on Real Property

Blackstone then proceeds, in the following twenty-two chapters, to give an account of the law of real property. Broadly, real property, as opposed to personal property (dealt with in the final nine chapters), was the law of immoveables as opposed to moveables, or land as opposed to chattels. Over the preceding seven centuries the common law judges and sergeants, assisted intermittently by parliamentary legislation (itself the work of common lawyers), had evolved separate bodies of law for real property and personal property. To make matters even more confusing, they had constructed in "chattels real"—typically, leases—a hybrid creature, which Blackstone discusses under the heading of real property. Since the twelfth century, the law of real property, that body of law involved in the resolution of land disputes, had been the predominant concern of the royal courts, where the common law was made, and the common law as an intellectual system evolved from the elaborate procedures through which rights in real property were challenged, tested, and vindicated. The name "real property" itself is taken from the procedures, the real actions, through which landowners' rights were specifically enforced. The dominant status of real property law, early established, long persisted, and in Blackstone's time that body of law, viewed as the mechanism either for the resolution of land disputes, or, as it was used by the expert conveyancers for the cooperative, consensual organization of land ownership, remained the most important and intellectually developed branch of the common law. Extreme intellectual development in law is not necessarily a virtue, and real property law had become the victim of too many able minds refining too many distinctions for too long.

It was of almost incredible complexity; cynics like Oliver Cromwell called it an ungodly jumble. It had become a mystery, unintelligible except to experts.

Its unintelligibility was aggravated by another feature. The basic scheme of concepts in which rights in land had come to be expressed had been settled in the early Middle Ages, when society had been organized feudally; land law was in origin feudal law. In the immense period which had elapsed between the world of Norman feudalism and the world of Blackstone there had of course been many important developments and changes in the law, but at no point had there been any radical break in continuity. Indeed to this very day, both in the country of its origin and in countries to which it was exported in the colonial and imperial periods, the common law remains an essentially medieval body of law that has been unsystematically modified and patched up so as to make the system work, if not always well, as least tolerably. Accidents of history have sometimes produced a situation in which real property law retains more archaic features outside England than at home. The major reforms date from the nineteenth century; in Blackstone's day all these lay in the future, so that the system was in many respects archaic. Its procedures and doctrines were of baffling complexity, and a fear existed that any tinkering with so venerable and ramshackle an edifice could collapse the structure and throw all property into confusion.

Blackstone made what was previously a dark mystery comprehensible to those who did not propose to acquire an understanding of the subject by years of study in conveyancing chambers or attorney's office. To have written, in so brief a compass, a clear, readable account of real property law was an extraordinary achievement. Blackstone's second volume exemplifies his remarkable ability to separate out the essentials, the elements of the subject, from matters of elaboration or refinement. With this ability he combined the equally important gift of succinct, economical expression. It is easy, from reading Blackstone, to be misled into thinking that the law of the time was as simple as he makes it seem; it must be emphasized that this was not the case. A good example of his technique is to be found in chapter 11, where he discusses the doctrines governing contingent remainders, which were soon, in 1772, to be made the subject of a celebrated but esoteric work, Fearne's *Essay on the Learning of Contingent Remainders and Executory*

Devises.[13] Blackstone, after setting out in a few pages the basic principles involved goes on, "It were endless to attempt to enter upon the particular subtilties and refinements, into which this doctrine, by the variety of cases which have occurred in the course of many centuries, has been spun out and subdivided: neither are they consonant to the design of these elementary disquisitions."[14] He knew what had to be cut out to hold his readers' attention.

Blackstone's Predecessors

Blackstone was not the first to compose a treatise on real property law: he had two celebrated predecessors. The first was Sir Thomas Littleton, a fifteenth-century lawyer and later judge, whose *Tenures*, a brief and mainly elementary statement of property law, was one of the earliest lawbooks printed in England, the first of its many editions appearing in about 1481.[15] Though according to tradition the *Tenures* was written for Littleton's son Richard,[16] I suspect that like the *Commentaries* it originated as lectures for students; this would explain its simplicity. Littleton's book was not, however, for laymen; indeed it was written not in English but in the Norman-French then used by lawyers as the private language of their mystery. For over a century it formed the staple diet of young law students.

Then in the early seventeenth century a fate typical of short successful lawbooks overtook the *Tenures,* it was made the subject of an elaborate gloss or commentary. The author was the most learned of all the black letter lawyers, Sir Edward Coke.[17] To Coke the *Tenures* was "the ornament of the common law, and the most perfect and absolute work that was ever written in any human science." In *The First Part of the Institutes of the Laws of England*, always known to lawyers as "Coke on Littleton," he expounded and dissected the words of the master with an incredible display of technical legal learning. Where Littleton's opening paragraph defines the fee simple in a hundred and ninety-four words, Coke's commentary on the same passage extends to over twenty thousand. Later commentators added further material, and in its final form, evolved in the late eighteenth century, Littleton's original text was submerged with notes by Francis Hargrave and Charles Butler superimposed on notes by Lord Nottingham and

Sir Matthew Hale expounding Coke's commentary. As a mine of learning on property law, "Coke on Littleton" was unrivaled, and its dominance continued until late in the nineteenth century. It was, however, a book to consult or study, being far too repulsive to read. If Blackstone's treatment of the subject owes anything to his predecessors, it must be to Littleton, not Coke, but there is no direct sense in which the *Tenures* formed a model.

Blackstone's Scheme

Blackstone himself acknowledged that an expositor of a complex subject, whose aim is simplicity, must hit on and adhere to a simple scheme.[18] After dealing with property in general, he treats of the objects of property (divided, in the case of real property, into corporeal things and incorporeal things), then with the tenures by which these forms of property are held, then with the interests those who hold them can have (the doctrine of estates), then with title to real property, and finally with modes of alienating real property. The scheme was not perfect, the principal difficulty being where to put that most characteristic of all the products of the ingenuity of English property lawyers, the trust. Blackstone's account of this institution is to be found principally in chapter 20, "Of Alienation by Deed,"[19] tucked away in an account of conveyancing forms. The subject is also discussed in chapter 8 ("Of Freeholds Not of Inheritance")[20] and in chapter 18 ("Of Title by Forfeiture").[21] Blackstone's account of the development of the trust from the use is inadequate, and he nowhere gives a clear account of the distinction between property rights established and recognized by the courts of common law as legal, and property rights—typically, the rights of a beneficiary under a trust—recognized in the Court of Chancery as equitable only. Essentially the distinction is that a legal property right is enforceable against the property into whomsoever's hands it has come, whereas an equitable right is liable to be defeated if the property comes into the hands of a purchaser in good faith for value of the legal estate without notice of the existence of the trust. The defective treatment of trusts is the only serious gap in Blackstone's comprehensiveness; it is a fault generated by his scheme of arrangement.

Blackstone and Feudalism

Blackstone's treatment of real property law within his scheme was essentially historical;[22] he believed that "It is impracticable to comprehend many rules of the modern law, in a scholarlike scientifical manner, without having recourse to the antient."[23] He seeks to explain existing law by setting out the manner of its evolution, using history for its explanatory and sometimes for its justificatory force; the majority of treatise writers have followed this technique ever since. Usually the picture is one of steady improvement, but at times Blackstone writes as if there was once a simple golden age of the common law, which thereafter suffered from new-fangled inventions.[24] Monks (Blackstone was hostile to monks) came in for a share of the blame.[25] Blackstone's historicism is particularly in evidence in his treatment of tenure. He emphasized, as he had to do, the feudal origins of English land law, and he begins with a somewhat idealized picture of "the nature and doctrine of feuds," whose principal legal expression is the dogma that all land is held of a feudal lord, and directly or ultimately of the monarch as supreme feudal lord. His historical views are largely derived from Sir Martin Wright's *Introduction to the Law of Tenures* (1730); Blackstone was not himself a historian, but a user of history. But in Blackstone's time the major and economically important consequences of tenure had largely vanished, as had the military tenures which were the typical expressions of Norman feudalism. Blackstone emphasizes feudalism partly because the structure and terminology of the law was still dominated by its origin, and partly because he was at pains to demonstrate that the common law, in spite of its feudal lineage, gave expression and protection to the natural right of individual private property. For feudalism seems, on the face of things, to deny this; subjects "hold" land conditionally from the monarch, they do not "own." Indeed it is part of the modern folklore of real property law that "the king owns all the land," a notion not, however, to be found in Blackstone. He is, however, anxious to demonstrate that feudalism (which he abominated)[26] had been largely deprived of its oppressive character, and that in spite of the survival of feudal elements and the universal doctrine of tenure, the common law does recognize individual private ownership.[27]

Blackstone on the Doctrine of Estates

The second leading characteristic of English land law is the doctrine of estates. The law of tenure having set out those rights, duties, and liabilities of the landholder which sprang from his relationship as tenant with his feudal lord, the doctrine of estates comprises an analysis of the quantum of interest of the landholder in terms of time. The most elegant statement of the doctrine, which Blackstone unfortunately does not quote, is to be found in the sixteenth-century *Walsingham's Case*: "The land itself is one thing and the estate in land is another thing: for an estate in the land is a time in the land, or land for a time: and there are diversities of estates, which are no more than diversities of time; for he who hath a fee simple in the land has a time in the land without end, or land for a time without end; and he who has land in tail has a time in land, or the land for a time, as long as he has issue of his body; and he who has an estate in land for life has no time in it longer than his own life; and so of one who has an estate in land for the life of another, or for years."[28]

The whole corpus of rules defining the estates which could exist, their incidents and manner of creation, and most importantly how they could be put together like an elaborate jigsaw, was enormously complex; Blackstone's simplification is remarkable. It is easy enough to grasp the notion of the fee simple—roughly, "ownership"—and of the estate for years, the familiar lease. What is more baffling is the scheme of estates associated with *family* land-ownership: the life estate, the entail, conditional and determinable fees, and estates in remainder and reversion. All the elaboration here was the product of aristocratic dynastic family landholding. To the wealthy landed classes, real property was the essential endowment not of individuals but of the family, a continuing but constantly changing entity forming and reforming around the basic family events—birth, the attainment of majority, marriage and death—and rendered continuous by the concepts of blood and inheritance. Land was to be exploited in the interests of the family, not the individual, but the mechanism for its exploitation was, paradoxically, a subtle manipulation of individual property rights; the family was never treated as an entity capable of itself owning or possessing rights, nor on the other hand were patriarchal notions carried to the point at which only the father of the family enjoyed rights. In the complex history of the subject was expressed a continuous tension between two strategies. According to one, the family endowment is best secured by permitting individuals, particularly the current head of the family, as little discretion and power of disposition over the family lands as possible. According to the other, the same end was better achieved by a flexible system under which the endowment can be reallocated so as to adapt to changes in the family, catering for personalities and uncovenanted family events. The compromise commonly employed in Blackstone's time, and evolved in the seventeenth century, was the strict settlement under which the land was managed by a succession of life tenants, the settlement being reconstituted each generation to ensure that no single individual ever acquired an unfettered power to appropriate the family capital for his individual purposes. It is remarkable that in spite of Blackstone's exaltation of private *individual* property rights, the landowning class in reality had little use for them.

Of the strict settlement, which all his readers would know in practice, Blackstone gives no general account, though in Appendix II his specimen conveyance by lease and release is a strict settlement of typical form on the occasion of a marriage. For an account of the institution it is necessary to go outside the *Commentaries*.

Blackstone on Title and Modes of Alienation

The remainder of Blackstone's account deals with the principles governing both the establishment of title to real property, and the mechanisms of transfer which themselves constitute steps in the establishment of title. Blackstone presents this intricate body of law, which in reality gave rise to extensive insecurity of title, in the form of a set of exceptions to title by inheritance, which he viewed as "the principal object of the laws of real property in England." A romantic attachment to the hereditary principle, and particularly to the principle of primogeniture, long persisted in England, though the truth of the matter was that the landowning classes, as paradoxically as they shied away from individual property rights, avoided, by settlements either by will or *inter vivos* (i.e., between the living, taking effect before death), the operation of the doctrine of inheritance wherever possible. To understand Blackstone one must appreciate this paradox.

Blackstone on Personal Property

The remainder of the volume deals with personal property, a branch of the law which was, in Blackstone's time, relatively less developed than that of real property, but one in which individual property rights were in reality more respected. The principal and historical reason for this was partly economic, partly social. The common law was essentially the law of the aristocratic landed classes, and in their world, as contrasted with the urban world of the mercantile classes, moveable, tangible property constituted a less significant form of wealth than land. In the main their personal property represented expenditure rather than investment. Blackstone himself makes much of the relative unimportance of chattels in his explanation for the way in which the law of moveables had evolved on quite different lines than real property law. In particular, moveables had never been subjected to the doctrines of tenure or estates, and consequently they could not be subjected to the elaborate scheme of the family strict settlement; relatively simple mechanisms were used to ensure that the more permanent forms of personal property devolved with the land. Blackstone's whole account of personal property, with its discussion of the problems of the beekeeper and the legal position of partridges in a mew, smells of the countryside; the law is the law of the country gentry, not Cheapside. The *Commentaries* reflects the essentially rural character of the high civilization of the eighteenth century.

Mercantile Custom and Personal Property

Today of course much wealth consists of various forms of intangible personal property: stocks and shares, life insurance policies, negotiable commercial instruments, copyrights, patents, commercial goodwill, and so forth. The legal institutions involved were essentially emanations of the urban commercial world of merchants, principally though not exclusively taking the form of offshoots of commercial contract law. Historically the law merchant had been conceived of as a body of law quite distinct from the common law, as a personal law of those of the merchant class. In Blackstone's time theory had changed; he tells us that the custom of merchants, "however different from the common law, is allowed for the benefit of trade, to be of the utmost validity in all commercial transactions . . . ."[29] Particularly with the chief justiceship of Lord Mansfield (1756–88),[30] there was a major reception of mercantile custom into the common law.

In Blackstone's treatment of personal property this area of law is not emphasized. There is a discussion of copyright and a short account of bills of exchange, promissory notes, and insurance, the first tucked away in the discussion of title by occupancy and the second in the section on title by gift, grant, and contract.[31] In Blackstone's basic analysis of personal property rights, the newer forms of commercial intangible property presented peculiar difficulty. He adopted a traditional distinction between "things in possession" and "things in action," the latter comprising objects of private property rights which are recoverable by legal action, as opposed to being in the actual possession of the owner; an example is a debt. Blackstone supposed that title to all "things in action" had its basis in contract, express or implied.[32] Given this defective scheme it is not easy to see where to place intangibles generally; copyright for example is intangible but not based on contract. Blackstone never thought through the analytical problems, and his scheme is rendered even more difficult by the distinction he draws between "absolute" and "qualified" property.[33] As in the case of the trust, the source of difficulty is the original scheme.

Blackstone on Contract

The received concept of a "thing in action" as a form of property fathered what seems to modern readers to be the most peculiar feature of Book II. Lurking unexpectedly in chapter 30, which is devoted to modes of acquisition of personal property, is Blackstone's account of the law of contract, dealing both with formal contracts by sealed instruments and with the so-called simple or parole contracts by word of mouth, some evidenced by written documents.[34] Contracts are here conceived of as a sort of conveyance; either they pass property in tangible things such as a horse or book (as in the case of chattel sales), or they pass intangible property recoverable in action, such as a debt. Contracts to perform services or other acts, such as marriage, do not fit the analysis, since the right to the services is not technically a "thing in action," and such contracts are consequently hardly mentioned. Blackstone's treatment of contract is unsatisfactory because again he falls victim to the deficiency of his basic scheme which, in its failure to reflect the sophistication of contemporary law, has misled many into supposing that the law of contract was in his time little developed. Blackstone's scheme does, however, reflect the fact that in eighteenth-century legal thought contract had not achieved the status it was to gain in the nineteenth century, when it came to be viewed as the principal civilizing force in social development, and consequently as the branch of the law of the profoundest social significance. Freedom of contract was to overtake freedom of property; Blackstone never of course mentions freedom of contract.

A. W. Brian Simpson

NOTES

1. (1609–76). Hale's best known works are his *History of the Pleas of the Crown,* and *The History of the Common Law of England,* available in a paperback edition by the University of Chicago Press (ed. C. M. Gray). His *General Analysis of the Civil Part of the Law* was first published posthumously in 1713.
2. Blackstone, *Commentaries* II:1.
3. Id. Introduction I:7.
4. Available in numerous editions, perhaps most usefully in that by P. Laslett (1963).
5. Blackstone ch. 1 of Book II. See also I:138.
6. A useful introduction is A. P. d'Entrèves, *Natural Law* (1951).
7. First published in 1672. Baron Pufendorf (1632–89) was professor of the law of nature and nations at Heidelberg and later professor of jurisprudence at Lund.
8. The term translates *occupatio* of Roman law texts; the equivalent term for moveables is *perceptio,* "taking."

9. The *Patriarcha* and other political writings of Filmer (c. 1588–1653) are available in a modern edition by P. Laslett (1949). His theory of property is set out in § VIII–X. The *Patriarcha* was first published posthumously in 1680.

10. Hugo Grotius (1583–1645), whose *De Iure Belli ac Pacis* appeared in 1625.

11. Blackstone II:10.

12. See on inheritance id. I:134, II:400, IV:9; on occupancy II:258ff, especially the discussion of copyright at 405–7. The long discussion of the legal position of game and the prerogative is at II:410ff. On slavery see I:123 and II:402, discussed in F. O. Shyllon, *Black Slaves in Britain* (1974), in ch. 5. The passage in I:123 was altered in the second edition (1766) to conform more to the doctrine set out for captives at II:402.

13. Fearne went through numerous editions, suffering the fate of the good lawbook; from an original size of under a hundred pages it expanded in the hands of editors to over a thousand.

14. Blackstone II:172.

15. Littleton (c. 1410–81) became a judge in 1466; his effigy may still be seen in Worcester Cathedral.

16. The traditional story to this effect is based on the use of the expression *"mon fils"* in the text, but this was at the time the way one addressed young students generally.

17. (1551–1633).

18. See Blackstone ch. 1 of Book I.

19. Id. II:327–39. Notice also 296–97.

20. Id. II:137.

21. Id. II:271–74.

22. See also id. IV:435, where are set out "some rude outlines of a plan of the history of our laws and liberties."

23. Id. II:44.

24. See, e.g., II:331.

25. See, e.g., id. II:48.

26. See id. II:52.

27. See id. II:104–6.

28. Plowden, *Commentaries* 555 (1578).

29. Blackstone I:75.

30. The only modern life discussing Mansfield's contribution as a lawyer is C. H. S. Fifoot's *Lord Mansfield* (1936).

31. Blackstone II:405 and 458ff.

32. Id. II:397.

33. Id. II:389–91.

34. Blackstone, following Hale's scheme, also discusses contract when dealing with private wrongs.

COMMENTARIES

ON THE

LAWS

OF

ENGLAND.

BOOK THE SECOND.

BY

WILLIAM BLACKSTONE, Esq.
SOLICITOR GENERAL TO HER MAJESTY.

OXFORD,
PRINTED AT THE CLARENDON PRESS.
M. DCC. LXVI.

CONTENTS.

BOOK II.

Of the RIGHTS *of* THINGS.

a 2   CHAP.

CONTENTS.

CHAP.

CONTENTS.

CONTENTS.

CHAP.

CONTENTS.

CHAP. XXXII.

Of TITLE by TESTAMENT, and ADMINISTRATION.

✿❀✿❀✿❀✿❀✿❀✿❀✿❀✿❀✿❀✿❀✿❀✿❀✿❀✿❀✿❀✿❀✿❀✿❀✿

APPENDIX.

E R R A T A.

Page 13, *line* 6 : *before* heir *insert* their immediate
21, *line* 4 : *for* and *read* or
96, *line* 4 : *after* was *insert* virtually
103, *line* 4 : *after* another *insert* and his heirs
121, *line* 3 : *for* specifice state *read* specific estate
149, *line* 17 : *for* at *read* as
199, *line* 9 : *for* alienes to *read* enfeoffs
272, *line* 25 : *for* 32 *read* 23
276, (*note* [a] *and* [b]) *for* 152, 153, *read* 252, 253,
309, (*note* [w]) *for* 90 *read* n°. 24. 1 Vern. 348.
473, *line* 30 : }
474, *line* 12 : } *for* tradesman *read* trader

COMMENTARIES

ON THE

LAWS of ENGLAND.

BOOK THE SECOND.

OF THE RIGHTS OF THINGS.

CHAPTER THE FIRST.

OF PROPERTY, IN GENERAL.

THE former book of thefe commentaries having treated at large of the *jura perfonarum*, or fuch rights and duties as are annexed to the perfons of men, the objects of our enquiry in this fecond book will be the *jura rerum*, or, thofe rights which a man may acquire in and to fuch external things as are unconnected with his perfon. Thefe are what the writers on natural law ftile the rights of dominion, or property, concerning the nature and original of which I fhall firft premife a few obfervations, before I proceed to diftribute and confider it's feveral objects.

THERE is nothing which so generally strikes the imagination, and engages the affections of mankind, as the right of property; or that sole and despotic dominion which one man claims and exercises over the external things of the world, in total exclusion of the right of any other individual in the universe. And yet there are very few, that will give themselves the trouble to consider the original and foundation of this right. Pleased as we are with the possession, we seem afraid to look back to the means by which it was acquired, as if fearful of some defect in our title; or at best we rest satisfied with the decision of the laws in our favour, without examining the reason or authority upon which those laws have been built. We think it enough that our title is derived by the grant of the former proprietor, by descent from our ancestors, or by the last will and testament of the dying owner; not caring to reflect that (accurately and strictly speaking) there is no foundation in nature or in natural law, why a set of words upon parchment should convey the dominion of land; why the son should have a right to exclude his fellow creatures from a determinate spot of ground, because his father had done so before him; or why the occupier of a particular field or of a jewel, when lying on his death-bed and no longer able to maintain possession, should be entitled to tell the rest of the world which of them should enjoy it after him. These enquiries, it must be owned, would be useless and even troublesome in common life. It is well if the mass of mankind will obey the laws when made, without scrutinizing too nicely into the reasons of making them. But, when law is to be considered not only as matter of practice, but also as a rational science, it cannot be improper or useless to examine more deeply the rudiments and grounds of these positive constitutions of society.

IN the beginning of the world, we are informed by holy writ, the all-bountiful creator gave to man "dominion over all "the earth; and over the fish of the sea, and over the fowl of "the air, and over every living thing that moveth upon the "earth [a]."

"earth[a]." This is the only true and folid foundation of man's dominion over external things, whatever airy metaphyfical notions may have been ftarted by fanciful writers upon this fubject. The earth therefore, and all things therein, are the general property of all mankind, exclufive of other beings, from the immediate gift of the creator. And, while the earth continued bare of inhabitants, it is reafonable to fuppofe, that all was in common among them, and that every one took from the public ftock to his own ufe fuch things as his immediate neceffities required.

THESE general notions of property were then fufficient to anfwer all the purpofes of human life; and might perhaps ftill have anfwered them, had it been poffible for mankind to have remained in a ftate of primaeval fimplicity: as may be collected from the manners of many American nations when firft difcovered by the Europeans; and from the antient method of living among the firft Europeans themfelves, if we may credit either the memorials of them preferved in the golden age of the poets, or the uniform accounts given by hiftorians of thofe times, wherein " *erant omnia communia et indivifa omnibus, veluti unum cunctis pa-* " *trimonium effet* [b]." Not that this communion of goods feems ever to have been applicable, even in the earlieft ages, to ought but the *fubftance* of the thing; nor could be extended to the *ufe* of it. For, by the law of nature and reafon, he who firft began to ufe it, acquired therein a kind of tranfient property, that lafted fo long as he was ufing it, and no longer [c]: or, to fpeak with greater precifion, the *right* of poffeffion continued for the fame time only that the *act* of poffeffion lafted. Thus the ground was in common, and no part of it was the permanent property of any man in particular: yet whoever was in the occupation of any determinate fpot of it, for reft, for fhade, or the like, acquired for the time a fort of ownerfhip, from which it would have been unjuft, and contrary to the law of nature, to have driven him by force; but the inftant that he quitted the ufe or occupation of it,

[a] Gen. 1. 28.
[b] Juftin. *l.* 43. *c.* 1.
[c] Barbeyr. Puff. l. 4. c. 4.

another

another might feife it without injuftice. Thus alfo a vine or other
tree might be faid to be in common, as all men were equally entitled to it's produce; and yet any private individual might gain
the fole property of the fruit, which he had gathered for his own
repaft. A doctrine well illuftrated by Cicero, who compares the
world to a great theatre, which is common to the public, and yet
the place which any man has taken is for the time his own [d].

BUT when mankind increafed in number, craft, and ambi-
tion, it became neceffary to entertain conceptions of more permanent dominion; and to appropriate to individuals not the immediate *ufe* only, but the very *fubftance* of the thing to be ufed.
Otherwife innumerable tumults muft have arifen, and the good
order of the world been continually broken and difturbed, while
a variety of perfons were ftriving who fhould get the firft occupation of the fame thing, or difputing which of them had actually gained it. As human life alfo grew more and more refined,
abundance of conveniences were devifed to render it more eafy,
commodious, and agreeable; as, habitations for fhelter and fafety,
and raiment for warmth and decency. But no man would be at
the trouble to provide either, fo long as he had only an ufufructuary property in them, which was to ceafe the inftant that he
quitted poffeffion; --- if, as foon as he walked out of his tent, or
pulled off his garment, the next ftranger who came by would
have a right to inhabit the one, and to wear the other. In the cafe
of habitations in particular, it was natural to obferve, that even
the brute creation, to whom every thing elfe was in common,
maintained a kind of permanent property in their dwellings, efpecially for the protection of their young; that the birds of the
air had nefts, and the beafts of the field had caverns, the invafion
of which they efteemed a very flagrant injuftice, and would fa-
crifice their lives to preferve them. Hence a property was foon
eftablifhed in every man's houfe and home-ftall; which feem to
have been originally mere temporary huts or moveable cabins,

[d] *Quemadmodum theatrum, cum commune fit, recte tamen dici poteft, ejus effe eum locum quem quifque occuparit. De Fin. l. 3. c. 20.*

fuited

suited to the defign of providence for more fpeedily peopling the earth, and fuited to the wandering life of their owners, before any extenfive property in the foil or ground was eftablifhed. And there can be no doubt, but that moveables of every kind became fooner appropriated than the permanent fubftantial foil : partly becaufe they were more fufceptible of a long occupancy, which might be continued for months together without any fenfible interruption, and at length by ufage ripen into an eftablifhed right; but principally becaufe few of them could be fit for ufe, till improved and meliorated by the bodily labour of the occupant ; which bodily labour, beftowed upon any fubject which before lay in common to all men, is univerfally allowed to give the faireft and moft reafonable title to an exclufive property therein.

THE article of food was a more immediate call, and therefore a more early confideration. Such, as were not contented with the fpontaneous product of the earth, fought for a more folid refrefhment in the flefh of beafts, which they obtained by hunting. But the frequent difappointments, incident to that method of provifion, induced them to gather together fuch animals as were of a more tame and fequacious nature ; and to eftablifh a permanent property in their flocks and herds, in order to fuftain themfelves in a lefs precarious manner, partly by the milk of the dams, and partly by the flefh of the young. The fupport of thefe their cattle made the article of *water* alfo a very important point. And therefore the book of Genefis (the moft venerable monument of antiquity, confidered merely with a view to hiftory) will furnifh us with frequent inftances of violent contentions concerning wells; the exclufive property of which appears to have been eftablifhed in the firft digger or occupant, even in fuch places where the ground and herbage remained yet in common. Thus we find Abraham, who was but a fojourner, afferting his right to a well in the country of Abimelech, and exacting an oath for his fecurity, " becaufe he had digged that well[c]." And Ifaac, about ninety years afterwards, re-claimed this his fa-

[c] Gen. 21. 30.

ther's

ther's property; and, after much contention with the Philiftines, was fuffered to enjoy it in peace [f].

ALL this while the foil and pafture of the earth remained ftill in common as before, and open to every occupant: except perhaps in the neighbourhood of towns, where the neceffity of a fole and exclufive property in lands (for the fake of agriculture) was earlier felt, and therefore more readily complied with. Otherwife, when the multitude of men and cattle had confumed every convenience on one fpot of ground, it was deemed a natural right to feife upon and occupy fuch other lands as would more eafily fupply their neceffities. This practice is ftill retained among the wild and uncultivated nations that have never been formed into civil ftates, like the Tartars and others in the eaft; where the climate itfelf, and the boundlefs extent of their territory, confpire to retain them ftill in the fame favage ftate of vagrant liberty, which was univerfal in the earlieft ages; and which Tacitus informs us continued among the Germans till the decline of the Roman empire [s]. We have alfo a ftriking example of the fame kind in the hiftory of Abraham and his nephew Lot [h]. When their joint fubftance became fo great, that pafture and other conveniences grew fcarce, the natural confequence was that a ftrife arofe between their fervants; fo that it was no longer practicable to dwell together. This contention Abraham thus endeavoured to compofe : "let there be no ftrife, "I pray thee, between thee and me. Is not the whole land be- "fore thee? Separate thyfelf, I pray thee, from me. If thou "wilt take the left hand, then I will go to the right; or if thou "depart to the right hand, then I will go to the left." This plainly implies an acknowleged right, in either, to occupy whatever ground he pleafed, that was not pre-occupied by other tribes. "And Lot lifted up his eyes, and beheld all the plain of Jordan, "that it was well watered every where, even as the garden of the "Lord. Then Lot chofe him all the plain of Jordan, and jour- "neyed eaft; and Abraham dwelt in the land of Canaan."

[f] Gen. 26. 15, 18, &c.

[g] *Colunt difcreti et diverfi; ut fons, ut* *campus, ut nemus placuit. De mor. Germ.* 16.

[h] Gen. c. 13.

UPON the same principle was founded the right of migration, or sending colonies to find out new habitations, when the mother-country was overcharged with inhabitants; which was practised as well by the Phaenicians and Greeks, as the Germans, Scythians, and other northern people. And, so long as it was confined to the stocking and cultivation of desart uninhabited countries, it kept strictly within the limits of the law of nature. But how far the seising on countries already peopled, and driving out or massacring the innocent and defenceless natives, merely because they differed from their invaders in language, in religion, in customs, in government, or in colour; how far such a conduct was consonant to nature, to reason, or to christianity, deserved well to be considered by those, who have rendered their names immortal by thus civilizing mankind.

As the world by degrees grew more populous, it daily became more difficult to find out new spots to inhabit, without encroaching upon former occupants; and, by constantly occupying the same individual spot, the fruits of the earth were consumed, and it's spontaneous produce destroyed, without any provision for a future supply or succession. It therefore became necessary to pursue some regular method of providing a constant subsistence; and this necessity produced, or at least promoted and encouraged, the art of agriculture. And the art of agriculture, by a regular connexion and consequence, introduced and established the idea of a more permanent property in the soil, than had hitherto been received and adopted. It was clear that the earth would not produce her fruits in sufficient quantities, without the assistance of tillage: but who would be at the pains of tilling it, if another might watch an opportunity to seise upon and enjoy the product of his industry, art, and labour? Had not therefore a separate property in lands, as well as moveables, been vested in some individuals, the world must have continued a forest, and men have been mere animals of prey; which, according to some philosophers, is the genuine state of nature. Whereas now (so graciously

has

has providence interwoven our duty and our happiness together)
the result of this very necessity has been the enobling of the human
species, by giving it opportunities of improving it's *rational* fa-
culties, as well as of exerting it's *natural*. Necessity begat property; and, in order to insure that property, recourse was had to
civil society, which brought along with it a long train of insepa-
rable concomitants; states, government, laws, punishments, and
the public exercise of religious duties. Thus connected together,
it was found that a part only of society was sufficient to provide,
by their manual labour, for the necessary subsistence of all; and
leisure was given to others to cultivate the human mind, to invent
useful arts, and to lay the foundations of science.

THE only question remaining is, how this property became
actually vested; or what it is that gave a man an exclusive right
to retain in a permanent manner that specific land, which before
belonged generally to every body, but particularly to nobody.
And, as we before observed that occupancy gave the right to the
temporary *use* of the soil, so it is agreed upon all hands that occupancy gave also the original right to the permanent property in
the *substance* of the earth itself; which excludes every one else
but the owner from the use of it. There is indeed some difference among the writers on natural law, concerning the reason
why occupancy should convey this right, and invest one with this
absolute property: Grotius and Puffendorf insisting, that this
right of occupancy is founded upon a tacit and implied assent of
all mankind, that the first occupant should become the owner;
and Barbeyrac, Titius, Mr Locke, and others, holding, that there
is no such implied assent, neither is it necessary that there should
be; for that the very act of occupancy, alone, being a degree of
bodily labour, is from a principle of natural justice, without any
consent or compact, sufficient of itself to gain a title. A dispute
that favours too much of nice and scholastic refinement! However, both sides agree in this, that occupancy is the thing by
which the title was in fact originally gained; every man seising
to his own continued use such spots of ground as he found most
agreeable

agreeable to his own convenience, provided he found them un-occupied by any one else.

PROPERTY, both in lands and moveables, being thus originally acquired by the firſt taker, which taking amounts to a declaration that he intends to appropriate the thing to his own uſe, it remains in him, by the principles of univerſal law, till ſuch time as he does ſome other act which ſhews an intention to abandon it: for then it becomes, naturally ſpeaking, *publici juris* once more, and is liable to be again appropriated by the next occupant. So if one is poſſeſſed of a jewel, and caſts it into the ſea or a public highway, this is ſuch an expreſs dereliction, that a property will be veſted in the firſt fortunate finder that will ſeiſe it to his own uſe. But if he hides it privately in the earth, or other ſecret place, and it is diſcovered, the finder acquires no property therein; for the owner hath not by this act declared any intention to abandon it, but rather the contrary: and if he loſes or drops it by accident, it cannot be collected from thence, that he deſigned to quit the poſſeſſion; and therefore in ſuch caſe the property ſtill remains in the loſer, who may claim it again of the finder. And this, we may remember, is the doctrine of the law of England, with relation to treaſure trove[i].

BUT this method, of one man's abandoning his property, and another's ſeiſing the vacant poſſeſſion, however well founded in theory, could not long ſubſiſt in fact. It was calculated merely for the rudiments of civil ſociety, and neceſſarily ceaſed among the complicated intereſts and artificial refinements of polite and eſtabliſhed governments. In theſe it was found, that what became inconvenient or uſeleſs to one man was highly convenient and uſeful to another; who was ready to give in exchange for it ſome equivalent, that was equally deſirable to the former proprietor. This mutual convenience introduced commercial traffic, and the reciprocal transfer of property by ſale, grant, or conveyance: which may be conſidered either as a con-

[i] See Book I. pag. 285.

tinuance of the original poffeffion which the firft occupant had ;
or as an abandoning of the thing by the prefent owner, and an
immediate fucceffive occupancy of the fame by the new proprietor.   The voluntary dereliction of the owner, and delivering the
poffeffion to another individual, amount to a transfer of the property ; the proprietor declaring his intention no longer to occupy
the thing himfelf, but that his own right of occupancy fhall be
vefted in the new acquirer.   Or, taken in the other light, if I
agree to part with an acre of my land to Titius, the deed of
conveyance is an evidence of my having abandoned the property,
and Titius, being the only or firft man acquainted with fuch my
intention, immediately fteps in and feifes the vacant poffeffion :
thus the confent expreffed by the conveyance gives Titius a good
right againft me ; and poffeffion, or occupancy, confirms that
right againft all the world befides.

THE moft univerfal and effectual way, of abandoning property, is by the death of the occupant ; when, both the actual
poffeffion and intention of keeping poffeffion ceafing, the property, which is founded upon fuch poffeffion and intention, ought
alfo to ceafe of courfe.   For, naturally fpeaking, the inftant a
man ceafes to be, he ceafes to have any dominion : elfe, if he
had a right to difpofe of his acquifitions one moment beyond his
life, he would alfo have a right to direct their difpofal for a million of ages after him ; which would be highly abfurd and inconvenient.   All property muft therefore ceafe upon death, confidering men as abfolute individuals, and unconnected with civil
fociety : for then, by the principles before eftablifhed, the next
immediate occupant would acquire a right in all that the deceafed
poffeffed.   But as, under civilized governments which are calculated for the peace of mankind, fuch a conftitution would be
productive of endlefs difturbances, the univerfal law of almoft
every nation (which is a kind of fecondary law of nature) has
either given the dying perfon a power of continuing his property,
by difpofing of his poffeffions by will ; or, in cafe he neglects to
difpofe of it, or is not permitted to make any difpofition at all,
the

the municipal law of the country then fteps in, and declares who
fhall be the fucceffor, reprefentative, or heir of the deceafed;
that is, who alone fhall have a right to enter upon this vacant
poffeffion, in order to avoid that confufion, which it's becoming
again common would occafion [i]. And farther, in cafe no teftament be permitted by the law, or none be made, and no heir can
be found fo qualified as the law requires, ftill, to prevent the ro-
buft title of occupancy from again taking place, the doctrine of
efcheats is adopted in almoft every country; whereby the fovereign of the ftate, and thofe who claim under his authority, are
the ultimate heirs, and fucceed to thofe inheritances, to which
no other title can be formed.

THE right of inheritance, or defcent to the children and *re-*
lations of the deceafed, feems to have been allowed much earlier
than the right of devifing by teftament. We are apt to conceive
at firft view that it has nature on it's fide; yet we often miftake
for nature what we find eftablifhed by long and inveterate cuftom.
It is certainly a wife and effectual, but clearly a political, eftablifhment; fince the permanent right of property, vefted in the anceftor himfelf, was no *natural*, but merely a *civil*, right. It is
true, that the tranfmiffion of one's poffeffions to pofterity has an
evident tendency to make a man a good citizen and a ufeful member of fociety: it fets the paffions on the fide of duty, and
prompts a man to deferve well of the public, when he is fure
that the reward of his fervices will not die with himfelf, but be
tranfmitted to thofe with whom he is connected by the deareft
and moft tender affections. Yet, reafonable as this foundation of
the right of inheritance may feem, it is probable that it's immediate original arofe not from fpeculations altogether fo delicate and
refined; and, if not from fortuitous circumftances, at leaft from
a plainer and more fimple principle. A man's children or neareft
relations are ufually about him on his death-bed, and are the

---

[i] It is principally to prevent any vacancy
of poffeffion, that the civil law confiders
father and fon as one perfon; fo that upon
the death of either the inheritance does not
fo properly defcend, as continue in the
hands of the furvivor. *Ff.* 28. 2. 11.

earlieft witneffes of his deceafe. They became therefore generally the next immediate occupants, till at length in procefs of
time this frequent ufage ripened into general law. And therefore
alfo in the earlieft ages, on failure of children, a man's fervants
born under his roof were allowed to be his heirs ; being immediately on the fpot when he died. For we find the old patriarch
Abraham expreffly declaring, that "fince God had given him no
"feed, his fteward Eliezer, one born in his houfe, was his heir[k]."

WHILE property continued only for life, teftaments were ufelefs and unknown; and, when it became inheritable, the inheritance was long indefeafible, and the children or heirs at law were
incapable of exclufion by will. Till at length it was found, that
fo ftrict a rule of inheritance made heirs difobedient and head-
ftrong, defrauded creditors of their juft debts, and prevented
many provident fathers from dividing or charging their eftates as
the exigence of their families required. This introduced pretty
generally the right of difpofing one's property, or a part of it,
by *teftament*; that is, by written or oral inftructions properly *witneffed* and authenticated, according to the *pleafure* of the deceafed ;
which we therefore emphatically ftile his *will*. This was eftablifhed in fome countries much later than in others. With us in
England, till modern times, a man could only difpofe of one
third of his moveables from his wife and children : and, in general, no will was permitted of lands till the reign of Henry the
eighth ; and then only of a certain portion : for it was not till
after the reftoration that the power of devifing real property became fo univerfal as at prefent.

WILLS therefore and teftaments, rights of inheritance and
fucceffions, are all of them creatures of the civil or municipal
laws, and accordingly are in all refpects regulated by them; every
diftinct country having different ceremonies and requifites to make
a teftament completely valid : neither does any thing vary more
than the right of inheritance under different national eftablifh-

[k] Gen. 15. 3.

ments.

ments. In England particularly, this diverfity is carried to fuch a length, as if it had been meant to point out the power of the laws in regulating the fucceffion to property, and how futile every claim muft be that has not it's foundation in the pofitive rules of the ftate. In perfonal eftates the father may fucceed to his children; in landed property he never can be heir, by any the remoteft poffibility: in general only the eldeft fon, in, fome places only the youngeft, in others all the fons together, have a right to fucceed to the inheritance: in real eftates males are preferred to females, and the eldeft male will ufually exclude the reft; in the divifion of perfonal eftates, the females of equal degree are admitted together with the males, and no right of primogeniture is allowed.

THIS one confideration may help to remove the fcruples of many well-meaning perfons, who fet up a miftaken confcience in oppofition to the rules of law. If a man difinherits his fon, by a will duly executed, and leaves his eftate to a ftranger, there are many who confider this proceeding as contrary to natural juftice: while others fo fcrupuloufly adhere to the fuppofed intention of the dead, that if a will of lands be attefted by only *two* witneffes inftead of *three*, which the law requires, they are apt to imagine that the heir is bound in confcience to relinquifh his title to the devifee. But both of them certainly proceed upon very erroneous principles: as if, on the one hand, the fon had by nature a right to fucceed to his father's lands; or as if, on the other hand, the owner was by nature intitled to direct the fucceffion of his property after his own deceafe. Whereas the law of nature fuggefts, that on the death of the poffeffor the eftate fhould again become common, and be open to the next occupant, unlefs otherwife ordered for the fake of civil peace by the pofitive law of fociety. The pofitive law of fociety, which is with us the municipal law of England, directs it to veft in fuch perfon as the laft proprietor fhall by will, attended with certain requifites, appoint; and, in defect of fuch appointment, to go to fome particular perfon, who, from the refult of certain local

confti-

conftitutions, appears to be the heir at law. Hence it follows, that, where the appointment is regularly made, there cannot be a fhadow of right in any one but the perfon appointed : and, where the neceffary requifites are omitted, the right of the heir is equally ftrong and built upon as folid a foundation, as the right of the devifee would have been, fuppofing fuch requifites were obferved.

But, after all, there are fome few things, which notwith-ftanding the general introduction and continuance of property, muft ftill unavoidably remain in common ; being fuch wherein nothing but an ufufructuary property is capable of being had ; and therefore they ftill belong to the firft occupant, during the time he holds poffeffion of them, and no longer. Such (among others) are the elements of light, air, and water ; which a man may occupy by means of his windows, his gardens, his mills, and other conveniences : fuch alfo are the generality of thofe animals which are faid to be *ferae naturae,* or of a wild and un-tameable difpofition ; which any man may feife upon and keep for his own ufe or pleafure. All thefe things, fo long as they re-main in poffeffion, every man has a right to enjoy without dif-turbance ; but if once they efcape from his cuftody, or he vo-luntarily abandons the ufe of them, they return to the common ftock, and any man elfe has an equal right to feife and enjoy them afterwards.

Again ; there are other things, in which a permanent pro-perty *may* fubfift, not only as to the temporary ufe, but alfo the folid fubftance ; and which yet would be frequently found with-out a proprietor, had not the wifdom of the law provided a re-medy to obviate this inconvenience. Such are forefts and other wafte grounds, which were omitted to be appropriated in the general diftribution of lands : fuch alfo are wrecks, eftrays, and that fpecies of wild animals, which the arbitrary conftitutions of pofitive law have diftinguifhed from the reft by the well-known appellation of game. With regard to thefe and fome others, as

diftur-

disturbances and quarrels would frequently arise among individuals, contending about the acquisition of this species of property by first occupancy, the law has therefore wisely cut up the root of dissension, by vesting the things themselves in the sovereign of the state; or else in his representatives, appointed and authorized by him, being usually the lords of manors. And thus the legislature of England has universally promoted the grand ends of civil society, the peace and security of individuals, by steadily pursuing that wise and orderly maxim, of assigning to every thing capable of ownership a legal and determinate owner.

CHAPTER THE SECOND.

OF REAL PROPERTY; AND, FIRST, OF
CORPOREAL HEREDITAMENTS.

THE objects of dominion or property are *things,* as contradiftinguifhed from *perfons:* and things are by the law
of England diftributed into two kinds; things *real,* and things
perfonal. Things real are fuch as are permanent, fixed, and immoveable, which cannot be carried out of their place; as lands
and tenements: things perfonal are goods, money, and all other
moveables; which may attend the owner's perfon wherever he
thinks proper to go.

IN treating of things real, let us confider, firft, their feveral
forts or kinds; fecondly, the tenures by which they may be holden; thirdly, the eftates which may be had in them; and,
fourthly, the title to them, and the manner of acquiring and
lofing it.

FIRST, with regard to their feveral forts or kinds, things
real are ufually faid to confift in lands, tenements, or hereditaments. *Land* comprehends all things of a permanent, fubftantial
nature; being a word of a very extenfive fignification, as will
prefently appear more at large. *Tenement* is a word of ftill greater
extent; and though in it's vulgar acceptation it is only applied to
houfes

houfes and other buildings, yet in it's original, proper, and legal
fenfe it fignifies every thing that may be *holden*, provided it be
of a permanent nature; whether it be of a fubftantial and fenfible,
or of an unfubftantial ideal kind. Thus *liberum tenementum*,
franktenement, or freehold, is applicable not only to lands and
other folid objects, but alfo to offices, rents, commons, and the
like[a]: and as lands and houfes are tenements, fo is an advowfon
a tenement; and a franchife, an office, a right of common, a
peerage, or other property of the like unfubftantial kind, are, all
of them, legally fpeaking, tenements[b]. But an *hereditament*, fays
fir Edward Coke[c], is by much the largeft and moft comprehenfive expreffion; for it includes not only lands and tenements, but
whatfoever may be *inherited*, be it corporeal, or incorporeal, real,
perfonal, or mixed. Thus an heir loom, or implement of furniture which by cuftom defcends to the heir together with an
houfe, is neither land, nor tenement, but a mere moveable; yet,
being inheritable, is comprized under the general word, hereditament: and fo a condition, the benefit of which may defcend
to a man from his anceftor, is alfo an hereditament[d].

HEREDITAMENTS then, to ufe the largeft expreffion, are
of two kinds, corporeal, and incorporeal. Corporeal confift of
fuch as affect the fenfes; fuch as may be feen and handled by
the body: incorporeal are not the object of fenfation, can neither
be feen nor handled. are creatures of the mind, and exift only in
contemplation.

CORPOREAL hereditaments confift wholly of fubftantial
and permanent objects; all which may be comprehended under
the general denomination of land only. For *land*, fays fir Edward
Coke[e], comprehendeth in it's legal fignification any ground,
foil, or earth whatfoever; as arable, meadows, paftures, woods,
moors, waters, marifhes, furzes, and heath. It legally includeth

[a] Co. Litt. 6.
[b] Co. Litt. 19, 20.
[c] 1 Inft. 6.
[d] 3 Rep. 2.
[e] 1 Inft. 4.

alfo

alfo all caftles, houfes, and other buildings : for they confift,
faith he, of two things; *land*, which is the foundation; and
ftruƈure thereupon : fo that, if I convey the land or ground, the
ftruƈture or building paffeth therewith. It is obfervable that *water*
is here mentioned as a fpecies of land, which may feem a kind
of folecifm ; but fuch is the language of the law : and I cannot
bring an aƈtion to recover poffeffion of a pool or other piece of
water, by the name of *water* only ; either by calculating it's capacity, as, for fo many cubical yards; or, by fuperficial meafure,
for twenty acres of water; or by general defcription, as for a
pond, a watercourfe, or a rivulet : but I muft bring my aƈtion
for the land that lies at the bottom, and muft call it twenty acres
of *land covered with water* [f]. For water is a moveable, wandering
thing, and muft of neceffity continue common by the law of nature ; fo that I can only have a temporary, tranfient, ufufruƈtuary
property therein : wherefore if a body of water runs out of my
pond into another man's, I have no right to reclaim it. But the
land, which that water covers, is permanent, fixed, and immoveable : and therefore in this I may have a certain, fubftantial property; of which the law will take notice, and not of the
other.

L A N D hath alfo, in it's legal fignification, an indefinite extent, upwards as well as downwards. *Cujus eft folum, ejus eft ufque ad coelum,* is the maxim of the law, upwards; therefore no
man may ereƈt any building, or the like, to overhang another's
land : and, downwards, whatever is in a direƈt line between the
furface of any land, and the center of the earth, belongs to the
owner of the furface; as is every day's experience in the mining
countries. So that the word "land" includes not only the face of
the earth, but every thing under it, or over it. And therefore if a
man grants all his lands, he grants thereby all his mines of metal
and other foffils, his woods, his waters, and his houfes, as well
as his fields and meadows. Not but the particular names of the
things are equally fufficient to pafs them, except in the inftance

[f] Brownl. 142.

of

of water; by a grant of which, nothing paſſes but a right of fiſhing [g] : but the capital diſtinction is this; that by the name of a caſtle, meſſuage, toft, croft, or the like, nothing elſe will paſs, except what falls with the utmoſt propriety under the term made uſe of; but by the name of land, which is *nomen generaliſſimum*, every thing terreſtrial will paſs [h].

[g] Co. Litt. 4.   [h] *Ibid.* 4, 5, 6.

CHAPTER THE THIRD.

OF INCORPOREAL HEREDITAMENTS.

AN incorporeal hereditament is a right iffuing out of a thing corporate (whether real or perfonal) or concerning, or annexed to, or exercifible within, the fame[a]. It is not the thing corporate itfelf, which may confift in lands, houfes, jewels, or the like; but fomething collateral thereto, as a rent iffuing out of thofe lands or houfes, or an office relating to thofe jewels. In fhort, as the logicians fpeak, corporeal hereditaments are the fubftance, which may be always feen, always handled: incorporeal hereditaments are but a fort of accidents, which inhere in and are fupported by that fubftance; and may belong, or not belong to it, without any vifible alteration therein. Their exiftence is merely in idea and abftracted contemplation; though their effects and profits may be frequently objects of our bodily fenfes. And indeed, if we would fix a clear notion of an incorporeal hereditament, we muft be careful not to confound together the profits produced, and the thing, or hereditament, which produces them. An annuity, for inftance, is an incorporeal hereditament: for though the money, which is the fruit or product of this annuity, is doubtlefs of a corporeal nature, yet the annuity itfelf, which produces that money, is a thing invifible, has only a mental exiftence, and cannot be delivered over from hand to hand. So tithes,

[a] Co. Litt. 19, 20.

if

if we confider the produce of them, as the tenth fheaf or tenth lamb, feem to be completely corporeal; yet they are indeed in-corporeal hereditaments: for they, being merely a contingent right, collateral to and iffuing out of lands, can never be the object of fenfe: they are neither capable of being fhewn to the eye, nor of being delivered into bodily poffeffion.

INCORPOREAL hereditaments are principally of ten forts; advowfons, tithes, commons, ways, offices, dignities, franchifes, corodies or penfions, annuities, and rents.

I. ADVOWSON is the right of prefentation to a church, or ecclefiaftical benefice. Advowfon, *advocatio*, fignifies *in clientelam recipere*, the taking into protection; and therefore is fynonymous with patronage, *patronatus:* and he who has the right of ad-vowfon is called the patron of the church. For, when lords of manors firft built churches on their own demefnes, and appointed the tithes of thofe manors to be paid to the officiating minifters, which before were given to the clergy in common (from whence, as was formerly mentioned [b], arofe the divifion of parifhes) the lord, who thus built a church, and endowed it with glebe or land, had of common right a power annexed of nominating fuch minifter as he pleafed (provided he were canonically qualified) to officiate in that church of which he was the founder, endower, maintainer, or, in one word, the patron [c].

THIS inftance of an advowfon will completely illuftrate the nature of an incorporeal hereditament. It is not itfelf the bodily poffeffion of the church and it's appendages; but it is a right to give fome other man a title to fuch bodily poffeffion. The ad-vowfon is the object of neither the fight, nor the touch; and yet it perpetually exifts in the mind's eye, and in contemplation of law. It cannot be delivered from man to man by any vifible bo-

---

[b] Vol. I. pag. 109.
[c] This original of the *jus patronatus*, by building and endowing the church, appears

alfo to have been allowed in the empire. *Nov.* 56. *t.* 12. *c.* 2. *Nov.* 118. *c.* 23.

dily transfer, nor can corporal poſſeſſion be had of it. If the patron takes corporal poſſeſſion of the church, the church-yard, the
glebe or the like, he intrudes on another man's property ; for to
theſe the parſon has an excluſive right. The patronage can therefore be only conveyed by operation of law, by verbal grant, either
oral or written, which is a kind of inviſible, mental transfer :
and being ſo veſted, it lies dormant and unnoticed, till occaſion
calls it forth ; when it produces a viſible, corporeal fruit, by in-
titling ſome clerk, whom the patron ſhall pleaſe to nominate, to
enter and receive bodily poſſeſſion of the lands and tenements of
the church.

ADVOWSONS are either advowſons *appendant*, or advowſons
in groſs. Lords of manors being originally the only founders,
and of courſe the only patrons, of churches [d], the right of patronage or preſentation, ſo long as it continues annexed to the
poſſeſſion of the manor, as ſome have done from the foundation
of the church to this day, is called an advowſon appendant [e] : and
it will paſs, or be conveyed, together with the manor, as incident and appendant thereto, by a grant of the manor only, without adding any other words [f]. But where the property of the advowſon has been once ſeparated from the property of the manor,
by legal conveyance, it is called an advowſon in groſs, or at large,
and never can be appendant any more ; but is for the future annexed to the perſon of it's owner, and not to his manor or lands [g].

ADVOWSONS are alſo either *preſentative*, *collative*, or *donative* [h]. An advowſon preſentative is where the patron hath a right
of preſentation to the biſhop or ordinary, and moreover to demand of him to inſtitute his clerk, if he find him canonically
qualified : and this is the moſt uſual advowſon. An advowſon
collative is where the biſhop and patron are one and the ſame
perſon : in which caſe the biſhop cannot preſent to himſelf ; but

[d] Co. Litt. 119.
[e] Ibid. 121.
[f] Ibid. 307.
[g] Ibid. 120.
[h] Ibid.

he

he does, by the one act of collation, or conferring the benefice, the whole that is done in common cafes, by both prefentation and inftitution. An advowfon donative is when the king, or any fubject by his licence, doth found a church or chapel, and ordains that it fhall be merely in the gift or difpofal of the patron; fubject to his vifitation only, and not to that of the ordinary; and vefted abfolutely in the clerk by the patron's deed of donation, without prefentation, inftitution, or induction [i]. This is faid to have been antiently the only way of conferring ecclefiaftical benefices in England; the method of inftitution by the bifhop not being eftablifhed more early than the time of arch-bifhop Becket in the reign of Henry II [k]. And therefore though pope Alexander III [l], in a letter to Becket, feverely inveighs againft the *prava confuetudo*, as he calls it, of inveftiture conferred by the patron only, this however fhews what was then the common ufage. Others contend, that the claim of the bifhops to inftitution is as old as the firft planting of chriftianity in this ifland; and in proof of it they allege a letter from the Englifh nobility, to the pope in the reign of Henry the third, recorded by Matthew Paris [m], which fpeaks of prefentation to the bifhop as a thing immemorial. The truth feems to be, that, where the benefice was to be conferred on a mere layman, he was firft prefented to the bifhop, in order to receive ordination, who was at liberty to examine and refufe him: but where the clerk was already in orders, the living was ufually vefted in him by the fole donation of the patron; till about the middle of the twelfth century, when the pope and his bifhops endeavoured to introduce a kind of feodal dominion over ecclefiaftical benefices, and, in confequence of that, began to claim and exercife the right of inftitution univerfally, as a fpecies of fpiritual inveftiture.

HOWEVER this may be, if, as the law now ftands, the true patron *once* waives this privilege of donation, and prefents to the bifhop, and his clerk is admitted and inftituted, the advow-

[i] Co. Litt. 344.
[k] Seld. tith. c. 12. §. 2.

[l] *Decretal. l. 3. t. 7. c. 3.*
[m] *A. D.* 1239.

son is now become for ever prefentative, and fhall never be donative any more. For thefe exceptions to general rules, and common right, are ever looked upon by the law in an unfavourable view, and conftrued as ftrictly as poffible. If therefore the patron, in whom fuch peculiar right refides, does once give up that right, the law, which loves uniformity, will interpret it to be done with an intention of giving it up for ever; and will thereupon reduce it to the ftandard of other ecclefiaftical livings.

II. A SECOND fpecies of incorporeal hereditaments is that of tithes; which are defined to be the tenth part of the increafe, yearly arifing and renewing from the profits of lands, the ftock upon lands, and the perfonal induftry of the inhabitants: the firft fpecies being ufually called *predial*, as of corn, grafs, hops, and wood[n]; the fecond *mixed*, as of wool, milk, pigs, &c[o], confifting of natural products, but nurtured and preferved in part by the care of man; and of thefe the tenth muft be paid in grofs: the third *perfonal*, as of manual occupations, trades, fifheries, and the like; and of thefe only the tenth part of the clear gains and profits is due[p].

IT is not to be expected from the nature of thefe general commentaries, that I fhould particularly fpecify, what things are tithable, and what not, the time when, or the manner and proportion in which, tithes are ufually due. For this I muft refer to fuch authors as have treated the matter in detail: and fhall only obferve, that, in general, tithes are to be paid for every thing that yields an annual increafe, as corn, hay, fruit, cattle, poultry, and the like; but not for any thing that is of the fubftance of the earth, or is not of annual increafe, as ftone, lime, chalk, and the like; nor for creatures that are of a wild nature, or *ferae naturae*, as deer, hawks, &c, whofe increafe, fo as to profit the owner, is not annual, but cafual[q]. It will rather be our bufinefs to confider, 1. The original of the right of tithes. 2. In whom

[n] 1 Roll. Abr. 635. 2 Inft. 649.
[o] *Ibid.*

[p] 1 Roll. Abr. 656.
[q] 2 Inft. 651.

that

that right at prefent fubfifts. 3. Who may be difcharged, either totally or in part, from paying them.

1. As to their original. I will not put the title of the clergy to tithes upon any divine right; though fuch a right certainly commenced, and I believe as certainly ceafed, with the Jewifh theocracy. Yet an honourable and competent maintenance for the minifters of the gofpel is, undoubtedly, *jure divino*; whatever the particular mode of that maintenance may be. For, befides the pofitive precepts of the new teftament, natural reafon will tell us, that an order of men, who are feparated from the world, and excluded from other lucrative profeffions, for the fake of the reft of mankind, have a right to be furnifhed with the neceffaries, conveniences, and moderate enjoyments of life, at their expenfe, for whofe benefit they forego the ufual means of providing them. Accordingly all municipal laws have provided a liberal and decent maintenance for their national priefts or clergy : ours in particular have eftablifhed this of tithes, probably in imitation of the Jewifh law : and perhaps, confidering the degenerate ftate of the world in general, it may be more beneficial to the Englifh clergy to found their title on the law of the land, than upon any divine right whatfoever, unacknowleged and unfupported by temporal fanctions.

We cannot precifely afcertain the time when tithes were firft introduced into this country. Poffibly they were cotemporary with the planting of chriftianity among the Saxons, by Auguftin the monk, about the end of the fixth century. But the firft mention of them, which I have met with in any written Englifh law, is in a conftitutional decree, made in a fynod held *A. D.* 786 [r], wherein the payment of tithes in general is ftrongly enjoined. This canon, or decree, which at firft bound not the laity, was effectually confirmed by two kingdoms of the heptarchy, in their parliamentary conventions of eftates, refpective-

[r] Selden, c. 8. §. 2.

ly confisting of the kings of Mercia and Northumberland, the bishops, dukes, senators, and people. Which was a few years later than the time that Charlemagne established the payment of them in France[s], and made that famous division of them into four parts; one to maintain the edifice of the church, the second to support the poor, the third the bishop, and the fourth the parochial clergy[t].

T H E next authentic mention of them is in the *foedus Edwardi et Guthruni* ; or the laws agreed upon between king Guthrun the Dane, and Alfred and his son Edward the elder, successive kings of England, about the year 900. This was a kind of treaty between those monarchs, which may be found at large in the Anglo-Saxon laws[u]; wherein it was necessary, as Guthrun was a pagan, to provide for the subsistence of the christian clergy under his dominion ; and, accordingly, we find[w] the payment of tithes not only *enjoined*, but a *penalty* added upon non-observance : which law is seconded by those of Athelstan[x], about the year 930. And this is as much as can certainly be traced out, with regard to their legal original.

ł. ỵ. W E are next to consider the persons to whom they are due. And upon their first introduction (as hath formerly been observed[y]) though every man was obliged to pay tithes in general, yet he might give them to what priests he pleased[z]; which were called *arbitrary* consecrations of tithes : or he might pay them into the hands of the bishop, who distributed among his diocesan clergy the revenues of the church, which were then in common[a]. But, when dioceses were divided into parishes, the tithes of each parish were allotted to it's own particular minister ; first by common consent, or the appointments of lords of manors, and afterwards by the written law of the land[b].

[s] *A. D.* 778.
[t] Book I. ch. 11. Seld. c. 6. §. 7. Sp. of laws, b. 31. c. 12.
[u] Wilkins, pag. 51.
[w] *cap.* 6.

[x] *cap.* 1.
[y] Book I. Introd. §. 4.
[z] 2 Inst. 646. Hob. 296.
[a] Seld. c. 9. §. 4.
[b] *LL. Edgar. c.* 1 & 2. *Canut. c.* 11.

How-

HOWEVER, arbitrary confecrations of tithes took place again afterwards, and became in general ufe till the time of king John[c]. Which was probably owing to the intrigues of the regular clergy, or monks of the Benedictine and other rules, under arch-bifhop Dunftan and his fuccefors; who endeavoured to wean the people from paying their dues to the fecular or parochial clergy, (a much more valuable fet of men than themfelves) and were then in hopes to have drawn, by fanctimonious pretences to extraordinary purity of life, all ecclefiaftical profits to the coffers of their own focieties. And this will naturally enough account for the number and riches of the monafteries and religious houfes, which were founded in thofe days, and which were frequently endowed with tithes. For a layman, who was obliged to pay his tithes fomewhere, might think it good policy to erect an abbey, and there pay them to his own monks; or grant them to fome abbey already erected; fince for this dotation, which really coft the patron little or nothing, he might, according to the fuperftition of the times, have maffes for ever fung for his foul. But, in procefs of years, the income of the poor laborious parifh priefts being fcandaloufly reduced by thefe arbitrary confecrations of tithes, it was remedied by pope Innocent the third[d] about the year 1200 in a decretal epiftle, fent to the arch-bifhop of Canterbury, and dated from the palace of Lateran : which has occafioned fir Henry Hobart and others to miftake it for a decree of the council of Lateran held *A.D.* 1179, which only prohibited what was called the infeodation of tithes, or their being granted to mere laymen[e]; whereas this letter of pope Innocent to the arch-bifhop enjoined the payment of tithes to the parfons of the refpective parifhes where every man inhabited, agreeable to what was afterwards directed by the fame pope in other countries[f]. This epiftle, fays fir Edward Coke[g], bound not the lay fubjects of this realm; but, being reafonable and juft (and, he might have added,

[c] Selden. c. 11.
[d] *Opera Innocent. III. tom.* 2. *pag.* 452.
[e] *Decretal. l.* 3. *t.* 30. *c.* 19.
[f] *Ibid. c.* 26.
[g] 2 Inft. 641.

being

being correspondent to the antient law) it was allowed of, and so became *lex terrae*. This put an effectual stop to all the arbitrary consecrations of tithes ; except some footsteps which still continue in those portions of tithes, which the parson of one parish hath, though rarely, a right to claim in another : for it is now universally held [h], that tithes are due, of common right, to the parson of the parish, unless there be a special exemption. This parson of the parish, we have formerly seen [i], may be either the actual incumbent, or else the appropriator of the benefice : appropriations being a method of endowing monasteries, which seems to have been devised by the regular clergy, by way of substitution to arbitrary consecrations of tithes [k].

3. WE observed that tithes are due to the parson of common right, unless by special exemption : let us therefore see, thirdly, who may be exempted from the payment of tithes, and how. Lands, and their occupiers, may be exempted or discharged from the payment of tithes, either in part or totally, first, by a real composition; or, secondly, by custom or prescription.

FIRST, a real composition is when an agreement is made between the owner of the lands, and the parson or vicar, with the consent of the ordinary and the patron, that such lands shall for the future be discharged from payment of tithes, by reason of some land or other real recompence given to the parson, in lieu and satisfaction thereof [l]. This was permitted by law, because it was supposed that the clergy would be no losers by such composition; since the consent of the ordinary, whose duty it is to take care of the church in general, and of the patron, whose interest it is to protect that particular church, were both made necessary to render the composition effectual : and hence have arisen all such compositions as exist at this day by force of the common law. But, experience shewing that even this caution was ineffectual, and

---

[h] Regist. 46. Hob. 296.
[i] Book I. pag. 372.
[k] In extraparochial places the king, by

his royal prerogative, has a right to all the tithes. See book I. pag. 110.
[l] 2 Inst. 490. Regist. 38. 13 Rep. 40.

the

the poffeffions of the church being, by this and other means, every day diminifhed, the difabling ftatute 13 Eliz. c. 10. was made; which prevents, among other fpiritual perfons, all parfons and vicars from making any conveyances of the eftates of their churches, other than for three lives or twenty one years. So that now, by virtue of this ftatute, no real compofition made fince the 13 Eliz. is good for any longer term than three lives or twenty one years, though made by confent of the patron and ordinary: which has indeed effectually demolifhed this kind of traffick; fuch compofitions being now rarely heard of, unlefs by authority of parliament.

SECONDLY, a difcharge by cuftom or prefcription, is where time out of mind fuch perfons or fuch lands have been, either partially or totally, difcharged from the payment of tithes. And this immemorial ufage is binding upon all parties, as it is in it's nature an evidence of univerfal confent and acquiefcence; and with reafon fuppofes a real compofition to have been formerly made. This cuftom or prefcription is either *de modo decimandi,* or *de non decimando.*

A *modus decimandi,* commonly called by the fimple name of a *modus* only, is where there is by cuftom a particular manner of tithing allowed, different from the general law of taking tithes in kind, which are the actual tenth part of the annual increafe. This is fometimes a pecuniary compenfation, as twopence an acre for the tithe of land: fometimes it is a compenfation in work and labour, as that the parfon fhall have only the twelfth cock of hay, and not the tenth, in confideration of the owner's making it for him: fometimes, in lieu of a large quantity of crude or imperfect tithe, the parfon fhall have a lefs quantity, when arrived to greater maturity, as a couple of fowls in lieu of tithe eggs; and the like. Any means, in fhort, whereby the general law of tithing is altered, and a new method of taking them is introduced, is called a *modus decimandi,* or fpecial manner of tithing.

To

To make a good and fufficient *modus*, the following rules muft be obferved.   1. It muft be *certain* and *invariable* [m], for payment of different fums will prove it to be no *modus*, that is, no original real compofition; becaufe that muft have been one and the fame, from it's firft original to the prefent time.   2. The thing given, in lieu of tithes, muft be beneficial to the *parfon*, and not for the emolument of *third perfons* only [n]: thus a *modus*, to repair the *church* in lieu of tithes, is not good, becaufe that is an advantage to the parifh only; but to repair the *chancel* is a good *modus*, for that is an advantage to the parfon.   3. It muft be fomething *different* from the thing compounded for [o]: one load of hay, in lieu of *all* tithe hay, is no good *modus*: for no parfon would, *bona fide*, make a compofition to receive lefs than his due in the fame fpecies of tithe; and therefore the law will not fuppofe it poffible for fuch compofition to have exifted.   4. One cannot be difcharged from payment of one fpecies of tithe, by paying a *modus* for another [p].   Thus a *modus* of 1 d. for every *milch* cow will difcharge the tithe of *milch* kine, but not of *barren* cattle: for tithe is, of common right, due for both; and therefore a *modus* for one fhall never be a difcharge for the other.   5. The recompence muft be in it's nature as durable as the tithes difcharged by it; that is, an inheritance certain [q]: and therefore a *modus* that every *inhabitant* of a houfe fhall pay 4 d. a year, in lieu of the owner's tithes, is no good *modus*; for poffibly the houfe may not be inhabited, and then the recompence will be loft.   6. The *modus* muft not be too large, which in law is called a *rank modus*: as if the real value of the tithes be 60 l. *per annum*, and a *modus* is fuggefted of 40 l. this *modus* will not be good; though one of 40 s. might have been valid [r].   For, in thefe cafes of prefcriptive or cuftomary *modus's*, the law fuppofes an original real compofition to have been regularly made; which being loft by length of time, the immemorial ufage is admitted

[m] 1 Keb. 602.
[n] 1 Roll. Abr. 649.
[o] 1 Lev. 179.

[p] Cro. Eliz. 446. Salk. 657.
[q] 2 P. W[ms]. 462.
[r] 11 Mod. 60.

as

as evidence to shew that it once did exist, and that from thence such usage was derived. Now time of memory hath been long ago ascertained by the law to commence from the reign of Richard the first [s]; and any custom may be destroyed by evidence of it's non-existence in any part of the long period from his days to the present: wherefore, as this real composition is supposed to have been an equitable contract, or the full value of the tithes, at the time of making it, if the *modus* set up is so rank and large, as that it beyond dispute exceeds the value of the tithes in the time of Richard the first, this *modus* is *felo de se* and destroys itself. For, as it would be destroyed by any direct evidence to prove it's non-existence at any time since that aera, so also it is destroyed by carrying in itself this internal evidence of a much later original.

A PRESCRIPTION *de non decimando* is a claim to be entirely discharged of tithes, and to pay no compensation in lieu of them. Thus the king by his prerogative is discharged from all tithes [t]. So a vicar shall pay no tithes to the rector, nor the rector to the vicar, for *ecclesia decimas non solvit ecclesiae* [u]. But these privileges are *personal* to both the king and the clergy; for their tenant or lessee shall pay tithes of the same land, though in their own occupation it is not tithable. And, generally speaking, it is an established rule, that in *lay* hands, *modus de non decimando non valet* [w]. But spiritual persons or corporations, as monasteries, abbots, bishops, and the like, were always capable of having their lands totally discharged of tithes, by various ways [x]: as, 1. By real composition: 2. By the pope's bull of exemption: 3. By unity of possession; as when the rectory of a parish, and lands in the same parish, both belonged to a religious house, those lands

---

[s] This rule was adopted, when by the statute of Westm. 1. (3 Edw. I. c. 39.) the reign of Richard I. was made the time of limitation in a writ of right. But, since by the statute 32 Hen. VIII. c 2. this period (in a writ of right) hath been very rationally reduced to sixty years, it seems unaccountable, that the date of legal prescription or memory should still continue to be reckoned from an aera so very antiquated. See 2 Roll. Abr. 269. pl. 16.

[t] Cro. Eliz. 511.

[u] *Ibid.* 479.

[w] *Ibid.* 511.

[x] Hob. 309. Cro. Jac. 308.

were difcharged of tithes by this unity of poffeffion : 4. By prefcription ; having never been liable to tithes, by being always in
fpiritual hands : 5. By virtue of their order; as the knights templars, ciftercians, and others, whofe lands were privileged by the
pope with a difcharge of tithes [y]. Though, upon the diffolution
of abbeys by Henry VIII, moft of thefe exemptions from tithes
would have fallen with them, and the lands become tithable a-
gain ; had they not been fupported and upheld by the ftatute
31 Hen. VIII. c. 13. which enacts, that all perfons who fhould
come to the poffeffion of the lands of any abbey then diffolved,
fhould hold them free and difcharged of tithes, in as large and
ample a manner as the abbeys themfelves formerly held them.
And from this original have fprung all the lands, which, being
in lay hands, do at prefent claim to be tithe-free : for, if a man
can fhew his lands to have been fuch abbey lands, and alfo immemorially difcharged of tithes by any of the means before-mentioned, this is now a good prefcription *de non decimando*. But he
muft fhew both thefe requifites : for abbey lands, without a fpecial ground of difcharge, are not difcharged of courfe; neither
will any prefcription *de non decimando* avail in total difcharge of
tithes, unlefs it relates to fuch abbey lands.

III. COMMON, or right of common, appears from it's very
definition to be an incorporeal hereditament : being a profit
which a man hath in the land of another ; as to feed his beafts,
to catch fifh, to dig turf, to cut wood, or the like [z]. And hence
common is chiefly of four forts ; common of pafture, of pifcary,
of turbary, and of eftovers.

1. COMMON of pafture is a right of feeding one's beafts on
another's land ; for in thofe wafte grounds, which are ufually
called commons, the property of the foil is generally in the lord
of the manor ; as in common fields it is in the particular tenants.
This kind of common is either appendant, appurtenant, becaufe
of vicinage, or in grofs [a].

[y] 2 Rep. 44. Seld. tith. c. 13. §. 2.   [a] Co. Litt. 122.
[z] Finch, law. 157.

COMMON *appendant* is a right, belonging to the owners or occupiers of arable land, to put commonable beafts upon the lord's wafte, and upon the lands of other perfons within the fame manor. Commonable beafts are either beafts of the plough, or fuch as manure the ground. This is a matter of moft univerfal right; and it was originally permitted [b], not only for the encouragement of agriculture, but for the neceffity of the thing. For, when lords of manors granted out parcels of land to tenants, for fervices either done or to be done, thefe tenants could not plough or manure the land without beafts; thefe beafts could not be fuftained without pafture; and pafture could not be had but in the lord's waftes, and on the uninclofed fallow grounds of themfelves and the other tenants. The law therefore annexed this right of common, as infeparably incident, to the grant of the lands; and this was the original of common appendant: which obtains in Sweden, and the other northern kingdoms, much in the fame manner as in England [c]. Common *appurtenant* is where the owner of land has a right to put in other beafts, befides fuch as are generally commonable; as hogs, goats, and the like, which neither plough nor manure the ground. This, not arifing from the neceffity of the thing, like common appendant, is therefore not of common right; but can only be claimed by immemorial ufage and prefcription [d], which the law efteems fufficient proof of a fpecial grant or agreement for this purpofe. Common *becaufe of vicinage*, or neighbourhood, is where the inhabitants of two townfhips, which lie contiguous to each other, have ufually intercommoned with one another; the beafts of the one ftraying mutually into the other's fields, without any moleftation from either. This is indeed only a permiffive right, intended to excufe what in ftrictnefs is a trefpafs in both, and to prevent a multiplicity of fuits: and therefore either townfhip may enclofe and bar out the other, though they have intercommoned time out of mind. Neither hath any perfon of one town a right to put his

b 2 Inft. 86.   d Co. Litt. 122.
c Stiernh. *de jure Sueonum. l. 2. c.* 6.

beafts originally into the other's common; but if they efcape, and ftray thither of themfelves, the law winks at the trefpafs[e]. Common *in grofs*, or at large, is fuch as is neither appendant nor appurtenant to land, but is annexed to a man's perfon; being granted to him and his heirs by deed: or it may be claimed by prefcriptive right, as by parfon of a church, or the like corporation fole. This is a feparate inheritance, entirely diftinct from any landed property, and may be vefted in one who has not a foot of ground in the manor.

ALL thefe fpecies, of pafturable common, may be and ufually are limited as to number and time; but there are alfo commons without ftint, and which laft all the year. By the ftatute of Merton however, and other fubfequent ftatutes[f], the lord of a manor may enclofe fo much of the wafte as he pleafes, for tillage or woodground, provided he leaves common fufficient for fuch as are entitled thereto. This enclofure, when juftifiable, is called in law " approving;" an antient expreffion fignifying the fame as " im- " proving [g]." The lord hath the fole intereft in the foil; but the intereft of the lord and commoner, in the common, are looked upon in law as mutual. They may both bring actions for damage done, either againft ftrangers, or each other; the lord for the public injury, and each commoner for his private damage[h].

2, 3. COMMON of pifcary is a liberty of fifhing in another man's waters; as common of turbary is a liberty of digging turf upon another's ground[i]. There is alfo a common of digging for coals, minerals, ftones, and the like. All thefe bear a refemblance to common of pafture in many refpects; though in one point they go much farther: common of pafture being only a right of feeding on the herbage and vefture of the foil, which renews annually; but common of turbary, and the reft, are a right of carrying away the very foil itfelf.

[e] Co. Litt. 122.
[f] 20 Hen. III. c. 4.   29 Geo. II. c. 36. and 31 Geo. II. c. 41.
[g] 2 Inft. 474.
[h] 9 Rep. 113.
[i] Co. Litt. 122.

4. COM-

4. COMMON of eftovers (from *eftoffer*, to furnifh) is a liberty of taking neceffary wood, for the ufe or furniture of a houfe or farm, from off another's eftate. The Saxon word, *bote*, is of the fame fignification with the French *eftovers*; and therefore houfe-bote is a fufficient allowance of wood, to repair, or to burn in, the houfe ; which latter is fometimes called fire-bote : plough-bote and cart-bote are wood to be employed in making and re-pairing all inftruments of hufbandry : and hay-bote or hedge-bote is wood for repairing of hays, hedges, or fences. Thefe botes or eftovers muft be reafonable ones; and fuch any tenant or leffee may take off the land let or demifed to him, without waiting for any leave, affignment, or appointment of the leffor, unlefs he be reftrained by fpecial covenant to the contrary [k].

THESE feveral fpecies of commons do all originally refult from the fame neceffity as common of pafture; viz. for the main-tenance and carrying on of hufbandry : common of pifcary being given for the fuftenance of the tenant's family; common of tur-bary and fire-bote for his fuel ; and houfe-bote, plough-bote, cart-bote, and hedge-bote, for repairing his houfe, his inftru-ments of tillage, and the neceffary fences of his grounds.

IV. A FOURTH fpecies of incorporeal hereditaments is that of *ways* ; or the right of going over another man's ground. I fpeak not here of the king's highways, which lead from town to town ; nor yet of common ways, leading from a village into the fields; but of private ways, in which a particular man may have an intereft and a right, though another be owner of the foil. This may be grounded on a fpecial permiffion ; as when the owner of the land grants to another a liberty of paffing over his grounds, to go to church, to market, or the like : in which cafe the gift or grant is particular, and confined to the grantee alone ; it dies with the perfon ; and, if the grantee leaves the country, he cannot affign over his right to any other ; nor can he juftify

[k] Co. Litt. 41.

taking

taking another perfon in his company[1]. A way may be alfo by prefcription ; as if all the owners and occupiers of fuch a farm have immemorially ufed to crofs another's ground : for this immemorial uiage fuppofes an original grant, whereby a right of way thus appurtenant to land may clearly be created. A right of way may alfo arife by act and operation of law : for, if a man grants me a piece of ground in the middle of his field, he at the fame time tacitly and impliedly gives me a way to come at it ; and I may crofs his land for that purpofe without trefpafs[m]. For when the law doth give any thing to one, it giveth impliedly whatfoever is neceffary for enjoying the fame[n]. By the law of the twelve tables at Rome, where a man had the right of way over another's land, and the road was out of repair, he who had the right of way might go over any part of the land he pleafed : which was the eftablifhed rule in public as well as private ways. And the law of England, in both cafes, feems to correfpond with the Roman[o].

V. Offices, which are a right to exercife a public or private employment, and the fees and emoluments thereunto belonging, are alfo incorporeal hereditaments : whether public, as thofe of magiftrates ; or private, as of bailiffs, receivers, and the like. For a man may have an eftate in them, either to him and his heirs, or for life, or for a term of years, or during pleafure only : fave only that offices of public truft cannot be granted for a term of years, efpecially if they concern the adminiftration of juftice, for then they might perhaps veft in executors or adminiftrators[p]. Neither can any *judicial* office be granted in reverfion ; becaufe, though the grantee may be able to perform it at the time of the grant, yet before the office falls he may become unable and infufficient : but *minifterial* offices may be fo granted[q] ; for thofe may be executed by deputy. Alfo, by ftatute 5 and 6 Edw. VI. c. 16. no public office fhall be fold, under pain of difability to difpofe of or hold it. For the law prefumes that he, who buys an

[1] Finch. law. 31.
[m] *Ibid.* 63.
[n] Co. Litt. 56.
[o] Lord Raym. 725. 1 Brownl. 212.

[2] Show. 28. 1 Jon. 297.
[p] 9 Rep. 97.
[q] 11 Rep. 4.

office,

office, will by bribery, extortion, or other unlawful means, make his purchafe good, to the manifeft detriment of the public.

VI. DIGNITIES bear a near relation to offices. Of the nature of thefe we treated at large in the former book [r] : it will therefore be here fufficient to mention them as a fpecies of incorporeal hereditaments, wherein a man may have a property or eftate.

VII. FRANCHISES are a feventh fpecies. Franchife and liberty are ufed as fynonymous terms : and their definition is [s], a royal privilege, or branch of the king's prerogative, fubfifting in the hands of a fubject. Being therefore derived from the crown, they muft arife from the king's grant; or, in fome cafes, may be held by prefcription, which, as has been frequently faid, prefuppofes a grant. The kinds of them are various, and almoft infinite : I will here briefly touch upon fome of the principal ; premifing only, that they may be vefted in either natural perfons or bodies politic ; in one man, or in many : but the fame identical franchife, that has before been granted to one, cannot be beftowed on another; for that would prejudice the former grant [t].

To be a county palatine is a franchife, vefted in a number of perfons. It is likewife a franchife for a number of perfons to be incorporated, and fubfift as a body politic, with a power to maintain perpetual fucceffion and do other corporate acts : and each individual member of fuch corporation is alfo faid to have a franchife or freedom. Other franchifes are, to hold a court leet : to have a manor or lordfhip ; or, at leaft, to have a lordfhip paramount : to have waifs, wrecks, eftrays, treafure-trove, royal fifh, fo feitures, and deodands : to have a court of one's own, or liberty of holding pleas, and trying caufes : to have the cognizance of pleas ; which is a ftill greater liberty, being an exclufive right, fo that no other court fhall try caufes arifing within that jurifdiction : to have a bailiwick, or liberty exempt from the fheriff of the county, wherein the grantee only, and his officers, are to

[r] See Book I. ch. 12.
[s] Finch. L. 164.
[t] 2 Roll. Abr. 191. Keilw 196.

exe-

execute all procefs : to have a fair or market ; with the right of taking toll, either there or at any other public places, as at bridges, wharfs, and the like ; which tolls muft have a reafonable caufe of commencement, (as in confideration of repairs, or the like) elfe the franchife is illegal and void [u] : or, laftly, to have a foreft, chafe, park, warren, or fifhery, endowed with privileges of royalty ; which fpecies of franchife may require a more minute difcuffion.

As to a *foreft* : this, in the hands of a fubject, is properly the fame thing with a chafe ; being fubject to the common law, and not to the foreft laws [v]. But a *chafe* differs from a park, in that it is not enclofed, and alfo in that a man may have a chafe in another man's ground as well as his own ; being indeed the liberty of keeping beafts of chafe or royal game therein, protected even from the owner of the land, with a power of hunting them thereon.   A *park* is an enclofed chafe, extending only over a man's own grounds.   The word *park* indeed properly fignifies any enclofure ; bnt yet it is not every field or common, which a gentleman pleafes to furround with a wall or paling, and to ftock with a herd of deer, that is thereby conftituted a legal park : for the king's grant, or at leaft immemorial prefcription, is neceffary to make it fo [w].   Though now the difference between a real park, and fuch enclofed grounds, is in many refpects not very material : only that it is unlawful at common law for any perfon to kill any beafts of park or chafe [x], except fuch as poffefs thefe franchifes of foreft, chafe, or park.   *Free-warren* is a fimilar franchife, erected for prefervation or cuftody (which the word fignifies) of beafts and fowls of warren [y] ; which, being *ferae naturae*, every one had a natural right to kill as he could :

<hr/>

[u] 2 Inft. 220.
[v] 4 Inft. 314.
[w] Co. Litt. 233. 2 Inft. 199. 11 Rep. 86.
[x] Thefe are properly buck, doe, fox, martin, and roe ; but in a common and legal fenfe extend likewife to all the beafts of the foreft : which, befides the other, are reckoned to be hart, hind, hare, boar, and

wolf, and in a word, all wild beafts of venary or hunting   (Co. Litt. 233.)
[y] The beafts are hares, conies, and roes : the fowls are either *campeftres*, as partridges, rails, and quails ; or *fylveftres*, as woodcocks and pheafants ; or *aquatiles*, as mallards and herons. *(Ibid.)*

but

but upon the introduction of the foreſt laws at the Norman conqueſt, as will be ſhewn hereafter, theſe animals being looked
upon as royal game and the ſole property of our ſavage monarchs,
this franchiſe of free-warren was invented to protect them ; by
giving the grantee a ſole and excluſive power of killing ſuch
game, ſo far as his warren extended, on condition of his preventing other perſons.   A man therefore that has the franchiſe
of warren, is in reality no more than a royal game-keeper : but
no man, not even a lord of a manor, could by common law juſtify
ſporting on another's ſoil, or even on his own, unleſs he had the
liberty of free-warren[z].   This franchiſe is almoſt fallen into diſ-
regard, ſince the new ſtatutes for preſerving the game ; the name
being now chiefly preſerved in grounds that are ſet apart for
breeding hares and rabbets.   There are many inſtances of keen
ſportſmen in antient times, who have ſold their eſtates, and reſerved the free-warren, or right of killing game, to themſelves ;
by which means it comes to paſs that a man and his heirs have
ſometimes free-warren over another's ground[a].   A *free fiſhery*,
or excluſive right of fiſhing in a public river, is alſo a royal franchiſe ; and is conſidered as ſuch in all countries where the feodal
polity has prevailed[b] : though the making ſuch grants, and by
that means appropriating what ſeems to be unnatural to reſtrain,
the uſe of running water, was prohibited for the future by king
John's great charter, and the rivers that were fenced in his time
were directed to be laid open, as well as the foreſts to be diſ-
afforeſted[c].   This opening was extended, by the ſecond[d] and
third[d] charters of Henry III, to thoſe alſo that were fenced under
Richard I ; ſo that a franchiſe of free fiſhery ought now to be at
leaſt as old as the reign of Henry II.   This differs from a *ſeveral*
fiſhery ; becauſe he that has a ſeveral fiſhery muſt alſo be the
owner of the ſoil, which in a free fiſhery is not requiſite.   It
differs alſo from a *common* of piſcary before-mentioned, in that

[z] Salk. 637.
[a] Bro. *Abr. tit. Warren.* 3.
[b] Seld. *Mar. clauſ. I* 24. Dufreſne. V.
503. Crag. *de Jur feod.* II. 8. 15.

[c] *cap.* 47. *edit. Oxon.*
[d] *cap.* 20.
[e] 9 Hen. III. c. 16.

the free fifhery is an exclufive right, the common of pifcary is
not fo : and therefore, in a free fifhery, a man has a property in
the fifh before they are caught ; in a common of pifcary, not till
afterwards [f].   Some indeed have confidered a *free* fifhery not as
a royal franchife, but merely as a private grant of a liberty to fifh
in the *feveral* fifhery of the grantor [g].   But the confidering fuch
right as originally a flower of the prerogative, till reftrained by
magna carta, and derived by royal grant (previous to the reign
of Richard I.) to fuch as now claim it by prefcription, may remove fome difficulties in refpect to this matter, with which our
books are embaraffed.

VIII. C o r o d i e s are a right of fuftenance, or to receive
certain allotments of victual and provifion for one's maintenance [h].
In lieu of which (efpecially when due from ecclefiaftical perfons)
a penfion or fum of money is fometimes fubftituted [i].   And thefe
may be reckoned another fpecies of incorporeal hereditaments ;
though not chargeable on, or iffuing from, any corporeal inheritance, but only charged on the perfon of the owner in refpect
of fuch his inheritance.   To thefe may be added,

IX. A n n u i t i e s, which are much of the fame nature ;
only that thefe arife from temporal, as the former from fpiritual,
perfons.   An annuity is a thing very diftinct from a rent-charge,
with which it is frequently confounded : a rent-charge being a
burthen impofed upon and iffuing out of *lands*, whereas an annuity
is a yearly fum chargeable only upon the *perfon* of the grantor [j].
Therefore, if a man by deed grant to another the fum of 20*l. per
annum*, without expreffing out of what lands it fhall iffue, no
land at all fhall be charged with it ; but it is a mere perfonal
annuity : which is of fo little account in the law, that, if granted to an eleemofynary corporation, it is not within the ftatutes
of mortmain [k] ; and yet a man may have a real eftate in it,
though his fecurity is merely perfonal.

---

[f] F. N. B. 88. Salk. 637.
[g] 2 Sid. 8.
[h] Finch. L. 162.

[i] See Book I. ch. 8.
[j] Co. Litt. 144.
[k] *Ibid.* 2.   X. R e n t s

X. RENTS are the laft fpecies of incorporeal hereditaments. The word, rent, or render, *reditus*, fignifies a compenfation, or return; it being in the nature of an acknowlegement given for the poffeffion of fome corporeal inheritance [1]. It is defined to be a certain profit iffuing yearly out of lands and tenements corporeal. It muft be a *profit*; yet there is no occafion for it to be, as it ufually is, a fum of money: for fpurs, capons, horfes, corn, and other matters may be rendered, and frequently are rendered, by way of rent [m]. It may alfo confift in fervices or manual operations; as, to plough fo many acres of ground, to attend the king or the lord to the wars, and the like; which fervices in the eye of the law are profits. This profit muft alfo be *certain*; or that which may be reduced to a certainty by either party. It muft alfo iffue *yearly*; though there is no occafion for it to iffue every fucceffive year; but it may be referved every fecond, third, or fourth year [n]: yet, as it is to be produced out of the profits of lands and tenements, as a recompenfe for being permitted to hold and enjoy them, it ought to be referved yearly, becaufe thofe profits do annually arife and are annually renewed. It muft *iffue out* of the thing granted, and not be part of the land or thing itfelf; wherein it differs from an exception in the grant, which is always of part of the thing granted [o]. It muft, laftly, iffue out of *lands and tenements corporeal*; that is, from fome inheritance whereunto the owner or grantee of the rent may have recourfe to diftrein. Therefore a rent cannot be referved out of an advowfon, a common, an office, a franchife, or the like [p]. But a grant of fuch annuity or fum may operate as a perfonal contract, and oblige the grantor to pay the money referved, or fubject him to an action of debt [q]; though it doth not affect the inheritance, and is no legal rent in contemplation of law.

THERE are at common law [r] three manner of rents; rentfervice, rent-charge, and rent-feck. *Rent-fervice* is fo called be-

[1] Co. Litt. 144.
[m] *Ibid.* 142.
[n] *Ibid.* 47.

[o] Plowd. 13. 8 Rep. 71.
[p] Co. Litt. 144.
[q] *Ibid.* 47.   [r] Litt. §. 213.

cause it hath some corporal service incident to it, as at the least fealty, or the feodal oath of fidelity [s]. For, if a tenant holds his land by fealty, and ten shillings rent; or by the service of plough-ing the lord's land, and five shillings rent; these pecuniary rents, being connected with personal services, are therefore called rent-service. And for these, in case they be behind, or arrere, at the day appointed, the lord may distrein of common right, without reserving any special power of distress; provided he hath in him-self the reversion, or future estate of the lands and tenements, after the lease or particular estate of the lessee or grantee is expired [t]. A *rent-charge,* is where the owner of the rent hath no future interest, or reversion expectant in the land; as where a man by deed maketh over to others his *whole* estate in fee simple, with a certain rent payable thereout, and adds to the deed a cove-nant or clause of distress, that if the rent be arrere, or behind, it shall be lawful to distrein for the same. In this case the land is liable to the distress, not of common right, but by virtue of the clause in the deed: and therefore it is called a rent-*charge,* because in this manner the land is charged with a distress for the payment of it [u]. *Rent-seck, reditus siccus,* or barren rent, is in effect nothing more than a rent reserved by deed, but without any clause of distress.

THERE are also other species of rents, which are reducible to these three. Rents *of assise* are the certain established rents of the freeholders and antient copyholders of a manor [w], which can-not be departed from or varied. Those of the freeholders are fre-quently called *chief* rents, *reditus capitales;* and both sorts are in-differently denominated *quit* rents, *quieti reditus;* because thereby the tenant goes quit and free of all other services. When these payments were reserved in silver or white money, they were an-tiently called *white*-rents, or *blanch-farms, reditus albi* [x]; in con-tradistinction to rents reserved in work, grain, &c. which were

[s] Co. Litt. 142.
[t] Litt. §. 215.
[u] Co. Litt. 143.
[w] 2 Inst. 19.

[x] In Scotland this kind of small pay-ment is called *blench-holding,* or *reditus albae firmae.*

called

called *reditus nigri*, or *black-maile*[y]. *Rack*-rent is only a rent of the full value of the tenement, or near it. A *feefarm*-rent is a rent-charge iſſuing out of an eſtate in fee; of at leaſt one fourth of the value of the lands, at the time of it's reſervation[z]: for a grant of lands, reſerving ſo conſiderable a rent, is indeed only letting lands to farm in fee ſimple inſtead of the uſual methods for life or years.

THESE are the general diviſions of rent; but the difference between them (in reſpect to the remedy for recovering them) is now totally aboliſhed; and all perſons may have the like remedy by diſtreſs for rents-ſeck, rents of aſſiſe, and chief-rents, as in caſe of rents reſerved upon leaſe[a].

RENT is regularly due and payable upon the land from whence it iſſues, if no particular place is mentioned in the reſervation[b]: but, in caſe of the king, the payment muſt be either to his officers at the exchequer, or to his receiver in the country[c]. And, ſtrictly, the rent is demandable and payable before the time of ſunſet of the day whereon it is reſerved[d]; though ſome have thought it not abſolutely due till midnight[e].

WITH regard to the original of rents, ſomething will be ſaid in the next chapter: and, as to diſtreſſes and other remedies for their recovery, the doctrine relating thereto, and the ſeveral proceedings thereon, theſe belong properly to the third part of our commentaries, which will treat of civil injuries, and the means whereby they are redreſſed.

[y] 2 Inſt. 19.
[z] Co. Litt. 143.
[a] Stat. 4 Geo. II. c. 28.
[b] Co. Litt. 201.
[c] 4 Rep. 73.
[d] Anderſ. 253.
[e] 1 Saund. 287. 1 Chan. Prec. 555.

CHAPTER THE FOURTH.

OF THE FEODAL SYSTEM.

IT is impoſſible to underſtand, with any degree of accuracy, either the civil conſtitution of this kingdom, or the laws which regulate it's landed property, without ſome general acquaintance with the nature and doctrine of feuds, or the feodal law : a ſyſtem ſo univerſally received throughout Europe, upwards of twelve centuries ago, that ſir Henry Spelman [a] does not ſcruple to call it the law of nations in our weſtern world. This chapter will be therefore dedicated to this inquiry. And though, in the courſe of our obſervations in this and many other parts of the preſent book, we may have occaſion to ſearch pretty highly into the antiquities of our Engliſh juriſprudence, yet ſurely no induſtrious ſtudent will imagine his time miſ-employed, when he is led to conſider that the obſolete doctrines of our laws are frequently the foundation, upon which what remains is erected ; and that it is impracticable to comprehend many rules of the modern law, in a ſcholarlike ſcientifical manner, without having recourſe to the antient. Nor will theſe reſearches be altogether void of rational entertainment as well as uſe : as in viewing the majeſtic ruins of Rome or Athens, of Balbec or Palmyra, it adminiſters both pleaſure and inſtruction to compare them with the draughts of the ſame edifices, in their priſtine proportion and ſplendor.

[a] of parliaments. 57.

THE

THE conſtitution of feuds[b] had it's original from the military policy of the northern or Celtic nations, the Goths, the Hunns, the Franks, the Vandals, and the Lombards, who all migrating from the ſame *officina gentium*, as Crag very juſtly entitles it[c], poured themſelves in vaſt quantities into all the regions of Europe, at the declenſion of the Roman empire. It was brought by them from their own countries, and continued in their reſpective colonies as the moſt likely means to ſecure their new acquiſitions : and, to that end, large diſtricts or parcels of land were allotted by the conquering general to the ſuperior officers of the army, and by them dealt out again in ſmaller parcels or allotments to the inferior officers and moſt deſerving ſoldiers[d]. Theſe allotments were called *feoda*, feuds, fiefs, or fees; which laſt appellation in the northern languages[e] ſignifies a conditional ſtipend or reward[f]. Rewards or ſtipends they evidently were; and the condition annexed to them was, that the poſſeſſor ſhould do ſervice. faithfully, both at home and in the wars, to him by whom they were given; for which purpoſe he took the *juramentum fidelitatis*, or oath of fealty[g] : and in caſe of the breach of this condition and oath, by not performing the ſtipulated ſervice, or by deſerting the lord in battle, the lands were again to revert to him who granted them[h].

ALLOTMENTS thus acquired, naturally engaged ſuch as accepted them to defend them : and, as they all ſprang from the

[b] See Spelman of feuds, and Wright of tenures, *per tot.*
[c] *De jure feod.* 19, 20.
[d] Wright.7.
[e] Spelm. *Gl.* 216.
[f] Pontoppidan in his hiſtory of Norway (page 290) obſerves, that in the northern languages **oꝺꝺ** ſignifies *proprietas* and **all** *totum.* Hence he derives the **oꝺꝺal** right in thoſe countries; and hence too perhaps is derived the *udal* right in Finland, &c. (See Mac Doual. Inſt. part. 2.) Now the tranſ-

poſition of theſe northern ſyllables, **allodꝺ**, will give us the true etymology of the *allodium*, or abſolute property of the feudiſts; as, by a ſimilar combination of the latter ſyllable with the word **fee** (which ſignifies, we have ſeen, a conditional reward or ſtipend) **feodꝺ** or *feodum* will denote ſtipendiary property.
[g] See this Oath explained at large in *Feud. l. 2. t.* 7.
[h] *Feud. l. 2. t.* 24.

same right of conqueft, no part could fubfift independent of the whole; wherefore all givers as well as receivers were mutually bound to defend each others poffeffions. But, as that could not effectually be done in a tumultuous irregular way, government, and to that purpofe fubordination, was neceffary. Every receiver of lands, or feudatory, was therefore bound, when called upon by his benefactor, or immediate lord of his feud or fee, to do all in his power to defend him. Such benefactor or lord was like-wife fubordinate to and under the command of his immediate benefactor or fuperior; and fo upwards to the prince or general himfelf. And the feveral lords were alfo reciprocally bound, in their refpective gradations, to protect the poffeffions they had given. Thus the feodal connection was eftablifhed, a proper military fubjection was naturally introduced, and an army of feudatories were always ready enlifted, and mutually prepared to mufter, not only in defence of each man's own feveral property, but alfo in defence of the whole, and of every part of this their newly acquired country [i]: the prudence of which conftitution was foon fufficiently vifible in the ftrength and fpirit, with which they maintained their conquefts.

The univerfality and early ufe of this feodal plan, among all thofe nations which in complaifance to the Romans we ftill call barbarous, may appear from what is recorded [k] of the Cimbri and Teutones, nations of the fame northern original as thofe whom we have been defcribing, at their firft irruption into Italy about a century before the chriftian aera. They demanded of the Romans, "*ut martius populus aliquid fibi terrae daret, quafi ftipen-* "*dium: caeterum, ut vellet, manibus atque armis fuis uteretur.*" The fenfe of which may be thus rendered; they defired ftipendiary lands (that is, feuds) to be allowed them, to be held by military and other perfonal fervices, whenever their lords fhould call upon them. This was evidently the fame conftitution, that difplayed itfelf more fully about feven hundred years afterwards; when the Salii, Burgundians, and Franks broke in upon Gaul,

[i] Wright. 8.　　　　　[k] *L. Florus. l. 3. c. 3.*

the

the Vifigoths on Spain, and the Lombards upon Italy, and introduced with themfelves this northern plan of polity, ferving at
once to diftribute, and to protect, the territories they had newly
gained. And from hence it is probable that the emperor Alexander Severus [1] took the hint, of dividing lands conquered from
the enemy among his generals and victorious foldiery, on condition of receiving military fervice from them and their heirs for
ever.

SCARCE had thefe northern conquerors eftablifhed themfelves
in their new dominions, when the wifdom of their conftitutions,
as well as their perfonal valour, alarmed all the princes of Europe;
that is, of thofe countries which had formerly been Roman provinces, but had revolted, or were deferted by their old mafters,
in the general wreck of the empire. Wherefore moft, if not all,
of them thought it neceffary to enter into the fame or a fimilar
plan of policy. For whereas, before, the poffeffions of their
fubjects were perfectly *allodial*; (that is, wholly independent,
and held of no fuperior at all) now they parcelled out their royal
territories, or perfuaded their fubjects to furrender up and retake
their own landed property, under the like feodal obligation of
military fealty [m]. And thus, in the compafs of a very few years,
the feodal conftitution, or the doctrine of tenure, extended itfelf
over all the weftern world. Which alteration of landed property,
in fo very material a point, neceffarily drew after it an alteration
of laws and cuftoms : fo that the feodal laws foon drove out the
Roman, which had hitherto univerfally obtained, but now became for many centuries loft and forgotten; and Italy itfelf (as
fome of the civilians, with more fpleen than judgment, have expreffed it) *belluinas, atque ferinas, immanefque Longobardorum leges
accepit* [n]

---

[1] " Sola, *quae de hoftibus capta funt, limi-*
" *taneis ducibus et militibus donavit; ita ut*
" *eorum ita effent, fi haeredes illorum militarent,*
" *nec unquam ad privatos pertinerent : dicens*
" *attentius illos militaturos, fi etiam fua rura*
" *defenderent. Addidit fane his et animalia et*
" *fervos, ut poffent colere quod acceperant ; ne*

" *per inopiam hominum vel per feneĉlutem defe-*
" *rerentur rura vicina barbariae, quod turpif-*
" *fimum ille ducebat.*" (Æl. Lamprid. *in vita*
Alex. Severi.)

[m] Wright. 10.

[n] Gravin. *Orig. l.* 1. §. 139.

B U T this feodal polity, which was thus by degrees eſtabliſhed over all the continent of Europe, ſeems not to have been received in this part of our iſland, at leaſt not univerſally and as a part of the national conſtitution, till the reign of William the Norman ° Not but that it is reaſonable to believe, from abundant traces in our hiſtory and laws, that even in the times of the Saxons, who were a ſwarm from what ſir William Temple calls the ſame northern hive, ſomething ſimilar to this was in uſe : yet not ſo extenſively, nor attended with all the rigour that was afterwards imported by the Normans. For the Saxons were firmly ſettled in this iſland, at leaſt as early as the year 600 : and it was not till two centuries after, that feuds arrived to their full vigour and maturity, even on the continent of Europe ᴾ.

T H I S introduction however of the feodal tenures into England, by king William, does not ſeem to have been effected immediately after the conqueſt, nor by the mere arbitrary will and power of the conqueror ; but to have been conſented to by the great council of the nation long after his title was eſtabliſhed. Indeed from the prodigious ſlaughter of the Engliſh nobility at the battle of Haſtings, and the fruitleſs inſurrections of thoſe who ſurvived, ſuch numerous forfeitures had accrued, that he was able to reward his Norman followers with very large and extenſive poſſeſſions : which gave a handle to the monkiſh hiſtorians, and ſuch as have implicitly followed them, to repreſent him as having by right of the ſword ſeiſed on all the lands of England, and dealt them out again to his own favourites. A ſuppoſition, grounded upon a miſtaken ſenſe of the word *conqueſt* ; which, in it's feodal acceptation, ſignifies no more than *acquiſition :* and this has led many haſty writers into a ſtrange hiſtorical miſtake, and one which upon the ſlighteſt examination will be found to be moſt untrue. However, certain it is, that the Normans now began to gain very large poſſeſſions in England : and their regard for the feodal law, under which they had long lived, together

° Spelm. *Gloſſ.* 218. Bract. *l.* 2. *c.* 16. §. 7. ᴾ Crag. *l.* 1. *t.* 4.

with

with the king's recommendation of this policy to the Englifh, as the beft way to put themfelves on a military footing, and thereby to prevent any future attempts from the continent, were probably the reafons that prevailed to effect it's eftablifhment here. And perhaps we may be able to afcertain the time of this great revolution in our landed property with a tolerable degree of exactnefs. For we learn from the Saxon Chronicle [q], that in the nineteenth year of king William's reign an invafion was apprehended from Denmark; and the military conftitution of the Saxons being then laid afide, and no other introduced in it's ftead, the kingdom was wholly defencelefs: which occafioned the king to bring over a large army of Normans and Bretons, who were quartered upon every landholder, and greatly oppreffed the people. This apparent weaknefs, together with the grievances occafioned by a foreign force, might co-operate with the king's remonftrances, and the better encline the nobility to liften to his propofals for putting them in a pofture of defence. For, as foon as the danger was over, the king held a great council to inquire into the ftate of the nation [r]; the immediate confequence of which was the compiling of the great furvey called domefday-book, which was finifhed in the next year: and in the latter end of that very year the king was attended by all his nobility at Sarum; where all the principal landholders fubmitted their lands to the yoke of military tenure, became the king's vafals, and did homage and fealty to his perfon [s]. This feems to have been the aera of formally introducing the feodal tenures by law; and probably the very law, thus made at the council of Sarum, is that which is ftill extant [t], and couched in thefe remarkable words: "*ftatuimus, ut omnes liberi* "*homines foedere et facramento affirment, quod intra et extra uni-* "*verfum regnum Angliae Wilhelmo regi domino fuo fideles effe volunt;* "*terras et honores illius omni fidelitate ubique fervare cum eo, et*

[q] *A. D.* 1085.

[r] *Rex tenuit magnum concilium, et graves fermones habuit cum fuis proceribus de hac terra, quo modo incoleretur, et a quibus hominibus. Chron. Sax. ibid.*

[s] *Omnes praedia tenentes, quotquot effent notae*

melioris per totam Angliam, ejus homines facti funt, et omnes fe illi fubdidere, ejufque facti funt vafalli, ac ei fidelitatis juramenta praeftiterunt, fe contra alios quofcunque illi fidos futuros. Chron. Sax. A. D. 1086.

[t] *cap.* 52. Wilk. 228.

" *contra inimicos et alienigenas defendere.*" The terms of this law (as fir Martin Wright has obferved[u]) are plainly feodal : for, firft, it requires the oath of fealty, which made in the fenfe of the feudifts every man that took it a tenant or vafal; and, fecondly, the tenants obliged themfelves to defend their lord's territories and titles againft all enemies foreign and domeftic. But what puts the matter out of difpute is another law of the fame collection[w], which exacts the performance of the military feodal fervices, as ordained by the general council. " *Omnes comites, et* " *barones, et milites, et fervientes, et univerfi liberi homines totius* " *regni noftri praedicti, habeant et tenoant fe femper bene in armis et* " *in equis, ut decet et oportet : et fint femper prompti et bene parati* " *ad fervitium fuum integrum nobis explendum et peragendum cum* " *opus fuerit ; fecundum quod nobis debent de feodis et tenementis fuis* " *de jure facere ; et ficut illis ftatuimus per commune concilium totius* " *regni noftri praedicti.*"

THIS new polity therefore feems not to have been *impofed* by the conqueror, but nationally and freely *adopted* by the general affembly of the whole realm, in the fame manner as other nations of Europe had before adopted it, upon the fame principle of felf-fecurity. And, in particular, they had the recent example of the French nation before their eyes ; which had gradually furrendered up all it's allodial or free lands into the king's hands, who reftored them to the owners as a *beneficium* or feud, to be held to them and fuch of their heirs as they previoufly nominated to the king : and thus by degrees all the allodial eftates of France were converted into feuds, and the freemen became the vafals of the crown[x]. The only difference between this change of tenures in France, and that in England, was, that the former was effected gradually, by the confent of private perfons ; the latter was done at once, all over England, by the common confent of the nation[y].

---

[u] Tenures. 66.
[w] *cap.* 58. Wilk. 228.
[x] Montefq. Sp. L. b. 31. c. 8.
[y] Pharoah thus acquired the dominion of all the lands in Egypt, and granted them out to the Egyptians, referving an annual render of the fifth part of their value. (Gen. c. 47.)

IN confequence of this change, it became a fundamental maxim and neceffary principle (though in reality a mere fiction) of our Englifh tenures, "that the king is the univerfal lord and original "proprietor of all the lands in his kingdom; and that no man "doth or can poffefs any part of it, but what has mediately or "immediately been derived as a gift from him, to be held upon "feodal fervices." For, this being the real cafe in pure, original, proper feuds, other nations who adopted this fyftem were obliged to act upon the fame fuppofition, as a fubftruction and foundation of their new polity, though the fact was indeed far otherwife. And indeed by thus confenting to the introduction of feodal tenures, our Englifh anceftors probably meant no more than to put the kingdom in a ftate of defence by eftablifhing a military fyftem; and to oblige themfelves (in refpect of their lands) to maintain the king's title and territories, with equal vigour and fealty, *as if* they had received their lands from his bounty upon thefe exprefs conditions, as pure, proper, beneficiary feudatories. But, whatever their meaning was, the Norman interpreters, fkilled in all the niceties of the feodal conftitutions, and well underftanding the import and extent of the feodal terms, gave a very different conftruction to this proceeding; and thereupon took a handle to introduce not only the rigorous doctrines which prevailed in the duchy of Normandy, but alfo fuch fruits and dependencies, fuch hardfhips and fervices, as were never known to other nations '; as if the Englifh had in fact, as well as theory, owed every thing they had to the bounty of their fovereign lord.

OUR anceftors therefore, who were by no means beneficiaries, but had barely confented to this fiction of tenure from the crown, as the bafis of a military difcipline, with reafon looked upon thefe deductions as grievous impofitions, and arbitrary conclufions from principles that, as to them, had no foundation in truth ᵃ. However, this king, and his fon William Rufus, kept up with

' Spelm. of feuds, c. 28.   ᵃ Wright. 81.

G 2   a high

a high hand all the rigours of the feodal doctrines : but their
fucceffor, Henry I, found it expedient, when he fet up his pretenfions to the crown, to promife a reftitution of the laws of king
Edward the confeffor, or antient Saxon fyftem ; and accordingly,
in the firft year of his reign, granted a charter[b], whereby he gave
up the greater grievances, but ftill referved the fiction of feodal
tenure, for the fame military purpofes which engaged his father
to introduce it. But this charter was gradually broke through,
and the former grievances were revived and aggravated, by himfelf and fucceeding princes ; till in the reign of king John they
became fo intolerable, that they occafioned his barons, or principal feudatories, to rife up in arms againft him : which at length
produced the famous great charter at Runing-mead, which, with
fome alterations, was confirmed by his fon Henry III. And,
though it's immunities (efpecially as altered on it's laft edition by
his fon[c]) are very greatly fhort of thofe granted by Henry I, it
was juftly efteemed at the time a vaft acquifition to Englifh liberty. Indeed, by the farther alteration of tenures that has fince
happened, many of thefe immunities may now appear, to a common obferver, of much lefs confequence than they really were
when granted : but this, properly confidered, will fhew, not
that the acquifitions under John were fmall, but that thofe under
Charles were greater. And from hence alfo arifes another infe-
rence ; that the liberties of Englifhmen are not (as fome arbitrary
writers would reprefent them) mere infringements of the king's
prerogative, extorted from our princes by taking advantage of
their weaknefs ; but a reftoration of that antient conftitution, of
which our anceftors had been defrauded by the art and fineffe of
the Norman lawyers, rather than deprived by the force of the
Norman arms.

HAVING given this fhort hiftory of their rife and progrefs,
we will next confider the nature, doctrine, and principal laws of
feuds ; wherein we fhall evidently trace the groundwork of many
parts of our public polity, and alfo the original of fuch of our

_____

[b] *LL. Hen. I. c. 1.*   [c] *9 Hen. III.*

OWN

own tenures, as were either abolished in the laſt century, or ſtill remain in force.

T H E grand and fundamental maxim of all feodal tenure is this; that all lands were originally granted out by the ſovereign, and are therefore holden, either mediately or immediately, of the crown. The grantor was called the proprietor, or *lord*; being he who retained the dominion or ultimate property of the feud or fee: and the grantee, who had only the uſe and poſſeſſion, ac-- cording to the terms of the grant, was ſtiled the feudatory or *vaſal*, which was only another name for the tenant or holder of the lands; though, on account of the prejudices we have juſtly conceived againſt the doctrines that were afterwards grafted on this ſyſtem, we now uſe the word *vaſal* opprobriouſly, as ſyno- nymous to ſlave or bondman. The manner of the grant was by words of gratuitous and pure donation, *dedi et conceſſi*; which are ſtill the operative words in our modern infeodations or deeds of feoffment. This was perfected by the ceremony of corporal in- veſtiture, or open and notorious delivery of poſſeſſion in the pre- ſence of the other vaſals, which perpetuated among them the aera of the new acquiſition, at a time when the art of writing was very little known: and therefore the evidence of property was repoſed in the memory of the neighbourhood; who, in caſe of a diſputed title, were afterwards called upon to decide the diffe- rence, not only according to external proofs, adduced by the par- ties litigant, but alſo by the internal teſtimony of their own pri- vate knowlege.

B E S I D E S an oath of *fealty*, or profeſſion of faith to the lord, which was the parent of our oath of allegiance, the vaſal or te- nant upon inveſtiture did uſually *homage* to his lord; openly and humbly kneeling, being ungirt, uncovered, and holding up his hands both together between thoſe of the lord, who ſate before him; and there profeſſing that " he did become his *man*, from " that day forth, of life and limb and earthly honour:" and then he received a kiſs from his lord [d]. Which ceremony was deno-

^d Litt. §. 85.

minated

minated *homagium,* or *manhood,* by the feudists, from the stated form of words, *devenio vester homo* [e].

WHEN the tenant had thus professed himself to be the man of his superior or lord, the next consideration was concerning the *service,* which, as such, he was bound to render, in recompense for the land he held. This, in pure, proper, and original feuds, was only twofold : to follow, or do *suit* to, the lord in his courts in time of peace; and in his armies or warlike retinue, when necessity called him to the field. The lord was, in early times, the legislator and judge over all his feudatories : and therefore the vasals of the inferior lords were bound by their fealty to attend their domestic courts baron [f], (which were instituted in every manor or barony, for doing speedy and effectual justice to all the tenants) in order as well to answer such complaints as might be alleged against themselves, as to form a jury or homage for the trial of their fellow-tenants; and upon this account, in all the feodal institutions both here and on the continent, they are distinguished by the appellation of the peers of the court ; *pares curtis,* or *pares curiae.* In like manner the barons themselves, or lords of inferior districts, were denominated peers of the king's court, and were bound to attend him upon summons, to hear causes of greater consequence in the king's presence and under the direction of his grand justiciary ; till in many countries the power of that officer was broken and distributed into other courts of judicature, the peers of the king's court still reserving to themselves (in almost every feodal government) the right of appeal from those subordinate courts in the last resort. The military branch of service consisted in attending the lord to the wars, if called upon, with such a retinue, and for such a number of days,

---

[e] It was an observation of Dr Arbuthnot, that tradition was no where preserved so pure and incorrupt as among children, whose games and plays are delivered down invariably from one generation to another. (Warburton's notes on Pope. vi. 134. 8°.) Perhaps it may be thought puerile to ob-serve (in confirmation of this remark) that in one of our antient pastimes (the *basilinda* of Julius Pollux, *Onomastic. l. 9. c. 7.*) the ceremonies and language of feodal homage are preserved with great exactness.

[f] *Feud. l. 2. t. 55.*

as

as were ſtipulated at the firſt donation, in proportion to the quantity of the land.

AT the firſt introduction of feuds, as they were gratuitous, ſo
alſo they were precarious and held at the *will* of the lord [g], who
was the ſole judge whether his vaſal performed his ſervices faithfully. Then they became certain, for one or more *years*. Among
the antient Germans they continued only from year to year ; an
annual diſtribution of lands being made by their leaders in their
general councils or aſſemblies [h]. This was profeſſedly done, leſt
their thoughts ſhould be diverted from war to agriculture ; leſt
the ſtrong ſhould incroach upon the poſſeſſions of the weak ; and
leſt luxury and avarice ſhould be encouraged by the erection of
permanent houſes, and too curious an attention to convenience
and the elegant ſuperfluities of life. But, when the general migration was pretty well over, and a peaceable poſſeſſion of their
new-acquired ſettlements had introduced new cuſtoms and manners ; when the fertility of the ſoil had encouraged the ſtudy of
huſbandry, and an affection for the ſpots they had cultivated began naturally to ariſe in the tillers ; a more permanent degree of
property was introduced, and feuds began now to be granted for
the *life* of the feudatory [i]. But ſtill feuds were not yet *hereditary*;
though frequently granted, by the favour of the lord, to the
children of the former poſſeſſor ; till in proceſs of time it became
unuſual, and was therefore thought hard, to reject the heir, if
he were capable to perform the ſervices [k] : and therefore infants,
women, and profeſſed monks, who were incapable of bearing
arms, were alſo incapable of ſucceeding to a genuine feud. But
the heir, when admitted to the feud which his anceſtor poſſeſſed,
uſed generally to pay a fine or acknowlegement to the lord, in

[g] *Feud. l.* 1. *t.* 1.
[h] Thus Tacitus : (*de mor. Germ. c.* 26.)
"*agri ab univerſis per vices occupantur : arva*
"*per annos mutant.*" And Caeſar yet more
fully ; (*de bell. Gall. l.* 6. *c.* 21.) "*Neque*
"*quiſquam agri modum certum, aut fines pro-*
"*prios habet ; ſed magiſtratus et principes, in*

"*annos ſingulos, gentibus et cognationibus ho-*
"*minum qui una coierunt, quantum eis et quo*
"*loco viſum eſt, attribuunt agri, atque anno*
"*poſt alio tranſire cogunt.*"
[i] *Feud. l.* 1. *t.* 1.
[k] Wright. 14.

horfes, arms, money, and the like, for fuch renewal of the feud : which was called a relief, becaufe it re-eftablifhed the inherit-ance, or, in the words of the feodal writers, " *incertam et cadu-* " *cam hereditatem relevabat.*" This relief was afterwards, when feuds became abfolutely hereditary, continued on the death of the tenant, though the original foundation of it had ceafed.

FOR in procefs of time feuds came by degrees to be univer-fally extended, beyond the life of the firft vafal, to his *fons*, or perhaps to fuch one of them, as the lord fhould name ; and in this cafe the form of the donation was ftrictly obferved : for if a feud was given to a man and his *fons*, all his fons fucceeded him in equal portions ; and as they died off, their fhares reverted to the lord, and did not defcend to their children, or even to their furviving brothers, as not being fpecified in the donation[1]. But when fuch a feud was given to a man, and his *heirs*, in general terms, then a more extended rule of fucceffion took place ; and when a feudatory died, his male defcendants *in infinitum* were ad-mitted to the fucceffion. When any fuch defcendant, who thus had fucceeded, died, his male defcendants were alfo admitted in the firft place ; and, in defect of them, fuch of his male collateral kindred as were of the blood or lineage of the firft feudatory, but no others. For this was an unalterable maxim in feodal fuc-ceffion, that " none was capable of inheriting a feud, but fuch " as was of the blood of, that is, lineally defcended from, the " firft feudatory[m]." And the defcent, being thus confined to males, originally extended to all the males alike ; all the fons, without any diftinction of primogeniture, fucceeding to equal portions of the father's feud. But this being found upon many accounts inconvenient, (particularly, by dividing the fervices, and thereby weakening the ftrength of the feodal union) and *honorary* feuds (or titles of nobility) being now introduced, which were not of a divifible nature, but could only be inherited by the eldeft fon[n] ; in imitation of thefe, *military* feuds (or thofe we are now defcribing) began alfo in moft countries to defcend ac-

[1] Wright. 17.   [n] *Feud.* 2. *t.* 55.
[m] *Ibid.* 183.

cording

cording to the fame rule of primogeniture, to the eldeft fon, in excluſion of all the reſt °.

OTHER qualities of feuds were, that the feudatory could not aliene or diſpoſe of his feud; neither could he exchange, nor yet mortgage, nor even deviſe it by will, without the conſent of the lord ᴾ. For, the reaſon of conferring the feud being the perſonal abilities of the feudatory to ſerve in war, it was not fit he ſhould be at liberty to transfer this gift, either from himſelf, or his poſterity who were preſumed to inherit his valour, to others who might prove leſs able. And, as the feodal obligation was looked upon as reciprocal, the feudatory being entitled to the lord's protection, in return for his own fealty and ſervice; therefore the lord could no more transfer his ſeignory or protection without conſent of his vaſal, than the vaſal could his feud without conſent of his lord ᑫ: it being equally unreaſonable, that the lord ſhould extend his protection to a perſon to whom he had exceptions, and that the vaſal ſhould owe ſubjection to a ſuperior not of his own chooſing.

THESE were the principal, and very ſimple, qualities of the genuine or original feuds; being then all of a military nature, and in the hands of military perſons: though the feudatories, being under frequent incapacities of cultivating and manuring their own lands, ſoon found it neceſſary to commit part of them to inferior tenants; obliging them to ſuch returns in ſervice, corn, cattle, or money, as might enable the chief feudatories to attend their military duties without diſtraction: which returns, or *reditus*, were the original of rents. And by this means the feodal polity was greatly extended; theſe inferior feudatories (who held what are called in the Scots law " rere-fiefs") being under ſimilar obligations of fealty, to do ſuit of court, to anſwer the ſtipulated renders or rent-ſervice, and to promote the welfare of their immediate ſuperiors or lords ʳ. But this at the ſame time demoliſhed

° Wright. 32.   ᑫ *Ibid.* 30.
ᴾ *Ibid.* 29.   ʳ Wright. 20.

the antient fimplicity of feuds; and an inroad being once made upon their conftitution, it fubjected them, in a courfe of time, to great varieties and innovations. Feuds came to be bought and fold, and deviations were made from the old fundamental rules of tenure and fucceffion; which were held no longer facred, when the feuds themfelves no longer continued to be purely military. Hence thefe tenures began now to be divided into *feoda propria et impropria*, proper and improper feuds; under the former of which divifions were comprehended fuch, and fuch only, of which we have before fpoken; and under that of improper or derivative feuds were comprized all fuch as do not fall within the other defcription: fuch, for inftance, as were originally bartered and fold to the feudatory for a price; fuch as were held upon bafe or lefs honourable fervices, or upon a rent, in lieu of military fervice; fuch as were in themfelves alienable, without mutual licence; and fuch as might defcend indifferently either to males or females. But, where a difference was not expreffed in the creation, fuch new-created feuds did in all other refpects follow the nature of an original, genuine, and proper feud[s].

B U T as foon as the feodal fyftem came to be confidered in the light of a civil eftablifhment, rather than as a military plan, the ingenuity of the fame ages, which perplexed all theology with the fubtilty of fcholaftic difquifitions, and bewildered philofophy in the mazes of metaphyfical jargon, began alfo to exert it's influence on this copious and fruitful fubject: in purfuance of which, the moft refined and oppreffive confequences were drawn from what originally was a plan of fimplicity and liberty, equally beneficial to both lord and tenant, and prudently calculated for their mutual protection and defence. From this one foundation, in different countries of Europe, very different fuperftructures have been raifed: what effect it has produced on the landed property of England will appear in the following chapters.

[s] *Feud.* 2. *t.* 7.

CHAPTER THE FIFTH.

OF THE ANTIENT ENGLISH TENURES.

IN this chapter we fhall take a fhort view of the antient tenures of our Englifh eftates, or the manner in which lands, tenements, and hereditaments might have been holden; as the fame ftood in force, till the middle of the laft century. In which we fhall eafily perceive, that all the particularities, all the feeming and real hardfhips, that attended thofe tenures, were to be accounted for upon feodal principles and no other; being fruits of, and deduced from, the feodal policy.

ALMOST all the real property of this kingdom is by the policy of our laws fuppofed to be granted by, dependent upon, and *holden* of fome fuperior or lord, by and in confideration of certain fervices to be rendered to the lord by the tenant or poffeffor of this property. The thing holden is therefore ftiled a *tenement*, the poffeffors thereof *tenants*, and the manner of their poffeffion a *tenure*. Thus all the land in the kingdom is fuppofed to be holden, mediately or immediately, of the king; who is ftiled the lord *paramount*, or above all. Such tenants as held under the king immediately, when they granted out portions of their lands to inferior perfons, became alfo lords with refpect to thofe inferior perfons, as they were ftill tenants with refpect to the king; and, thus partaking of a middle nature, were called *mefne*, or middle, lords. So that if the king granted a manor to A, and he granted a portion of the land to B, now B was faid to hold

H 2   of

of A, and A of the king; or, in other words, B held his lands immediately of A, but mediately of the king. The king therefore was ftiled lord paramount; A was both tenant and lord, or was a mefne lord; and B was called tenant *paravail*, or the loweft tenant; being he who is fuppofed to make avail, or profit, of the land[a]. In this manner are all the lands of the kingdom holden, which are in the hands of fubjects: for, according to fir Edward Coke[b], in the law of England we have not properly *allodium*; which, we have feen[c], is the name by which the feudifts abroad diftinguifh fuch eftates of the fubject, as are not holden of any fuperior. So that at the firft glance we may obferve, that our lands are either plainly feuds, or partake very ftrongly of the feodal nature.

ALL tenures being thus derived, or fuppofed to be derived, from the king, thofe that held immediately under him, in right of his crown and dignity, were called his tenants *in capite*, or in chief; which was the moft honourable fpecies of tenure, but at the fame time fubjected the tenants to greater and more burthenfome fervices, than inferior tenures did[d]. This diftinction ran through all the different forts of tenure; of which I now proceed to give an account.

I. THERE feem to have fubfifted among our anceftors four principal fpecies of lay tenures, to which all others may be reduced: the grand criteria of which were the natures of the feveral fervices or renders, that were due to the lords from their tenants. The fervices, in refpect of their quality, were either *free* or *bafe* fervices; in refpect of their quantity and the time of exacting them, were either *certain* or *uncertain*. *Free* fervices fuch as were not unbecoming the character of a foldier, or a free-

---

[a] 2 Inft. 296.
[b] 1 Inft. 1.
[c] pag. 47.
[d] In the Germanic conftitution, the electors, the bifhops, the fecular princes, the imperial cities, &c, which hold directly from the emperor, are called the *immediate* ftates of the empire; all other landholders being denominated *mediate* ones. Mod. Un. Hift. xlii. 61.

man, to perform; as to serve under his lord in the wars, to pay a sum of money, and the like. *Base* services were such as were fit only for peasants, or persons of a servile rank; as to plough the lord's land, to make his hedges, to carry out his dung, or other mean employments. The *certain* services, whether free or base, were such as were stinted in quantity, and could not be exceeded on any pretence; as, to pay a stated annual rent, or to plough such a field for three days, The *uncertain* depended upon unknown contingencies; as to do military service in person, or pay an assessment in lieu of it, when called upon; or to wind a horn whenever the Scots invaded the realm; which are free services: or to do whatever the lord should command; which is a base or villein service.

FROM the various combinations of these services have arisen the four kinds of lay tenure which subsisted in England, till the middle of the last century; and three of which subsist to this day. Of these Bracton (who wrote under Henry the third) seems to give the clearest and most compendious account, of any author antient or modern [e]; of which the following is the outline or abstract [f]. "Tenements are of two kinds, *frank-tenement*, and " *villenage.* And, of frank-tenements, some are held freely in " consideration of homage and *knight-service*; others in *free-socage* " with the service of fealty only." And again [g], " of villenages " some are pure, and others privileged. He that holds in *pure* " *villenage* shall do whatsoever is commanded him, and always be " bound to an uncertain service. The other kind of villenage is " called *villein-socage*; and these villein-socmen do villein services, " but such as are certain and determined." Of which the sense seems to be as follows: first, where the service was *free*, but *uncertain*, as military service with homage, that tenure was called

<hr/>

[e] *l. 4. tr. 1. c. 28.*

[f] *Tenementorum aliud liberum, aliud ville-nagium. Item, liberorum aliud tenetur libere pro homagio et servitio militari; aliud in libero socagio cum fidelitate tantum. §. 1.*

[g] *Villenagiorum aliud purum, alium privile-* *giatum. Qui tenet in puro villenagio faciet quicquid ei praeceptum fuerit, et semper tenebi-tur ad incerta. Aliud genus vil'enagii di itur villanum socagium; et hujusmodi villani soc-manni — villana faciunt servitia, sed certa et determinata. §. 5.*

the

the tenure in chivalry, *per servitium militare*, or by knight-service. Secondly, where the service was not only *free*, but also *certain*, as by fealty only, by rent and fealty, &c, that tenure was called *liberum socagium*, or free socage. These were the only *free* holdings or tenements; the others were *villenous* or servile : as, thirdly, where the service was *base* in it's nature, and *uncertain* as to time and quantity, the tenure was *purum villenagium*, absolute or pure villenage. Lastly, where the service was *base* in it's nature, but reduced to a *certainty*, this was still villenage, but distinguished from the other by the name of privileged villenage, *villenagium privilegiatum*; or it might be still called socage (from the *certainty* of it's services) but degraded by their *baseness* into the inferior title of *villanum socagium*, villein-socage.

I. THE first, most universal, and esteemed the most honourable species of tenure, was that by knight-service, called in Latin *servitium militare*, and in law French *chivalry*, or *service de chivaler*, answering to the *fief d' haubert* of the Normans[h], which name is expressly given it by the mirrour[i]. This differed in very few points, as we shall presently see, from a pure and proper feud, being entirely military, and the genuine effect of the feodal establishment in England. To make a tenure by knight-service, a determinate quantity of land was necessary, which was called a knight's fee, *feodum militare*; the value of which, not only in the reign of Edward II[k], but also of Henry II[l], and therefore probably at it's original in the reign of the conqueror, was stated at 20 *l. per annum*; and a certain number of these knight's fees were requisite to make up a barony. And he who held this proportion of land (or a whole fee) by knight-service, was bound to attend his lord to the wars for forty days in every year, if called upon : which attendance was his *reditus* or return, his rent or service, for the land he claimed to hold. If he held only half a knight's fee, he was only bound to attend twenty days, and so in proportion[m]. And there is reason to apprehend, that this ser-

h Spelm. *Gloss.* 219.
i c. 2. §. 27.
k Stat. *de milit.* 1 Edw. II. Co. Litt. 69.

l Glanvil. *l.* 9. *c.* 4.
m Litt. §. 95.

vice was the whole that our anceftors meant to fubject themfelves to; the other fruits and confequences of this tenure being fraudulently fuperinduced, as the regular (though unforefeen) appendages of the feodal fyftem.

THIS tenure of knight-fervice had all the marks of a ftrict and regular feud : it was granted by words of pure donation, *dedi et conceffi*[n]; was transferred by inveftiture or delivering corporal poffeffion of the land, ufually called livery of feifin; and was perfected by homage and fealty. It alfo drew after it thefe feven fruits and confequences, as infeparably incident to the tenure in chivalry; *viz.* aids, relief, primer feifin, wardfhip, marriage, fines for alienation, and efcheat : all which I fhall endeavour to explain, and fhew to be of feodal original.

1. AIDS were originally mere benevolences granted by the tenant to his lord, in times of difficulty and diftrefs[o]; but in procefs of time they grew to be confidered as a matter of right, and not of difcretion. Thefe aids were principally three : firft, to ranfom the lord's perfon, if taken prifoner; a neceffary confequence of the feodal attachment and fidelity; infomuch that the neglect of doing it, whenever it was in the vafal's power, was, by the ftrict rigour of the feodal law, an abfolute forfeiture of his eftate[p]. Secondly, to make the lord's eldeft fon a knight; a matter that was formerly attended with great ceremony, pomp, and expenfe. This aid could not be demanded till the heir was fifteen years old, or capable of bearing arms[q]: the intention of it being to breed up the eldeft fon, and heir apparent of the feignory, to deeds of arms and chivalry, for the better defence of the nation. Thirdly, to marry the lord's eldeft daughter, by giving her a fuitable portion : for daughters' portions were in thofe days extremely flender; few lords being able to fave much out of their

[n] Co. Litt. 9.

[o] *Auxilia fiunt de gratia et non de jure,* — *cum dependeant ex gratia tenentium et non ad voluntatem dominorum.* Bracton. *l.* 2. *tr.* 1. *c.* 16. §. 8.

[p] Feud. *l.* 2. *t.* 24.

[q] 2 Inft. 233.

income

income for this purpofe; nor could they acquire money by other means, being wholly converfant in matters of arms; nor, by the nature of their tcnure, could they charge their lands with this, or any other incumbrances. From bearing their proportion to thefe aids no rank or profeffion was exempted: and therefore even the monafteries, till the time of their diffolution, contributed to the knighting of their founder's male heir (of whom their lands were holden) and the marriage of his female defcendants[r]. And one cannot but obferve, in this particular, the great refemblance which the lord and vafal of the feodal law bore to the patron and client of the Roman republic; between whom alfo there fubfifted a mutual fealty, or engagement of defence and protection. With regard to the matter of aids, there were three which were ufually raifed by the client; *viz.* to marry the patron's daughter; to pay his debts; and to redeem his perfon from captivity[s].

BUT befides thefe antient feodal aids, the tyranny of lords by degrees exacted more and more; as, aids to pay the lord's debts, (probably in imitation of the Romans) and aids to enable him to pay aids or reliefs to his fuperior lord; from which laft indeed the king's tenants *in capite* were, from the nature of their tenure, excufed, as they held immediately of the king who had no fuperior. To prevent this abufe, king John's *magna carta*[t] ordained, that no aids be taken by the king without confent of parliament, nor in any wife by inferior lords, fave only the three antient ones above-mentioned. But this provifion was omitted in Henry III's charter, and the fame oppreffions were continued till the 25 Edw. I; when the ftatute called *confirmatio chartarum* was enacted; which in this refpect revived king John's charter, by ordaining that none but the antient aids fhould be taken. But though the fpecies of aids was thus reftrained, yet the quantity

---

[r] Philips's life of Pole. I. 223.

[s] *Erat autem haec inter utrofque officiorum viciffitudo, — ut clientes ad collocandas fenatorum filias de fuo conferrent; in aeris alieni dif-* *folutionem gratuitam pecuniam erogarent; et ab hoftibus in bello captos redimerent.* Paul. Manutius *de fenatu Romano. c.* 1.

[t] *cap.* 12. 15.

of

of each aid remained arbitrary and uncertain. King John's charter indeed ordered, that all aids taken by inferior lords should be
reasonable [u]; and that the aids taken by the king of his tenants
in capite should be settled by parliament [w]. But they were never
completely ascertained and adjusted till the statute Westm. 1.
3 Edw. I. c. 36. which fixed the aids of inferior lords at twenty
shillings, or the supposed twentieth part of every knight's fee,
for making the eldest son a knight, or marrying the eldest daughter; and the same was done with regard to the king's tenants *in
capite* by statute 25 Edw. III. c. 11. The other aid, for ransom
of the lord's person, being not in it's nature capable of any certainty, was therefore never ascertained.

2. RELIEF, *relevium,* was before mentioned as incident to
every feodal tenure, by way of fine or composition with the lord
for taking up the estate, which was lapsed or fallen in by the
death of the last tenant. But, though reliefs had their original
while feuds were only life-estates, yet they continued after feuds
became hereditary; and were therefore looked upon, very justly,
as one of the greatest grievances of tenure: especially when, at
the first, they were merely arbitrary and at the will of the lord;
so that, if he pleased to demand an exorbitant relief, it was in
effect to disinherit the heir [x]. The English ill brooked this consequence of their new adopted policy; and therefore William the
conqueror by his laws [y] *ascertained* the relief, by directing (in imitation of the Danish heriots) that a certain quantity of arms and
habiliments of war should be paid by the earls, barons, and va-
vasours respectively; and, if the latter had no arms, they should
pay 100 *s.* William Rufus broke through this composition, and
again demanded arbitrary uncertain reliefs, as due by the feodal
laws; thereby in effect obliging every heir to new-purchase or *redeem* his land [z]: but his brother Henry I by the charter before-
mentioned restored his father's law; and ordained, that the relief

[u] *cap.* 15.
[w] *Ibid.* 14.
[x] Wright. 99.

[y] C. 22, 23, 24.
[z] 2 Roll. Abr. 514.

to be paid fhould be according to the law fo eftablifhed, and not an arbitrary redemption[a]. But afterwards, when, by an ordinance in 27 Hen. II. called the affife of arms, it was provided that every man's armour fhould defcend to his heir, for defence of the realm; and it thereby became impracticable to pay thefe acknowlegements in arms, according to the laws of the conqueror, the compofition was univerfally accepted of 100s. for every knight's fee; as we find it ever after eftablifhed[b]. But it muft be remembered, that this relief was only then payable, if the heir at the death of his anceftor had attained his full age of one and twenty years.

3. PRIMER *feifin* was a feodal burthen, only incident to the king's tenants *in capite*, and not to thofe who held of inferior or mefne lords. It was a right which the king had, when any of his tenants *in capite* died feifed of a knight's fee, to receive of the heir (provided he were of full age) one whole year's profits of the lands, if they were in immediate poffeffion; and half a year's profits, if the lands were in reverfion expectant on an eftate for life[c]. This feems to be little more than an additional relief: but grounded upon this feodal reafon; that, by the antient law of feuds, immediately upon a death of a vafal the fuperior was intitled to enter and take feifin or poffeffion of the land, by way of protection againft intruders, till the heir appeared to claim it, and receive inveftiture: and, for the time the lord fo held it, he was entitled to take the profits; and, unlefs the heir claimed within a year and day, it was by the ftrict law a forfeiture[d]. This practice however feems not to have long obtained in England, if ever, with regard to tenures under inferior lords; but, as to the king's tenures *in capite*, this *prima feifina* was exprefsly declared, under Henry III and Edward II, to belong to the king by prerogative, in contradiftinction to other lords[e]. And the king was intitled to enter and receive the whole profits of the land, till livery was

[a] " *Hæres non redimet terram fuam, ficut*
" *faciebat tempore fratris mei, fed legitima et*
" *jufta relevatione relevabit eam.*" (*Text.*
Roffens. cap. 34.)

[b] Glanv. *l.* 9. *c.* 4. Litt. §. 112.
[c] Co. Litt. 77.
[d] Feud. *l.* 2. *t.* 24.
[e] Stat. Marlbr. c. 16. 17 Edw. II. c. 3.

                                                    fued;

sued; which suit being commonly within a year and day next after the death of the tenant, therefore the king used to take at an average the *first fruits*, that is to say, one year's profits of the land[f]. And this afterwards gave a handle to the popes, who claimed to be feodal lords of the church, to claim in like manner from every clergyman in England the first year's profits of his benefice, by way of *primitiae*, or first fruits.

4. THESE payments were only due if the heir was of full age; but if he was under the age of twenty one, being a male, or fourteen, being a female[g], the lord was intitled to the *wardship* of the heir, and was called the guardian in chivalry. This wardship consisted in having the custody of the body and lands of such heir, without any account of the profits, till the age of twenty one in males, and sixteen in females. For the law supposed the heir-male unable to perform knight-service till twenty one; but as for the female, she was supposed capable at fourteen to marry, and then her husband might perform the service. The lord therefore had no wardship, if at the death of the ancestor the heir-male was of the full age of twenty one, or the heir-female of fourteen: yet, if she was then under fourteen, and the lord once had her in ward, he might keep her so till sixteen, by virtue of the statute of Westm. 1. 3 Edw. I. c. 22. the two additional years being given by the legislature for no other reason but merely to benefit the lord[h].

THIS wardship, so far as it related to land, though it was not nor could be part of the law of feuds, so long as they were arbitrary, temporary, or for life only; yet, when they became hereditary, and did consequently often descend upon infants, who by reason of their age could neither perform nor stipulate for the services of the feud, does not seem upon feodal principles to have been unreasonable. For the wardship of the land, or custody of the feud, was retained by the lord, that he might out of the profits thereof provide a fit person to supply the infant's services,

[f] Staundf. Prerog. 12.
[g] Litt. §. 103.
[h] *Ibid.*

till]

till he fhould be of age to perform them himfelf. And, if we confider a feud in it's original import, as a ftipend, fee, or reward for actual fervice, it could not be thought hard that the lord fhould withhold the ftipend, fo long as the fervice was fufpended. Though undoubtedly to our Englifh anceftors, where fuch ftipendiary donation was a mere fuppofition or figment, it carried abundance of hardfhip ; and accordingly it was relieved by the charter of Henry I before-mentioned, which took this cuftody from the lord, and ordained that the cuftody, both of the land and the children, fhould belong to the widow or next of kin. But this noble immunity did not continue many years.

THE wardfhip of the body was a confequence of the wardfhip of the land ; for he who enjoyed the infant's eftate was the propereft perfon to educate and maintain him in his infancy : and alfo, in a political view, the lord was moft concerned to give his tenant a fuitable education, in order to qualify him the better to perform thofe fervices which in his maturity he was bound to render.

WHEN the male heir arrived to the age of twenty one, or the heir-female to that of fixteen, they might fue out their livery or *oufterlemain*[i] ; that is, the delivery of their lands out of their guardian's hands. For this they were obliged to pay a fine, namely, half a year's profits of the land ; though this feems exprefily contrary to *magna carta*[k]. However, in confideration of their lands having been fo long in ward, they were excufed all reliefs, and the king's tenants alfo all primer feifins[l]. In order to afcertain the profits that arofe to the crown by thefe fruits of tenure, and to grant the heir his livery, the itinerant juftices, or juftices in eyre, had it formerly in charge to make inquifition concerning them by a jury of the county[m], commonly called an *inquifitio poft mortem* ; which was inftituted to enquire (at the death of any man of fortune) the value of his eftate, the tenure by which it

i Co. Litt. 77.   l Co. Litt. 77.
k 9 Hen. III. c. 3.   m Hoveden. *fub Ric. I.*

was holden, and who, and of what age, his heir was; thereby to ascertain the relief and value of the primer seisin, or the wardship and livery accruing to the king thereupon. A manner of proceeding that came in process of time to be greatly abused, and at length an intolerable grievance; it being one of the principal accusations against Empson and Dudley, the wicked engines of Henry VII, that by colour of false inquisitions they compelled many persons to sue out livery from the crown, who by no means were tenants thereunto [n]. And, afterwards, a court of wards and liveries was erected [o], for conducting the same enquiries in a more solemn and legal manner.

WHEN the heir thus came of full age, provided he held a knight's fee, he was to receive the order of knighthood, and was compellable to take it upon him, or else pay a fine to the king. For, in those heroical times, no person was qualified for deeds of arms and chivalry who had not received this order, which was conferred with much preparation and solemnity. We may plainly discover the footsteps of a similar custom in what Tacitus relates of the Germans, who in order to qualify their young men to bear arms, presented them in a full assembly with a shield and lance; which ceremony, as was formerly hinted [p], is supposed to have been the original of the feodal knighthood [q]. This prerogative, of compelling the vasals to be knighted, or to pay a fine, was expressly recognized in parliament, by the statute *de militibus*, 1 Edw. II; was exerted as an expedient of raising money by many of our best princes, particularly by Edward VI and queen Elizabeth; but yet was the occasion of heavy murmurs when exerted by Charles I: among whose many misfortunes it was, that neither himself nor his people seemed able to distinguish between the arbitrary stretch, and the legal exertion, of prerogative. However,

[n] 4 Inst. 198.
[o] Stat. 32 Hen. VIII. c. 46.
[p] Vol. I. pag. 392.
[q] " *In ipso concilio vel principum aliquis,* " *vel pater, vel propinquus, scuto frameaque*

" *juvenem ornant. Haec apud illos toga, hic* " *primus juventae honos: ante hoc domus pars* " *videntur; mox reipublicae* " *de mor. Germ. cap.* 13.

among

among the other conceſſions made by that unhappy prince, before the fatal recourſe to arms, he agreed to diveſt himſelf of this un-doubted flower of his crown, and it was accordingly aboliſhed by ſtatute 16 Car. I. c. 20.

5. BUT, before they came of age, there was ſtill another piece of authority, which the guardian was at liberty to exer-ciſe over his infant wards; I mean the right of *marriage, (ma-ritagium,* as contradiſtinguiſhed from *matrimonium)* which in it's feodal ſenſe ſignifies the power, which the lord or guardian in chivalry had of diſpoſing of his infant ward in matrimony. For, while the infant was in ward, the guardian had the power of tendering him or her a ſuitable match, without *diſparage-ment,* or inequality: which if the infants refuſed, they for-feited the value of the marriage, *valorem maritagii,* to their guardian [r]; that is, ſo much as a jury would aſſeſs, or any one would *bona fide* give to the guardian for ſuch an alliance [s]: and, if the infants married themſelves without the guardian's con-ſent, they forfeited double the value, *duplicem valorem maritagii* [t]. This ſeems to have been one of the greateſt hardſhips of our an-tient tenures. There are indeed ſubſtantial reaſons why the lord ſhould have the *reſtraint* and *controll* of the ward's marriage, eſ-pecially of his female ward; becauſe of their tender years, and the danger of ſuch female ward's intermarrying with the lord's enemy [u]. But no tolerable pretence could be aſſigned why the lord ſhould have the *ſale,* or *value,* of the marriage. Nor indeed is this claim of ſtrictly feodal original; the moſt probable account of it ſeeming to be this: that by the cuſtom of Normandy the lord's conſent was neceſſary to the marriage of his *female*-wards [w]; which was introduced into England, together with the reſt of the Nor-man doctrine of feuds: and it is likely that the lords uſually took money for ſuch their conſent, ſince in the often-cited charter of Henry the firſt, he engages for the future to take nothing for *his* conſent; which alſo he promiſes in general to give, provided ſuch

[r] Litt. §. 110.
[s] Stat. Mert. c.6. Co. Litt. 82.
[t] Litt. §. 110.
[u] Bract. *l.* 2. *c.* 37. §. 6.
[w] Gr. Cuſt. 55.

female

female ward were not married to his enemy. But this, among other beneficial parts of that charter, being difregarded, and guardians ftill continuing to difpofe of their wards in a very arbitrary unequal manner, it was provided by king John's great charter, that heirs fhould be married without difparagement, the next of kin having previous notice of the contract[x]; or, as it was expreffed in the firft draught of that charter, *ita maritentur ne difparagentur, et per confilium propinquorum de confanguinitate fua*[y]. But thefe claufes in behalf of the relations were omitted in the charter of Henry III; wherein[z] the claufe ftands merely thus, "*haeredes maritentur abfque difparagatione;*" meaning certainly, by *haeredes*, heirs female, as there are no traces before this to be found of the lord's claiming the marriage of heirs male; and as Glanvil[a] expreffly confines it to heirs female. But the king and his great lords thenceforward took a handle from the ambiguity of this expreffion to claim them both, *five fit mafculus five foemina*, as Bracton more than once expreffes it[b]; and alfo, as nothing but difparagement was reftrained by *magna carta*, they thought themfelves at liberty to make all other advantages that they could[c]. And afterwards this right, of felling the ward in marriage or elfe receiving the price or value of it, was expreffly declared by the ftatute of Merton[d]; which is the firft direct mention of it that I have met with, in our own or in any other law.

6. ANOTHER attendant or confequence of tenure by knight-fervice was that of *fines* due to the lord for every *alienation*, whenever the tenant had occafion to make over his land to another. This depended on the nature of the feodal connexion; it not being reafonable nor allowed, as we have before feen, that a feudatory fhould transfer his lord's gift to another, and fubftitute a new tenant to do the fervice in his own ftead, without the confent of the lord: and, as the feodal obligation was confidered as

[x] *cap. 6. edit. Oxon.*
[y] *cap. 3. ibid.*
[z] *cap. 6.*
[a] *l. 9. c. 9. & 12. & l. 9. c. 4.*
[b] *l. 2. c. 38. §. 1.*
[c] Wright. 97.
[d] 20 Hen. III. c. 6.

reciprocal,

reciprocal, the lord alſo could not alienate his ſeignory without the conſent of his tenant, which conſent of his was called an *attornment*. This reſtraint upon the lords ſoon wore away; that upon the tenants continued longer. For, when every thing came in proceſs of time to be bought and ſold, the lords would not grant a licence to their tenants to aliene, without a fine being paid; apprehending that, if it was reaſonable for the heir to pay a fine or relief on the renovation of his paternal eſtate, it was much more reaſonable that a ſtranger ſhould make the ſame acknowlegement on his admiſſion to a newly purchaſed feud. With us in England, theſe fines ſeem only to have been exacted from the king's tenants *in capite*, who were never able to aliene without a licence: but, as to common perſons, they were at liberty, by *magna carta*ᵉ, and the ſtatute of *quia emptores*ᶠ, (if not earlier) to aliene the whole of their eſtate, to be holden of the ſame lord, as they themſelves held it of before. But the king's tenants *in capite*, not being included under the general words of theſe ſtatutes, could not aliene without a licence: for if they did, it was in antient ſtrictneſs an abſolute forfeiture of the landsᵍ; though ſome have imagined otherwiſe. But this ſeverity was mitigated by the ſtatute 1 Edw. III. c. 12. which ordained, that in ſuch caſe the lands ſhould not be forfeited, but a reaſonable fine be paid to the king. Upon which ſtatute it was ſettled, that one third of the yearly value ſhould be paid for a licence of alienation; but, if the tenant preſumed to aliene without a licence, a full year's value ſhould be paidʰ.

7. THE laſt conſequence of tenure in chivalry was eſcheat; which is the determination of the tenure, or diſſolution of the mutual bond between the lord and tenant, from the extinction of the blood of the latter by either natural or civil means: if he died without heirs of his blood, or if his blood was corrupted and ſtained by commiſſion of treaſon or felony; whereby every inheritable quality was intirely blotted out and aboliſhed. In ſuch

ᵉ *cap.* 32.   ᵍ 2 Inſt. 66.
ᶠ 18 Edw. I. c. 1.   ʰ *Ibid.* 67.

cafes the land efcheated, or fell back, to the lord of the fee[i] ;
that is, the tenure was determined by breach of the original
condition, expreffed or implied in the feodal donation.   In the
one cafe, there were no heirs fubfifting of the blood of the firft
feudatory or purchafer, to which heirs alone the grant of the
feud extended : in the other, the tenant, by perpetrating an
atrocious crime, fhewed that he was no longer to be trufted as a
vafal, having forgotten his duty as a fubject ; and therefore forfeited his feud, which he held under the implied condition that
he fhould not be a traitor or a felon.   The confequence of which
in both cafes was, that the gift, being determined, refulted back
to the lord who gave it[k].

THESE were the principal qualities, fruits, and confequences
of the tenure by knight-fervice : a tenure, by which the greateft
part of the lands in this kingdom were holden, and that principally of the king *in capite,* till the middle of the laft century ;
and which was created, as fir Edward Coke expreffly teftifies[l],
for a military purpofe ; *viz.* for defence of the realm by the
king's own principal fubjects, which was judged to be much better than to truft to hirelings or foreigners.   The defcription here
given is that of knight-fervice proper ; which was to attend the
king in his wars.   There were alfo fome other fpecies of knight-
fervice ; fo called, though improperly, becaufe the fervice or
render was of a free and honourable nature, and equally uncertain as to the time of rendering as that of knight-fervice proper,
and becaufe they were attended with fimilar fruits and confequences.   Such was the tenure by *grand ferjeanty, per magnum
fervitium,* whereby the tenant was bound, inftead of ferving the
king *generally* in his wars, to do fome fpecial honorary fervice to
the king in perfon; as to carry his banner, his fword, or the like ;
or to be his butler, champion, or other officer at his coronation[m].
It was in moft other refpects like knight-fervice[n] ; only he was

[i] Co. Litt. 13.
[k] *Feud. l. 2. t.* 86.
[l] 4 Inft. 192.

[m] Litt. §. 153.
[n] *Ibid.* §. 158.

not bound to pay aid[o], or escuage[p]; and, when tenant by knight-service paid five pounds for a relief on every knight's fee, tenant by grand serjeanty paid one year's value of his land, were it much or little[q]. Tenure by *cornage*, which was, to wind a horn when the Scots or other enemies entered the land, in order to warn the king's subjects, was (like other services of the same nature) a species of grand serjeanty[r].

THESE services, both of chivalry and grand serjeanty, were all personal, and uncertain as to their quantity or duration. But, the personal attendance in knight-service growing troublesome and inconvenient in many respects, the tenants found means of compounding for it; by first sending others in their stead, and in process of time making a pecuniary satisfaction to the lords in lieu of it. This pecuniary satisfaction at last came to be levied by assessments, at so much for every knight's fee; and therefore this kind of tenure was called *scutagium* in Latin, or *servitium scuti*; *scutum* being then a well-known denomination of money: and, in like manner it was called, in our Norman French, *escuage*; being indeed a pecuniary, instead of a military, service. The first time this appears to have been taken was in the 5 Hen. II. on account of his expedition to Toulouse; but it soon came to be so universal, that personal attendance fell quite into disuse. Hence we find in our antient histories that, from this period, when our kings went to war, they levied scutages on their tenants, that is, on all the landholders of the kingdom, to defray their expenses, and to hire troops: and these assessments, in the time of Henry II, seem to have been made arbitrarily and at the king's pleasure. Which prerogative being greatly abused by his successors, it became matter of national clamour, and king John was obliged to consent, by his *magna carta*, that no scutage should be imposed without consent of parliament[s]. But this clause was omitted in his son Henry III's charter; where we only find[t], that

[o] 2 Inst. 233.
[p] Litt. §. 158.
[q] Litt. §. 154.
[r] *Ibid.* §. 156.
[s] *Nullum scutagium ponatur in regno nostro, nisi per commune consilium regni nostri. cap.*12.
[t] *cap.* 37.

scutages

scutages or escuage should be taken as they were used to be taken in the time of Henry II; that is, in a reasonable and moderate manner. Yet afterwards by statute 25 Edw. I. c. 5 & 6. and many subsequent statutes [u] it was enacted, that the king should take no aids or tasks but by the common assent of the realm. Hence it is held in our old books, that escuage or scutage could not be levied but by consent of parliament [w]; such scutages being indeed the groundwork of all succeeding subsidies, and the land-tax of later times.

SINCE therefore escuage differed from knight-service in nothing, but as a compensation differs from actual service, knight-service is frequently confounded with it. And thus Littleton [x] must be understood, when he tells us, that tenant by homage, fealty, and escuage was tenant by knight-service : that is, that this tenure (being subservient to the military policy of the nation) was respected [y] as a tenure in chivalry [z]. But as the actual service was uncertain, and depended upon emergences, so it was necessary that this pecuniary compensation should be equally uncertain, and depend on the assessments of the legislature suited to those emergences. For had the escuage been a settled invariable sum, payable at certain times, it had been neither more nor less than a mere pecuniary rent; and the tenure, instead of knight-service, would have then been of another kind, called socage [a], of which we shall speak in the next chapter.

FOR the present, I have only to observe, that by the degenerating of knight-service, or personal military duty, into escuage, or pecuniary assessments, all the advantages (either promised or real) of the feodal constitution were destroyed, and nothing but the hardships remained. Instead of forming a national militia composed of barons, knights, and gentlemen, bound by their interest, their honour, and their oaths, to defend their king and

[u] See Vol. I. pag. 136.
[w] Old Ten. *tit. Escuage.*
[x] §. 103.
[y] Wright. 122.

[z] *Pro feodo. militari reputatur.* Flet. *l.* 2. *c.* 14. §. 7.
[a] Litt. §. 97. 120.

K 2

country, the whole of this fyftem of tenures now tended to nothing elfe, but a wretched means of raifing money to pay an army of occafional mercenaries. In the mean time the families of
all our nobility and gentry groaned-under the intolerable burthens,
which (in confequence of the fiction adopted after the conqueft)
were introduced and laid upon them by the fubtlety and fineffe
of the Norman lawyers. For, befides the fcutages they were
liable to in defect of perfonal attendance, which however were
affeffed by themfelves in parliament, they might be called upon
by the king or lord paramount for *aids,* whenever his eldeft fon
was to be knighted, or his eldeft daughter married; not to for-
get the ranfom of his own perfon. The heir, on the death of
his anceftor, if of full age, was plundered of the firft emoluments
arifing from his inheritance, by way of *relief* and *primer feifin;*
and, if under age, of the whole of his eftate during infancy.
And then, as fir Thomas Smith [b] very feelingly complains, "when
" he came to his own, after he was out of *wardfhip,* his woods
" decayed, houfes fallen down, ftock wafted and gone, lands let
" forth and ploughed to be barren," to make amends he was yet
to pay half a year's profits as a fine for fuing out his *livery;* and
alfo the price or value of his *marriage,* if he refufed fuch wife as
his lord and guardian had bartered for, and impofed upon him;
or twice that value, if he married another woman. Add to this,
the untimely and expenfive honour of *knighthood,* to make his
poverty more completely fplendid. And when by thefe deductions his fortune was fo fhattered and ruined, that perhaps he was
obliged to fell his patrimony, he had not even that poor privilege
allowed him, without paying an exorbitant fine for a *licence* of
alienation.

A SLAVERY fo complicated, and fo extenfive as this, called
aloud for a remedy in a nation that boafted of her freedom. Pal-
liatives were from time to time applied by fucceffive acts of parliament, which affwaged fome temporary grievances. Till at
length the humanity of king James I confented [c] for a proper

equivalent to abolish them all; though the plan then proceeded not to effect: in like manner as he had formed a scheme, and began to put it in execution, for removing the feodal grievance of heretable jurisdictions in Scotland [d], which has since been pursued and effected by the statute 20 Geo. II. c. 43. [e] King James's plan for exchanging our military tenures seems to have been nearly the same as that which has been since pursued; only with this difference, that, by way of compensation for the loss which the crown and other lords would sustain, an annual feefarm rent should be settled and inseparably annexed to the crown, and assured to the inferior lords, payable out of every knight's fee within their respective signories. An expedient, seemingly much better than the hereditary excise, which was afterwards made the principal equivalent for these concessions. For at length the military tenures, with all their heavy appendages, were destroyed at one blow by the statute 12 Car. II. c. 24. which enacts, " that the court of " wards and liveries, and all wardships, liveries, primer seisins, " and ousterlemains, values and forfeitures of marriages, by rea- " son of any tenure of the king or others, be totally taken away. " And that all fines for alienations, tenures by homage, knights- " service, and escuage, and also aids for marrying the daughter " or knighting the son, and all tenures of the king *in capite*, be " likewise taken away. And that all sorts of tenures, held of the " king or others, be turned into free and common socage; save " only tenures in frankalmoign, copyholds, and the honorary ser- " vices (without the slavish part) of grand serjeanty." A statute, which was a greater acquisition to the civil property of this kingdom than even *magna carta* itself: since that only pruned the luxuriances that had grown out of the military tenures, and thereby preserved them in vigour; but the statute of king Charles extirpated the whole, and demolished both root and branches.

---

[d] Dalrymp of feuds. 292.

[e] By another statute of the same year (20 Geo. II. c. 50.) the tenure of *wardhold-*

ing (equivalent to the knight-service of England) is for ever abolished in Scotland.

CHAPTER THE SIXTH.

OF THE MODERN ENGLISH TENURES.

ALTHOUGH, by the means that were mentioned in
the preceding chapter, the oppreffive or military part of
the feodal conftitution was happily done away, yet we are not to
imagine that the conftitution itfelf was utterly laid afide, and a
new one introduced in it's room ; fince by the ftatute 12 Car. II.
the tenures of focage and frankalmoign, the honorary fervices of
grand ferjeanty, and the tenure by copy of court roll were referved ; nay all tenures in general, except frankalmoign, grand
ferjeanty, and copyhold, were reduced to one general fpecies of
tenure, then well known and fubfifting, called free and common
focage. And this, being fprung from the fame feodal original as
the reft, demonftrates the neceffity of fully contemplating that
antient fyftem ; fince it is that alone, to which we can recur to
explain any feeming, or real, difficulties, that may arife in our
prefent mode of tenure.

THE military tenure, or that by knight-fervice, confifted of
what were reputed the moft free and honourable fervices ; but
which in their nature were unavoidably uncertain in refpect to the
time of their performance. The fecond fpecies of tenure, or
free-focage, confifted alfo of free and honourable fervices ; but
fuch as were liquidated and reduced to an abfolute certainty. And
this tenure not only fubfifts to this day, but has in a manner ab-
forbed and fwallowed up (fince the ftatute of Charles the fecond)
almoft

almoſt every other ſpecies of tenure. And to this we are next to proceed.

II. SOCAGE, in it's moſt general and extenſive ſignification, ſeems to denote a tenure by any certain and determinate ſervice. And in this ſenſe it is by our antient writers conſtantly put in op-poſition to chivalry, or knight-ſervice, where the render was pre-carious and uncertain. Thus Braɕton[a]; if a man holds by a rent in money, without any eſcuage or ſerjeanty, "*id tenementum dici* "*poteſt ſocagium:*" but if you add thereto any royal ſervice, or eſcuage to any, the ſmalleſt, amount, "*illud dici poterit feodum* "*militare.*" So too the author of Fleta[b]; "*ex donationibus ſer-* "*vitia militaria vel magnae ſerjantiae non continentibus, oritur no-* "*bis quoddam nomen generale, quod eſt ſocagium.*" Littleton alſo[c] defines it to be, where the tenant holds his tenement of the lord by any *certain* ſervice, in lieu of all other ſervices; ſo that they be not ſervices of chivalry, or knight-ſervice. And therefore af-terwards[d] he tells us, that whatſoever is not tenure in chivalry is tenure in ſocage: in like manner as it is defined by Finch[e], a tenure to be done out of war. The ſervice muſt therefore be cer-tain, in order to denominate it ſocage; as to hold by fealty and 20 *s.* rent; or, by homage, fealty, and 20 *s.* rent; or, by homage and fealty without rent; or, by fealty and certain corporal ſer-vice, as ploughing the lord's land for three days; or, by fealty only without any other ſervice: for all theſe are tenures in ſocage[f].

BUT ſocage, as was hinted in the laſt chapter, is of two ſorts: *free*-ſocage, where the ſervices are not only certain, but honour-able; and *villein*-ſocage, where the ſervices, though certain, are of a baſer nature. Such as hold by the former tenure are called in Glanvil[g], and other ſubſequent authors, by the name of *liberi ſokemanni,* or tenants in free-ſocage. Of this tenure we are firſt

[a] *l.* 2. *c.* 16. §. 9.
[b] *l.* 3. *c.* 14. § 9.
[c] §. 117.
[d] §. 118.
[e] L. 147.
[f] Litt. §. 117, 118, 119.
[g] *l.* 3. *c.* 7.

to fpeak ; and this, both in the nature of it's fervice, and the fruits and confequences appertaining thereto, was always by much the moft free and independent fpecies of any. And therefore I cannot but affent to Mr Somner's etymology of the word [h]; who derives it from the Saxon appellation, *foc*, which fignifies liberty or privilege, and, being joined to a ufual termination, is called *focage*, in Latin *focagium*; fignifying thereby a free or privileged tenure [i]. This etymology feems to be much more juft than that of our common lawyers in general, who derive it from *foca*, an old Latin word denoting (as they tell us) a plough : for that in antient time this focage tenure confifted in nothing elfe but fervices of hufbandry, which the tenant was bound to do to his lord, as to plough, fow, or reap for him ; but that, in procefs of time, this fervice was changed into an annual rent by confent of all parties, and that, in memory of it's original, it ftill retains the name of focage or plough-fervice [k]. But this by no means agrees with what Littleton himfelf tells us [l], that to hold by fealty only, without paying any rent, is tenure in focage ; for here is plainly no commutation for plough-fervice. Befides, even fervices, con- feffedly of a military nature and original, (as efcuage itfelf, which while it remained uncertain was equivalent to knight-fervice) the inftant they were reduced to a certainty changed both their name and nature, and were called focage [m]. It was the certainty there- fore that denominated it a focage tenure ; and nothing fure could be a greater liberty or privilege, than to have the fervice afcer- tained, and not left to the arbitrary calls of the lord, as in the te- nures of chivalry. Wherefore alfo Britton, who defcribes focage tenure under the name of *fraunke ferme* [n], tells us, that they are " lands and tenements, whereof the nature of the fee is changed " by feoffment *out of chivalry* for *certain* yearly fervices, and in " refpect whereof neither homage, ward, marriage, nor relief can " be demanded." Which leads us alfo to another obfervation,

---

[h] Gavelk. 138.

[i] In like manner Skene in his expofition of the Scots' law, title *focage*, tells us that it is "anè kind of holding of lands, quhen "ony man is infeft *freely*," &c.

[k] Litt. §. 119.

[l] §. 118.

[m] Litt. §. 98. 120.

[n] c. 65.

that,

that, if focage tenures were of fuch bafe and fervile original, it
is hard to account for the very great immunities which the tenants of them always enjoyed ; fo highly fuperior to thofe of the
tenants by chivalry, that it was thought, in the reigns of both
Edward I and Charles II, a point of the utmoft importance and
value to the tenants, to reduce the tenure by knight-fervice to
fraunk ferme or tenure by focage. We may therefore, I think,
fairly conclude in favour of Somner's etymology, and the liberal
extraction of the tenure in free focage, againft the authority even
of Littleton himfelf.

TAKING this then to be the meaning of the word, it feems
probable that the focage tenures were the relicks of Saxon liberty,
retained by fuch perfons, as had neither forfeited them to the
king, nor been obliged to exchange their tenure for the more
honourable, as it was called, but at the fame time more burthenfome, tenure of knight-fervice. This is peculiarly remarkable in
the tenure which prevails in Kent, called gavelkind, which is
generally acknowleged to be a fpecies of focage tenure°; the prefervation whereof inviolate from the innovations of the Norman
conqueror is a fact univerfally known. And thofe who thus preferved their liberties were faid to hold in *free* and *common* focage.

AS therefore the grand criterion and diftinguifhing mark of
this fpecies of tenure are the having it's renders or fervices afcertained, it will include under it all other methods of holding free
lands by certain and invariable rents and duties : and, in particular, *petit ferjeanty,* tenure in *burgage,* and *gavelkind.*

WE may remember, that by the ftatute 12 Car. II. grand ferjeanty is not itfelf totally abolifhed, but only the flavifh appendages belonging to it ; for the honorary fervices (fuch as carrying
the king's fword or banner, officiating as his butler, carver, &c,
at the coronation) are ftill referved. Now *petit ferjeanty* bears a
great refemblance to grand ferjeanty ; for as the one is a perfonal

° Wright. 211.

service, so the other is a rent or render, both tending to some purpose relative to the king's person. Petit serjeanty, as defined by Littleton[p], consists in holding lands of the king by the service of rendering to him annually some small implement of war, as a bow, a sword, a lance, an arrow, or the like. This, he says[q], is but socage in effect; for it is no personal service, but a certain rent: and, we may add, it is clearly no predial service, or service of the plough, but in all respects *liberum et commune socagium;* only, being held of the king, it is by way of eminence dignified with the title of *parvum servitium regis*, or petit serjeanty. And *magna carta* respects it in this light, when it enacts[r], that no wardship of the lands or body shall be claimed by the king in virtue of a tenure by petit serjeanty.

TENURE in *burgage* is described by Glanvil[s], and is expressly said by Littleton[t], to be but tenure in socage; and it is where the king or other person is lord of an antient borough, in which the tenements are held by a rent certain[u]. It is indeed only a kind of town socage; as common socage, by which other lands are holden, is usually of a rural nature. A borough, as we have formerly seen, is distinguished from other towns by the right of sending members to parliament; and, where the right of election is by burgage tenure, that alone is a proof of the antiquity of the borough. Tenure in burgage therefore, or burgage tenure, is where houses, or lands which were formerly the scite of houses, in an antient borough, are held of some lord in common socage, by a certain established rent. And these seem to have withstood the shock of the Norman encroachments principally on account of their insignificancy, which made it not worth while to compel them to an alteration of tenure; as an hundred of them put together would scarce have amounted to a knight's fee. Besides, the owners of them, being chiefly artificers and persons engaged in trade, could not with any tolerable propriety be put on such a

[p] §. 159.
[q] §. 160.
[r] cap. 27.

[s] *lib.* 7. *cap.* 3.
[t] §. 162.
[u] Litt. §. 162, 163.

military

military eſtabliſhment, as the tenure in chivalry was. And here also we have again an inſtance, where a tenure is confeſſedly in ſocage, and yet is impoſſible ever to have been held by plough-ſervice; ſince the tenants muſt have been citizens or burghers, the ſituation frequently a walled town, the tenement a ſingle houſe; ſo that none of the owners was probably maſter of a plough, or was able to uſe one, if he had it. The free ſocage therefore, in which theſe tenements are held, ſeems to be plainly a remnant of Saxon liberty; which may alſo account for the great variety of cuſtoms, affecting theſe tenements ſo held in antient burgage: the principal and moſt remarkable of which is that called *Borough-Engliſh*, ſo named in contradiſtinction as it were to the Norman cuſtoms, and which is taken notice of by Glanvil [w], and by Littleton [x]; *viz.* that the youngeſt ſon, and not the eldeſt, ſucceeds to the burgage tenement on the death of his father. For which Littleton [y] gives this reaſon; becauſe the youngeſt ſon, by reaſon of his tender age, is not ſo capable as the reſt of his brethren to help himſelf. Other authors [z] have indeed given a much ſtranger reaſon for this cuſtom, as if the lord of the fee had antiently a right to break the ſeventh commandment with his tenant's wife on her wedding-night; and that therefore the tene-ment deſcended not to the eldeſt, but the youngeſt, ſon; who was more certainly the offspring of the tenant. But I cannot learn that ever this cuſtom prevailed in England, though it cer-tainly did in Scotland, (under the name of *mercheta* or *marcheta*) till aboliſhed by Malcolm III [a]. And perhaps a more rational ac-count than either may be fetched (though at a ſufficient diſtance) from the practice of the Tartars; among whom, according to father Duhalde, this cuſtom of deſcent to the youngeſt ſon alſo prevails. That nation is compoſed totally of ſhepherds and herdſ-men; and the elder ſons, as ſoon as they are capable of leading a paſtoral life, migrate from their father with a certain allotment of cattle; and go to ſeek a new habitation. The youngeſt ſon

[w] *ubi ſupra.*
[x] §. 165.
[y] §. 211.

[z] 3 Mod. Pref.
[a] Seld. tit. of hon. z. 1. 47. *Reg. Mag.* *l.* 4. *c.* 31.

therefore,

therefore, who continues lateſt with the father, is naturally the heir of his houſe, the reſt being already provided for. And thus we find that, among many other northern nations, it was the cuſtom for all the ſons but one to migrate from the father, which one became his heir [b]. So that poſſibly this cuſtom, wherever it prevails, may be the remnant of that paſtoral ſtate of our Britiſh and German anceſtors, which Caeſar and Tacitus deſcribe. Other ſpecial cuſtoms there are in burgage tenures; as that the wife ſhall be endowed of *all* her huſband's tenements [c], and not of the third part only, as at the common law: and that a man might diſpoſe of his tenements by will [d], which, in general, was not permitted after the conqueſt till the reign of Henry the eighth; though in the Saxon times it was allowable [e]. A pregnant proof that theſe liberties of ſocage tenure were fragments of Saxon liberty.

THE nature of the tenure in *gavelkind* affords us a ſtill ſtronger argument. It is univerſally known what ſtruggles the Kentiſhmen made to preſerve their antient liberties; and with how much ſucceſs thoſe ſtruggles were attended. And as it is principally here that we meet with the cuſtom of gavelkind, (though it was and is to be found in ſome other parts of the kingdom [f]) we may fairly conclude that this was a part of thoſe liberties; agreeably to Mr Selden's opinion, that gavelkind before the Norman conqueſt was the general cuſtom of the realm [g]. The diſtinguiſhing properties of this tenure are various: ſome of the principal are theſe; 1. The tenant is of age ſufficient to aliene his eſtate by feoffment at the age of fifteen [h]. 2. The eſtate does not eſcheat in caſe of an attainder and execution for felony; their maxim being, "the "father to the bough, the ſon to the plough [i]." 3. In moſt places

[b] *Pater cunctos filios adultos a ſe pellebat, praeter unum quem heredem ſui juris relinquebat. (Walſingh. Upodigm. Neuſtr. c. 1.)*
[c] Litt. §. 166.
[d] §. 167.
[e] Wright. 172.
[f] Stat. 32 Hen. VIII. c. 29. Kitch. of courts, 200.

[g] *In toto regno, ante ducis adventum, frequens et uſitata fuit: poſtea caeteris adempta, ſed privatis quorundam locorum conſuetudinibus alibi poſtea regerminans: Cantianis ſolum integra et inviolata remanſit. (Analect. l.2. c.7.)*
[h] Lamb. Peramb. 614.
[i] Lamb. 634.

he

he had a power of devising lands by will, before the statute for
that purpose was made [k]. 4. The lands descend, not to the eldest,
youngest, or any one son only, but to all the sons together [l];
which was indeed antiently the most usual course of descent all
over England [m], though in particular places particular customs
prevailed. These, among other properties, distinguished this tenure in a most remarkable manner : and yet it is held to be only
a species of a socage tenure, modified by the custom of the country ; being holden by suit of court and fealty, which is a service
in it's nature certain [n]. Wherefore, by a charter of king John [o],
Hubert arch-bishop of Canterbury was authorized to *exchange*
the gavelkind tenures holden of the see of Canterbury into tenures by knight-service ; and by statute 31 Hen. VIII. c. 3. for
disgavelling the lands of divers lords and gentlemen in the county
of Kent, they are directed to be descendible for the future *like other
lands, which were never holden by service of socage.* Now the immunities which the tenants in gavelkind enjoyed were such, as
we cannot conceive should be conferred upon mere ploughmen,
or peasants : from all which I think it sufficiently clear, that tenures in free socage are in general of a nobler original than is af-
signed by Littleton, and after him by the bulk of our common
lawyers.

H A V I N G thus distributed and distinguished the several species
of tenure in free socage, I proceed next to shew that this also
partakes very strongly of the feodal nature. Which may probably
arise from it's antient Saxon original ; since (as was before observed [p]) feuds were not unknown among the Saxons, though they
did not form a part of their military policy, nor were drawn out
into such arbitrary consequences as among the Normans. It seems
therefore reasonable to imagine, that socage tenure existed in
much the same state before the conquest as after ; that in Kent it
was preserved with a high hand, as our histories inform us it was ;

[k] F. N. B. 198. Cro. Car. 561.   [n] Wright. 211.
[l] Litt. §. 210.   [o] Spelm. *cod vet. leg.* 355.
[m] Glanv. *l. 7. c. 3*   [p] pag. 48.

and I

and that the rest of the socage tenures dispersed through England escaped the general fate of other property, partly out of favour and affection to their particular owners, and partly from their own insignificancy; since I do not apprehend the number of socage tenures soon after the conquest to have been very considerable, nor their value by any means large; till by successive charters of enfranchisement granted to the tenants, which are particularly mentioned by Britton [q], their number and value began to swell so far, as to make a distinct, and justly envied, part of our English system of tenures.

HOWEVER this may be, the tokens of their feodal original will evidently appear from a short comparison of the incidents and consequences of socage tenure with those of tenure in chivalry; remarking their agreement or difference as we go along.

1. IN the first place, then, both were held of superior lords; of the king as lord paramount, and sometimes of a subject or mesne lord between the king and the tenant.

2. BOTH were subject to the feodal return, render, rent, or service, of some sort or other, which arose from a supposition of an original grant from the lord to the tenant. In the military tenure, or more proper feud, this was from it's nature uncertain; in socage, which was a feud of the improper kind, it was certain, fixed, and determinate, (though perhaps nothing more than bare fealty) and so continues to this day.

3. BOTH were, from their constitution, universally subject (over and above all other renders) to the oath of fealty, or mutual bond of obligation between the lord and tenant [r]. Which oath of fealty usually draws after it suit to the lord's court. And this oath every lord, of whom tenements are holden at this day, may and ought to call upon his tenants to take in his court baron; if it be only for the reason given by Littleton [s], that if it be ne-

[q] c. 66.
[r] Litt. §. 117. 131.
[s] §. 130.

glected,

glected, it will by long continuance of time grow out of memory (as doubtlefs it frequently has) whether the land be holden of the lord or not; and fo he may lofe his feignory, and the profit which may accrue to him by efcheats and other contingences [t].

4. THE tenure in focage was fubject, of common right, to aids for knighting the fon and marrying the eldeft daughter [u]: which were fixed by the ftatute Weftm. 1. c. 36. at 20 *s.* for every 20 *l. per annum* fo held; as in knight-fervice. Thefe aids, as in tenure by chivalry, were originally mere benevolences, though afterwards claimed as matter of right; but were all abolifhed by the ftatute 12 Car. II.

5. RELIEF is due upon focage tenure, as well as upon tenure in chivalry: but the manner of taking it is very different. The relief on a knight's fee was 5 *l.* or one quarter of the fuppofed value of the land; but a focage relief is one year's rent or render, payable by the tenant to the lord, be the fame either great or fmall [w]: and therefore Bracton [x] will not allow this to be properly a relief, but *quaedam praeftatio loco relevii in recognitionem domini.* So too the ftatute 28 Edw. I. c. 1. declares, that a free fokeman fhall give *no relief,* but fhall double his rent after the death of his anceftor, according to that which he hath ufed to pay his lord, and fhall not be grieved above meafure. Reliefs in knight-fervice were only payable, if the heir at the death of his anceftor was of full age: but in focage they were due, even though the heir was under age, becaufe the lord has no wardfhip over him [y]. The ftatute of Charles II referves the reliefs incident to focage tenures; and therefore, wherever lands in fee fimple are holden by a rent, relief is ftill due of common right upon the death of the tenant [z].

---

[t] *Eo maxime praeftandum eft, ne dubium reddatur jus domini et vetuftate temporis obfcuretur. (Corvin. jus feud. l. 2. t. 7.)*
[u] Co. Litt. 91.
[w] Litt. §. 126.
[x] *l.* 2. *c.* 37. §. 8.
[y] Litt. §. 127.
[z] 3 Lev. 145.

6. PRIMER

6. PRIMER feifin was incident to the king's focage tenants *in capite*, as well as to thofe by knight-fervice [a]. But tenancy *in capite* as well as primer feifins, are alfo, among the other feodal burthens, intirely abolifhed by the ftatute.

7. WARDSHIP is alfo incident to tenure in focage; but of a nature very different from that incident to knight-fervice. For if the inheritance defcend to an infant under fourteen, the wardfhip of him fhall not belong to the lord of the fee; becaufe, in this tenure no military or other perfonal fervice being required, there is no occafion for the lord to take the profits, in order to provide a proper fubftitute for his infant tenant: but his neareft relation (to whom the inheritance cannot defcend) fhall be his guardian in focage, and have the cuftody of his land and body till he arrives at the age of fourteen. The guardian muft be fuch a one, to whom the inheritance by no poffibility can defcend; as was fully explained, together with the reafons for it, in the former book of thefe commentaries [b]. At fourteen this wardfhip in focage ceafes, and the heir may ouft the guardian, and call him to account for the rents and profits [c]: for at this age the law fuppofes him capable of chufing a guardian for himfelf. It was in this particular, of wardfhip, as alfo in that of marriage, and in the certainty of the render or fervice, that the focage tenures had fo much the advantage of the military ones. But as the wardfhip ceafed at fourteen, there was this difadvantage attending it; that young heirs, being left at fo tender an age to chufe their own guardians till twenty one, they might make an improvident choice. Therefore, when almoft all the lands of the kingdom were turned into focage tenures, the fame ftatute 12 Car. II. c. 24. enacted, that it fhould be in the power of any father by will to appoint a guardian, till his child fhould attain the age of twenty one. And, if no fuch appointment be made, the court of chancery will frequently interpofe, to prevent an infant heir from improvidently expofing himfelf to ruin.

[a] Co. Litt. 77.
[b] page 449.

[c] Litt. §. 123. Co. Litt. 89.

8. MAR-

8. MARRIAGE, or the *valor maritagii*, was not in focage tenure any perquifite or advantage to the guardian, but rather the reverfe. For, if the guardian married his ward under the age of fourteen, he was bound to account to the ward for the value of the marriage, even though he took nothing for it, unlefs he married him to advantage[d]. For the law, in favour of infants, is always jealous of guardians, and therefore in this cafe it made them account, not only for what they *did*, but alfo for what they *might*, receive on the infant's behalf; left by fome collufion the guardian fhould have received the value, and not brought it to account: but, the ftatute having deftroyed all values of marriages, this doctrine of courfe is ceafed with them. At fourteen years of age the ward might have difpofed of himfelf in marriage, without any confent of his guardian, till the late act for preventing clandeftine marriages. Thefe doctrines of wardfhip and marriage in focage tenure were fo diametrically oppofite to thofe in knight-fervice, and fo entirely agree with thofe parts of king Edward's laws, that were reftored by Henry the firft's charter, as might alone convince us that focage was of a higher original than the Norman conqueft.

9. FINES for alienations were, I apprehend, due for lands holden of the king *in capite* by focage tenure, as well as in cafe of tenure by knight-fervice: for the ftatutes that relate to this point, and fir Edward Coke's comment on them[e], fpeak generally of all tenants *in capite*, without making any diftinction; though now all fines for alienation are demolifhed by the ftatute of Charles the fecond.

10. ESCHEATS are equally incident to tenure in focage, as they were to tenure by knight-fervice; except only in gavelkind lands, which are (as is before-mentioned) fubject to no efcheats for felony, though they are to efcheats for want of heirs[f].

[d] Litt. §. 123.   [f] Wright. 210.
[e] 1 Inft. 43.   2 Inft. 65, 66, 67.

THUS much for the two grand species of tenure, under which almost all the free lands of the kingdom were holden till the reftoration in 1660, when the former was abolished and funk into the latter: fo that lands of both forts are now holden by the one univerfal tenure of free and common focage.

THE other grand divifion of tenure, mentioned by Bracton as cited in the preceding chapter, is that of *villenage*, as contradiftinguifhed from *liberum tenementum*, or frank tenure. And this (we may remember) he fubdivides into two claffes, *pure*, and *privileged*, villenage: from whence have arifen two other fpecies of our modern tenures.

III. FROM the tenure of pure villenage have fprung our prefent *copyhold* tenures, or tenure by copy of court roll at the will of the lord; in order to obtain a clear idea of which, it will be previoufly neceffary to take a fhort view of the original and nature of manors.

MANORS are in fubftance as antient as the Saxon conftitution, though perhaps differing a little, in fome immaterial circumftances, from thofe that exift at this day[g]: juft as we obferved of feuds, that they were partly known to our anceftors, even before the Norman conqueft. A manor, *manerium, a manendo*, becaufe the ufual refidence of the owner, feems to have been a diftrict of ground, held by lords or great perfonages; who kept in their own hands fo much land as was neceffary for the ufe of their families, which were called *terrae dominicales*, or *demefne* lands; being occupied by the lord, or *dominus manerii*, and his fervants. The other *tenemental* lands they diftributed among their tenants; which from the different modes of tenure were called and diftinguifhed by two different names. Firft, *book-land*, or charter-land, which was held by deed under certain rents and free fervices, and in effect differed nothing from free focage lands[h]: and from

[g] Co. Cop. §. 2, & 10.   [h] Co. Cop. §. 3.

hence

hence have arifen all the freehold tenants which hold of particular manors, and owe fuit and fervice to the fame. The other fpecies was called *folk-land*, which was held by no affurance in writing, but diftributed among the common folk or people at the pleafure of the lord, and refumed at his difcretion; being indeed land held in villenage, which we fhall prefently defcribe more at large. The refidue of the manor, being uncultivated, was termed the lord's wafte, and ferved for public roads, and for common of pafture to the lord and his tenants. Manors were formerly called baronies, as they ftill are lordfhips: and each lord or baron was empowered to hold a domeftic court, called the court-baron, for redreffing mifdemefnors and nufances within the manor, and for fettling difputes of property among the tenants. This court is an infeparable ingredient of every manor; and if the number of fuitors fhould fo fail, as not to leave fufficient to make a jury or homage, that is, two tenants at the leaft, the manor itfelf is loft.

BEFORE the ftatute of *quia emptores*, 18 Edw. I. the king's greater barons, who had a large extent of territory held under the crown, granted out frequently fmaller manors to inferior perfons to be held of themfelves; which do therefore now continue to be held under a fuperior lord, who is called in fuch cafes the lord paramount over all thefe manors: and his feignory is frequently termed an honour, not a manor, efpecially if it hath belonged to an antient feodal baron, or hath been at any time in the hands of the crown. In imitation whereof, thefe inferior lords began to carve out and grant to others ftill more minute eftates, to be held as of themfelves, and were fo proceeding downwards *in infinitum*; till the fuperior lords obferved, that by this method of fubinfeudation they loft all their feodal profits, of wardfhips, marriages, and efcheats, which fell into the hands of thefe mefne or middle lords, who were the immediate fuperiors of the *terre-tenant*, or him who occupied the land. This occafioned the ftatute of Weftm. 3. or *quia emptores*, 18 Edw. I. to be made; which directs, that, upon all fales or feoffments of land, the feoffee

fhall

fhall hold the fame, not of his immediate feoffor, but of the chief lord of the fee, of whom fuch feoffor himfelf held it. And from hence it is held, that all manors exifting at this day, muft have exifted by immemorial prefcription; or at leaft ever fince the 18 Edw. I. when the ftatute of *quia emptores* was made. For no new manor can have been created fince that ftatute: becaufe it is effential to a manor, that there be tenants who hold of the lord, and that ftatute enacts, that for the future no fubject fhall create any new tenants to hold of himfelf.

N o w with regard to the folk-land, or eftates held in villen-age, this was a fpecies of tenure neither ftrictly feodal, Norman, or Saxon; but mixed and compounded of them all [i]: and which alfo, on account of the heriots that ufually attend it, may feem to have fomewhat Danifh in it's compofition. Under the Saxon government there were, as fir William Temple fpeaks [k], a fort of people in a condition of downright fervitude, ufed and employed in the moft fervile works, and belonging, both they, their child-ren, and effects, to the lord of the foil, like the reft of the cattle or ftock upon it. Thefe feem to have been thofe who held what was called the folk-land, from which they were removeable at the lord's pleafure. On the arrival of the Normans here, it feems not improbable, that they, who were ftrangers to any other than a feodal ftate, might give fome fparks of enfranchifement to fuch wretched perfons as fell to their fhare, by admitting them, as well as others, to the oath of fealty; which conferred a right of protection, and raifed the tenant to a kind of eftate fuperior to downright flavery, but inferior to every other condition [l]. This they called villenage, and the tenants villeins, either from the word *vilis*, or elfe, as fir Edward Coke tells us [m], *a villa*; becaufe they lived chiefly in villages, and were employed in ruftic works of the moft fordid kind: like the Spartan *helotes*, to whom alone the culture of the lands was configned; their rugged mafters, like our northern anceftors, efteeming war the only honourable employment of mankind.

[i] Wright. 215.
[k] Introd. Hift. Engl. 59.
[l] Wright. 217.
[m] 1 Inft. 116.

Thefe

THESE villeins, belonging principally to lords of manors, were either villeins *regardant*, that is, annexed to the manor or land; or elfe they were *in grofs*, or at large, that is, annexed to the perfon of the lord, and transferrable by deed from one owner to another [n]. They could not leave their lord without his per-miffion; but, if they ran away, or were purloined from him, might be claimed and recovered by action, like beafts or other chattels. They held indeed fmall portions of land by way of fuf-taining themfelves and families; but it was at the mere will of the lord, who might difpoffefs them whenever he pleafed; and it was upon villein fervices, that is, to carry out dung, to hedge and ditch the lord's demefnes, and any other the meaneft offices [o]: and thefe fervices were not only bafe, but uncertain both as to their time and quantity [p]. A villein, in fhort, was in much the fame ftate with us, as lord Molefworth [q] defcribes to be that of the boors in Denmark, and Stiernhook [r] attributes alfo to the *traals* or flaves in Sweden; which confirms the probability of their being in fome degree monuments of the Danifh tyranny. A villein could acquire no property either in lands or goods; but, if he purchafed either, the lord might enter upon them, ouft the villein, and feife them to his own ufe, unlefs he contrived to dif-pofe of them again before the lord had feifed them; for the lord had then loft his opportunity [s].

IN many places alfo a fine was payable to the lord, if the vil-lein prefumed to marry his daughter to any one without leave from the lord [t]: and, by the common law, the lord might alfo bring an action againft the hufband for damages in thus purloin-ing his property [u]. For the children of villeins were alfo in the fame ftate of bondage with their parents; whence they were

---

[n] Litt. § 181.

[o] Ibid. §. 172.

[p] *Ille qui tenet in villenagio faciet quicquid ei praeceptum fuerit, nec fcire debet fero quid facere debet in craftino, et femper tenebitur ad incerta.* (Bracton. *l. 4. tr. 1. c. 28.*)

[q] c. 8.

[r] *de jure Sueonum. l. 2. c. 4.*

[s] Litt. §. 177.

[t] Co. Litt. 40.

[u] Litt. §. 202.

called

called in Latin, *nativi*, which gave rife to the female appellation of a villein, who was called a *neife* [w]. In cafe of a marriage between a freeman and a neife, or a villein and a freewoman, the iffue followed the condition of the father, being free if he was free, and villein if he was villein ; contrary to the maxim of the civil law, that *partus fequitur ventrem*. But no baftard could be born a villein, becaufe by another maxim of our law he is *nullius filius* ; and as he can *gain* nothing by inheritance, it were hard that he fhould *lofe* his natural freedom by it [x]. The law however protected the perfons of villeins, as the king's fubjects, againft atrocious injuries of the lord : for he might not kill, or maim his villein [y] ; though he might beat him with impunity, fince the villein had no action or remedy at law againft his lord, but in cafe of the murder of his anceftor or the maim of his own perfon. Niefes indeed had alfo an appeal of rape, in cafe the lord violated them by force [z].

Villeins might be enfranchifed by manumiffion, which is either exprefs or implied : exprefs ; as where a man granted to the villein a deed of manumiffion [a] : implied ; as where a man bound himfelf in a bond to his villein for a fum of money, granted him an annuity by deed, or gave him an eftate in fee, for life, or years [b] : for this was dealing with his villein on the footing of a freeman ; it was in fome of the inftances giving him an action againft his lord, and in others vefting an ownerfhip in him entirely inconfiftent with his former ftate of bondage. So alfo if the lord brought an action againft his villein, this enfranchifed him [c] ; for, as the lord might have a fhort remedy againft his villein, by feifing his goods, (which was more than equivalent to any damages he could recover) the law, which is always ready to catch at any thing in favour of liberty, prefumed that by bringing this action he meant to fet his villein on the fame footing

[w] Litt. §. 187.
[x] *Ibid.* §. 187, 188.
[y] *Ibid.* §. 189. 194.
[z] *Ibid.* §. 190.

[a] *Ibid* §. 204.
[b] §. 204, 5, 6.
[c] §. 208.

with

with himfelf, and therefore held it an implied manumiffion. But, in cafe the lord indicted him for felony, it was otherwife; for the lord could not inflict a capital punifhment on his villein, without calling in the affiftance of the law.

VILLEINS, by this and many other means, in procefs of time gained confiderable ground on their lords; and in particular ftrengthened the tenure of their eftates to that degree, that they came to have in them an intereft in many places full as good, in others better than their lords. For the goodnature and benevolence of many lords of manors having, time out of mind, permitted their villeins and their children to enjoy their poffeffions without interruption, in a regular coufe of defcent, the common law, of which cuftom is the life, now gave them title to prefcribe againft their lords; and, on performance of the fame fervices, to hold their lands, in fpight of any determination of the lord's will. For, though in general they are ftill faid to hold their eftates at the will of the lord, yet it is fuch a will as is agreeable to the cuftom of the manor; which cuftoms are preferved and evidenced by the rolls of the feveral courts baron in which they are entered, or kept on foot by the conftant immemorial ufage of the feveral manors in which the lands lie. And, as fuch tenants had nothing to fhew for their eftates but thefe cuftoms, and admiffions in purfuance of them, entered on thofe rolls, or the copies of fuch entries witneffed by the fteward, they now began to be called *tenants by copy of court roll*, and their tenure itfelf a *copyhold*[d].

THUS copyhold tenures, as fir Edward Coke obferves[e], although very meanly defcended, yet come of an antient houfe; for, from what has been premifed it appears, that copyholders are in truth no other but villeins, who, by a long feries of immemorial encroachments on the lord, have at laft eftablifhed a cuftomary right to thofe eftates, which before were held abfolutely at the lord's will. Which affords a very fubftantial reafon for the great variety

[d] F. N. B. 12.　　　　　　　　[e] Cop. §. 32.

of

of cuſtoms that prevail in different manors, with regard both to the deſcent of the eſtates, and the privileges belonging to the tenants. And theſe encroachments grew to be ſo univerſal, that when tenure in villenage was aboliſhed, (though copyholds were reſerved) by the ſtatute of Charles II, there was hardly a pure villein left in the nation. For ſir Thomas Smith ꜰ teſtifies, that in all his time (and he was ſecretary to Edward VI) he never knew any villein in groſs throughout the realm ; and the few villeins regardant that were then remaining were ſuch only as had belonged to biſhops, monaſteries, or other eccleſiaſtical corporations, in the preceding times of popery. For he tells us, that " the holy fathers, monks, and friars, had in their confeſſions, " and ſpecially in their extreme and deadly ſickneſs, convinced the " laity how dangerous a practice it was, for one chriſtian man to " hold another in bondage : ſo that temporal men, by little and " little, by reaſon of that terror in their conſciences, were glad " to manumit all their villeins. But the ſaid holy fathers, with " the abbots and priors, did not in like ſort by theirs ; for they " alſo had a ſcruple in conſcience to empoveriſh and deſpoil the " church ſo much, as to manumit ſuch as were bond to their " churches, or to the manors which the church had gotten ; and " ſo kept their villeins ſtill." By theſe ſeveral means the generality of villeins in the kingdom have long ago ſprouted up into copyholders : their perſons being enfranchiſed by manumiſſion or long acquieſcence ; but their eſtates, in ſtrictneſs, remaining ſubject to the ſame ſervile conditions and forfeitures as before; though, in general, the villein ſervices are uſually commuted for a ſmall pecuniary quit-rent ᵍ.

ꜰ Commonwealth. b. 3. c. 10.

ᵍ In ſome manors the copyholders were bound to perform the moſt ſervile offices, as to hedge and ditch the lord's grounds, to lop his trees, to reap his corn, and the like; the lord uſually finding them meat and drink, and ſometimes (as is ſtill the uſe in the highlands of Scotland) a minſtrell or piper for their diverſion. *(Rot. Maner. de Edgware Com. Midd.)* As in the kingdom of Whidah, on the ſlave coaſt of Africa, the people are bound to cut and carry in the king's corn from off his demeſne lands, and are attended by muſic during all the time of their labour. (Mod. Un. Hiſt. xvi. 429.)

A ſ

As a farther confequence of what has been premifed, we may collect thefe two main principles, which are held[h] to be the fupporters of a copyhold tenure, and without which it cannot exift; 1. That the lands be parcel of, and fituate within, that manor, under which it is held. 2. That they have been demifed, or demifable, by copy of court roll immemorially. For immemorial cuftom is the life of all tenures by copy; fo that no new copyhold can, ftrictly fpeaking, be granted at this day.

In fome manors, where the cuftom hath been to permit the heir to fucceed the anceftor in his tenure, the eftates are ftiled copyholds of inheritance; in others, where the lords have been more vigilant to maintain their rights, they remain copyholds for life only: for the cuftom of the manor has in both cafes fo far fuperfeded the will of the lord, that, provided the fervices be performed or ftipulated for by fealty, he cannot, in the firft inftance, refufe to admit the heir of his tenant upon his death; nor, in the fecond, can he remove his prefent tenant fo long as he lives, though he holds nominally by the precarious tenure of his lord's will.

The fruits and appendages of a copyhold tenure, that it hath in common with free tenures, are fealty, fervices (as well in rents as otherwife) reliefs, and efcheats. The two latter belong only to copyholds of inheritance; the former to thofe for life alfo. But, befides thefe, copyholds have alfo heriots, wardfhip, and fines. Heriots, which I think are agreed to be a Danifh cuftom, and of which we fhall fay more hereafter, are a render of the beft beaft or other good (as the cuftom may be) to the lord on the death of the tenant. This is plainly a relic of villein tenure; there being originally lefs hardfhip in it, when all the goods and chattels belonged to the lord, and he might have feifed them even in the villein's lifetime. Thefe are incident to both fpecies of copyhold; but wardfhip and fines to thofe of inheritance only.

[h] Co. Litt. 58.

Wardſhip, in copyhold eſtates, partakes both of that in chivalry and that in ſocage. Like that in chivalry, the lord is the legal guardian, who uſually aſſigns ſome relation of the infant tenant to act in his ſtead : and he, like guardian in ſocage, is accountable to his ward for the profits. Of fines, ſome are in the nature of primer ſeiſins, due on the death of each tenant, others are mere fines for alienation of the lands ; in ſome manors only one of theſe ſorts can be demanded, in ſome both, and in others neither. They are ſometimes arbitrary and at the will of the lord, ſometimes fixed by cuſtom : but, even when arbitrary, the courts of law, in favour of the liberty of copyholders, have tied them down to be *reaſonable* in their extent ; otherwiſe they might amount to a diſheriſon of the eſtate. No fine therefore is allowed to be taken upon deſcents and alienations, (unleſs in particular circumſtances) of more than two years improved value of the eſtate [i]. From this inſtance we may judge of the favourable diſpoſition, that the law of England (which is a law of liberty) hath always ſhewn to this ſpecies of tenants ; by removing, as far as poſſible, every real badge of ſlavery from them, however ſome nominal ones may continue. It ſuffered cuſtom very early to get the better of the expreſs terms upon which they held their lands ; by declaring, that the will of the lord was to be interpreted by the cuſtom of the manor : and, where no cuſtom has been ſuffered to grow up to the prejudice of the lord, as in this caſe of arbitrary fines, the law itſelf interpoſes in an equitable method, and will not ſuffer the lord to extend his power ſo far, as to diſinherit the tenant.

THUS much for the antient tenure of *pure* villenage, and the modern one of *copyhold at the will of the lord*, which is lineally deſcended from it.

IV. THERE is yet a fourth ſpecies of tenure, deſcribed by Bracton under the name ſometimes of *privileged* villenage, and ſometimes of *villein-ſocage*. This, he tells us [k], is ſuch as has been held of

[i] 2 Ch. Rep. 134.   [k] *l.* 4. *tr.* 1. *c.* 28.

the

the kings of England from the conqueſt downwards; that the tenants herein "*villana faciunt ſervitia, ſed certa et determinata;*" that they cannot aliene or transfer their tenements by grant or feoffment, any more than pure villeins can; but muſt ſurrender them to the lord or his ſteward, to be again granted out and held in villenage. And from theſe circumſtances we may collect, that what he here deſcribes is no other than an exalted ſpecies of copyhold, ſubſiſting at this day, *viz.* the tenure in *antient demeſne*: to which, as partaking of the baſeneſs of villenage in the nature of it's ſervices, and the freedom of ſocage in their certainty, he has therefore given a name compounded out of both, and calls it *villanum ſocagium.*

ANTIENT demeſne conſiſts of thoſe lands or manors, which, though now perhaps granted out to private ſubjects, were actually in the hands of the crown in the time of Edward the confeſſor, or William the conqueror; and ſo appear to have been by the great ſurvey in the exchequer called domeſday book[1]. The tenants of theſe lands, under the crown, were not all of the ſame order or degree. Some of them, as Britton teſtifies[m], continued for a long time pure and abſolute villeins, dependent on the will of the lord: and thoſe who have ſucceeded them in their tenures now differ from common copyholders in only a few points[n]. Others were in great meaſure enfranchiſed by the royal favour: being only bound in reſpect of their lands to perform ſome of the better ſort of villein ſervices, but thoſe determinate and certain; as, to plough the king's land, to ſupply his court with proviſions, and the like; all of which are now changed into pecuniary rents: and in conſideration hereof they had many immunities and privileges granted to them[o]; as, to try the right of their property in a peculiar court of their own, called a court of antient demeſne, by a peculiar proceſs denominated a writ of *right cloſe*[p]; not to pay toll or taxes; not to contribute to the expenſes of knights of the ſhire; not to be put on juries, and the like[q].

[1] F. N. B. 14. 16.
[m] c. 66.
[n] F. N. B. 228.
[o] 4 Inſt. 269.
[p] F. N. B. 11.
[q] *Ibid.* 14.

THESE

T H E S E tenants therefore, though their *tenure* be abfolutely copyhold, yet have an *intereft* equivalent to a freehold : for, though their fervices were of a bafe and villenous original [r], yet the tenants were efteemed in all other refpects to be highly privileged villeins ; and efpecially in this, that their fervices were fixed and determinate, and that they could not be compelled (like pure villeins) to relinquifh thefe tenements at the lord's will, or to hold them againft their own : "*et ideo,* fays Bracton, *dicuntur liberi.*" Britton alfo, from fuch their freedom, calls them abfolutely *fokemans,* and their tenure *fokemanries* ; which he defcribes [s] to be " lands and tenements, which are not held by knight-fervice, nor " by grand ferjeanty, nor by petit, but by fimple fervices, being " as it were lands enfranchifed by the king or his predeceffors " from their antient demefne." And the fame name is alfo given them in Fleta [t]. Hence Fitzherbert obferves [u], that no lands are antient demefne, but lands holden in focage : that is, not in free and common focage, but in this amphibious, fubordinate clafs, of villein-focage. And it is poffible, that as this fpecies of focage tenure is plainly founded upon predial fervices, or fervices of the plough, it may have given caufe to imagine that all focage tenures arofe from the fame original ; for want of diftinguifhing, with Bracton, between free-focage or focage of frank-tenure, and villan-focage or focage of antient demefne.

L A N D S held by this tenure are therefore a fpecies of copyhold, and as fuch preferved and exempted from the operation of the ftatute of Charles II. Yet they differ from common copyholds, principally in the privileges before-mentioned : as alfo they differ from freeholders by one efpecial mark and tincture of villenage, noted by Bracton and remaining to this day ; *viz.* that they cannot be conveyed from man to man by the general common law conveyances of feoffment, and the reft ; but muft pafs by furrender to the lord or his fteward, in the manner of common

[r] Gilb. hift. of the exch. 16. & 30.
[s] c. 66.
[t] *l.* 1. *c.* 8.
[u] N. B. 13.

copyholds :

copyholds : yet with this difference [w], that, in thefe furrenders of lands in antient demefne of frank tenure, it is not ufed to fay " *to* " *hold at the will of the lord*" in their copies, but only " *to hold* " *according to the cuftom of the manor.*"

THUS have we taken a compendious view of the principal and fundamental points of the doctrine of tenures, both antient and modern, in which we cannot but remark the mutual connexion and dependence that all of them have upon each other. And upon the whole it appears, that, whatever changes and alterations thefe tenures have in procefs of time undergone, from the Saxon aera to the 12 Car. II, all lay tenures are now in effect reduced to two fpecies ; *free* tenure in common focage ; and *bafe* tenure by copy of court roll.

I MENTIONED *lay* tenures only ; becaufe there is ftill behind one other fpecies of tenure, referved by the ftatute of Charles II, which is of a *fpiritual* nature, and called the tenure in frankalmoign.

V. TENURE in *frankalmoign, in libera eleemofyna,* or free alms, is that, whereby a religious corporation, aggregate or fole, holdeth lands of the donor to them and their fucceffors for ever [x]. The fervice, which they were bound to render for thefe lands was not certainly defined ; but only in general to pray for the fouls of the donor and his heirs, dead or alive ; and therefore they did no fealty, (which is incident to all other fervices but this [y]) becaufe this divine fervice was of a higher and more exalted nature [z]. This is the tenure, by which almoft all the antient monafteries and religious houfes held their lands ; and by which the parochial clergy, and very many ecclefiaftical and eleemofynary foundations, hold them at this day [a]; the nature of the fervice being upon the reformation altered, and made conformable to the purer doctrines

[w] Kitchen on courts. 194.
[x] Litt. §. 133.
[y] *Ibid.* 131.
[z] *Ibid.* 135.
[a] Bracton. *l.* 4. *tr.* 1. *c.* 28. §. 1.

of

of the church of England. It was an old Saxon tenure; and continued under the Norman revolution, through the great refpect that was fhewn to religion and religious men in antient times. Which is alfo the reafon that tenants in *frankalmoign* were difcharged of all other fervices, except the *trinoda neceſſitas*, of repairing the highways, building caſtles, and repelling invafions [b]: juft as the druids, among the antient Britons, had *omnium rerum immunitatem* [c]. And, even at prefent, this is a tenure of a nature very diftinct from all others; being not in the leaft feodal, but merely fpiritual. For if the fervice be neglected, the law gives no remedy by diftrefs or otherwife to the lord of whom the lands are holden; but merely a complaint to the ordinary or vifitor to correct it [d]. Wherein it materially differed from what was called *tenure by divine fervice :* in which the tenants were obliged to do fome fpecial divine fervices in certain; as to fing fo many maffes, to diftribute fuch a fum in alms, and the like; which, being expreſſly defined and prefcribed, could with no kind of propriety be called *free* alms; efpecially as for this, if unperformed, the lord might diftrein, without any complaint to the vifitor [e]. All fuch donations are indeed now out of ufe: for, fince the ftatute of *quia emptores*, 18 Edw. I, none but the king can give lands to be holden by this tenure [f]. So that I only mention them, becaufe *frankalmoign* is excepted by name in the ftatute of Charles II, and therefore fubfifts in many inftances at this day. Which is all that fhall be remarked concerning it; herewith concluding our obfervations on the nature of tenures.

[b] Seld. *Jan.* 1. 42.
[c] Caefar *de bell. Gall. l.* 6. *c.* 13.
[d] Litt. §. 136.
[e] *Ibid.* 137.
[f] *Ibid.* 140.

CHAPTER THE SEVENTH.

OF FREEHOLD ESTATES, OF INHERITANCE.

THE next objects of our difquifitions are the nature and properties of *eſtates*. An eſtate in lands, tenements, and hereditaments, ſignifies ſuch intereſt as the tenant hath therein : ſo that if a man grants all *his eſtate* to another, every thing that he can poſſibly grant ſhall paſs thereby [a]. It is called in Latin, *ſtatus*; it ſignifying the condition, or circumſtance, in which the owner ſtands, with regard to his property. And, to aſcertain this with proper preciſion and accuracy, eſtates may be conſidered in a threefold view : firſt, with regard to the *quantity of intereſt* which the tenant has in the tenement : ſecondly, with regard to the *time* at which that quantity of intereſt is to be enjoyed : and, thirdly, with regard to the *number* and *connexions* of the tenants.

FIRST, with regard to the *quantity of intereſt* which the tenant has in the tenement, this is meaſured by it's duration and extent. Thus, either his right of poſſeſſion is to ſubſiſt for an uncertain period, during his own life, or the life of another man ; to determine at his own deceaſe, or to remain to his deſcendants after him : or it is circumſcribed within a certain number of years, months, or days : or, laſtly, it is infinite and unlimited, being veſted in him and his repreſentatives for ever. And this

[a] Co. Litt. 345.

occaſions

occafions the primary divifion of eftates, into fuch as are *free-hold*, and fuch as are *lefs than freehold*.

AN eftate of freehold, *liberum tenementum*, or franktenement, is defined by Britton [b] to be " the *poffeffion* of the foil by a free-"man." And St. Germyn [c] tells us, that " the *poffeffion* of the "land is called in the law of England the franktenement or free-"hold." Such eftate therefore, and no other, as requires actual poffeffion of the land, is legally fpeaking freehold : which actual poffeffion can, by the courfe of the common law, be only given by the ceremony called livery of feifin, which is the fame as the feodal inveftiture. And from thefe principles we may extract this defcription of a freehold; that it is fuch an eftate in lands as is conveyed by livery of feifin; or, in tenements of an incorporeal nature, by what is equivalent thereto. And accordingly it is laid down by Littleton [d], that where a freehold fhall pafs, it behoveth to have livery of feifin. As therefore eftates of inheritance and eftates for life could not by common law be conveyed without livery of feifin, thefe are properly eftates of freehold; and, as no other eftates were conveyed with the fame folemnity, therefore no others are properly freehold eftates.

ESTATES of freehold then are divifible into eftates *of inheritance*, and eftates *not of inheritance*. The former are again divided into inheritances *abfolute* or fee-fimple; and inheritances *limited*, one fpecies of which we ufually call fee-tail.

I. TENANT in fee-fimple (or, as he is frequently ftiled, tenant in fee) is he that hath lands, tenements, or hereditaments, to hold to him and his heirs for ever [e]; generally, abfolutely, and fimply; without mentioning *what* heirs, but referring that to his own pleafure, or to the difpofition of the law. The true meaning of the word fee *(feodum)* is the fame with that of feud or fief, and in it's original fenfe it is taken in contradiftinction to

[b] c. 32.
[c] Dr & Stud. b. 2. d. 22.
[d] §. 59.
[e] Litt. §. 1.

allodium [f];

allodium[f]; which latter the writers on this subject define to be every man's own land, which he possesseth merely in his own right, without owing any rent or service to any superior. This is property in it's highest degree; and the owner thereof hath *absolutum et directum dominium*, and therefore it is said to be seised thereof absolutely *in dominico suo*, in his own demesne. But *feodum*, or fee, is that which is held of some superior, on condition of rendering him service; in which superior the ultimate property of the land resides. And therefore sir Henry Spelman[g] defines a feud or fee to be the right which the vasal or tenant hath in lands, to *use* the same, and take the profits thereof to him and his heirs, rendering to the lord his due services; the mere allodial *propriety* of the soil always remaining in the lord. This allodial property no subject in England has[h]; it being a received, and now undeniable, principle in the law, that all the lands in England are holden mediately or immediately of the king. The king therefore only hath *absolutum et directum dominium*[i]; but all subjects' lands are in the nature of *feodum* or fee; whether derived to them by descent from their ancestors, or purchased for a valuable consideration; for they cannot come to any man by either of those ways, unless accompanied with those feodal clogs, which were laid upon the first feudatory when it was originally granted. A subject therefore hath only the usufruct, and not the absolute property of the soil; or, as sir Edward Coke expresses it[k], he hath *dominium utile*, but not *dominium directum*. And hence it is that, in the most solemn acts of law, we express the strongest and highest estate, that any subject can have, by these words; "he is seised "thereof *in his demesne, as of fee.*" It is a man's demesne, *dominicum*, or property, since it belongs to him and his heirs for ever: yet this *dominicum*, property, or demesne, is strictly not absolute or allodial, but qualified or feodal: it is his demesne, *as of fee*; that is, it is not purely and simply his own, since it is held of a superior lord, in whom the ultimate property resides.

---

[f] See pag. 45, 47.
[g] of feuds, c. 1.
[h] Co. Litt. 1.

[i] *Praedium domini regis est directum dominium, cujus nullus est author nisi Deus. Ibid.*
[k] *Ibid.*

THIS is the primary fenfe and acceptation of the word *fee*. But (as fir Martin Wright very juftly obferves[1]) the doctrine, " that all lands are holden," having been for fo many ages a fixed and undeniable axiom, our Englifh lawyers do very rarely (of late years efpecially) ufe the word *fee* in this it's primary original fenfe, in contradiftinction to *allodium* or abfolute property, with which they have no concern; but generally ufe it to exprefs the continuance or quantity of eftate. A *fee* therefore, in general, fignifies an eftate of inheritance; being the higheft and moft ex-tenfive intereft that a man can have in a feud : and, when the term is ufed fimply, without any other adjunct, or has the adjunct of *fimple* annexed to it, (as, a fee, or, a fee-fimple) it is ufed in contradiftinction to a fee conditional at the common law, or a fee-tail by the ftatute; importing an abfolute inheritance, clear of any condition, limitation, or reftrictions to particular heirs, but defcendible to the heirs general, whether male or female, lineal or collateral. And in no other fenfe than this is the king faid to be feifed in fee, he being the feudatory of no man [m].

TAKING therefore *fee* for the future, unlefs where otherwife explained, in this it's fecondary fenfe, as a ftate of inheritance, it is applicable to, and may be had in, any kind of hereditaments either corporeal or incorporeal [n]. But there is this diftinction be-tween the two fpecies of hereditaments; that, of a corporeal in-heritance a man fhall be faid to be feifed *in his demefne, as of fee*; of an incorporeal one he fhall only be faid to be feifed *as of fee*, and not in his demefne [o]. For, as incorporeal hereditaments are in their nature collateral to, and iffue out of, lands and houfes [p], their owner hath no property, *dominicum*, or demefne, in the *thing* itfelf, but hath only fomething derived out of it; refembling the *fervitutes*, or fervices, of the civil law [q]. The *dominicum* or pro-

[1] pag. 148.
[m] Co. Litt. 1.
[n] *Feodum eft quod quis tenet fibi et heredibus fuis, five fit tenementum, five reditus, &c.* Flet. *l.* 5. *c.* 5. §. 7.

[o] Litt. §. 10.
[p] See pag. 20.
[q] *Servitus eft jus, quo res mea alterius rei vel perfonae fervit.* Ff. 8. 1. 1.

perty

perty is frequently in one man, while the appendage or fervice is in another. Thus Gaius may be feifed *as of fee*, of a way going over the land, of which Titius is feifed *in his demefne as of fee*.

THE fee-fimple or inheritance of lands and tenements is generally vefted and refides in fome perfon or other ; though divers inferior eftates may be carved out of it. As if one grants a leafe for twenty one years, or for one or two lives, the fee-fimple remains vefted in him and his heirs ; and after the determination of thofe years or lives, the land reverts to the grantor or his heirs, who fhall hold it again in fee-fimple. Yet fometimes the fee may be in *abeyance*, that is (as the word fignifies) in expectation, remembrance, and contemplation of law ; there being no perfon *in effe*, in whom it can veft and abide ; though the law confiders it as always potentially exifting, and ready to veft whenever a proper owner appears. Thus, in a grant to John for life, and afterwards to the heirs of Richard, the inheritance is plainly neither granted to John nor Richard, nor can it veft in the heirs of Richard till his death, *nam nemo eft haeres viventis :* it remains therefore in waiting, or abeyance, during the life of Richard [r]. This is likewife always the cafe of a parfon of a church, who hath only an eftate therein for the term of his life : and the inheritance remains in abeyance [s]. And not only the fee, but the freehold alfo, may be in abeyance ; as, when a parfon dies, the freehold of his glebe is in abeyance, until a fucceffor be named, and then it vefts in the fucceffor [t].

THE word, heirs, is neceffary in the grant or donation in order to make a fee, or inheritance. For if land be given to a man for ever, or to him and his affigns for ever, this vefts in him but an eftate for life [u]. This very great nicety about the infertion of the word "heirs" in all feoffments and grants, in order to veft a fee, is plainly a relic of the feodal ftrictnefs : by which we may remember [w] it was required, that the form of the donation fhould

[r] Co. Litt. 342.
[s] Litt. §. 646.
[t] Litt. §. 647.

[u] Litt. §. 1.
[w] See pag. 56.

be

be punctually purfued; or that, as Crag[x] expreffes it, in the words of Baldus, "*donationes fint ftricti juris, ne quis plus donaffe prae-*"*fumatur quam in donatione exprefferit.*" And therefore, as the perfonal abilities of the donee were originally fuppofed to be the only inducements to the gift, the donee's eftate in the land extended only to his own perfon, and fubfifted no longer than his life; unlefs the donor, by an exprefs provifion in the grant, gave it a longer continuance, and extended it alfo to his heirs. But this rule is now foftened by many exceptions[y].

FOR, 1. It does not extend to devifes by will; in which, as they were introduced at the time when the feodal rigor was apace wearing out, a more liberal conftruction is allowed: and therefore by a devife to a man for ever, or to one and his affigns for ever, or to one in fee-fimple, the devifee hath an eftate of inheritance; for the intention of the devifor is fufficiently plain from the words of perpetuity annexed, though he hath omitted the legal words of inheritance. But if the devife be to a man and his affigns, without annexing words of perpetuity, there the devifee fhall take only an eftate for life; for it does not appear that the devifor intended any more. 2. Neither does this rule extend to fines or recoveries, confidered as a fpecies of conveyance; for thereby an eftate in fee paffes by act and operation of law without the word "heirs:" as it does alfo, for particular reafons, by certain other methods of conveyance, which have relation to a former grant or eftate, wherein the word "heirs" was expreffed[z]. 3. In creations of nobility by writ, the peer fo created hath an inheritance in his title, without expreffing the word, "heirs;" for they are implied in the creation, unlefs it be otherwife fpecially provided: but in creations by patent, which are *ftricti juris*, the word "heirs" muft be inferted, otherwife there is no inheritance. 4. In grants of lands to fole corporations and their fucceffors, the word "fucceffors" fupplies the place of "heirs;" for as heirs take from the anceftor, fo doth the fucceffor from

[x] *l.* 1. *t.* 9. §. 17.
[y] Co. Litt. 9, 10.
[z] *Ibid.* 9.

the

the predeceſſor. Nay, in a grant to a biſhop, or other ſole ſpiritual corporation, in *frankalmoign*, the word "*frankalmoign*" ſupplies the place of both " heirs" and " ſucceſſors," *ex vi termini*; and in all theſe caſes a fee-ſimple veſts in ſuch ſole corporation. But, in a grant of lands to a corporation aggregate, the word " ſucceſſors" is not neceſſary, though uſually inſerted : for, albeit ſuch ſimple grant be ſtrictly only an eſtate for life, yet, as that corporation never dies, ſuch eſtate for life is perpetual, or equivalent to a fee-ſimple, and therefore the law allows it to be one[a]. Laſtly, in the caſe of the king, a fee-ſimple will veſt in him, without the words " heirs" or " ſucceſſors" in the grant; partly from prerogative royal, and partly from a reaſon ſimilar to the laſt, becauſe the king in judgment of law never dies[b]. But the general rule is, that the word " heirs" is neceſſary to create an eſtate of inheritance.

II. WE are next to conſider limited fees, or ſuch eſtates of inheritance as are clogged and confined with conditions, or qualifications, of any ſort. And theſe we may divide into two ſorts : 1. *Qualified*, or *baſe* fees; and 2. Fees *conditional*, ſo called at the common law; and afterwards fees-*tail*, in conſequence of the ſtatute *de donis*.

1. A BASE, or qualified, fee is ſuch a one as has a qualification ſubjoined thereto, and which muſt be determined whenever the qualification annexed to it is at an end. As, in the caſe of a grant to A and his heirs, *tenants of the manor of Dale*; in this inſtance, whenever the heirs of A ceaſe to be tenants of that manor, the grant is intirely defeated. So, when Henry VI granted to John Talbot, lord of the manor of Kingſton-Liſle in Berks, that he and his heirs, lords of the ſaid manor, ſhould be peers of the realm, by the title of barons of Liſle; here John Talbot had a baſe or qualified fee in that dignity[c]; and the inſtant he or his heirs quitted the ſeignory of this manor, the dignity was at an

[a] See Vol. I. pag. 472.
[b] *Ibid.* 242.

[c] Co. Litt. 27.

end.

end. This eftate is a fee, becaufe by poffibility it may endure for ever in a man and his heirs; yet as that duration depends upon the concurrence of collateral circumftances, which qualify and debafe the purity of the donation, it is therefore a qualified or bafe fee.

2. A CONDITIONAL fee, at the common law, was a fee reftrained to fome particular heirs, exclufive of others : " *donatio* " *ftricta et coarctata* [d]; *ficut certis haeredibus, quibufdam a fucceffione* " *exclufis* :" as, to the heirs *of a man's body*, by which only his lineal defcendants were admitted, in exclufion of collateral heirs ; or, to the heirs *male of his body*, in exclufion both of collaterals, and lineal females alfo. It was called a conditional fee, by reafon of the condition expreffed or implied in the donation of it, that if the donee died without fuch particular heirs, the land fhould revert to the donor. For this was a condition annexed by law to all grants whatfoever ; that on failure of the heirs fpecified in the grant, the grant fhould be at an end, and the land return to it's antient proprietor [e]. Such conditional fees were ftrictly agreeable to the nature of feuds, when they firft ceafed to be mere eftates for life, and were not yet arrived to be abfolute eftates in fee-fimple. And we find ftrong traces of thefe limited, conditional fees, which could not be alienated from the lineage of the firft purchafor, in our earlieft Saxon laws [f].

Now, with regard to the condition annexed to thefe fees by the common law, our anceftors held, that fuch a gift (to a man and the heirs of his body) was a gift upon condition, that it fhould revert to the donor, if the donee had no heirs of his body; but, if he had, it fhould then remain to the donee. They there-fore called it a fee-fimple, on condition that he had iffue. Now we muft obferve, that, when any condition is performed, it is thenceforth intirely gone; and the thing, to which it was before

[d] Flet. *l.* 3. *c.* 3. §. 5.
[e] Plowd. 241.
[f] *Si quis terram haereditariam habeat, eam*

non vendat a cognatis haeredibus fuis, fi illi viro prohibitum fit, qui eam ab initio acquifi-vit, ut ita facere nequeat. LL. *Aelfred. c.*37.

annexed,

annexed, becomes abfolute, and wholly unconditional. So that, as foon as the grantee had any iffue born, his eftate was fuppofed to become abfolute, by the performance of the condition; at leaft, for thefe three purpofes: 1. To enable the tenant to aliene the land, and thereby to bar not only his own iffue, but alfo the donor of his intereft in the reverfion [g]. 2. To fubject him to forfeit it for treafon : which he could not do, till iffue born, longer than for his own life; left thereby the inheritance of the iffue, and reverfion of the donor, might have been defeated [h]. 3. To empower him to charge the land with rents, commons, and certain other incumbrances, fo as to bind his iffue [i]. And this was thought the more reafonable, becaufe, by the birth of iffue, the poffibility of the donor's reverfion was rendered more diftant and precarious : and *his* intereft feems to have been the only one which the law, as it then ftood, was folicitous to protect; without much regard to the right of fucceffion intended to be vefted in the iffue. However, if the tenant did not in fact aliene the land, the courfe of defcent was not altered by this performance of the condition : for if the iffue had afterwards died, and then the tenant, or original grantee, had died, without making any alienation; the land, by the terms of the donation, could defcend to none but the heirs *of his body*, and therefore, in default of them, muft have reverted to the donor. For which reafon, in order to fubject the lands to the ordinary courfe of defcent, the donees of thefe conditional fee-fimples took care to aliene as foon as they had performed the condition by having iffue; and afterwards re-purchafed the lands, which gave them a fee-fimple abfolute, that would defcend to the heirs general, according to the courfe of the common law. And thus ftood the old law with regard to conditional fees : which things, fays fir Edward Coke [k], though they feem antient, are yet neceffary to be known; as well for the declaring how the common law ftood in fuch cafes, as for the fake of annuities, and fuch like inheritances, as are not within the ftatutes of entail, and therefore remain as at the common law.

[g] Co. Litt. 19. 2 Inft. 233.
[h] Co. Litt. *Ibid.* 2 Inft. 234.
[i] Co. Litt. 19.
[k] 1 Inft. 19.

THE

THE inconvenience, which attended thefe limited and fettered inheritances, were probably what induced the judges to give way to this fubtle finefſe, (for fuch it undoubtedly was) in order to fhorten the duration of thefe conditional eſtates. But, on the other hand, the nobility, who were willing to perpetuate their poſſeſſions in their own families, to put a ſtop to this practice, procured the ſtatute of Weſtminſter the ſecond[1] (commonly called the ſtatute *de donis conditionalibus*) to be made ; which pays a greater regard to the private will and intentions of the donor, than to the propriety of fuch intentions, or any public confiderations whatſoever. This ſtatute revives in ſome ſort the antient feodal reſtraints which were originally laid on alienations, by enacting, that from thenceforth the will of the donor be obſerved ; and that the tenements fo given (to a man and the heirs of his body) ſhould at all events go to the iſſue, if there were any ; or, if none, ſhould revert to the donor.

UPON the conſtruction of this act of parliament, the judges determined that the donee had no longer a conditional fee-ſimple, which became abſolute and at his own difpoſal, the inſtant any iſſue was born ; but they divided the eſtate into two parts, leaving in the donee a new kind of particular eſtate, which they denominated a *fee-tail*[m] ; and veſting in the donor the ultimate fee-ſimple of the land, expectant on the failure of iſſue ; which expectant eſtate is what we now call a reverſion[n]. And hence it is that Littleton tells us[o], that tenant in fee-tail is by virtue of the ſtatute of Weſtminſter the ſecond.

HAVING thus ſhewn the *original* of eſtates-tail, I now proceed to conſider, *what things* may, or may not, be entailed under

---

[1] 13 Edw. I. c. 1.

[m] The expreſſion *fee-tail*, or *feodum talliatum*, was borrowed from the feudiſts ; (See Crag. *l. 1. t. 10. §. 24, 25.*) among whom it ſignified any mutilated or truncated inheritance, from which the heirs general were *cut* off; being derived from the barbarous verb *taliare*, to cut ; from which the French *tailler* and the Italian *tagliare* are formed. (Spelm. *Gloſſ.* 531.)

[n] 2 Inſt. 335.

[o] §. 13.

the

the ftatute *de donis*. *Tenements* is the only word ufed in the ftatute : and this fir Edward Coke [p] expounds to comprehend all
corporeal hereditaments whatfoever; and alfo all incorporeal hereditaments which favour of the realty, that is, which iffue out
of corporeal ones, or which concern, or are annexed to, or may
be exercifed within the fame ; as, rents, eftovers, commons, and
the like. Alfo offices and dignities, which concern lands, or have
relation to fixed and certain places, may be entailed [q]. But mere
perfonal chattels, which favour not at all of the realty, cannot
be entailed. Neither can an office, which merely relates to fuch
perfonal chattels; nor an annuity, which charges only the perfon,
and not the lands, of the grantor. But in them, if granted to a
man and the heirs of his body, the grantee hath ftill a fee conditional at common law, as before the ftatute; and by his alienation may bar the heir or reverfioner [r]. An eftate to a man and his
heirs for another's life cannot be entailed [s]; for this is ftrictly no
eftate of inheritance (as will appear hereafter) and therefore not
within the ftatute *de donis*. Neither can a copyhold eftate be entailed by virtue of the *ftatute* ; for that would tend to encroach
upon and reftrain the will of the lord : but, by the *fpecial cuftom*
of the manor, a copyhold may be limited to the heirs of the
body [t]; for here the cuftom afcertains and interprets the lord's will.

NEXT, as to the feveral *fpecies* of eftates-tail, and how they
are refpectively created. Eftates-tail are either *general*, or *fpecial*.
Tail-general is where lands and tenements are given to one, and
the *heirs of his body begotten:* which is called tail-general, becaufe,
how often foever fuch donee in tail be married, his iffue in general by all and every fuch marriage is, in fucceffive order, capable
of inheriting the eftate-tail, *per formam doni* [u]. Tenant in tail-
fpecial is where the gift is reftrained to certain heirs of the donee's body, and does not go to all of them in general. And this

[p] 1 Inft. 19, 20.
[q] 7 Rep. 33.
[r] Co. Litt. 19, 20.

[s] 2 Vern. 225.
[t] 3 Rep. 8.
[u] Litt. §. 14, 15.

may happen feveral ways ᵂ. I fhall inftance in only one : as where lands and tenements are given to a man and the *heirs of his body, on Mary his now wife to be begotten*; here no iffue can inherit, but fuch fpecial iffue as is engendered between them two; not fuch as the hufband may have by another wife : and therefore it is called fpecial tail. And here we may obferve, that the words of inheritance (to him and his *heirs*) give him an eftate in fee; but they being heirs *to be by him begotten*, this makes it a fee-tail; and the perfon being alfo limited, on whom fuch heirs fhall be begotten, (viz. *Mary his prefent wife*) this makes it a fee-tail fpecial.

E s t a t e s, in general and fpecial tail, are farther diverfified by the diftinction of fexes in fuch entails; for both of them may either be in tail *male* or tail *female*. As if lands be given to a man, and his *heirs male of his body begotten*, this is an eftate in tail male general; but if to a man and the *heirs female of his body on his prefent wife begotten*, this is an eftate in tail female fpecial. And, in cafe of an entail male, the heirs female fhall never inherit, nor any derived from them; nor, *e converfo*, the heirs male, in cafe of a gift in tail female ˣ. Thus, if the donee in tail male hath a daughter, who dies leaving a fon, fuch grandfon in this cafe cannot inherit the eftate-tail; for he cannot deduce his defcent wholly by heirs male ʸ. And as the heir male muft convey his defcent wholly by males, fo muft the heir female wholly by females. And therefore if a man hath two eftates-tail, the one in tail male, the other in tail female; and he hath iffue a daughter, which daughter hath iffue a fon; this grandfon can fucceed to neither of the eftates: for he cannot convey his defcent wholly either in the male or female line ᶻ.

A s the word *heirs* is neceffary to create a fee, fo, in farther imitation of the ftrictnefs of the feodal donation, the word *body*, or fome other words of procreation, are neceffary to make it a

ᵂ Litt. §. 16, 26, 27, 28, 29.   ʸ *Ibid.* §. 24.
ˣ *Ibid.* §. 21, 22.   ᶻ Co. Litt. 25.

fee-tail;

fee-tail, and afcertain to what heirs in particular the fee is limited. If therefore either the words of inheritance or words of
procreation be omitted, albeit the others are inferted in the grant,
this will not make an eftate-tail. As, if the grant be to a man and
his *iffue of his body*, to a man and his *feed*, to a man and his
children, or *offspring*; all thefe are only eftates for life, there
wanting the words of inheritance, his heirs [a]. So, on the other
hand, a gift to a man, and his *heirs male*, or *female*, is an eftate
in fee-fimple, and not in fee-tail; for there are no words to afcertain the body out of which they fhall iffue [b]. Indeed, in laft wills
and teftaments, wherein greater indulgence is allowed, an eftate-
tail may be created by a devife to a man and his *feed*, or to a man
and his *heirs male*; or by other irregular modes of expreffion [c].

THERE is ftill another fpecies of entailed eftates, now indeed
grown out of ufe, yet ftill capable of fubfifting in law; which
are eftates *in libero maritagio*, or *frankmarriage*. Thefe are defined [d] to be, where tenements are given by one man to another,
together with a wife, who is the daughter or coufin of the donor,
to hold in frankmarriage. Now by fuch gift, though nothing
but the word *frankmarriage* is expreffed, the donees fhall have
the tenements to them, and the heirs of their two bodies begotten; that is, they are tenants in fpecial tail. For this one word,
frankmarriage, does *ex vi termini* not only create an inheritance,
like the word *frankalmoign*, but likewife limits that inheritance;
fupplying not only words of defcent, but of procreation alfo.
Such donees in frankmarriage are liable to no fervice but fealty;
for a rent referved thereon is void, until the fourth degree of confanguinity be paft between the iffues of the donor and donee [e].

THE *incidents* to a tenancy in tail, under the ftatute Weftm. 2.
are chiefly thefe [f]. 1. That a tenant in tail may commit *wafte* on
the eftate-tail, by felling timber, pulling down houfes, or the

[a] Co. Litt. 20.
[b] Litt. §. 31. Co. Litt. 27.
[c] Co. Litt. 9. 27.

[d] Litt. §. 17.
[e] *Ibid.* §. 19, 20.
[f] Co. Litt. 224.

like,

like, without being impeached, or called to account, for the fame. 2. That the wife of the tenant in tail fhall have her *dower*, or thirds, of the eftate-tail. 3. That the hufband of a female tenant in tail may be tenant by the *curtefy* of the eftate-tail. 4. That an eftate-tail may be *barred*, or deftroyed, by a fine, by a common recovery, or by lineal warranty defcending with affets to the heir. All which will hereafter be explained at large.

THUS much for the nature of eftates-tail: the eftablifhment of which family law (as it is properly ftiled by Pigott[g]) occafioned infinite difficulties and difputes [h]. Children grew difobedient when they knew they could not be fet afide: farmers were oufted of their leafes made by tenants in tail; for, if fuch leafes had been valid, then under colour of long leafes the iffue might have been virtually difinherited: creditors were defrauded of their debts; for, if tenant in tail could have charged his eftate with their payment, he might alfo have defeated his iffue, by mortgaging it for as much as it was worth: innumerable latent entails were produced to deprive purchafers of the lands they had fairly bought; of fuits in confequence of which our antient books are full: and treafons were encouraged; as eftates-tail were not liable to forfeiture, longer than for the tenant's life. So that they were juftly branded, as the fource of new contentions, and mifchiefs unknown to the common law; and almoft univerfally confidered as the common grievance of the realm [i]. But, as the nobility were always fond of this ftatute, becaufe it preferved their family eftates from forfeiture, there was little hope of procuring a repeal by the legiflature; and therefore, by the connivance of an active and politic prince, a method was devifed to evade it.

ABOUT two hundred years intervened between the making of the ftatute *de donis*, and the application of common recoveries to this intent, in the twelfth year of Edward IV: which were then openly declared by the judges to be a fufficient bar of an eftate-

g Com. Recov. 5.   i Co. Litt. 19. Moor. 156. 10 Rep. 38.
h 1 Rep. 131.

tail[k].

tail[k]. For though the courts had, so long before as the reign of
Edward III, very frequently hinted their opinion that a bar might
be effected upon these principles[l], yet it never was carried into
execution; till Edward IV obferving[m] (in the difputes between
the houfes of York and Lancafter) how little effect attainders for
treafon had on families, whofe eftates were protected by the fanc-
tuary of entails, gave his countenance to this proceeding, and
fuffered Taltarum's cafe to be brought before the court[n]: wherein,
in confequence of the principles then laid down, it was in effect
determined, that a common recovery fuffered by tenant in tail
fhould be an effectual deftruction thereof. What common recoveries are, both in their nature and confequences, and why they
are allowed to be a bar to the eftate-tail, muft be referved to a
fubfequent enquiry. At prefent I fhall only fay, that they are
fictitious proceedings, introduced by a kind of *pia fraus*, to elude
the ftatute *de donis*, which was found fo intolerably mifchievous,
and which yet one branch of the legiflature would not then confent to repeal: and, that thefe recoveries, however clandeftinely
begun, are now become by long ufe and acquiefcence a moft
common affurance of lands; and are looked upon as the legal
mode of conveyance, by which tenant in tail may difpofe of his
lands and tenements: fo that no court will fuffer them to be
fhaken or reflected on, and even acts of parliament[o] have by a
fidewind countenanced and eftablifhed them.

THIS expedient having greatly abridged eftates-tail with regard to their duration, others were foon invented to ftrip them of
other privileges. The next that was attacked was their freedom
from forfeitures for treafon. For, notwithftanding the large ad-
vances made by recoveries, in the compafs of about threefcore
years, towards unfettering thefe inheritances, and thereby fubjecting the lands to forfeiture, the rapacious prince then reigning,

k 1 Rep. 131. 6 Rep. 40.
l 10 Rep. 37, 38.
m Pigott. 8.
f Year Book. 12 Edw. IV. 14. 19. Fitzh.
Abr. tit. faux recov. 20. Bro. *Abr. ibid.* 30.

tit. recov. in value. 19. *tit. taile.* 36.
o 11 Hen. VII. c. 20. 7 Hen. VIII. c. 4.
34 & 35 Hen. VIII. c. 20. 14 Eliz. c. 8.
4 & 5 Ann. c. 16. 14 Geo. II. c. 20.
                                finding

finding them frequently re-fetttled in a fimilar manner to fuit the convenience of families, had addrefs enough to procure a ftatute[p], whereby all eftates of inheritance (under which general words eftates-tail were covertly included) are declared to be forfeited to the king upon any conviction of high treafon.

THE next attack which they fuffered, in order of time, was by the ftatute 32 Hen. VIII. c. 28. whereby certain leafes made by tenants in tail, which do not tend to the prejudice of the iffue, were allowed to be good in law, and to bind the iffue in tail. But they received a more violent blow, in the fame feffion of parliament, by the conftruction put upon the ftatute of fines[q], by the ftatute 32 Hen. VIII. c. 36. which declares a fine duly levied by tenant in tail to be a complete bar to him and his heirs, and all other perfons, claiming under fuch entail. This was evidently agreeable to the intention of Henry VII, whofe policy it was (before common recoveries had obtained their full ftrength and authority) to lay the road as open as poffible to the alienation of landed property, in order to weaken the overgrown power of his nobles. But as they, from the oppofite reafons, were not eafily brought to confent to fuch a provifion, it was therefore couched, in his act, under covert and obfcure expreffions. And the judges, though willing to conftrue that ftatute as favourably as poffible for the defeating of entailed eftates, yet hefitated at giving fines fo extenfive a power by mere implication, when the ftatute *de donis* had expreffly declared, that they fhould *not* be a bar to eftates-tail. But the ftatute of Henry VIII, when the doctrine of alienation was better received, and the will of the prince more implicitly obeyed than before, avowed and eftablifhed that intention. Yet, in order to preferve the property of the crown from any danger of infringement, all eftates-tail created by the crown, and of which the crown has the reverfion, are excepted out of this ftatute. And the fame was done with regard to common recoveries, by the ftatute 34 & 35 Hen. VIII. c. 20. which enacts, that no feigned recovery had againft tenants

[p] 26 Hen. VIII. c. 13.   [q] 4 Hen. VII. c. 24.

in

in tail, where the eſtate was created by the crown [r], and the remainder or reverſion continues ſtill in the crown, ſhall be of any force or effect. Which is allowing, indirectly and collaterally, their full force and effect with reſpect to ordinary eſtates-tail, where the royal prerogative is not concerned.

LASTLY, by a ſtatute of the ſucceeding year [s], all eſtates-tail are rendered liable to be charged for payment of debts due to the king by record or ſpecial contract; as, ſince, by the bankrupt laws [t], they are alſo ſubjected to be ſold for the debts contracted by a bankrupt. And, by the conſtruction put on the ſtatute 43 Eliz. c. 4. an appointment [u] by tenant in tail of the lands entailed, to a charitable uſe, is good without fine or recovery.

ESTATES-TAIL, being thus by degrees unfettered, are now reduced again to almoſt the ſame ſtate, even before iſſue born, as conditional fees were in at common law, after the condition was performed, by the birth of iſſue. For, firſt, the tenant in tail is now enabled to aliene his lands and tenements by fine, by recovery, or by certain other means; and thereby to defeat the intereſt as well of his own iſſue, though unborn, as alſo of the reverſioner, except in the caſe of the crown: ſecondly, he is now liable to forfeit them for high treaſon: and, laſtly, he may charge them with reaſonable leaſes, and alſo with ſuch of his debts as are due to the crown on ſpecialties, or have been contracted with his fellow-ſubjects in a courſe of extenſive commerce.

[r] Co. Litt. 372.

[s] 33 Hen. VIII. c. 39. §. 75.

[t] Stat. 21 Jac. I. c. 19.

[u] 2 Vern. 453. Chan. Prec 16

C H A P T E R T H E E I G H T H.

Of FREEHOLDS, NOT of INHERITANCE.

WE are next to difcourfe of fuch eftates of freehold, as are not of inheritance, but *for life* only. And, of thefe eftates for life, fome are *conventional*, or expreffly created by the act of the parties; others merely *legal*, or created by conftruction and operation of law[a]. We will confider them both in their order.

I. ESTATES for life, expreffly created by deed or grant, (which alone are properly conventional) are where a leafe is made of lands or tenements to a man, to hold for the term of his own life, or for that of any other perfon, or for more lives than one: in any of which cafes he is ftiled tenant for life; only, when he holds the eftate by the life of another, he is ufually called tenant *pur auter vie*[b]. Thefe eftates for life are, like inheritances, of a feodal nature; and were, for fome time, the higheft eftate that any man could have in a feud, which (as we have before feen[c]) was not in it's original hereditary. They are given or conferred by the fame feodal rites and folemnities, the fame inveftiture or livery of feifin, as fees themfelves are; and they are held by fealty, if demanded, and fuch conventional rents and fervices as the lord or leffor, and his tenant or leffee, have agreed on.

[a] Wright. 190.
[b] Litt. §.56.

[c] pag. 55.

ESTATES

ESTATES for life may be created, not only by the exprefs words before-mentioned, but alfo by a general grant, without defining or limiting any fpecifice ftate. As, if one grants to A. B. the manor of Dale, this makes him tenant for life[d]. For though, as there are no words of inheritance, or *heirs*, mentioned in the grant, it cannot be conftrued to be a fee, it fhall however be conftrued to be as large an eftate as the words of the donation will bear, and therefore an eftate for life. Alfo fuch a grant at large, or a grant for term of life generally, fhall be conftrued to be an eftate for the life *of the grantee*[e]; in cafe the grantor hath authority to make fuch a grant : for an eftate for a man's own life is more beneficial and of a higher nature than for any other life ; and the rule of law is, that all grants are to be taken moft ftrongly againft the grantor[f], unlefs in the cafe of the king.

SUCH eftates for life will, generally fpeaking, endure as long as the life for which they are granted : but there are fome eftates for life, which may determine upon future contingencies, before the life, for which they are created, expires. As, if an eftate be granted to a woman during her widowhood, or to a man until he be promoted to a benefice ; in thefe, and fimilar cafes, whenever the contingency happens, when the widow marries, or when the grantee obtains a benefice, the refpective eftates are abfolutely determined and gone[g]. Yet, while they fubfift, they are reckoned eftates for life ; becaufe, the time for which they will endure being uncertain, they may by poffibility laft for life, if the contingencies upon which they are to determine do not fooner happen. And, moreover, in cafe an eftate be granted to a man for his life, generally, it may alfo determine by his *civil* death ; as if he enters into a monaftery, whereby he is dead in law[h] : for which reafon in conveyances the grant is ufually made "for the "term of a man's *natural* life;" which can only determine by his *natural* death[i].

[d] Co. Litt. 42.
[e] *Ibid.*
[f] *Ibid.* 36.

[g] Co. Litt. 42.   3 Rep. 20.
[h] 2 Rep. 48.
[i] See Vol. I. pag. 129.

THE *incidents* to an estate for life, are principally the following; which are applicable not only to that species of tenants for life, which are expressly created by deed; but also to those, which are created by act and operation of law.

1. EVERY tenant for life, unless restrained by covenant or agreement, may of common right take upon the land demised to him reasonable *estovers* [k] or *botes* [l]. For he hath a right to the full enjoyment and use of the land, and all it's profits, during his estate therein. But he is not permitted to cut down timber or do other waste upon the premises [m] : for the destruction of such things, as are not the temporary profits of the tenement, is not necessary for the tenant's complete enjoyment of his estate; but tends to the permanent and lasting loss of the person entitled to the inheritance.

2. TENANT for life, or his representatives, shall not be prejudiced by any sudden determination of his estate, because such determination is contingent and uncertain [n]. Therefore if a tenant for his own life sows the lands, and dies before harvest, his executors shall have the *emblements,* or profits of the crop : for the estate was determined by the *act of God*; and it is a maxim in the law, that *actus Dei nemini facit injuriam.* The representatives therefore of the tenant for life shall have the emblements, to compensate for the labour and expense of tilling, manuring, and sowing, the lands; and also for the encouragement of husbandry, which being a public benefit, tending to the increase and plenty of provisions, ought to have the utmost security and privilege that the law can give it. Wherefore, by the feodal law, if a tenant for life died between the beginning of September and the end of February, the lord, who was entitled to the reversion, was also entitled to the profits of the whole year; but, if he died between the beginning of March and the end of August, the

[k] See pag 35.
[l] Co. Litt. 41.

[m] Ibid. 53.
[n] Ibid. 55.

heirs

heirs of the tenant received the whole [o]. From hence our law of emblements ſeems to have been derived, but with very conſiderable improvements. So it is alſo, if a man be tenant for the life of another, and *ceſtuy que vie*, or he on whoſe life the land is held, dies after the corn ſown, the tenant *pur auter vie* ſhall have the emblements. The ſame is alſo the rule, if a life-eſtate be determined by the *act of law*. Therefore, if a leaſe be made to huſband and wife during coverture, (which gives them a determinable eſtate for life) and the huſband ſows the land, and afterwards they are divorced *a vinculo matrimonii*, the huſband ſhall have the emblements in this caſe; for the ſentence of divorce is the act of law [p]. But if an eſtate for life be determined by the tenant's *own act*, (as, by forfeiture for waſte committed; or, if a tenant during widowhood thinks proper to marry) in theſe, and ſimilar caſes, the tenants, having thus determined the eſtate by their own acts, ſhall not be entitled to take the emblements [q]. The doctrine of emblements extends not only to corn ſown, but to roots planted, or other annual artificial profit: but it is otherwiſe of fruit-trees, graſs, and the like; which are not planted annually at the expenſe and labour of the tenant, but are either the permanent, or natural, profit of the earth [r]. For even when a man plants a tree, he cannot be preſumed to plant it in contemplation of any preſent profit; but merely with a proſpect of it's being uſeful to future ſucceſſions of tenants. The advantages alſo of emblements are particularly extended to the parochial clergy by the ſtatute 28 Hen. VIII. c. 11. For all perſons, who are preſented to any eccleſiaſtical benefice, or to any civil office, are conſidered as tenants for their own lives, unleſs the contrary be expreſſed in the form of donation.

3. A THIRD incident to eſtates for life relates to the under-tenants or leſſees. For they have the ſame, nay greater indulgences, than their leſſors, the original tenants for life. The ſame; for the law of eſtovers and emblements, with regard to the tenant

[o] *Feud. l. 2. t. 28.*

[p] 5 Rep. 116.

[q] Co. Litt. 55.

[r] Co. Litt. 55, 56. 1 Roll. Abr. 728.

for life, is alſo law with regard to his under-tenant, who repreſents him and ſtands in his place[s]: and greater; for in thoſe caſes where tenant for life ſhall not have the emblements, becauſe the eſtate determines by his own act, the exception ſhall not reach his leſſee who is a third perſon. As in the caſe of a woman who holds *durante viduitate*; her taking huſband is her own act, and therefore deprives her of the emblements: but if ſhe leaſes her eſtate to an under-tenant, who ſows the land, and ſhe then marries, this her act ſhall not deprive the tenant of his emblements, who is a ſtranger and could not prevent her[t]. The leſſees of tenants for life had alſo at the common law another moſt unreaſonable advantage; for, at the death of their leſſors the tenants for life, theſe under-tenants might if they pleaſed quit the premiſes, and pay no rent to any body for the occupation of the land ſince the laſt quarter day, or other day aſſigned for payment of rent[u]. To remedy which it is now enacted[v], that the executors or adminiſtrators of tenant for life, on whoſe death any leaſe determined, ſhall recover of the leſſee a ratable proportion of rent, from the laſt day of payment to the death of ſuch leſſor.

II. THE next eſtate for life is of the legal kind, as contradiſtinguiſhed from conventional; *viz.* that of tenant *in tail after poſſibility of iſſue extinct.* This happens, where one is tenant in ſpecial tail, and a perſon, from whoſe body the iſſue was to ſpring, dies without iſſue; or, having left iſſue, that iſſue becomes extinct; in either of theſe caſes the ſurviving tenant in ſpecial tail becomes tenant in tail after poſſibility of iſſue extinct. As, where one has an eſtate to him and his heirs on the body of his preſent wife to be begotten, and the wife dies without iſſue[w]; in this caſe the man has an eſtate-tail, which cannot poſſibly deſcend to any one; and therefore the law makes uſe of this long periphraſis, as abſolutely neceſſary to give an adequate idea of his eſtate. For if it had called him barely *tenant in fee-tail ſpecial*, that would

[s] Co. Litt. 55.
[t] Cro. Eliz. 461.   1 Roll. Abr. 727.
[u] 10 Rep. 127.

[v] Stat. 11 Geo. II. c. 19. §. 15.
[w] Litt. §. 32.

not

not have diftinguifhed him from others ; and befides he has no longer an eftate of inheritance, or fee[x], for he can have no heirs, capable of taking *per formam doni*. Had it called him *tenant in tail without iffue*, this had only related to the prefent fact, and would not have excluded the poffibility of future iffue. Had he been ftiled *tenant in tail without poffibility of iffue*, this would exclude time paft as well as prefent, and he might under this defcription never have had any poffibility of iffue. No definition therefore could fo exactly mark him out, as this of tenant *in tail after poffibility of iffue extinct*, which (with a precifion peculiar to our own law) not only takes in the poffibility of iffue in tail which he once had, but alfo ftates that this poffibility is now extinguifhed and gone.

THIS eftate muft be created by the act of God, that is, by the death of that perfon out of whofe body the iffue was to fpring ; for no limitation, conveyance, or other human act can make it. For, if land be given to a man and his wife, and the heirs of their two bodies begotten, and they are divorced *a vinculo matrimonii*, they fhall neither of them have this eftate, but be barely tenants for life, notwithftanding the inheritance once vefted in them[y]. A poffibility of iffue is always fuppofed to exift, in law, unlefs extinguifhed by the death of the parties ; even though the donees be each of them an hundred years old[z].

THIS eftate is of an amphibious nature, partaking partly of an eftate-tail, and partly of an eftate for life. The tenant is, in truth, only tenant for life, but with many of the privileges of a tenant in tail ; as, not to be punifhable for wafte, &c[a]: or, he is tenant in tail, with many of the reftrictions of a tenant for life ; as, to forfeit his eftate if he aliencs it in fee-fimple[b] : whereas fuch alienation by tenant in tail, though voidable by the iffue, is no forfeiture of the eftate to the reverfioner ; who is not concerned in intereft, till all poffibility of iffue be extinct. But, in

[x] 1 Roll. Rep. 184. 11 Rep. 80.
[y] Co. Litt. 28.
[z] Litt. §. 34. Co. Litt. 28.

[a] Co. Litt. 27.
[b] Ibid. 28.

general, the law looks upon this eſtate as equivalent to an eſtate for life only; and, as ſuch, will permit this tenant to exchange his eſtate with a tenant for life; which exchange can only be made, as we ſhall ſee hereafter, of eſtates that are equal in their nature.

III. TENANT *by the curteſy of England,* is where a man marries a woman ſeiſed of lands or tenements in fee-ſimple or fee-tail; that is, of any eſtate of inheritance; and has by her iſſue, born alive, which was capable of inheriting her eſtate. In this caſe, he ſhall, on the death of his wife, hold the lands for his life, as tenant by the curteſy of England[c].

THIS eſtate, according to Littleton, has it's denomination, becauſe it is uſed within the realm of England only; and it is ſaid in the mirrour[d] to have been introduced by king Henry the firſt: but it appears alſo to have been the eſtabliſhed law of Scotland, wherein it was called *curialitas*[e]: ſo that probably our word *curteſy* was underſtood to ſignify rather an attendance upon the lord's *court* or *curtis*, (that is, being his vaſal or tenant) than to denote any peculiar favour belonging to this iſland. And therefore it is laid down[f] that, by having iſſue, the huſband ſhall be intitled to do homage to the lord, for the wife's lands, alone. It is likewiſe uſed in Ireland, by virtue of an ordinance of king Henry III[g]. It alſo appears[h] to have obtained in Normandy; and was likewiſe uſed among the antient Almains or Germans[i]. And yet it is not generally apprehended to have been a conſequence of feodal tenure[k], though I think ſome ſubſtantial feodal reaſons may be given for it's introduction. For, if a woman ſeiſed of lands hath iſſue by her huſband, and dies, the huſband is the natural guardian of the child, and as ſuch is in reaſon entitled to the profits of the lands in order to maintain it: and therefore the

---

[c] Litt. §. 35, 52.
[d] c. 1. §. 3.
[e] Crag. *l.* 2. *t.* 19. §. 4.
[f] Litt. §. 90. Co. Litt. 30. 67.

[g] *Pat.* 11*H.III. m.*30. in 2 Bac. Abr.659.
[h] *Grand Couſtum. c.* 119.
[i] Lindenbrog. LL. *Alman. t.*92.
[k] Wright. 294.

heir

heir apparent of a tenant by the curtefy could not be in ward to the lord of the fee, during the life of fuch tenant [1]. As foon therefore as any child was born, the father began to have a permanent intereſt in the lands, he became one of the *pares curtis*, and was called tenant by the curtefy *initiate*; and this eſtate being once veſted in him by the birth of the child, was not liable to be determined by the fubfequent death or coming of age of the infant.

THERE are four requiſites neceſſary to make a tenancy by the curtefy; marriage, feiſin of the wife, iſſue, and death of the wife [m]. 1. The marriage muſt be canonical, and legal. 2. The feiſin of the wife muſt be an actual feiſin, or poſſeſſion of the lands; not a bare right to poſſefs, which is a feiſin in law, but an actual poſſeſſion, which is a feiſin in deed. And therefore a man ſhall not be tenant by the curtefy of a remainder or reverſion. But of fome incorporeal hereditaments a man may be tenant by the curtefy, though there have been no actual feiſin of the wife; as in cafe of an advowfon, where the church has not become void in the life time of the wife, which a man may hold by the curtefy, becaufe it is impoſſible to have had actual feiſin of it; and *impotentia excufat legem* [n]. If the wife be an idiot, the huſband ſhall not be tenant by the curtefy of her lands; for the king by prerogative is entitled to them, the inſtant ſhe herſelf has any title: and ſince ſhe could never be rightfully feiſed of theſe lands, and the huſband's title depends entirely upon her feiſin, the huſband can have no title as tenant by the curtefy [o]. 3. The iſſue muſt be born alive. Some have had a notion that it muſt be heard to cry; but that is a miſtake. Crying indeed is the *ſtrongeſt* evidence of it's being born alive; but it is not the *only* evidence [p].

ıe iſſue alſo muſt be born during the life of the mother; for, ıf the mother dies in labour, and the Caefarean operation is performed, the huſband in this cafe ſhall not be tenant by the cur-

[1] F. N. B. 143.
[m] Co. Litt. 30.
[n] *Ibid.* 29.

[o] Co. Litt. 30. Plowd. 263.
[p] Dyer. 25. 8 Rep. 34.

tefy : becaufe, at the inftant of the mother's death, he was clearly not entitled, as having had no iffue born, but the land defcended to the child, while he was yet in his mother's womb ; and the eftate, being once fo vefted, fhall not afterwards be taken from him [q]. In gavelkind lands, a hufband may be tenant by the curtefy without having any iffue [r]. But in general there muft be iffue born ; and fuch iffue muft alfo be capable of inheriting the mother's eftate [s]. Therefore if a woman be tenant in tail *male*, and hath only a *daughter* born, the hufband is not thereby entitled to be tenant by the curtefy ; becaufe fuch iffue female can never inherit the eftate in tail male [t]. And this feems to be the true reafon, why the hufband cannot be tenant by the curtefy of any lands of which the wife was not actually feifed : becaufe, in order to intitle himfelf to fuch eftate, he muft have begotten iffue that may be heir to the wife ; but no one, by the ftanding rule of law, can be heir to the anceftor of any land, whereof the anceftor was not actually feifed ; and therefore, as the hufband hath never begotten any iffue that can be heir to thofe lands, he fhall not be tenant of them by the curtefy [u]. And hence we may obferve, with how much nicety and confideration the old rules of law were framed ; and how clofely they are connected and interwoven together, fupporting, illuftrating, and demonftrating one another. The time when the iffue was born is immaterial, provided it were during the coverture : for, whether it were born before or after the wife's feifin of the lands, whether it be living or dead at the time of the feifin, or at the time of the wife's deceafe, the hufband fhall be tenant by the curtefy [w]. The hufband by the birth of the child becomes (as was before obferved) tenant by the curtefy *initiate* [x], and may do many acts to charge the lands ; but his eftate is not *confummate* till the death of the wife ; which is the fourth and laft requifite to make a complete tenant by the curtefy [y].

[q] Co. Litt. 29.
[r] *Ibid* 30.
[s] Litt. §. 56.
[t] Co. Litt. 29.

[u] *Ibid.* 40.
[w] *Ibid.* 29.
[x] *Ibid.* 30.
[y] *Ibid.*

IV. TENANT

IV. TENANT in *dower* is where the hufband of a woman is feifed of an eftate of inheritance, and dies; in this cafe, the wife fhall have the third part of all the lands and tenements whereof he was feifed during the coverture, to hold to herfelf for the term of her natural life [z].

DOWER is called in Latin by the foreign jurifts *doarium*, but by Bracton and our Englifh writers *dos*; which among the Romans fignified the marriage portion, which the wife brought to her hufband; but with us is applied to fignify this kind of eftate, to which the civil law, in it's original ftate, had nothing that bore a refemblance: nor indeed is there any thing in general more different, than the regulation of landed property according to the Englifh, and Roman laws. Dower out of lands feems alfo to have been unknown in the early part of our Saxon conftitution; for, in the laws of king Edmond [a], the wife is directed to be fupported wholly out of the perfonal eftate. Afterwards, as may be feen in gavelkind tenure, the widow became entitled to a conditional eftate in one half of the lands, with a provifo that fhe remained chafte and unmarried [b]; as is ufual alfo in copyhold dowers, or free bench. Yet fome [c] have afcribed the introduction of dower to the Normans, as a branch of *their* local tenures; though we cannot expect any feodal reafon for it's invention, fince it was not a part of the pure, primitive, fimple law of feuds, but was firft of all introduced into that fyftem (wherein it was called *triens*, *tertia* [d], and *dotalitium*) by the emperor Frederick the fecond [e]; who was cotemporary with our king Henry III. It is poffible therefore that it might be with us the relic of a Danifh cuftom: fince, according to the hiftorians of that country, dower was introduced into Denmark by Swein, the father of our Canute the great, out of gratitude to the Danifh ladies, who fold all their

[z] Litt. §. 36.
[a] Wilk. 75.
[b] Somner. Gavelk. 51. Co. Litt. 33. Bro. *Dower*. 70.
[c] Wright. 192.
[d] Crag. *l. 2. t.* 22. §. 9.
[e] *Ibid.*

jewels

jewels to ranfom him when taken prifoner by the Vandals [f]. However this be, the reafon, which our law gives for adopting it, is
a very plain and a fenfible one ; for the fuftenance of the wife,
and the nurture and education of the younger children [g].

I N treating of this eftate, let us, firft, confider, *who* may be
endowed ; fecondly, of *what* fhe may be endowed ; thirdly, the
manner *how* fhe fhall be endowed ; and, fourthly, how dower
may be *barred* or prevented.

1. W H o may be endowed. She muft be the actual wife of
the party at the time of his deceafe. If fhe be divorced *a vinculo matrimonii,* fhe fhall not be endowed ; for *ubi nullum matrimonium, ibi nulla dos* [h]. But a divorce *a menfa et thoro* only doth
not deftroy the dower [i] ; no, not even for adultery itfelf, by the
common law [k]. Yet now by the ftatute Weftm. 2. [l] if a woman
elopes from her hufband, and lives with an adulterer, fhe fhall
lofe her dower, unlefs her hufband be voluntarily reconciled to
her. It was formerly held, that the wife of an idiot might be
endowed, though the hufband of an idiot could not be tenant by
the curtefy [m] : but as it feems to be at prefent agreed, upon principles of found fenfe and reafon, that an idiot cannot marry, being incapable of confenting to any contract, this doctrine cannot
now take place. By the antient law the wife of a perfon attainted
of treafon or felony could not be endowed ; to the intent, fays
Staunforde [n], that, if the love of a man's own life cannot reftrain
him from fuch atrocious acts, the love of his wife and children
may : though Britton [o] gives it another turn ; *viz.* that it is prefumed the wife was privy to her hufband's crime. However, the
ftatute 1 Edw. VI. c. 12. abated the rigor of the common law in

[f] Mod. Un. Hift. xxxii. 91.
[g] Bract. *l.* 2. *c.* 39.   Co. Litt. 30.
[h] Bract. *l.* 2. *c.* 39. §. 4.
[i] Co. Litt. 32.
[k] Yet, among the antient Goths, an a-
dulterefs was punifhed by the lofs of her

dotalitii et trientis ex bonis mobilibus viri:
(Stiernh. *l.* 3. *c.* 2.)
[l] 13 Edw. I. c. 34.
[m] Co. Litt. 31.
[n] P. C. b. 3. c. 3.
[o] c. 110.

this

this particular, and allowed the wife her dower.   But a fubfequent ftatute [p] revived this feverity againft the widows of traitors,
who are now barred of their dower, but not the widows of felons.
An alien alfo cannot be endowed, unlefs fhe be queen confort;
for no alien is capable of holding lands [q].   The wife muft be above
nine years old at her hufband's death, otherwife fhe fhall not be
endowed [r] :. though in Bracton's time the age was indefinite, and
dower was then only due, "*fi uxor poffit dotem promereri, et vi-*
"*rum fuftinere* [s]."

2. WE are next to enquire, of what a wife may be endowed.
And fhe is now by law entitled to be endowed of all lands and
tenements, of which her hufband was feifed in fee-fimple or fee-
tail at any time during the coverture; and of which any iffue,
which fhe might have had, might by poffibility have been heir [t].
Therefore if a man, feifed in fee-fimple, hath a fon by his firft
wife, and after marries a fecond wife, fhe fhall be endowed of
his lands; for her iffue might by poffibility have been heir, on
the death of the fon by the former wife.   But, if there be a
donee in fpecial tail, who holds lands to him and the heirs of his
body begotten on Jane his wife; though Jane may be endowed
of thefe lands, yet if Jane dies, and he marries a fecond wife,
that fecond wife fhall never be endowed of the lands entailed;
for no iffue, that fhe could have, could by any poffibility inherit
them [u].   A feifin in law of the hufband will be as effectual as a
feifin in deed, in order to render the wife dowable; for it is not
in the wife's power to bring the hufband's title to an actual feifin,
as it is in the hufband's power to do with regard to the wife's
lands : which is one reafon why he fhall not be tenant by the
curtefy, but of fuch lands whereof the wife, or he himfelf in
her right, was actually feifed in deed [w].   The feifin of the hufband, for a tranfitory inftant only, when the fame act which gives

[p] 5 & 6 Edw. VI. c. 11.
[q] Co. Litt. 31.
[r] Litt. §. 36.
[s] *l. 2. c. 9. §. 3.*

[t] Litt. §. 36. 53.
[u] *Ibid.* §. 53.
[w] Co. Litt. 31.

him the eftate conveys it alfo out of him again, (as where by a fine land is granted to a man, and he immediately renders it back by the fame fine) fuch a feifin will not intitle the wife to dower [x] : for the land was merely *in tranfitu*, and never refted in the hufband. But, if the land abides in him for a fingle moment, it feems that the wife fhall be endowed thereof [y]. And, in fhort, a widow may be endowed of all her hufband's lands, tenements, and hereditaments, corporeal or incorporeal, under the reftrictions before-mentioned ; unlefs there be fome fpecial reafon to the contrary. Thus, a woman fhall not be endowed of a caftle, built for defence of the realm [z] : nor of a common without ftint ; for, as the heir would then have one portion of this common, and the widow another, and both without ftint, the common would be doubly ftocked [a]. Copyhold eftates alfo are not liable to dower, being only eftates at the lord's will ; unlefs by the fpecial cuftom of the manor, in which cafe it is ufually called the widow's free-bench [b]. But, where dower is allowable, it matters not, though the hufband aliene the lands during the coverture ; for he alienes them liable to dower [c].

3. NEXT, as to the manner in which a woman is to be endowed. There are now fubfifting four fpecies of dower ; the fifth, mentioned by Littleton [d], *de la plus belle,* having been abolifhed together with the military tenures, of which it was a confequence. 1. Dower by the *common law* ; or that which is before defcribed. 2. Dower by particular *cuftom* [e] ; as that the wife fhall have half the hufband's lands, or in fome places the whole, and in fome only a quarter. 3. Dower *ad oftium ecclefiae* [f] : which is

---

[x] Cro. Jac. 615. 2 Rep. 67. Co. Litt. 31.

[y] This doctrine was extended very far by a jury in Wales, where the father and fon were both hanged in one cart, but the fon was fuppofed to have furvived the father, by appearing to ftruggle longeft ; whereby he became feifed of an eftate by furvivorfhip, in confequence of which feifin his widow

had a verdict for her dower. (Cro. Eliz. 503.)

[z] Co. Litt. 31. 3 Lev. 401.

[a] Co. Litt. 32. 1 Jon. 315.

[b] 4 Rep. 22.

[c] Co. Litt. 32.

[d] §. 48, 49.

[e] Litt. §. 37.

[f] *Ibid.* §. 39.

where

where tenant in fee-fimple of full age, openly at the church door, where all marriages were formerly celebrated, after affiance made and (fir Edward Coke in his tranflation adds) troth plighted between them, doth endow his wife with the whole, or fuch quantity as he fhall pleafe, of his lands; at the fame time fpecifying and afcertaining the fame : on which the wife, after her hufband's death, may enter without farther ceremony. 4. Dower *ex affenfu patris*[g]; which is only a fpecies of dower *ad oftium ecclefiae*, made when the hufband's father is alive, and the fon by his confent, expreffly given, endows his wife with parcel of his father's lands. In either of thefe cafes, they muft (to prevent frauds) be made[h] *in facie ecclefiae et ad oftium ecclefiae; non enim valent facta in lecto mortali, nec in camera, aut alibi ubi clandeftina fuere conjugia.*

IT is curious to obferve the feveral revolutions which the doctrine of dower has undergone, fince it's introduction into England. It feems firft to have been of the nature of the dower in gavelkind, before-mentioned; *viz.* a moiety of the hufband's lands, but forfeitable by incontinency or a fecond marriage. By the famous charter of Henry I, this condition, of widowhood and chaftity, was only required in cafe the hufband left any iffue[i]: and afterwards we hear no more of it. Under Henry the fecond, according to Glanvil[k], the dower *ad oftium ecclefiae* was the moft ufual fpecies of dower; and here, as well as in Normandy[l], it was binding upon the wife, if by her confented to at the time of marriage. Neither, in thofe days of feodal rigour, was the hufband allowed to endow her *ad oftium ecclefiae* with more than the third part of the lands whereof he then was feifed, though he might endow her with lefs; left by fuch liberal endowments the lord fhould be defrauded of his wardfhips and other feodal profits[m]. But if no

---

[g] *Ibid.* §. 40.
[h] Bracton. *l.* 2. *c.* 39. §. 4.
[i] *Si mortuo viro uxor ejus remanferit, et fine liberis fuerit, dotem fuam habebit; — fi vero uxor cum liberis remanferit, dotem quidem habebit, dum corpus fuum legitime fervaverit.*

(*Cart. Hen. I. A. D.* 1101. Introd. to great charter, *edit. Oxon.* pag. iv.)
[k] *l.* 6. *c.* 1. & 2.
[l] *Gr. Couftum. c.* 101.
[m] Bract. *l.* 2. *c.* 39. §. 6.

fpecific

fpecific dotation was made at the church porch, then fhe was endowed *by the common law* of the third part (which was called her *dos rationabilis*) of fuch lands and tenements, as the hufband was feifed of at the time of the efpoufals, and no other; unlefs he fpecially engaged before the prieft to endow her of his future acquifitions [n] : and, if the hufband had no lands, an endowment in goods, chattels, or money, at the time of efpoufals, was a bar of any dower [o] in lands which he afterwards acquired [p]. In king John's *magna carta,* and the firft charter of Henry III [q], no mention is made of any alteration of the common law, in refpect of the lands fubject to dower : but in thofe of 1217, and 1224, it is particularly provided, that a widow fhall be intitled for her dower to the third part of *all* fuch lands as the hufband had held in his life time [r] : yet, in cafe of a fpecific endowment of lefs *ad oftium ecclefiae,* the widow had ftill no power to waive it after her hufband's death. And this continued to be law, during the reigns of Henry III and Edward I [s]. In Henry IV's time it was denied to be law, that a woman can be endowed of her hufband's goods and chattels [t] : and, under Edward IV, Littleton lays it down ex-

[n] *De queftu fuo.* (Glanv. *ibid.*) *de terris acquifitis et acquirendis.* (Bract. *ibid.*)

[o] Glanv. *c.* 2.

[p] When fpecial endowments were made *ad oftium ecclefiae,* the hufband, after affiance made, and troth plighted, ufed to declare with what fpecific lands he meant to endow his wife, *(quod dotat eam de tali manerio cum pertinentiis, &c.* Bract. *ibid)* and therefore in the old York ritual (Seld. *Ux. Hebr. l. 2. c.* 27) there is, at this part of the matrimonial fervice, the following rubric; "*fa-* "*cerdos interroget dotem mulieris ; et, fi terra* "*ei in dotem detur, tunc dicatur pfalmus ifte,* "*&c.*" When the wife was endowed generally *(ubi quis uxorem fuam dotaverit in generali, de omnibus terris et tenementis ;* Bract. *ibid.)* the hufband feems to have faid, "with "all my lands and tenements I thee endow;" and then they all became liable to her dower. When he endowed her with perfonalty only,

he ufed to fay, "with all my worldly goods "(or, as the Salifbury ritual has it, *with all* "*my worldly chatel)* I thee endow ;" which intitled the wife to her thirds, or *pars rationabil:s,* of his perfonal eftate, which is provided for by *magna carta, cap.* 26. and will be farther treated of in the concluding chapter of this book : though the retaining this laft expreffion in our modern liturgy, if of any meaning at all, can now refer only to the right of maintenance, which fhe acquires during coverture, out of her hufband's perfonalty.

[q] *A. D.* 1216. *c.* 7. *edit. Oxon.*

[r] *Affignetur autem ei pro dote fua tertia pars totius terrae mariti fui quae fua fuit in vita fua, nifi de minori dotata fuerit ad oftium ecclefiae. c.* 7. *(Ibid.)*

[s] Bract. *ubi fupr.* Britton. *c.* 101, 102. Flet. *l.* 5. *c.* 23. §. 11, 12.

[t] *P.* 7 *Hen. IV.* 13, 14.

preffly,

preſſly, that a woman may be endowed *ad oſtium ecclefiae* with more than a third part [u]; and ſhall have her election, after her huſband's death, to accept ſuch dower, or refuſe it and betake herſelf to her dower at common law [w]. Which ſtate of uncertainty was probably the reaſon, that theſe ſpecific dowers, *ad oſtium ecclefiae* and *ex aſſenſu patris*, have ſince fallen into total diſuſe.

I PROCEED therefore to conſider the method of endowment, or aſſigning dower, by the common law, which is now the only uſual ſpecies. By the old law, grounded on the feodal exactions, a woman could not be endowed without a fine paid to the lord: neither could ſhe marry again without his licence; leſt ſhe ſhould contract herſelf, and ſo convey part of the feud, to the lord's enemy [x]. This licence the lords took care to be well paid for; and, as it ſeems, would ſometimes force the dowager to a ſecond marriage, in order to gain the fine. But, to remedy theſe oppreſſions, it was provided, firſt by the charter of Henry I [y], and afterwards by *magna carta* [z], that the widow ſhall pay nothing for her marriage, nor ſhall be diſtreined to marry afreſh, if ſhe chooſes to live without a huſband; but ſhall not however marry againſt the conſent of the lord: and farther, that nothing ſhall be taken for aſſignment of the widow's dower, but that ſhe ſhall remain in her huſband's capital manſion-houſe for forty days after his death, during which time her dower ſhall be aſſigned. Theſe forty days are called the widow's *quarentine*; a term made uſe of in law to ſignify the number of forty days, whether applied to this occaſion, or any other [a]. The particular lands to be held in dower, muſt be aſſigned [b] by the heir of the huſband, or his guardian; not only for the ſake of notoriety, but alſo to entitle the lord of the fee to demand his ſervices of the heir, in reſpect of the lands ſo held. For the heir by this entry becomes tenant

[u] §. 39 F. N. B. 150.
[w] §. 41.
[x] Mirr. c. 1. §. 3.
[y] *ubi ſupra.*
[z] *cap.* 7.

[a] It ſignifies, in particular, the forty days, which perſons coming from infected countries are obliged to wait, before they are permitted to land in England.
[b] Co. Litt. 34, 35.

thereof

thereof to the lord, and the widow is immediate tenant to the heir, by a kind of fubinfeudation or under-tenancy, completed by this inveftiture or affignment : which tenure may ftill be created, notwithftanding the ftatute of *quia emptores*, becaufe the heir parts not with the fee-fimple, but only with an eftate for life. If the heir or his guardian do not affign her dower within the term of quarentine, or do affign it unfairly, fhe has her remedy at law, and the fheriff is appointed to affign it[c]. If the thing of which fhe is endowed be divifible, her dower muft be fet out by metes and bounds ; but, if it be indivifible, fhe muft be endowed fpecially ; as, of the third prefentation to a church, the third toll-difh of a mill, the third part of the profits of an office, the third fheaf of tithe, and the like[d].

UPON preconcerted marriages, and in eftates of confiderable confequence, tenancy in dower happens very feldom : for, the claim of the wife to her dower at the common law diffufing itfelf fo extenfively, it became a great clog to alienations, and was otherwife inconvenient to families. Wherefore, fince the alteration of the antient law refpecting dower *ad oftium ecclefiae*, which hath occafioned the intire difufe of that fpecies of dower, jointures have been introduced in their ftead, as a bar to the claim at common law. Which leads me to enquire, laftly,

4. HOW dower may be *barred* or prevented. A widow may be barred of her dower not only by elopement, divorce, being an alien, the treafon of her hufband, and other difabilities beforementioned, but alfo by detaining the title deeds, or evidences of the eftate from the heir ; until fhe reftores them[e] : and, by the ftatute of Glocefter[f], if a dowager alienes the land affigned her for dower, fhe forfeits it *ipfo facto*, and the heir may recover it by action. A woman alfo may be barred of her dower, by levying a fine or fuffering a recovery of the lands, during her cover-

[c] Co. Litt. 34. 35.
[d] *Ibid.* 32.

[e] *Ibid.* 39.
[f] 6 Edw. I. c. 7.

ture[g].

ture[g]. But the moſt uſual method of barring dowers is by jointures, as regulated by the ſtatute 27 Hen.VIII. c. 10.

A JOINTURE, which ſtrictly ſpeaking ſignifies a joint eſtate,
limited to both huſband and wife, but in common acceptation
extends alſo to a ſole eſtate, limited to the wife only, is thus defined by ſir Edward Coke[h]; " a competent livelyhood of freehold
" for the wife, of lands and tenements; to take effect, in profit
" or poſſeſſion, preſently after the death of the huſband; for the
" life of the wife at leaſt." This deſcription is framed from the
purview of the ſtatute 27 Hen.VIII. c. 10. before-mentioned;
commonly called the ſtatute of *uſes*, of which we ſhall ſpeak
fully hereafter. At preſent I have only to obſerve, that, before
the making of that ſtatute, the greateſt part of the land of England was conveyed to uſes; the property or poſſeſſion of the ſoil
being veſted in one man, and the *uſe*, or profits thereof, in another; whoſe directions, with regard to the diſpoſition thereof,
the former was in conſcience obliged to follow, and might be
compelled by a court of equity to obſerve. Now, though a huſband had the *uſe* of lands in abſolute fee-ſimple, yet the wife was
not entitled to any dower therein; he not being *ſeiſed* thereof:
wherefore it became uſual, on marriage, to ſettle by expreſs deed
ſome ſpecial eſtate to the uſe of the huſband and his wife, for
their lives, in joint-tenancy or jointure; which ſettlement would
be a proviſion for the wife in caſe ſhe ſurvived her huſband. At
length the ſtatute of uſes ordained, that ſuch as had the *uſe* of
lands, ſhould, to all intents and purpoſes, be reputed and taken
to be abſolutely *ſeiſed* and poſſeſſed of the ſoil itſelf. In conſequence of which legal ſeiſin, all wives would have become dowable of ſuch lands as were held to the uſe of their huſbands, and
alſo entitled at the ſame time to any ſpecial lands that might be
ſettled in jointure; had not the ſame ſtatute provided, that upon
making ſuch an eſtate in jointure to the wife before marriage,
ſhe ſhall be for ever precluded from her dower[i]. But then theſe

[g] Pig. of recov. 66.
[h] 1 Inſt. 36.

[i] 4 Rep. 1, 2.

four requisites must be punctually observed. 1. The jointure must take effect immediately on the death of the husband. 2. It must be for her own life at least, and not *pur auter vie*, or for any term of years, or other smaller estate. 3. It must be made to herself, and no other in trust for her. 4. It must be made, and so in the deed particularly expressed to be, in satisfaction of her whole dower, and not of any particular part of it. If the jointure be made to her *after* marriage, she has her election after her husband's death, as in dower *ad ostium ecclesiae*, and may either accept it, or refuse it and betake herself to her dower at common law; for she was not capable of consenting to it during coverture. And if, by any fraud or accident, a jointure made before marriage proves to be on a bad title, and the jointress is evicted, or turned out of possession, she shall then (by the provisions of the same statue) have her dower *pro tanto* at the common law [k].

THERE are some advantages attending tenants in dower that do not extend to jointresses; and so, *vice versa*, jointresses are in some respects more privileged than tenants in dower. Tenant in dower by the old common law is subject to no tolls or taxes; and hers is almost the only estate on which, when derived from the king's debtor, the king cannot distrain for his debt; if contracted during the coverture [l]. But, on the other hand, a widow may enter at once, without any formal process, on her jointure land; as she also might have done on dower *ad ostium ecclesiae*, which a

---

[k] These settlements, previous to marriage, seem to have been in use among the antient Germans, and their kindred nation the Gauls. Of the former Tacitus gives us this account. "*Dotem non uxor marito, sed* "*uxori maritus affert: intersunt parentes et* "*propinqui, et munera probant.*" (*de mer. Germ. c.* 18.) And Caesar, (*de bello Gallico, l.* 6. *c.* 18.) has given us the terms of a marriage settlement among the Gauls, as nicely calculated as any modern jointure. "*Viri, quantas pecunias ab uxoribus dotis no-* "*mine acceperunt, tantas ex suis bonis, aesti-*

"*matione facta, cum dotibus communicant.* "*Hujus omnis pecuniae conjunctim ratio habe-* "*tur, fructusque servantur. Uter eorum vita* "*superarit, ad eum pars utriusque cum fruc-* "*tibus superiorum temporum pervenit.*" The dauphin's commentator on Caesar supposes that this Gaulish custom was the ground of the new regulations made by Justinian (*Nov.* 97.) with regard to the provision for widows among the Romans: but surely there is as much reason to suppose, that it gave the hint for our statutable jointures.

[l] Co. Litt. 31. a. F. N. B. 150.

jointure

jointure in many points refembles; and the refemblance was ftill greater, while that fpecies of dower continued in it's primitive ftate: whereas no fmall trouble, and a very tedious method of proceeding, is neceffary to compel a legal affignment of dower [m]. And, what is more, though dower be forfeited by the treafon of the hufband, yet lands fettled in jointure remain unimpeached to the widow [n]. Wherefore fir Edward Coke very juftly gives it the preference, as being more fure and fafe to the widow, than even dower *ad oftium ecclefiae,* the moft eligible fpecies of any.

[m] Co. Litt. 36.   [n] *Ibid.* 37.

CHAPTER THE NINTH.

OF ESTATES, LESS THAN FREEHOLD.

O F eftates, that are lefs than freehold, there are three forts ;
1. Eftates for years: 2. Eftates at will: 3. Eftates by
fufferance.

I. AN eftate for *years* is a contract for the poffeffion of lands
or tenements, for fome determinate period: and it happens where
a man letteth them to another for the term of a certain number
of years, agreed upon between the leffor and the leffee [a], and
the leffee enters thereon [b]. If the leafe be but for half a year,
or a quarter, or any lefs time, this leffee is refpected as a tenant
for years, and is ftiled fo in fome legal proceedings ; a year being
the fhorteft term which the law in this cafe takes notice of [c].
And this may, not improperly, lead us into a fhort explanation
of the divifion and calculation of time by the Englifh law.

THE fpace of a year is a determinate and well-known period,
confifting commonly of 365 days: for, though in biffextile or

---

[a] We may here remark, once for all, that
the terminations of "—or" and "—ee"
obtain, in law, the one an active, the other
a paffive fignification ; the former ufually
denoting the doer of any act, the latter him
to whom it is done. The feoffor is he that
maketh a feoffment ; the feoffee is he to

whom it is made: the donor is one that
giveth lands in tail; the donee is he who
receiveth it : he that granteth a leafe is denominated the leffor ; and he to whom it
is granted the leffee. (Litt. §. 57.)

[b] *Ibid.* 58.
[c] *Ibid.* 67.

leap-years

leap-years it confifts properly of 366, yet by the ftatute 21 Hen. III. the increafing day in the leap-year, together with the preceding day, fhall be accounted for one day only. That of a month is more ambiguous: there being, in common ufe, two ways of calculating months; either as lunar, confifting of twenty eight days, the fuppofed revolution of the moon, thirteen of which make a year; or, as calendar months, of unequal lengths, according to the Julian divifion in our common almanacs, commencing at the calends of each month, whereof in a year there are only twelve. A month in law is a lunar month, or twenty eight days, unlefs otherwife expreffed; not only becaufe it is always one uniform period, but becaufe it falls naturally into a quarterly divifion by weeks. Therefore a leafe for "twelve months" is only for forty eight weeks; but if be for "*a* twelve-month" in the fingular number, it is good for the whole year[d]. For herein the law recedes from it's ufual calculation, becaufe the ambiguity between the two methods of computation ceafes; it being generally underftood that by the fpace of time called thus, in the fingular number, a twelvemonth, is meant the whole year, confifting of one folar revolution. In the fpace of a day all the twenty four hours are ufually reckoned; the law generally rejecting all fractions of a day, in order to avoid difputes[e]. Therefore, if I am bound to pay money on any certain day, I difcharge the obligation if I pay it before twelve o'clock at night; after which the following day commences. But to return to eftates for years.

THESE eftates were originally granted to mere farmers or hufbandmen, who every year rendered fome equivalent in money, provifions, or other rent, to the leffors or landlords; but, in order to encourage them to manure and cultivate the ground, they had a permanent intereft granted them, not determinable at the will of the lord. And yet their poffeffion was efteemed of fo little confequence, that they were rather confidered as the bailiffs or fervants of the lord, who were to receive and account for the

[d] 6 Rep. 61.   [e] Co. Litt. 135.

profits,

profits at a fettled price, than as having any property of their
own. And therefore they were not allowed to have a freehold
eftate : but their intereft (fuch as it was) vefted after their deaths
in their executors, who were to make up the accounts of their
teftator with the lord, and his other creditors, and were intitled
to the ftock upon the farm. The leffee's eftate might alfo, by
the antient law, be at any time defeated, by a common recovery
fuffered by the tenant of the freehold [f] ; which annihilated all
leafes for years then fubfifting, unlefs afterwards renewed by the
recoveror, whofe title was fuppofed fuperior to his by whom
thofe leafes were granted.

WHILE eftates for years were thus precarious, it is no wonder
that they were ufually very fhort, like our modern leafes upon
rack rent ; and indeed we are told [g] that by the antient law no
leafes for more than forty years were allowable, becaufe any longer
poffeffion (efpecially when given without any livery declaring the
nature and duration of the eftate) might tend to defeat the inheritance. Yet this law, if it ever exifted, was foon antiquated :
for we may obferve, in Madox's collection of antient inftru-
ments, fome leafes for years of a pretty early date, which confiderably exceed that period [h] ; and long terms, for three hundred
years at leaft, were certainly in ufe in the time of Edward III [i],
and probably of Edward I [k]. But certainly, when by the ftatute
21 Hen. VIII. c. 15. the termor (that is, he who is intitled to the
term of years) was protected againft thefe fictitious recoveries,
and his intereft rendered fecure and permanent, long terms began
to be more frequent than before ; and were afterwards extenfively
introduced, being found extremely convenient for family fettlements and mortgages : continuing fubject, however, to the fame
rules of fucceffion, and with the fame inferiority to freeholds,

[f] Co. Litt. 46.
[g] Mirror. c. 2. §. 27. Co. Litt. 45, 46.
[h] Madox *Formulare Anglican.* n°. 239.
*fol.*140. Demife for eighty years, 21 Ric. II.
.... *Ibid.* n°. 245. *fol.* 146: for the like
term, *A. D.* 1429. ..... *Ibid.* n°. 248.
fol. 148. for fifty years, 7 Edw. IV.
[i] 32 Aff. pl. 6.
[k] Stat. of mortmain, 7 Edw. I.

as

as when they were little better than tenancies at the will of the landlord.

EVERY eftate which muft expire at a period certain and pre-fixed, by whatever words created, is an eftate for years. And therefore this eftate is frequently called a term, *terminus*, becaufe it's duration or continuance is bounded, limited, and determined: for every fuch eftate muft have a certain beginning, and certain end[1]. But *id certum eft, quod certum reddi poteft :* therefore if a man make a leafe to another, for fo many years as J. S. fhall name, it is a good leafe for years[m]; for though it is at prefent uncertain, yet when J. S. hath named the years, it is then re-duced to a certainty. If no day of commencement is named in the creation of this eftate, it begins from the making, or delivery, of the leafe[n]. A leafe for fo many years as J. S. fhall live, is void from the beginning[o]; for it is neither certain, nor can ever be reduced to a certainty, during the continuance of the leafe. And the fame doctrine holds, if a parfon make a leafe of his glebe for fo many years as he fhall continue parfon of Dale; for this is ftill more uncertain. But a leafe for twenty or more years, if J. S. fhall fo long live, or if he fhall fo long continue parfon, is good[p]: for there is a certain period fixed, beyond which it cannot laft; though it may determine fooner, on the death of J. S. or his ceafing to be parfon there.

WE have before remarked, and endeavoured to affign the rea-fon of, the inferiority in which the law places an eftate for years, when compared with an eftate for life, or an inheritance: ob-ferving, that an eftate for life, even it be *pur auter vie*, is a free-hold; but that an eftate for a thoufand years is only a chattel, and reckoned part of the perfonal eftate[q]. Hence it follows, that a leafe for years may be made to commence *in futuro*, though a leafe for life cannot. As, if I grant lands to Titius to hold from

[1] Co. Litt. 45.
[m] 6 Rep. 35.
[n] Co. Litt. 46

[o] *Ibid.* 45.
[p] *Ibid.*
[q] *Ibid.* 46.

Michaelmas

Michaelmas next for twenty years, this is good; but to hold from Michaelmas next for the term of his natural life, is void. For no eſtate of freehold can commence *in futuro*; becauſe it cannot be created at common law without livery of ſeiſin, or corporal poſſeſſion of the land : and corporal poſſeſſion cannot be given of an eſtate now, which is not to commence now, but hereafter[r]. And, becauſe no livery of ſeiſin is neceſſary to a leaſe for years, ſuch leſſee is not ſaid to be *ſeiſed*, or to have true legal ſeiſin, of the lands. Nor indeed does the bare leaſe veſt any eſtate in the leſſee; but only gives him a right of entry on the tenement, which right is called his *intereſt in the term*, or *intereſſe termini :* but when he has actually ſo entered, and thereby accepted the grant, the eſtate is then and not before veſted in him, and he is *poſſeſſed*, not properly of the land, but of the term of years[s] : the poſſeſſion or ſeiſin of the *land* remaining ſtill in him who hath the freehold. Thus the word, *term*, does not merely ſignify the time ſpecified in the leaſe, but the eſtate alſo and intereſt that paſſes by that leaſe : and therefore the *term* may expire, during the continuance of the *time*; as by ſurrender, forfeiture, and the like. For which reaſon, if I grant a leaſe to A for the term of three years, and after the expiration of the ſaid *term* to B for ſix years, and A ſurrenders or forfeits his leaſe at the end of *one* year, B's intereſt ſhall immediately take effect : but if the remainder had been to B from and after the expiration of the ſaid *three years*, or from and after the expiration of the ſaid *time*, in this caſe B's intereſt will not commence till the time is fully elapſed, whatever may become of A's term[t].

TENANT for term of years hath incident to, and inſeparable from his eſtate, unleſs by ſpecial agreement, the ſame eſtovers, which we formerly obſerved[u] that tenant for life was entitled to; that is to ſay, houſe-bote, fire-bote, plough-bote, and hay-bote[w]: terms which have been already explained[x].

[r] 5 Rep. 94.
[s] Co. Litt. 46.
[t] *Ibid.* 45.

[u] pag. 122.
[w] Co. Litt. 45.
[x] pag. 35.

WITH

WITH regard to emblements, or profits of land fowed by tenant for years, there is this difference between him, and tenant for life : that where the term of tenant for years depends upon a certainty, as if he holds from midfummer for ten years, and in the laft year he fows a crop of corn, and it is not ripe and cut before midfummer, the end of his term, the landlord fhall have it ; for the tenant knew the expiration of his term, and therefore it was his own folly to fow what he never could reap the profits of[y]. But where the leafe for years depends upon an uncertainty ; as, upon the death of the leffor, being himfelf only tenant for life, or being a hufband feifed in right of his wife ; or if the term of years be determinable upon a life or lives ; in all thefe cafes, the eftate for years not being certainly to expire at a time foreknown, but merely by the act of God, the tenant, or his executors, fhall have the emblements in the fame manner, that a tenant for life or his executors fhall be intitled thereto[z]. Not fo, if it determine by the act of the party himfelf ; as if tenant for years does any thing that amounts to a forfeiture : in which cafe the emblements fhall go to the leffor, and not to the leffee, who hath determined his eftate by his own default[a].

II. THE fecond fpecies of eftates not freehold are eftates at *will*. An eftate at will is where lands and tenements are let by one man to another, to have and to hold at the will of the leffor ; and the tenant by force of this leafe obtains poffeffion[b]. Such tenant hath no certain indefeafible eftate, nothing that can be affigned by him to any other ; for that the leffor may determine his will, and put him out whenever he pleafes. But every eftate at will is at the will of both parties, landlord and tenant, fo that either of them may determine his will, and quit his connexions with the other at his own pleafure[c]. Yet this muft be underftood with fome reftriction. For, if the tenant at will fows his land,

[y] Litt. §. 68.
[z] Co. Litt. 56.
[a] *Ibid.* 55.

[b] Litt. §. 68.
[c] Co. Litt. 55.

and the landlord before the corn is ripe, or before it is reaped, puts him out, yet the tenant ſhall have the emblements, and free ingreſs, egreſs, and regreſs, to cut and carry away the profits[d]. And this for the ſame reaſon, upon which all the caſes of emblements turn; *viz.* the point of uncertainty : ſince the tenant could not poſſibly know when his landlord would determine his will, and therefore could make no proviſion againſt it; and having ſown the land, which is for the good of the public, upon a reaſonable preſumption, the law will not ſuffer him to be a loſer by it. But it is otherwiſe, and upon reaſon equally good, where the tenant himſelf determines the will; for in this caſe the landlord ſhall have the profits of the land[e].

WHAT act does, or does not, amount to a determination of the will on either ſide, has formerly been matter of great debate in our courts. But it is now, I think, ſettled, that (beſides the expreſs determination of the leſſor's will, by declaring that the leſſee ſhall hold no longer; which muſt either be made upon the land[f], or notice muſt be given to the leſſee[g]) the exertion of any act of ownerſhip by the leſſor, as entring upon the premiſes and cutting timber[h], taking a diſtreſs for rent and impounding them thereon[i], or making a feoffment, or leaſe for years of the land to commence immediately[k]; any act of deſertion by the leſſee, as aſſigning his eſtate to another, or committing waſte, which is an act inconſiſtent with ſuch a tenure[l]; or, which is *inſtar omnium*, the death or outlawry, of either leſſor or leſſee[m]; puts an end to or determines the eſtate at will.

THE law is however careful, that no ſudden determination of the will by one party ſhall tend to the manifeſt and unforeſeen prejudice of the other. This appears in the caſe of emblements

---

[d] Co. Litt. 56.
[e] *Ibid.* 55.
[f] *Ibid.*
[g] 1 Ventr. 248.
[h] Co. Litt. 55.

[i] *Ibid.* 57.
[k] 1 Roll. Abr. 860. 2 Lev. 88.
[l] Co. Litt. 57.
[m] 5 Rep. 116. Co. Litt. 57. 62.

before-

before-mentioned; and, by a parity of reason, the lessee after the determination of the lessor's will, shall have reasonable ingress and egress to fetch away his goods and utensils [n]. And, if rent be payable quarterly or half-yearly, and the lessee determines the will, the rent shall be paid to the end of the current quarter or half-year [o]. And, upon the same principle, courts of law have of late years leant as much as possible against construing demises, where no certain term is mentioned, to be tenancies at will; but have rather held them to be tenancies from year to year so long as both parties please, especially where an annual rent is reserved: in which case they will not suffer either party to determine the tenancy even at the end of the year, without reasonable notice to the other.

THERE is one species of estates at will, that deserves a more particular regard than any other; and that is, an estate held by copy of court roll; or, as we usually call it, a *copyhold* estate. This, as was before observed [p], was in it's original and foundation nothing better than a mere estate at will. But, the kindness and indulgence of successive lords of manors having permitted these estates to be enjoyed by the tenants and their heirs, according to particular customs established in their respective districts; therefore, though they still are held at the will of the lord, and so are in general expressed in the court rolls to be, yet that will is qualified, restrained, and limited, to be exerted according to the custom of the manor. This custom, being suffered to grow up by the lord, is looked upon as the evidence and interpreter of his will: his will is no longer arbitrary and precarious; but fixed and ascertained by the custom to be the same, and no other, that has time out of mind been exercised and declared by his ancestors. A copyhold tenant is therefore now full as properly a tenant by the custom, as a tenant at will, the custom having arisen from a series of uniform wills. And therefore it is rightly observed by Calthorpe [q], that " copyholders and customary tenants differ not

---

[n] Litt. §. 69.
[o] Salk. 414. 1 Sid. 339.

[p] pag. 93.
[q] on copyholds. 51. 54.

" so

" fo much in nature as in name : for although fome be called
" copyholders, fome cuftomary, fome tenants by the virge, fome
" bafe tenants, fome bond tenants, and fome by one name and
" fome by another, yet do they all agree in fubftance and kind of
" tenure : all the faid lands are holden in one general kind, that
" is, by cuftom and continuance of time ; and the diverfity of
" their names doth not alter the nature of their tenure."

ALMOST every copyhold tenant being therefore thus tenant
at the will of the lord according to the cuftom of the manor ;
which cuftoms differ as much as the humour and temper of the
refpective antient lords, (from whence we may account for their
great variety) fuch tenant, I fay, may have, fo far as the cuftom
warrants, any other of the eftates or quantities of intereft, which
we have hitherto confidered, or may hereafter confider, to hold
united with this cuftomary eftate at will. A copyholder may, in
many manors, be tenant in fee-fimple, in fee-tail, for life, by
the curtefy, in dower, for years, at fufferance, or on condition :
fubject however to be deprived of thefe eftates upon the concurrence of thofe circumftances which the will of the lord, promul-
ged by immemorial cuftom, has declared to be a forfeiture or abfolute determination of thofe interefts ; as in fome manors the
want of iffue male, in others the cutting down timber, the non-
payment of a fine, and the like. Yet none of thefe interefts
amount to freehold ; for the freehold of the whole manor abides
always in the lord only [r], who hath granted out the ufe and occupation, but not the corporal feifin or true poffeffion, of certain parts and parcels thereof, to thefe his cuftomary tenants at
will.

THE reafon of originally granting out this complicated kind
of intereft, fo that the fame man fhall, with regard to the fame
land, be at one and the fame time tenant in fee-fimple and alfo
tenant at the lord's will, feems to have arifen from the nature of
villenage tenure ; in which a grant of any eftate of freehold, or

[r] Litt. §. 81. 2 Inft. 325.

even for years abfolutely, was an immediate enfranchifement of
the villein[s]. The lords therefore, though they were willing to
enlarge the intereft of their villeins, by granting them eftates
which might endure for their lives, or fometimes be defcendible
to their iffue, yet did not care to manumit them entirely; and
for that reafon it feems to have been contrived, that a power of
refumption at the will of the lord fhould be annexed to thefe
grants, whereby the tenants were ftill kept in a ftate of villenage,
and no freehold at all was conveyed to them in their refpective
lands: and of courfe, as the freehold of all lands muft neceffarily reft and abide fomewhere, the law fuppofes it to continue and
remain in the lord. Afterwards, when thefe villeins became
modern copyholders, and had acquired by cuftom a fure and indefeafible eftate in their lands, on performing the ufual fervices,
but yet continued to be ftiled in their admiffions tenants at the
will of the lord,---the law ftill fuppofed it an abfurdity to allow,
that fuch at were thus nominally tenants at will could have any
freehold intereft: and therefore continued, and ftill continues,
to determine, that the freehold of lands fo holden abides in the
lord of the manor, and not in the tenant; for though he *really*
holds to him and his heirs for ever, yet he is alfo *faid* to hold at
another's will. But, with regard to certain other copyholders, of
free or privileged tenure, which are derived from the antient tenants in villein-focage[t], and are not faid to hold *at the will of the
lord*, but only *according to the cuftom of the manor*, there is no
fuch abfurdity in allowing them to be capable of enjoying a freehold intereft; and therefore the law doth not fuppofe the freehold
of fuch lands to reft in the lord of whom they are holden, but in
the tenants themfelves[u]; who are allowed to have a freehold *intereft*, though not a freehold *tenure*.

HOWEVER, in common cafes, copyhold eftates are ftill
ranked (for the reafons above-mentioned) among tenancies at

---

[s] Mirr. c. 2. §. 28. Litt. §. 204, 5, 6.
[t] See page 98, &c.
[u] Fitzh. *Abr. tit. corone.* 310. *cuftom.* 12.
Bro. *Abr. tit. cuftom.* 2. 17. *tenant per copie.* 22.

9 Rep. 76. Co. Litt. 59. Co. Copyh. §. 32.
Cro. Car. 229. 1 Roll. Abr. 562. 2 Ventr.
143. Carth. 432. Lord Raym. 1225.

will; though cuftom, which is the life of the common law, has eftablifhed a permanent property in the copyholders, who were formerly nothing better than bondmen, equal to that of the lord himfelf, in the tenements holden of the manor: nay fometimes even fuperior; for we may now look upon a copyholder of inheritance, with a fine certain, to be little inferior to an abfolute freeholder in point of intereft, and in other refpects, particularly in the clearnefs and fecurity of his title, to be frequently in a better fituation.

III. An eftate at *fufferance*, is where one comes into poffeffion of land by lawful title, but keeps it afterwards without any title at all. As if a man takes a leafe for a year, and, after the year is expired, continues to hold the premifes without any frefh leave from the owner of the eftate. Or, if a man maketh a leafe at will, and dies, the eftate at will is thereby determined; but if the tenant continueth poffeffion, he is tenant at fufferance [w]. But no man can be tenant at fufferance againft the king, to whom no *laches*, or neglect, in not entering and oufting the tenant, is ever imputed by law: but his tenant, fo holding over, is confidered as an abfolute intruder [x]. But, in the cafe of a fubject, this eftate may be deftroyed whenever the true owner fhall make an actual entry on the lands and ouft the tenant; for, before entry, he cannot maintain an action of trefpafs againft the tenant by fufferance, as he might againft a ftranger [y]: and the reafon is, becaufe the tenant being once in by a lawful title, the law (which prefumes no wrong in any man) will fuppofe him to continue upon a title equally lawful; unlefs the owner of the land by fome public and avowed act, fuch as entry is, will declare his continuance to be tortious, or, in common language, wrongful.

Thus ftands the law, with regard to tenants by fufferance; and landlords are obliged in thefe cafes to make formal entries upon their lands [z], and recover poffeffion by the legal procefs of

[w] Co. Litt. 57.
[x] *Ibid.*
[y] *Ibid.*
[z] 5 Mod. 384.

ejectment:

ejectment : and at the utmoft, by the common law, the tenant was bound to account for the profits of the land fo by him detained. But now, by ftatute 4 Geo. II. c. 28. in cafe any tenant for life or years, or other perfon claiming under or by collufion with fuch tenant, fhall wilfully hold over after the determination of the term, and demand made in writing for recovering the poffeffion of the premifes, by him to whom the remainder or reverfion thereof fhall belong; fuch perfon, fo holding over, fhall pay, for the time he continues, at the rate of double the yearly value of the lands fo detained. This has almoft put an end to the practice of tenancy by fufferance, unlefs with the tacit confent of the owner of the tenement.

CHAPTER THE TENTH.

OF ESTATES UPON CONDITION.

BESIDES the feveral divifions of eftates, in point of intereft, which we have confidered in the three preceding
chapters, there is alfo another fpecies ftill remaining, which is
called an eftate *upon condition*; being fuch whofe exiftence depends upon the happening or not happening of fome uncertain
event, whereby the eftate may be either originally created, or enlarged, or finally defeated [a]. And thefe conditional eftates I have
chofen to referve till laft, becaufe they are indeed more properly
qualifications of other eftates, than a diftinct fpecies of themfelves; feeing that any quantity of intereft, a fee, a freehold, or
a term of years, may depend upon thefe provifional reftrictions.
Eftates then upon condition, thus underftood, are of two forts:
1. Eftates upon condition *implied*: 2. Eftates upon condition
expreffed: under which laft may be included, 3. Eftates held in
vadio, gage, or *pledge*: 4. Eftates by *ftatute merchant* or *ftatute
ftaple*: 5. Eftates held by *elegit*.

I. ESTATES upon condition implied in law, are where a
grant of an eftate has a condition annexed to it infeparably, from
it's effence and conftitution, although no condition be expreffed
in words. As if a grant be made to a man of an office, generally,
without adding other words; the law tacitly annexes hereto a
fecret condition, that the grantee fhall duly execute his office [b],

[a] Co. Litt. 201.   [b] Litt. §. 378.

on

on breach of which condition it is lawful for the grantor, or his heirs, to ouſt him, and grant it to another perſon[c]. For an office, either public or private, may be forfeited by *miſ-uſer* or *non-uſer*; both of which are breaches of this implied condition. 1. By *miſ-uſer*, or abuſe; as if a judge takes a bribe, or a park-keeper kills deer without authority. 2. By *non-uſer*, or neglect; which in public offices, that concern the adminiſtration of juſtice, or the commonwealth, is of itſelf a direct and immediate cauſe of forfeiture: but non-uſer of a private office is no cauſe of forfeiture, unleſs ſome ſpecial damage is proved to be occaſioned thereby[d]. For in the one caſe delay muſt neceſſarily be occaſioned in the affairs of the public, which require a conſtant attention; but, private offices not requiring ſo regular and unremitted a ſervice, the temporary neglect of them is not neceſſarily productive of miſchief; upon which account ſome ſpecial loſs muſt be proved, in order to vacate theſe. Franchiſes alſo, being regal privileges in the hands of a ſubject, are held to be granted on the ſame condition of making a proper uſe of them; and therefore they may be loſt and forfeited, like offices, either by abuſe or by neglect[e].

UPON the ſame principle proceed all the forfeitures which are given by law of life eſtates and others; for any acts done by the tenant himſelf, that are incompatible with the eſtate which he holds. As if tenants for life or years enfeoff a ſtranger in fee-ſimple: this is, by the common law, a forfeiture of their ſeveral eſtates; being a breach of the condition which the law annexes thereto, *viz.* that they ſhall not attempt to create a greater eſtate than they themſelves are entitled to[f]. So if any tenants for years, for life, or in fee, commit a felony; the king or other lord of the fee is entitled to have their tenements, becauſe their eſtate is determined by the breach of the condition, "that they ſhall not "commit felony," which the law tacitly annexes to every feodal donation.

[c] Litt. §. 379.
[d] Co. Litt. 233.
[e] 9 Rep. 50.
[f] Co. Litt. 215.

II. An estate on condition expressed in the grant itself, is where an estate is granted, either in fee-simple or otherwise, with an express qualification annexed, whereby the estate granted shall either commence, be enlarged, or be defeated, upon performance or breach of such qualification or condition [g]. These conditions are therefore either *precedent*, or *subsequent*. Precedent are such as must happen or be performed before the estate can vest or be enlarged; subsequent are such, by the failure or nonperformance of which an estate already vested may be defeated. Thus, if an estate for life be limited to A upon his marriage with B, the marriage is a precedent condition, and till that happens no estate [h] is vested in A. Or, if a man grant to his lessee for years, that upon payment of a hundred marks within the term he shall have the fee, this also is a condition precedent, and the fee-simple passeth not till the hundred marks be paid [i]. But if a man grant an estate in fee-simple, reserving to himself and his heirs a certain rent; and that, if such rent be not paid at the times limited, it shall be lawful for him and his heirs to re-enter, and avoid the estate; in this case the grantee and his heirs have an estate upon condition subsequent, which is defeasible if the condition be not strictly performed [k]. To this class may also be referred all base fees, and fee-simples conditional at the common law [l]. Thus an estate to a man and his heirs, *tenants of the manor of Dale*, is an estate on condition that he and his heirs continue tenants of that manor. And so, if a personal annuity be granted at this day to a man and the heirs of his body; as this is no tenement within the statute of Westminster the second, it remains, as at common law, a fee-simple on condition that the grantee has heirs of his body. Upon the same principle depend all the determinable estates of freehold, which we mentioned in the eighth chapter; as *durante viduitate, &c:* these are estates upon condition that the grantees do not marry, and the like. And, on the breach of any

[g] Co. Litt. 201.
[h] Show. Parl. Caf. 83, &c.
[i] Co. Litt. 217.

[k] Litt. §. 325.
[l] See pag. 109, 110, 111.

of

of thefe fubfequent conditions by the failure of thefe contingencies; by the grantee's not continuing tenant of the manor of
Dale, by not having heirs of his body, or by not continuing fole;
the eftates which were refpectively vefted in each grantee are
wholly determined and void.

A DISTINCTION is however made between a *condition in
deed* and a *limitation*, which Littleton [m] denominates alfo a *condition in law*. For when an eftate is fo exprefly confined and limited by the words of it's creation, that it cannot endure for any
longer time than till the contingency happens upon which the
eftate is to fail, this is denominated a *limitation :* as when land is
granted to a man, *fo long as* he is parfon of Dale, or *while* he
continues unmarried, or *until* out of the rents and profits he fhall
have made 500 *l.* and the like [n]. In fuch cafes the eftate determines as foon as the contingency happens, (when he ceafes to be
parfon, marries a wife, or has received the 500 *l.*) and the next
fubfequent eftate, which depends upon fuch determination, becomes immediately vefted, without any act to be done by him
who is next in expectancy. But when an eftate is, ftrictly fpeaking, upon *condition in deed* (as if granted exprefly *upon condition*
to be void upon the payment of 40 *l.* by the grantor, or *fo that*
the grantee continues unmarried, or *provided* he goes to York,
&c. [o]) the law permits it to endure beyond the time when fuch
contingency happens, unlefs the grantor or his heirs or affigns
take advantage of the breach of the condition, and make either
an entry or a claim in order to avoid the eftate [p]. But, though
ftrict words of condition be ufed in the creation of the eftate, yet
if on breach of the condition the eftate be limited over to a third
perfon, and does not immediately revert to the grantor or his reprefentatives, (as if an eftate be granted by A to B, on condition
that within two years B intermarry with C, and on failure thereof
then to D and his heirs) this the law conftrues to be a limitation

[m] §. 380. 1 Inft. 234.
[n] 10 Rep. 41.

[o] *Ibid.* 42.
[p] Litt. §. 347. Stat. 32 Hen.VIII. c.34.

and

and not a condition[q]: becaufe, if it were a condition, then, upon the breach thereof, only A or his reprefentatives could avoid the eftate by entry, and fo D's remainder might be defeated by their neglecting to enter; but, when it is a limitation, the eftate of B determines, and that of D commences, the inftant that the failure happens. So alfo, if a man by his will devifes land to his heir at law, on condition that he pays a fum of money, and for non-payment devifes it over, this fhall be confidered as a limitation; otherwife no advantage could be taken of the non-payment, for none but the heir himfelf could have entered for a breach of condition[r].

I N all thefe inftances, of limitations or conditions fubfequent, it is to be obferved, that fo long as the condition, either exprefs or implied, either in deed or in law, remains unbroken, the grantee may have an eftate of freehold, provided the eftate upon which fuch condition is annexed be in itfelf of a freehold nature; as if the original grant exprefs either an eftate of inheritance, or for life, or no eftate at all, which is conftructively an eftate for life. For the breach of thefe conditions being contingent and uncertain, this uncertainty preferves the freehold[s]; becaufe the eftate is capable to laft for ever, or at leaft for the life of the tenant, fuppofing the condition to remain unbroken. But where the eftate is at the utmoft a chattel intereft, which muft determine at a time certain, and may determine fooner, (as a grant for ninety nine years, provided A, B, and C, and the furvivor of them, fhall fo long live) this ftill continues a mere chattel, and is not, by it's uncertainty, ranked among eftates of freehold.

T H E S E exprefs conditions, if they be *impoffible* at the time of their creation, or afterwards become impoffible by the act of God or the act of the feoffor himfelf, or if they be *contrary to law*, or *repugnant* to the nature of the eftate, are void. In any of which cafes, if they be conditions *fubfequent*, that is, to be per-

q 1 Ventr. 202.   s Co. Litt. 42.
r Cro. Eliz. 205. 1 Roll. Abr. 411.

formed after the eftate is vefted, the eftate fhall become abfolute in the tenant. As, if a feoffment be made to a man in fee-fimple, on condition that unlefs he goes to Rome in twenty four hours; or unlefs he marries with Jane S. by fuch a day; (within which time the woman dies, or the feoffor marries her himfelf) or unlefs he kills another; or in cafe he alienes in fee; then and in any of fuch cafes the eftate fhall be vacated and determine: here the condition is void, and the eftate made abfolute in the feoffee. For he hath by the grant the eftate vefted in him, which fhall not be defeated afterwards by a condition either impoffible, illegal, or repugnant [t]. But if the condition be *precedent,* or to be performed before the eftate vefts, as a grant to a man that, if he kills another or goes to Rome in a day, he fhall have an eftate in fee; here, the void condition being precedent, the eftate which depends thereon is alfo void, and the grantee fhall take nothing by the grant: for he hath no eftate until the condition be performed [u].

THERE are fome eftates defeafible upon condition fubfequent, that require a more peculiar notice. Such are

III. ESTATES held *in vadio,* in *gage,* or pledge; which are of two kinds, *vivum vadium,* or living pledge; and *mortuum vadium,* dead pledge, or *mortgage.*

VIVUM *vadium,* or living pledge, is when a man borrows a fum (fuppofe 200 *l.*) of another; and grants him an eftate, as, of 20 *l. per annum,* to hold till the rents and profits fhall repay the fum fo borrowed. This is an eftate conditioned to be void, as foon as fuch fum is raifed. And in this cafe the land or pledge is faid to be living: it fubfifts, and furvives the debt; and, immediately on the difcharge of that, refults back to the borrower [w]. But *mortuum vadium,* a dead pledge, or *mortgage,* (which is much more common than the other) is where a man borrows of another

[t] Co. Litt. 206.   [w] *Ibid.* 205.
[u] *Ibid.*

a fpecific

a fpecific fum (*e. g.* 200 *l.*) and grants him an eftate in fee, on
condition that if he, the mortgagor, fhall repay the mortgagee
the faid fum of 200 *l.* on a certain day mentioned in the deed,
that then the mortgagor may re-enter on the eftate fo granted in
pledge; or, as is now the more ufual way, that the mortgagee
fhall re-convey the eftate to the mortgagor: in this cafe the land,
which is fo put in pledge, is by law, in cafe of non-payment at
the time limited, for ever dead and gone from the mortgagor;
and the mortgagee's eftate in the lands is then no longer conditional, but abfolute. But, fo long as it continues conditional,
that is, between the time of lending the money, and the time
allotted for payment, the mortgagee is called tenant in mortgage[x].
But, as it was formerly a doubt[y], whether, by taking fuch e-
ftate in fee, it did not become liable to the wife's dower, and
other incumbrances of the mortgagee (though that doubt has
been long ago over-ruled by our courts of equity[z]) it therefore
became ufual to grant only a long term of years, by way of mortgage; with condition to be void on re-payment of the mortgage-
money: which courfe has been fince continued, principally becaufe on the death of the mortgagee fuch term becomes vefted in
his perfonal reprefentatives, who alone are intitled in equity to
receive the money lent, of whatever nature the mortgage may
happen to be.

As foon as the eftate is created, the mortgagee may immediately enter on the lands; but is liable to be difpoffeffed, upon
performance of the condition by payment of the mortgage-money
at the day limited. And therefore the ufual way is to agree that
the mortgagor fhall hold the land till the day affigned for payment; when, in cafe of failure, whereby the eftate becomes
abfolute, the mortgagee may enter upon it and take poffeffion,
without any poffibility *at law* of being afterwards evicted by the
mortgagor, to whom the land is now for ever dead. But here
again the courts of equity interpofe; and, though a mortgage

[x] Litt. §. 332.   [z] Hardr. 466.
[y] *Ibid.* §. 357. Cro. Car. 191.

be

be thus forfeited, and the estate absolutely vested in the mortgagee at the common law, yet they will consider the real value
of the tenements compared with the sum borrowed. And, if the
estate be of greater value than the sum lent thereon, they will
allow the mortgagor at any reasonable time to re-call or redeem
his estate; paying to the mortgagee his principal, interest, and
expenses : for otherwise, in strictness of law, an estate worth
1000 *l.* might be forfeited for non-payment of 100 *l.* or a less
sum. This reasonable advantage, allowed to mortgagors, is called
the *equity of redemption :* and this enables a mortgagor to call
on the mortgagee, who has possession of his estate, to deliver it
back and account for the rents and profits received, on payment
of his whole debt and interest; thereby turning the *mortuum* into
a kind of *vivum vadium.* But, on the other hand, the mortgagee
may either compel the sale of the estate, in order to get the whole
of his money immediately; or else call upon the mortgagor to
redeem his estate presently, or, in default thereof, to be for ever
foreclosed from redeeming the same; that is, to lose his equity of
redemption without possibility of re-call. And also, in some cases
of fraudulent mortgages [a], the fraudulent mortgagor forfeits all
equity of redemption whatsoever. It is not therefore usual for
mortgagees to take possession of the mortgaged estate, unless
where the security is precarious, or small; or where the mortgagor neglects even the payment of interest : when the mortgagee is frequently obliged to bring an ejectment, and take the
land into his own hands, in the nature of a pledge, or the *pig-
nus* of the Roman law : whereas, while it remains in the hands
of the mortgagor, it more resembles their *hypotheca,* which was
where the possession of the thing pledged remained with the
debtor [b]. But, by statute 7 Geo. II. c. 20. after payment or tender by the mortgagor of principal, interest, and costs, the mortgagee can maintain no ejectment; but may be compelled to re-
assign his securities. In Glanvil's time, when the universal me-

---

[a] Stat. 4 & 5 W. & M. c. 16.
[b] *Pignoris appellatione eam proprie rem contineri dicimus, quae simul etiam traditur cre-*

*ditori. At eam, quae sine traditione nuda con-
ventione tenetur, proprie hypothecae appellatione
contineri dicimus. Inst. l. 4. t. 6. §. 7.*

thod

thod of conveyance was by livery of feifin or corporal tradition of the lands, no gage or pledge of lands was good unlefs poffeffion was alfo delivered to the creditor; *"fi non fequatur ipfius va-* " *dii traditio, curia domini regis hujufmodi privatas conventiones tueri* " *non folet:"* for which the reafon given is, to prevent fubfequent and fraudulent pledges of the fame land; " *cum in tali cafu* " *poffit eadem res pluribus aliis creditoribus tum prius tum pofterius* " *invadiari*[c]. And the frauds which have arifen, fince the exchange of thefe public and notorious conveyances for more private and fecret bargains, have well evinced the wifdom of our antient law.

IV. A FOURTH fpecies of eftates, defeafible on condition fubfequent, are thofe held by *ftatute merchant*, and *ftatute ftaple*; which are very nearly related to the *vivum vadium* before-mentioned, or eftate held till the profits thereof fhall difcharge a debt liquidated or afcertained. For both the ftatute merchant and ftatute ftaple are fecurities for money; the one entered into purfuant to the ftatute 13 Edw. I. *de mercatoribus*, and thence called a ftatute merchant; the other purfuant to the ftatute 27 Edw. III. c. 9. before the mayor of the ftaple, that is to fay, the grand mart for the principal commodities or manufactures of the kingdom, formerly held by act of parliament in certain trading towns[d], and thence this fecurity is called a ftatute ftaple. They are both, I fay, fecurities for debts, originally permitted only among traders, for the benefit of commerce; whereby the lands of the debtor are conveyed to the creditor, till out of the rents and profits of them his debt may be fatisfied: and during fuch time as the creditor fo holds the lands, he is tenant by ftatute merchant or ftatute ftaple. There is alfo a fimilar fecurity, the recognizance in the nature of a ftatute ftaple, which extends the benefit of this mercantile tranfaction to all the king's fubjects in general, by virtue of the ftatute 23 Hen. VIII. c. 6.

V. ANOTHER fimilar conditional eftate, created by operation of law, for fecurity and fatisfaction of debts, is called an eftate

[c] *l.* 10. *c.* 8.   [d] See Book I. ch. 8.

by

by *elegit*. What an *elegit* is, and why so called, will be explained in the third part of these commentaries. At present I need only mention, that it is the name of a writ, founded on the statute[e] of Westm. 2. by which, after a plaintiff has obtained judgment for his debt at law, the sheriff gives him possession of one half of the defendant's lands and tenements, to be held, occupied, and enjoyed, until his debt and damages are fully paid : and, during the time he so holds them, he is called tenant by *elegit*. It is easy to observe, that this is also a mere conditional estate, defeasible as soon as the debt is levied. But it is remarkable, that the feodal restraints of alienating lands, and charging them with the debts of the owner, were softened much earlier and much more effectually for the benefit of trade and commerce, than for any other consideration. Before the statute of *quia emptores*[f], it is generally thought that the proprietor of lands was enabled to alienate no more than a moiety of them : the statute therefore of Westm. 2. permits only so much of them to be affected by the process of law, as a man was capable of alienating by his own deed. But by the statute *de mercatoribus* (passed in the same year[g]) the *whole* of a man's lands was liable to be pledged in a statute merchant, for a debt contracted in trade ; though only *half* of them was liable to be taken in execution for any other debt of the owner.

I SHALL conclude what I had to remark of these estates, by statute merchant, statute staple, and *elegit*, with the observation of sir Edward Coke[h]. " These tenants have uncertain interests " in lands and tenements, and yet they have but chattels and no " freeholds ;" (which makes them an exception to the general rule) " because though they may hold an estate of inheritance, " or for life, *ut liberum tenementum*, until their debt be paid ; yet " it shall go to their executors : for *ut* is similitudinary ; and " though, to recover their estates, they shall have the same remedy " (by assise) as a tenant of the freehold shall have, yet it is but

[e] 13 Edw. I. c. 18.
[f] 18 Edw. I.
[g] 13 Edw. I.
[h] 1 Inst. 42, 43.

" the fimilitude of a freehold, and *nullum fimile eft idem*." This indeed only proves them to be chattel interefts, becaufe they go to the executors, which is inconfiftent with the nature of a freehold : but it does not affign the reafon why thefe eftates, in contradiftinction to other uncertain interefts, fhall veft in the executors of the tenant and not the heir ; which is probably owing to this : that, being a fecurity and remedy provided for perfonal debts owing to the deceafed, to which debts the executor is intitled, the law has therefore thus directed their fucceffion ; as judging it reafonable, from a principle of natural equity, that the fecurity and remedy fhould be vefted in them, to whom the debts if recovered would belong. And, upon the fame principle, if lands be devifed to a man's executor, until out of their profits the debts due from the teftator be difcharged, this intereft in the lands fhall be a chattel intereft, and on the death of fuch executor fhall go to *his* executors[i] : becaufe they, being liable to pay the original teftator's debts, fo far as his affets will extend, are in reafon intitled to poffefs that fund, out of which he has directed them to be paid.

[i] Co. Litt. 42.

CHAPTER THE ELEVENTH.

OF ESTATES IN POSSESSION, REMAINDER, AND REVERSION.

HITHERTO we have confidered eftates folely with regard to their duration, or the *quantity of intereft* which the
owners have therein. We are now to confider them in another
view; with regard to the *time of their enjoyment*, when the actual
pernancy of the profits (that is, the taking, perception, or receipt,
of the rents and other advantages arifing therefrom) begins. E-
ftates therefore, with refpect to this confideration, may either be
in *poffeffion*, or in *expectancy:* and of expectancies there are two
forts; one created by act of the parties, called a *remainder*; the
other by act of law, and called a *reverfion*.

I. OF eftates in *poffeffion*, (which are fometimes called eftates
executed, whereby a prefent intereft paffes to and refides in the
tenant, not depending on any fubfequent circumftance or contingency, as in the cafe of eftates *executory*) there is little or nothing
peculiar to be obferved. All the eftates we have hitherto fpoken
of are of this kind; for, in laying down general rules, we ufually
apply them to fuch eftates as are then actually in the tenant's
poffeffion. But the doctrine of eftates in expectancy contains
fome of the niceft and moft abftrufe learning in the Englifh law.
Thefe will therefore require a minute difcuffion, and demand
fome degree of attention.

II. AN

II. A N eſtate then in remainder may be defined to be, an eſtate limited to take effect and be enjoyed after another eſtate is determined. As if a man ſeiſed in fee-ſimple granteth lands to A for twenty years, and, after the determination of the ſaid term, then to B and his heirs for ever : here A is tenant for years, remainder to B in fee. In the firſt place an eſtate for years is created or carved out of the fee, and given to A ; and the reſidue or remainder of it is given to B. But both theſe intereſts are in fact only one eſtate ; the preſent term of years and the remainder afterwards, when added together, being equal only to one eſtate in fee [a]. They are indeed different *parts*, but they conſtitute only one *whole* : they are carved out of one and the ſame inheritance : they are both created, and may both ſubſiſt, together ; the one in poſſeſſion, the other in expectancy. So if land be granted to A for twenty years, and after the determination of the ſaid term to B for life ; and, after the determination of B's eſtate for life, it be limited to C and his heirs for ever : this makes A tenant for years, with remainder to B for life, remainder over to C in fee. Now here the eſtate of inheritance undergoes a diviſion into three portions : there is firſt A's eſtate for years carved out of it ; and after that B's eſtate for life ; and then the whole that remains is limited to C and his heirs. And here alſo the firſt eſtate, and both the remainders, for life and in fee, are one eſtate only ; being nothing but parts or portions of one entire inheritance : and if there were a hundred remainders, it would ſtill be the ſame thing ; upon a principle grounded on mathematical truth, that all the parts are equal, and no more than equal, to the whole. And hence alſo it is eaſy to collect, that no remainder can be limited after the grant of an eſtate in fee-ſimple [b]: becauſe a fee-ſimple is the higheſt and largeſt eſtate, that a ſubject is capable of enjoying ; and he that is tenant in fee hath in him the *whole* of the eſtate : a remainder therefore, which is only a portion, or reſiduary *part*, of the eſtate, cannot be reſerved after the whole is diſpoſed of. A particular eſtate, with all the remain-

[a] Co. Litt. 143.   [b] Plowd. 29.

ders

ders expectant thereon, is only one fee-fimple ; as 40 *l.* is part of
100 *l.* and 60 *l.* is the remainder of it : wherefore, after a fee-
fimple once vefted, there can no more be a remainder limited
thereon, than after the whole 100 *l.* is appropriated there can be
any refidue fubfifting.

THUS much being premifed, we fhall be the better enabled
to comprehend the rules that are laid down by law to be obferved
in the creation of remainders, and the reafons upon which thofe
rules are founded.

1. AND, firft, there muft neceffarily be fome particular eftate,
precedent to the eftate in remainder[c]. As, an eftate for years to
A, remainder to B for life ; or, an eftate for life to A, remainder to B in tail. This precedent eftate is called the *particular*
eftate, as being only a fmall part, or *particula,* of the inheritance ; the refidue or remainder of which is granted over to another. The neceffity of creating this preceding particular eftate,
in order to make a good remainder, arifes from this plain reafon ;
that *remainder* is a relative expreffion, and implies that fome part
of the thing is previoufly difpofed of : for, where the whole is
conveyed at once, there cannot poffibly exift a remainder ; but
the intereft granted, whatever it be, will be an eftate in poffeffion.

AN eftate created to commence at a diftant period of time,
without any intervening eftate, is therefore properly no remainder : it is the whole of the gift, and not a refiduary part. And
fuch future eftates can only be made of chattel interefts, which
were confidered in the light of mere contracts by the antient
law[d], to be executed either now or hereafter, as the contracting
parties fhould agree : but an eftate of freehold muft be created
to commence immediately. For it is an antient rule of the common law, that no eftate of freehold can be created to commence
in futuro ; but it ought to take effect prefently either in poffeffion
or remainder[e] : becaufe at common law no freehold in lands

[c] Co. Litt. 49. Plowd. 25.   [e] 5 Rep. 94.
[d] Raym. 151.   could

could pafs without livery of feifin; which muft operate either
immediately, or not at all. It would therefore be contradictory,
if an eftate, which is not to commence till hereafter, could be
granted by a conveyance which imports an immediate poffeffion.
Therefore, though a leafe to A for feven years, to commence
from next Michaelmas, is good; yet a conveyance to B of lands,
to hold to him and his heirs for ever from the end of three years
next enfuing, is void. So that when it is intended to grant an
eftate of freehold, whereof the enjoyment fhall be deferred till a
future time, it is neceffary to create a previous particular eftate,
which may fubfift till that period of time it completed; and for
the grantor to deliver immediate poffeffion of the land to the tenant of this particular eftate, which is conftrued to be giving
poffeffion to him in remainder, fince his eftate and that of the
particular tenant are one and the fame eftate in law. As, where
one leafes to A for three years, with remainder to B in fee, and
makes livery of feifin to A; here by the livery the freehold is
immediately created, and vefted in B, during the continuance of
A's term of years. The whole eftate paffes at once from the
grantor to the grantees, and the remainder-man is feifed of his
remainder at the fame time that the termor is poffeffed of his
term. The enjoyment of it muft indeed be deferred till hereafter; but it is to all intents and purpofes an eftate commencing *in
praefenti*, though to be occupied and enjoyed *in futuro*.

As no remainder can be created, without fuch a precedent
particular eftate, therefore the particular eftate is faid to *fupport*
the remainder. But a leafe at will is not held to be fuch a particular eftate, as will fupport a remainder over [f]. For an eftate at
will is of a nature fo flender and precarious, that it is not looked
upon as a portion of the inheritance; and a portion muft firft be
taken out of it, in order to conftitute a remainder. Befides, if
it be a freehold remainder, livery of feifin muft be given at the
time of it's creation; and the entry of the grantor, to do this,
determines the eftate at will in the very inftant in which it is

[f] 8 Rep. 75.

made [g].

made [g] : or, if it be a chattel interest, though perhaps it might operate as a *future contract*, if the tenant for years be a party to the deed of creation, yet it is void by way of *remainder :* for it is a separate independent contract, distinct from the precedent estate at will ; and every remainder must be part of one and the same estate, out of which the preceding particular estate is taken [h]. And hence it is generally true, that if the particular estate is void in it's creation, or by any means is defeated afterwards, the remainder supported thereby shall be defeated also [i]: as where the particular estate is an estate for the life of a person not *in esse* [k] ; or an estate for life upon condition, on breach of which condition the grantor enters and avoids the estate [l] ; in either of these cases the remainder over is void.

2 A SECOND rule to be observed is this ; that the remainder must commence or pass out of the grantor at the time of the creation of the particular estate [m]. As, where there is an estate to A for life, with remainder to B in fee : here B's remainder in fee passes from the grantor at the same time that seisin is delivered to A of his life estate in possession. And it is this, which induces the necessity at common law of livery of seisin being made on the particular estate, whenever a *freehold* remainder is created. For, if it be limited even on an estate for years, it is necessary that the lessee for years should have livery of seisin, in order to convey the freehold from and out of the grantor ; otherwise the remainder is void [n]. Not that the livery is necessary to strengthen the estate for years ; but, as livery of the land is requisite to convey the freehold, and yet cannot be given to him in remainder without infringing the possession of the lessee for years, therefore the law allows such livery, made to the tenant of the particular estate, to relate and enure to him in remainder, as both are but one estate in law [o].

[g] Dyer. 18.
[h] Raym. 151.
[i] Co. Litt. 298.
[k] 2 Roll. Abr. 415.

[l] 1 Jon. 58.
[m] Litt. §. 671. Plowd. 25.
[n] Litt. §. 60.
[o] Co. Litt. 49.

3. A THIRD

3. A THIRD rule refpecting remainders is this; that the remainder muft veft in the grantee during the continuance of the
particular eftate, or *eo inftanti* that it determines[p]. As, if A be
tenant for life, remainder to B in tail; here B's remainder is
vefted in him, at the creation of the particular eftate to A for
life : or, if A and B be tenants for their joint lives, remainder
to the furvivor in fee ; here, though during their joint lives the
remainder is vefted in neither, yet on the death of either of them,
the remainder vefts inftantly in the furvivor : wherefore both
thefe are good remainders. But, if an eftate be limited to A for
life, remainder to the eldeft fon of B in tail, and A dies before B
hath any fon ; here the remainder will be void, for it did not
veft in any one during the continuance, nor at the determination,
of the particular eftate : and, even fuppofing that B fhould afterwards have a fon, he fhall not take by this remainder ; for, as it
did not veft at or before the end of the particular eftate, it never
can veft at all, but is gone for ever[q]. And this depends upon the
principle before laid down, that the precedent particular eftate
and the remainder are one eftate in law; they muft therefore
fubfift and be *in effe* at one and the fame inftant of time, either
during the continuance of the firft eftate or at the very inftant
when that determines, fo that no other eftate can poffibly come
between them. For there can be no intervening eftate between
the particular eftate, and the remainder fupported thereby[r] : the
thing fupported muft fall to the ground, if once it's fupport be
fevered from it.

IT is upon thefe rules, but principally the laft; that the doctrine of *contingent* remainders depends. For remainders are either
vefted or *contingent*. *Vefted* remainders (or remainders *executed*,
whereby a prefent intereft paffes to the party, though to be enjoyed *in futuro*) are where the eftate is invariably fixed, to remain
to a determinate perfon, after the particular eftate is fpent. As

[p] Plowd. 25. 1 Rep. 66.   [r] 3 Rep. 21.
[q] 1 Rep. 138.

if

if A be tenant for twenty years, remainder to B in fee; here B's is a vested remainder, which nothing can defeat, or set aside.

CONTINGENT or *executory* remainders (whereby no present interest passes) are where the estate in remainder is limited to take effect, either to a dubious and uncertain *person*, or upon a dubious and uncertain *event*; so that the particular estate may chance to be determined, and the remainder never take effect[s].

FIRST, they may be limited to a dubious and uncertain *person*. As if A be tenant for life, with remainder to B's eldest son (then unborn) in tail; this is a contingent remainder, for it is uncertain whether B will have a son or no: but the instant that a son is born, the remainder is no longer contingent, but vested. Though, if A had died before the contingency happened, that is, before B's son was born, the remainder would have been absolutely gone; for the particular estate was determined before the remainder could vest. Nay, by the strict rule of law, if A were tenant for life, remainder to his own eldest son in tail, and A died without issue born, but leaving his wife *enseint* or big with child, and after his death a posthumous son was born, this son could not take the land, by virtue of this remainder; for the particular estate determined before there was any person *in esse*, in whom the remainder could vest[t]. But, to remedy this hardship, it is enacted by statute 10 & 11 W. III. c. 16. that posthumous children shall be capable of taking in remainder, in the same manner as if they had been born in their father's lifetime: that is, the remainder is allowed to vest in them, while yet in their mother's womb[u].

THIS species of contingent remainders, to a person not in being, must however be limited to some one, that may by common possibility, or *potentia propinqua*, be *in esse* at or before the particular estate determines[w]. As if an estate be made to A for

---

[s] 3 Rep. 20.
[t] Salk. 228. 4 Mod. 282.
[u] See Vol. I. pag. 126.
[w] 2 Rep. 51.

life,

life, remainder to the heirs of B : now, if A dies before B, the remainder is at an end ; for during B's life he has no heir, *nema est haeres viventis :* but if B dies firſt, the remainder then immediately veſts in his heir, who will be entitled to the land on the death of A. This is a good contingent remainder, for the poſſibility of B's dying before A is *potentia propinqua,* and therefore allowed in law·[x]. But a remainder to the right heirs of B (if there be no ſuch perſon as B *in eſſe*) is void[y] For here there muſt two contingencies happen ; firſt, that ſuch a perſon as B ſhall be born ; and, ſecondly, that he ſhall alſo die during the continuance of the particular eſtate ; which make it *potentia remotiſſima,* a moſt improbable poſſibility. A remainder to a man's eldeſt ſon, who hath none, (we have ſeen) is good ; for by common poſſibility he may have one ; but if it be limited in particular to his ſon John, or Richard, it is bad, if he have no ſon of that name ; for it is too remote a poſſibility that he ſhould not only have a ſon, but a ſon of a particular name[z]. A limitation of a remainder to a baſtard before it is born, is not good[a] : for though the law allows the poſſibility of having baſtards, it preſumes it to be a very remote and improbable contingency. Thus may a remainder be contingent, on account of the uncertainty of the *perſon* who is to take it.

A REMAINDER may alſo be contingent, where the perſon to whom it is limited is fixed and certain, but the *event* upon which it is to take effect is vague and uncertain. As, where land is given to A for life, and in caſe B ſurvives him, then with remainder to B in fee : here B is a certain perſon, but the remainder to him is a contingent remainder, depending upon a dubious event, the uncertainty of his ſurviving A. During the joint lives of A and B it is contingent ; and if B dies firſt, it never can veſt in his heirs, but is for ever gone ; but if A dies firſt, the remainder to B becomes veſted.

[x] Co. Litt. 378.
[y] Hob. 33.

[z] 5 Rep. 51.
[a] Cro. Eliz. 509.

CONTINGENT remainders of either kind, if they amount to a freehold, cannot be limited on an eftate for years, or any other particular eftate, lefs than a freehold. Thus if land be granted to A for ten years, with remainder in fee to the right heirs of B, this remainder is void [b]: but if granted to A for life, with a like remainder, it is good. For, unlefs the freehold paffes out of the grantor at the time when the remainder is created, fuch freehold remainder is void : it cannot pafs out of him, without vefting fomewhere; and in the cafe of a contingent remainder it muft veft in the particular tenant, elfe it can veft no where : unlefs therefore the eftate of fuch particular tenant be of a freehold nature, the freehold cannot veft in him, and confequently the remainder is void.

CONTINGENT remainders may be *defeated*, by deftroying or determining the particular eftate upon which they depend, before the contingency happens whereby they become vefted [c]. Therefore when there is tenant for life, with divers remainders in contingency, he may, not only by his death, but by alienation, furrender, or other methods, deftroy and determine his own lifeeftate, before any of thofe remainders veft; the confequence of which is that he utterly defeats them all. As, if there be tenant for life, with remainder to his eldeft fon unborn in tail, and the tenant for life, before any fon is born, furrenders his life-eftate, he by that means defeats the remainder in tail to his fon : for his fon not being *in effe*, when the particular eftate determined, the remainder could not then veft; and, as it could not veft then, by the rules before laid down, it never can veft at all. In thefe cafes therefore it is neceffary to have truftees appointed to preferve the contingent remainders; in whom there is vefted an eftate in remainder for the life of the tenant for life, to commence when his determines. If therefore his eftate for life determines otherwife than by his death, their eftate, for the refidue of his natural life, will then take effect, and become a particular estate in possession, sufficient to support the remainders depending in contingency. This method is said to have been invented by sir Orlando Bridgman, sir Geoffery Palmer, and other eminent council, who betook themselves to conveyancing during the time of the civil wars; in order thereby to secure in family settlements a provision for the future children of an intended marriage, who before were usually left at the mercy of the particular tenant for life [d] : and when, after the restoration, those gentlemen came to fill the first offices of the law, they supported this invention within reasonable and proper bounds, and introduced it into general use.

THUS the student will observe how much nicety is required in creating and securing a remainder; and I trust he will in some measure see the general reasons, upon which this nicety is founded. It were endless to attempt to enter upon the particular subtilties and refinements, into which this doctrine, by the variety of cases which have occurred in the course of many centuries, has been spun out and subdivided: neither are they consonant to the design of these elementary disquisitions. I must not however omit, that in devises by last will and testament, (which, being often drawn up when the party is *inops concilii*, are always more favoured in construction than formal deeds, which are presumed to be made with great caution, fore-thought, and advice) in these devises, I say, remainders may be created in some measure contrary to the rules before laid down: though our lawyers will not allow such dispositions to be strictly remainders; but call them by another name, that of *executory devises*, or devises hereafter to be executed.

AN executory devise of lands is such a disposition of them by will, that thereby no estate vests at the death of the devisor, but only on some future contingency. It differs from a remainder in three very material points: 1. That it needs not any particular

---

[d] See Moor. 486. 2 Roll. Abr. 797. pl. 12. 2 Sid. 159. 2 Chan. Rep. 170.

estate

estate to support it. 2. That by it a fee-simple or other less e-
state, may be limited after a fee-simple. 3. That by this means
a remainder may be limited of a chattel interest, after a particular estate for life created in the same.

1. THE first case happens when a man devises a future estate,
to arise upon a contingency; and, till that contingency happens,
does not dispose of the fee-simple, but leaves it to descend to his
heir at law. As if one devises land to a feme-sole and her heirs,
upon her day of marriage : here is in effect a contingent remainder without any particular estate to support it; a freehold commencing *in futuro*. This limitation, though it would be void
in a deed, yet is good in a will, by way of executory devise [e].
For, since by a devise a freehold may pass without corporal tradition or livery of seisin, (as it must do, if it passes at all) therefore it may commence *in futuro*; because the principal reason
why it cannot commence *in futuro* in other cases, is the necessity
of actual seisin, which always operates *in praesenti*. And, since
it may thus commence *in futuro*, there is no need of a particular
estate to support it; the only use of which is to make the remainder, by it's unity with the particular estate, a present interest.
And hence also it follows, that such an executory devise, not being a present interest, cannot be barred by a recovery, suffered
before it commences [f].

2. BY executory devise a fee, or other less estate, may be limited
after a fee. And this happens where a devisor devises his whole
estate in fee, but limits a remainder thereon to commence on a
future contingency. As if a man devises land to A and his heirs;
but, if he dies before the age of twenty one, then to B and his
heirs : this remainder, though void in a deed, is good by way of
executory devise [g]. But, in both these species of executory devises,
the contingencies ought to be such as may happen within a reasonable time; as within one or more life or lives in being, or within

e 1 Sid. 153.   g 2 Mod. 289.
f Cro. Jac. 593.

a moderate

a moderate term of years ; for courts of juſtice will not indulge even wills, ſo as to create a perpetuity, which the law abhors[h]: becauſe by perpetuities, (or the ſettlement of an intereſt, which ſhall go in the ſucceſſion preſcribed, without any power of alienation[i]) eſtates are made incapable of anſwering thoſe ends, of ſocial commerce, and providing for the ſudden contingencies of private life, for which property was at firſt eſtabliſhed. The utmoſt length that has been hitherto allowed, for the contingency of an executory deviſe of either kind to happen in, is that of a life or lives in being, and one and twenty years afterwards. As when lands are deviſed to ſuch unborn ſon of a feme-covert, as ſhall firſt attain the age of twenty one, and his heirs; the utmoſt length of time that can happen before the eſtate can veſt, is the life of the mother and the ſubſequent infancy of her ſon : and this hath been decreed to be a good executory deviſe[k].

3. By executory deviſe a term of years may be given to one man for his life, and afterwards limited over in remainder to another, which could not be done by deed : for by law the firſt grant of it, to a man for life, was a total diſpoſition of the whole term ; a life eſtate being eſteemed of a higher and larger nature than any term of years[l]. And, at firſt, the courts were tender, even in the caſe of a will, of reſtraining the deviſee for life from aliening the term ; but only held, that in caſe he died without exerting that act of ownerſhip, the remainder over ſhould then take place[m]: for the reſtraint of the power of alienation, eſpecially in very long terms, was introducing a ſpecies of perpetuity. But, ſoon afterwards, it was held[n], that the deviſee for life hath no power of aliening the term, ſo as to bar the remainder-man : yet in order to prevent the danger of perpetuities, it was ſettled[o], that, though ſuch remainders may be limited to as many perſons ſucceſſively as the deviſor thinks proper, yet they muſt all be *in eſſe*

[h] 12 Mod. 287. 1 Vern. 164.
[i] Salk 229.
[k] Forr. 232.
[l] 8 Rep. 95.
[m] Bro. *tit. chatteles.* 23. Dyer 74.
[n] Dyer. 358. 8 Rep. 96.
[o] 1 Sid. 451.

during

during the life of the firſt deviſee ; for then all the candles are lighted and are conſuming together, and the ultimate remainder is in reality only to that remainder-man who happens to ſurvive the reſt : or, that ſuch remainder may be limited to take effect upon ſuch contingency only, as muſt happen (if at all) during the life of the firſt deviſee [p].

Thus much for ſuch eſtates in expectancy, as are created by the expreſs words of the parties themſelves ; the moſt intricate title in the law. There is yet another ſpecies, which is created by the act and operation of the law itſelf, and this is called a reverſion.

III. An eſtate in *reverſion* is the reſidue of an eſtate left in the grantor, to commence in poſſeſſion after the determination of ſome particular eſtate granted out by him [q]. Sir Edward Coke [r] deſcribes a reverſion to be the returning of land to the grantor or his heirs after the grant is over. As, if there be a gift in tail, the reverſion of the fee is, without any ſpecial reſervation, veſted in the donor by act of law : and ſo alſo the reverſion, after an eſtate for life, years, or at will, continues in the leſſor. For the fee-ſimple of all lands muſt abide ſomewhere ; and if he, who was before poſſeſſed of the whole, carves out of it any ſmaller eſtate, and grants it away, whatever is not ſo granted remains in him. A reverſion is therefore never created by deed or writing, but ariſes from conſtruction of law ; a remainder can never be limited, unleſs by either deed or deviſe. But both are equally transferable, when actually veſted, being both eſtates *in praeſenti*, though taking effect *in futuro*.

The doctrine of reverſions is plainly derived from the feodal conſtitution. For, when a feud was granted to a man for life, or to him and his iſſue male, rendering either rent, or other ſervices ; then, on his death or the failure of iſſue male, the feud was de-

---

[p] Skinn. 341. 3 P. W^{ms}. 258.   [r] 1 Inſt. 142.
[q] Co. Litt. 22.

termined

termined and refulted back to the lord or proprietor, to be again
difpofed of at his pleafure. And hence the ufual *incidents* to reverfions are faid to be *fealty* and *rent*. When no rent is referved
on the particular eftate, fealty however refults of courfe, as an
incident quite infeparable, and may be demanded as a badge of
tenure, or acknowlegement of fuperiority ; being frequently the
only evidence that the lands are holden at all. Where rent is referved, it is alfo incident, though not infeparably fo, to the reverfion ˢ. The rent may be granted away, referving the reverfion ;
and the reverfion may be granted away, referving the rent ; by
fpecial words : but by a *general* grant of the reverfion, the rent
will pafs with it, as incident thereunto ; though by the grant of
the rent generally, the reverfion will not pafs. The incident
paffes by the grant of the principal, but not *e converfo* : for the
maxim of law is, " *accefforium non ducit, fed fequitur, fuum prin-*
" *cipale* ᵗ."

THESE *incidental* rights of the reverfioner, and the refpective
modes of defcent, in which remainders very frequently differ from
reverfions, have occafioned the law to be careful in diftinguifhing
the one from the other, however inaccurately the parties themfelves may defcribe them. For if one, feifed of a paternal eftate
in fee, makes a leafe for life, with remainder to himfelf and
his heirs, this is properly a mere reverfion ᵘ, to which rent and
fealty fhall be incident ; and which fhall only defcend to the
heirs of his father's blood, and not to his heirs general, as a remainder limited to him by a third perfon would have done ʷ :
for it is the old eftate, which was originally in him, and never
yet was out of him. And fo likewife, if a man grants a leafe
for life to A, referving rent, with reverfion to B and his heirs,
B hath a remainder defcendible to his heirs general, and not a
reverfion to which the rent is incident ; but the grantor fhall be
intitled to the rent, during the continuance of A's eftate ˣ.

ˢ Co. Litt. 143.
ᵗ *Ibid.* 151, 152.
ᵘ Cro. Eliz. 321.

ʷ 3 Lev. 407.
ˣ 1 And. 23.

IN

IN order to affift fuch perfons as have any eftate in remainder, reverfion, or expectancy, after the death of others, againft fraudulent concealments of their deaths, it is enacted by the ftatute 6 Ann. c. 18. that all perfons on whofe lives any lands or tenements are holden, fhall (upon application to the court of chancery and order made thereupon) once in every year, if required, be produced to the court, or it's commiffioners; or, upon neglect or refufal, they fhall be taken to be actually dead, and the perfon entitled to fuch expectant eftate may enter upon and hold the lands and tenements, till the party fhall appear to be living.

BEFORE we conclude the doctrine of remainders and reverfions, it may be proper to obferve, that whenever a greater eftate and a lefs coincide and meet in one and the fame perfon, without any intermediate eftate [y], the lefs is immediately annihilated; or, in the law phrafe, is faid to be *merged*, that is, funk or drowned, in the greater. Thus, if there be tenant for years, and the reverfion in fee-fimple defcends to or is purchafed by him, the term of years is merged in the inheritance, and fhall never exift any more. But they muft come to one and the fame perfon in one and the fame right; elfe, if the freehold be in his own right, and he has a term in right of another *(en auter droit)* there is no merger. Therefore, if tenant for years dies, and makes him who hath the reverfion in fee his executor, whereby the term of years vefts alfo in him, the term fhall not merge; for he hath the fee in his own right, and the term of years in the right of the teftator, and fubject to his debts and legacies. So alfo, if he who hath the reverfion in fee marries the tenant for years, there is no merger; for he hath the inheritance in his own right, the leafe in the right of his wife [z]. An eftate-tail is an exception to this rule: for a man may have in his own right both an eftate-tail and a reverfion in fee; and the eftate-tail, though a lefs eftate, fhall not merge in the fee [a]. For eftates-tail are protected and preferved from

[y] 3 Lev. 437.
[z] Plow. 418. Cro. Jac. 275. Co. Litt. 338.
[a] 2 Rep. 61. 8 Rep. 74.

merger

merger by the operation and conſtruction, though not by the expreſs words, of the ſtatute *de donis :* which operation and conſtruction have probably ariſen upon this conſideration ; that, in
the common caſes of *merger* of eſtates for life or years by uniting
with the inheritance, the particular tenant hath the ſole intereſt
in them, and hath full power at any time to defeat, deſtroy, or
ſurrender them to him that hath the reverſion ; therefore, when
ſuch an eſtate unites with the reverſion in fee, the law conſiders
it in the light of a virtual ſurrender of the inferior eſtate [b]. But,
in an eſtate-tail, the caſe is otherwiſe : the tenant for a long time
had no power at all over it, ſo as to bar or to deſtroy it ; and
now can only do it by certain ſpecial modes, by a fine, a recovery, and the like [c]: it would therefore have been ſtrangely improvident, to have permitted the tenant in tail, by purchaſing
the reverſion in fee, to merge his particular eſtate, and defeat the
inheritance of his iſſue : and hence it has become a maxim, that
a tenancy in tail, which cannot be ſurrendered, cannot alſo be
merged in the fee.

[b] Cro. Eliz. 302.   [c] See pag. 116.

CHAPTER THE TWELFTH.

OF ESTATES IN SEVERALTY, JOINT-TENANCY, COPARCENARY, AND COMMON.

WE come now to treat of eftates, with refpect to the number and connexions of their owners, the tenants who occupy and hold them. And, confidered in this view, eftates of any quantity or length of duration, and whether they be in actual poffeffion or expectancy, may be held in four different ways; in feveralty, in joint-tenancy, in coparcenary, and in common.

I. HE that holds lands or tenements in *feveralty*, or is fole tenant thereof, is he that holds them in his own right only, without any other perfon being joined or connected with him in point of intereft, during his eftate therein. This is the moft common and ufual way of holding an eftate; and therefore we may make the fame obfervations here, that we did upon eftates in poffeffion, as contradiftinguifhed from thofe in expectancy, in the preceding chapter: that there is little or nothing peculiar to be remarked concerning it, fince all eftates are fuppofed to be of this fort, unlefs where they are exprefsly declared to be otherwife; and that, in laying down general rules and doctrines, we ufually apply them to fuch eftates as are held in feveralty. I fhall therefore proceed to confider the other three fpecies of eftates, in which there are always a plurality of tenants.

II. AN

II. An eftate in *joint-tenancy* is where lands or tenements are granted to two or more perfons, to hold in fee-fimple, fee-tail, for life, for years, or at will. In confequence of fuch grants the eftate is called an eftate in joint-tenancy[a], and fometimes an eftate in *jointure*, which word as well as the other fignifies a union or conjunction of intereft; though in common fpeech the term, *jointure*, is now ufually confined to that joint eftate, which by virtue of the ftatute 27 Hen. VIII. c. 10. is frequently vefted in the hufband and wife before marriage, as a full fatisfaction and bar of the woman's dower[b].

In unfolding this title, and the two remaining ones in the prefent chapter, we will firft enquire, how thefe eftates may be *created*; next, their *properties* and refpective *incidents*; and laftly, how they may be *fevered* or *deftroyed*.

1. The *creation* of an eftate in joint-tenancy depends on the wording of the deed or devife, by which the tenants claim title; for this eftate can only arife by purchafe or grant, that is, by the act of the parties, and never by the mere act of law. Now, if an eftate be given to a plurality of perfons, without adding any re-ftrictive, exclufive, or explanatory words, as if an eftate be granted to A and B and their heirs, this makes them immediately joint-tenants in fee of the lands. For the law interprets the grant fo as to make all parts of it take effect, which can only be done by creating an equal eftate in them both. As therefore the grantor has thus united their names, the law gives them a thorough union in all other refpects. For,

2. The *properties* of a joint eftate are derived from it's unity, which is fourfold; the unity of *intereft*, the unity of *title*, the unity of *time*, and the unity of *poffeffion:* or, in other words, joint-tenants have one and the fame intereft, accruing by one and the fame conveyance, commencing at one and the fame time, and held by one and the fame undivided poffeffion.

[a] Litt. §. 277.   [b] See pag. 137.   First,

FIRST, they muſt have one and the ſame *intereſt*. One joint-tenant cannot be entitled to one period of duration or quantity of intereſt in lands, and the other to a different : one cannot be tenant for life, and the other for years : one cannot be tenant in fee, and the other in tail [c]. But, if land be limited to A and B for their lives, this makes them joint-tenants of the freehold ; if to A and B and their heirs, it makes them joint-tenants of the inheritance [d]. If land be granted to A and B for their lives and to the heirs of A ; here A and B are joint-tenants of the freehold during their reſpective lives, and A has the remainder of the fee in ſeveralty : or, if land be given to A and B, and the heirs of the body of A ; here both have a joint eſtate for life, and A hath a ſeveral remainder in tail [e]. Secondly, joint-tenants muſt alſo have an unity of *title :* their eſtate muſt be created by one and the ſame act, whether legal or illegal ; as by one and the ſame grant, or by one and the ſame diſſeiſin [f]. Joint-tenancy cannot ariſe by deſcent or act of law ; but merely by purchaſe, or acquiſition by the act of the party : and, unleſs that act be one and the ſame, the two tenants would have different titles ; and if they had different titles, one might prove good, and the other bad, which would abſolutely deſtroy the jointure. Thirdly, there muſt alſo be an unity of *time :* their eſtates muſt be veſted at one and the ſame period, as well as by one and the ſame title. As in caſe of a preſent eſtate made to A and B ; or a remainder in fee to A and B after a particular eſtate ; in either caſe A and B are joint tenants of this preſent eſtate, or this veſted remainder. But if, after a leaſe for life, the remainder be limited to the heirs of A and B ; and during the continuance of the particular eſtate A dies, which veſts the remainder of one moiety in his heir ; and then B dies, whereby the other moiety becomes veſted in the heir of B : now A's heir and B's heir are not joint-tenants of this remainder, but tenants in common ; for one moiety veſted at one time, and the other moiety veſted at another [g]. Yet, where

[c] Co. Litt. 188.
[d] Litt. §. 277.
[e] *Ibid.* §. 285.

[f] *Ibid.* §. 278.
[g] Co. Litt. 188.

a feoffment

a feoffment was made to the ufe of a man, and fuch wife as he fhould afterwards marry, for term of their lives, and he afterwards married; in this cafe it feems to have been held that the hufband and wife had a joint eftate, though vefted at different times [h] : becaufe the *ufe* of the wife's eftate was in abeyance and dormant till the intermarriage; and, being then awakened, had relation back, and took effect from the original time of creation. Laftly, in joint-tenancy, there muft be an unity of *poffeffion*. Joint-tenants are faid to be feifed *per my et per tout*, by the *half* or *moiety*, and by *all*; that is, they each of them have the entire poffeffion, as well of every *parcel* as of the *whole* [i]. They have not, one of them a feifin of one half or moiety, and the other of the other moiety; neither can one be exclufively feifed of one acre, and his companion of another; but each has an undivided moiety of the whole, and not the whole of an undivided moiety [k].

UPON thefe principles, of a thorough and intimate union of intereft and poffeffion, depend many other confequences and incidents to the joint-tenant's eftate. If two joint-tenants let a verbal leafe of their land, referving rent to be paid to one of them, it fhall enure to both, in refpect of the joint reverfion [l]. If their leffee furrenders his leafe to one of them, it fhall alfo enure to both, becaufe of the privity, or relation of their eftate [m]. On the fame reafon, livery of feifin, made to one joint-tenant, fhall enure to both of them [n]: and the entry, or re-entry, of one joint-tenant is as effectual in law as if it were the act of both [o]. In all actions alfo relating to their joint eftate, one joint-tenant cannot fue or be fued without joining the other [p]. But if two or more joint-tenants be feifed of an advowfon, and they prefent different clerks, the bifhop may refufe to admit either; becaufe neither joint-tenant hath a feveral right of patronage, but each is feifed of the

---

[h] Dyer. 340. [l] Rep. 101.
[i] Litt. §. 288. 5 Rep. 10.
[k] *Quilibet totum tenet et nihil tenet; fcilicet, totum in communi, et nihil feparatim per fe.* Bract. *l. 5. tr. 5. c. 26.*

[l] Co. Litt. 214.
[m] Ibid. 192.
[n] Ibid. 49.
[o] Ibid. 319. 364.
[p] Ibid. 195.

whole :

whole: and, if they do not both agree within six months, the right of prefentation fhall lapfe. But the ordinary may, if he pleafes, admit a clerk prefented by either, for the good of the church, that divine fervice may be regularly performed; which is no more than he otherwife would be entitled to do, in cafe their difagreement continued, fo as to incur a lapfe : and, if the clerk of one joint-tenant be fo admitted, this fhall keep up the title in both of them; in refpect of the privity and union of their eftate[q]. Upon the fame ground it is held, that one joint-tenant cannot have an action againft another for trefpafs, in refpect of his land[r]; for each has an equal right to enter on any part of it. But one joint-tenant is not capable by himfelf to do any act, which may tend to defeat or injure the eftate of the other; as to let leafes, or to grant copyholds[s] : and, if any wafte be done, which tends to the deftruction of the inheritance, one joint-tenant may have an action of wafte againft the other, by conftruction of the ftatute Weftm. 2. c. 22[t]. So too, though at common law no action of account lay for one joint-tenant againft another, unlefs he had conftituted him his bailiff or receiver[u], yet now by the ftatute 4 Ann. c. 16. joint-tenants may have actions of account againft each other, for receiving more than their due fhare of the profits of the tenements held in joint-tenancy.

FROM the fame principle alfo arifes the remaining grand incident of joint eftates; *viz.* the doctrine of *furvivorfhip :* by which, when two or more perfons are feifed of a joint eftate of inheritance, for their own lives, or *pur auter vie,* or are jointly poffeffed of any chattel intereft, the entire tenancy upon the deceafe of any of them remains to the furvivors, and at length to the laft furvivor; and he fhall be entitled to the whole eftate, whatever it be, whether an inheritance or a common freehold only, or even a lefs eftate[w]. This is the natural and regular confequence of the union and entirety of their intereft. The intereft of two joint-

---

[q] Co. Litt. 185.
[r] 3 Leon. 262.
[s] 1 Leon. 234.
[t] 2 Inft. 403.
[u] Co. Litt. 200.
[w] Litt. §. 280, 281.

tenants is not only equal or fimilar, but alfo is one and the fame. One has not originally a diftinct moiety from the other; but, if by any fubfequent act (as by alienation or forfeiture of either) the intereft becomes feparate and diftinct, the joint-tenancy inftantly ceafes. But, while it continues, each of two joint-tenants has a concurrent intereft in the whole; and therefore, on the death of his companion, the fole intereft in the whole remains to the fur-vivor. For the intereft, which the furvivor originally had, is clearly not devefted by the death of his companion; and no other perfon can now claim to have a *joint* eftate with him, for no one can now have an intereft in the whole, accruing by the fame title, and taking effect at the fame time with his own; neither can any one claim a *feparate* intereft in any part of the tenements; for that would be to deprive the furvivor of the right which he has in all, and every part. As therefore the furvivor's original intereft in the whole ftill remains; and as no one can now be ad-mitted, either jointly or feverally, to any fhare with him there-in; it follows, that his own intereft muft now be entire and feve-ral, and that he fhall alone be entitled to the whole eftate (what-ever it be) that was created by the original grant.

THIS right of furvivorfhip is called by our antient authors[x] the *jus accrefcendi*, becaufe the right, upon the death of one joint-tenant, accumulates and increafes to the furvivors; or, as they themfelves exprefs it, "*pars illa communis accrefcit fuperftitibus,* "*de perfona in perfonam, ufque ad ultimum fuperftitem.*" And this *jus accrefcendi* ought to be mutual; which I apprehend to be the reafon why neither the king[y], nor any corporation[z], can be a joint-tenant with a private perfon. For here is no mutuality: the private perfon has not even the remoteft chance of being feifed of the entirety, by benefit of furvivorfhip, for the king and the corporation can never die.

[x] Bracton, *l.* 4. *tr.* 3. *c.* 9. §. 3. Fleta. *l.* 3. *c.* 4.

[y] Co. Litt. 190. Finch L. 83.
[z] 2 Lev. 12.

3. WE

3. WE are, laftly, to enquire, how an eftate in joint-tenancy may be *fevered* and *deftroyed*. And this may be done by deftroying any of it's conftituent unities. 1. That of *time*, which refpects only the original commencement of the joint eftate, cannot indeed (being now paft) by affected by any fubfequent tranfactions. But, 2. the joint-tenants' eftate may be deftroyed, without any alienation, by merely difuniting their *poffeffion*. For joint-tenants being feifed *per my et per tout*, every thing that tends to narrow that intereft, fo that they fhall not be feifed throughout the whole, and throughout every part, is a feverance or deftruction of the jointure. And therefore, if two joint-tenants agree to part their lands, and hold them in feveralty, they are no longer joint-tenants ; for they have now no joint intereft in the whole, but only a feveral intereft refpectively in the feveral parts. And, for that reafon alfo, the right of furvivorfhip is by fuch feparation deftroyed[a]. By common law all the joint-tenants might agree to make partition of the lands, but one of them could not compel the others fo to do[b] : for, this being an eftate originally created by the act and agreement of the parties, the law would not permit any one or more of them to deftroy the united poffeffion without a fimilar univerfal confent. But now by the ftatutes 31 Hen.VIII. c. 1. and 32 Hen.VIII. c. 32. joint-tenants, either of inheritances or other lefs eftates, are compellable by writ of partition to divide their lands. 3. The jointure may be deftroyed, by deftroying the unity of *title*. As if one joint-tenant alienes and conveys his eftate to a third perfon : here the joint-tenancy is fevered, and turned into tenancy in common[d] ; for the grantee and the remaining joint-tenant hold by different titles, (one derived from the original, the other from the fubfequent, grantor) though, till partition made, the unity of poffeffion conti-

---

[a] Co. Litt. 188. 193.
[b] Litt. §. 290.
[c] Thus, by the civil law, *nemo invitus compellitur ad communionem. (Ff.* 12. 6. 26. §. 4.) And again : *fi non omnes qui rem*

communem habent, fed certi ex his, dividere defiderant ; hoc judicium inter eos accipi poteft. (Ff. 10. 3. 8.)
[d] Litt. §. 292.

nues. But a devife of one's fhare by will is no feverance of the jointure : for no teftament takes effect till after the death of the teftator, and by fuch death the right of the furvivor (which accrued at the original creation of the eftate, and has therefore a priority to the other ^e) is already vefted ^f. 4. It may alfo be deftroyed, by deftroying the unity of *intereft.* And therefore, if there be two joint-tenants for life, and the inheritance is purchafed by or defcends upon either, it is a feverance of the jointure ^g: though, if an eftate is originally limited to two for life, and after to the heirs of one of them, the freehold fhall remain in jointure, without merging in the inheritance ; becaufe, being created by one and the fame conveyance, they are not feparate eftates, (which is requifite in order to a merger) but branches of one intire eftate ^h. In like manner, if a joint-tenant in fee makes a leafe for life of his fhare, this defeats the jointure ⁱ; for it deftroys the unity both of title and of intereft. And, whenever or by whatever means the jointure ceafes or is fevered, the right of furvivorfhip or *jus accrefcendi* the fame inftant ceafes with it ^k. Yet, if one of three joint-tenants alienes his fhare, the two remaining tenants ftill hold their parts by joint-tenancy and furvivorfhip ^l: and, if one of three joint-tenants releafes his fhare to one of his companions, though the joint-tenancy is deftroyed with regard to that part, yet the two remaining parts are ftill held in jointure ^m; for they ftill preferve their original conftituent unities. But when, by any act or event, different interefts are created in the feveral parts of the eftate, or they are held by different titles, or if merely the poffeffion is feparated ; fo that the tenants have no longer thefe four indifpenfable properties, a famenefs of intereft, an undivided poffeffion, a title vefting at one and the fame time, and by one and the fame act or grant ; the jointure is inftantly diffolved.

^e *Jus accrefcendi præfertur ultimæ voluntati.* Co. Litt. 185.

^f Litt. §. 287.

^g Cro. Eliz. 470.

^h 2 Rep. 60. Co. Litt. 182.

ⁱ Litt. §. 302, 303.

^k *Nihil de re accrefcit ei, qui nihil in re quando jus accrefceret habet.* Co. Litt. 188.

^l Litt. §. 294.

^m *Ibid.* §. 304.

IN

In general it is advantageous for the joint-tenants to diffolve the jointure; fince thereby the right of furvivorfhip is taken away, and each may tranfmit his own part to his own heirs. Sometimes however it is difadvantageous to diffolve the joint eftate : as if there be joint-tenants for life, and they make partition, this diffolves the jointure; and, though before they each of them had an eftate in the whole for their own lives and the life of their companion, now they have an eftate in a moiety only for their own lives merely; and, on the death of either, the reverfioner fhall enter on his moiety[n]. And therefore, if there be two joint-tenants for life, and one grants away his part for the life of his companion, it is a forfeiture[o] : for, in the firft place, by the feverance of the jointure he has given himfelf in his own moiety only an eftate for his own life; and then he grants the fame land for the life of another : which grant, by a tenant for his own life merely, is a forfeiture of his eftate[p]; for it is creating an eftate which may by poffibility laft longer than that which he is legally entitled to.

III. An eftate held in *coparcenary* is where lands of inheritance defcend from the anceftor to two or more perfons. It *arifes* either by common law, or particular cuftom. By common law : as where a perfon feifed in fee-fimple or in fee-tail dies, and his next heirs are two or more females, his daughters, fifters, aunts, coufins, or their reprefentatives; in this cafe they fhall all inherit, as will be more fully fhewn, when we treat of defcents hereafter : and thefe co-heirs are then called *coparceners*; or, for brevity, *parceners* only[q]. Parceners by particular cuftom are where lands defcend, as in gavelkind, to all the males in equal degree, as fons, brothers, uncles, &c[r]. And, in either of thefe cafes, all the parceners put together make but one heir; and have but one eftate among them[s].

[n] 1 Jones. 55.
[o] 4 Leon. 237.
[p] Co. Litt. 252.

[q] Litt. §. 241, 242.
[r] *Ibid.* §. 265.
[s] Co. Litt. 163.

THE *properties* of parceners are in some respects like those of joint-tenants; they having the same unities of *interest, title,* and *possession*. They may sue and be sued jointly for matters relating to their own lands[t]: and the entry of one of them shall in some cases enure as the entry of them all[u]. They cannot have an action of trespass against each other: but herein they differ from joint-tenants, that they are also excluded from maintaining an action of waste[w]; for coparceners could at all times put a stop to any waste by a writ of partition, but till the statute of Henry the eighth joint-tenants had no such power. Parceners also differ materially from joint-tenants in four other points: 1. They always claim by descent, whereas joint-tenants always claim by purchase. Therefore if two sisters purchase lands, to hold to them and their heirs, they are not parceners, but joint-tenants[x]: and hence it likewise follows, that no lands can be held in coparcenary, but estates of inheritance, which are of a descendible nature; whereas not only estates in fee and in tail, but for life or years, may be held in joint-tenancy. 2. There is no unity of *time* necessary to an estate in coparcenary. For if a man hath two daughters, to whom his estate descends in coparcenary, and one dies before the other; the surviving daughter and the heir of the other, or, when both are dead, their two heirs, are still parceners[y]; the estates vesting in each of them at different times, though it be the same quantity of interest, and held by the same title. 3. Parceners, though they have a *unity*, have not an *entirety,* of interest. They are properly intitled each to the whole of a distinct moiety[z]; and of course there is no *jus accrescendi,* or survivorship between them: for each part descends severally to their respective heirs, though the unity of possession continues. And as long as the lands continue in a course of descent, and united in possession, so long are the tenants thereof, whether male or female, called parceners. But if the possession be once severed

[t] Co. Litt. 164.
[u] *Ibid.* 188.
[w] 2 Inst. 403.

[x] Litt. §. 254.
[y] Co. Litt. 164. 174.
[z] *Ibid.* 163, 164.

by

by partition, they are no longer parceners, but tenants in feveralty; or if one parcener aliens her fhare, though no partition be made, then are the lands no longer held in *coparcenary*, but in *common* [a].

PARCENERS are fo called, faith Littleton [b], becaufe they may be conftrained to make *partition*. And he mentions many methods of making it [c]; four of which are by confent, and one by compulfion. The firft is, where they agree to divide the lands into equal parts in feveralty, and that each fhall have fuch a determinate part. The fecond is, when they agree to chufe fome friend to make partition for them, and then the fifters fhall chufe each of them her part according to feniority of age; or otherwife, as fhall be agreed. But this privilege of feniority is then perfonal; for if the eldeft fifter be dead, her iffue fhall not chufe firft, but the next fifter. But, if an advowfon defcend in coparcenary, and the fifters cannot agree in the prefentation, the eldeft and her iffue, nay her hufband, or her affigns, fhall prefent alone, before the younger [d]. And the reafon given is that the former privilege, of priority in choice upon a divifion, arifes from an act of her own, the agreement to make partition; and therefore is merely perfonal: the latter, of prefenting to the living, arifes from the act of the law, and is annexed not only to her perfon, but to her eftate alfo. A third method of partition is, where the eldeft divides, and then fhe fhall chufe laft; for the rule of law is, *cujus eft divifio, alterius eft electio*. The fourth method is where the fifters agree to caft lots for their fhares. And thefe are the methods by confent. That by compulfion is, where one or more fue out a writ of partition againft the others, whereupon the fheriff fhall go to the lands, and make partition thereof by the verdict of a jury there impanneled, and affign to each of the parceners her part in feveralty [e]. But there are fome things which

[a] Litt. §. 309.
[b] §. 241.
[c] §. 243 to 264.
[d] Co. Litt. 166. 3 Rep. 22.
[e] By ftatute 8 & 9 W. III. c. 3. An eafier method of carrying on the proceedings on a writ of partition, of lands held either in joint-tenancy, parcenary, or common, than was ufed at the common law, is chalked out and provided.

are

are in their nature impartible. The manfion-houfe, common of eftovers, common of pifcary uncertain, or any other common without ftint, fhall not be divided; but the eldeft fifter, if fhe pleafes, fhall have them, and make the others a reafonable fatisfaction in other parts of the inheritance; or, if that cannot be, then they fhall have the profits of the thing by turns, in the fame manner as they take the advowfon [f].

THERE is yet another confideration attending the eftate in coparcenary; that if one of the daughters has had an eftate given with her in *frankmarriage* by her anceftor (which we may remember was a fpecies of eftates-tail, freely given by a relation for advancement of his kinfwoman in marriage [g]) in this cafe, if lands defcend from the *fame* anceftor to her and her fifters in fee-fimple, fhe or her heirs fhall have no fhare of them, unlefs they will agree to divide the lands fo given in frankmarriage in equal proportion with the reft of the lands defcending [h]. This general divifion was known in the law of the Lombards [i], which direct the woman fo preferred in marriage, and claiming her fhare of the inheritance, *mittere in confufum cum fororibus, quantum pater aut frater ei dederit, quando ambulaverit ad maritum.* With us it is denominated bringing thofe lands into *botchpot* [k]; which term I fhall explain in the very words of Littleton [l]: " it " feemeth that this word, hotchpot, is in Englifh, a pudding; " for in a pudding is not commonly put one thing alone, but one " thing with other things together." By this houfewifely metaphor our anceftors meant to inform us [m], that the lands, both thofe given in frankmarriage and thofe defcending in fee-fimple, fhould be mixed and blended together, and then divided in equal portions among all the daughters. But this was left to the choice of the donee in frankmarriage, and if fhe did not chufe to put her lands in hotchpot, fhe was prefumed to be fufficiently provi-

[f] Co. Litt. 164, 165.
[g] See pag. 115.
[h] Bracton. *l.* 2. *c.* 34. Litt. §. 266 to 273.
[i] *l.* 2. *t.* 14. *c.* 15.
[k] Britton. *c.* 72.
[l] §. 267.
[m] Litt. §. 268.

ded

ded for, and the reſt of the inheritance was divided among
her other ſiſters. The law of hotchpot took place then only,
when the other lands deſcending from the anceſtor were fee-
ſimple; for, if they deſcended in tail, the donee in frankmarriage
was entitled to her ſhare, without bringing her lands ſo given into
hotchpot [n]. And the reaſon is, becauſe lands deſcending in fee-
ſimple are diſtributed by the policy of law, for the maintenance
of all the daughters; and, if one has a ſufficient proviſion out of
the ſame inheritance, equal to the reſt, it is not reaſonable that
ſhe ſhould have more: but lands, deſcending in tail, are not diſtributed by the operation of law, ſo properly as *per formam doni*;
it matters not therefore how unequal this diſtribution may be.
Alſo no lands, but ſuch as are given in frankmarriage, ſhall be
brought into hotchpot; for no others are looked upon in law as
given for the advancement of the woman, or by way of marriage-
portion [o]. And therefore, as gifts in frankmarriage are fallen into
diſuſe, I ſhould hardly have mentioned the law of hotchpot, had
not this method of diviſion been revived and copied by the ſtatute
for diſtribution of perſonal eſtates, which we ſhall hereafter conſider at large.

THE eſtate in coparcenary may be *diſſolved*, either by partition;
which diſunites the poſſeſſion; by alienation of one parcener,
which diſunites the title, and may diſunite the intereſt; or by
the whole at laſt deſcending to and veſting in one ſingle perſon,
which brings it to an eſtate in ſeveralty.

IV. TENANTS in *common* are ſuch as hold by ſeveral and
diſtinct titles, but by unity of poſſeſſion; becauſe none knoweth
his own ſeveralty, and therefore they all occupy promiſcuouſly [p].
This tenancy therefore happens, where there is an unity of poſſeſſion merely, but perhaps an entire diſunion of intereſt, of title,
and of time. For, if there be two tenants in common of lands,
one may hold his part in fee-ſimple, the other in tail, or for life;

[n] Litt. §. 274.　　　[p] *Ibid.* 292.
[o] *Ibid.* 275.

fo

so that there is no necessary unity of interest : one may hold by
descent, the other by purchase; or the one by purchase from A,
the other by purchase from B; so that there is no unity of title :
one's estate may have been vested fifty years, the other's but yes-
terday; so there is no unity of time. The only unity there is,
is that of possession; and for this Littleton gives the true reason,
because no man can certainly tell which part is his own : otherwise even this would be soon destroyed.

TENANCY in common may be created, either by the destruction of the two other estates, in joint-tenancy and coparcenary, or by special limitation in a deed. By the destruction of
the two other estates, I mean such destruction as does not sever
the unity of possession, but only the unity of title or interest.
As, if one of two joint-tenants in fee alienes his estate for the
life of the alienee, the alienee and the other joint-tenant are tenants in common : for they now have several titles, the other
joint-tenant by the original grant, the alienee by the new alienation [q]; and they also have several interests, the former joint-
tenant in fee-simple, the alienee for his own life only. So, if one
joint-tenant give his part to A in tail, and the other gives his to
B in tail, the donees are tenants in common, as holding by different titles and conveyances [r]. If one of two parceners alienes,
the alienee and the remaining parcener are tenants in common [s];
because they hold by different titles, the parcener by descent, the
alienee by purchase. So likewise, if there be a grant to two *men*,
or two *women*, and the heirs of their bodies, here the grantees
shall be joint-tenants of the life-estate, but they shall have several inheritances; because they cannot possibly have one heir of
their two bodies, as might have been the case had the limitation
been to *a man and woman*, and the heirs of their bodies begotten [t]:
and in this, and the like cases, their issues shall be tenants in
common; because they must claim by different titles, one as heir
of A, and the other as heir of B; and those too not titles by

[q] Litt. §. 293.
[r] Ibid. 295.
[s] Ibid. 309.
[t] Ibid. 283.

purchase,

purchafe, but defcent. In fhort, whenever an eftate in joint-tenancy or coparcenary is diffolved, fo that there be no partition made, but the unity of poffeffion continues, it is turned into a tenancy in common.

A TENANCY in common may alfo be created by exprefs li-mitation in a deed: but here care muft be taken not to infert words which imply a joint eftate; and then if lands be given to two or more, and it be not joint-tenancy, it muft be a tenancy in common. But the law is apt in it's conftructions to favour joint-tenancy rather than tenancy in common [u]; becaufe the di-vifible fervices iffuing from land (as rent, &c) are not divided, nor the entire fervices (as fealty) multiplied, by joint-tenancy, as they muft neceffarily be upon a tenancy in common. Land given to two, to be holden the one moiety to one, and the other moiety to the other, is an eftate in common [w]; and, if one grants to an-other *half* his land, the grantor and grantee are alfo tenants in common [x]: becaufe, as has been before [y] obferved, joint-tenants do not take by diftinct halves or moieties; and by fuch grants the divifion and feveralty of the eftate is fo plainly expreffed, that it is impoffible they fhould take a joint intereft in the whole of the tenements. But a *devife* to two perfons, to hold *jointly and feverally*, is a joint-tenancy; becaufe that is implied in the word "jointly," even though the word "feverally" feems to im-ply the direct reverfe [z]: and an eftate given to A and B, *equally to be divided* between them, though in *deeds* it hath been faid to be a joint-tenancy [a], (for it implies no more than the law has annexed to that eftate, *viz.* divifibility [b]) yet in *wills* it is cer-tainly a tenancy in common [c]; becaufe the devifor may be pre-fumed to have meant what is moft beneficial to both the devifees, though his meaning is imperfectly expreffed. And this nicety in the wording of grants makes it the moft ufual as well as the fafeft

---

[u] Salk. 392.
[w] Litt. §. 298.
[x] *Ibid.* 299.
[y] See pag. 182.

[z] Poph. 52.
[a] 1 Equ. Caf. abr. 291.
[b] 1 P. W[ms]. 17.
[c] 3 Rep. 39. 1 Ventr. 32.

way, when a tenancy in common is meant to be created, to add
exprefs words of excluſion as well as defcription, and limit the eſtate
to A and B, to hold *as tenants in common, and not as joint-tenants.*

A s to the *incidents* attending a tenancy in common : tenants
in common (like joint-tenants) are compellable by the ſtatutes
of Henry VIII and William III, before-mentioned [d], to make partition of their lands ; which they were not at common law. They
properly take by diſtinct moieties, and have no entirety of intereſt ;
and therefore there is no ſurvivorſhip between tenants in common.
Their other incidents are fuch as merely ariſe from the unity of
poſſeſſion ; and are therefore the ſame as appertain to joint-tenants
merely upon that account : ſuch as being liable to reciprocal actions of waſte, and of account, by the ſtatutes of Weſtm. 2. c. 22.
and 4 Ann. c. 16. For by the common law no tenant in common
was liable to account to his companion for embezzling the profits
of the eſtate [e] ; though, if one actually turns the other out of
poſſeſſion, an action of ejectment will lie againſt him [f]. But, as
for other incidents of joint-tenants, which ariſe from the privity
of title, or the union and entirety of intereſt, (ſuch as joining
or being joined in actions [g], unleſs in the caſe where ſome intire
or indiviſible thing is to be recovered [h]) theſe are not applicable
to tenants in common, whoſe intereſts are diſtinct, and whoſe
titles are not joint but ſeveral.

E s T A T E s in common can only be *diſſolved* two ways : 1. By
uniting all the titles and intereſts in one tenant, by purchaſe or
otherwiſe ; which brings the whole to one ſeveralty : 2. By making partition between the ſeveral tenants in common, which
gives them all reſpective ſeveralties. For indeed tenancies in common differ in nothing from ſole eſtates, but merely in the blend-
ing and unity of poſſeſſion. And this finiſhes our enquiries with
reſpect to the nature of *eſtates.*

[d] pag. 185, & 186.   [g] Litt. §. 311.
[e] Co. Litt. 199.   [h] Co. Litt. 197.
[f] *Ibid.* 200.

CHAPTER THE THIRTEENTH.

)F THE TITLE TO THINGS REAL,

IN GENERAL.

THE foregoing chapters having been principally employed in defining the *nature* of things real, in defcribing the *tenures* by which they may be holden, and in diftinguifhing the feveral kinds of *eftate* or intereft that may be had therein, I come now to confider, laftly, the *title* to things real, with the manner of acquiring and lofing it. A title is thus defined by fir Edward Coke[a], *titulus eft jufta caufa poffidendi id quod noftrum eft* ; or, it is the means whereby the owner of lands hath the juft poffeffion of his property.

THERE are feveral ftages or degrees requifite to form a complete title to lands and tenements. We will confider them in a progreffive order.

I. THE loweft and moft imperfect degree of title confifts in the mere *naked poffeffion,* or actual occupation of the eftate ; without any apparent right, or any fhadow or pretence of right, to hold and continue fuch poffeffion. This may happen, when one man invades the poffeffion of another, and by force or furprize turns him out of the occupation of his lands ; which is termed a *diffeifin,* being a deprivation of that actual feifin, or corporal

[a] 1 Inft. 345.

A a 2

freehold

freehold of the lands, which the tenant before enjoyed. Or it may happen, that after the death of the anceſtor and before the entry of the heir, or after the death of a particular tenant and before the entry of him in remainder or reverſion, a ſtranger may contrive to get poſſeſſion of the vacant land, and hold out him that had a right to enter. In all which caſes, and many others that might be here ſuggeſted, the wrongdoer has only a mere naked poſſeſſion, which the rightful owner may put an end to, by a variety of legal remedies, as will more fully appear in the third book of theſe commentaries. But in the mean time, till ſome act be done by the rightful owner to deveſt this poſſeſſion and aſſert his title, ſuch actual poſſeſſion is, *prima facie*, evidence of a legal title in the poſſeſſor; and it may, by length of time, and negligence of him who hath the right, by degrees ripen into a perfect and indefeaſible title. And, at all events, without ſuch actual poſſeſſion no title can be completely good.

II. THE next ſtep to a good and perfect title is the *right of poſſeſſion*, which may reſide in one man, while the actual poſſeſſion is either in himſelf or in another. For if a man be diſſeiſed, or otherwiſe kept out of poſſeſſion, by any of the means beforementioned, though the *actual* poſſeſſion be loſt, yet he has ſtill remaining in him the *right* of poſſeſſion; and may exert it whenever he thinks proper, by entering upon the diſſeiſor, and turning him out of that occupancy which he has ſo illegally gained. But this right of poſſeſſion is of two ſorts: an *apparent* right of poſſeſſion, which may be defeated by proving a better; and an *actual* right of poſſeſſion, which will ſtand the teſt againſt all opponents. Thus if the diſſeiſor, or other wrongdoer, dies poſſeſſed of the land whereof he ſo became ſeiſed by his own unlawful act, and the ſame deſcends to his heir; now the heir hath obtained an *apparent* right, though the *actual* right of poſſeſſion reſides in the perſon diſſeiſed; and it ſhall not be lawful for the perſon diſſeiſed to deveſt this apparent right by mere entry or other act of his own, but only by an action at law [b]. For, until

[b] Litt. §. 386.

the

the contrary be proved by legal demonſtration, the law will rather preſume the right to reſide in the heir, whoſe anceſtor died ſeiſed, than in one who has no ſuch preſumptive evidence to urge in his own behalf. Which doctrine in ſome meaſure aroſe from the principles of the feodal law, which, after feuds became hereditary, much favoured the right of deſcent; in order that there might be a perſon always on the ſpot to perform the feodal duties and ſervices[c]: and therefore, when a feudatory died in battle, or otherwiſe, it preſumed always that his children were entitled to the feud, till the right was otherwiſe determined by his fellow-ſoldiers and fellow-tenants, the peers of the feodal court. But if he, who has the actual right of poſſeſſion, puts in his claim and brings his action within a reaſonable time, and can prove by what unlawful means the anceſtor became ſeiſed, he will then by ſentence of law recover that poſſeſſion, to which he hath ſuch actual right. Yet, if he omits to bring this his poſſeſſory action within a competent time, his adverſary may imperceptibly gain an actual right of poſſeſſion, in conſequence of the other's negligence. And by this, and certain other means, the party kept out of poſſeſſion may have nothing left in him, but what we are next to ſpeak of; *viz.*

III. THE mere *right of property*, the *jus proprietatis*, without either poſſeſſion or even the right of poſſeſſion. This is frequently ſpoken of in our books under the name of the *mere right*, *jus merum*; and the eſtate of the owner is in ſuch caſes ſaid to be totally deveſted, and *put to a right*[d]. A perſon in this ſituation may have the true ultimate property of the lands in himſelf: but by the intervention of certain circumſtances, either by his own negligence, the ſolemn act of his anceſtor, or the determination of a court of juſtice, the preſumptive evidence of that right is ſtrongly in favour of his antagoniſt; who has thereby obtained the abſolute right of poſſeſſion. As, in the firſt place, if a perſon diſſeiſed, or turned out of poſſeſſion of his eſtate, neglects to purſue his remedy within the time limited by law; by this means

[c] Gilb. Ten. 18. [d] Co. Litt. 345.

the

the diſſeiſor or his heirs gain the actual right of poſſeſſion : for the law preſumes that either he had a good right originally, in virtue of which he entered on the lands on queſtion, or that ſince ſuch his entry he has procured a ſufficient title ; and therefore, after ſo long an acquieſcence, the law will not ſuffer his poſſeſſion to be diſturbed without enquiring into the abſolute right of property. Yet, ſtill, if the perſon diſſeiſed or his heir hath the true right of property remaining in himſelf, his eſtate is indeed ſaid to be turned into a mere right ; but, by proving ſuch his better right, he may at length recover the lands. Again ; if a tenant in tail diſcontinues his eſtate-tail, by alienating the lands to a ſtranger in fee, and dies ; here the iſſue in tail hath no right of *poſſeſſion*, independent of the right of *property* : for the law preſumes *prima facie* that the anceſtor would not diſinherit, or attempt to diſinherit, his heir, unleſs he had power ſo to do ; and therefore, as the anceſtor had in himſelf the right of poſſeſſion, and has transferred the ſame to a ſtranger, the law will not permit that poſſeſſion now to be diſturbed, unleſs by ſhewing the abſolute right of property to reſide in another perſon. The heir therefore in this caſe has only a *mere right*, and muſt be ſtrictly held to the proof of it, in order to recover the lands. Laſtly, if by accident, neglect, or otherwiſe, judgment is given for either party in any *poſſeſſory* action, (that is, ſuch wherein the right of poſſeſſion only, and not that of property, is conteſted) and the other party hath indeed in himſelf the right of property, this is now turned to a *mere right* ; and upon proof thereof in a ſubſequent action, denominated a writ of right, he ſhall recover his ſeiſin of the lands.

THUS, if a diſſeiſor turns me out of poſſeſſion of my lands, he thereby gains a *mere naked poſſeſſion*, and I ſtill retain the *right of poſſeſſion*, and *right of property*. If the diſſeiſor dies, and the lands deſcend to his ſon, the ſon gains an *apparent* right of *poſſeſſion* ; but I ſtill retain the *actual* right both of *poſſeſſion* and *property*. If I acquieſce for thirty years, without bringing any action to recover poſſeſſion of the lands, the ſon gains the *actual right*

right of poſſeſſion, and I retain nothing but the *mere right of pro-perty.* And even this right of property will fail, or at leaſt it will be without a remedy, unleſs I purſue it within the ſpace of ſixty years. So alſo if the father be tenant in tail, and alienes the eſtate-tail to a ſtranger in fee, the alienee thereby gains the *right of poſſeſſion,* and the ſon hath only the *mere right* or *right of property.* And hence it will follow, that one man may have the *poſſeſſion,* another the *right of poſſeſſion,* and a third the *right of property.* For if tenant in tail alienes to A in fee-ſimple, and dies, and B diſſeiſes A ; now B will have the *poſſeſſion,* A the *right of poſſeſ-ſion,* and the iſſue in tail the *right of property :* A may recover the poſſeſſion againſt B; and afterwards the iſſue in tail may evict A, and unite in himſelf the poſſeſſion, the right of poſſeſſion, and alſo the right of property. In which union conſiſts,

IV. A COMPLETE title to lands, tenements, and heredita-ments. For it is an antient maxim of the law[e], that no title is completely good, unleſs the right of poſſeſſion be joined with the right of property ; which right is then denominated a double right, *jus duplicatum,* or *droit droit*[f]. And when to this double right the actual poſſeſſion is alſo united, when there is, according to the expreſſion of Fleta[g], *juris et ſeiſinae conjunctio,* then, and then only, is the title completely legal.

[e] Mirr. *l.* 2. *c.* 27.
[f] Co. Litt. 266. Bract. *l.* 5. *tr.* 3. *c.* 5
[g] *l.* 3. *c.* 15. §. 5.

C H A P T E R　T H E　F O U R T E E N T H.

O f　T I T L E　b y　D E S C E N T.

THE feveral gradations and ftages, requifite to form a complete title to lands, tenements, and hereditaments, having
been briefly ftated in the preceding chapter, we are next to confider the feveral manners, in which this complete title (and therein
principally the right of *propriety*) may be reciprocally loft and acquired : whereby the dominion of things real is either continued,
or transferred from one man to another. And here we muft firft
of all obferve, that (as gain and lofs are terms of relation, and
of a reciprocal nature) by whatever method one man gains an
eftate, by that fame method or it's correlative fome other man
has loft it. As where the heir acquires by defcent, the anceftor
has firft loft or abandoned the eftate by his death : where the
lord gains land by efcheat, the eftate of the tenant is firft of all
loft by the natural or legal extinction of all his hereditary blood :
where a man gains an intereft by occupancy, the former owner
has previoufly relinquifhed his right of poffeffion : where one
man claims by prefcription or immemorial ufage, another man
has either parted with his right by an antient and now forgotten
grant, or has forfeited it by the fupinenefs or neglect of himfelf
and his anceftors for ages : and fo, in cafe of forfeiture, the tenant
by his own mifbehaviour or neglect has renounced his intereft in
the eftate ; whereupon it devolves to that perfon who by law may
take advantage of fuch default : and, in alienation by common
affurances, the two confiderations of lofs and acquifition are fo
interwoven,

interwoven, and fo conftantly contemplated together, that we never hear of a conveyance, without at once receiving the idea as well of the grantor as the grantee.

THE methods therefore of acquiring on the one hand, and of lofing on the other, a title to eftates in things real, are reduced by our law to two: *defcent*, where the title is vefted in a man by the fingle operation of law; and *purchafe*, where the title is vefted in him by his own act or agreement[a].

DESCENT, or hereditary fucceffion, is the title whereby a man on the death of his anceftor acquires his eftate by right of reprefentation, as his heir at law. An heir therefore is he upon whom the law cafts the eftate immediately on the death of the anceftor: and an eftate, fo defcending to the heir, is in law called the inheritance.

THE doctrine of defcents, or law of inheritances in fee-fimple, is a point of the higheft importance; and is indeed the principal object of the laws of real property in England. All the rules relating to purchafes, whereby the legal courfe of defcents is broken and altered, perpetually refer to this fettled law of inheritance, as a *datum* or firft principle univerfally known, and upon which their fubfequent limitations are to work. Thus a gift in tail, or to a man and the heirs of his body, is a limitation that cannot be perfectly underftood without a previous knowlege of the law of defcents in fee-fimple. One may well perceive, that this is an eftate confined in it's defcent to fuch heirs only of the donee, as have fprung or fhall fpring from his body; but who thofe heirs are, whether all his children both male and female, or the male only, and (among the males) whether the eldeft, youngeft, or other fon alone, or all the fons together, fhall be his heir; this is a point, that we muft refult back to the ftanding law of defcents in fee-fimple to be informed of.

[a] Co. Litt. 18.

IN order therefore to treat a matter of this univerfal confe-quence the more clearly, I fhall endeavour to lay afide fuch mat-ters as will only tend to breed embaraffment and confufion in our enquiries, and fhall confine myfelf entirely to this one object. I fhall therefore decline confidering at prefent who are, and who are not, capable of being heirs; referring that for the chapter of *efcheats*. I fhall alfo pafs over the frequent divifion of defcents, into thofe by *cuftom*, *ftatute*, and *common law:* for defcents by *particular cuftom*, as to all the fons in gavelkind, and to the youngeft in borough-englifh, have already been often[b] hinted at, and may alfo be incidentally touched upon again; but will not make a fe-parate confideration by themfelves, in a fyftem fo general as the prefent: and defcents by *ftatute*, or fee-tail *per formam doni*, in purfuance of the ftatute of Weftminfter the fecond, have alfo been already[c] copioufly handled; and it has been feen that the defcent in tail is reftrained and regulated according to the words of the original donation, and does not intirely purfue the common law doctrine of inheritance; which, and which only, it will now be our bufinefs to explain.

AND, as this depends not a little on the nature of kindred, and the feveral degrees of confanguinity, it will be previoufly ne-ceffary to ftate, as briefly as poffible, the true notion of this kind-red or alliance in blood[d].

CONSANGUINITY, or kindred, is defined by the writers on thefe fubjects to be " *vinculum perfonarum ab eodem ftipite defcen-* " *dentium;*" the connexion or relation of perfons defcended from the fame ftock or common anceftor. This confanguinity is either lineal, or collateral.

---

[b] See Vol. I. pag. 74, 75. Vol. II. pag. 83, 85.
[c] See pag. 112, &c.
[d] For a fuller explanation of the doctrine of confanguinity, and the confequences re-fulting from a right apprehenfion of it's na-ture, fee *an effay on collateral confanguinity*, in the firft volume of law tracts. *Oxon.* 1762. 8°.

LINEAL

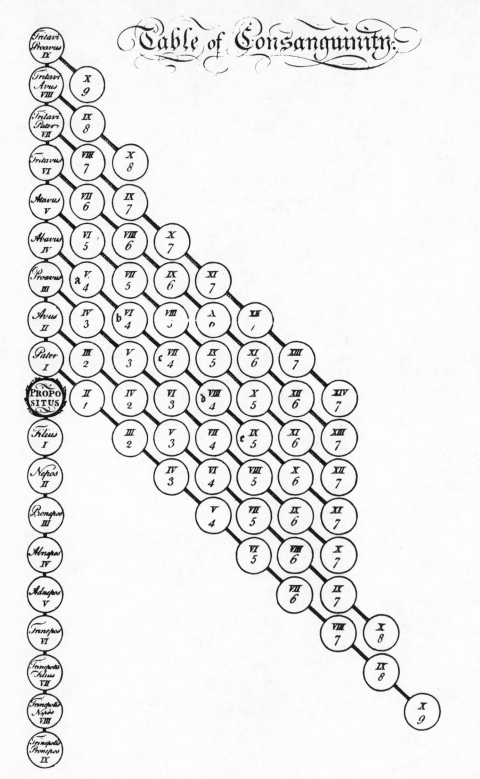

Table of Consanguinity.

LINEAL confanguinity is that which fubfifts between perfons, of whom one is defcended in a direct line from the other : as between John Stiles (the *propofitus* in the table of confanguinity) and his father, grandfather, great-grandfather, and fo upwards in the direct afcending line ; or between John Stiles and his fon, grandfon, great-grandfon, and fo downwards in the direct defcending line. Every generation, in this lineal direct confanguinity, conftitutes a different degree, reckoning either upwards or downwards : the father of John Stiles is related to him in the firft degree, and fo likewife is his fon ; his grandfire and grandfon in the fecond ; his great-grandfire, and great-grandfon in the third. This is the only natural way of reckoning the degrees in the direct line, and therefore univerfally obtains, as well in the civil [e], and canon [f], as in the common law [g].

THE doctrine of lineal confanguinity is fufficiently plain and obvious ; but it is at the firft view aftonifhing to confider the number of lineal anceftors which every man has, within no very great number of degrees : and fo many different bloods [h] is a man faid to contain in his veins, as he hath lineal anceftors. Of thefe he hath two in the firft afcending degree, his own parents ; he hath four in the fecond, the parents of his father and the parents of his mother ; he hath eight in the third, the parents of his two grandfathers and two grandmothers ; and, by the fame rule of progreffion, he hath an hundred and twenty eight in the feventh ; a thoufand and twenty four in the tenth ; and at the twentieth degree, or the diftance of twenty generations, every man hath above a million of anceftors, as common arithmetic will demonftrate [i]. This lineal confanguinity, we may obferve, falls ftrictly within the definition of *vinculum perfonarum ab eodem ftipite def-*

---

[e] *Ff.* 38. 10. 10.
[f] *Decretal. l.* 4. *tit.* 14.
[g] Co. Litt. 23.
[h] *Ibid.* 12.
[i] This will feem furprizing to thofe who are unacquainted with the encreafing power of progreffive numbers ; but is palpably evident from the following table of a geometrical progreffion, in which the firft term is 2, and the denominator alfo 2 : or, to

ſpeak

cendentium; fince lineal relations are fuch as defcend one from the other, and both of courfe from the fame common anceftor.

COLLATERAL kindred anfwers to the fame defcription: collateral relations agreeing with the lineal in this, that they de-fcend from the fame ftock or anceftor; but differing in this, that they do not defcend from each other. Collateral kinfmen as fuch then as lineally fpring from one and the fame anceftor, who is the *ftirps*, or root, the *ftipes*, trunk, or common ftock, from whence thefe relations are branched out. As if John Stiles hath

fpeak more intelligibly, it is evident, for that each of us has two anceftors in the firft degree; the number of whom is doubled at every remove, becaufe each of our an-ceftors has alfo two immediate anceftors of his own.

Lineal Degrees.	Number of Anceftors.
1	2
2	4
3	8
4	16
5	32
6	64
7	128
8	256
9	512
10	1024
11	2048
12	4096
13	8192
14	16384
15	32768
16	65536
17	131072
18	262144
19	524288
20	1048576

A fhorter method of finding the number of anceftors at any even degree is by fquaring the number of anceftors at half that num-ber of degrees. Thus 16 (the number of anceftors at four degrees) is the fquare of 4, the number of anceftors at two; 256 is the fquare of 16; 65536 of 256; and the number of anceftors at 40 degrees would be the fquare of 1048576, or upwards of a million millions.

two

two sons, who have each a numerous issue; both these issues are lineally descended from John Stiles as their common ancestor; and they are collateral kinsmen to each other, because they are all descended from this common ancestor, and all have a portion of his blood in their veins, which denominates them *consanguineos*.

WE must be careful to remember, that the very being of collateral consanguinity consists in this descent from one and the same common ancestor. Thus *Titius* and his brother are related; why? because both are derived from one father: *Titius* and his first cousin are related; why? because both descend from the same grandfather: and his second cousin's claim to consanguinity is this, that they both are derived from one and the same great-grandfather. In short, as many ancestors as a man has, so many common stocks he has, from which collateral kinsmen may be derived. And as we are taught by holy writ, that there is one couple of ancestors belonging to us all, from whom the whole race of mankind is descended, the obvious and undeniable consequence is, that all men are in some degree related to each other. For indeed, if we only only suppose each couple of our ancestors to have left, one with another, two children; and each of those children on an average to have left two more; (and, without such a supposition, the human species must be daily diminishing) we shall find that all of us have now subsisting near two hundred and seventy millions of kindred in the fifteenth degree, at the same distance from the several common ancestors as ourselves are; besides those that are one or two descents nearer to or farther from the common stock, who may amount to as many more [k]. And, if this calculation should appear incompatible with the number of inhabitants on the earth, it is because, by intermarriages among the several descendants from the same ancestor, a hundred or a thousand modes of consanguinity may be consolidated in one person, or he may be related to us a hundred or a thousand different ways.

[k] This will swell more considerably than the former calculation: for here, though the first term is but 1, the denominator is 4; that is, there is *one* kinsman (a brother) in the first degree, who makes, together with the *proposuus*, the two descendants from the first couple of ancestors; and in every other degree the number of kindred must be

THE method of computing thefe degrees in the canon law [1], which our law has adopted [m], is as follows. We begin at the common anceftor, and reckon downwards; and in whatfoever degree the two perfons, or the moft remote of them, is diftant

be the *quadruple* of thofe in the degree which immediately precedes it. For, fince each couple of anceftors has two defcendants, who encreafe in a duplicate *ratio*, it will follow that the *ratio*, in which all the defcendants encreafe downwards, muft be double to that

in which the anceftors encreafe upwards: but we have feen that the anceftors encreafe in a duplicate *ratio*: therefore the defcendants muft encreafe in a double duplicate, that is, in a quadruple, *ratio*.

Collateral Degrees.	*Number of Kindred.*
1	1
2	4
3	16
4	64
5	256
6	1024
7	4096
8	16384
9	65536
10	262144
11	1048576
12	4194304
13	16777216
14	67108864
15	268435456
16	1073741824
17	4294967296
18	17179869184
19	68719476736
20	274877906944

This calculation may alfo be formed by a more compendious procefs, *viz.* by fquaring the couples, or half the number, of anceftors at any given degree; which will furnifh us with the number of kindred we have in the fame degree, at equal diftance with ourfelves from the common ftock, befides thofe at unequal diftances. Thus, in the tenth lineal degree, the number of anceftors is 1024; it's half, or the couples, amount to 512; the number of kindred in the tenth collateral degree amounts therefore

to 262144, or the fquare of 512. And if we will be at the trouble to recollect the ftate of the feveral families within our own knowlege, and obferve how far they agree with this account; that is, whether, on an average, every man has not one brother or fifter, four firft coufins, fixteen fecond confins, and fo on; we fhall find that the prefent calculation is very far from being overcharged.

[1] *Decretal.* 4. 14. 3 & 9.
[m] Co. Litt. 23.

from

from the common anceftor, that is the degree in which they are related to each other. Thus *Titius* and his brother are related in the firft degree; for from the father to each of them is counted only one: *Titius* and his nephew are related in the fecond degree; for the nephew is two degrees removed from the common anceftor; *viz.* his own grandfather, the father of *Titius*. Or, (to give a more illuftrious inftance from our Englifh annals) king Henry the feventh, who flew Richard the third in the battle of Bofworth, was related to that prince in the fifth degree. Let the *propofitus* therefore in the table of confanguinity reprefent king Richard the third, and the clafs marked (е) king Henry the feventh. Now their common ftock or anceftor was king Edward the third, the *abavus* in the fame table: from him to Edmond duke of York, the *proavus*, is one degree; to Richard earl of Cambridge, the *avus*, two; to Richard duke of York, the *pater*, three; to king Richard the third, the *propofitus*, four: and from king Edward the third to John of Gant (а) is one degree; to John earl of Somerfet (b) two; to John duke of Somerfet (с) three; to Margaret countefs of Richmond (d) four; to king Henry the feventh (е) five. Which laft mentioned prince, being the fartheft removed from the common ftock, gives the denomination to the degree of kindred in the canon and municipal law. Though according to the computation of the civilians, (who count upwards, from either of the perfons related, to the common ftock, and then downwards again to the other; reckoning a degree for each perfon both afcending and defcending) thefe two princes were related in the ninth degree: for from king Richard the third to Richard duke of York is one degree; to Richard earl of Cambridge, two; to Edmond duke of York, three; to king Edward the third, the common anceftor, four; to John of Gant, five; to John earl of Somerfet, fix; to John duke of Somerfet, feven; to Margaret countefs of Richmond, eight; to king Henry the feventh, nine[n].

[n] See the table of confanguinity annexed; wherein all the degrees of collateral kindred to the *propofitus* are computed, fo far as the tenth of the civilians and the feventh of the canonifts inclufive; the former being diftinguifhed by the numeral letters, the latter by the common ciphers.

THE

Th e nature and degrees of kindred being thus in fome meafure explained, I fhall next proceed to lay down a feries of rules,
or canons of inheritance, according to which eftates are tranfmitted from the anceftor to the heir ; together with an explanatory comment, remarking their original and progrefs, the reafons
upon which they are founded, and in fome cafes their agreement
with the laws of other nations.

I. Th e firft rule is, that inheritances fhall lineally defcend to
the iffue of the perfon laft actually feifed, *in infinitum;* but fhall
never lineally afcend.

To explain the more clearly both this and the fubfequent
rules, it muft firft be obferved, that by law no inheritance can
veft, nor can any perfon be the actual complete heir of another,
till the anceftor is previoufly dead. *Nemo eft haeres viventis.* Before that time the perfon who is next in the line of fucceffion is
called an heir apparent, or heir prefumptive. Heirs apparent are
fuch, whofe right of inheritance is indefeafible, provided they
outlive the anceftor ; as the eldeft fon or his iffue, who muft by
the courfe of the common law be heirs to the father whenever
he happens to die. Heirs prefumptive are fuch, who, if the anceftor fhould die immediately, would in the prefent circumftances of things be his heirs ; but whofe right of inheritance may
be defeated by the contingency of fome nearer heir being born :
as a brother, or nephew, whofe prefumptive fucceffion may be
deftroyed by the birth of a child ; or a daughter, whofe prefent
hopes may be hereafter cut off by the birth of a fon. Nay, even
if the eftate hath defcended, by the death of the owner, to fuch
brother, or nephew, or daughter ; in the former cafes the eftate
fhall be devefted and taken away by the birth of a pofthumous
child ; and, in the latter, it fhall alfo be totally devefted by the
birth of a pofthumous fon [o].

[o] Bro. *tit. defcent.* 58.

We

WE muſt alſo remember, that no perſon can be properly ſuch an anceſtor, as that an inheritance in lands or tenements can be derived from him, unleſs he hath had actual ſeiſin of ſuch lands, either by his own entry, or by the poſſeſſion of his own or his anceſtor's leſſee for years, or by receiving rent from a leſſee of the freehold [p]: or unleſs he hath had what is equivalent to corporal ſeiſin in hereditaments that are incorporeal; ſuch as the receipt of rent, a preſentation to the church in caſe of an advowſon [q], and the like. But he ſhall not be accounted an anceſtor, who hath had only a bare right or title to enter or be otherwiſe ſeiſed. And therefore all the caſes, which will be mentioned in the preſent chapter, are upon the ſuppoſition that the deceaſed (whoſe inheritance is now claimed) was the laſt perſon actually ſeiſed thereof. For the law requires this notoriety of poſſeſſion, as evidence that the anceſtor had that property in himſelf, which is now to be tranſmitted to his heir. Which notoriety hath ſucceeded in the place of the antient feodal inveſtiture, whereby, while feuds were precarious, the vaſal on the deſcent of lands was formerly admitted in the lord's court (as is ſtill the practice in Scotland) and there received his ſeiſin, in the nature of a renewal of his anceſtors grant, in the preſence of the feodal peers: till at length, when the right of ſucceſſion became indefeaſible, an entry on any part of the lands within the county (which if diſputed was afterwards to be tried by thoſe peers) or other notorious poſſeſſion, was admitted as equivalent to the formal grant of ſeiſin, and made the tenant capable of tranſmitting his eſtate by deſcent. The ſeiſin therefore of any perſon, thus underſtood, makes him the root or ſtock, from which all future inheritance by right of blood muſt be derived: which is very briefly expreſſed in this maxim, *ſeiſina facit ſtipitem* [r].

[p] Co. Litt. 15.
[q] *Ibid.* 11.

[r] Flet. *l.* 6. *c.* 2. §. 2.

WHEN therefore a person dies so seised, the inheritance first goes to his issue: as if there be Geoffrey, John, and Matthew, grandfather, father, and son; and John purchases land and dies; his son Matthew shall succeed him as heir, and not the grandfather Geoffrey; to whom the land shall never ascend, but shall rather escheat to the lord[s].

THIS rule, so far as it is affirmative and relates to lineal descents, is almost universally adopted by all nations; and it seems founded on a principle of natural reason, that (whenever a right of property transmissible to representatives is admitted) the possessions of the parents should go, upon their decease, in the first place to their children, as those to whom they have given being, and for whom they are therefore bound to provide. But the negative branch, or total exclusion of parents and all lineal ancestors from succeeding to the inheritance of their offspring, is peculiar to our own laws, and such as have been deduced from the same original. For, by the Jewish law, on failure of issue the father succeeded to the son, in exclusion of brethren, unless one of them married the widow and raised up seed to his brother[t]. And, by the laws of Rome, in the first place the children or lineal descendants were preferred; and, on failure of these, the father and mother or lineal ascendants succeeded together with the brethren and sisters[v]; though by the law of the twelve tables the mother was originally, on account of her sex, excluded[u]. Hence this rule of our laws has been censured and declaimed against, as absurd and derogating from the maxims of equity and natural justice[w]. Yet that there is nothing unjust or absurd in it, but that on the contrary it is founded upon very good reason, may appear from considering as well the nature of the rule itself, as the occasion of introducing it into our laws.

[s] Litt. §. 3.
[t] Selden. *de succeß. Ebraeor. c.* 12.
[v] *Ff.* 38. 15. 1. *Nov.* 118. 127.

[u] *Inst.* 3. 3. 1.
[w] Craig. *de jur. feud. l.* 2. *t.* 13. §. 15.
Locke on gov. part. 1. §. 90.

WE

WE are to reflect, in the first place, that all rules of succession to estates are creatures of the civil polity, and *juris positivi* merely. The right of property, which is gained by occupancy, extends naturally no farther than the life of the present possessor; after which the land by the law of nature would again become common, and liable to be seised by the next occupant: but society, to prevent the mischiefs that might ensue from a doctrine so productive of contention, has established conveyances, wills, and successions; whereby the property originally gained by possession is continued, and transmitted from one man to another, according to the rules which each state has respectively thought proper to prescribe. There is certainly therefore no injustice done to individuals, whatever be the path of descent marked out by the municipal law.

IF we next consider the time and occasion of introducing this rule into our law, we shall find it to have been grounded upon very substantial reasons. I think there is no doubt to be made, but that it was introduced at the same time with, and in consequence of, the feodal tenures. For it was an express rule of the feodal law [x], that *successionis feudi talis est natura, quod ascendentes non succedunt*; and therefore the same maxim obtains also in the French law to this day [y]. Our Henry the first indeed, among other restorations of the old Saxon laws, restored the right of succession in the ascending line [z]: but this soon fell again into disuse; for so early as Glanvil's time, who wrote under Henry the second, we find it laid down as established law [a], that *haereditas nunquam ascendit*; which has remained an invariable maxim ever since. These circumstances evidently shew this rule to be of feodal original; and, taken in that light, there are some arguments in it's favour, besides those which are drawn merely from the reason of the thing. For if the feud, of which the son died

[x] 2 *Feud.* 50.
[y] *Domat. p.* 2. *l.* 2. *t.* 2. Montesqu. *Esp. L. l.* 31. *c.* 33.
[z] *LL. Hen. I. c.* 70.
[a] *l.* 7. *c.* 1.

seised,

feifed, was really *feudum antiquum*, or one defcended to him from
his anceftors, the father could not poffibly fucceed to it, becaufe
it muft have paffed him in the courfe of defcent, before it could
come to the fon ; unlefs it were *feudum maternum*, or one defcended from his mother, and then for other reafons (which will
appear hereafter) the father could in no wife inherit it. And if
it were *feudum novum*, or one newly acquired by the fon, then
only the defcendants from the body of the feudatory himfelf
could fucceed, by the known maxim of the early feodal conftitutions [b] ; which was founded as well upon the perfonal merit of
the vafal, which might be tranfmitted to his children but could
not afcend to his progenitors, as alfo upon this confideration of
military policy, that the decrepit grandfire of a vigorous vafal
would be but indifferently qualified to fucceed him in his feodal
fervices. Nay, even if this *feudum novum* were held by the fon
ut feudum antiquum, or with all the qualities annexed of a feud
defcended from his anceftors, fuch feud muft in all refpects have
defcended as if it had been really an antient feud ; and therefore
could not go to the father, becaufe, if it had been an antient
feud, the father muft have been dead before it could have come
to the fon. Thus whether the feud was ftrictly *novum*, or ftrictly
antiquum, or whether it was *novum* held *ut antiquum*, in none of
thefe cafes the father could poffibly fucceed. Thefe reafons, drawn
from the hiftory of the rule itfelf, feem to be more fatisfactory
than that quaint one of Bracton [c], adopted by fir Edward Coke [d],
which regulates the defcent of lands acccording to the laws of
gravitation.

II. A SECOND general rule or canon is, that the male iffue
fhall be admitted before the female.

---

[b] 1 *Feud.* 20.

[c] *Defcendit itaque jus, quafi ponderofum quid,* *cadens deorfum recta linea, et nunquam reafcen-*
dit. l. 2. c. 29.

[d] 1 Inft. 11.

THUS

THUS fons fhall be admitted before daughters; or, as our male lawgivers have fomewhat uncomplaifantly expreffed it, the worthieft of blood fhall be preferred[e]. As if John Stiles hath two fons, Matthew and Gilbert, and two daughters, Margaret and Charlotte, and dies; firft Matthew, and (in cafe of his death without iffue) then Gilbert, fhall be admitted to the fucceffion in preference to both the daughters.

THIS preference of males to females is entirely agreeable to the law of fucceflion among the Jews[f], and alfo among the ftates of Greece, or at leaft among the Athenians[g]; but was totally unknown to the laws of Rome[h], (fuch of them, I mean, as are at prefent extant) wherein brethren and fifters were allowed to fucceed to equal portions of the inheritance. I fhall not here enter into the comparative merit of the Roman and the other conftitutions in this particular, nor examine into the greater dignity of blood in the male or female fex; but fhall only obferve, that our prefent preference of males to females feems to have arifen entirely from the feodal law. For though our Britifh anceftors, the Welfh, appear to have given a preference to males[i], yet our fubfequent Danifh predeceffors feem to have made no diftinction of fexes, but to have admitted all the children at once to the inheritance[k]. But the feodal law of the Saxons on the continent (which was probably brought over hither, and firft altered by the law of king Canute) gives an evident preference of the male to the female fex. " *Pater aut mater, defuncti, filio non* " *filiae haereditatem relinquent. . . . . Qui defunctus non filios fed* " *filias reliquerit, ad eas omnis haereditas pertineat*[l]." It is poffible therefore that this preference might be a branch of that imperfect fyftem of feuds, which obtained here before the conqueft; efpe-

[e] Hal. H. C. L. 235.
[f] Numb. c. 27.
[g] Petit. LL. *Attic. l.* 6. *t.* 6.
[h] *Inft.* 3. 1. 6.

[i] *Stat. Wall.* 12 Edw. 1.
[k] LL. *Canut. c.* 68.
[l] *tit.* 7. §. 1 & 4.

cially

cially as it fubfifts among the cuftoms of gavelkind, and as, in the charter or laws of king Henry the firft, it is not (like many Norman innovations) given up, but rather enforced [m]. The true reafon of preferring the males muft be deduced from feodal principles : for, by the genuine and original policy of that conftitution, no female could ever fucceed to a proper feud [n], inafmuch as they were incapable of performing thofe military fervices, for the fake of which that fyftem was eftablifhed. But our law does not extend to a total exclufion of females, as the Salic law, and others, where feuds were moft ftrictly retained : it only poftpones them to males ; for, though daughters are excluded by fons, yet they fucceed before any collateral relations : our law, like that of the Saxon feudifts before-mentioned, thus fteering a middle courfe, between the abfolute rejection of females, and the putting them on a footing with males.

III. A THIRD rule, or canon of defcent, is this ; that, where there are two or more males in equal degree, the eldeft only fhall inherit ; but the females all together.

As if a man hath two fons, Matthew and Gilbert, and two daughters, Margaret and Charlotte, and dies ; Matthew his eldeft fon fhall alone fucceed to his eftate, in exclufion of Gilbert the fecond fon and both the daughters : but, if both the fons die without iffue before the father, the daughters Margaret and Charlotte fhall both inherit the eftate as coparceners [o].

THIS right of primogeniture in males feems antiently to have only obtained among the Jews, in whofe conftitution the eldeft fon had a double portion of the inheritance [p] ; in the fame manner as with us, by the laws of king Henry the firft [q], the eldeft fon had the capital fee or principal feud of his father's poffeffions,

[m] *c.* 70.
[n] 1 *Feud.* 8.
[o] Litt. §. 5. Hale. H. C. L. 238.

[p] Selden. *de fucc. Ebr. c.* 5.
[q] *c.* 70.

and

and no other pre-eminence; and as the eldeſt daughter had afterwards the principal manſion, when the eſtate deſcended in coparcenary [r]. The Greeks, the Romans, the Britons, the Saxons, and
even originally the feudiſts, divided the lands equally; ſome
among all the children at large, ſome among the males only.
This is certainly the moſt obvious and natural way; and has the
appearance, at leaſt in the opinion of younger brothers, of the
greateſt impartiality and juſtice. But when the emperors began
to create honorary feuds, or titles of nobility, it was found neceſſary (in order to preſerve their dignity) to make them impartible [s], or (as they ſtiled them) *feuda individua*, and in conſequence
deſcendible to the eldeſt ſon alone. This example was farther enforced by the inconveniences that attended the ſplitting of eſtates;
namely, the diviſion of the military ſervices, the multitude of
infant tenants incapable of performing any duty, the conſequen-
tial weakening of the ſtrength of the kingdom, and the inducing
younger ſons to take up with the buſineſs and idleneſs of a country life, inſtead of being ſerviceable to themſelves and the public,
by engaging in mercantile, in military, in civil, or in eccleſiaſtical employments [t]. Theſe reaſons occaſioned an almoſt total change
in the method of feodal inheritances abroad; ſo that the eldeſt
male began univerſally to ſucceed to the whole of the lands in all
military tenures: and in this condition the feodal conſtitution was
eſtabliſhed in England by William the conqueror.

Y ET we find, that ſocage eſtates frequently deſcended to all
the ſons equally, ſo lately as when Glanvil [u] wrote, in the reign
of Henry the ſecond; and it is mentioned in the mirror [w] as a
part of our antient conſtitution, that knights' fees ſhould deſcend
to the eldeſt ſon, and ſocage fees ſhould be partible among the
male children. However in Henry the third's time we find by
Bracton [x] that ſocage lands, in imitation of lands in chivalry, had

[r] Glanvil. *l.* 7. *c.* 3.
[s] 2 *Feud.* 55.
[t] Hale. H. C. L. 221.
[u] *l.* 7. *c.* 3.
[w] *c.* 1. §. 3.
[x] *l* 2. *c.* 30, 31.

almoſt

almoft entirely fallen into the right of fucceffion by primogeniture, as the law now ftands : except in Kent, where they gloried
in the prefervation of their antient gavelkind tenure, of which a
principal branch was the joint inheritance of all the fons [y]; and
except in fome particular manors and townfhips, where their local cuftoms continued the defcent, fometimes to all, fometimes
to the youngeft fon only, or in other more fingular methods of
fucceffion.

As to the females, they are ftill left as they were by the antient law: for they were all equally incapable of performing any
perfonal fervice; and therefore, one main reafon of preferring
the eldeft ceafing, fuch preference would have been injurious to
the reft : and the other principal purpofe, the prevention of the
too minute fubdivifion of eftates, was left to be confidered and
provided for by the lords, who had the difpofal of thefe female
heireffes in marriage. However, the fucceffion by primogeniture,
even among females, took place as to the inheritance of the
crown [z]; wherein the neceffity of a fole and determinate fucceffion is as great in the one fex as the other. And the right of fole
fucceffion, though not of primogeniture, was alfo eftablifhed with
refpect to female dignities and titles of honour. For if a man
holds an earldom to him and the heirs of his body, and dies,
leaving only daughters; the eldeft fhall not of courfe be countefs,
but the dignity is in fufpenfe or abeyance till the king fhall declare his pleafure; for he, being the fountain of honour, may
confer it on which of them he pleafes [a]. In which difpofition is
preferved a ftrong trace of the antient law of feuds, before their
defcent by primogeniture even among the males was eftablifhed;
namely, that the lord might beftow them on which of the fons
he thought proper : --- " *progreffum eft, ut ad filios deveniret, in*
" *quem fcilicet dominus hoc vellet beneficium confirmare* [b]."

[y] Somner. Gavelk. 7.
[z] C . Litt. 165.
[a] *Ibid.*
[b] 1 *Feud.* 1.

IV. A FOURTH

IV. A FOURTH rule, or canon of defcents, is this; that the lineal defcendants, *in infinitum*, of any perfon deceafed fhall reprefent their anceftor; that is, fhall ftand in the fame place as the perfon himfelf would have done, had he been living.

THUS the child, grandchild, or great-grandchild (either male or female) of the eldeft fon fucceeds before the younger fon, and fo *in infinitum*[c]. And thefe reprefentatives fhall take neither more nor lefs, but juft fo much as their principals would have done. As if there be two fifters, Margaret and Charlotte; and Margaret dies, leaving fix daughters; and then John Stiles the father of the two fifters dies, without other iffue: thefe fix daughters fhall take among them exactly the fame as their mother Margaret would have done, had fhe been living; that is, a moiety of the lands of John Stiles in coparcenary: fo that, upon partition made, if the land be divided into twelve parts, thereof Charlotte the furviving fifter fhall have fix, and her fix neices, the daughters of Margaret, one apiece.

THIS taking by reprefentation is called a fucceffion *in flirpes*, according to the roots; fince all the branches inherit the fame fhare that their root, whom they reprefent, would have done. And in this manner alfo was the Jewifh fucceffion directed[d]; but the Roman fomewhat differed from it. In the defcending line the right of reprefentation continued *in infinitum*, and the inheritance ftill defcended *in flirpes*: as if one of three daughters died, leaving ten children, and then the father died; the two furviving daughters had each one third of his effects, and the ten grandchildren had the remaining third divided between them. And fo among collaterals, if any perfons of equal degree with the perfons reprefented were ftill fubfifting, (as if the deceafed left one brother, and two nephews the fons of another brother) the fucceffion was ftill guided by the *roots*: but, if both the brethren were dead leaving iffue, then (I apprehend) their repre-

---

[c] Hale. H. C. L. 236, 237.   [d] Selden. *de fucc. Ebr. c.* 1.

fentatives in equal degree became themfelves principals, and fhared the inheritance *per capita*, that is, fhare and fhare alike; they being themfelves now the next in degree to the anceftor, in their own right, and not by right of reprefentation[c]. So, if the next heirs of *Titius* be fix nieces, three by one fifter, two by another, and one by a third; his inheritance by the Roman law was divided into fix parts, and one given to each of the nieces: whereas the law of England in this cafe would ftill divide it only into three parts, and diftribute it *per ftirpes*, thus; one third to the three children who reprefent one fifter, another third to the two who reprefent the fecond, and the remaining third to the one child who is the fole reprefentative of her mother.

THIS mode of reprefentation is a neceffary confequence of the double preference given by our law, firft to the male iffue, and next to the firftborn among the males, to both which the Roman law is a ftranger. For if all the children of three fifters were in England to claim *per capita*, in their own rights as next of kin to the anceftor, without any refpect to the ftocks from whence they fprung, and thofe children were partly male and partly female; then the eldeft male among them would exclude not only his own brethren and fifters, but all the iffue of the other two daughters; or elfe the law in this inftance muft be inconfiftent with itfelf, and depart from the preference which it conftantly gives to the males, and the firftborn, among perfons in equal degree. Whereas, by dividing the inheritance according to the roots or *ftirpes*, the rule of defcent is kept uniform and fteady: the iffue of the eldeft fon excludes all other pretenders, as the fon himfelf (if living) would have done; but the iffue of two daughters divide the inheritance between them, provided their mothers (if living) would have done the fame: and among thefe feveral iffues, or reprefentatives of the refpective roots, the fame preference to males and the fame right of primogeniture obtain, as would have obtained at the firft among the roots themfelves, the fons or daughters of the deceafed. As if a man hath

[c] *Nov.* 118. *c.* 3. *Inft.* 3. 1. 6.

two

two fons, A and B, and A dies leaving two fons, and then the grandfather dies; now the eldeft fon of A fhall fucceed to the whole of his grandfather's eftate : and if A had left only two daughters, they fhould have fucceeded alfo to equal moieties of the whole, in exclufion of B and his iffue. But if a man hath only three daughters, C, D, and E; and C dies leaving two fons, D leaving two daughters, and E leaving a daughter and a fon who is younger than his fifter : here, when the grandfather dies, the eldeft fon of C fhall fucceed to one third, in exclufion of the younger; the two daughters of D to another third in partnerfhip; and the fon of E to the remaining third, in exclufion of his elder fifter. And the fame right of reprefentation, guided and reftrained by the fame rules of defcent, prevails downwards *in infinitum.*

YET this right does not appear to have been thoroughly eftablifhed in the time of Henry the fecond, when Glanvil wrote; and therefore, in the title to the crown efpecially, we find frequent contefts between the younger (but furviving) brother, and his nephew (being the fon and reprefentative of the elder deceafed) in regard to the inheritance of their common anceftor : for the uncle is certainly nearer of kin to the common ftock, by one degree, than the nephew; though the nephew, by reprefenting his father, has in him the right of primogeniture. The uncle alfo was ufually better able to perform the fervices of the fief; and befides had frequently fuperior intereft and ftrength, to back his pretenfions and crufh the right of his nephew. And even to this day, in the lower Saxony, proximity of blood takes place of reprefentative primogeniture; that is, the younger furviving brother is admitted to the inheritance before the fon of an elder deceafed : which occafioned the difputes between the two houfes of Mecklenburg, Schwerin and Strelitz, in 1692[f]. Yet Glanvil, with us, even in the twelfth century, feems[g] to declare for the right of the nephew by reprefentation; provided the eldeft fon had not received a provifion in lands from his father, (or as the

[f] Mod. Un. Hift. xlii. 334.   [g] *l.* 7. *c.* 3.

civil

civil law would call it) had not been forisfamiliated, in his life-time. King John, however, who kept his nephew Arthur from the throne, by difputing this right of reprefentation, did all in his power to abolifh it throughout the realm [h] : but in the time of his fon, king Henry the third, we find the rule indifputably fettled in the manner we have here laid it down [i], and fo it has continued ever fince. And thus much for lineal defcents.

V. A FIFTH rule is, that, on failure of lineal defcendants, or iffue, of the perfon laft feifed, the inheritance fhall defcend to the blood of the firft purchafor; fubjeÐ to the three preceding rules.

THUS if Geoffrey Stiles purchafes land, and it defcends to John Stiles his fon, and John dies feifed thereof without iffue; whoever fucceeds to this inheritance muft be of the blood of Geoffrey the firft purchafor of this family [k]. The firft purchafor, *perquifitor,* is he who firft acquired the eftate to his family, whether the fame was transferred to him by fale, or by gift, or by any other method, except only that of defcent.

THIS is a rule almoft peculiar to our own laws, and thofe of a fimilar original. For it was entirely unknown among the Jews, Greeks, and Romans : none of whofe laws looked any farther than the perfon himfelf who died feifed of the eftate; but af-figned him an heir, without confidering by what title he gained it, or from what anceftor he derived it. But the law of Nor-mandy [l] agrees with our law in this refpeÐ : nor indeed is that agreement to be wondered at, fince the law of defcents in both is of feodal original; and this rule or canon cannot otherwife be accounted for than by recurring to feodal principles.

WHEN feuds firft began to be hereditary, it was made a ne-ceffary qualification of the heir, who would fucceed to a feud, that he fhould be of the blood of, that is lineally defcended from,

[h] Hale. H. C. L. 217, 229. [k] Co. Litt. 12.
[i] BraÐon. *l.* 2. *c.* 30. §. 2. [l] *Gr. Couftum. c.* 25.

the firſt feudatory or purchaſor. In conſequence whereof, if a
vaſal died poſſeſſed of a feud of his own acquiring, or *feudum
novum*, it could not deſcend to any but his own offspring ; no,
not even to his brother, becauſe he was not deſcended, nor derived his blood, from the firſt acquirer. But if it was *feudum
antiquum*, that is, one deſcended to the vaſal from his anceſtors,
then his brother, or ſuch other collateral relation as was deſcended
and derived his blood from the firſt feudatory, might ſucceed to
ſuch inheritance. To this purpoſe ſpeaks the following rule ;
" *frater fratri ſine legitimo haerede defuncto, in beneficio quod eorum*
" *patris fuit, ſuccedat : ſin autem unus e fratribus a domino feu-*
" *dum acceperit, eo defuncto ſine legitimo haerede, frater ejus in feu-*
" *dum non ſuccedit* [m]." The true feodal reaſon for which rule was
this ; that what was given to a man, for his perſonal ſervice and
perſonal merit, ought not to deſcend to any but the heirs of his
perſon. And therefore, as in eſtates-tail, (which a proper feud
very much reſembled) ſo in the feodal donation, " *nomen haeredis,*
" *in prima inveſtitura expreſſum, tantum ad deſcendentes ex corpore*
" *primi vaſalli extenditur ; et non ad collaterales, niſi ex corpore*
" *primi vaſalli ſive ſtipitis deſcendant* [n] :" the will of the donor, or
original lord, (when feuds were turned from life eſtates into inheritances) not being to make them abſolutely hereditary, like
the Roman *allodium*, but hereditary only *ſub modo* ; not hereditary to the collateral relations, or lineal anceſtors, or huſband, or
wife of the feudatory, but to the iſſue deſcended from his body
only.

HOWEVER, in proceſs of time, when the feodal rigour was
in part abated, a method was invented to let in the collateral relations of the grantee to the inheritance, by granting him a *feudum novum* to hold *ut feudum antiquum* ; that is, with all the
qualities annexed of a feud derived from his anceſtors ; and then
the collateral relations were admitted to ſucceed even *in infinitum*,
becauſe they might have been of the blood of, that is deſcended
from, the firſt imaginary purchaſor. For ſince it is not aſcertained

[m] 1 *Feud.* 1. §. 2.   [n] Crag. *l.* 1. *t.* 9. §. 36.

in fuch general grants, whether this feud fhall be held *ut feudum paternum*, or *feudum avitum*, but *ut feudum antiquum* merely, as a feud of indefinite antiquity; that is, fince it is not afcertained from which of the anceftors of the grantee this feud fhall be fuppofed to have defcended; the law will not afcertain it, but will fuppofe *any* of his anceftors, *pro re nata*, to have been the firft purchafor : and therefore it admits *any* of his collateral kindred (who have the other neceffary requifites) to the inheritance, becaufe every collateral kinfman muft be defcended from fome one of his lineal anceftors.

O F this nature are all the grants of fee-fimple eftates of this kingdom; for there is now in the law of England no fuch thing as a grant of a *feudum novum*, to be held *ut novum* ; unlefs in the cafe of a fee-tail, and there we fee that this rule is ftrictly obferved, and none but the lineal defcendants of the firft donee (or purchafor) are admitted : but every grant of lands in fee-fimple is with us a *feudum novum* to be held *ut antiquum*, as a feud whofe antiquity is indefinite ; and therefore the collateral kindred of the grantee, or defcendants from any of his lineal anceftors, by whom the lands might have poffibly been purchafed, are capable of being called to the inheritance.

YE T, when an eftate hath really defcended in a courfe of inheritance to the perfon laft feifed, the ftrict rule of the feodal law is ftill obferved ; and none are admitted, but the heirs of thofe through whom the inheritance hath paffed : for all others have demonftrably none of the blood of the firft purchafor in them, and therefore fhall never fucceed. As, if lands come to John Stiles by defcent from his mother Lucy Baker, no relation of his father (as fuch) fhall ever be his heir of thefe lands ; and, *vice verfa*, if they defcended from his father Geoffrey Stiles, no relation of his mother (as fuch) fhall ever be admitted thereto ; for his father's kindred have none of his mother's blood, nor have his mother's relations any fhare of his father's blood. And fo, if the eftate defcended from his father's father, George Stiles ;

the

the relations of his father's mother, Cecilia Kempe, fhall for the fame reafon never be admitted, but only thofe of his father's father. This is alfo the rule of the French law°, which is derived from the fame feodal fountain.

HERE we may obferve, that, fo far as the feud is really *antiquum*, the law traces it back, and will not fuffer any to inherit but the blood of thofe anceftors, from whom the feud was conveyed to the late proprietor. But when, through length of time, it can trace it no farther; as if it be not known whether his grandfather, George Stiles, inherited it from his father Walter Stiles, or his mother Chriftian Smith; or if it appear that his grandfather was the firft grantee, and fo took it (by the general law) as a feud of indefinite antiquity; in either of thefe cafes the law admits the defcendants of any anceftor of George Stiles, either paternal or maternal, to be in their due order the heirs to John Stiles of this eftate: becaufe in the firft cafe it is really uncertain, and in the fecond cafe it is fuppofed to be uncertain, whether the grandfather derived his title from the part of his father or his mother.

THIS then is the great and general principle, upon which the law of collateral inheritances depends; that, upon failure of iffue in the laft proprietor, the eftate fhall defcend to the blood of the firft purchafor; or, that it fhall refult back to the heirs of the body of that anceftor, from whom it either really has, or is fuppofed by fiction of law to have, originally defcended: according to the rule laid down in the yearbooks P, Fitzherbert q, Brook r, and Hale s; "that he who would have been heir to the "father of the deceafed" (and, of courfe, to the mother, or any other purchafing anceftor) "fhall alfo be heir to the fon."

THE remaining rules are only rules of evidence, calculated to inveftigate who that purchafing anceftor was; which, *in feudis*

° Domat. *part.* 2. *pr.*
P *M.* 12 *Edw. IV.* 14.
q *Abr. t. difcent.* 2.

r *Ibid.* 38.
s H. C. L. 243.

vere

vere antiquis, has in procefs of time been forgotten, and is fuppofed fo to be in feuds that are held *ut antiquis.*

VI. A SIXTH rule or canon therefore is, that the collateral
heir of the perfon laft feifed muft be his next collateral kinfman,
of the whole blood.

FIRST, he muft be his next collateral kinfman, either perfonally or *jure reprefentationis;* which proximity is reckoned according to the canonical degrees of confanguinity before-mentioned.
Therefore, the brother being in the firft degree, he and his defcendants fhall exclude the uncle and his iffue, who is only in the fecond.
And herein confifts the true reafon of the different methods of
computing the degrees of confanguinity, in the civil law on the
one hand, and in the canon and common laws on the other. The
civil law regards confanguinity principally with refpect to fucceffions, and therein very naturally confiders only the perfon deceafed, to whom the relation is claimed : it therefore counts the degrees of kindred according to the number of perfons through
whom the claim muft be derived from him ; and makes not only
his great-nephew but alfo his firft-coufin to be both related to
him in the fourth degree; becaufe there are three perfons between
him and each of them. The canon law regards confanguinity
principally with a view to prevent inceftuous marriages, between
thofe who have a large portion of the fame blood running in their
refpective veins; and therefore looks up to the author of that
blood, or the common anceftor, reckoning the degrees from him :
fo that the great-nephew is related in the third canonical degree
to the perfon propofed, and the firft-coufin in the fecond ; the
former being diftant three degrees from the common anceftor,
and therefore deriving only one fourth of his blood from the fame
fountain with the *propofitus;* the latter, and alfo the *propofitus,*
being each of them diftant only two degrees from the common
anceftor, and therefore having one half of each of their bloods
the fame. The common law regards confanguinity principally
with refpect to defcents; and, having therein the fame object in
view

view as the civil, it may feem as if it ought to proceed according
to the civil computation.   But as it alfo refpects the purchafing
anceftor, from whom the eftate was derived, it therein refembles
the canon law, and therefore counts it's degrees in the fame
manner. Indeed the defignation of perfon (in feeking for the next
of kin) will come to exactly the fame end (though the degrees
will be differently numbered) whichever method of computation
we fuppofe the law of England to ufe; fince the right of reprefentation (of the father by the fon, &c) is allowed to prevail *in
infinitum*.   This allowance was abfolutely neceffary, elfe there
would have frequently been many claimants in exactly the fame
degree of kindred, as (for inftance) uncles and nephews of the
deceafed; which multiplicity, though no inconvenience in the
Roman law of partible inheritances, yet would have been productive of endlefs confufion where the right of fole fucceffion, as
with us, is eftablifhed. The iffue or defcendants therefore of
John Stiles's brother are all of them in the firft degree of kindred
with refpect to inheritances, as their father alfo, when living,
was; thofe of his uncle in the fecond; and fo on; and are feverally called to the fucceffion in right of fuch their reprefentative
proximity.

THE right of reprefentation being thus eftablifhed, the former
part of the prefent rule amounts to this; that, on failure of iffue
of the perfon laft feifed, the inheritance fhall defcend to the iffue
of his next immediate anceftor. Thus if John Stiles dies without iffue, his eftate fhall defcend to Francis his brother, who is
lineally defcended from Geoffrey Stiles his next immediate anceftor, or father. On failure of brethren, or fifters, and their iffue,
it fhall defcend to the uncle of John Stiles, the lineal defcendant
of his grandfather George, and fo on *in infinitum*. Very fimilar
to which was the law of inheritance among the antient Germans,
our progenitors: "*haeredes fuccefforefque fui cuique liberi, et nullum
*"teftamentum: fi liberi non funt, proximus gradus in poffeffione,
"fratres, patrui, avunculi*[t]."

Now here it muft be obferved, that the lineal anceftors, though (according to the firft rule) incapable themfelves of fucceeding to the eftate, becaufe it is fuppofed to have already paffed them, are yet the common ftocks from which the next fucceffor muft fpring. And therefore in the Jewifh law, which in this refpect entirely correfponds with ours[u], the father or other lineal anceftor is him-felf faid to be the heir, though long fince dead, as being repre-fented by the perfons of his iffue; who are held to fucceed not in their own rights, as brethren, uncles, *&c*, but in right of repre-fentation, as the fons of the father, grandfather, *&c*, of the de-ceafed[v]. But, though the common anceftor be thus the root of the inheritance, yet with us it is not neceffary to *name* him in making out the pedigree or defcent. For the defcent between two brothers is held to be an *immediate* defcent; and therefore title may be made by one brother or his reprefentatives *to* or *through* another, without mentioning their common father[w]. If Geoffrey Stiles hath two fons, John and Francis, Francis may claim as heir to John, without naming their father Geoffrey: and fo the fon of Francis may claim as coufin and heir to Matthew the fon of John, without naming the grandfather; viz. as fon of Francis, who was the brother of John, who was the father of Matthew. But though the common anceftors are not named in deducing the pedigree, yet the law ftill refpects them as the foun-tains of inheritable blood : and therefore in order to afcertain the collateral heir of John Stiles, it is in the firft place neceffary to recur to his anceftors in the firft degree; and if they have left any other iffue befides John, that iffue will be his heir. On default of fuch, we muft afcend one ftep higher to the anceftors in the fecond de-gree, and then to thofe in the third, and fourth, and fo upwards *in infinitum*; till fome anceftors be found, who have other iffue defcending from them befides the deceafed, in a parallel or colla-teral line. From thefe anceftors the heir of John Stiles muft derive his defcent; and in fuch derivation the fame rules muft

[u] Numb. c. 27.   [w] 1 Sid. 193. 1 Lev. 60. 12 Mod. 619.
[v] Selden. *de fucc. Ebr. c.* 12.

be

be obferved, with regard to fex, primogeniture, and reprefentation, that have juft been laid down with regard to lineal defcents
from the perfon of the laft proprietor.

BUT, fecondly, the heir need not be the neareft kinfman abfolutely, but only *fub modo*; that is, he muft be the neareft kinfman of the whole blood; for, if there be a much nearer kinfman of the half blood, a diftant kinfman of the whole blood
fhall be admitted, and the other entirely excluded.

A KINSMAN of the whole blood is he that is derived, not
only from the fame anceftor, but from the fame couple of anceftors. For, as every man's own blood is compounded of the bloods
of his refpective anceftors, he only is properly of the whole or
entire blood with another, who hath (fo far as the diftance of degrees will permit) all the fame ingredients in the compofition of
his blood that the other hath. Thus, the blood of John Stiles
being compofed of thofe of Geoffrey Stiles his father and Lucy
Baker his mother, therefore his brother Francis, being defcended
from both the fame parents, hath entirely the fame blood with
John Stiles; or, he is his brother of the whole blood. But if,
after the death of Geoffrey, Lucy Baker the mother marries a
fecond hufband, Lewis Gay, and hath iffue by him; the blood
of this iffue, being compounded of the blood of Lucy Baker (it
is true) on the one part, but of that of Lewis Gay (inftead of
Geoffrey Stiles) on the other part, it hath therefore only half the
fame ingredients with that of John Stiles; fo that he is only his
brother of the half blood, and for that reafon they fhall never
inherit to each other. So alfo, if the father has two fons, A and
B, by different venters or wives; now thefe two brethren are
not brethren of the whole blood, and therefore fhall never inherit to each other, but the eftate fhall rather efcheat to the lord.
Nay, even if the father dies, and his lands defcend to his eldeft
fon A, who enters thereon, and dies feifed without iffue; ftill B
fhall not be heir to this eftate, becaufe he is only of the half
blood to A, the perfon laft feifed: but, had A died without entry

try

try, then B might have inherited ; not as heir to A his half-bro-
ther, but as heir to their common father, who was the perfon
laft actually feifed [x].

TH I S total exclufion of the half blood from the inheritance,
being almoft peculiar to our own law, is looked upon as a ftrange
hardfhip by fuch as are unacquainted with the reafons on which
it is grounded. But thefe cenfures arife from a mifapprehenfion
of the rule ; which is not fo much to be confidered in the light
of a rule of defcent, as of a rule of evidence ; an auxiliary rule,
to carry a former into execution. And here we muft again remember, that the great and moft univerfal principle of collateral
inheritances being this, that an heir to a *feudum antiquum* muft
be of the blood of the firft feudatory or purchafor, that is, derived in a lineal defcent from him ; it was originally requifite, as
upon gifts in tail it ftill is, to make out the pedigree of the heir
from the firft donee or purchafor, and to fhew that fuch heir was
his lineal reprefentative. But when, by length of time and a long
courfe of defcents, it came (in thofe rude and unlettered ages) to
be forgotten who was really the firft feudatory or purchafor, and
thereby the proof of an actual defcent from him became impoffible ; then the law fubftituted what fir Martin Wright [y] calls a
reafonable, in the ftead of an *impoffible*, proof : for it remits the
proof of an actual defcent from the firft purchafor ; and only requires, in lieu of it, that the claimant be next of the whole blood
to the perfon laft in poffeffion ; (or derived from the fame couple
of anceftors) which will probably anfwer the fame end as if he
could trace his pedigree in a direct line from the firft purchafor.
For he who is my kinfman of the whole blood can have no anceftors beyond or higher than the common ftock, but what are
equally my anceftors alfo ; and mine are *vice verfa* his : he therefore is very likely to be derived from that unknown anceftor of
mine, from whom the inheritance defcended. But a kinfman
of the half blood has but one half of his anceftors above the
common ftock the fame as mine ; and therefore there is not the

[x] Hale. H. C. L. 238.   [y] Tenures. 186.

fame

fame probability of that ftanding requifite in the law, that he be derived from the blood of the firft purchafor.

To illuftrate this by example. Let there be John Stiles, and Francis, brothers by the fame father and mother, and another fon of the fame mother by Lewis Gay a fecond hufband. Now, if John dies feifed of lands, but it is uncertain whether they defcended to him from his father or mother; in this cafe his brother Francis, of the whole blood, is qualified to be his heir; for he is fure to be in the line of defcent from the firft purchafor, whether it were the line of the father or the mother. But if Francis fhould die before John, without iffue, the mother's fon by Lewis Gay (or brother of the half blood) is utterly incapable of being heir; for he cannot prove his defcent from the firft purchafor, who is unknown, nor has he that fair probability which the law admits as prefumptive evidence, fince he is to the full as likely *not to be* defcended from the line of the firft purchafor, as *to be* defcended: and therefore the inheritance fhall go to the neareft relation poffeffed of this prefumptive proof, the whole blood.

And, as this is the cafe *in feudis antiquis,* where there really did once exift a purchafing anceftor, who is forgotten; it is alfo the cafe *in feudis novis* held *ut antiquis,* where the purchafing anceftor is merely ideal, and never exifted but only in fiction of law. Of this nature are all grants of lands in fee-fimple at this day, which are inheritable as if they defcended from fome uncertain indefinite anceftor, and therefore any of the collateral kindred of the real modern purchafor (and not his own offspring only) may inherit them, provided they be of the whole blood; for all fuch are, in judgment of law, likely enough to be derived from this indefinite anceftor: but thofe of the half blood are excluded, for want of the fame probability. Nor fhould this be thought hard, that a brother of the purchafor, though only of the half blood, muft thus be difinherited, and a more remote relation of the whole blood admitted, merely upon a fuppofition and

fiction

fiction of law; since it is only upon a like supposition and fiction, that brethren of purchasors (whether of the whole or half blood) are entitled to inherit at all : for we have seen that in *feudis strictè novis* neither brethren nor any other collaterals were admitted. As therefore *in feudis antiquis* we have seen the reasonableness of excluding the half blood, if by a fiction of law a *feudum novum* be made descendible to collaterals as if it was *feudum antiquum*, it is just and equitable that it should be subject to the same re-strictions as well as the same latitude of descent.

PERHAPS by this time the exclusion of the half blood does not appear altogether so unreasonable, as at first sight it is apt to do. It is certainly a very fine-spun and subtile nicety : but, con-sidering the principles upon which our law is founded, it is nei-ther an injustice nor a hardship; since even the succession of the whole blood was originally a beneficial indulgence, rather than the strict right of collaterals : and, though that indulgence is not extended to the demi-kindred, yet they are rarely abridged of any right which they could possibly have enjoyed before. The doctrine of whole blood was calculated to supply the frequent impossibility of proving a descent from the first purchasor, with-out some proof of which (according to our fundamental maxim) there can be no inheritance allowed of. And this purpose it an-swers, for the most part, effectually enough. I speak with these restrictions, because it does not, neither can any other method, answer this purpose entirely. For though all the ancestors of John Stiles, above the common stock, are also the ancestors of his col-lateral kinsman of the whole blood; yet, unless that common stock be in the first degree, (that is, unless they have the same father and mother) there will be intermediate ancestors below the common stock, that may belong to either of them respectively, from which the other is not descended, and therefore can have none of their blood. Thus, though John Stiles and his brother of the whole blood can each have no other ancestors, than what are in common to them both; yet with regard to his uncle, where the common stock is removed one degree higher, (that is,
the

the grandfather and grandmother) one half of John's anceftors will not be the anceftors of his uncle: his *patruus*, or father's brother, derives not his defcent from John's maternal anceftors; nor his *avunculus*, or mother's brother, from thofe in the paternal line. Here then the fupply of proof is deficient, and by no means amounts to a certainty: and, the higher the common ftock is removed, the more will even the probability decreafe. But it muft be obferved, that (upon the fame principles of calculation) the half blood have always a much lefs chance to be defcended from an unknown indefinite anceftor of the deceafed, than the whole blood in the fame degree. As, in the firft degree, the whole brother of John Stiles is fure to be defcended from that unknown anceftor; his half brother has only an even chance, for half John's anceftors are not his. So, in the fecond degree, John's uncle of the whole blood has an even chance; but the chances are three to one againft his uncle of the half blood, for three fourths of John's anceftors are not his. In like manner, in the third degree, the chances are only three to one againft John's great uncle of the whole blood, but they are feven to one againft his great uncle of the half blood, for feven eighths of John's anceftors have no connexion in blood with him. Therefore the much lefs probability of the half blood's defcent from the firft purchafor, compared with that of the whole blood, in the feveral degrees, has occafioned a general exclufion of the half blood in all.

B u t, while I thus illuftrate the reafon of excluding the half blood in general, I muft be impartial enough to own, that, in fome inftances, the practice is carried farther than the principle upon which it goes will warrant. Particularly, when a man has two fons by different venters, and the eftate on his death defcends from him to the eldeft, who enters, and dies without iffue: now the younger fon cannot inherit this eftate, becaufe he is not of the whole blood to the laft proprietor. This, it muft be owned, carries a hardfhip with it, even upon feodal principles: for the rule was introduced only to fupply the proof of a defcent from the firft purchafor; but here, as this eftate notorioufly defcended from the

the father, and as both the brothers confessedly sprung from him, it is demonstrable that the half brother must be of the blood of the first purchasor, who was either the father or some of the father's anceſtors. When therefore there is actual demonſtration of the thing to be proved, it is hard to exclude a man by a rule ſubſtituted to ſupply that proof when deficient. So far as the inheritance can be evidently traced back, there ſeems no need of calling in this preſumptive proof, this rule of probability, to inveſtigate what is already certain. Had the elder brother indeed been a purchaſor, there would have been no hardſhip at all, for the reaſons already given : or had the *frater uterinus* only, or brother by the mother's ſide, been excluded from an inheritance which deſcended from the father, it had been highly reaſonable.

INDEED it is this very inſtance, of excluding a *frater conſanguineus*, or brother by the father's ſide, from an inheritance which deſcended *a patre*, that Craig[z] has ſingled out, on which to ground his ſtrictures on the Engliſh law of half blood. And, really, it ſhould ſeem, as if the cuſtom of excluding the half blood in Normandy[a] extended only to exclude a *frater uterinus*, when the inheritance deſcended *a patre*, and *vice verſa :* as even with us it remained a doubt, in the time of Bracton[b], and of Fleta[c], whether the half blood on the father's ſide were excluded from the inheritance which originally deſcended from the common father, or only from ſuch as deſcended from the reſpective mothers, and from newly purchaſed lands. And the rule of law, as laid down by our Forteſcue[d], extends no farther than this ; *frater fratri uterino non ſuccedet in haereditate paterna.* It is moreover worthy of obſervation, that by our law, as it now ſtands, the crown (which is the higheſt inheritance in the nation) may deſcend to the half blood of the preceding ſovereign[e], ſo as it be the blood of the firſt monarch, purchaſor, or (in the feodal language) conqueror, of the reigning family. Thus it actually

[z] *l. 2. t.* 15. §. 14.
[a] *Gr. Couſtum. c.* 25.
[b] *l. 2. c.* 30. §. 3.
[c] *l. 6. c.* 1. §. 14.
[d] *de laud. LL. Angl.* 5.
[e] Plowd. 245. Co. Litt. 15.

did

did defcend from king Edward the fixth to queen Mary, and from her to queen Elizabeth, who were refpectively of the half blood to each other. For, the royal pedigree being always a matter of fufficient notoriety, there is no occafion to call in the aid of this prefumptive rule of evidence, to render probable the defcent from the royal flock; which was formerly king William the Norman, and is now (by act of parliament[f]) the princefs Sophia of Hanover. Hence alfo it is, that in eftates-tail, where the pedigree from the firft donee muft be ftrictly proved, half blood is no impediment to the defcent[g]: becaufe, when the lineage is clearly made out, there is no need of this auxiliary proof. How far it might be defirable for the legiflature to give relief, by amending the law of defcents in this fingle inftance, and ordaining that the half blood might inherit, where the eftate notoriously defcended from it's own proper anceftor, but not otherwife; or how far a private inconvenience fhould be fubmitted to, rather than a long eftablifhed rule fhould be fhaken; it is not for me to determine.

THE rule then, together with it's illuftration, amounts to this: that, in order to keep the eftate of John Stiles as nearly as poffible in the line of his purchafing anceftor, it muft defcend to the iffue of the neareft couple of anceftors that have left defcendants behind them; becaufe the defcendants of one anceftor only are not fo likely to be in the line of that purchafing anceftor, as thofe who are defcended from two.

BUT here another difficulty arifes. In the fecond, third, fourth, and every fuperior degree, every man has many couples of anceftors, increafing according to the diftances in a geometrical progreffion upwards[h], the defcendants of all which refpective couples are (reprefentatively) related to him in the fame degree. Thus in the fecond degree, the iffue of George and Cecilia Stiles and of Andrew and Efther Baker, the two grandfires and grand-

[f] 12 Will. III. c. 2.
[g] Litt. §. 14, 15.
[h] See pag. 204.

mothers of John Stiles, are each in the fame degree of propinquity; in the third degree, the refpective iffues of Walter and Chriftian Stiles, of Luke and Frances Kempe, of Herbert and Hannah Baker, and of James and Emma Thorpe, are (upon the extinction of the two inferior degrees) all equally entitled to call themfelves the next kindred of the whole blood to John Stiles. To which therefore of thefe anceftors muft we firft refort, in order to find out defcendants to be preferably called to the inheritance? In anfwer to this, and to avoid the confufion and uncertainty that muft arife between the feveral ftocks, wherein the purchafing anceftor may be fought for,

VII. THE feventh and laft rule or canon is, that in collateral inheritances the male ftocks fhall be preferred to the female; (that is, kindred derived from the blood of the male anceftors fhall be admitted before thofe from the blood of the female) --- unlefs where the lands have, in fact, defcended from a female.

THUS the relations on the father's fide are admitted *in infinitum*, before thofe on the mother's fide are admitted at all [i]; and the relations of the father's father, before thofe of the father's mother; and fo on. And in this the Englifh law is not fingular, but warranted by the examples of the Hebrew and Athenian laws, as ftated by Selden [k], and Petit [l]; though among the Greeks, in the time of Hefiod [m], when a man died without wife or children, all his kindred (without any diftinction) divided his eftate among them. It is likewife warranted by the example of the Roman laws; wherein the *agnati*, or relations by the father, were preferred to the *cognati*, or relations by the mother, till the edict of the emperor Juftinian [n] abolifhed all diftinction between them. It is alfo conformable to the cuftomary law of Normandy [o], which indeed in moft refpects agrees with our law of inheritance.

[i] Litt. §. 4.
[k] *de fucc. Ebraeor.* c. 12.
[l] *LL. Attic. l.* 1. t. 6.
[m] Θεογον. 606.
[n] *Nov.* 118.
[o] *Gr. Couftum.* c. 25.

HOWEVER

HOWEVER, I am inclined to think, that this rule of our laws does not owe it's immediate original to any view of conformity to thofe which I have juft now mentioned; but was eftablifhed in order to effectuate and carry into execution the fifth rule or canon before laid down; that every heir muft be of the blood of the firft purchafor. For, when fuch firft purchafor was not eafily to be difcovered after a long courfe of defcents, the lawyers not only endeavoured to inveftigate him by taking the next relation of the whole blood to the perfon laft in poffeffion; but alfo, confidering that a preference had been given to males (by virtue of the fecond canon) through the whole courfe of lineal defcent from the firft purchafor to the prefent time, they judged it more likely that the lands fhould have defcended to the laft tenant from his male than from his female anceftors; from the father (for inftance) rather than from the mother; from the father's father, rather than the father's mother: and therefore they hunted back the inheritance (if I may be allowed the expreffion) through the male line; and gave it to the next relations on the fide of the father, the father's father, and fo upwards; imagining with reafon that this was the moft probable way of continuing it in the line of the firft purchafor. A conduct much more rational than the preference of the *agnati* by the Roman laws: which, as they gave no advantage to the males in the firft inftance or direct lineal fucceffion, had no reafon for preferring them in the tranfverfe collateral one: upon which account this preference was very wifely abolifhed by Juftinian.

THAT this was the true foundation of the preference of the *agnati* or male ftocks, in our law, will farther appear if we confider, that, whenever the lands have notorioufly defcended to a man from his mother's fide, this rule is totally reverfed, and no relation of his by the father's fide, as fuch, can ever be admitted to them; becaufe he cannot poffibly be of the blood of the firft purchafor. And fo, *e converfo*, if the lands defcended from the father's fide, no relation of the mother, as fuch, fhall ever in-

F f 2 herit

herit. So also, if they in fact defcended to John Stiles from his father's mother Cecilia Kempe; here not only the blood of Lucy Baker his mother, but alfo of George Stiles his father's father, is perpetually excluded. And, in like manner, if they be known to have defcended from Frances Holland the mother of Cecilia Kempe, the line not only of Lucy Baker, and of George Stiles, but alfo of Luke Kempe the father of Cecilia, is excluded. Whereas when the fide from which they defcended is forgotten, or never known, (as in the cafe of an eftate newly purchafed to be holden *ut feudum antiquum*) here the right of inheritance firft runs up all the father's fide, with a preference to the male ftocks in every inftance; and, if it finds no heirs there, it then, and then only, reforts to the mother's fide; leaving no place untried, in order to find heirs that may by poffibility be derived from the original purchafor. The greateft probability of finding fuch was among thofe defcended from the male anceftors; but, upon failure of iffue there, they may poffibly be found among thofe derived from the females.

THIS I take to be the true reafon of the conftant preference of the agnatic fucceffion, or iffue derived from the male anceftors, through all the ftages of collateral inheritance; as the ability for perfonal fervice was the reafon for preferring the males at firft in the direct lineal fucceffion. We fee clearly, that, if males had been perpetually admitted, in utter exclufion of females, the tracing the inheritance back through the male line of anceftors muft at laft have inevitably brought us up to the firft purchafor: but, as males have not been *perpetually admitted*, but only *generally preferred*; as females have not been *utterly excluded*, but only *generally poftponed* to males; the tracing the inheritance up through the male ftocks will not give us abfolute demonftration, but only a ftrong probability, of arriving at the firft purchafor; which, joined with the other probability, of the wholenefs or entirety of blood, will fall little fhort of a certainty.

BEFORE we conclude this branch of our enquiries, it may not be amiss to exemplify these rules by a short sketch of the manner in which we must search for the heir of a person, as *John Stiles*, who dies seised of land which he acquired, and which therefore he held as a feud of indefinite antiquity [P].

IN the first place succeeds the eldest son, Matthew Stiles, or his issue : (n° 1.) --- if his line be extinct, then Gilbert Stiles and the other sons, respectively, in order of birth, or their issue : (n° 2.) --- in default of these, all the daughters together, Margaret and Charlotte Stiles, or their issue. (n° 3.) --- On failure of the descendants of *John Stiles* himself, the issue of Geoffrey and Lucy Stiles, his parents, is called in : *viz.* first, Francis Stiles, the eldest brother of the whole blood, or his issue : (n° 4.) --- then Oliver Stiles, and the other whole brothers, respectively, in order of birth, or their issue : (n 5.) --- then the sisters of the whole blood, all together, Bridget and Alice Stiles, or their issue. (n° 6.) --- In defect of these, the issue of George and Cecilia Stiles, his father's parents; respect being still had to their age and sex : (n° 7.) --- then the issue of Walter and Christian Stiles, the parents of his paternal grandfather : (n° 8.) --- then the issue of Richard and Anne Stiles, the parents of his paternal grandfather's father : (n° 9.) --- and so on in the paternal grandfather's paternal line, or blood of Walter Stiles, *in infinitum.* In defect of these, the issue of William and Jane Smith, the parents of his paternal grandfather's mother : (n° 10.) --- and so on in the paternal grandfather's maternal line, or blood of Christian Smith, *in infinitum*; till both the immediate bloods of George Stiles, the paternal grandfather, are spent. --- Then we must resort to the issue of Luke and Frances Kempe, the parents of *John Stiles's* paternal grandmother : (n° 11.) --- then to the issue of Thomas and Sarah Kempe, the parents of his paternal grandmother's father : (n° 12.) --- and so on in the paternal grandmother's paternal line, or blood of Luke Kempe, *in infinitum.* ---

[P] See the table of descents annexed.

In default of which, we muft call in the iffue of Charles and Mary Holland, the parents of his paternal grandmother's mother: (n° 13.) --- and fo on in the paternal grandmother's maternal line, or blood of Frances Holland, *in infinitum*; till both the immediate bloods of Cecilia Kempe, the paternal grandmother, are alfo fpent. --- Whereby the paternal blood of *John Stiles* entirely failing, recourfe muft then, and not before, be had to his maternal relations; or the blood of the Bakers, (n° 14, 15, 16.) Willis's, (n° 17.) Thorpes, (n° 18, 19.) and Whites; (n° 20.) in the fame regular fucceffive order as in the paternal line.

THE ftudent fhould however be informed, that the clafs, n° 10, would be poftponed to n° 11, in confequence of the doctrine laid down, *arguendo*, by juftice Manwoode, in the cafe of Clere and Brooke[q]; from whence it is adopted by lord Bacon[r], and fir Matthew Hale[s]. And yet, notwithftanding thefe refpectable authorities, the compiler of this table hath ventured to give the preference therein to n° 10 before n° 11; for the following reafons: 1. Becaufe this point was not the principal queftion in the cafe of Clere and Brooke; but the law concerning it is delivered *obiter* only, and in the courfe of argument, by juftice Manwoode; though afterwards faid to be confirmed by the three other juftices in feparate, extrajudicial, conferences with the reporter. 2. Becaufe the chief-juftice, fir James Dyer, in reporting the refolution of the court in what feems to be the fame cafe[t], takes no notice of this doctrine. 3. Becaufe it appears, from Plowden's report, that very many gentlemen of the law were diffatisfied with this pofition of juftice Manwoode. 4. Becaufe the pofition itfelf deftroys the otherwife entire and regular fymmetry of our legal courfe of defcents, as is manifeft by infpecting the table; and deftroys alfo that conftant preference of the male ftocks in the law of inheritance, for which an additional reafon is before given, befides the mere dignity of blood. 5. Becaufe it introduces all that uncertainty and contradiction, which is pointed

[q] Plowd. 450.
[r] Elem. c. 1.
[s] H. C. L. 240, 244.
[t] Dyer. 314.

out

out by an ingenious author[u]; and eftablifhes a collateral doctrine, incompatible with the principal point refolved in the cafe of Clere and Brooke, viz. the preference of n° 11 to n° 14. And, though that learned writer propofes to refcind the principal point then refolved, in order to clear this difficulty; it is apprehended, that the difficulty may be better cleared, by rejecting the collateral doctrine, which was never yet refolved at all. 6. Becaufe by the reafon that is given for this doctrine, in Plowden, Bacon, and Hale, (viz. that in any degree, paramount the firft, the law refpecteth proximity, and not dignity of blood) n° 18 ought alfo to be preferred to n° 16; which is directly contrary to the eighth rule laid down by Hale himfelf[w]. 7. Becaufe this pofition feems to contradict the allowed doctrine of fir Edward Ccke[x]; who lays it down (under different names) that the blood of the Kempes (*alias* Sandies) fhall not inherit till the blood of the Stiles's (*alias* Fairfields) fail. Now the blood of the Stiles's does certainly not fail, till both n° 9 and n° 10 are extinct. Wherefore n° 11 (being the blood of the Kempes) ought not to inherit till then. 8. Becaufe in the cafe, Mich. 12 Edw. IV. 14[y]. (much relied on in that of Clere and Brooke) it is laid down as a rule, that " *cefluy, que doit inheriter al pere, doit inheriter al fits.*" And fo fir Matthew Hale[z] fays, " that though the law excludes the father from in-" heriting, yet it fubftitutes and directs the defcent, as it fhould " have been, had the father inherited." Now it is fettled, by the refolution in Clere and Brooke, that n° 10 fhould have inherited to Geoffrey Stiles, the father, before n° 11; and therefore n° 10 ought alfo to be preferred in inheriting to *John Stiles*, the fon.

IN cafe *John Stiles* was not himfelf the purchafor, but the eftate in fact came to him by defcent from his father, mother, or any higher anceftor, there is this difference; that the blood of that line of anceftors, from which it did not defcend, can never

[u] Law of inheritances. 2ᵈ edit. pag. 30, 38, 61, 62, 66.
[w] Hift. C. L. 247.
[x] Co. Litt. 12. Hawk. abr. *in loc.*
[y] Fitzh. abr. tit. *difcent.* 2. Bro. abr. t. *difcent.* 3.
[z] Hift. C. L. 243.

inherit

inherit. Thus, if it defcended from Geoffrey Stiles, the father, the blood of Lucy Baker, the mother, is perpetually excluded : and fo, *vice verfa*, if it defcended from Lucy Baker, it cannot defcend to the blood of Geoffrey Stiles. This, in either cafe, cuts off one half of the table from any poffible fucceffion. And farther, if it can be fhewn to have defcended from George Stiles, this cuts off three fourths ; for now the blood, not only of Lucy Baker, but alfo of Cecilia Kempe, is excluded. If, laftly, it defcended from Walter Stiles, this narrows the fucceffion ftill more, and cuts off feven eighths of the table ; for now, neither the blood of Lucy Baker, nor of Cecilia Kempe, nor of Chriftian Smith, can ever fucceed to the inheritance. And the like rule will hold upon defcents from any other anceftors.

THE ftudent fhould bear in mind, that, during this whole procefs, *John Stiles* is the perfon fuppofed to have been laft actually feifed of the eftate. For if ever it comes to veft in any other perfon, as heir to *John Stiles*, a new order of fucceffion muft be obferved upon the death of fuch heir ; fince he, by his own feifin, now becomes himfelf an anceftor, or *ftipes*, and muft be put in the place of *John Stiles*. The figures therefore denote the order, in which the feveral claffes would fucceed to *John Stiles*, and not to each other : and, before we fearch for an heir in any of the higher figures, (as n° 8.) we muft be firft affured that all the lower claffes (from n° 1 to 7.) were extinct, at *John Stiles*'s deceafe.

CHAPTER THE FIFTEENTH.

OF TITLE BY PURCHASE, AND FIRST BY ESCHEAT.

PURCHASE, *perquifitio,* taken in it's largeſt and moſt extenſive ſenſe, is thus defined by Littleton[a]; the poſſeſſion of lands and tenements, which a man hath by his own act or agreement; and not by deſcent from any of his anceſtors or kindred. In this ſenſe it is contradiſtinguiſhed from acquiſition by right of blood, and includes every other method of coming to an eſtate, but merely that by inheritance; wherein the title is veſted in a perſon, not by his own act or agreement, but by the ſingle operation of law[b].

PURCHASE, indeed, in it's vulgar and confined acceptation, is applied only to ſuch acquiſitions of land, as are obtained by way of bargain and ſale, for money, or ſome other valuable conſideration. But this falls far ſhort of the legal idea of purchaſe: for, if I *give* land freely to another, he is in the eye of the law a purchaſor[c]; and falls within Littleton's definition, for he comes to the eſtate by his own agreement, that is, he conſents to the gift. A man who has his father's eſtate ſettled upon him in tail, before he is born, is alſo a purchaſor; for he takes quite another eſtate than the law of deſcents would have given him. Nay even if the anceſtor deviſes his eſtate to his heir at law by will, with other limitations or in any other ſhape than the courſe of deſcents would direct, ſuch heir ſhall take by purchaſe[d]. But if a man, ſeiſed in fee, deviſes his whole eſtate to his heir at law, ſo that the heir takes neither a greater nor a leſs eſtate by the deviſe than

[a] §. 12.
[b] Co. Litt. 18.
[c] *Ibid.*
[d] Lord Raym. 728.

PATERNAL LINE

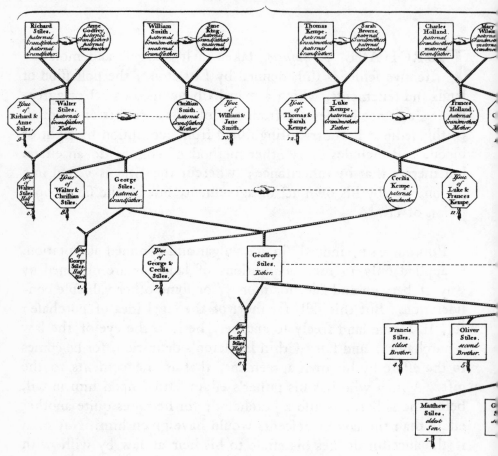

MATERNAL LINE

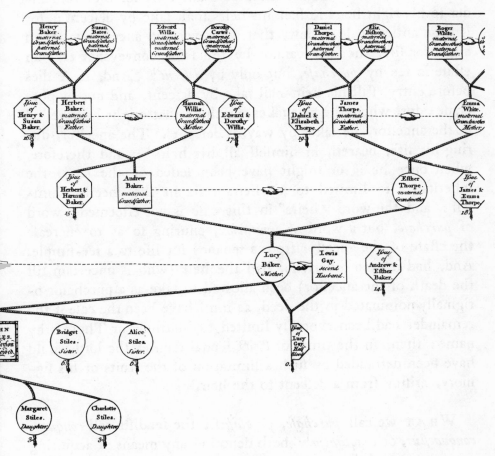

he would have done without it, he fhall be adjudged to take by defcent[e], even though it be charged with incumbrances[f]; for the benefit of creditors, and others, who have demands on the eftate of the anceftor. If a remainder be limited to *the heirs* of Sempronius, here Sempronius himfelf takes nothing; but, if he dies during the continuance of the particular eftate, his heirs fhall take as purchafors[g]. But, if an eftate be made to A for life, remainder to his right heirs in fee, his heirs fhall take by defcent: for it is an antient rule of law, that wherever the anceftor takes an eftate for life, the heir cannot by the fame conveyance take an eftate in fee by *purchafe*, but only by *defcent*[h]. And, if A dies before entry, ftill his heir fhall take by defcent, and not by purchafe; for, where the heir takes any thing that might have vefted in the anceftor, he takes by way of defcent[i]. The anceftor, during his life, beareth in himfelf all his heirs[k]; and therefore, when once he is or might have been feifed of the land, the inheritance fo limited to his heirs vefts in the anceftor himfelf: and the word "heirs" in this cafe is not efteemed a word of *purchafe*, but a word of *limitation*, enuring fo as to encreafe the eftate of the anceftor from a tenancy for life to a fee-fimple. And, had it been otherwife, had the heir (who is uncertain till the death of the anceftor) been allowed to take as a purchafor originally nominated in the deed, as muft have been the cafe if the remainder had been exprefsly limited to Matthew or Thomas by name; then, in the times of ftrict feodal tenure, the lord would have been defrauded by fuch a limitation of the fruits of his figniory, arifing from a defcent to the heir.

WHAT we call *purchafe, perquifitio,* the feudifts call *conqueft, conquaeftus,* or *conquifitio*[l]: both denoting any means of acquiring an eftate out of the common courfe of inheritance. And this is ftill the proper phrafe in the law of Scotland[m]; as it was, among

[e] 1 Roll. Abr. 626.
[f] Salk. 241. Lord Raym. 728.
[g] 1 Roll. Abr. 627.
[h] 1 Rep. 104. 2 Lev. 60. Raym. 334.

[i] 1 Rep. 98.
[k] Co. Litt. 23.
[l] Crag. *l.* 1. *t.* 10. §. 18.
[m] Dalrymple of feuds. 210.

the

the Norman jurifts, who ftiled the firft purchafor (that is, he who firft brought the eftate into the family which at prefent owns it) the conqueror or *conquereur* [n]. Which feems to be all that was meant by the appellation which was given to William the Norman, when his manner of afcending the throne of England was, in his own and his fucceffors' charters, and by the hiftorians of the times, entitled *conquaeftus*, and himfelf *conquaeftor* or *conquifitor* [o]; fignifying, that he was the firft of his family who acquired the crown of England, and from whom therefore all future claims by defcent muft be derived : though now, from our difufe of the feodal fenfe of the word, together with the reflexion on his forcible method of acquifition, we are apt to annex the idea of *victory* to this name of *conqueft* or *conquifition* ; a title which, however juft with regard to the *crown*, the conqueror never pretended with regard to the *realm* of England, nor, in fact, ever had [p].

THE difference in effect, between the acquifition of an eftate by defcent and by purchafe, confifts principally in thefe two points : 1. That by purchafe the eftate acquires a new inheritable quality, and is defcendible to the owner's blood in general, and not the blood only of fome particular anceftor. For, when a man takes an eftate by purchafe, he takes it not *ut feudum paternum* or *maternum*, which would defcend only to the heirs by the father's or the mother's fide : but he takes it *ut feudum antiquum*, as a feud of indefinite antiquity ; whereby it becomes inheritable to his heirs general, firft of the paternal, and then of the maternal line [q]. 2. An eftate taken by purchafe will not make the heir anfwerable for the acts of the anceftor, as an eftate by defcent will. For, if the anceftor by any deed, obligation, covenant, or the like, bindeth himfelf and his heirs, and dieth ; this deed, obligation, or covenant, fhall be binding upon the heir, fo far forth only as he had any eftate of inheritance vefted in him (or in fome other in truft for him [r]) by defcent from that

[n] *Gr. Couftum. Gloff. c. 25. pag.* 40.
[o] Spelm. *Gloff.* 145.
[p] See Book I. ch. 3.

[q] See pag 236.
[r] Stat. 29 Car. II. c. 3.

anceftor,

anceſtor, ſufficient to anſwer the charge[s]; whether he remains in poſſeſſion, or hath aliened it before action brought[t]: which ſufficient eſtate is in law called *aſſets*; from the French word, *aſſez*, enough[u]. Therefore if a man covenants, for himſelf and his heirs, to keep my houſe in repair, I can then (and then only) compel his heir to perform this covenant, when he has an eſtate ſufficient for this purpoſe, or *aſſets*, by deſcent from the covenantor: for though the covenant deſcends to the heir, whether he inherits any eſtate or no, it lies dormant, and is not compulſory, until he has aſſets by deſcent[v].

THIS is the legal ſignification of the word *perquiſitio*, or purchaſe; and in this ſenſe it includes the five following methods of acquiring a title to eſtates: 1. Eſcheat. 2. Occupancy. 3 Preſcription. 4. Forfeiture. 5. Alienation. Of all theſe in their order.

I. ESCHEAT, we may remember[w], was one of the fruits and conſequences of feodal tenure. The word itſelf is originally French or Norman[x], in which language it ſignifies chance or accident; and with us denotes an obſtruction of the courſe of deſcent, and a conſequent determination of the tenure, by ſome unforeſeen contingency: in which caſe the land naturally reſults back, by a kind of reverſion, to the original grantor or lord of the fee[y].

ESCHEAT therefore being a title frequently veſted in the lord by inheritance, as being the fruit of a ſigniory to which he was intitled by deſcent, (for which reaſon the lands eſcheating ſhall attend the ſigniory, and be inheritable by ſuch only of his heirs as are capable of inheriting the other[z]) it may ſeem in ſuch caſes to fall more properly under the former general head of acquiring title to eſtates, *viz.* by deſcent, (being veſted in him by act of

[s] 1 P. W[ms]. 777.
[t] Stat. 3 & 4 W. & M. c. 14.
[u] Finch. law. 119.
[v] Finch. Rep. 86.
[w] See pag. 72.

[x] *Eſchet* or *échet*, formed from the verb *eſchoir* or *échoir*, to happen.
[y] 1 *Feud.* 86. Co. Litt. 13.
[z] Co. Litt. 13.

law,

law, and not by his own act or agreement) than under the prefent, by purchafe. But it muft be remembered that in order to
complete this title by efcheat, it is neceffary that the lord perform
an act of his own, by *entering* on the lands and tenements fo efcheated, or fuing out a *writ of efcheat*[a] : on failure of which,
or by doing any act that amounts to an implied waiver of his
right, as by accepting homage or rent of a ftranger who ufurps
the poffeffion, his title by efcheat is barred[b]. It is therefore in
fome refpect a title acquired by his own act, as well as by act of
law. Indeed this may alfo be faid of defcents themfelves, in
which an entry or other feifin is required, in order to make a
complete title; and therefore this diftribution by our legal writers feems in this refpect rather inaccurate : for, as efcheats muft
follow the nature of the figniory to which they belong, they may
veft by either purchafe or defcent, according as the figniory is
vefted. And, though fir Edward Coke confiders the lord by efcheat as in fome refpects the affignee of the laft tenant[c], and
therefore taking by purchafe; yet, on the other hand, the lord
is more frequently confidered as being *ultimus haeres*, and therefore taking by defcent in a kind of caducary fucceffion.

THE law of efcheats is founded upon this fingle principle,
that the blood of the perfon laft feifed in fee-fimple is, by fome
means or other, utterly extinct and gone : and, fince none can
inherit his eftate but fuch as are of his blood and confanguinity,
it follows as a regular confequence, that when fuch blood is extinct, the inheritance itfelf muft fail; the land muft become
what the feodal writers denominate *feudum apertum*; and muft
refult back again to the lord of the fee, by whom, or by thofe
whofe eftate he hath, it was given.

ESCHEATS are frequently divided into thofe *propter defectum
fanguinis* and thofe *propter delictum tenentis :* the one fort, if the
tenant dies without heirs; the other, if his blood be attainted[d].

---

[a] Bro. *Abr. tit. efcheat.* 26.   [c] 1 Inft. 215.
[b] *Ibid. tit. acceptance.* 25. Co. Litt. 268.   [d] Co. Litt. 13. 92.

But

But both thefe fpecies may well be comprehended under the firft denomination only; for he that is attainted fuffers an extinction of his blood, as well as he that dies without relations. The inheritable quality is expunged in one inftance, and expires in the other; or, as the doctrine of efcheats is very fully expreffed in Fleta.[c], " *dominus capitalis feodi loco haeredis habetur, quoties per* " *defeƈtum vel deliƈtum extinguitur fanguis tenentis.*"

E s c h e a t s therefore arifing merely upon the deficiency of the blood, whereby the defcent is impeded, their doctrine will be better illuftrated by confidering the feveral cafes wherein hereditary blood may be deficient, than by any other method whatfoever.

1, 2, 3. T h e firft three cafes, wherein inheritable blood is wanting, may be collected from the rules of defcent laid down and explained in the preceding chapter, and therefore will need very little illuftration or comment. Firft, when the tenant dies without any relations on the part of any of his anceftors: fecondly, when he dies without any relations on the part of thofe anceftors from whom his eftate defcended: thirdly, when he dies without any relations of the whole blood. In two of thefe cafes the blood of the firft purchafor is certainly, in the other it is probably, at an end; and therefore in all of them the law directs, that the land fhall efcheat to the lord of the fee: for the lord would be manifeftly prejudiced, if, contrary to the inherent condition tacitly annexed to all feuds, any perfon fhould be fuffered to fucceed to lands, who is not of the blood of the firft feudatory, to whom for his perfonal merit the eftate is fuppofed to have been granted.

4. A m o n s t e r, which hath not the fhape of mankind, but in any part evidently bears the refemblance of the brute creation, hath no inheritable blood, and cannot be heir to any land, albeit it be brought forth in marriage: but, although it hath deformity

[c] *l. 6. c. 1.*

in

in any part of it's body, yet if it hath human fhape, it may be heir[f]. This is a very antient rule in the law of England[g]; and it's reafon is too obvious, and too fhocking, to bear a minute difcuffion. The Roman law agrees with our own in excluding fuch births from fucceffions[h] : yet accounts them, however, children in fome refpects, where the parents, or at leaft the father, could reap any advantage thereby[i]; (as the *jus trium liberorum*, and the like) efteeming them the misfortune, rather than the fault, of that parent. But our law will not admit a birth of this kind to be fuch an iffue, as fhall intitle the hufband to be tenant by the curtefy[k]; becaufe it is not capable of inheriting. And therefore, if there appears no other heir than fuch a prodigious birth, the land fhall efcheat to the lord.

5. BASTARDS are incapable of being heirs. Baftards, by our law, are fuch children as are not born either in lawful wedlock, or within a competent time after it's determination[l]. Such are held to be *nullius filii*, the fons of nobody ; for the maxim of law is, *qui ex damnato coitu nafcuntur, inter liberos non computantur*[m]. Being thus the fons of nobody, they have no blood in them, at leaft no inheritable blood ; confequently, none of the blood of the firft purchafor : and therefore, if there be no other claimant than fuch illegitimate children, the land fhall efcheat to the lord[n]. The civil law differs from ours in this point, and allows a baftard to fucceed to an inheritance, if after it's birth the mother was married to the father[o] : and alfo, if the father had no lawful wife or child, then, even if the concubine was never married to the father, yet fhe and her baftard fon were admitted each to one twelfth of the inheritance[p], and a baftard was like-

[f] Co. Litt. 7, 8.

[g] *Qui contra formam humani generis converfo more procreantur, ut fi mulier monftrofum vel prodigiofum enixa fit, inter liberos non computentur. Partus tamen, cui natura aliquantulum addiderit vel diminuerit, ut fi fex vel tantum quatuor digitos habuerit, bene debet inter liberos connumerari : et, fi membra fint inutilia aut tortuofa, non tamen eft partus mon-* *ftrofus.* Bracton. *l.*1. *c.*6. *& l.*5. *tr.*5. *c.*30.

[h] *Ff.* 1. 5. 14.

[i] *Ff.* 50. 16. 135. Paul. 4 *fent.* 9. §. 63.

[k] Co. Litt. 29.

[l] See Book I. ch. 16.

[m] Co. Litt. 8.

[n] Finch. law. 117.

[a] *Nov.* 89. *c.* 8.

[o] *Ibid. c.* 12.

wife

wife capable of fucceeding to the whole of his mother's eftate, although fhe was never married; the mother being fufficiently certain, though the father is not[q]. But our law, in favour of marriage, is much lefs indulgent to baftards.

THERE is indeed one inftance, in which our law has fhewn them fome little regard; and that is ufually termed the cafe of *baftard eignè* and *mulier puifnè*. This happens when a man has a baftard fon, and afterwards marries the mother, and by her has a legitimate fon, who in the language of the law is called a *mulier*, or as Glanvil[r] expreffes it in his Latin, *filius mulieratus*; the woman before marriage being *concubina*, and afterwards *mulier*. Now here the eldeft fon is baftard, or *baftard eignè*; and the younger fon is legitimate, or *mulier puifnè*. If then the father dies, and the *baftard eignè* enters upon his land, and enjoys it to his death, and dies feifed thereof, whereby the inheritance defcends to his iffue; in this cafe the *mulier puifnè*, and all other heirs, (though minors, feme-coverts, or under any incapacity whatfoever) are totally barred of their right[s]. And this, 1. As a punifhment on the *mulier* for his negligence, in not entering during the *baftard*'s life, and evicting him. 2. Becaufe the law will not fuffer a man to be baftardized after his death, who entered as heir and died feifed, and fo paffed for legitimate in his lifetime. 3. Becaufe the canon law (following the civil) did allow fuch *baftard eignè* to be legitimate, on the fubfequent marriage of his mother : and therefore the laws of England (though they would not admit either the civil or canon law to rule the inheritances of this kingdom, yet) paid fuch a regard to a perfon thus peculiarly circumftanced, that, after the land had defcended to his iffue, they would not unravel the matter again, and fuffer his eftate to be fhaken. But this indulgence was fhewn to no other kind of baftard; for, if the mother was never married to the father, fuch baftard could have no colourable title at all[t].

[q] *Cod.* 6. 57. 5.   [s] Litt. §. 399. Co. Litt. 244.
[r] *l.* 7. *c.* 1.   [t] Litt. §. 400.

As

As baſtards cannot be heirs themſelves, ſo neither can they have any heirs but thoſe of their own bodies. For, as all collateral kindred conſiſts in being derived from the ſame common anceſtor, and as a baſtard has no legal anceſtors, he can have no collateral kindred; and, conſequently, can have no legal heirs, but ſuch as claim by a lineal deſcent from himſelf. And therefore if a baſtard purchaſes land, and dies ſeiſed thereof without iſſue, and inteſtate, the land ſhall eſcheat to the lord of the fee[u].

6. ALIENS alſo are incapable of taking by deſcent, or inheriting[w]: for they are not allowed to have any inheritable blood in them; rather indeed upon a principle of national or civil policy, than upon reaſons ſtrictly feodal. Though, if lands had been ſuffered to fall into their hands who owe no allegiance to the crown of England, the deſign of introducing our feuds, the defence of the kingdom, would have been defeated. Wherefore if a man leaves no other relations but aliens, his land ſhall eſcheat to the lord.

As aliens cannot inherit, ſo far they are on a level with baſtards; but, as they are alſo diſabled to hold by purchaſe[x], they are under ſtill greater diſabilities. And, as they can neither hold by purchaſe, nor by inheritance, it is almoſt ſuperfluous to ſay that they can have no heirs, ſince they can have nothing for an heir to inherit: but ſo it is expreſſly holden[y], becauſe they have not in them any inheritable blood.

AND farther, if an alien be made a denizen by the king's letters patent, and then purchaſes lands, (which the law allows ſuch a one to do) his ſon, born before his denization, ſhall not (by the common law) inherit thoſe lands; but a ſon born afterwards may, even though his elder brother be living; for the father, before denization, had no inheritable blood to communicate

u Bract. *l.* 2. *c.* 7. Co. Litt. 244.   x *Ibid.* 2.
w Co. Litt. 8.   y *Ibid.* 1 Lev. 59.

to his eldeſt ſon ; but by denization it acquires an hereditary
quality, which will be tranſmitted to his ſubſequent poſterity.
Yet, if he had been naturalized by act of parliament, ſuch eldeſt
ſon might then have inherited ; for that cancels all defects, and
is allowed to have a retroſpective energy, which ſimple denization has not [z].

Sir Edward Coke [a] alſo holds, that if an alien cometh into
England, and there hath iſſue two ſons, who are thereby natural
born ſubjects ; and one of them purchaſes land, and dies ; yet
neither of theſe brethren can be heir to the other. For the *com-*
mune vinculum, or common ſtock of their conſanguinity, is the
father ; and, as he had no inheritable blood in him, he could
communicate none to his ſons; and, when the ſons can by no poſſibility be heirs to the father, the one of them ſhall not be heir
to the other. And this opinion of his ſeems founded upon ſolid
principles of the antient law ; not only from the rule before
cited [b], that *ceſtuy, que doit inheriter al pere, doit inheriter al fits* ;
but alſo becauſe we have ſeen that the only feodal foundation
upon which newly purchaſed land can poſſibly deſcend to a brother, is the ſuppoſition and fiction of law, that it deſcended from
ſome one of his anceſtors : but in this caſe as the immediate anceſtor was an alien, from whom it could by no poſſibility deſcend,
this ſhould deſtroy the ſuppoſition, and impede the deſcent, and
the land ſhould be inherited *ut feudum ſtricte novum* ; that is, by
none but the lineal deſcendants of the purchaſing brother ; and,
on failure of them, ſhould eſcheat to the lord of the fee. But
this opinion hath been ſince overruled [c] : and it is now held for
law, that the ſons of an alien, born here, may inherit to each
other. And reaſonably enough upon the whole : for, as (in
common purchaſes) the whole of the ſuppoſed deſcent from indefinite anceſtors is but fictitious, the law may as well ſuppoſe
the requiſite anceſtor as ſuppoſe the requiſite deſcent.

[z] Co. Litt. 129.
[a] 1 Inſt. 8.

[b] See pag. 223 and 239.
[c] 1 Ventr. 473. 1 Lev. 59. 1 Sid. 193.

I T

IT is alfo enacted, by the ftatute 11 & 12 W. III. c. 6. that all perfons, being natural-born fubjects of the king, may inherit and make their titles by defcent from any of their anceftors lineal or collateral; although their father, or mother, or other anceftor, by, from, through, or under whom they derive their pedigrees, were born out of the king's allegiance. But inconveniences were afterwards apprehended, in cafe perfons fhould thereby gain a future capacity to inherit, who did not exift at the death of the perfon laft feifed. As, if Francis the elder brother of John Stiles be an alien, and Oliver the younger be a natural-born fubject, upon John's death without iffue his lands will defcend to Oliver the younger brother: now, if afterwards Francis hath a child, it was feared that, under the ftatute of king William, this new-born child might defeat the eftate of his uncle Oliver. Where-fore it is provided, by the ftatute 25 Geo. II. c. 39. that no right of inheritance fhall accrue by virtue of the former ftatute to any perfons whatfoever, unlefs they are in being and capable to take as heirs at the death of the perfon laft feifed : --- with an excep-tion however to the cafe, where lands fhall defcend to the daugh-ter of an alien; which daughter fhall refign fuch inheritance to her after-born brother, or divide it with her after-born fifters, according to the ufual rule [d] of defcents by the common law.

7. BY attainder alfo, for treafon or other felony, the blood of the perfon attainted is fo corrupted, as to be rendered no longer inheritable.

GREAT care muft be taken to diftinguifh between forfeiture of lands to the king, and this fpecies of efcheat to the lord; which, by reafon of their fimilitude in fome circumftances, and becaufe the crown is very frequently the immediate lord of the fee and therefore entitled to both, have been often confounded together. Forfeiture of lands, and of whatever elfe the offender poffeffed, was the doctrine of the old Saxon law [e], as a part of

---

[d] See pag. 208 and 214.   [e] *LL. Aelfred. c.* 4. *LL. Canut. c.* 54.

punifhment

punifhment for the offence ; and does not at all relate to the feodal fyftem, nor is the confequence of any figniory or lordfhip paramount [f] : but, being a prerogative vefted in the crown, was
neither fuperfeded nor diminifhed by the introduction of the Norman tenures ; a fruit and confequence of which efcheat muft undoubtedly be reckoned. Efcheat therefore operates in fubordination to this more antient and fuperior law of forfeiture.

T H E doctrine of efcheat upon attainder, taken fingly, is this :
that the blood of the tenant, by the commiffion of any felony,
(under which denomination all treafons were formerly comprized [g])
is corrupted and ftained, and the original donation of the feud is
thereby determined, it being always granted to the vafal on the
implied condition of *dum bene fe gefferit.* Upon the thorough
demonftration of which guilt, by legal attainder, the feodal covenant and mutual bond of fealty are held to be broken, the eftate
inftantly falls back from the offender to the lord of the fee, and
the inheritable quality of his blood is extinguifhed and blotted
out for ever. In this fituation the law of feodal efcheat was
brought into England at the conqueft ; and in general fuperadded
to the antient law of forfeiture. In confequence of which corruption and extinction of hereditary blood, the land of all felons
would immediately reveft in the lord, but that the fuperior law
of forfeiture intervenes, and intercepts it in it's paffage ; in cafe
of treafon, for ever ; in cafe of other felony, for only a year and
a day, after which time it goes to the lord in a regular courfe of
efcheat [h], as it would have done to the heir of the felon in cafe
the feodal tenures had never been introduced. And that this is
the true operation and genuine hiftory of efcheats will moft evidently appear from this incident to gavelkind lands, (which feem
to be the old Saxon tenure) that they are in no cafe fubject
to efcheat for felony, though they are liable to forfeiture for
treafon [i].

[f] 2 Inft. 64. Salk. 85.
[g] 3 Inft. 15. Stat. 25 Edw. III. c. 2. § 12.
[h] 2 Inft. 36.
[i] Somner. 53. Wright. Ten. 118.

A s

As a confequence of this doctrine of efcheat, all lands of in-heritance immediately revefting in the lord, the wife of the felon was liable to lofe her dower, till the ftatute 1 Edw. VI. c. 12. enacted, that albeit any perfon be attainted of mifprifion of trea-fon, murder, or felony, yet his wife fhall enjoy her dower. But fhe has not this indulgence where the antient law of forfeiture operates, for it is exprefsly provided by the ftatute 5 & 6 Edw. VI. c. 11. that the wife of one attaint of high treafon fhall not be endowed at all.

HITHERTO we have only fpoken of eftates vefted in the of-fender, at the time of his offence, or attainder.. And here the law of forfeiture ftops; but the law of efcheat purfues the mat-ter ftill farther. For, the blood of the tenant being utterly cor-rupted and extinguifhed, it follows, not only that all he now has fhould efcheat from him, but alfo that he fhould be incapable of inheriting any thing for the future. This may farther illuftrate the diftinction between forfeiture and efcheat. If therefore a fa-ther be feifed in fee, and the fon commits treafon and is attainted, and then the father dies : here the land fhall efcheat to the lord; becaufe the fon, by the corruption of his blood, is incapable to be heir, and there can be no other heir during his life : but no-thing fhall be forfeited to the king, for the fon never had any in-tereft in the lands to forfeit [k]. In this cafe the efcheat operates, and not the forfeiture; but in the following inftance the forfeit-ure works, and not the efcheat. As where a new felony is crea-ted by act of parliament, and it is provided (as is frequently the cafe) that it fhall not extend to corruption of blood : here the lands of the felon fhall not efcheat to the lord, but yet the pro-fits of them fhall be forfeited to the king fo long as the offender lives [l].

THERE is yet a farther confequence of the corruption and extinction of hereditary blood, which is this: that the perfon

[k] Co. Litt. 13.   [l] 3 Inft. 47.

attainted

attainted fhall not only be incapable himfelf of inheriting, or tranfmitting his own property by heirfhip, but fhall alfo obftruct the defcent of lands or tenements to his pofterity, in all cafes where they are obliged to derive their title through him from any remoter anceftor. The chanel, which conveyed the heredi-tary blood from his anceftors to him, is not only exhaufted for the prefent, but totally dammed up and rendered impervious for the future. This is a refinement upon the antient law of feuds, which allowed that the grandfon might be heir to his grandfather, though the fon in the intermediate generation was guilty of fe-lony [m]. But, by the law of England, a man's blood is fo uni-verfally corrupted by attainder, that his fons can neither inherit to him nor to any other anceftor [n], at leaft on the part of their attainted father.

THIS corruption of blood cannot be abfolutely removed but by authority of parliament. The king may excufe the public punifhment of an offender; but cannot abolifh the private right, which has accrued or may accrue to individuals as a confequence of the criminal's attainder. He may remit a forfeiture, in which the intereft of the crown is alone concerned: but he cannot wipe away the corruption of blood; for therein a third perfon hath an intereft, the lord who claims by efcheat. If therefore a man hath a fon, and is attainted, and afterwards pardoned by the king; this fon can never inherit to his father, or father's anceftors; becaufe his paternal blood, being once throughly corrupted by his father's attainder, muft continue fo: but if the fon had been born after the pardon, he might inherit; becaufe by the pardon the father is made a new man, and may convey new inheritable blood to his after-born children [o].

HEREIN there is however a difference between aliens and perfons attainted. Of aliens, who could never by any poffibility be heirs, the law takes no notice: and therefore we have feen,

[m] Van Leeuwen *in* 2 *Feud.* 31.   [o] *Ibid.* 392.
[n] Co. Litt. 391.

that

that an alien elder brother fhall not impede the defcent to a natural-born younger brother. But in attainders it is otherwife : for if a man hath iffue a fon, and is attainted, and afterwards pardoned, and then hath iffue a fecond fon, and dies ; here the corruption of blood is not removed from the eldeft, and therefore he cannot be heir : neither can the youngeft be heir, for he hath an elder brother living, of whom the law takes notice, as he once had a poffibility of being heir; and therefore the younger brother fhall not inherit, but the land fhall efcheat to the lord : though, had the elder died without iffue in the life of the father, the younger fon born after the pardon might well have inherited, for he hath no corruption of blood P. So if a man hath iffue two fons, and the elder in the lifetime of the father hath iffue, and then is attainted and executed, and afterwards the father dies, the lands of the father fhall not defcend to the younger fon : for the iffue of the elder, which had once a poffibility to inherit, fhall impede the defcent to the younger, and the land fhall efcheat to the lord q. Sir Edward Coke in this cafe allows r, that if the anceftor be attainted, his fons born before the attainder may be heirs to each other; and diftinguifhes it from the cafe of the fons of an alien, becaufe in this cafe the blood was inheritable when imparted to them from the father : but he makes a doubt (upon the fame principles, which are now overruled s) whether fons, born after the attainder, can inherit to each other; for they never had any inheritable blood in them.

UPON the whole it appears, that a perfon attainted is neither allowed to retain his former eftate, nor to inherit any future one, nor to tranfmit any inheritance to his iffue, either immediately from himfelf, or mediately through himfelf from any remoter anceftor; for his inheritable blood, which is neceffary either to hold, to take, or to tranfmit any feodal property, is blotted out, corrupted, and extinguifhed for ever : the confequence of which is, that eftates, thus impeded in their defcent, refult back and efcheat to the lord.

P Co. Litt. 8.
q Dyer. 48.
r Co. Litt. 8.
h 1 Hal. P. C. 357.

THIS

THIS corruption of blood, thus arifing from feodal principles, but perhaps extended farther than even thofe principles will warrant, has been long looked upon as a peculiar hardfhip: becaufe, the oppreffive parts of the feodal tenures being now in general abolifhed, it feems unreafonable to referve one of their moft inequitable confequences; namely, that the children fhould not only be reduced to prefent poverty, (which, however fevere, is fufficiently juftified upon reafons of public policy) but alfo be laid under future difficulties of inheritance, on account of the guilt of their anceftors. And therefore in moft (if not all) of the new felonies, created by parliament fince the reign of Henry the eighth, it is declared that they fhall not extend to any corruption of blood: and by the ftatute 7 Ann. c. 21. (the operation of which is poftponed by the ftatute 17 Geo. II. c. 39.) it is enacted, that, after the death of the pretender, and his fons, no attainder for treafon fhall extend to the difinheriting any heir, nor the prejudice of any perfon, other than the offender himfelf: which provifions have indeed carried the remedy farther, than was required by the hardfhip above complained of; which is only the future obftruction of defcents, where the pedigree happens to be deduced through the blood of an attainted anceftor.

BEFORE I conclude this head, of efcheat, I muft mention one fingular inftance in which lands held in fee-fimple are not liable to efcheat to the lord, even when their owner is no more, and hath left no heirs to inherit them. And this is the cafe of a corporation: for if that comes by any accident to be diffolved, the donor or his heirs fhall have the land again in reverfion, and not the lord by efcheat: which is perhaps the only inftance where a reverfion can be expectant on a grant in fee-fimple abfolute. But the law, we are told[t], doth tacitly annex a condition to every fuch gift or grant, that if the corporation be diffolved, the donor or grantor fhall re-enter; for the caufe of the gift or grant

[t] Co. Litt. 13.

faileth.

faileth. This is indeed founded upon the felf-fame principle as the law of efcheat; the heirs of the donor being only fubftituted inftead of the chief lord of the fee : which was formerly very frequently the cafe in fubinfeudations, or alienations of lands by a vafal to be holden as of himfelf; till that practice was reftrained by the ftatute of *quia emptores,* 18 Edw. I. ft. 1. to which this very fingular inftance ftill in fome degree remains an exception.

THERE is one more incapacity of taking by defcent, which, not being productive of any efcheat, is not properly reducible to this head, and yet muft not be paffed over in filence. It is enacted by the ftatute 11 & 12 Will. III. c. 4. that every papift who fhall not abjure the errors of his religion by taking the oaths to the government, and making the declaration againft tranfubftantiation, within fix months after he has attained the age of eighteen years, fhall be incapable of inheriting, or taking, by defcent as well as purchafe, any real eftates whatfoever; and his next of kin, being a proteftant, fhall hold them to his own ufe till fuch time as he complies with the terms impofed by the act. This incapacity is merely perfonal; it affects himfelf only, and does not deftroy the inheritable quality of his blood, fo as to impede the defcent to others of his kindred. In like manner as, even in the times of popery, one who entered into religion and became a monk profeffed was incapable of inheriting lands, both in our own [u] and the feodal law; *eo quod defiit effe miles feculi qui factus eft miles Chrifti; nec beneficium pertinet ad eum qui non debet gerere officium* [w]. But yet he was accounted only *civiliter mortuus*; he did not impede the defcent to others, but the next heir was entitled to his or his anceftor's eftate.

THESE are the feveral deficiencies of hereditary blood, recognized by the law of England; which, fo often as they happen, occafion lands to efcheat to the original proprietary or lord.

[u] Co. Litt. 132.   [w] 2 *Feud.* 21.

Chapter the sixteenth.

Of TITLE by OCCUPANCY.

OCCUPANCY is the taking poffeffion of thofe things, which before belonged to nobody. This, as we have feen[a], is the true ground and foundation of all property, or of holding thofe things in feveralty, which by the law of nature, unqualified by that of fociety, were common to all mankind. But, when once it was agreed that every thing capable of ownerfhip fhould have an owner, natural reafon fuggefted, that he who could firft declare his intention of appropriating any thing to his own ufe, and, in confequence of fuch intention, actually took it into pof-feffion, fhould thereby gain the abfolute property of it; according to that rule of the law of nations, recognized by the laws of Rome[b], *quod nullius eft, id ratione naturali occupanti conceditur.*

THIS right of occupancy, fo far as it concerns real property, (for of perfonal chattels I am not in this place to fpeak) hath been confined by the laws of England within a very narrow com-pafs; and was extended only to a fingle inftance : namely, where a man was tenant *pur auter vie*, or had an eftate granted to him-felf only (without mentioning his heirs) for the life of another man, and died during the life of *ceftuy que vie*, or him by whofe life it was holden : in this cafe he, that could firft enter on the land, might lawfully retain the poffeffion fo long as *ceftuy que vie* lived, by right of occupancy[c].

[a] See pag. 3 & 8.
[b] *Ff*. 41. 1. 3.
[c] Co. Litt. 41.

THIS

THIS seems to have been recurring to first principles, and calling in the law of nature to ascertain the property of the land, when left without a legal owner. For it did not revert to the grantor; who had parted with all his interest, so long as *cestuy que vie* lived: it did not escheat to the lord of the fee; for all escheats must be of the absolute entire fee, and not of any particular estate carved out of it; much less of so minute a remnant as this: it did not belong to the grantee; for he was dead: it did not descend to his heirs; for there were no words of inheritance in the grant: nor could it vest in his executors; for no executors could succeed to a freehold. Belonging therefore to nobody, like the *haereditas jacens* of the Romans, the law left it open to be seised and appropriated by the first person that could enter upon it, during the life of *cestuy que vie*, under the name of an occupant. But there was no right of occupancy allowed, where the king had the reversion of the lands; for the reversioner hath an equal right with any other man to enter upon the vacant possession, and where the king's title and a subject's concur, the king's shall be always preferred: against the king therefore there could be no prior occupant, because *nullum tempus occurrit regi*[d]. And, even in the case of a subject, had the estate *pur auter vie* been granted to a man *and his heirs* during the life of *cestuy que vie*, there the heir might, and still may, enter and hold possession, and is called in law a *special occupant*; as having a special exclusive right, by the terms of the original grant, to enter upon and occupy this *haereditas jacens*, during the residue of the estate granted: though some have thought him so called with no very great propriety[e]; and that such estate is rather a descendible freehold. But the title of common occupancy is now reduced almost to nothing by two statutes; the one, 29 Car. II. c. 3. which enacts, that where there is no special occupant, in whom the estate may vest, the tenant *pur auter vie* may devise it by will, or it shall go to the executors and be assets in their hands for payment of debts: the other that of 14 Geo. II. c. 20. which enacts, that it shall vest not only in the

[d] *Ibid.*   [e] Vaugh. 201.

I i 2   executors,

executors, but, in cafe the tenant dies inteftate, in the adminiftrators alfo; and go in a courfe of diftribution like a chattel
intereft.

B Y thefe two ftatutes the title of *common* occupancy is utterly
extinct and abolifhed : though that of *fpecial* occupancy, by the
heir at law, continues to this day; fuch heir being held to fucceed to the anceftor's eftate, not by defcent, for then he muft
take an eftate of inheritance, but as an occupant, fpecially marked
out and appointed by the original grant. The doctrine of common occupancy may however be ufefully remembered on the following account, among others : that, as by the common law no
occupancy could be of incorporeal hereditaments, as of rents,
tithes, advowfons, commons, or the like ᶠ, (becaufe, with refpect
to them, there could be no actual entry made, or corporal feifin
had; and therefore by the death of the grantee *pur auter vie* a
grant of fuch hereditaments was entirely determined ᵍ) fo now,
I apprehend, notwithftanding thefe ftatutes, fuch grant would be
determined likewife; and the hereditaments would not be devifable, nor veft in the executors, nor go in a courfe of diftribution.
For the ftatutes muft not be conftrued fo as to create any new e-
ftate, or to keep that alive which by the common law was determined, and thereby to defer the grantor's reverfion; but merely
to difpofe of an intereft in being, to which by law there was no
owner, and which therefore was left open to the firft occupant.
When there is a refidue left, the ftatutes give it to the executors,
&c, inftead of the firft occupant; but they will not *create* a refidue, on purpofe to give it the executors. They only meant to
provide an appointed inftead of a cafual, a certain inftead of an
uncertain, owner, of lands which before were nobody's; and
thereby to fupply this *cafus omiffus*, and render the difpofition of
law in all refpects entirely uniform : this being the only inftance
wherein a title to a real eftate could ever be acquired by occupancy.

ᶠ Co. Litt. 41.　　　　　　　　　ᵍ Vaugh. 201.

T H I S

THIS, I fay, was the only inftance; for I think there can be no other cafe devifed, wherein there is not fome owner of the land appointed by the law. In the cafe of a fole corporation, as a parfon of a church, when he dies or refigns, though there is no *actual* owner of the land till a fucceffor be appointed, yet there is a *legal, potential* ownerfhip, fubfifting in contemplation of law; and when the fucceffor is appointed, his appointment fhall have a retrofpect and relation backwards, fo as to entitle him to all the profits from the inftant that the vacancy commenced. And, in all other inftances, when the tenant dies inteftate, and no other owner of the lands is to be found in the common courfe of de-fcents, there the law vefts an ownerfhip in the king, or in the fubordinate lord of the fee, by efcheat.

So alfo in fome cafes, where the laws of other nations give a right by occupancy, as in lands newly created, by the rifing of an ifland in a river, or by the alluvion or dereliction of the fea; in thefe inftances the law of England affigns them an immediate owner. For Bracton tells us [h], that if an ifland arife in the *middle* of a *river*, it belongs in common to thofe who have lands on each fide thereof; but if it be nearer to one bank than the other, it belongs only to him who is proprietor of the neareft fhore: which is agreeable to, and probably copied from, the civil law [i]. Yet this feems only to be reafonable, where the foil of the river is equally divided between the owners of the oppofite fhores: for if the whole foil is the freehold of any one man, as it muft be whenever a feveral fifhery is claimed [k], there it feems juft (and fo is the ufual practice) that the eyotts or little iflands, arifing in any part of the river, fhall be the property of him who owneth the pif-cary and the foil. However, in cafe a new ifland rife in the *fea*, though the civil law gives it to the firft occupant [l], yet ours gives it to the king [m]. And as to lands gained from the fea, either by *allu-*

[h] *l. 2. c. 2.*
[i] *Inft. 2. 1. 22.*
[k] Salk. 637.

[l] *Inft. 2. 1. 18.*
[m] Bract. *l. 2. c. 2.* Callis of fewers. 22.

vion,

vion, by the wafhing up of fand and earth, fo as in time to make *terra firma*; or by *dereliction*, as when the fea fhrinks back below the ufual watermark; in thefe cafes the law is held to be, that if this gain be by little and little, by fmall and imperceptible degrees, it fhall go to the owner of the land adjoining. For *de minimis non curat lex*: and, befides, thefe owners being often lofers by the breaking in of the fea, or at charges to keep it out, this poffible gain is therefore a reciprocal confideration for fuch poffible charge or lofs. But, if the alluvion or dereliction be fudden and confider-able, in this cafe it belongs to the king: for, as the king is lord of the fea, and fo owner of the foil while it is covered with water, it is but reafonable he fhould have the foil, when the water has left it dry[n]. So that the quantity of ground gained, and the time during which it is gaining, are what make it either the king's, or the fubject's property. In the fame manner if a river, running between two lordfhips, by degrees gains upon the one, and thereby leaves the other dry; the owner who lofes his ground thus imperceptibly has no remedy: but if the courfe of the river be changed by a fudden and violent flood, or other hafty means, and thereby a man lofes his ground, he fhall have what the river has left in any other place, as a recompence for this fudden lofs[o]. And this law of alluvions and derelictions, with regard to *rivers*, is nearly the fame in the imperial law[p]; from whence indeed thofe our determinations feem to have been drawn and adopted: but we ourfelves, as iflanders, have applied them to *marine* increafes; and have given our fovereign the prerogative he enjoys, as well upon the particular reafons before-mentioned, as upon this other general ground of prerogative, which was for-merly remarked[q], that whatever hath no other owner is vefted by law in the king.

[n] Callis. 24. 28.   [p] *Inft.* 2. 1. 20, 21, 22, 23, 24.
[o] Callis. 28.   [q] See Vol. I. pag. 289.

CHAPTER THE SEVENTEENTH.

OF TITLE BY PRESCRIPTION.

A THIRD method of acquiring real property by purchafe is
that by *prefcription*; as when a man can fhew no other
title to what he claims, than that he, and thofe under whom he
claims, have immemorially ufed to enjoy it. Concerning cuftoms,
or immemorial ufages, in general, with the feveral requifites and
rules to be obferved, in order to prove their exiftence and validity, we enquired at large in the preceding part of thefe commentaries[a]. At prefent therefore I fhall only, firft, diftinguifh
between *cuftom*, ftrictly taken, and *prefcription*; and then fhew,
what fort of things may be prefcribed for.

AND, firft, the diftinction between cuftom and prefcription is
this; that cuftom is properly a *local* ufage, and not annexed to
any *perfon*; fuch as, a cuftom in the manor of Dale that lands
fhall defcend to the youngeft fon: prefcription is merely a *perfonal*
ufage; as, that Sempronius, and his anceftors, or thofe whofe eftate
he hath, have ufed time out of mind to have fuch an advantage
or privilege[b]. As for example: if there be a ufage in the parifh of
Dale, that all the inhabitants of that parifh may dance on a certain clofe, at all times, for their recreation; (which is held[c] to
be a lawful ufage) this is ftrictly a cuftom, for it is applied to
the *place* in general, and not to any particular *perfons* : but if the

[a] See Vol. I. pag. 75, &c.   [c] 1 Lev. 176.
[b] Co. Litt. 113.

tenant,

tenant, who is feifed of the manor of Dale in fee, alleges that he and his anceftors, or all thofe whofe eftate he hath in the faid manor, have ufed time out of mind to have common of pafture in fuch a clofe, this is properly called a prefcription; for this is a ufage annexed to the *perfon* of the owner of this eftate. All prefcription muft be either in a man and his anceftors, or in a man and thofe whofe eftate he hath [d]; which laft is called prefcribing in a *que eftate.* And formerly a man might, by the common law, have prefcribed for a right which had been enjoyed by his anceftors or predeceffors at any diftance of time, though his or their enjoyment of it had been fufpended [e] for an indefinite feries of years. But by the ftatute of limitations, 32 Hen. VIII. c. 2. it is enacted, that no perfon fhall make any prefcription by the feifin or poffeffion of his anceftor or predeceffor, unlefs fuch feifin or poffeffion hath been within threefcore years next before fuch prefcription made [f].

SECONDLY, as to the feveral fpecies of things which may, or may not, be prefcribed for: we may in the firft place, obferve, that nothing but incorporeal hereditaments can be claimed by prefcription; as a right of way, a common, *&c*; but that no prefcription can give a title to lands, and other corporeal fubftances, of which more certain evidence may be had [g]. For no man can be faid to prefcribe, that he and his anceftors have immemorially ufed to hold the caftle of Arundel: for this is clearly another fort of title; a title by corporal feifin and inheritance, which is more permanent, and therefore more capable of proof, than that of prefcription. But, as to a right of way, a common, or the like, a man may be allowed to prefcribe; for of thefe there is no corporal feifin, the enjoyment will be frequently by intervals, and therefore the right to enjoy them can depend on nothing elfe but immemorial ufage. 2. A prefcription muft

[d] 4 Rep. 32.
[e] Co. Litt. 113.
[f] This title, of prefcription, was well known in the Roman law by the name of

ufucapio; (*Ff.* 41. 3. 3.) fo called, becaufe a man, that gains a title by prefcription, may be faid *ufu rem capere.*
[g] Dr & St. dial. 1. c. 8. Finch. 132.

always

always be laid in him that is tenant of the fee. A tenant for life, for years, at will, or a copyholder, cannot prefcribe, by reafon of the imbecillity of their eftates [h]. For, as prefcription is ufage beyond time of memory, it is abfurd that they fhould pretend to prefcribe, whofe eftates commenced within the remembrance of man. And therefore the copyholder muft prefcribe under cover of his lord's eftate, and the tenant for life under cover of the tenant in fee-fimple. As, if tenant for life of a manor would prefcribe for a right of common as appurtenant to the fame, he muft prefcribe under cover of the tenant in fee-fimple; and muft plead, that John Stiles and his anceftors had immemorially ufed to have this right of common, appurtenant to the faid manor, and that John Stiles demifed the faid manor, with it's appurtenances, to him the faid tenant for life. 3. A prefcription cannot be for a thing which cannot be raifed by grant. For the law allows prefcription only in fupply of the lofs of a grant, and therefore every prefcription prefuppofes a grant to have exifted. Thus a lord of a manor cannot prefcribe to raife a tax or toll upon ftrangers; for, as fuch claim could never have been good by any grant, it fhall not be good by prefcription [i]. 4. A fourth rule is, that what is to arife by matter of record cannot be prefcribed for, but muft be claimed by grant, entered on record: fuch as, for inftance, the royal franchifes of deodands, felons' goods, and the like. Thefe, not being forfeited till the matter on which they arife is found by the inquifition of a jury, and fo made a matter of record, the forfeiture itfelf cannot be claimed by any inferior title. But the franchifes of treafure-trove, waifs, eftrays, and the like, may be claimed by prefcription; for they arife from private contingencies, and not from any matter of record [k]. 5. Among things incorporeal, which may be claimed by prefcription, a diftinction muft be made with regard to the manner of prefcribing; that is, whether a man fhall prefcribe in a *que eftate*, or in himfelf and his anceftors. For, if a man prefcribes in a *que eftate*, (that is, in himfelf and thofe whofe eftate he holds) nothing is claim-

[h] 4 Rep. 31, 32.   [k] Co. Litt. 114.
[i] 1 Ventr. 387.

able by this prefcription, but fuch things as are incident, appendant, or appurtenant to lands; for it would be abfurd to claim
any thing as the confequence, or appendix, of an eftate, with
which the thing claimed has no connexion: but, if he prefcribes
in himfelf and his anceftors, he may prefcribe for any thing whatfoever that lies in grant; not only things that are appurtenant,
but alfo fuch as may be in grofs[1]. Therefore a man may prefcribe,
that he, and thofe whofe eftate he hath in the manor of Dale, have
ufed to hold the advowfon of Dale, as *appendant* to that manor:
but, if the advowfon be a diftinct inheritance, and not appendant,
then he can only prefcribe in his anceftors. So alfo a man may
prefcribe in a *que eftate* for a common *appurtenant* to a manor;
but, if he would prefcribe for a common *in grofs*, he muft prefcribe in himfelf and his anceftors. 6. Laftly, we may obferve,
that eftates gained by prefcription are not, of courfe, defcendible
to the heirs general, like other purchafed eftates, but are an exception to the rule. For, properly fpeaking, the prefcription is
rather to be confidered as an evidence of a former acquifition,
than as an acquifition *de novo:* and therefore, if a man prefcribes for a right of way in himfelf and his anceftors, it will
defcend only to the blood of that line of anceftors in whom he fo
prefcribes; the prefcription in this cafe being indeed a fpecies of
defcent. But, if he prefcribes for it in a *que eftate*, it will follow
the nature of that eftate in which the prefcription is laid, and be
inheritable in the fame manner, whether that were acquired by
defcent or purchafe: for every acceffory followeth the nature of
it's principal.

[1] Litt. §. 183. Finch. L. 104.

CHAPTER THE EIGHTEENTH.

OF TITLE BY FORFEITURE.

FORFEITURE is a punifhment annexed by law to fome illegal act, or negligence, in the owner of lands, tenements, or hereditaments; whereby he lofes all his intereft therein, and they go to the party injured, as a recompenfe for the wrong which either he alone, or the public together with himfelf, hath fuftained.

LANDS, tenements, and hereditaments, may be forfeited in various degrees and by various means: 1. By crimes and mifdemefnors. 2. By alienation contrary to law. 3. By non-prefentation to a benefice, when the forfeiture is denominated a *lapfe*. 4. By fimony. 5. By non-performance of conditions. 6. By wafte. 7. By breach of copyhold cuftoms. 8. By bankruptcy.

I. THE foundation and juftice of forfeitures for *crimes and mifdemefnors*, and the feveral degrees of thofe forfeitures, proportioned to the feveral offences, have been hinted at in the preceding volume[a]; but will be more properly confidered, and more at large, in the fourth book of thefe commentaries. At prefent I fhall only obferve in general, that the offences which induce a forfeiture of lands and tenements to the crown are principally the following fix; 1. Treafon. 2. Felony. 3. Mifprifion of

[a] Vol. I. pag. 289.

K k 2

treafon.

treafon. 4. Praemunire. 5. Drawing a weapon on a judge, or ftriking any one in the prefence of the king's principal courts of juftice. 6. Popifh recufancy, or non-obfervance of certain laws enacted in reftraint of papifts. But at what time they feverally commence, how far they extend, and how long they endure, will with greater propriety be referved as the object of our future enquiries.

II. L A N D s and tenements may be forfeited by *alienation*, or conveying them to another, contrary to law. This is either alienation in *mortmain*, alienation to an *alien*, or alienation by *particular tenants*; in the two former of which cafes the forfeiture arifes from the incapacity of the alienee to take, in the latter from the incapacity of the alienor to grant.

1. A L I E N A T I O N in *mortmain, in mortua manu*, is an alienation of lands or tenements to any corporation, fole or aggregate, ecclefiaftical or temporal. But thefe purchafes having been chiefly made by religious houfes, in confequence whereof the lands became perpetually inherent in one dead hand, this hath occafioned the general appellation of mortmain to be applied to fuch alienations [b], and the religious houfes themfelves to be principally confidered in forming the ftatutes of mortmain : in deducing the hiftory of which ftatutes, it will be matter of curiofity to obferve the great addrefs and fubtil contrivance of the ecclefiaftics in eluding from time to time the laws in being, and the zeal with which fucceffive parliaments have purfued them through all their fineffes; how new remedies were ftill the parents of new evafions; till the legiflature at laft, though with difficulty, hath obtained a decifive victory.

B Y the common law any man might difpofe of his lands to any other private man at his own difcretion, efpecially when the feodal reftraints of alienation were worn away. Yet in confequence of thefe it was always, and is ftill, neceffary [c], for corpo-

[b] See Vol. I. pag. 467.   [c] F. N. B. 121.

rations

rations to have a licence of mortmain from the crown, to enable them to purchafe lands : for as the king is the ultimate lord of every fee, he ought not, unlefs by his own confent, to lofe his privilege of efcheats and other feodal profits, by the vefting of lands in tenants that can never be attainted or die. And fuch licences of mortmain feem to have been neceffary among the Saxons, above fixty years before the Norman conqueft [d]. But, befides this general licence from the king, as lord paramount of the kingdom, it was alfo requifite, whenever there was a mefne or intermediate lord between the king and the alienor, to obtain his licence alfo (upon the fame feodal principles) for the alienation of the fpecific land. And if no fuch licence was obtained, the king or other lord might refpectively enter on the lands fo aliened in mortmain, as a forfeiture. The neceffity of this licence from the crown was acknowleged by the conftitutions of Clarendon [e], in refpect of advowfons, which the monks always greatly coveted, as being the groundwork of fubfequent appropriations [f]. Yet fuch were the influence and ingenuity of the clergy, that (notwithftanding this fundamental principle) we find that the largeft and moft confiderable dotations of religious houfes happened within lefs than two centuries after the conqueft. And (when a licence could not be obtained) their contrivance feems to have been this : that, as the forfeiture for fuch alienations accrued in the firft place to the immediate lord of the fee, the tenant who meant to alienate firft conveyed his lands to the religious houfe, and inftantly took them back again, to hold as tenant to the monaftery ; which kind of inftantaneous feifin was probably held not to occafion any forfeiture : and then, by pretext of fome other forfeiture, furrender, or efcheat, the fociety entered into thofe lands in right of fuch their newly acquired figniory, as immediate lords of the fee. But, when thefe dotations began to grow numerous, it was obferved that the feodal fervices, ordained for the defence of the kingdom, were every day vifibly withdrawn ; that the circulation of landed property from man to man began to

---

[d] Selden. Jan. Angl. l. 2. §. 45.
[e] *Ecclefiae de feudo domini regis non poffunt in perpetuum dari, abfque affenfu et confenfione*

ipfius. c. 2. A. D. 1164.
[f] See Vol. I. pag. 373.

ftagnate ;

ftagnate; and that the lords were curtailed of the fruits of their figniories, their efcheats, wardfhips, reliefs, and the like : and therefore, in order to prevent this, it was ordained by the fecond of king Henry III's great charters[g], and afterwards by that printed in our common ftatute-books, that all fuch attempts fhould be void, and the land forfeited to the lord of the fee [h].

BUT, as this prohibition extended only to religious *houfes*, bifhops and other fole corporations were not included therein ; and the aggregate ecclefiaftical bodies (who, fir Edward Coke obferves [i], in this were to be commended, that they ever had of their counfel the beft learned men that they could get) found many means to creep out of this ftatute, by buying in lands that were *bona fide* holden of themfelves as lords of the fee, and thereby evading the forfeiture ; or by taking long leafes for years, which firft introduced thofe extenfive terms, for a thoufand or more years, which are now fo frequent in conveyances. This produced the ftatute *de religiofis*, 7 Edw. I; which provided, that no *perfon*, religious or other whatfoever, fhould buy, or fell, or receive, under pretence of a gift, or term of years, or any other title whatfoever, nor fhould by any art or ingenuity appropriate to himfelf, any lands or tenements in mortmain ; upon pain that the immediate lord of the fee, or, on his default for one year, the lords paramount, and, in default of all of them, the king, might enter thereon as a forfeiture.

THIS feemed to be a fufficient fecurity againft all alienations in mortmain : but, as thefe ftatutes extended only to gifts and conveyances between the parties, the religious houfes now began to fet up a fictitious title to the land, which it was intended they fhould have, and to bring an action to recover it againft the tenant ;

---

g *A. D.* 1217. *cap.* 43. *edit. Oxon.*

h *Non licet alicui de caetero dare terram fuam alicui domui religiofae, ita quod illam refumat tenendum de eadem domo ; nec liceat alicui domui religiofae terram alicujus fic accipere, quod tradat illam ei a quo ipfam recepit tenendam:* *fi quis autem autem de caetero terram fuam domui religiofae fic dederit, et fuper hoc convincatur, donum fuum penitus caffetur, et terra illa domino fuo illius feodi incurratur. Mag. Cart.* 9 *Hen. III. c.* 36.

i 2 Inft. 75.

who,

who, by fraud and collusion, made no defence, and thereby judgment was given for the religious house, which then *recovered* the
land by sentence of law upon a supposed prior title. And thus
they had the honour of inventing those fictitious adjudications of
right, which are since become the great assurance of the kingdom, under the name of *common recoveries*. But upon this the
statute of Westminster the second, 13 Edw. I. c. 32. enacted,
that in such cases a jury shall try the true right of the demand-
ants or plaintiffs to the land, and if the religious house or corporation be found to have it, they shall still recover seisin; otherwise
it shall be forfeited to the immediate lord of the fee, or else to the
next lord, and finally to the king, upon the immediate or other
lord's default. And the like provision was made by the succeeding chapter[k], in case the tenants set up crosses upon their lands
(the badges of knights templars and hospitallers) in order to protect them from the feodal demands of their lords, by virtue of
the privileges of those religious and military orders. And so careful was this provident prince to prevent any future evasions, that
when the statute of *quia emptores*, 18 Edw. I. abolished all sub-
infeudations, and gave liberty for all men to alienate their lands
to be holden of the next immediate lord[l], a proviso was inserted[m]
that this should not extend to authorize any kind of alienation in
mortmain. And when afterwards the method of obtaining the
king's licence by writ of *ad quod damnum* was marked out, by
the statute 27 Edw. I. st. 2. it was farther provided by statute
34 Edw. I. st. 3. that no such licence should be effectual, without the consent of the mesne or intermediate lords.

YET still it was found difficult to set bounds to ecclesiastical
ingenuity: for when they were driven out of all their former
holds, they devised a new method of conveyance, by which the
lands were granted, not to themselves directly, but to nominal
feoffees *to the use of* the religious houses; thus distinguishing between the *possession* and the *use*, and receiving the actual profits,

[k] *cap.* 33.   [m] *cap.* 3.
[l] 2 Inst. 501.

while

while the feifin of the land remained in the nominal feoffee: who was held by the courts of equity (then under the direction of the clergy) to be bound in confcience to account to his *ceftuy que ufe* for the rents and emoluments of the eftate. And it is to thefe inventions that our practifers are indebted for the introduction of ufes and trufts, the foundation of modern conveyancing. But, unfortunately for the inventors themfelves, they did not long en-joy the advantage of their new device, for the ftatute 15 Ric. II. c. 5. enacts, that the lands which had been fo purchafed to ufes fhould be amortifed by licence from the crown, or elfe be fold to private perfons; and that, for the future, ufes fhall be fubject to the ftatutes of mortmain, and forfeitable like the lands them-felves. And whereas the ftatutes had been eluded by purchafing large tracts of land, adjoining to churches, and confecrating them by the name of church-yards, fuch fubtile imagination is alfo de-clared to be within the compafs of the ftatutes of mortmain. And civil or lay corporations, as well as ecclefiaftical, are alfo declared to be within the mifchief, and of courfe within the remedy pro-vided by thofe falutary laws. And, laftly, as during the times of popery lands were frequently given to fuperftitious ufes, though not to any corporate bodies; or were made liable in the hands of heirs and devifees to the charge of obits, chaunteries, and the like, which were equally pernicious in a well-governed ftate as actual alienations in mortmain; therefore, at the dawn of the reformation, the ftatute $\frac{27}{32}$ Hen. VIII. c. 10. declares, that all fu-ture grants of lands for any of the purpofes aforefaid, if granted for any longer term than twenty years, fhall be void.

But, during all this time, it was in the power of the crown, by granting a licence of mortmain, to remit the forfeiture, fo far as related to it's own rights; and to enable any fpiritual or other corporation to purchafe and hold any lands or tenements in per-petuity: which prerogative is declared and confirmed by the fta-tute 18 Edw. III. ft. 3. c. 3. But, as doubts were conceived at the time of the revolution how far fuch licence was valid[n], fince

[n] 2 Hawk. P. C. 391.

the

the king had no power to difpenfe with the ftatutes of mortmain by a claufe of *non obftante*[o], which was the ufual courfe, though it feems to have been unneceffary[p]; and as, by the gradual declenfion of mefne figniories through the long operation of the ftatute of *quia emptores*, the rights of intermediate lords were reduced to a very fmall compafs; it was therefore provided by the ftatute 7 & 8 W. III. c. 37. that the crown for the future at it's own difcretion may grant licences to aliene or take in mortmain, of whomfoever the tenements may be holden.

After the diffolution of monafteries under Henry VIII, though the policy of the next popifh fucceffor affected to grant a fecurity to the poffeffors of abbey lands, yet, in order to regain fo much of them as either the zeal or timidity of their owners might induce them to part with, the ftatutes of mortmain were fufpended for twenty years by the ftatute 1 & 2 P. & M. c. 8. and, during that time, any lands or tenements were allowed to be granted to any fpiritual corporation without any licence whatfoever. And, long afterwards, for a much better purpofe, the augmentation of poor livings, it was enacted by the ftatute 17 Car. II. c. 3. that appropriators may annex the great tithes to the vicarages; and that all benefices under 100 *l. per annum* may be augmented by the purchafe of lands, without licence of mortmain in either cafe: and the like provifion hath been fince made, in favour of the governors of queen Anne's bounty[q]. It hath alfo been held[r], that the ftatute 23 Hen. VIII. before-mentioned did not extend to any thing but *fuperftitious* ufes; and that therefore a man may give lands for the maintenance of a fchool, an hofpital, or any other *charitable* ufes. But as it was apprehended from recent experience, that perfons on their deathbeds might make large and improvident difpofitions even for thefe good purpofes, and defeat the political ends of the ftatutes of mortmain; it is therefore enacted by the ftatute 9 Geo. II. c. 36. that no lands or tenements, or money to be laid out thereon,

[o] Stat. 1. W. & M. ft. 2. c. 2.　　　[q] Stat. 2 & 3 Ann. c. 11.
[p] Co. Litt. 99.　　　[r] 1 Rep. 24.

fhall be given for or charged with any *charitable* ufes whatfoever, unlefs by deed indented, executed in the prefence of two wit-neffes twelve calendar months before the death of the donor, and enrolled in the court of chancery within fix months after it's exe-cution, (except ftocks in the public funds, which may be trans-ferred within fix months previous to the donor's death) and un-lefs fuch gift be made to take effect immediately, and be with-out power of revocation : and that all other gifts fhall be void. The two univerfities, their colleges, and the fcholars upon the foundation of the colleges of Eaton, Winchefter, and Weftmin-fter, are excepted out of this act : but fuch exemption was grant-ed with this provifo, that no college fhall be at liberty to purchafe more advowfons, than are equal in number to one moiety of the fellows or ftudents, upon the refpective foundations.

2. SECONDLY, alienation *to an alien* is alfo a caufe of for-feiture to the crown of the lands fo alienated, not only on ac-count of his incapacity to hold them, which occafions him to be paffed by in defcents of land[s], but likewife on account of his prefumption in attempting, by an act of his own, to acquire any real property ; as was obferved in the preceding volume[t].

3. LASTLY, alienations *by particular tenants*, when they are greater than the law entitles them to make, and deveft the re-mainder or reverfion[v], are alfo forfeitures to him whofe right is attacked thereby. As, if tenant for his own life alienes by feoff-ment or fine for the life of another, or in tail, or in fee ; thefe being eftates, which either muft or may laft longer than his own, the creating them is not only beyond his power, and inconfiftent with the nature of his intereft, but is alfo a forfeiture of his own particular eftate to him in remainder or reverfion[u]. For which there feem to be two reafons. Firft, becaufe fuch alienation amounts to a renuntiation of the feodal connexion and dependence ; it im-plies a refufal to perform the due renders and fervices to the lord

[s] See pag. 249, 250.
[t] Book I. ch. 10.

[v] Co. Litt. 251.
[u] Litt. §. 415.

of

of the fee, of which fealty is conftantly one; and it tends in it's confequences to defeat and deveft the remainder or reverfion expectant: as therefore that is put in jeopardy, by fuch act of the particular tenant, it is but juft that, upon difcovery, the particular eftate fhould be forfeited and taken from him, who has fhewn fo manifeft an inclination to make an improper ufe of it. The other reafon is, becaufe the particular tenant, by granting a larger eftate than his own, has by his own act determined and put an entire end to his own original intereft; and on fuch determination the next taker is intitled to enter regularly, as in his remainder or reverfion. The fame law, which is thus laid down with regard to tenants for life, holds alfo with refpect to all tenants of the mere freehold, or of chattel interefts; but if tenant in tail alienes in fee, this is no immediate forfeiture to the remainder-man, but a mere *difcontinuance* (as it is called [w]) of the eftate-tail, which the iffue may afterwards avoid by due courfe of law [x]: for he in remainder or reverfion hath only a very remote and barely poffible intereft therein, until the iffue in tail is extinct. But, in cafe of fuch forfeitures by particular tenants, all legal eftates by them before created, as if tenant for twenty years grants a leafe for fifteen, and all charges by him lawfully made on the lands, fhall be good and available in law [y]. For the law will not hurt an innocent leffee for the fault of his leffor; nor permit the leffor, after he has granted a good and lawful eftate, by his own act to avoid it, and defeat the intereft which he himfelf has created.

EQUIVALENT, both in it's nature and it's confequences, to an illegal alienation by the particular tenant, is the civil crime of *difclaimer*; as where a tenant, who holds of any lord, neglects to render him the due fervices, and, upon an action brought to recover them, difclaims to hold of his lord. Which difclaimer of tenure in any court of record is a forfeiture of the lands to the lord [z], upon reafons moft apparently feodal. And fo likewife, if

[w] See Book III.
[x] Litt. §. 595, 6, 7.
[y] Co. Litt. 233.
[z] Finch. 270, 271.

in any court of record the particular tenant does any act which amounts to a virtual difclaimer; if he claims any greater eftate than was granted him at the firft infeodation, or takes upon himfelf thofe rights which belong only to tenants of a fuperior clafs[a]; if he affirms the reverfion to be in a ftranger, by accepting his fine, attorning as his tenant, collufive pleading, and the like[b]; fuch behaviour amounts to a forfeiture of his particular eftate.

III. L A P S E is a fpecies of forfeiture, whereby the right of prefentation to a church accrues to the ordinary by neglect of the patron to prefent, to the metropolitan by neglect of the ordinary, and to the king by neglect of the metropolitan. For it being for the intereft of religion, and the good of the public, that the church fhould be provided with an officiating minifter, the law has therefore given this right of lapfe, in order to quicken the patron; who might otherwife, by fuffering the church to remain vacant, avoid paying his ecclefiaftical dues, and fruftrate the pious intentions of his anceftors. This right of lapfe was firft eftablifhed about the time (though not by the authority[c]) of the council of Lateran[d], which was in the reign of our Henry the fecond, when the bifhops firft began to exercife univerfally the right of inftitution to churches[e]. And therefore, where there is no right of inftitution, there is no right of lapfe: fo that no donative can lapfe to the ordinary[f], unlefs it hath been augmented by the queen's bounty[g]. But no right of lapfe can accrue, when the original prefentation is in the crown[h].

T H E term, in which the title to prefent by lapfe accrues from the one to the other fucceffively, is fix calendar months[i]; (following in this cafe the computation of the church, and not the ufual one of the common law) and this exclufive of the day of

[a] Co. Litt. 152.
[b] *Ibid.* 153.
[c] 2 Roll. Abr. 336. pl. 10.
[d] Bracton. *l.* 4. *tr.* 2. *c.* 3.
[e] See pag. 23.

[f] Bro. *Abr. tit. Quar. Imped.* 131. Cro. Jac. 518.
[g] Stat. 1 Geo. I. ft. 2. c. 10.
[h] Stat. 17 Edw. II. c. 8. 2 Inft. 273.
[i] 6 Rep. 62. Regiftr. 42.

the

the avoidance [k]. But, if the bifhop be both patron and ordinary, he fhall not have a double time allowed him to collate in [l]; for the forfeiture accrues by law, whenever the negligence has continued fix months in the fame perfon. And alfo, if the bifhop doth not collate his own clerk immediately to the living, and the patron prefents, though after the fix months are lapfed, yet his prefentation is good, and the bifhop is bound to inftitute the patron's clerk [m]. For as the law only gives the bifhop this title by lapfe, to punifh the patron's negligence, there is no reafon that, if the bifhop himfelf be guilty of equal or greater negligence, the patron fhould be deprived of his turn. If the bifhop fuffer the prefentation to lapfe to the metropolitan, the patron alfo has the fame advantage if he prefents before the arch-bifhop has filled up the benefice; and that for the fame reafon. Yet the ordinary cannot, after lapfe to the metropolitan, collate his own clerk to the prejudice of the arch-bifhop [n]. For he had no permanent right and intereft in the advowfon, as the patron hath, but merely a temporary one; which having neglected to make ufe of during the time, he cannot afterwards retrieve it. But if the prefentation lapfes to the king, prerogative here intervenes and makes a difference; and the patron fhall never recover his right, till the king has fatisfied his turn by prefentation : for *nullum tempus occurrit regi* [o]. And therefore it may feem, as if the church might continue void for ever, unlefs the king fhall be pleafed to prefent; and a patron thereby be abfolutely defeated of his advowfon. But to prevent this inconvenience, the law has lodged a power in the patron's hands, of as it were compelling the king to prefent. For if, during the delay of the crown, the patron himfelf prefents, and his clerk is inftituted, the king indeed by prefenting another may turn out the patron's clerk; but if he does not, and the patron's clerk dies incumbent, or is canonically deprived, the king hath loft his right, which was only to the next or firft prefentation [p].

[k] 2 Inft. 361.
[l] Gibf. Cod. 769.
[m] 2 Inft. 273.

[n] 2 Roll. Abr. 368.
[o] Dr & St. d. 2. c. 36.   Cro. Car. 355.
[p] 7 Rep. 28.   Cro. Eliz. 44.

IN

I N cafe the benefice becomes void by death, or ceffion through plurality of benefices, there the patron is bound to take notice of the vacancy at his own peril; for thefe are matters of equal notoriety to the patron and ordinary : but in cafe of a vacancy by refignation, or canonical deprivation, or if a clerk prefented be refufed for infufficiency, thefe being matters of which the bifhop alone is prefumed to be cognizant, here the law requires him to give notice thereof to the patron, otherwife he can take no advantage by way of lapfe[q]. Neither fhall any lapfe thereby accrue to the metropolitan or to the king; for it is univerfally true, that neither the arch-bifhop or the king fhall ever prefent by lapfe, but where the immediate ordinary might have collated by lapfe, within the fix months, and hath exceeded his time : for the firft ftep or beginning faileth, *et quod non habet principium, non habet finem*[r]. If the bifhop refufe or negleⅭt to examine and admit the patron's clerk, without good reafon affigned or notice given, he is ftiled a difturber by the law, and fhall not have any title to prefent by lapfe; for no man fhall take advantage of his own wrong[s]. Alfo if the right of prefentation be litigious or contefted, and an aⅭtion be brought againft the bifhop to try the title, no lapfe fhall incur till the queftion of right be decided[t].

IV. B Y *fimony*, the right of prefentation to a living is forfeited, and vefted *pro hac vice* in the crown. Simony is the corrupt prefentation of any one to an ecclefiaftical benefice for money, gift, or reward. It is fo called from the refemblance it is faid to bear to the fin of Simon Magus, though the purchafing of holy orders feems to approach nearer to his offence. It was by the canon law a very grievous crime : and is fo much the more odious, becaufe, as fir Edward Coke obferves[u], it is ever accompanied with perjury; for the prefentee is fworn to have committed no fimony. However it is not an offence punifhable in a cri-

[q] 4 Rep. 75. 2 Inft. 632.
[r] Co. Litt. 344, 345.
[s] 2 Roll. Abr. 369.
[t] Co. Litt. 344.
[u] 3 Inft. 156.

minal

minal way at the common law [w]; it being thought fufficient to leave the clerk to ecclefiaftical cenfures. But as thefe did not affect the fimoniacal patron, nor were efficacious enough to repel the notorious practice of the thing, divers acts of parliament have been made to reftrain it by means of civil forfeitures; which the modern prevailing ufage, with regard to fpiritual preferments, calls aloud to be put in execution. I fhall briefly confider them in this place, becaufe they diveft the corrupt patron of the right of prefentation, and veft a new right in the crown.

By the ftatute 31 Eliz. c. 6. it is for avoiding of fimony enacted, that if any patron for any corrupt confideration, by gift or promife, directly or indirectly, fhall prefent or collate any perfon to an ecclefiaftical benefice or dignity; fuch prefentation fhall be void, and the prefentee be rendered incapable of ever enjoying the fame benefice: and the crown fhall prefent to it for that turn only [x]. Alfo by the ftatute 12 Ann. ftat. 2. c. 12. if any perfon for money or profit fhall procure, in his own name or the name of any other, the next prefentation to any living ecclefiaftical, and fhall be prefented thereupon, this is declared to be a fimoniacal contract; and the party is fubjected to all the ecclefiaftical penalties of fimony, is difabled from holding the benefice, and the prefentation devolves to the crown.

Upon thefe ftatutes many queftions have arifen, with regard to what is, and what is not fimony. And, among others, thefe points feem to be clearly fettled : 1. That to purchafe a prefentation, the living being actually vacant, is open and notorious fimony [y]; this being expreffly in the face of the ftatute. 2. That for a clerk to bargain for the next prefentation, the incumbent being fick and about to die, was fimony, even before the ftatute of queen Anne [z]: and now, by that ftatute, to purchafe, either in his own name or another's, the next prefentation, and be

---

[w] Moor. 564.
[x] For other penalties inflicted by this ftatute, fee Book IV.

[y] Cro. Eliz. 788. Moor. 914.
[z] Hob. 165.

thereupon prefented at any future time to the living, is direct
and palpable fimony. But, 3. It is held that for a father to purchafe fuch a prefentation, in order to provide for his fon, is not
fimony : for the fon is not concerned in the bargain, and the father is by nature bound to make a provifion for him[a]. 4. That
if a fimoniacal contract be made with the patron, the clerk not
being privy thereto, the prefentation for that turn fhall indeed
devolve to the crown, as a punifhment of the guilty patron; but
the clerk, who is innocent, does not incur any difability or forfeiture[b]. 5. That bonds given to pay money to charitable ufes,
on receiving a prefentation to a living, are not fimoniacal[c], provided the patron or his relations be not benefited thereby[d]; for
this is no corrupt confideration, moving to the patron. 6. That
bonds of refignation, in cafe of non-refidence or taking any other
living, are not fimoniacal[e]; there being no corrupt confideration
herein, but fuch only as is for the good of the public. So alfo
bonds to refign, when the patron's fon comes to canonical age,
are legal; upon the reafon before given, that the father is bound
to provide for his fon[f]. 7. Laftly, general bonds to refign at the
patron's requeft are held to be legal[g] : for they may poffibly be
given for one of the legal confiderations before-mentioned; and
where there is a poffibility that a tranfaction may be fair, the
law will not fuppofe it iniquitous without proof. But, if the
party can prove the contract to have been a corrupt one, fuch
proof will be admitted, in order to fhew the bond fimoniacal,
and therefore void. Neither will the patron be fuffered to make
an ill ufe of fuch a general bond of refignation; as by extorting
a compofition for tithes, procuring an annuity for his relation,
or by demanding a refignation wantonly and without good caufe,
fuch as is approved by the law; as, for the benefit of his own
fon, or on account of non-refidence, plurality of livings, or grofs
immorality in the incumbent[h].

[a] Cro Eliz. 686. Moor. 916.
[b] 3 Inft. 154. Cro. Jac. 385.
[c] Noy 142.
[d] Stra. 534.
[e] Cro. Car. 180.

[f] Cro. Jac. 248. 274
[g] Cro. Car. 180. Stra. 227.
[h] 1 Vern. 411. 1 Equ. Caf. abr. 86, 87.
Stra. 534.

V. THE

V. THE next kind of forfeitures are thofe by *breach* or non-performance of a *condition* annexed to the eftate, either expreffly by deed at it's original creation, or impliedly by law from a principle of natural reafon. Both which we confidered at large in a former chapter [i].

VI. I THEREFORE now proceed to another fpecies of forfeiture, viz. by *wafte*. Wafte, *vaftum*, is a fpoil or deftruction in houfes, gardens, trees, or other corporeal hereditaments, to the difherifon of him that hath the remainder or reverfion in fee-fimple or fee-tail [k].

WASTE is either *voluntary*, which is a crime of commiffion, as by pulling down a houfe; or it is *permiffive*, which is a matter of omiffion only, as by fuffering it to fall for want of neceffary reparations. Whatever does a lafting damage to the freehold or inheritance is wafte [l]. Therefore removing wainfcot, floors, or other things once fixed to the freehold of a houfe, is wafte [m]. If a houfe be deftroyed by tempeft, lightening, or the like, which is the act of providence, it is no wafte: but otherwife, if the houfe be burnt by the careleffnefs or negligence of the leffee; though now by the ftatute 6 Ann. c. 3. no action will lie againft a tenant for an accident of this kind, left misfortune be added to misfortune. Wafte may alfo be committed in ponds, dove-houfes, warrens, and the like; by fo reducing the number of the creatures therein, that there will not be fufficient for the reverfioner when he comes to the inheritance [n]. Timber alfo is part of the inheritance [o]. Such are oak, afh, and elm in all places: and in fome particular countries, by local cuftom, where other trees are generally ufed for building, they are thereupon confidered as timber; and to cut down fuch trees, or top them, or do any other act whereby the timber may decay, is wafte [p]. But underwood

[i] See chap. 10. pag. 152.
[k] Co. Litt. 53.
[l] Hetl. 35.
[m] 4 Rep. 64.
[n] Co. Litt. 53.
[o] 4 Rep. 62.
[p] Co. Litt. 53.

the tenant may cut down at any feafonable time that he pleafes[q]; and may take fufficient eftovers of common right for houfe-bote and cart-bote; unlefs reftrained (which is ufual) by particular covenants or exceptions[r]. The converfion of land from one fpecies to another is wafte. To convert wood, meadow, or pafture, into arable; to turn arable, meadow, or pafture into woodland; or to turn arable or woodland into meadow or pafture; are all of them wafte[s]. For, as fir Edward Coke obferves[t], it not only changes the courfe of hufbandry, but the evidence of the eftate; when fuch a clofe, which is conveyed and defcribed as pafture, is found to be arable, and *e converfo*. And the fame rule is obferved, for the fame reafon, with regard to converting one fpecies of edifice into another, even though it is improved in it's value[u]. To open the land to fearch for mines of metal, coal, &c, is wafte; for that is a detriment to the inheritance[w]: but, if the pits or mines were open before, it is no wafte for the tenant to continue digging them for his own ufe[x]; for it is now become the mere annual profit of the land. Thefe three are the general heads of wafte, viz. in houfes, in timber, and in land. Though, as was before faid, whatever tends to the deftruction, or depreciating the value, of the inheritance, is confidered by the law as wafte.

L E T us next fee, who are liable to be punifhed for committing wafte. And by the feodal law, feuds being originally granted for life only, we find that the rule was general for all vafals or feudatories; "*fi vafallus feudum diffipaverit, aut infigni detrimento* "*deterius fecerit, privabitur*[y]." But in our antient common law the rule was by no means fo large; for not only he that was feifed of an eftate of inheritance might do as he pleafed with it, but alfo wafte was not punifhable in any tenant, fave only in three perfons; guardian in chivalry, tenant in dower, and tenant by

[q] 2 Roll. Abr. 817.
[r] Co. Litt. 41.
[s] Hob. 296.
[t] 1 Inft. 53.

[u] 1 Lev. 309.
[w] 5 Rep. 12.
[x] Hob. 295.
[y] Wright. 44.

the

the curtefy[z]; and not in tenant for life or years[a]. And the reafon of the diverfity was, that the eftate of the three former was
created by the act of the law itfelf, which therefore gave a remedy againft them : but tenant for life, or for years, came in
by the demife and leafe of the owner of the fee, and therefore
he might have provided againft the committing of wafte by his
leffee ; and if he did not, it was his own default. But, in favour
of the owners of the inheritance, the ftatutes of Marlbridge[b] and
Glocefter[c] provided, that the writ of wafte fhall not only lie
againft tenants by the law of England, (or curtefy) and thofe in
dower, but againft any farmer or other that holds in any manner for
life or years. So that, for above five hundred years paft, all tenants
for life or for any lefs eftate, have been punifhable or liable to be
impeached for wafte, both voluntary and permiffive ; unlefs their
leafes be made, as fometimes they are, without impeachment of
wafte, *abfque impetitione vafti*; that is, with a provifion or protection
that no man fhall *impetere*, or fue him, for wafte committed.

THE punifhment for wafte committed was, by common law and
the ftatute of Marlbridge, only fingle damages[d]; except in the cafe
of a guardian, who alfo forfeited his wardfhip[e] by the provifions
of the great charter[f]: but the ftatute of Glocefter directs, that the
other four fpecies of tenants fhall lofe and forfeit the place wherein
the wafte is committed, and alfo treble damages, to him that
hath the inheritance. The expreffion of the ftatute is, " he fhall
" forfeit the *thing* which he hath wafted ;" and it hath been determined, that under thefe words the *place* is alfo included[g].
And if wafte be done *fparfim*, or here and there, all over a wood,
the whole wood fhall be recovered ; or if in feveral rooms of a
houfe, the whole houfe fhall be forfeited[h] ; becaufe it is impracticable for the reverfioner to enjoy only the identical places wafted,

---

[z] It was however a doubt whether wafte
was punifhable at the common law in tenant by the curtefy. Regift. 72. Bro. Abr.
tit. *wafte*. 88. 2 Inft. 301.

[a] 2 Inft. 299.

[b] 52 Hen. III. c. 24.

[c] 6 Edw. I. c. 5.

[d] 2 Inft. 146.

[e] *Ibid.* 300.

[f] 9 Hen. III. c. 4.

[g] 2 Inft. 303.

[h] Co. Litt. 51.

when

when lying interfperfed with the other. But if wafte be done only in one end of a wood (or perhaps in one room of a houfe) if that can be conveniently feparated from the reft, that part only is the *locus vaftatus*, or thing wafted, and that only fhall be forfeited to the reverfioner[i].

VII. A SEVENTH fpecies of forfeiture is that of *copyhold* eftates, by *breach* of the *cuftoms* of the manor. Copyhold eftates are not only liable to the fame forfeitures as thofe which are held in focage, for treafon, felony, alienation, and wafte; whereupon the lord may feife them without any prefentment by the homage[k]; but alfo to peculiar forfeitures, annexed to this fpecies of tenure, which are incurred by the breach of either the general cuftoms of all copyholds, or the peculiar local cuftoms of certain particular manors. And we may obferve that, as thefe tenements were originally holden by the loweft and moft abject vafals, the marks of feodal dominion continue much the ftrongeft upon this mode of property. Moft of the offences, which occafioned a refumption of the fief by the feodal law, and were denominated *feloniae, per quas vafallus amitteret feudum*[l], ftill continue to be caufes of forfeiture in many of our modern copyholds. As, by fubtraction of fuit and fervice[m]; *fi dominum deservire noluerit*[n]: by difclaiming to hold of the lord, or fwearing himfelf not his copyholder[o]; *fi dominum ejuravit, i. e. negavit fe a domino feudum habere*[p]: by neglect to be admitted tenant within a year and a day[q]; *fi per annum et diem ceffaverit in petenda inveftitura*[r]: by contumacy in not appearing in court after three proclamations[s]; *fi a domino ter citatus non comparuerit*[t]: or by refufing, when fworn of the homage, to prefent the truth according to his oath[u]; *fi pares veritatem noverint, et dicant fe nefcire, cum fciant*[w]. In

i 2 Inft. 304.
k 2 Ventr. 38. Cro. Eliz. 499.
l *Feud. l. 2. t. 26. in calc.*
m 3 Leon. 108. Dyer. 211.
n *Feud. l. 1. t. 21.*
o Co. Copyh. §. 57.
p *Feud. l. 2. t. 34. & t. 26. §. 3.*

q Plowd. 372.
r *Feud. l. 2. t. 24.*
s 8 Rep. 99. Co. Copyh. §. 57.
t *Feud. l. 2. t. 22.*
u Co. Copyh. §. 57.
w *Feud. l. 2. t. 58.*

thefe,

thefe, and a variety of other cafes, which it is impoffible here to enumerate, the forfeiture does not accrue to the lord till after the offences are prefented by the homage, or jury of the lord's court baron [x]; *per laudamentum parium fuorum* [y] : or, as it is more fully expreffed in another place [z], *nemo miles adimatur de poffeffione fui beneficii, nifi convicta culpa, quae fit laudanda* [a] *per judicium parium fuorum.*

VIII. THE eighth and laft method, whereby lands and tenements may become forfeited, is that of *bankruptcy*, or the act of becoming a bankrupt : which unfortunate perfon may, from the feveral defcriptions given of him in our ftatute law, be thus defined ; a trader, who fecretes himfelf, or does certain other acts, tending to defraud his creditors.

WHO fhall be fuch a trader, or what acts are fufficient to denominate him a bankrupt, with the feveral connected confequences refulting from that unhappy fituation, will be better confidered in a fubfequent chapter ; when we fhall endeavour more fully to explain it's nature, as it moft immediately relates to perfonal goods and chattels. I fhall only here obferve the manner in which the property of lands and tenements are transferred, upon the fuppofition that the owner of them is clearly and indifputably a bankrupt, and that a commiffion of bankrupt is awarded and iffued againft him.

BY the ftatute 13 Eliz. c.7. the commiffioners for that purpofe, when a man is declared a bankrupt, fhall have full power to difpofe of all his lands and tenements, which he had in his own right at the time when he became a bankrupt, or which fhall defcend or come to him at any time afterwards, before his debts are fatisfied or agreed for ; and all lands and tenements which were purchafed by him jointly with his wife or children to his own

[x] Co. Copyh. §. 58.
[y] *Feud. l. 1. t. 21.*
[z] *Ibid. t. 22.*

[a] *i. e. arbitranda, definienda.* Du Frefne. IV. 79.

ufe,

ufe, (or fuch intereft therein as he may lawfully part with) or purchafed with any other perfon upon fecret truft for his own ufe ; and to caufe them to be appraifed to their full value, and to fell the fame by deed indented and inrolled, or divide them proportionably among the creditors. The ftatute expreffly includes not only free, but copyhold, lands : but did not extend to eftates-tail, farther than for the bankrupt's life ; nor to equities of redemption on a mortgaged eftate, wherein the bankrupt has no legal intereft, but only an equitable reverfion. Whereupon the ftatute 21 Jac. I. c. 19. enacts, that the commiffioners fhall be impowered to fell or convey, by deed indented and inrolled, any lands or tenements of the bankrupt, wherein he fhall be feifed of an eftate-tail in poffeffion, remainder, or reverfion, unlefs the remainder or reverfion thereof fhall be in the crown ; and that fuch fale fhall be good againft all fuch iffues in tail, remainder-men, and reverfioners, whom the bankrupt himfelf might have barred by a common recovery, or other means : and that all equities of redemption upon mortgaged eftates, fhall be at the difpofal of the commiffioners ; for they fhall have power to redeem the fame, as the bankrupt himfelf might have done, and after redemption to fell them. And alfo, by this and a former act[b], all fraudulent conveyances to defeat the intent of thefe ftatutes are declared void ; but that no purchafer *bona fide*, for a good or valuable confideration, fhall be affected by the bankrupt laws, unlefs the commiffion be fued forth within five years after the act of bankruptcy committed.

By virtue of thefe ftatutes a bankrupt may lofe all his real eftates ; which may at once be transferred by his commiffioners to their affignees, without his participation or confent.

[b] 1 Jac. I. c. 15.

CHAPTER THE NINETEENTH.

OF TITLE BY ALIENATION.

THE moſt uſual and univerſal method of acquiring a title to real eſtates is that of alienation, conveyance, or pur-chaſe in it's limited ſenſe : under which may be comprized any method wherein eſtates are voluntarily reſigned by one man, and accepted by another ; whether that be effected by ſale, gift, mar-riage ſettlement, deviſe, or other tranſmiſſion of property by the mutual conſent of the parties.

THIS means of taking eſtates, by alienation, is not of equal antiquity in the law of England with that of taking them by deſcent. For we may remember that, by the feodal law[a], a pure and genuine feud could not be transferred from one feudatory to another without the conſent of the lord ; leſt thereby a feeble or ſuſpicious tenant might have been ſubſtituted and impoſed upon him, to perform the feodal ſervices, inſtead of one on whoſe abi-lities and fidelity he could depend. Neither could the feudatory then ſubject the land to his debts ; for, if he might, the feodal reſtraint of alienation would have been eaſily fruſtrated and eva-ded[b]. And, as he could not aliene it in his lifetime, ſo neither could he by will defeat the ſucceſſion, by deviſing his feud to an-other family ; nor even alter the courſe of it, by impoſing parti-cular limitations, or preſcribing an unuſual path of deſcent. Nor, in ſhort, could he aliene the eſtate, even with the conſent of the lord, unleſs he had alſo obtained the conſent of his own next ap-parent, or preſumptive, heir[c]. And therefore it was very uſual in antient feoffments to expreſs, that the alienation was made by con-

---

[a] See pag. 57.   [c] Co. Litt. 94. Wright. 168.
[b] *Feud. l. 1. t. 27.*

fent of the heirs of the feoffor; or fometimes for the heir apparent himfelf to join with the feoffor in the grant[d]. And, on the other hand, as the feodal obligation was looked upon to be reciprocal, the lord could not aliene or transfer his figniory without the confent of his vafal: for it was efteemed unreafonable to fubjeƈ a feudatory to a new fuperior, with whom he might have a deadly enmity, without his own approbation; or even to transfer his fealty, without his being thoroughly apprized of it, that he might know with certainty to whom his renders and fervices were due, and be able to diftinguifh a lawful diftrefs for rent from a hoftile feifing of his cattle by the lord of a neighbouring clan[e]. This confent of the vafal was expreffed by what was called *attorning*[f], or profeffing to become the tenant of the new lord; which doƈtrine of attornment was afterwards extended to all leffees for life or years. For if one bought an eftate with any leafe for life or years ftanding out thereon, and the leffee or tenant refufed to attorn to the purchafor, and to become his tenant, the grant or contraƈt was in moft cafes void, or at leaft incomplete[g]: which was alfo an additional clog upon alienations.

But by degrees this feodal feverity is worn off; and experience hath fhewn, that property beft anfwers the purpofes of civil life, efpecially in commercial countries, when it's transfer and circulation are totally free and unreftrained. The road was cleared in the firft place by a law of king Henry the firft, which allowed a man to fell and difpofe of lands which he himfelf had purchafed; for over thefe he was thought to have a more extenfive power, than over what had been tranfmitted to him in a courfe of defcent from his anceftors[h]: a doƈtrine, which is coun-

[d] Madox, *Formul. Angl.* n°. 316.319.427.
[e] Gilb. Ten. 75.
[f] The fame doƈtrine and the fame denomination prevailed in Bretagne. —— *poffef-fiones in jurifdiƈionalibus non aliter apprehendi poffe, quam per attournances et avirances, ut loqui folent; cum vafallus, ejurato prioris domini obfequio et fide, novo fe facramento novo*

item domino acquirenti obftringebat; idque juffu auƈoris. D'Argentre *Antiq. Confuet. Brit.* apud Dufrefne. i. 819, 820.
[g] Litt. §. 551.
[h] *Emptiones vel acquifitiones fuas det cui magis velit. Terram autem quam ei parentes dederunt, non mittat extra cognationem fuam.* LL. Hen. I. c. 70.

tenanced

tenanced by the feodal conftitutions themfelves[j]: but he was not allowed to fell the whole of his own acquirements, fo as totally to difinherit his children, any more than he was at liberty to aliene his paternal eftate[i]. Afterwards a man feems to have been at liberty to part with all his own acquifitions, if he had previoufly purchafed to him and his *affigns* by name ; but, if his *affigns* were not fpecified in the purchafe deed, he was not empowered to aliene[k] : and alfo he might part with one fourth of the inheritance of his anceftors without the confent of his heir[l]. By the great charter of Henry III[m], no fubinfeudation was permitted of part of the land, unlefs fufficient was left to anfwer the fervices due to the fuperior lord, which fufficiency was probably interpreted to be one half or moiety of the land[n]. But thefe reftrictions were in general removed by the ftatute of *quia emptores*[o], whereby all perfons, except the king's tenants *in capite*, were left at liberty to aliene all or any part of their lands at their own difcretion[p]. And even thefe tenants *in capite* were by the ftatute 1 Edw. III. c. 12. permitted to aliene, on paying a fine to the king[q]. By the temporary ftatutes 11 Hen. VII. c. 3. and 3 Hen.VIII. c.4. all perfons attending the king in his wars were allowed to aliene their lands without licence, and were relieved from other feodal burdens. And, laftly, thefe very fines for alienations were, in all cafes of freehold tenure, entirely abolifhed by the ftatute 12 Car. II. c. 24. As to the power of *charging* lands with the debts of the owner, this was introduced fo early as ftatute Weftm. 2. which[r] fubjected a *moiety* of the tenant's lands to executions, for debts recovered by law ; as the *whole* of them was likewife fubjected to be pawned in a ftatute merchant by the ftatute *de mercatoribus*, made the fame year, and in a ftatute ftaple by ftatute 27 Edw. III. c. 9. and in other fimilar recognizances

[j] *Feud. l. 2. t. 39.*

[i] *Si queftum tantum habuerit is, qui partem terrae fuae donare voluerit, tunc quidem hoc ei licet; fed non totum queftum, quia non poteft filium fuum baeredem exbaeredare.* Glanv. *l. 7. c. 1.*

[k] Mirr. c. 1. §. 3. This is alfo borrowed from the feodal law. *Feud. l. 2. t. 48.*

[l] Mirr. *ibid.*

[m] 9 Hen. III. c. 32.

[n] Dalrymple of feuds. 95.

[o] 18 Edw. I. c. 1.

[p] See pag. 72.

[q] 2 Inft. 67.

[r] 13 Edw. I. c. 18.

by ftatute 23 Hen. VIII. c. 6. And, now, the whole of them is not only fubject to be *pawned* for the debts of the owner, but likewife to be abfolutely *fold* for the benefit of trade and commerce by the feveral ftatutes of bankruptcy. The reftraint of *devifing* lands by will, except in fome places by particular cuftom, lafted longer; that not being totally removed, till the abolition of the military tenures. The doctrine of *attornments* continued ftill later than any of the reft, and became extremely troublefome, though many methods were invented to evade them; till, at laft, they were made no longer neceffary, by ftatutes 4 & 5 Ann. c. 16. and 11 Geo. II. c. 19.

IN examining the nature of alienation, let us firft enquire, briefly, *who* may aliene and to *whom*; and then, more largely, *how* a man may aliene, or the feveral modes of conveyance.

I. WHO may aliene, and to whom; or, in other words, who is capable of conveying and who of purchafing. And herein we muft confider rather the incapacity, than capacity, of the feveral parties: for all perfons in *poffeffion* are, *prima facie*, capable both of conveying and purchafing, unlefs the law has laid them under any particular difabilites. But, if a man has only in him the *right* of either poffeffion or property, he cannot convey it to any other, left pretended titles might be granted to great men, whereby juftice might be trodden down, and the weak oppreffed'. Yet reverfions and vefted remainders may be granted; becaufe the poffeffion of the particular tenant is the poffeffion of him in reverfion or remainder: but *contingencies*, and mere *poffibilities*, though they may be releafed, or devifed by will, or may pafs to the heir or executor, yet cannot (it hath been faid) be affigned to a ftranger, unlefs coupled with fome prefent intereft ͬ.

PERSONS attainted of treafon, felony, and *praemunire*, are incapable of conveying, from the time of the offence committed,

---

' Co. Litt. 214.   ͬ Sheppard's touchftone. 238, 239, 322.
                                11 Mod. 152. 1 P. Wᵐ. 574. Stra. 132.

provided

provided attainder follows[t]: for such conveyance by them may tend to defeat the king of his forfeiture, or the lord of his escheat. But they may *purchase* for the benefit of the crown, or the lord of the fee, though they are disabled to *hold :* the lands so purchased, if after attainder, being subject to immediate forfeiture ; if before, to escheat as well as forfeiture, according to the nature of the crime [u]. So also corporations, religious or others, may purchase lands ; yet, unless they have a licence to hold in mortmain, they cannot retain such purchase ; but it shall be forfeited to the lord of the fee.

IDIOTS and persons of nonsane memory, infants, and persons under duress, are not totally disabled either to convey or purchase, but *sub modo* only. For their conveyances and purchases are voidable, but not actually void. The king indeed, on behalf of an idiot, may avoid his grants or other acts [w]. But it hath been said, that a *non compos* himself, though he be afterwards brought to a right mind, shall not be permitted to allege his own insanity in order to avoid such grant : for that no man shall be allowed to stultify himself, or plead his own disability. The progress of this notion is somewhat curious. In the time of Edward I, *non compos* was a sufficient plea to avoid a man's own bond [x]: and there is a writ in the register [y] for the alienor himself to recover lands aliened by him during his insanity ; *dum fuit non compos mentis suae, ut dicit, &c.* But under Edward III a scruple began to arise, whether a man should be permitted to *blemish* himself, by pleading his own insanity [z]: and, afterwards, a defendant in assise having pleaded a release by the plaintiff since the last continuance, to which the plaintiff replied (*ore tenus,* as the manner then was) that he was out of his mind when he gave it, the court adjourned the assise ; doubting, whether as the plaintiff was sane both then and at the commencement of the suit, he should be permitted to plead an intermediate deprivation of reason ; and the question

[t] Co. Litt. 42.
[u] *Ibid.* 2.
[w] *Ibid.* 247.

[x] Britton, *c.* 28. *fol.* 66.
[y] *fol.* 228.
[z] 5 *Edw. III.* 70.

　　　　　　　　　　　　　　　was

was aſked, how he came to remember the releaſe, if out of his ſenſes when he gave it [a]. Under Henry VI this way of reaſoning (that a man ſhall not be allowed to diſable himſelf, by pleading his own incapacity, becauſe he cannot know what he did under ſuch a ſituation) was ſeriouſly adopted by the judges in argument [b]; upon a queſtion, whether the heir was barred of his right of entry by the feoffment of his inſane anceſtor. And from theſe looſe authorities, which Fitzherbert does not ſcruple to reject as being contrary to reaſon [c], the maxim that a man ſhall not ſtultify himſelf hath been handed down as ſettled law [d]: though later opinions, feeling the inconvenience of the rule, have in many points endeavoured to reſtrain it [e]. And, clearly, the next heir, or other perſon intereſted, may, after the death of the idiot or *non compos*, take advantage of his incapacity and avoid the grant [f]. And ſo too, if he purchaſes under this diſability, and does not afterwards upon recovering his ſenſes agree to the purchaſe, his heir may either waive or accept the eſtate at his option [g]. In like manner, an infant may waive ſuch purchaſe or conveyance, when he comes to full age; or, if he does not then actually agree to it, his heirs may waive it after him [h]. Perſons alſo, who purchaſe or convey under dureſs, may affirm or avoid ſuch tranſaction, whenever the dureſs is ceaſed [i]. For all theſe are under the protection of the law; which will not ſuffer them to be impoſed upon, through the imbecillity of their preſent condition; ſo that their acts are only binding, in caſe they be afterwards agreed to, when ſuch imbecillity ceaſes.

THE caſe of a feme-covert is ſomewhat different. She may *purchaſe* an eſtate without the conſent of her huſband, and the conveyance is good during the coverture, till he avoids it by ſome act declaring his diſſent [k]. And, though he does nothing to avoid

[a] 35 *Aſſiſ. pl.* 10.
[b] 39 *Hen. VI.* 42.
[c] F. N. B. 202.
[d] Litt. §. 405. Cro. Eliz. 398. 4 Rep. 123.
[e] Comb. 469. 3 Mod. 310, 311. 1 Equ. caſ. abr. 279.

[f] Perkins. §. 21.
[g] Co. Litt. 2.
[h] *Ibid.*
[i] 2 Inſt. 483. 5 Rep. 119.
[k] Co. Litt. 3.

it,

it, or even if he actually confents, the feme-covert herfelf may, after the death of her hufband, waive or difagree to the fame: nay, even her heirs may waive it after her, if fhe dies before her hufband, or if in her widowhood fhe does nothing to exprefs her confent or agreement[1]. But the *conveyance* or other contract of a feme-covert (except by fome matter of record) is abfolutely void, and not merely voidable[m]; and therefore cannot be affirmed or made good by any fubfequent agreement.

THE cafe of an alien born is alfo peculiar. For he may purchafe any thing; but after purchafe he can *hold* nothing, except a leafe for years of a houfe for convenience of merchandize, in cafe he be an alien-friend: all other purchafes (when found by an inqueft of office) being immediately forfeited to the king[n].

PAPISTS, laftly, and perfons profeffing the popifh religion, are by ftatute 11 & 12 W. III. c. 4. difabled to purchafe any lands, rents, or hereditaments; and all eftates made to their ufe, or in truft for them, are void. But this ftatute is conftrued to extend only to papifts above the age of eighteen; fuch only being abfolutely difabled to purchafe: yet the next proteftant heir of a papift under eighteen fhall have the profits, during his life; unlefs he renounces his errors within the time limited by law[o].

II. WE are next, but principally, to enquire, *how* a man may aliene or convey; which will lead us to confider the feveral modes of conveyance.

IN confequence of the admiffion of property, or the giving a feparate right by the law of fociety to thofe things which by the law of nature were in common, there was neceffarily fome means to be devifed, whereby that feparate right or exclufive property fhould be originally acquired; which, we have more than once obferved, was that of occupancy or firft poffeffion. But this pof-

---

[1] *Ibid.*
[m] Perkins. §. 154. 1 Sid. 120.

[n] Co. Litt. 2.
[o] 1 P. W[ms]. 354.

feffion, when once gained, was alfo neceffarily to be continued ;
or elfe, upon one man's derelidtion of the thing he had feifed, it
would again become common, and all thofe mifchiefs and contentions would enfue, which property was introduced to prevent.
For this purpofe therefore, of continuing the poffeffion, the municipal law has eftablifhed *defcents* and *alienations :* the former to
continue the poffeffion in the heirs of the proprietor, after his
involuntary derelidtion of it by his death ; the latter to continue
it in thofe perfons, to whom the proprietor, by his own *voluntary*
adt, fhall choofe to relinquifh it in his lifetime. A tranflation,
or transfer, of property being thus admitted by law, it became
neceffary that this transfer fhould be properly evidenced : in order to prevent difputes, either about the fadt, as whether there
was any transfer at all ; or concerning the perfons, by whom and
to whom it was transferred ; or with regard to the fubjedtmatter,
as what the thing transferred confifted of ; or, laftly, with relation to the mode and quality of the transfer, as for what period
of time (or, in other words, for what eftate and intereft) the
conveyance was made. The legal evidences of this tranflation of
property are called the *common affurances* of the kingdom ; whereby every man's eftate is affured to him, and all controverfies,
doubts, and difficulties are either prevented or removed.

THESE common affurances are of four kinds : 1. By matter
in pais, or deed ; which is an affurance tranfadted between two
or more private perfons *in pais,* in the country ; that is (according to the old common law) upon the very fpot to be transferred.
2. By matter of *record,* or an affurance tranfadted only in the
king's public courts of record. 3. By fpecial *cuftom,* obtaining
in fome particular places, and relating only to fome particular
fpecies of property. Which three are fuch as take effedt during
the life of the party conveying or affuring. 4. The fourth takes
no effedt, till after his death ; and that is by *devife,* contained in
his laft will and teftament. We fhall treat of each in it's order.

CHAPTER THE TWENTIETH.

OF ALIENATION BY DEED.

IN treating of deeds I shall consider, first, their general nature; and, next, the several sorts or kinds of deeds, with their respective incidents. And in explaining the former, I shall examine, first, what a deed is; secondly, it's requisites; and, thirdly, how it may be avoided.

I. FIRST then, a deed is a writing sealed and delivered by the parties [a]. It is sometimes called a charter, *carta*, from it's materials; but most usually, when applied to the transactions of private subjects, it is called a deed, in Latin *factum*, κατ᾽ ἐξοχην, because it is the most solemn and authentic act that a man can possibly perform, with relation to the disposal of his property; and therefore a man shall always be *estopped* by his own deed, or not permitted to aver or prove any thing in contradiction to what he has once so solemnly and deliberately avowed [b]. If a deed be made by more parties than one, there ought to be regularly as many copies of it as there are parties, and each should be cut or indented (formerly in acute angles *instar dentium*, but at present in a waving line) on the top or side, to tally or correspond with the other; which deed, so made, is called an indenture. Formerly, when deeds were more concise than at present, it was usual to write both parts on the same piece of parchment, with some word or letters of the alphabet written between them; through which the parchment was cut, either in a strait or indented line, in such

[a] Co. Litt. 171.   [b] Plowd. 434.

a man-a manner as to leave half the word on one part and half on the other. Deeds thus made were denominated *ſyngrapha* by the canoniſts [c]; and with us *chirographa*, or hand-writings [d]; the word *cirographum* or *cyrographum* being uſually that which was divided in making the indenture: and this cuſtom is ſtill preſerved in making out the indentures of a fine, whereof hereafter. But at length indenting only has come into uſe, without cutting through any letters at all; and it ſeems at preſent to ſerve for little other purpoſe, than to give name to the ſpecies of the deed. When the ſeveral parts of an indenture are interchangeably executed by the ſeveral parties, that part or copy which is executed by the grantor is uſually called the *original*, and the reſt are *counterparts:* though of late it is moſt frequent for all the parties to execute every part; which renders them all originals. A deed made by one party only is not indented, but *polled* or ſhaved quite even; and is therefore called a *deed-poll*, or a ſingle deed [e].

II. WE are in the next place to conſider the *requiſites* of a deed. The firſt of which is, that there be perſons able to contract and be contracted with, for the purpoſes intended by the deed; and alſo a thing, or ſubject matter to be contracted for; all which muſt be expreſſed by ſufficient names [f]. So as in every grant there muſt be a grantor, a grantee, and a thing granted; in every leaſe a leſſor, a leſſee, and a thing demiſed.

SECONDLY; the deed muſt be founded upon good and ſufficient *conſideration*. Not upon an uſurious contract [g]; nor upon fraud or colluſion, either to deceive purchaſors *bona fide* [h], or juſt and lawful creditors [i]; any of which bad conſiderations will vacate the deed. A deed alſo, or other grant, made without any conſideration, is, as it were, of no effect; for it is conſtrued to enure, or to be effectual, only to the uſe of the grantor himſelf [k].

[c] Lyndew. *l.* 1. *t.* 10. *c.* 1.   [g] Stat. 13 Eliz. c. 8.
[d] Mirror. c. 2. §. 27.   [h] Stat. 27 Eliz. c. 4.
[e] *Ibid.* Litt. §. 371, 372.   [i] Stat. 13 Eliz. c. 5.
[f] Co. Litt. 35.   [k] Perk. §. 533.

The

The confideration may be either a *good,* or a *valuable* one. A good confideration is fuch as that of blood, or of natural love and affection, when a man grants an eftate to a near relation; being founded in motives of generofity, prudence, and natural duty: a valuable confideration is fuch as money, marriage, or the like, which the law efteems an equivalent given for the grant[1]; and is therefore founded in motives of juftice. Deeds, made upon good confideration only, are confidered as merely voluntary, and are frequently fet afide in favour of creditors, and *bona fide* purchafors.

THIRDLY; the deed muft be *written,* or I prefume *printed*; for it may be in any character or any language; but it muft be upon paper, or parchment. For if it be written on ftone, board, linen, leather, or the like, it is no deed[m]. Wood or ftone may be more durable, and linen lefs liable to rafures; but writing on paper or parchment unites in itfelf, more perfectly than any other way, both thofe defirable qualities: for there is nothing elfe fo durable, and at the fame time fo little liable to alteration; nothing fo fecure from alteration, that is at the fame time fo durable. It muft alfo have the regular ftamps, impofed on it by the feveral ftatutes for the increafe of the public revenue; elfe it cannot be given in evidence. Formerly many conveyances were made by parol, or word of mouth only, without writing; but this giving a handle to a variety of frauds, the ftatute 29 Car. II. c. 3. enacts, that no leafe or eftate in lands, tenements, or hereditaments, (except leafes, not exceeding three years from the making, and whereon the referved rent is at leaft two thirds of the real value) fhall be looked upon as of greater force than a leafe or eftate at will; unlefs put in writing, and figned by the party granting, or his agent lawfully authorized in writing.

FOURTHLY; the matter written muft be *legally* and *orderly* fet forth: that is, there muft be words fufficient to fpecify the agreement and bind the parties: which fufficiency muft be left to

---

[1] 3 Rep. 83.   [m] Co. Litt. 229. F. N. B. 122.

the courts of law to determine [n]. For it is not abſolutely neceſſary in law, to have all the formal parts that are uſually drawn out in deeds, ſo as there be ſufficient words to declare clearly and legally the party's meaning. But, as theſe formal and orderly parts are calculated to convey that meaning in the cleareſt, diſtincteſt, and moſt effectual manner, and have been well conſidered and ſettled by the wiſdom of ſucceſſive ages, it is prudent not to depart from them without good reaſon or urgent neceſſity; and therefore I will here mention them in their uſual [o] order.

1. THE *premiſes* may be uſed to ſet forth the number and names of the parties, with their additions or titles. They alſo contain the recital, if any, of ſuch deeds, agreements, or matters of fact, as are neceſſary to explain the reaſons upon which the preſent tranſaction is founded: and herein alſo is ſet down the conſideration upon which the deed is made. And then follows the certainty of the grantor, grantee, and thing granted [p].

2. 3. NEXT come the *habendum* and *tenendum* [q]. The office of the *habendum* is properly to determine what eſtate or intereſt is granted by the deed: though this may be performed, and ſometimes is performed, in the premiſes. In which caſe the *habendum* cannot *leſſen*, but it may *enlarge*, the eſtate granted in the premiſes; as if a grant be "to A and the heirs of his body" in the premiſes, *habendum* "to him and his heirs for ever," here A has an eſtate-tail, and a fee-ſimple expectant thereon [r]. But had it been in the premiſes "to him and his heirs," *habendum* "to him "and the heirs of his body," the *habendum* would be utterly void [s]; for the larger and more beneficial eſtate is veſted in him before the *habendum* comes, and ſhall not afterwards be narrowed, or deveſted, by it. The *tenendum*, "and to hold," is now of very little uſe, and is only kept in by cuſtom. It was ſometimes formerly uſed to ſignify the tenure, by which the eſtate granted was

[n] Co. Litt. 225.

[o] *Ibid.* 6.

[p] See appendix, N°. 2. §. 2. pag. v.

[q] *Ibid.*

[r] Co. Litt. 21.

[s] 8 Rep. 154.

to

to be holden; viz. "*tenendum per servitium militare, in burgagio,* "*in libero socagio, &c.*" But, all these being now reduced to free and common socage, the tenure is never specified. Before the statute of *quia emptores,* 18 Edw. I. it was also sometimes used to denote the lord of whom the land should be holden; but that statute directing all future purchasers to hold, not of the immediate grantor, but of the chief lord of the fee, this use of the *tenendum* hath been also antiquated; though for a long time after we find it mentioned in antient charters, that the tenements shall be holden *de capitalibus dominis feodi* [t]: but, as this expressed nothing more than the statute had already provided for, it gradually grew out of use.

4. NEXT follow the terms or stipulations, if any, upon which the grant is made: the first of which is the *reddendum* or reservation, whereby the grantor doth create or reserve some new thing to himself out of what he had before granted. As "rendering "therefore yearly the sum of ten shillings, or a pepper corn, or "two days ploughing, or the like [u]." This render, *reditus,* return, or rent, under the pure feodal system consisted, in chivalry, principally of military services; in villenage, of the most slavish offices; and, in socage, it usually consists of money, though it may consist of services still, or of any other certain profit [w]. To make a *reddendum* good, if it be of any thing newly created by the deed, the reservation must be to the grantors, or some, or one of them, and not to any stranger to the deed [x]. But if it be of antient services or the like, annexed to the land, then the reservation may be to the lord of the fee [y].

5. ANOTHER of the terms upon which a grant may be made is a *condition;* which is a clause of contingency, on the happening of which the estate granted may be defeated; as "provided "always, that if the mortgagor shall pay the mortgagee 500 *l.*

[t] Append. N°. I. Madox. *Formul. passim.*
[u] Append. N°. II. §. 1. pag. iii.
[w] See pag. 41.

[x] Plowd. 13. 8 Rep. 71.
[y] Append. N°. I. pag. i.

"upon

" upon fuch a day, the whole eftate granted fhall determine;"
and the like^z.

6. NEXT may follow the claufe of *warranty*; whereby the
grantor doth, for himfelf and his heirs, warrant and fecure to the
grantee the eftate fo granted^a. By the feodal conftitution, if the
vafal's title to enjoy the feud was difputed, he might vouch, or
call, the lord or donor to warrant or infure his gift; which if he
failed to do, and the vafal was evicted, the lord was bound to
give him another feud of equal value in recompenfe^b. And fo,
by our antient law, if before the ftatute of *quia emptores* a man
enfeoffed another in fee, by the feodal verb *dedi*, to hold of himfelf and his heirs by certain fervices; the law annexed a warranty to this grant, which bound the feoffor and his heirs, to
whom the fervices (which were the confideration and equivalent
for the gift) were originally ftipulated to be rendered^c. Or if a
man and his anceftors had immemorially holden land of another
and his anceftors by the fervice of homage (which was called
homage aunceftrel) this alfo bound the lord to warranty^d; the
homage being an evidence of fuch a feodal grant. And, upon a
fimilar principle, in cafe, after a partition or exchange of lands
of inheritance, either party or his heirs be evicted of his fhare,
the other and his heirs are bound to warranty^e, becaufe they
enjoy the equivalent. And fo, even at this day, upon a gift in
tail or leafe for life, rendering rent, the donor or leffor and his
heirs (to whom the rent is payable) are bound to warrant the
title^f. But in a feoffment in fee by the verb *dedi*, fince the ftatute of *quia emptores*, the feoffor only is bound to the implied
warranty, and not his heirs^g; becaufe it is a mere perfonal contract on the part of the feoffor, the tenure (and of courfe the antient fervices) refulting back to the fuperior lord of the fee. And
in other forms of alienation, gradually introduced fince that fta-

^z Append. N°. II. §. 2. pag. viii.   ^d Litt. §. 143.
^a *Ibid.* N^o. I. pag. i.   ^e Co. Litt. 174.
^b *Feud. l* 2. *t.* 8, & 25.   ^f *Ibid.* 384.
^c Co. Litt. 384.   ^g *Ibid.*

tute,

tute, no warranty whatfoever is implied[h]; they bearing no fort of analogy to the original feodal donation. And therefore in fuch cafes it became neceffary to add an exprefs claufe of warranty, to bind the grantor and his heirs; which is a kind of covenant real, and can only be created by the verb *warrantizo* or *warrant*[i].

THESE exprefs warranties were introduced, even prior to the ftatute of *quia emptores*, in order to evade the ftrictnefs of the feodal doctrine of non-alienation without the confent of the heir. For, though he, at the death of his anceftor, might have entered on any tenements that were aliened without his concurrence, yet, if a claufe of warranty was added to the anceftor's grant, this covenant defcending upon the heir infured the grantee; not fo much by confirming his title, as by obliging fuch heir to yield him a recompenfe in lands of equal value: the law, in favour of alienations, fuppofing that no anceftor would wantonly difinherit his next of blood[k]; and therefore prefuming that he had received a valuable confideration, either in land, or in money which had purchafed land, and that this equivalent defcended to the heir together with the anceftor's warranty. So that when either an anceftor, being the rightful tenant of the freehold, conveyed the land to a ftranger and his heirs, or releafed the right in fee-fimple to one who was already in poffeffion, and fuperadded a warranty to his deed, it was held that fuch warranty not only bound the warrantor himfelf to protect and affure the title of the warrantee, but it alfo bound his heir: and this, whether that warranty was *lineal*, or *collateral* to the title of the land. *Lineal* warranty was where the heir derived, or might by poffibility have derived, his title to the land warranted, either from or through the anceftor who made the warranty; as, where a father, or an elder fon in the life of the father, releafed to the diffeifor of either themfelves or the grandfather, with warranty, this was lineal to the younger fon[l]. *Collateral* warranty was where the heir's title to the land neither was, nor could have been, derived from

---

[h] Co. Litt. 102.
[i] Litt. §. 733.

[k] Co. Litt. 373.
[l] Litt. §. 703. 706..707.

the

the warranting anceftor; as, where a younger brother releafed
to his father's diffeifor, with warranty, this was collateral to the
elder brother ᵐ. But where the very conveyance, to which the
warranty was annexed, immediately followed a diffeifin, or operated itfelf as fuch (as, where a father tenant for years, with
remainder to his fon in fee, aliened in fee-fimple with warranty)
this, being in it's original manifeftly founded on the *tort* or wrong
of the warrantor himfelf, was called a warranty *commencing by
diffeifin*; and, being too palpably injurious to be fupported, was
not binding upon any heir of fuch tortious warrantor ⁿ.

I N both lineal and collateral warranty, the obligation of the
heir (in cafe the warrantee was evicted, to yield him other lands
in their ftead) was only on condition that he had other fufficient lands by defcent from the warranting anceftor ᵒ. But
though, without affets, he was not bound to infure the title of
another, yet, in cafe of lineal warranty, whether affets defcended
or not, the heir was perpetually barred from claiming the land
himfelf; for, if he could fucceed in fuch claim, he would then
gain affets by defcent (if he had them not before) and muft fulfil
the warranty of his anceftor : and the fame rule ᵖ was with lefs
juftice adopted alfo in refpect of collateral warranties, which likewife (though no affets defcended) barred the heir of the warrantor
from claiming the land by any collateral title; upon the prefumption of law that he might hereafter have affets by defcent either
from or through the fame anceftor. The inconvenience of this
latter branch of the rule was felt very early, when tenants by the
curtefy took upon them to aliene their lands with warranty ;
which collateral warranty of the father defcending upon his fon
(who was the heir of both his parents) barred him from claiming his maternal inheritance : to remedy which the ftatute of
Glocefter, 6 Edw. I. c. 3. declared, that fuch warranty fhould
be no bar to the fon, unlefs affets defcended from the father. It
was afterwards attempted in 50 Edw. III. to make the fame pro-

ᵐ Litt. §. 705. 707. ᵒ Co. Litt. 102.
ⁿ *Ibid.* §. 698. 702. ᵖ Litt. §. 711. 712.

vifion

vision universal, by enacting that no collateral warranty should be a bar, unless where assets descended from the same ancestor[q], but it then proceeded not to effect. However, by the statute 11 Hen. VII. c. 20. notwithstanding any alienation with warranty by tenant in dower, the heir of the husband is not barred, though he be also heir to the wife. And by statute 4 & 5 Ann. c. 16. all warranties by any tenant for life shall be void against those in remainder or reversion; and all collateral warranties by any ancestor who has no estate of inheritance in possession shall be void against his heir. By the wording of which last statute it should seem, that the legislature meant to allow, that the collateral warranty of tenant in tail, descending (though without assets) upon a remainder-man or reversioner, should still bar the remainder or reversion. For though the judges, in expounding the statute *de donis*, held that, by analogy to the statute of Glocester, a lineal warranty by the tenant in tail without assets should not bar the issue in tail, yet they held such warranty with assets to be a sufficient bar[r]: which was therefore formerly mentioned[s] as one of the ways whereby an estate tail might be destroyed; it being indeed nothing more in effect, than exchanging the lands entailed for others of equal value. They also held that collateral warranty was not within the statute *de donis*; as that act was principally intended to prevent the tenant in tail from disinheriting his own issue: and therefore collateral warranty (though without assets) was allowed to be, as at common law, a sufficient bar of the estate-tail and all remainders and reversions expectant thereon[t]. And so it still continues to be, notwithstanding the statute of queen Anne, if made by tenant in tail in possession: who therefore may now, without the forms of a fine or recovery, in some cases make a good conveyance in fee-simple, by superadding a warranty to his grant; which, if accompanied with assets, bars his own issue, and without them bars such of his heirs as may be in remainder or reversion.

[q] Co. Litt. 373.
[r] Litt. §. 712. 2 Inst. 293.
[s] pag. 116.
[t] Co. Litt. 374. 2 Inst. 335.

7. AFTER warranty ufually follow *covenants*, or conventions; which are claufes of agreement contained in a deed, whereby either party may ftipulate for the truth of certain facts, or may bind himfelf to perform, or give, fomething to the other. Thus the grantor may covenant that he hath a right to convey; or for the grantee's quiet enjoyment; or the like: the grantee may covenant to pay his rent, to repair the premifes, &c [u]. If the covenantor covenants for himfelf and his *heirs*, it is then a covenant real, and defcends upon the heirs; who are bound to perform it, provided they have affets by defcent, but not otherwife: if he covenants alfo for his *executors* and *adminiftrators*, his perfonal affets, as well as his real, are likewife pledged for the performance of the covenant; which makes fuch covenant a better fecurity than any warranty, and it has therefore in modern practice totally fuperfeded the other.

8. LASTLY, comes the *conclufion*, which mentions the execution and date of the deed, or the time of it's being given or executed, either expreffly, or by reference to fome day and year before-mentioned [w]. Not but a deed is good, although it mention no date; or hath a falfe date; or even if it hath an impoffible date, as the thirtieth of February; provided the real day of it's being dated or given, that is, delivered, can be proved [x].

I PROCEED now to the *fifth* requifite for making a good deed; the *reading* of it. This is neceffary, wherever any of the parties defire it; and, if it be not done on his requeft, the deed is void as to him. If he can, he fhould read it himfelf: if he be blind or illiterate, another muft read it to him. If it be read falfely, it will be void; at leaft for fo much as is mifrecited: unlefs it be agreed by collufion that the deed fhall be read falfe, on purpofe to make it void; for in fuch cafe it fhall bind the fraudulent party [y].

---

[u] Append. Nº. II. §. 2. pag. viii.
[w] *Ibid.* pag. xii.

[x] Co. Litt. 46. Dyer. 28.
[y] 2 Rep. 3. 9. 11 Rep. 27.

SIXTHLY,

SIXTHLY, it is requifite that the party, whofe deed it is, fhould *feal*, and in moft cafes I apprehend fhould *fign* it alfo. The ufe of feals, as a mark of authenticity to letters and other inftruments in writing, is extremely antient. We read of it among the Jews and Perfians in the earlieft and moft facred records of hiftory². And in the book of Jeremiah there is a very remarkable inftance, not only of an atteftation by feal, but alfo of the other ufual formalities attending a Jewifh purchafe². In the civil law alfo ᵇ, feals were the evidence of truth; and were required, on the part of the witneffes at leaft, at the atteftation of every teftament. But in the times of our Saxon anceftors, they were not much in ufe here. For though fir Edward Coke ᶜ relies on an inftance of king Edwyn's making ufe of a feal about an hundred years before the conqueft, yet it does not follow that this was the ufage among the whole nation : and perhaps the charter he mentions may be of doubtful authority, from this very circumftance, of being fealed; fince we are affured by all our antient hiftorians, that fealing was not then in common ufe. The method of the Saxons was for fuch as could write to fubfcribe their names, and, whether they could write or not, to affix the fign of the crofs : which cuftom our illiterate vulgar do, for the moft part, to this day keep up; by figning a crofs for their mark, when unable to write their names. And indeed this inability to write, and therefore making a crofs in it's ftead, is honeftly avowed by Caedwalla, a Saxon king, at the end of one of his charters ᵈ. In like manner, and for the fame unfurmountable reafon, the Normans, a brave but

---

² 1 Kings. c. 21. Daniel. c. 6. Efther. c. 8.
ᵃ "And I bought the field of Hanameel, "and weighed him the money, even feven-"teen fhekels of filver. And I fubfcribed "the evidence, and fealed it, and took wit-"neffes, and weighed him the money in the "ballances. And I took the evidence of "the purchafe, both that which was fealed "according to the law and cuftom, and "alfo that which was open." c. 32.

ᵇ *Inft.* 2. 10. 2 & 3.
ᶜ 1 Inft. 7.
ᵈ "*Propria manu pro ignorantia literarum.* "*fignum fanctae crucis expreffi et fubfcripfi.*" Seld. *Jan. Angl. l.* 1. §. 42. And this (according to Procopius) the emperor Juftin in the eaft, and Theodoric king of the Goths in Italy, had before authorized by their example, on account of their inability to write.

illiterate nation, at their firſt ſettlement in France, uſed the practice of ſealing only, without writing their names : which cuſtom
continued, when learning made it's way among them, though
the reaſon for doing it had ceaſed ; and hence the charter of Edward the confeſſor to Weſtminſter abbey, himſelf being brought
up in Normandy, was witneſſed only by his ſeal, and is generally
thought to be the oldeſt ſealed charter of any authenticity in
England[e]. At the conqueſt, the Norman lords brought over
into this kingdom their own faſhions ; and introduced waxen ſeals
only, inſtead of the Engliſh method of writing their names, and
ſigning with the ſign of the croſs[f]. The impreſſions of theſe
ſeals were ſometimes a knight on horſeback, ſometimes other
deviſes : but coats of arms were not introduced into ſeals, nor
indeed into any other uſe, till about the reign of Richard the
firſt, who brought them from the croiſade in the holy land ;
where they were firſt invented and painted on the ſhields of the
knights, to diſtinguiſh the variety of perſons of every chriſtian
nation who reſorted thither, and who could not, when clad in
complete ſteel, be otherwiſe known or aſcertained.

THIS neglect of ſigning, and reſting only upon the authenticity of ſeals, remained very long among us ; for it was held in
all our books that ſealing alone was ſufficient to authenticate a
deed : and ſo the common form of atteſting deeds, --- "*ſealed*
and delivered," continues to this day ; notwithſtanding the ſtatute 29 Car. II. c. 3. before-mentioned revives the Saxon cuſtom, and expreſſly directs the ſigning, in all grants of lands, and
many other ſpecies of deeds ; in which therefore ſigning ſeems
to be now as neceſſary as ſealing, though it hath been ſometimes
held, that the one includes the other[g].

A SEVENTH requiſite to a good deed is that it be *delivered*,
by the party himſelf or his certain attorney : which therefore is

---

[e] Lamb. *Archeion.* 51.
[f] " *Normanni chirographorum confectionem,*
" *cum crucibus aureis, aliiſque ſignaculis ſacris,*
" *in Anglia firmari ſolitam, in ceram impreſ-*
" *ſam mutant, modumque ſcribendi Anglicum*
" *rejiciunt.*" Ingulph.
[g] 3 Lev. 1. Stra. 764.

also

alſo expreſſed in the atteſtation; "ſealed and *delivered*." A deed takes effect only from this tradition or delivery; for, if the date be falſe or impoſſible, the delivery aſcertains the time of it. And if another perſon ſeals the deed, yet if the party delivers it him-ſelf, he thereby adopts the ſealing[h], and by a parity of reaſon the ſigning alſo, and makes them both his own. A delivery may be either abſolute, that is, to the party or grantee himſelf; or to a third perſon, to hold till ſome conditions be performed on the part of the grantee: in which laſt caſe it is not delivered as a *deed*, but as an *eſcrow*; that is, as a ſcrowl or writing, which is not to take effect as a deed till the conditions be performed; and then it is a deed to all intents and purpoſes[i].

THE *laſt* requiſite to the validity of a deed is the *atteſtation*, or execution of it *in the preſence of witneſſes:* though this is neceſſary, rather for preſerving the evidence, than for conſtituting the eſſence, of the deed. Our modern deeds are in reality nothing more than an improvement or amplification of the *brevia teſtata* mentioned by the feodal writers[k]; which were written memorandums, intro-duced to perpetuate the tenor of the conveyance and inveſtiture, when grants by parol only became the foundation of frequent diſ-pute and uncertainty. To this end they regiſtered in the deed the perſons who attended as witneſſes, which was formerly done without their ſigning their names (that not being always in their power) but they only heard the deed read; and then the clerk or ſcribe added their names, in a ſort of memorandum; thus; " *hijs teſtibus, Johanne Moore, Jacobo Smith, et aliis ad hanc rem* " *convocatis*[l]." This, like all other ſolemn tranſactions, was ori-ginally done only *coram paribus*[m], and frequently when aſſembled in the court baron, hundred, or county court; which was then expreſſed in the atteſtation, *teſte comitatu, hundredo, &c*[n]. After-wards the atteſtation of other witneſſes was allowed, the trial in

[h] Perk. §. 130.
[i] Co. Litt. 36.
[k] *Feud. l.* 1. *t.* 4.
[l] Co. Litt. 7.

[m] *Feud. l.* 2. *t.* 32.
[n] Spelm. *Gloſſ.* 228. Madox. *Formul.* n°. 221. 322. 660.

caſe

cafe of a difpute being ftill referved to the *pares;* with whom the witneffes (if more than one) were affociated, and joined in the verdict[o]: till that alfo was abrogated by the ftatute of York, 12 Edw. II. ft. 1. c. 2. And in this manner, with fome fuch claufe of *hijs teftibus,* are all old deeds and charters, particularly *magna carta,* witneffed. And, in the time of fir Edward Coke, creations of nobility were ftill witneffed in the fame manner[p]. But in the king's common charters, writs, or letters patent, the ftile is now altered : for, at prefent, the king is his own witnefs, and attefts his letters patent thus ; " *tefte meipfo,* witnefs ourfelf at Weftminfter, *&c :*" a form which was introduced by Richard the firft[q], but not commonly ufed till about the beginning of the fifteenth century ; nor the claufe of *hijs teftibus* intirely difcontinued till the reign of Henry the eighth[r] : which was alfo the aera of difcontinuing it in the deeds of fubjects, learning being then revived, and the faculty of writing more general : and therefore ever fince that time the witneffes have fubfcribed their atteftation, either at the bottom, or on the back, of the deed[s].

III. WE are next to confider, how a deed may be *avoided,* or rendered of no effect. And from what has been before laid down it will follow, that if a deed wants any of the effential requifites before-mentioned ; either, 1. Proper parties, and a proper fubject matter : 2. A good and fufficient confideration : 3. Writing, on paper or parchment, duly ftamped : 4. Sufficient and legal words, properly difpofed : 5. Reading, if defired, before the execution : 6. Sealing ; and, by the ftatute, in many cafes figning alfo : or, 7. Delivery : it is a void deed *ab initio.* It may alfo be avoided by matter *ex poft facto :* as, 1. By rafure, interlining, or other alteration in any material part ; unlefs a memorandum be made thereof at the time of the execution and atteftation[t]. 2. By breaking off, or defacing, the feal[u]. 3. By

[o] Co. Litt. 6.
[p] 2 Inft. 77.
[q] Madox, *Formul.* n[o]. 515.
[r] *Ibid.* Differt. fol. 32.

[s] 2 Inft. 78.
[t] 11 Rep. 27.
[u] 5 Rep. 23.

delivering

delivering it up to be cancelled; that is to have lines drawn over it, in the form of lattice work or *cancelli*; though the phrase is now used figuratively for any manner of obliteration or defacing it. 4. By the disagreement of such, whose concurrence is necessary, in order for the deed to stand: as, the husband, where a feme covert is concerned; an infant, or person under duress, when those disabilities are removed; and the like. 6. By the judgment or decree of a court of judicature. This was antiently the province of the court of star chamber, and now of the chancery: when it appears that the deed was obtained by fraud, force, or other foul practice; or is proved to be an absolute forgery ᵂ. In any of these cases the deed may be voided, either in part or totally, according as the cause of avoidance is more or less extensive.

A N D, having thus explained the general nature of deeds, we are next to consider their several species, together with their respective incidents. And herein I shall only examine the particulars of those, which, from long practice and experience of their efficacy, are generally used in the alienation of *real* estates: for it would be tedious, nay infinite, to descant upon all the several instruments made use of in *personal* concerns, but which fall under our general definition of a deed; that is, a writing sealed and delivered. The former, being principally such as serve to *convey* the property of lands and tenements from man to man, are commonly denominated *conveyances*: which are either conveyances at *common law*, or such as receive their force and efficacy by virtue of the *statute of uses*.

I. O F conveyances by the common law, some may be called *original*, or *primary* conveyances; which are those by means whereof the benefit or estate is created or first arises: others are *derivative* or *secondary*; whereby the benefit or estate, originally created, is enlarged, restrained, transferred, or extinguished.

ᵂ Toth. 90.

ORIGINAL

ORIGINAL conveyances are the following; 1. Feoffment: 2. Gift; 3. Grant; 4. Leaſe; 5. Exchange; 6. Partition: *derivative* are, 7. Releaſe; 8. Confirmation; 9. Surrender; 10. Aſſignment; 11. Defeazance.

1. A FEOFFMENT, *feoffamentum,* is a ſubſtantive derived from the verb, to enfeoff, *feoffare* or *infeudare,* to give one a feud; and therefore feoffment is properly *donatio feudi*ˣ. It is the moſt antient method of conveyance, the moſt ſolemn and public, and therefore the moſt eaſily remembered and proved. And it may properly be defined, the gift of any corporeal hereditament to another. He that ſo gives, or enfeoffs, is called the *feoffor;* and the perſon enfeoffed is denominated the *feoffee.*

THIS is plainly derived from, or is indeed itſelf the very mode of the antient feodal donation; for though it may be performed by the word "enfeoff" or "grant," yet the apteſt word of feoffment is "*do* or *dedi*ʸ." And it is ſtill directed and governed by the ſame feodal rules; inſomuch that the principal rule relating to the extent and effect of a feodal grant, "*tenor eſt* "*qui legem dat feudo,*" is in other words become the maxim of our law with relation to feoffments, "*modus legem dat donationi*ᶻ." And therefore as in pure feodal donations the lord, from whom the feud moved, muſt expreſſly limit and declare the continuance or quantity of eſtate he meant to confer, "*ne quis plus donaſſe* "*praeſumatur, quam in donatione expreſſerit*ᵃ;" ſo, if one grants by feoffment lands or tenements to another, and limits or expreſſes no eſtate, the grantee (due ceremonies of law being performed) hath barely an eſtate for lifeᵇ. For, as the perſonal abilities of the feoffee were originally preſumed to be the immediate or principal inducements to the feoffment, the feoffee's eſtate ought to be confined to his perſon, and ſubſiſt only for his

ˣ Co. Litt. 9.
ʸ *Ibid.*
ᶻ Wright. 21.

ᵃ pag. 108.
ᵇ Co. Litt. 42.

life;

life; unlefs the feoffor, by exprefs provifion in the creation and conftitution of the eftate, hath given it a longer continuance. Thefe exprefs provifions are indeed generally made; for this was for ages the only conveyance, whereby our anceftors were wont to create an eftate in fee-fimple [c], by giving the land to the feoffee, to hold to him and his heirs for ever; though it ferves equally well to convey any other eftate of freehold [d].

BUT by the mere words of the deed the feoffment is by no means perfected. There remains a very material ceremony to be performed, called *livery of feifin*; without which the feoffee has but a mere eftate at will [e]. This livery of feifin is no other than the pure feodal inveftiture, or delivery of corporal poffeffion of the land or tenement; which was held abfolutely neceffary to complete the donation. "*Nam feudum fine inveftitura nullo modo* "*conftitui potuit* [f] :" and an eftate was then only perfect, when, as Fleta expreffes it in our law, "*fit juris et feifinae conjunctio* [g]."

INVESTITURES, in their original rife, were probably intended to demonftrate in conquered countries the actual poffeffion of the *lord*; and that he did not grant a bare litigious right, which the foldier was ill qualified to profecute, but a peaceable and firm poffeffion. And, at a time when writing was feldom practifed, a mere oral gift, at a diftance from the fpot that was given, was not likely to be either long or accurately retained in the memory of by-ftanders, who were very little interefted in the grant. Afterwards they were retained as a public and notorious act, that the country might take notice of and teftify the transfer of the eftate; and that fuch as claimed title by other means might know againft whom to bring their actions.

IN all well-governed nations, fome notoriety of this kind has been ever held requifite, in order to acquire and afcertain the

[c] See Appendix. Nº. I.
[d] Co. Litt. 9.
[e] Litt. §. 66.
[f] Wright. 37.
[g] *l.* 3. *c.* 15. §. 5.

property

property of lands. In the Roman law *plenum dominium* was not
said to subfist, unless where a man hath both the *right*, and the
corporal possession; which possession could not be acquired without both an actual intention to possess, and an actual seisin, or
entry into the premises, or part of them in the name of the
whole [h]. And even in ecclesiastical promotions, where the freehold passes to the person promoted, corporal possession is required at this day, to vest the property completely in the new proprietor; who, according to the distinction of the canonists [i], acquires the *jus ad rem*, or inchoate and imperfect right, by nomination and institution; but not the *jus in re*, or complete and
full right, unless by corporal possession. Therefore in dignities
possession is given by installment; in rectories and vicarages by
induction, without which no temporal rights accrue to the minister, though every ecclesiastical power is vested in him by institution. So also even in descents of lands, by our law, which
are cast on the heir by act of the law itself, the heir has not *plenum dominium,* or full and complete ownership, till he has made
an actual corporal entry into the lands: for if he dies before *entry*
made, *his* heir shall not be intitled to take the possession, but the
heir of the person who was last actually seised [k]. It is not therefore only a mere right to enter, but the actual entry, that makes
a man complete owner; so as to transmit the inheritance to his
own heirs: *non jus, sed seisina, facit stipitem* [l].

Y E T, the corporal tradition of lands being sometimes inconvenient, a symbolical delivery of possession was in many cases
antiently allowed; by transferring something near at hand, in the
presence of credible witnesses, which by agreement should serve
to represent the very thing designed to be conveyed; and an oc-

---

[h] *Nam apiscimur possessionem corpore et animo: neque per se corpore; neque per se animo.
Non autem ita accipiendum est, ut qui fundum
possidere velit, omnes glebas circumambulet; sed
sufficit quamlibet partem ejus fundi introire.*
(*Ff.* 41. 2. 3.) And again: *traditionibus do-*
minia rerum, non nudis pactis, transferuntur.
(Cod. 2. 3. 20.)

[i] Decretal. *l.* 3. *t.* 4. *c.* 40.

[k] See pag. 209. 227, 228.

[l] Flet. *l.* 6. *c.* 2. §. 2.

cupancy

cupancy of this fign or fymbol was permitted as equivalent to occupancy of the land itfelf. Among the Jews we find the evidence of a purchafe thus defined in the book of Ruth[m] : " now " this was the manner in former time in Ifrael, concerning re- " deeming and concerning changing, for to confirm all things : " a man plucked off his fhoe, and gave it to his neighbour ; and " this was a teftimony in Ifrael." Among the antient Goths and Swedes, contracts for the fale of lands were made in the prefence of witnefses, who extended the cloak of the buyer, while the feller caft a clod of the land into it, in order to give poffeffion : and a ftaff or wand was alfo delivered from the vendor to the vendee, which paffed through the hands of the witnefses[n]. With our Saxon anceftors the delivery of a turf was a necefsary folemnity, to eftablifh the conveyance of lands[o]. And, to this day, the conveyance of our copyhold eftates is ufually made from the feller to the lord or his fteward by delivery of a rod or virge, and then from the lord to the purchafor by re-delivery of the fame, in the prefence of a jury of tenants.

CONVEYANCES in writing were the laft and moft refined improvement. The mere delivery of poffeffion, either actual or fymbolical, depending on the ocular teftimony and remembrance of the witnefses, was liable to be forgotten or mifreprefented, and became frequently incapable of proof. Befides, the new occafions and neceffities, introduced by the advancement of commerce, required means to be devifed of charging and incumbering eftates, and of making them liable to a multitude of conditions and minute defignations for the purpofes of raifing money, without an abfolute fale of the land; and fometimes the like proceedings were found ufeful in order to make a decent and competent provifion for the numerous branches of a family, and for other domeftic views. None of which could be effected by a mere, fimple, corporal transfer of the foil from one man to another, which was principally calculated for conveying an abfolute

[m] ch. 4. v. 7.
[n] Stiernhook. *de jure Sueon. l. 2. c. 4.*
[o] Hickes. *Differt. epiftolar.* 8;.

unlimited dominion. Written deeds were therefore introduced, in order to fpecify and perpetuate the peculiar purpofes of the party who conveyed : yet ftill, for a very long feries of years, they were never made ufe of, but in company with the more antient and notorious method of transfer, by delivery of corporal poffeffion.

LIVERY of feifin, by the common law, is neceffary to be made upon every grant of an eftate of freehold in hereditaments corporeal, whether of inheritance or for life only. In hereditaments incorporeal it is impoffible to be made ; for they are not the object of the fenfes : and in leafes for years, or other chattel interefts, it is not neceffary. In leafes for years indeed an actual *entry* is neceffary, to veft the eftate in the leffee : for the bare leafe gives him only a right to enter, which is called his intereft in the term, or *intereffe termini*; and, when he enters in purfuance of that right, he is then and not before in poffeffion of his term, and complete tenant for years[p]. This entry by the tenant himfelf ferves the purpofe of notoriety, as well as livery of feifin from the grantor could have done ; which it would have been improper to have given in this cafe, becaufe that folemnity is appropriated to the conveyance of a freehold. And this is one reafon why freeholds cannot be made to commence *in futuro*, becaufe they cannot be made but by livery of feifin ; which livery, being an actual manual tradition of the land, muft take effect *in praefenti*, or not at all[q].

ON the creation of a *freehold* remainder, at one and the fame time with a particular eftate for years, we have before feen that at the common law livery muft be made to the particular tenant[r]. But if fuch a remainder be created afterwards, expectant on a leafe for years now in being, the livery muft not be made to the leffee for years, for then it operates nothing ; " *nam quod femel* " *meum eft, amplius meum effe non poteft*[s] :" but it muft be made

[p] Co. Litt. 46.
[q] See pag. 165.

[r] pag. 167.
[s] Co. Litt. 49.

to the remainder-man himself, by consent of the lessee for years : for without his consent no livery of the possession can be given[t]; partly because such forcible livery would be an ejectment of the tenant from his term, and partly for the reasons before given[u] for introducing the doctrine of attornments.

LIVERY of seisin is either in *deed*, or in *law*. Livery in *deed* is thus performed. The feoffor, lessor, or his attorney, together with the feoffee, lessee, or his attorney, (for this may as effectually be done by deputy or attorney, as by the principals themselves in person) come to the land, or to the house; and there, in the presence of witnesses, declare the contents of the feoffment or lease, on which livery is to be made. And then the feoffor, if it be of land, doth deliver to the feoffee, all other persons being out of the ground, a clod or turf, or a twig or bough there growing, with words to this effect. "I deliver these to you in the name "of seisin of all the lands and tenements contained in this deed." But, if it be of a house, the feoffor must take the ring, or latch of the door, the house being quite empty, and deliver it to the feoffee in the same form; and then the feoffee must enter alone, and shut to the door, and then open it, and let in the others[w]. If the conveyance or feoffment be of divers lands, lying scattered in one and the same county, then in the feoffor's possession, livery of seisin of any parcel, in the name of the rest, sufficeth for all[x]; but, if they be in several counties, there must be as many liveries as there are counties. For, if the title to these lands comes to be disputed, there must be as many trials as there are counties, and the jury of one county are no judges of the notoriety of a fact in another. Besides, antiently this seisin was obliged to be delivered *coram paribus de vicineto*, before the peers or freeholders of the neighbourhood, who attested such delivery in the body or on the back of the deed; according to the rule of the feodal law[y], *pares debent interesse investiturae feudi, et non alii :* for which

[t] Co. Litt. 48.
[u] pag. 288.
[w] Co. Litt. 48. West. Symb. 251.

[x] Litt. §. 414.
[y] Feud. *l.* 2. *t.* 58.

this reafon is exprefsly given; becaufe the peers or vafals of the lord, being bound by their oath of fealty, will take care that no fraud be committed to his prejudice, which ftrangers might be apt to connive at. And though, afterwards, the ocular attefta-tion of the *pares* was held unneceffary, and livery might be made before any credible witneffes, yet the trial, in cafe it was difpu-ted, (like that of all other atteftations[z]) was ftill referved to the *pares* or jury of the county[a]. Alfo, if the lands be out on leafe, though all lie in the fame county, there muft be as many liveries as there are tenants : becaufe no livery can be made in this cafe, but by the confent of the particular tenant; and the confent of one will not bind the reft[b]. And in all thefe cafes it is prudent, and ufual, to endorfe the livery of feifin on the back of the deed, fpecifying the manner, place, and time of making it; together with the names of the witneffes[c]. And thus much for livery in deed.

LIVERY in *law* is where the fame is not made *on* the land, but *in fight of it* only; the feoffor faying to the feoffee, "I give "you yonder land, enter and take poffeffion." Here, if the feoffee enters during the life of the feoffor, it is a good livery, but not otherwife; unlefs he dares not enter, through fear of his life or bodily harm: and then his continual claim, made yearly, in due form of law, as near as poffible to the lands[d], will fuffice with-out an entry[e]. This livery in law cannot however be given or received by attorney, but only by the parties themfelves[f].

2. THE conveyance by *gift*, *donatio*, is properly applied to the creation of an eftate-tail, as feoffment is to that of an eftate in fee, and leafe to that of an eftate for life or years. It differs in nothing from a feoffment, but in the nature of the eftate paff-ing by it : for the operative words of conveyance in this cafe are *do* or *dedi*[g]; and gifts in tail are equally imperfect without livery

[z] See pag. 307.
[a] Gilb. Ten. 35.
[b] Dyer. 18.
[c] See appendix. N°. I.

[d] Litt. §. 421, &c.
[e] Co. Litt. 48.
[f] *Ibid.* 52.
[g] Weft's Symbol. 256.

of

of feifin, as feoffments in fee-fimple [h]. And this is the only diftinction that Littleton feems to take, when he fays [i], "it is to be
"underftood that there is feoffor and feoffee, donor and donee,
"leffor and leffee;" viz. feoffor is applied to a feoffment in fee-
fimple, donor to a gift in tail, and leffor to a leafe for life, or for
years, or at will. In common acceptation gifts are frequently
confounded with the next fpecies of deeds: which are,

3. GRANTS, *conceffiones*; the regular method by the common law of transferring the property of *incorporeal* hereditaments, or, fuch things whereof no livery can be had [k]. For
which reafon all corporeal hereditaments, as lands and houfes,
are faid to lie *in livery*; and the others, as advowfons, commons,
rents, reverfions, &c, to lie *in grant* [l]. And the reafon is given
by Bracton [m]: "*traditio*, or livery, *nihil aliud eft quam rei corpo-*
"*ralis de perfona in perfonam, de manu in manum, tranflatio aut in*
"*poffeffionem inductio; fed res incorporales, quae funt ipfum jus rei*
"*vel corpori inhaerens, traditionem non patiuntur.*" Thefe therefore pafs merely by the delivery of the deed. And in figniories,
or reverfions of lands, fuch grant, together with the attornment
of the tenant (while attornments were requifite) were held to be
of equal notoriety with, and therefore equivalent to, a feoffment
and livery of lands in immediate poffeffion. It therefore differs
but little from a feoffment, except in it's fubject matter: for the
operative words therein commonly ufed are *dedi et conceffi*, "have
given and granted."

4. A LEASE is properly a conveyance of any lands or tenements, (ufually in confideration of rent or other annual recompenfe) made for life, for years, or at will, but always for
a *lefs* time than the leffor hath in the premifes: for if it be
for the *whole* intereft, it is more properly an affignment than
a leafe. The ufual words of operation in it are, "demife, grant,

[h] Litt. §. 59.
[i] §. 57.
[k] Co. Litt 9.

[l] *Ibid.* 172.
[m] *l.* 2. *c.* 18.

"and

"and to farm let; *dimifi, conceffi, et ad firmam tradidi.*" *Farm,*
or *feorme,* is an old Saxon word fignifying provifions [n] : and
it came to be ufed inftead of rent or render, becaufe antiently the greater part of rents were referved in provifions ; in
corn, in poultry, and the like; till the ufe of money became
more frequent. So that a farmer, *firmarius,* was one who held
his lands upon payment of a rent or *feorme* : though at prefent, by a gradual departure from the original fenfe, the word
farm is brought to fignify the very eftate or lands fo held upon
farm or rent. By this conveyance an eftate for life, for years,
or at will, may be created, either in corporeal or incorporeal
hereditaments : though livery of feifin is indeed incident and neceffary to one fpecies of leafes, *viz.* leafes for life of corporeal
hereditaments ; but to no other.

WHATEVER reftrictions, by the feverity of the feodal law,
might in times of very high antiquity be obferved with regard to
leafes ; yet by the common law, as it has ftood for many centuries, all perfons feifed of any eftate might let leafes to endure
fo long as their own intereft lafted, but no longer. Therefore
tenant in fee-fimple might let leafes of any duration ; for he hath
the whole intereft : but tenant in tail, or tenant for life, could
make no leafes which fhould bind the iffue in tail or reverfioner;
nor could a hufband, feifed *jure uxoris,* make a firm or valid leafe
for any longer term than the joint lives of himfelf and his wife,
for then his intereft expired. Yet fome tenants for life, where
the fee-fimple was in abeyance, might (with the concurrence of
fuch as have the guardianfhip of the fee) make leafes of equal
duration with thofe granted by tenants in fee-fimple : fuch as
parfons and vicars with confent of the patron and ordinary [o]. So
alfo bifhops, and deans, and fuch other fole ecclefiaftical corporations as are feifed of the fee-fimple of lands in their corporate
right, might, with the concurrence and confirmation of fuch
perfons as the law requires, have made leafes for years, or for
life, eftates in tail, or in fee, without any limitation or controll.

[n] Spelm. *Gl.* 229.   [o] Co. Litt. 44.

And

And corporations aggregate might have made what eftates they pleafed, without the confirmation of any other perfon whatfoever. Whereas now, by feveral ftatutes, this power where it was unreafonable, and might be made an ill ufe of, is reftrained ; and, where in the other cafes the reftraint by the common law feemed too hard, it is in fome meafure removed. The former ftatutes are called the *reftraining*, the latter the *enabling* ftatute. We will take a view of them all, in order of time.

AND, firft, the *enabling* ftatute, 32 Hen. VIII. c. 28. empowers three manner of perfons to make leafes, to endure for three lives or one and twenty years, which could not do fo before. As, firft, tenant in tail, may by fuch leafes bind his iffue in tail, but not thofe in remainder or reverfion. Secondly, a hufband feifed in right of his wife, in fee-fimple or fee-tail, provided the wife joins in fuch leafe, may bind her and her heirs thereby. Laftly, all perfons feifed of an eftate of fee-fimple in right of their churches, except parfons and vicars, may (without the concurrence of any other perfon) bind their fucceffors. But then there muft many requifites be obferved, which the ftatute fpecifies, otherwife fuch leafes are not binding [f]. 1. The leafe muft be by indenture ; and not by deed poll, or by parol. 2. It muft begin from the making, or day of the making, and not at any greater diftance of time. 3. If there be any old leafe in being, it muft be firft abfolutely furrendered, or be within a year of expiring. 4. It muft be *either* for twenty one years, *or* three lives ; and not for both. 5. It muft not exceed the term of three lives, or twenty one years, but may be for a fhorter term. 6. It muft be of corporeal hereditaments, and not of fuch things as lie merely in grant ; for no rent can be referved thereout by the common law, as the leffor cannot refort to them to diftrein [q]. 7. It muft be of

[f] Co. Litt. 44.

[q] But now by the ftatute 5 Geo. III. c. 17. a leafe of tithes or other incorporeal hereditaments, alone, may be granted by any bifhop or ecclefiaftical or eleemofynary corporation, and the fucceffor fhall be intitled to recover the rent by an action of debt, which (in cafe of a freehold leafe) he could not have brought at the common law.

lands

lands and tenements moſt commonly letten for twenty years paſt; ſo that if they have been let for above half the time (or eleven years out of the twenty) either for life, for years, at will, or by copy of court roll, it is ſufficient. 8. The moſt uſual and cuſtomary feorm or rent, for twenty years paſt, muſt be reſerved yearly on ſuch leaſe. 9. Such leaſes muſt not be made without impeachment of waſte. Theſe are the guards, impoſed by the ſtatute (which was avowedly made for the ſecurity of farmers and the conſequent improvement of tillage) to prevent unreaſonable abuſes, in prejudice of the iſſue, the wife, or the ſucceſſor, of the reaſonable indulgence here given.

NEXT follows, in order of time, the *diſabling* or *reſtraining* ſtatute, 1 Eliz. c. 19. (made entirely for the benefit of the ſucceſſor) which enacts, that all grants by archbiſhops and biſhops (which include even thoſe confirmed by the dean and chapter; the which, however long or unreaſonable, were good at common law) other than for the term of one and twenty years or three lives from the making, or without reſerving the uſual rent, ſhall be void. Concurrent leaſes, if confirmed by the dean and chapter, are held to be within the exception of this ſtatute, and therefore valid; provided they do not exceed (together with the leaſe in being) the term permitted by the act[r]. But, by a ſaving expreſſly made, this ſtatute of 1 Eliz. did not extend to grants made by any biſhop to the crown; by which means queen Elizabeth procured many fair poſſeſſions to be made over to her by the prelates, either for her own uſe, or with intent to be granted out again to her favourites, whom ſhe thus gratified without any expenſe to herſelf. To prevent which[s] for the future, the ſtatute 1 Jac. I. c. 3. extends the prohibition to grants and leaſes made to the king, as well as to any of his ſubjects.

NEXT comes the ſtatute 13 Eliz. c. 10. explained and enforced by the ſtatutes 14 Eliz. c. 11 & 14. 18 Eliz. c. 11. and 43 Eliz. c. 29. which extend the reſtrictions, laid by the laſt

[r] Co. Litt. 45.   [s] 11 Rep. 71.

mentioned ſtatute on biſhops, to certain other inferior corporations, both ſole and aggregate. From laying all which together
we may collect, that all colleges, cathedrals, and other eccleſiaſtical, or eleemoſynary corporations, and all parſons and vicars,
are reſtrained from making any leaſes of their lands, unleſs under
the following regulations : 1. They muſt not exceed twenty one
years, or three lives, from the making. 2. The accuſtomed
rent, or more, muſt be yearly reſerved thereon. 3. Houſes in
corporations, or market towns, may be let for forty years ; provided they be not the manſion-houſes of the leſſors, nor have
above ten acres of ground belonging to them ; and provided the
leſſee be bound to keep them in repair : and they may alſo be
aliened in fee-ſimple for lands of equal value in recompenſe.
4. Where there is an old leaſe in being, no concurrent leaſe ſhall
be made, unleſs where the old one will expire within three
years. 5. No leaſe (by the equity of the ſtatute) ſhall be made
without impeachment of waſte[t]. 6. All bonds and covenants
tending to fruſtrate the proviſions of the ſtatutes 13 & 18 Eliz.
ſhall be void.

CONCERNING theſe reſtrictive ſtatutes there are two obſervations to be made. Firſt, that they do not, by any conſtruction,
enable any perſons to make ſuch leaſes as they were by common
law diſabled to make. Therefore a parſon, or vicar, though he
is reſtrained from making longer leaſes than for twenty one years
or three lives, even *with* the conſent of patron and ordinary, yet
is not enabled to make any leaſe at all, ſo as to bind his ſucceſſor, *without* obtaining ſuch conſent[u]. Secondly, that though
leaſes contrary to theſe acts are declared void, yet they are good
againſt the *leſſor* during his life, if he be a ſole corporation ;
and are alſo good againſt an aggregate corporation ſo long as the
head of it lives, who is preſumed to be the moſt concerned in
intereſt. For the act was intended for the benefit of the ſucceſſor only ; and no man ſhall make an advantage of his own wrong[w].

[t] Co. Litt. 45.   [w] *Ibid.* 45.
[u] *Ibid.* 44.

THERE is yet another reſtriction with regard to college leaſes, by ſtatute 18 Eliz. c. 6. which directs, that one third of the old rent, then paid, ſhould for the future be reſerved in wheat or malt, reſerving a quarter of wheat for each 6 s 8 d, or a quarter of malt for every 5 s; or that the leſſees ſhould pay for the ſame according to the price that wheat and malt ſhould be ſold for, in the market next adjoining to the reſpective colleges, on the market-day before the rent becomes due. This is ſaid[x] to have been an invention of lord treaſurer Burleigh, and ſir Thomas Smith, then principal ſecretary of ſtate; who, obſerving how greatly the value of money had ſunk, and the price of all proviſions riſen, by the quantity of bullion imported from the newfound Indies, (which effects were likely to increaſe to a greater degree) deviſed this method for upholding the revenues of colleges. Their foreſight and penetration has in this reſpect been very apparent: for, though the rent ſo reſerved in corn was at firſt but one third of the old rent, or half of what was ſtill reſerved in money, yet now the proportion is nearly inverted; and the money ariſing from corn rents is, *communibus annis*, almoſt double to the rents reſerved in money.

THE leaſes of beneficed clergymen are farther reſtrained, in caſe of their non-reſidence, by ſtatutes 13 Eliz. c. 20. 14 Eliz. c. 11. and 18 Eliz. c. 11. which direct, that, if any beneficed clergyman be abſent from his cure above fourſcore days in any one year, he ſhall not only forfeit one year's profit of his benefice, to be diſtributed among the poor of the pariſh; but that all leaſes made by him, of the profits of ſuch benefice, and all covenants and agreements of like nature, ſhall ceaſe and be void: except in the caſe of licenſed pluraliſts, who are allowed to demiſe the living, on which they are non-reſident, to their curates only; provided ſuch curates do not abſent themſelves above forty days in any one year. And thus much for leaſes, with their ſeveral enlargements and reſtrictions[y].

[x] Strype's annals of Eliz.
[y] For the other learning relating to leaſes,

which is very curious and diffuſive, I muſt refer the ſtudent to 3 Bac. abridg. 295. (title, *leaſes*

5. AN *exchange* is a mutual grant of equal interests, the one in consideration of the other. The word "exchange" is so individually requisite and appropriated by law to this case, that it cannot be supplied by any other word or expressed by any circumlocution[z]. The estates exchanged must be equal in quantity[a]; not of *value*, for that is immaterial, but of *interest*; as fee-simple for fee-simple, a lease for twenty years for a lease for twenty years, and the like. And the exchange may be of things that lie either in grant or in livery[b]. But no livery of seisin, even in exchanges of freehold, is necessary to perfect the conveyance[c]: for each party stands in the place of the other and occupies his right, and each of them hath already had corporal possession of his own land. But entry must be made on both sides; for, if either party die before entry, the exchange is void, for want of sufficient notoriety[d]. And so also, if two parsons, by consent of patron and ordinary, exchange their preferments; and the one is presented, instituted, and inducted, and the other is presented, and instituted, but dies before induction; the former shall not keep his new benefice, because the exchange was not completed, and therefore he shall return back to his own . For if, after an exchange of lands or other hereditaments, either party be evicted of those which were taken by him in exchange, through defect of the other's title; he shall return back to the possession of his own, by virtue of the implied warranty contained in all exchanges[f].

6. A PARTITION, is when two or more joint-tenants, coparceners, or tenants in common, agree to divide the lands so held among them in severalty, each taking a distinct part. Here, as in some instances there is a unity of interest, and in all a unity

---

leases and terms for years) where the subject is treated in a perspicuous and masterly manner; being supposed to be extracted from a manuscript of sir Geoffrey Gilbert.

[z] Co. Litt. 50, 51.

[a] Litt. §. 64, 65.

[b] Co Litt. 51.

[c] Litt. §. 62.

[d] Co. Litt. 50.

[e] Perk. §. 288.

[f] pag. 301.

of poffeffion, it is neceffary that they all mutually convey and affure to each other the feveral eftates, which they are to take and enjoy feparately. By the common law coparceners, being compellable to make partition, might have made it by parol only; but joint-tenants and tenants in common muft have done it by deed : and in both cafes the conveyance muft have been perfected by livery of feifin [g]. And the ftatutes of 31 Hen.VIII. c. 1. and 32 Hen.VIII. c.32. made no alteration in this point. But the ftatute of frauds 29 Car. II. c. 3. hath now abolifhed this diftinction, and made a deed in all cafes neceffary.

THESE are the feveral fpecies of *primary*, or *original* conveyances. Thofe which remain are of the *fecondary*, or *derivative* fort; which prefuppofe fome other conveyance precedent, and only ferve to enlarge, confirm, alter, reftrain, reftore, or transfer the intereft granted by fuch original conveyance. As,

7. RELEASES; which are a difcharge or conveyance of a man's right in lands or tenements, to another that hath fome former eftate in poffeffion. The words generally ufed therein are " remifed, releafed, and for ever quit-claimed [h]." And thefe releafes may enure either, 1. By way of *enlarging an eftate*, or *enlarger l' eftate* : as, if there be tenant for life or years, remainder to another in fee, and he in remainder releafes all his right to the particular tenant and his heirs, this gives him the eftate in fee [i]. But in this cafe the releffee muft be in *poffeffion* of fome eftate, for the releafe to work upon; for if there be leffee for years, and, before he enters and is in poffeffion, the leffor releafes to him all his right in the reverfion, fuch releafe is void for want of poffeffion in the releffee [k]. 2. By way of *paffing an eftate*, or *mitter l' eftate* : as when one of two coparceners releafeth all her right to the other, this paffeth the fee-fimple of the whole [l]. And in both thefe cafes there muft be a privity of eftate between the releffor and releffee [m]; that is, one of their eftates muft be

[g] Litt. §. 250. Co. Litt. 169.
[h] Litt. §. 445.
[i] Ibid. §. 465.
[k] Ibid. §. 459.
[l] Co. Litt. 273.
[m] Ibid. 272, 273.

fo

ſo related to the other, as to make but one and the ſame eſtate in law. 3. By way of *paſſing a right*, or *mitter le droit :* as if a man be diſſeiſed, and releaſeth to his diſſeiſor all his right; hereby the diſſeiſor acquires a new right, which changes the quality of his eſtate, and renders that lawful which before was tortious[n]. 4. By way of *extinguiſhment :* as if my tenant for life makes a leaſe to A for life, remainder to B and his heirs, and I releaſe to A; this extinguiſhes my right to the reverſion, and ſhall enure to the advantage of B's remainder as well as of A's particular eſtate[o]. 5. By way of *entry and feoffment :* as if there be two joint diſſeiſors, and the diſſeiſee releaſes to one of them, he ſhall be ſole ſeiſed, and ſhall keep out his former companion ; which is the ſame in effect as if the diſſeiſee had entered, and thereby put an end to the diſſeiſin, and afterwards had enfeoffed one of the diſſeiſors in fee[p]. And hereupon we may obſerve, that when a man has in himſelf the poſſeſſion of lands, he muſt at the common law convey the freehold by feoffment and livery ; which makes a notoriety in the country : but if a man has only a right or a future intereſt, he may convey that right or intereſt by a mere releaſe to him that is in poſſeſſion of the land : for the occupancy of the releſſee is a matter of ſufficient notoriety already.

8. A CONFIRMATION is of a nature nearly allied to a releaſe. Sir Edward Coke defines it[q] to be a conveyance of an eſtate or right *in eſſe*, whereby a voidable eſtate is made ſure and unavoidable, or whereby a particular eſtate is encreaſed : and the words of making it are theſe, " have given, granted, rati- " fied, approved, and confirmed[r]." An inſtance of the firſt branch of the definition is, if tenant for life leaſeth for forty years, and dieth during that term ; here the leaſe for years is voidable by him in reverſion : yet, if he hath confirmed the eſtate of the leſſee for years, before the death of tenant for life, it is no longer voidable but ſure[s]. The latter branch, or that which tends

[a] Litt. §. 466.
[o] *Ibid.* §. 470.
[p] Co. Litt. 278.

[q] 1 Inſt. 295.
[r] Litt. §. 515. 531.
[s] *Ibid.* §. 516.

to the encrease of a particular estate, is the same in all respects with that species of release, which operates by way of enlargement.

9. A SURRENDER, *sursumredditio*, or rendering up, is of a nature directly opposite to a release; for, as that operates by the greater estate's descending upon the less, a surrender is the falling of a less estate into a greater by deed. It is defined[t], a yielding up of an estate for life or years to him that hath the immediate reversion or remainder, wherein the particular estate may merge or drown, by mutual agreement between them. It is done by these words, "hath surrendered, granted, and yielded up." The surrenderor must be in possession[u]; and the surrenderee must have a higher estate, in which the estate surrendered may merge: therefore tenant for life cannot surrender to him in remainder for years[w]. In a surrender there is no occasion for livery of seisin[x]; for there is a privity of estate between the surrenderor, and the surrenderee; the one's particular estate, and the other's remainder are one and the same estate; and livery having been once made at the creation of it, there is no necessity for having it afterwards. And, for the same reason, no livery is required on a release or confirmation in fee to tenant for years or at will, though a freehold thereby passes; since the reversion of the relessor, or confirmor, and the particular estate of the relessee, or confirmee, are one and the same estate; and where there is already a possession, derived from such a privity of estate, any farther delivery of possession would be vain and nugatory[y].

10. AN *assignment* is properly a transfer, or making over to another, of the right one has in *any* estate; but it is usually applied to an estate for life or years. And it differs from a lease only in this: that by a lease one grants an interest less than his own, reserving to himself a reversion; in assignments he parts with the whole

[t] Co. Litt. 337.
[u] *Ibid.* 338.
[w] Perk. §. 589.

[x] Co. Litt. 50.
[y] Litt. §. 460.

property,

property, and the affignee ftands to all intents and purpofes in the place of the affignor.

11. A DEFEAZANCE is a collateral deed, made at the fame time with a feoffment or other conveyance, containing certain conditions, upon the performance of which the eftate then created may be *defeated*[z] or totally undone. And in this manner mortgages were in former times ufually made; the mortgagor enfeoffing the mortgagee, and he at the fame time executing a deed of defeazance, whereby the feoffment was rendered void on re-payment of the money borrowed at a certain day. And this, when executed at the fame time with the original feoffment, was confidered as part of it by the antient law[a]; and, therefore only, indulged: no fubfequent fecret revocation of a folemn conveyance, executed by livery of feifin, being allowed in thofe days of fimplicity and truth; though. when ufes were afterwards introduced, a revocation of fuch ufes was permitted by the courts of equity. But things that were merely executory, or to be completed by matter fubfequent, (as rents, of which no feifin could be had till the time of payment; and fo alfo annuities, conditions, warranties, and the like) were always liable to be recalled by defeazances made fubfequent to the time of their creation[b].

II. THERE yet remain to be fpoken of fome few conveyances, which have their force and operation by virtue of the *ftatute of ufes.*

USES and *trufts* are in their original of a nature very fimilar, or rather exactly the fame: anfwering more to the *fidei-commiffum* than the *ufus-fructus*, of the civil law; which latter was the temporary right of ufing a thing, without having the ultimate property, or full dominion of the fubftance[c]. But the *fidei-commiffum*, which ufually was created by will, was the difpofal of an inheritance to one, in confidence that he fhould convey it or dif-

---

[z] From the French verb *defaire, infectum reddere.*

[a] Co. Litt. 236.

[b] *Ibid.* 237.

[c] *Ff.* 7. 1. 1.

pofe of the profits at the will of another. And it was the bufinefs of a particular magiftrate, the *praetor fidei-commiffarius*, inftituted by Auguftus, to enforce the obfervance of this confidence[d].
So that the right thereby given was looked upon as a vefted right,
and entitled to a remedy from a court of juftice: which occafioned that known divifion of rights by the Roman law, into *jus
legitimum*, a legal right, which was remedied by the ordinary
courfe of law; *jus fiduciarium*, a right in truft, for which there
was a remedy in confcience; and *jus precarium*, a right in cour-
tefy, for which the remedy was only by intreaty or requeft[e]. In
our law, a ufe might be ranked under the rights of the fecond
kind; being a confidence repofed in another who was tenant of
the land, or *terre-tenant*, that he fhould difpofe of the land according to the intentions of *ceftuy que ufe*, or him to whofe ufe it
was granted, and fuffer him to take the profits[f]. As, if a feoffment was made to A and his heirs, to the ufe of (or in truft for) B
and his heirs; here at the common law A the *terre-tenant* had the
legal property and poffeffion of the land, but B the *ceftuy que ufe*
was in confcience and equity to have the profits and difpofal of it.

THIS notion was tranfplanted into England from the civil law,
about the clofe of the reign of Edward III[g], by means of the
foreign ecclefiaftics; who introduced it to evade the ftatutes of
mortmain, by obtaining grants of lands, not to their religious houfes
directly, but to *the ufe of* the religious houfes[h]: which the cleri-
cal chancellors of thofe times held to be *fidei-commiffa*, and binding in confcience; and therefore affumed the jurifdiction, which
Auguftus had vefted in his *praetor*, of compelling the execution
of fuch trufts in the court of chancery. And, as it was moft
eafy to obtain fuch grants from dying perfons, a maxim was eftablifhed, that though by law the lands themfelves were not devifable, yet if a teftator had enfeoffed another to his own ufe,
and fo was poffeffed of the ufe only, fuch ufe was devifable by

[d] *Inft.* 2. *tit.* 23.
[e] *Ff.* 43. 26. 1. Bacon on ufes. 8°. 306.
[f] Plowd. 352.

[g] Stat. 50 Edw. III. c.6. 1 Ric. II. c.9.
[h] See pag. 271.

will.

will. But we have seen [i] how this evasion was crushed in it's infancy, by statute 15 Ric. II. c. 5. with respect to religious houses.

YET, the idea being once introduced, however fraudulently, it afterwards continued to be often innocently, and sometimes very laudably, applied to a number of civil purposes : particularly as it removed the restraint of alienations by will, and permitted the owner of lands in his lifetime to make various designations of their profits, as prudence, or justice, or family convenience, might from time to time require. Till at length, during our long wars in France and the subsequent civil commotions between the houses of York and Lancaster, uses grew almost universal : through the desire that men had (when their lives were continually in hazard) of providing for their children by will, and of securing their estates from forfeitures; when each of the contending parties, as they became uppermost, alternately attainted the other. Wherefore about the reign of Edward IV, (before whose time, lord Bacon remarks [k], there are not six cases to be found relating to the doctrine of uses) the courts of equity began to reduce them to something of a regular system.

ORIGINALLY it was held that the chancery could give no relief, but against the very person himself intrusted for *cestuy que use*, and not against his heir or alienee. This was altered in the reign of Henry VI, with respect to the heir [l]; and afterwards the same rule, by a parity of reason, was extended to such alienees as had purchased either without a valuable consideration, or with an express notice of the use [m]. But a purchasor for a valuable consideration, without notice, might hold the land discharged of any trust or confidence. And also it was held, that neither the king or queen, on account of their dignity royal [n], nor any corporation aggregate, on account of it's limited capacity [o], could be seised to any use but their own; that is, they

[i] pag. 272.
[k] on uses. 313.
[l] Keilw. 42. Yearbook 22 Edw. IV. 6.
[m] Keilw. 46. Bacon of uses. 312.

[n] Bro. *Abr. tit. Feoffm. al uses.* 31. Bacon of uses. 346, 347.
[o] Bro. *Abr. tit. Feoffm. al uses.* 40. Bacon. 347.

might hold the lands, but were not compellable to execute the truſt. And, if the feoffee to uſes died without heir, or committed a forfeiture, or married, neither the lord who entered for his eſcheat or forfeiture, nor the huſband who retained the poſſeſſion as tenant by the curteſy, nor the wife who was aſſigned her dower, were liable to perform the uſe[p]; becauſe they were not parties to the truſt, but came in by act of law: though doubtleſs their title in reaſon was no better than that of the heir.

On the other hand the uſe itſelf, or intereſt of *ceſtuy que uſe*, was learnedly refined upon with many elaborate diſtinctions. And, 1. It was held that nothing could be granted to a uſe, whereof the uſe is inſeparable from the poſſeſſion; as annuities, ways, commons, and authorities, *quae ipſo uſu conſumuntur*[q]: or whereof the ſeiſin could not be inſtantly given[r]. 2. A uſe could not be raiſed without a ſufficient conſideration. For where a man makes a feoffment to another without any conſideration, equity preſumes that he meant it to the uſe of himſelf[s]: unleſs he expreſſly declares it to be to the uſe of another, and then nothing ſhall be preſumed contrary to his own expreſſions[t]. But, if either a good or a valuable conſideration appears, equity will immediately raiſe a uſe correſpondent to ſuch conſideration[u]. 3. Uſes were deſcendible according to the rules of the common law, in the caſe of inheritances in poſſeſſion[w]; for in this and many other reſpects *aequitas ſequitur legem*, and cannot eſtabliſh a different rule of property from that which the law has eſtabliſhed. 4. Uſes might be aſſigned by ſecret deeds between the parties[x], or be deviſed by laſt will and teſtament[y]: for, as the legal eſtate in the ſoil was not transferred by theſe tranſactions, no livery of ſeiſin was neceſſary; and, as the intention of the parties was the leading principle in this ſpecies of property, any inſtrument declaring that intention was allowed to be binding in

[p] 1 Rep. 122.
[q] 1 Jon. 127.
[r] Cro. Eliz. 401.
[s] See pag 296.
[t] 1 And. 37.

[u] Moor. 684.
[w] 2 Roll. Abr. 780.
[x] Bacon of uſes. 312.
[y] *Ibid.* 308.

equity.

equity. But *ceftuy que ufe* could not at common law aliene the legal intereft of the lands, without the concurrence of his feoffee[z]; to whom he was accounted by law to be only tenant at fufferance[a]. 5. Ufes were not liable to any of the feodal burthens; and particularly did not efcheat for felony or other defeĉt of blood; for efcheats, *&c*, are the confequence of *tenure*, and ufes are *held* of nobody: but the land itfelf was liable to efcheat, whenever the blood of the feoffee to ufes was extinguifhed by crime or by defeĉt; and the lord (as was before obferved) might hold it difcharged of the ufe[b]. 6. No wife could be endowed, or hufband have his curtefy, of a ufe[c]: for no truft was declared for their benefit, at the original grant of the eftate. And therefore it became cuftomary, when moft eftates were put in ufe, to fettle before marriage fome joint eftate to the ufe of the hufband and wife for their lives; which was the original of modern jointures[d]. 7. A ufe could not be extended by writ of *elegit*, or other legal procefs, for the debts of *ceftuy que ufe*[e]. For, being merely a creature of equity, the common law, which looked no farther than to the perfon aĉtually feifed of the land, could award no procefs againft it.

I T is impraĉticable, upon our prefent plan, to purfue the doctrine of ufes through all the refinements and niceties, which the ingenuity of the times (abounding in fubtile difquifitions) deduced from this child of the imagination; when once a departure was permitted from the plain fimple rules of property eftablifhed by the antient law. Thefe principal outlines will be fully fufficient to fhew the ground of lord Bacon's complaint[f], that this courfe of proceeding " was turned to deceive many of their juft and " reafonable rights. A man, that had caufe to fue for land, knew " not againft whom to bring his aĉtion, or who was the owner " of it. The wife was defrauded of her thirds; the hufband of

[z] Stat. 1 Ric. III. c. 1.
[a] Bro. *Abr. ibid.* 23.
[b] Jenk. 190.
[c] 4 Rep. 1. 2 And. 75.

[d] See pag. 137.
[e] Bro. *Abr. tit. executions.* 90.
[f] Ufe of the law. 153.

" his

" his curtefy; the lord of his wardfhip, relief, heriot, and ef-
" cheat; the creditor of his extent for debt; and the poor te-
" nant of his leafe." To remedy thefe inconveniences abundance
of ftatutes were provided, which made the lands liable to be extended by the creditors of *ceftuy que ufe*[g]; allowed actions for
the freehold to be brought againft him, if in the actual pernancy
or enjoyment of the profits[h]; made him liable to actions of
wafte[i]; eftablifhed his conveyances and leafes made without the
concurrence of his feoffees[k]; and gave the lord the wardfhip
of his heir, with certain other feodal perquifites[l].

T H E S E provifions all tended to confider *ceftuy que ufe* as the
real owner of the eftate; and at length that idea was carried into
full effect by the ftatute 27 Hen. VIII. c. 10. which is ufually
called the *ftatute of ufes*, or, in conveyances and pleadings, the
ftatute *for transferring ufes into poffeffion*. The hint feems to have
been derived from what was done at the acceffion of king Richard III; who having, when duke of Glocefter, been frequently
made a feoffee to ufes, would upon the affumption of the crown (as
the law was then underftood) have been intitled to hold the lands
difcharged of the ufe. But, to obviate fo notorious an injuftice,
an act of parliament was immediately paffed[m], which ordained
that, where he had been fo infeoffed jointly with other perfons,
the land fhould veft in the other feoffees, as if he had never been
named; and that, where he ftood folely infeoffed, the eftate
itfelf fhould veft in *ceftuy que ufe* in like manner as he had the
ufe. And fo the ftatute of Henry VIII, after reciting the various
inconveniences before-mentioned and many others, enacts, that
" when any perfon fhall be *feifed* of lands, &c, to the ufe, confi-
" dence, or truft, of any other perfon or body politick, the perfon
" or corporation intitled to the ufe in fee-fimple, fee-tail, for life,

---

[g] Stat. 50 Edw III. c.6. 2 Ric. II. feff.2.
c. 3. 19 Hen V 1 c. 15.
[h] Stat 1 Ric. II. c 9. 4 Hen. IV. c. 7.
11 Hen VI. c. 3. 1 Hen. VII. c. 1.
[i] Stat. 11 Hen. VI. c. 5.

[k] Stat. 1 Ric. III. c. 1.
[l] Stat. 4 Hen. VII. c. 17. 19 Hen. VII.
c. 15.
[m] 1 Ric. III. c. 5.

" or

" or years, or otherwife, fhall from thenceforth ftand and be feifed
" or poffeffed of the land, *&c*, of and in the like eftates as they
" have in the ufe, truft, or confidence; and that the eftate of
" the perfon fo feifed to ufes fhall be deemed to be in him or
" them that have the ufe, in fuch quality, manner, form, and
" condition, as they had before in the ufe." The ftatute thus
executes the ufe, as our lawyers term it; that is, it conveys the
poffeffion to the ufe, and transfers the ufe into poffeffion : thereby
making *ceftuy que ufe* complete owner of the lands and tenements,
as well at law as in equity.

THE ftatute having thus, not abolifhed the conveyance to
ufes, but only annihilated the intervening eftate of the feoffee,
and turned the intereft of *ceftuy que ufe* into a legal inftead of an
equitable ownerfhip ; the courts of common law began to take
cognizance of ufes, inftead of fending the party to feek his relief in chancery. And, confidering them now as merely a mode
of conveyance, very many of the rules before eftablifhed in equity
were adopted with improvements by the judges of the common
law. The fame perfons only were held capable of being feifed
to a ufe, the fame confiderations were neceffary for raifing it,
and it could only be raifed of the fame hereditaments, as formerly. But as the ftatute, the inftant it was raifed, converted it
into an actual poffeffion of the land, a great number of the incidents, that formerly attended it in it's fiduciary ftate, were now
at an end. The land could not efcheat or be forfeited by the act
or defect of the feoffee, nor be aliened to any purchafor difcharged of the ufe, nor be liable to dower or curtefy on account of
the feifin of fuch feoffee ; becaufe the legal eftate never refts in
him for a moment, but is inftantaneoufly transferred to *ceftuy que
ufe*, as foon as the ufe is declared. And, as the ufe and the land
were now convertible terms, they became liable to dower, curtefy,
and efcheat, in confequence of the feifin of *ceftuy que ufe*, who
was now become the *terre-tenant* alfo; and they likewife were
no longer devifable by will.

THE

THE various neceffities of mankind induced alfo the judges very foon to depart from the rigour and fimplicity of the rules of the common law, and to allow a more minute and complex conftruction upon conveyances to ufes than upon others. Hence it was adjudged, that the ufe need not always be executed the inftant the conveyance is made : but, if it cannot take effect at that time, the operation of the ftatute may wait till the ufe fhall arife upon fome future contingency, to happen within a reafonable period of time; and in the mean while the antient ufe fhall remain in the original grantor : as, when lands are conveyed to the ufe of A and B, after a marriage fhall be had between them[n], or to the ufe of A and his heirs till B fhall pay him a fum of money, and then to the ufe of B and his heirs[o]. Which doctrine, when devifes by will were again introduced, and confidered as equivalent in point of conftruction to declarations of ufes, was alfo adopted in favour of *executory devifes*[p]. But herein thefe, which are called *contingent* or *fpringing*, ufes differ from an executory devife; in that there muft be a perfon feifed to fuch ufes at the time when the contingency happens, elfe they can never be executed by the ftatute; and therefore, if the eftate of the feoffee to fuch ufe be deftroyed by alienation or otherwife, before the contingency arifes, the ufe is deftroyed for ever[q]: whereas by an executory devife the freehold itfelf is transferred to the future devifee. And, in both thefe cafes, a fee may be limited to take effect after a fee[r]; becaufe, though that was forbidden by the common law in favour of the lord's efcheat, yet, when the legal eftate was not extended beyond one fee-fimple, fuch fubfequent ufes (after a ufe in fee) were before the ftatute permitted to be limited in equity; and then the ftatute executed the legal eftate in the fame manner as the ufe before fubfifted. It was alfo held that a ufe, though executed, may change from one to another by circumftances *ex poft facto*[s]; as, if A makes a feoffment

[n] 2 Roll. Abr. 791. Cro. Eliz. 439.
[o] Bro. *Abr. tit. Feoffm. al ufes.* 30.
[p] See pag. 173.
[q] 1 Rep. 134. 138. Cro. Eliz. 439.
[r] Pollexf. 78. 10 Mod. 423.
[s] Bro. *Abr. tit. Feoffm. al ufes.* 30.

to the use of his intended wife and her eldest son for their
lives, upon the marriage the wife takes the whole use in severalty; and, upon the birth of a son, the use is executed jointly
in them both[t]. This is sometimes called a *secondary*, sometimes
a *shifting*, use. And, whenever the use limited by the deed expires,
or cannot vest, it returns back to him who raised it, after such
expiration or during such impossibility, and is stiled a *resulting*
use. As, if a man makes a feoffment to the use of his intended
wife for life, with remainder to the use of her first-born son in
tail : here, till he marries the use results back to himself; after
marriage, it is executed in the wife for life; and, if she dies without issue, the whole results back to him in fee[u]. It was likewise
held, that the uses originally declared may be revoked at any future time, and new uses be declared of the land, provided the
grantor reserved to himself such a power at the creation of the
estate; whereas the utmost that the common law would allow,
was a deed of defeazance coeval with the grant itself (and therefore esteemed a part of it) upon events specifically mentioned[w].
And, in case of such a revocation, the old uses were held instantly
to cease, and the new ones to become executed in their stead[x].
And this was permitted, partly to indulge the convenience, and
partly the caprice of mankind; who (as lord Bacon observes[y])
have always affected to have the disposition of their property revocable in their own time, and irrevocable ever afterwards.

BY this equitable train of decisions in the courts of law, the
power of the court of chancery over landed property was greatly
curtailed and diminished. But one or two technical scruples, which
the judges found it hard to get over, restored it with tenfold increase. They held in the first place, that " no use could be li-
" mited on a use[z]," and that when a man bargains and sells his
land for money, which raises a use by implication to the bargainee, the limitation of a farther use to another person is re-

[t] Bacon of uses. 351.

[u] *Ibid.* 350. 1 Rep. 120.

[w] See pag. 327.

[x] Co. Litt. 237.

[y] on uses. 316.

[z] Dyer. 155.

pugnant

pugnant and therefore void[a]. And therefore, on a feoffment to A and his heirs, to the ufe of B and his heirs, in truft for C and his heirs, they held that the ftatute executed only the firft ufe, and that the fecond was a mere nullity : not adverting, that the inftant the firft ufe was executed in B, he became feifed to the ufe of C, which fecond ufe the ftatute might as well be permitted to execute as it did the firft; and fo the legal eftate might be inftantaneoufly tranfmitted down, through a hundred ufes upon ufes, till finally executed in the laft *ceftuy que ufe*. Again; as the ftatute mentions only fuch perfons as were *feifed* to the ufe of others, this was held not to extend to terms of years, or other chattel interefts, whereof the termor is not *feifed*, but only *poffeffed*[b]; and therefore, if a term of one thoufand years be limited to A, to the ufe of (or in truft for) B, the ftatute does not execute this ufe, but leaves it as at common law[c]. And laftly, (by more modern refolutions) where lands are given to one and his heirs, in truft to receive and pay over the profits to another, this ufe is not executed by the ftatute : for the land muft remain in the truftee to enable him to perform the truft[d].

O F the two more antient diftinctions the courts of equity quickly availed themfelves. In the firft cafe it was evident, that B was never intended by the parties to have any beneficial intereft; and, in the fecond, the *ceftuy que ufe* of the term was expreffly driven into the court of chancery to feek his remedy : and therefore that court determined, that though thefe were not *ufes*, which the ftatute could execute, yet ftill they were *trufts* in equity, which in confcience ought to be performed. To this the reafon of mankind affented, and the doctrine of ufes was revived, under the denomination of *trufts :* and thus, by this ftrict conftruction of the courts of law, a ftatute made upon great deliberation, and introduced in the moft folemn manner, has had little other effect than to make a flight alteration in the formal words of a conveyance[e].

[a] 1 And. 37. 136.
[b] Bacon law of ufes. 335. Jenk. 244.
[c] Poph. 76. Dyer. 369.
[d] 1 Equ. Caf. abr. 383, 384.
[e] Vaugh. 50. Atk. 591

HOWEVER,

HOWEVER, the courts of equity, in the exercife of this new jurifdiction, have wifely avoided in a great degree thofe mifchiefs which made ufes intolerable. They now confider a truft-eftate (either when exprefly declared or refulting by neceffary implication) as equivalent to the legal ownerfhip, governed by the fame rules of property, and liable to every charge in equity, which the other is fubject to in law: and, by a long feries of uniform determinations, for now near a century paft, with fome affiftance from the legiflature, they have raifed a new fyftem of rational jurifprudence, by which trufts are made to anfwer in general all the beneficial ends of ufes, without their inconvenience or frauds. The truftee is confidered as merely the inftrument of conveyance, and can in no fhape affect the eftate, unlefs by alienation for a valuable confideration to a purchafor without notice[f]; which, as *ceftuy que ufe* is generally in poffeffion of the land, is a thing that can rarely happen. The truft will defcend, may be aliened, is liable to debts, to forfeiture, to leafes and other incumbrances, nay even to the curtefy of the hufband, as if it was an eftate at law. It has not yet indeed been fubjected to dower, more from a cautious adherence to fome hafty precedents[g], than from any well-grounded principle. It hath alfo been held not liable to efcheat to the lord, in confequence of attainder or want of heirs[h]: becaufe the truft could never be intended for his benefit. But let us now return to the ftatute of ufes.

THE only fervice, as was before obferved, to which this ftatute is now configned, is in giving efficacy to certain new and fecret fpecies of conveyances; introduced in order to render tranf-actions of this fort as private as poffible, and to fave the trouble of making livery of feifin, the only antient conveyance of corporeal freeholds: the fecurity and notoriety of which public inveftiture abundantly overpaid the labour of going to the land, or of fending an attorney in one's ftead. But this now has given way to

---

[f] 2 Freem. 43.
[g] 1 Chanc. Rep. 254. 2 P. W^ms. 640.
[h] Hardr. 494. Burgefs & Wheate. Hil. 32 Geo. II. in Canc.

12. A TWELFTH fpecies of conveyance, called a *covenant to ftand feifed to ufes*: by which a man, feifed of lands, covenants in confideration of blood or marriage that he will ftand feifed of the fame to the ufe of his child, wife, or kinfman; for life, in tail, or in fee. Here the ftatute executes at once the eftate; for the party intended to be benefited, having thus acquired the ufe, is thereby put at once into corporal poffeffion of the land[i], without ever feeing it, by a kind of parliamentary magic. But this conveyance can only operate, when made upon fuch weighty and interefting confiderations as thofe of blood or marriage.

13. A THIRTEENTH fpecies of conveyance, introduced by this ftatute, is that of a *bargain and fale* of lands; which is a kind of a real contract, whereby the bargainor for fome pecuniary confideration bargains and fells, that is, contracts to convey, the land to the bargainee; and becomes by fuch bargain a truftee for, or feifed to the ufe of, the bargainee; and then the ftatute of ufes completes the purchafe[j]: or, as it hath been well expreffed[k], the bargain firft vefts the ufe, and then the ftatute vefts the poffeffion. But as it was forefeen that conveyances, thus made, would want all thofe benefits of notoriety, which the old common law affurances were calculated to give; to prevent therefore clandeftine conveyances of freeholds, it was enacted in the fame feffion of parliament by ftatute 27 Hen. VIII. c. 16. that fuch bargains and fales fhould not enure to pafs a freehold, unlefs the fame be made by indenture, and *enrolled* within fix months in one of the courts of Weftminfter-hall or with the *cuftos rotulorum* of the county. Clandeftine bargains and fales of chattel interefts, or leafes for years, were thought not worth regarding, as fuch interefts were very precarious till about fix years before[l]; which alfo occafioned them to be overlooked in framing the ftatute of ufes: and therefore fuch bargains and fales are not directed to be enrolled. But how impoffible is it to forefee, and

---

[i] Bacon. Ufe of the law. 151.   [k] Cro. Jac. 696.
 Ibid. 150.   [l] See pag. 142.

provide

provide againſt, *all* the conſequences of innovations! This omiſ-
ſion has given riſe to

14. A FOURTEENTH ſpecies of conveyance, *viz.* by *leaſe
and releaſe*; firſt invented by ſerjeant Moore, ſoon after the ſtatute of uſes, and now the moſt common of any, and therefore
not to be ſhaken; though very great lawyers (as, particularly,
Mr Noy) have formerly doubted it's validity[m]. It is thus contrived. A leaſe, or rather bargain and ſale, upon ſome pecuniary
conſideration, for one year, is made by the tenant of the freehold
to the leſſee or bargainee. Now this, without any enrollment,
makes the bargainor ſtand ſeiſed to the uſe of the bargainee, and
veſts in the bargainee the *uſe* of the term for a year; and then
the ſtatute immediately annexes the *poſſeſſion*. He therefore, being thus in poſſeſſion, is capable of receiving a releaſe of the freehold and reverſion; which, we have ſeen before[n], muſt be made
to a tenant in poſſeſſion: and accordingly, the next day, a releaſe
is granted to him[o]. This is held to ſupply the place of livery of
ſeiſin; and ſo a conveyance by leaſe and releaſe is ſaid to amount
to a feoffment[p].

15. To theſe may be added deeds to *lead* or *declare the uſes* of
other more direct conveyances, as feoffments, fines, and recoveries; of which we ſhall ſpeak in the next chapter: and,

16. DEEDS of *revocation of uſes*; hinted at in a former page[q],
and founded in a previous power, reſerved at the raiſing of the
uſes[r], to revoke ſuch as were then declared; and to appoint others
in their ſtead, which is incident to the power of revocation[s].
And this may ſuffice for a ſpecimen of conveyances founded upon
the ſtatute of uſes; and will finiſh our obſervations upon ſuch
deeds as ſerve to *transfer* real property.

[m] 2 Mod. 252.
[n] pag. 324.
[o] See Appendix. Nº. II. §. 1, 2.
[p] Co. Litt. 270. Cro. Jac. 604.
[q] pag. 335.
[r] See Appendix. Nº. II. pag. xi.
[s] Co. Litt. 237.

BEFORE we conclude, it will not be improper to fubjoin a few remarks upon fuch deeds as are ufed not to *convey*, but to *charge* or incumber, lands, and *difcharge* them again : of which nature are, *obligations* or bonds, *recognizances*, and *defeazances* upon them both.

1. AN *obligation*, or bond, is a deed[t] whereby the obligor obliges himfelf, his heirs, executors, and adminiftrators, to pay a certain fum of money to another at a day appointed. If this be all, the bond is called a fingle one, *fimplex obligatio* ; but there is generally a condition added, that if the obligor does fome particular act, the obligation fhall be void, or elfe fhall remain in full force : as, payment of rent ; performance of covenants in a deed ; or repayment of a principal fum of money borrowed of the obligee, with intereft, which principal fum is ufually one half of the penal fum fpecified in the bond. In cafe this condition is not performed, the bond becomes forfeited, or abfolute at law, and charges the obligor while living ; and after his death the obligation defcends upon his heir, who (on defect of perfonal affets) is bound to difcharge it, provided he has real affets by defcent as a recompenfe. So that it may be called, though not a *direct*, yet a *collateral*, charge upon the lands. How it affects the perfonal property of the obligor, will be more properly confidered hereafter.

IF the condition of a bond be impoffible at the time of making it, or be to do a thing contrary to fome rule of law that is merely pofitive, or be uncertain, or infenfible, the condition alone is void, and the bond fhall ftand fingle and unconditional : for it is the folly of the obligor to enter into fuch an obligation, from which he can never be releafed. If it be to do a thing that is *malum in fe*, the obligation itfelf is void : for the whole is an unlawful contract, and the obligee fhall take no advantage from fuch a tranfaction. And if the condition be poffible at the time

[t] See Appendix. N°. III. pag. xiii.

of

of making it, and afterwards becomes impoffible by the act of
God, the act of law, or the act of the obligee himfelf, there the
penalty of the obligation is faved : for no prudence or forefight
of the obligor could guard againft fuch a contingency ᵘ. On the
forfeiture of a bond, or it's becoming fingle, the whole penalty
was recoverable at law : but here the courts of equity interpofed,
and would not permit a man to take more than in confcience he
ought ; *viz.* his principal, intereft, and expenfes, in cafe the forfeiture accrued by non-payment of money borrowed ; the damages fuftained, upon non-performance of covenants ; and the like.
And the ftatute 4 & 5 Ann. c. 16. hath alfo enacted, in the fame
fpirit of equity, that in cafe of a bond, conditioned for the payment of money, the payment or tender of the principal fum
due, with intereft, and cofts, even though the bond be forfeited
and a fuit commenced thereon, fhall be a full fatisfaction and
difcharge.

2. A *recognizance* is an obligation of record, which a man enters into before fome court of record or magiftrate duly authorized ʷ, with condition to do fome particular act ; as to appear at
the affifes, to keep the peace, to pay a debt, or the like. It is
in moft refpects like another bond : the difference being chiefly
this ; that the bond is the creation of a frefh debt or obligation
de novo, the recognizance is an acknowlegement of a former debt
upon record ; the form whereof is, " that A. B. doth acknow-
" lege to owe to our lord the king, to the plaintiff, to C. D. or
" the like, the fum of ten pounds," with condition to be void on
performance of the thing ftipulated : in which cafe the king,
the plaintiff, C. D. *&c*, is called the cognizee, " *is cui cognofci-*
" *tur;*" as he that enters into the recognizance is called the cognizor, " *is qui cognofcit.*" This, being either certified to, or taken
by the officer of fome court, is witneffed only by the record of
that court, and not by the party's feal : fo that it is not in ftrict
propriety a deed, though the effects of it are greater than a common obligation ; being allowed a priority in point of payment,

ᵘ Co. Litt. 206.   ʷ Bro. *Abr. tit. recognizance.* 24.

                                                                    and

and binding the lands of the cognizor, from the time of enrollment on record[x]. There are alſo other recognizances, of a private kind, *in nature of a ſtatute ſtaple,* by virtue of the ſtatute
23 Hen. VIII. c. 6. which have been already explained[y], and
ſhewn to be a charge upon real property.

3. A DEFEAZANCE, on a bond, or recognizance, or judgment recovered, is a condition which, when performed, defeats
or undoes it, in the ſame manner as a defeazance of an eſtate
before-mentioned. It differs only from the common condition of
a bond, in that the one is always inſerted in the deed or bond
itſelf, the other is made between the ſame parties by a ſeparate
and frequently a ſubſequent deed[z]. This, like the condition of
a bond, when performed, diſcharges and diſincumbers the eſtate
of the obligor.

THESE are the principal ſpecies of deeds or matter *in pais,*
by which eſtates may be either conveyed, or at leaſt affected.
Among which the conveyances to uſes are by much the moſt frequent of any; though in theſe there is certainly one palpable defect, the want of ſufficient notoriety: ſo that purchaſors or creditors cannot know with any abſolute certainty, what the eſtate,
and the title to it, in reality are, upon which they are to lay out
or to lend their money. In the antient feodal method of conveyance (by giving corporal ſeiſin of the lands) this notoriety was in
ſome meaſure anſwered; but all the advantages reſulting from
thence are now totally defeated by the introduction of death-bed
deviſes and ſecret conveyances: and there has never been yet any
ſufficient guard provided againſt fraudulent charges and incumbrances; ſince the diſuſe of the old Saxon cuſtom of tranſacting
all conveyances at the county court, and entering a memorial of
them in the chartulary or leger-book of ſome adjacent monaſtery[a];
and the failure of the general regiſter eſtabliſhed by king Richard
the firſt, for mortgages made to Jews, in the *capitula de Judaeis,*

[x] Stat. 29 Car. II. c. 3. §. 18.
[y] See pag. 160.
[z] Co. Litt. 237. 2 Saund. 47.
[a] Hickes *Diſſertat. epiſtolar.* 9.

of

of which Hoveden has preserved a copy. How far the establishment of a like general register, for deeds, and wills, and other
acts affecting real property, would remedy this inconvenience,
deserves to be well considered. In Scotland every act and event,
regarding the transmission of property, is regularly entered on
record [b]. And some of our own provincial divisions, particularly
the extended county of York, and the populous county of Mid-
dlesex, have prevailed with the legislature [c] to erect such registers
in their several districts. But, however plausible these provisions
may appear in theory, it hath been doubted by very competent
judges, whether more disputes have not arisen in those counties
by the inattention and omissions of parties, than prevented by
the use of registers.

[b] Dalrymple on feodal property. 262, &c.
[c] Stat. 2 & 3 Ann. c. 4. 6 Ann. c. 35. 7 Ann. c. 20. 8 Geo. II. c. 6.

CHAPTER THE TWENTY FIRST.

Of ALIENATION by matter of RECORD.

ASSURANCES by *matter of record* are fuch as do not entirely depend on the act or confent of the parties them-felves: but the fanction of a court of record is called in, to fub-ftantiate, preferve, and be a perpetual teftimony of, the transfer of property from one man to another; or of it's eftablifhment, when already transferred. Of this nature are, 1. Private acts of parliament. 2. The king's grants. 3. Fines. 4. Common re-coveries.

I. PRIVATE *acts of parliament* are, efpecially of late years, become a very common mode of affurance. For it may fome-times happen, that, by the ingenuity of fome, and the blunders of other practitioners, an eftate is moft grievoufly entangled by a multitude of contingent remainders, refulting trufts, fpringing ufes, executory devifes, and the like artificial contrivances; (a confufion unknown to the fimple conveyances of the common law) fo that it is out of the power of either the courts of law or equity to relieve the owner. Or it may fometimes happen, that, by the ftrictnefs or omiffions of family fettlements, the te-nant of the eftate is abridged of fome reafonable power, (as let-ting leafes, making a jointure for a wife, or the like) which power cannot be given him by the ordinary judges either in com-mon law or equity. Or it may be neceffary, in fettling an e-ftate, to fecure it againft the claims of infants or other perfons

under

under legal difabilities; who are not bound by any judgments or decrees of the ordinary courts of juftice. In thefe, or other cafes of the like kind, the tranfcendent power of parliament is called in, to cut the Gordian knot; and by a particular law, enacted for this very purpofe, to unfetter an eftate; to give it's tenant reafonable powers; or to affure it to a purchafor, againft the remote or latent claims of infants or difabled perfons, by fettling a proper equivalent in proportion to the intereft fo barred. This practice was carried to a great length in the year fucceeding the reftoration; by fetting afide many conveyances alleged to have been made by conftraint, or in order to fcreen the eftates from being forfeited during the ufurpation. And at laft it proceeded fo far, that, as the noble hiftorian expreffes it [a], every man had raifed an equity in his own imagination, that he thought ought to prevail againft any defcent, teftament, or act of law, and to find relief in parliament : which occafioned the king at the clofe of the feffion to remark [b], that the good old rules of law are the beft fecurity; and to wifh, that men might not have too much caufe to fear, that the fettlements which they make of their eftates fhall be too eafily unfettled when they are dead, by the power of parliament.

ACTS of this kind are however at prefent carried on, in both houfes, with great deliberation and caution; particularly in the houfe of lords they are ufually referred to two judges, to examine and report the facts alleged, and to fettle all technical forms. Nothing alfo is done without the confent, expreffly given, of all parties in being and capable of confent, that have the remoteft intereft in the matter; unlefs fuch confent fhall appear to be perverfely and without any reafon withheld. And, as was before hinted, an equivalent in money or other eftate is ufually fettled upon infants, or perfons not *in effe*, or not of capacity to act for themfelves, who are to be concluded by this act. And a general faving is conftantly added, at the clofe of. the bill, of the right and intereft of all perfons whatfoever; except thofe whofe con-

[a] Lord Clar. Contin. 162. [b] *Ibid.* 163.

fent is fo given or purchafed, and who are therein particularly named.

A law, thus made, though it binds all parties to the bill, is yet looked upon rather as a private conveyance, than as the folemn act of the legiflature. It is not therefore allowed to be a *public*, but a mere *private* ftatute; it is not printed or publifhed among the other laws of the feffion; and no judge or jury is bound to take notice of it, unlefs the fame be fpecially fet forth and pleaded to them. It remains however enrolled among the public records of the nation, to be for ever preferved as a perpetual teftimony of the conveyance or affurance fo made or eftablifhed.

II. The *king's grants* are alfo matter of public record. For, as St. Germyn fays[c], the king's excellency is fo high in the law, that no freehold may be given to the king, nor derived from him, but by matter of record. And to this end a variety of offices are erected, communicating in a regular fubordination one with another, through which all the king's grants muft pafs, and be tranfcribed, and enrolled; that the fame may be narrowly infpected by his officers, who will inform him if any thing contained therein is improper, or unlawful to be granted. Thefe grants, whether of lands, honours, liberties, franchifes, or ought befides, are contained in charters, or letters *patent*, that is, open letters, *literae patentes:* fo called becaufe they are not fealed up, but expofed to open view, with the great feal pendant at the bottom; and are ufually directed or addreffed by the king to all his fubjects at large. And therein they differ from certain other letters of the king, fealed alfo with his great feal, but directed to particular perfons, and for particular purpofes: which therefore, not being proper for public infpection, are clofed up and fealed on the outfide, and are thereupon called writs *clofe, literae claufae*; and are recorded in the *clofe-rolls*, in the fame manner as the others are in the *patent-rolls*.

[c] Dr & Stud. l. 1. d. 8.

GRANTS or letters patent muſt firſt paſs by *bill:* which is prepared by the attorney and ſolicitor general, in conſequence of a warrant from the crown; and is then ſigned, that is, ſuper-ſcribed at the top, with the king's own *ſign manual,* and ſealed with his *privy ſignet,* which is always in the cuſtody of the prin-cipal ſecretary of ſtate; and then ſometimes it immediately paſſes under the great ſeal, in which caſe the patent is ſubſcribed in theſe words, " *per ipſum regem,* by the king himſelf[d]." Otherwiſe the courſe is to carry an extract of the bill to the keeper of the *privy ſeal,* who makes out a writ or warrant thereupon to the chancery; ſo that the ſign manual is the warrant to the privy ſeal, and the privy ſeal is the warrant to the great ſeal: and in this laſt caſe the patent is ſubſcribed, " *per breve de privato ſigillo,* by writ of privy " ſeal[e]." But there are ſome grants, which only paſs through certain offices, as the admiralty or treaſury, in conſequence of a *ſign manual,* without the confirmation of either the *ſignet,* the *great,* or the *privy* ſeal.

THE *manner* of granting by the king, does not more differ from that by a ſubject, than the *conſtruction* of his grants, when made. 1. A grant made by the king, *at the ſuit of the grantee,* ſhall be taken moſt beneficially *for* the king, and *againſt* the par-ty: whereas the grant of a ſubject is conſtrued moſt ſtrongly *a-gainſt the grantor.* Wherefore is is uſual to inſert in the king's grants, that they are made, not at the ſuit of the grantee, but " *ex ſpeciali gratia, certa ſcientia, et mero motu regis;*" and then they have a more liberal conſtruction[f]. 2. A ſubject's grant ſhall be conſtrued to include many things, beſides what are expreſſed, if neceſſary for the operation of the grant. Therefore, in a pri-vate grant of the profits of land for one year, free ingreſs, egreſs, and regreſs, to cut and carry away thoſe profits, are alſo inclu-ſively granted[g]: and if a feoffment of land was made by a lord

9 Rep. 18.
[e] *Ibid.* 2 Inſt. 555.

[f] Finch. L. 100. 10 Rep. 112.
[g] Co. Litt. 56.

to his villein, this operated as a manumiffion [h]; for he was other-wife unable to hold it. But the king's grant fhall not enure to any other intent, than that which is precifely expreffed in the grant. As, if he grants land to an alien, it operates nothing; for fuch grant fhall not alfo enure to make him a denizen, that fo he may be capable of taking by grant [i]. 3. When it appears, from the face of the grant, that the king is miftaken, or deceived, either in matter of fact or matter of law, as in cafe of falfe fug-geftion, mifinformation, or mifrecital of former grants; or if his own title to the thing granted be different from what he fuppofes; or if the grant be informal; or if he grants an eftate contrary to the rules of law; in any of thefe cafes the grant is abfolutely void [k]. For inftance; if the king grants lands to one and his *heirs male*, this is merely void: for it fhall not be an eftate-tail, becaufe there want words of procreation, to afcertain the body, out of which the heirs fhall iffue: neither is it a fee-fimple, as in common grants it would be; becaufe it may reafonably be fuppofed, that the king meant to give no more than an eftate-tail [l]: the grantee is therefore (if any thing) nothing more than tenant at will [m]. And, to prevent deceits of the king, with re-gard to the value of the eftate granted, it is particularly provided by the ftatute 1 Hen. IV. c. 6. that no grant of his fhall be good, unlefs, in the grantee's petition for them, exprefs mention be made of the real value of the lands.

III. WE are next to confider a very ufual fpecies of affurance, which is alfo of record; viz. a *fine* of lands and tenements. In which it will be neceffary to explain, 1. The *nature* of a fine; 2. It's feveral *kinds*; and 3. It's *force* and *effect*.

1. A FINE is fometimes faid to be a feoffment of record [n]: though it might with more accuracy be called, an acknowledge-ment of a feoffment on record. By which is to be underftood,

---

[h] Litt. §. 206.
[i] Bro. *Abr. tit Patent*. 62. Finch. L. 110.
[k] Freem. 172.
[l] Finch. 101, 102.

[m] Bro. *Abr. tit. Eftates*. 34. *tit. Patents*. 104. Dyer 270. Dav. 45.
[n] Co. Litt. 50.

that

that it has at leaſt the ſame force and effect with a feoffment, in the conveying and aſſuring of lands : though it is one of thoſe methods of transferring eſtates of freehold by the common law, in which livery of ſeiſin is not neceſſary to be actually given ; the ſuppoſition and acknowlegement thereof in a court of record, however fictitious, inducing an equal notoriety.   But, more particularly, a fine may be deſcribed to be an amicable compoſition or agreement of a ſuit, either actual or fictitious, by leave of the king or his juſtices ; whereby the lands in queſtion become, or are acknowleged to be, the right of one of the parties[o]. In it's original it was founded on an actual ſuit, commenced at law for recovery of the poſſeſſion of land ; and the poſſeſſion thus gained by ſuch compoſition was found to be ſo ſure and effectual, that fictitious actions were, and continue to be, every day commenced, for the ſake of obtaining the ſame ſecurity.

A FINE is ſo called becauſe it puts an *end,* not only to the ſuit thus commenced, but alſo to all other ſuits and controverſies concerning the ſame matter.   Or, as it is expreſſed in an antient record of parliament[p], 18 Edw. I. " *non in regno Angliae provide-* " *tur, vel eſt, aliqua ſecuritas major vel ſolennior, per quam aliquis* " *ſtatum certiorem habere poſſit, neque ad ſtatum ſuum verificandum* " *aliquod ſolennius teſtimonium producere, quam finem in curia domini* " *regis levatum : qui quidem finis ſic vocatur, eo quod finis et con-* " *ſummatio omnium placitorum eſſe debet, et hac de cauſa provideba-* " *tur.*"   Fines indeed are of equal antiquity with the firſt rudiments of the law itſelf ; are ſpoken of by Glanvil[q] and Bracton[r] in the reigns of Henry II, and Henry III, as things then well known and long eſtabliſhed ; and inſtances have been produced of them even before the Norman invaſion[s].   So that the ſtatute 18 Edw. I. called *modus levandi fines,* did not give them original, but only declared and regulated the manner in which they ſhould be levied, or carried on.   And that is as follows :

[o] Co. Litt. 120.
[p] 2 Roll. Abr. 13.
[q] *l.* 8. *c.* 1.

[r] *l.* 5. *t.* 5. *c.* 28.
[s] Plowd. 369.

I. THE

1. THE party, to whom the land is to be conveyed or assured, commences an action or suit at law against the other, generally an action of covenant, by suing out a writ or *praecipe*, called a writ of covenant[t]: the foundation of which is a supposed agreement or covenant, that the one shall convey the lands to the other; on the breach of which agreement the action is brought. On this writ there is due to the king, by antient prerogative, a *primer fine*, or a noble for every five marks of land sued for; that is, one tenth of the annual value[u]. The suit being thus commenced, then follows,

2. THE *licentia concordandi*, or leave to agree the suit[w]. For, as soon as the action is brought, the defendant, knowing himself to be in the wrong, is supposed to make overtures of peace and accommodation to the plaintiff. Who, accepting them, but having, upon suing out the writ, given pledges to prosecute his suit, which he endangers if he now deserts it without licence, he therefore applies to the court for leave to make the matter up. This leave is readily granted, but for it there is also another fine due to the king by his prerogative; which is an antient revenue of the crown, and is called the *king's silver*, or sometimes the *post fine*, with respect to the *primer fine* before-mentioned. And it is as much as the *primer fine*, and half as much more, or ten shillings for every five marks of land; that is, three twentieths of the supposed annual value[x].

3. NEXT comes the *concord*, or agreement itself[y], after leave obtained from the court; which is usually an acknowlegement from the deforciants (or those who keep the other out of possession) that the lands in question are the right of the complainant. And from this acknowlegement, or recognition of right, the party levying the fine is called the *cognizor*, and he to whom it is levied

[t] See Appendix, Nº. IV. §. 1.
[u] 2 Inst. 511.
[w] Append. Nº. IV. §. 2.
[x] 5 Rep. 39. 2 Inst. 511.
[y] Append. Nº .IV. §. 3.

the

the *cognizee*. This acknowlegement muſt be made either openly in the court of common pleas, or before one of the judges of that court, or elſe before commiſſioners in the country, empowered by a ſpecial authority called a writ of *dedimus poteſtatem*; which judges and commiſſioners are bound by ſtatute 18 Edw. I. ſt. 4. to take care that the cognizors be of full age, ſound memory, and out of priſon. If there be any feme-covert among the cognizors, ſhe is privately examined whether ſhe does it willingly and freely, or by compulſion of her huſband.

By theſe acts all the eſſential parts of a fine are completed; and, if the cognizor dies the next moment after the fine is acknowleged, provided it be ſubſequent to the day on which the writ is made returnable[z], ſtill the fine ſhall be carried on in all it's remaining parts: of which the next is

4. THE *note* of the fine[a]: which is only an abſtract of the writ of covenant, and the concord; naming the parties, the parcels of land, and the agreement. This muſt be enrolled of record in the proper office, by direction of the ſtatute 5 Hen. IV. c. 14.

5. THE fifth part is the *foot* of the fine, or concluſion of it: which includes the whole matter, reciting the parties, day, year, and place, and before whom it was acknowleged or levied[b]. Of this there are indentures made, or engroſſed, at the chirographer's office, and delivered to the cognizor and the cognizee; uſually beginning thus, " *haec eſt finalis concordia*, this is the final agree-" ment," and then reciting the whole proceeding at length. And thus the fine is completely levied at common law.

By ſeveral ſtatutes ſtill more ſolemnities are ſuperadded, in order to render the fine more univerſally public, and leſs liable to be levied by fraud or covin. And, firſt, by 27 Edw. I. c. 1. the

[z] Comb. 71.
[a] Append. Nº. IV. §. 4.
[b] *Ibid.* §. 5.

note of the fine fhall be openly read in the court of common pleas, at two feveral days in one week, and during fuch reading all pleas fhall ceafe. By 5 Hen. IV. c. 14. and 23 Eliz. c. 3. all the proceedings on fines either at the time of acknowlegement, or previous, or fubfequent thereto, fhall be enrolled of record in the court of common pleas. By 1 Ric. III. c. 7. confirmed and enforced by 4 Hen. VII. c. 24. the fine, after engroffment, fhall be openly read and proclaimed in court fixteen times ; viz. four times in the term in which it is made, and four times in each of the three fucceeding terms ; during which time all pleas fhall ceafe : but this is reduced to once in each term by 31 Eliz. c. 2. and thefe proclamations are endorfed on the back of the record [c]. It is alfo enacted by 23 Eliz. c. 3. that the chirographer of fines fhall every term write out a table of the fines levied in each county in that term, and fhall affix them in fome open part of the court of common pleas all the next term : and fhall alfo deliver the contents of fuch table to the fheriff of every county, who fhall at the next affifes fix the fame in fome open place in the court, for the more public notoriety of the fine.

2. FINES, thus levied, are of four kinds. 1. What in our law French is called a fine "*fur cognizance de droit, come ceo que il ad de fon done ;*" or, a fine upon acknowlegement of the right of the cognizee, as that which he hath of the gift of the cognizor [d]. This is the beft and fureft kind of fine ; for thereby the deforciant, in order to keep his covenant with the plaintiff, of conveying to him the lands in queftion, and at the fame time to avoid the formality of an actual feoffment and livery, acknowleges in court a former feoffment, or gift in poffeffion, to have been made by him to the plaintiff. This fine is therefore faid to be a feoffment of record ; the livery thus acknowleged in court, being equivalent to an actual livery : fo that this affurance is rather a confeffion of a former conveyance, than a conveyance now originally made ; for the deforciant, or cognizor, acknowleges,

[c] Append. No. IV. §. 6.

[d] This is that fort, of which an example is given in the appendix, No. IV.

cognofcit,

cognofcit, the right to be in the plaintiff, or cognizee, as that which he hath *de fon done*, of the proper gift of himfelf, the cognizor. 2. A fine "*fur cognizance de droit tantum*," or, upon acknowlegement of the right merely; not with the circumftance of a preceding gift from the cognizor. This is commonly ufed to pafs a *reverfionary* intereft, which is in the cognizor. For of fuch reverfions there can be no feoffment, or donation with livery, fuppofed; as the poffeffion during the particular eftate belongs to a third perfon [e]. It is worded in this manner; "that "the cognizor acknowleges the right to be in the cognizee; and "grants for himfelf and his heirs, that the reverfion, after the "particular eftate determines, fhall go to the cognizee [f]. 3. A fine "*fur conceffit*" is where the cognizor, in order to make an end of difputes, though he acknowleges no precedent right, yet grants to the cognizee an eftate *de novo*, ufually for life or years, by way of fuppofed compofition. And this may be done referving a rent, or the like: for it operates as a new grant [s]. 4. A fine "*fur done, grant, et render*," is a double fine, comprehending the fine *fur cognizance de droit come ceo, &c*, and the fine *fur conceffit*; and may be ufed to create particular limitations of eftate: whereas the fine *fur cognizance de droit come ceo, &c*, conveys nothing but an abfolute eftate, either of inheritance or at leaft of freehold [h]. In this laft fpecies of fine, the cognizee, after the right is acknowleged to be in him, grants back again, or renders to the cognizor, or perhaps to a ftranger, fome other eftate in the premifes. But, in general, the firft fpecies of fine, "*fur cogni*- "*zance de droit come ceo, &c*," is the moft ufed, as it conveys a clean and abfolute freehold, and gives the cognizee a feifin in law, without any actual livery; and is therefore called a fine executed, whereas the others are but executory.

3. WE are next to confider the *force* and *effect* of a fine. Thefe principally depend, at this day, on the common law, and the two ftatutes, 4 Hen. VII. c. 24. and 32 Hen. VIII. c. 36. The

[e] Moor. 629.
[f] Weft. Symb. p. 2. §. 95.
[s] Weft. p. 2. §. 66.
[h] Salk 340.

antient common law, with refpect to this point, is very forcibly declared by the ftatute 18 Edw. I. in thefe words. " And the " reafon, why fuch folemnity is required in the paffing of a fine, " is this ; becaufe the fine is fo high a bar, and of fo great force, " and of a nature fo powerful in itfelf, that it precludes not only " thofe which are parties and privies to the fine, and their heirs, " but all other perfons in the world, who are of full age, out of " prifon, of found memory, and within the four feas the day of " the fine levied ; unlefs they put in their claim within a year " and a day." But this doctrine, of barring the right by *non-claim*, was abolifhed for a time by a ftatute made in 34 Edw. I. c. 16. which admitted perfons to claim, and falfify a fine, at any indefinite diftance [i] : whereby, as fir Edward Coke obferves [k], great contention arofe, and few men were fure of their poffeffions, till the parliament held 4 Hen. VII reformed that mifchief, and excellently moderated between the latitude given by the ftatute and the rigour of the common law. For the ftatute, then made [l], reftored the doctrine of non claim ; but extended the time of claim. So that now, by that ftatute, the right of all ftrangers whatfoever is bound, unlefs they make claim, not within *one* year and a day, as by the common law, but within *five* years after proclamations made : except *feme-coverts*, infants, prifoners, perfons beyond the feas, and fuch as are not of whole mind ; who have five years allowed to them and their heirs, after the death of their hufbands, their attaining full age, recovering their liberty, returning into England, or being reftored to their right mind.

IT feems to have been the intention of that politic prince, king Henry VII, to have covertly by this ftatute extended fines to have been a bar of eftates-tail, in order to unfetter the more eafily the eftates of his powerful nobility, and lay them more open to alienations ; being well aware that power will always accompany property. But doubts having arifen whether they could, by mere implication, be adjudged a fufficient bar, (which they

[i] Litt. §. 441.
[k] 2 Inft. 518.

[l] 4 Hen. V' 24.

were

were expreſſly declared *not* to be by the ſtatute *de donis*) the ſtatute 32 Hen.VIII. c. 36. was thereupon made; which removes
all difficulties, by declaring that a fine levied by any perſon of
full age, to whom or to whoſe anceſtors lands have been entailed,
ſhall be a perpetual bar to them and their heirs claiming by force
of ſuch entail: unleſs the fine be levied by a woman after the
death of her huſband, of lands which were, by the gift of him
or his anceſtor, aſſigned to her in tail for her jointure ᵐ; or unleſs it be of lands entailed by act of parliament or letters patent,
and whereof the reverſion belongs to the crown.

FROM this view of the common law, regulated by theſe ſtatutes, it appears, that a fine is a ſolemn conveyance on record from
the cognizor to the cognizee, and that the perſons bound by a
fine are *parties*, *privies*, and *ſtrangers*.

THE *parties* are either the cognizors, or cognizees; and theſe
are immediately concluded by the fine, and barred of any latent
right they might have, even though under the legal impediment
of coverture. And indeed, as this is almoſt the only act that a
feme-covert, or married woman, is permitted by law to do, (and
that becauſe ſhe is privately examined as to her voluntary conſent, which removes the general ſuſpicion of compulſion by her
huſband) it is therefore the uſual and almoſt the only ſafe method, whereby ſhe can join in the ſale, ſettlement, or incumbrance, of any eſtate.

PRIVIES to a fine are ſuch as are any way related to the
parties who levy the fine, and claim under them by any right of
blood, or other right of repreſentation. Such as are the heirs
general of the cognizor, the iſſue in tail ſince the ſtatute of Henry
the eighth, the vendee, the deviſee, and all others who muſt
make title by the perſons who levied the fine. For the act of the
anceſtor ſhall bind the heir, and the act of the principal his ſub-

ᵐ See ſtatute 11 Hen.VII. c. 20.

ftitute, or fuch as claim under any conveyance made by him fubfequent to the fine fo levied [n].

S T R A N G E R S to a fine are all other perfons in the world,
except only parties and privies. And thefe are alfo bound by a
fine, unlefs, within five years after proclamations made, they
interpofe their claim; provided they are under no legal impediments, and have then a prefent intereft in the eftate. The impediments, as hath before been faid, are coverture, infancy, imprifonment, infanity, and abfence beyond fea : and perfons, who
are thus incapacitated to profecute their rights, have five years
allowed them to put in their claims after fuch impediments are
removed. Perfons alfo that have not a prefent, but a future intereft only, as thofe in remainder or reverfion, have five years allowed them to claim in, from the time that fuch right accrues [o].
And if within that time they neglect to claim, or (by the ftatute
4 Ann. c. 16.) if they do not bring an action to try the right,
within one year after making fuch claim, and profecute the fame
with effect, all perfons whatfoever are barred of whatever right
they may have, by force of the ftatute of non-claim.

B u t, in order to make a fine of any avail at all, it is neceffary that the parties fhould have fome intereft or eftate in the
lands to be affected by it. Elfe it were poffible that two ftrangers, by a mere confederacy, might without any rifque defraud
the owners by levying fines of their lands; for if the attempt be
difcovered, they can be no fufferers, but muft only remain *in ftatu
quo :* whereas if a tenant for life or years levies a fine, it is an
abfolute forfeiture of his eftate to the remainder-man or reverfioner [p], if claimed in proper time. It is not therefore to be
fuppofed that fuch tenants will frequently run fo great a hazard;
but if they do, and the claim is not duly made within five years
after their refpective terms expire [q], the eftate is for ever barred

[n] 3 Rep. 87.
[o] Co. Litt. 372.
[p] *Ibid.* 251.
[q] 2 Lev. 52.

by

by it. Yet where a stranger, whose presumption cannot thus be punished, officiously interferes in an estate which in no wise belongs to him, his fine is of no effect; and may at any time be set aside (unless by such as are parties or privies thereunto[r]) by pleading that "*partes finis nihil habuerunt.*" And thus much for the conveyance or assurance by fine: which not only like other conveyances binds the grantor himself, and his heirs; but also all mankind, whether concerned in the transfer or no, if they fail to put in their claims within the time allotted by law.

IV. THE fourth species of assurance, by matter of record, is a *common recovery.* Concerning the original of which, it was formerly observed[s], that common recoveries were invented by the ecclesiastics to elude the statutes of mortmain; and afterwards encouraged by the finesse of the courts of law in 12 Edw. IV. in order to put an end to all fettered inheritances, and bar not only estates-tail, but also all remainders and reversions expectant thereon. I am now therefore only to consider, first, the *nature* of a common recovery; and, secondly, it's *force* and *effect.*

1. AND, first, the *nature* of it; or what a common recovery is. A common recovery is so far like a fine, that it is a suit or action, either actual or fictitious: and in it the lands are *recovered* against the tenant of the freehold; which recovery, being a supposed adjudication of the right, binds all persons, and vests a free and absolute fee-simple in the recoveror. A recovery therefore being in the nature of an action at law, not immediately compromised like a fine, but carried on through every regular stage of proceeding, I am greatly apprehensive that it's form and method will not be easily understood by the student, who is not yet acquainted with the course of judicial proceedings; which cannot be thoroughly explained, till treated of at large in the third book of these commentaries. However I shall endeavour to state it's nature and progress, as clearly and concisely as I can; avoid-

[r] Hob. 334.   [s] pag. 117. 271.

ing

ing, as far as poffible, all technical terms, and phrafes not hitherto interpreted.

LET us, in the firft place, fuppofe David Edwards [t] to be tenant of the freehold, and defirous to fuffer a common recovery, in order to bar all entails, remainders, and reverfions, and to convey the fame in fee-fimple to Francis Golding. To effect this, Golding is to bring an action againft him for the lands; and he accordingly fues out a writ, called a *praecipe quod reddat*, becaufe thofe were it's initial or moft operative words, when the law proceedings were in Latin. In this writ the demandant Golding alleges, that the defendant Edwards (here called the tenant) has no legal title to the land; but that he came into poffeffion of it after one Hugh Hunt had turned the demandant out of it [v]. The fubfequent proceedings are made up into a record or recovery roll [u], in which the writ and complaint of the demandant are firft recited: whereupon the tenant appears, and calls upon one Jacob Morland, who is fuppofed, at the original purchafe, to have warranted the title to the tenant; and thereupon he prays, that the faid Jacob Morland may be called in to defend the title which he fo warranted. This is called the *voucher*, *vocatio*, or calling of Jacob Morland to warranty; and Morland is called the *vouchee*. Upon this, Jacob Morland, the vouchee, appears, is impleaded, and defends the title. Whereupon Golding, the demandant, defires leave of the court to *imparl*, or confer with the vouchee in private; which is (as ufual) allowed him. And foon afterwards the demandant, Golding, returns to court, but Morland the vouchee difappears, or makes default. Whereupon judgment is given for the demandant, Golding, now called the recoveror, to recover the lands in queftion againft the tenant, Edwards, who is now the recoveree: and Edwards has judgment to recover of Jacob Morland lands of equal value, in recompenfe for the lands fo warranted by him, and now loft by his default; which is agreeable to the doctrine of warranty mentioned in the preceding

[t] See appendix, N°. V.   [u] §. 2.
[v] §. 1.

chapter [w].

chapter ᵂ. This is called the recompenfe, or *recovery in value*. But Jacob Morland having no lands of his own, being ufually the cryer of the court (who, from being frequently thus vouched, is called the *common vouchee*) it is plain that Edwards has only a nominal recompenfe for the lands fo recovered againft him by Golding ; which lands are now abfolutely vefted in the faid re-coveror by judgment of law, and feifin thereof is delivered by the fheriff of the county. So that this collufive recovery operates merely in the nature of a conveyance in fee-fimple, from Ed-wards the tenant in tail, to Golding the purchafor.

THE recovery, here defcribed, is with a *fingle* voucher only ; but fometimes it is with *double*, *treble*, or farther voucher, as the exigency of the cafe may require. And indeed it is now ufual always to have a recovery with double voucher at the leaft ; by firft conveying an eftate of freehold to any indifferent perfon, againft whom the *praecipe* is brought ; and then he vouches the tenant in tail, who vouches over the common vouchee ˣ. For, if a recovery be had immediately againft tenant in tail, it bars only fuch eftate in the premifes of which he is then actually feifed ; whereas if the recovery be had againft another perfon, and the tenant in tail be vouched, it bars every latent right and intereft which he may have in the lands recovered ʸ. If Edwards there-fore be tenant of the freehold in poffeffion, and John Barker be tenant in tail in remainder, here Edwards doth firft vouch Bar-ker, and then Barker vouches Jacob Morland the common vouchee; who is always the laft perfon vouched, and always makes default : whereby the demandant Golding recovers the land againft the tenant Edwards, and Edwards recovers a recompenfe of equal value againft Barker the firft vouchee ; who recovers the like againft Morland the common vouchee, againft whom fuch ideal recovery in value is always ultimately awarded.

ᵂ pag. 301.
ˣ See appendix, pag. xviii.

ʸ Bro. *Abr.* tit. *Taile* 32. Plowd. 8.

THIS

THIS suppofed recompenfe in value is the reafon why the iffue in tail is held to be barred by a common recovery. For, if the recoveree fhould ever obtain a recompenfe in lands from the common vouchee (which there is a poffibility in contemplation of law, though a very improbable one, of his doing) thefe lands would fupply the place of thofe fo recovered from him by collufion, and would defcend to the iffue in tail [z]. This reafon will alfo hold, with equal force, as to *moft* remainder-men and reverfioners; to whom the poffibility will remain and revert, as a full recompenfe for the reality, which they were otherwife entitled to : but it will not *always* hold; and therefore, as Pigott fays [a], the judges have been even *aftuti*, in inventing other reafons to maintain the authority of recoveries. And, in particular, it hath been faid, that, though the eftate-tail is gone from the recoveree, yet it is not *deftroyed*, but only *transferred*; and ftill fubfifts, and will ever continue to fubfift (by conftruction of law) in the recoveror, his heirs, and affigns : and, as the eftate-tail fo continues to fubfift for ever, the remainders or reverfions expectant on the determination of fuch eftate-tail can never take place.

To fuch awkward fhifts, fuch fubtile refinements, and fuch ftrange reafoning, were our anceftors obliged to have recourfe, in order to get the better of that ftubborn ftatute *de donis*. The defign, for which thefe contrivances were fet on foot, was certainly laudable; the unrivetting the fetters of eftates-tail, which were attended with a legion of mifchiefs to the commonwealth : but, while we applaud the end, we cannot but admire the means. Our modern courts of juftice have indeed adopted a more manly way of treating the fubject; by confidering common recoveries in no other light, than as the formal mode of conveyance, by which tenant in tail is enabled to aliene his lands. But, fince the ill confequences of fettered inheritances are now generally feen and allowed, and of courfe the utility and expedience of fetting them at liberty are apparent; it hath often been wifhed, that the procefs of this conveyance was fhortened, and rendered lefs fubject to niceties, by either totally repealing the ftatute *de donis*, which perhaps, by reviving the old doctrine of conditional fees, might give birth to many litigations : or by vefting in every tenant in tail of full age the fame abfolute fee-fimple at once, which now he may obtain whenever he pleafes, by the collufive fiction of a common recovery; though this might poffibly bear hard upon thofe in remainder or reverfion, by abridging the chances they would otherwife frequently have, as no recovery can be fuffered in the intervals between term and term, which fometimes continue for near five months together : or, laftly, by empowering the tenant in tail to bar the eftate-tail by a folemn deed, to be made in term time and enrolled in fome court of record ; which is liable to neither of the other objections, and is warranted not only by the ufage of our American colonies, but by the precedent of the ftatute[b] 21 Jac. I. c. 19. which, in cafe of a bankrupt tenant in tail, empowers his commiffioners to fell the eftate at any time, by deed indented and enrolled. And if, in fo national a concern, the emoluments of the officers, concerned in paffing recoveries, are thought to be worthy attention, thofe might be provided for in the fees to be paid upon each enrollment.

2. THE *force* and *effect* of common recoveries may appear, from what has been faid, to be an abfolute bar not only of all eftates-tail, but of remainders and reverfions expectant on the determination of fuch eftates. So that a tenant in tail may, by this method of affurance, convey the lands held in tail to the recoveror his heirs and affigns, abfolutely free and difcharged of all conditions and limitations in tail, and of all remainders and reverfions. But, by ftatute 34 & 35 Hen.VIII. c. 20. no recovery had againft tenant in tail, of the king's gift, whereof the remainder or reverfion is in the king, fhall bar fuch eftate-tail, or the remainder or reverfion of the crown. And by the ftatute 11 Hen.VII. c. 20. no woman, after her hufband's death, fhall fuffer a recovery of lands fettled on her in tail by way of jointure

b See pag. 286.

by her hufband or any of his anceftors. And by ftatute 14 Eliz.
c. 8. no tenant for life, of any fort, can fuffer a recovery, fo as
to bind them in remainder or reverfion. For which reafon, if
there be tenant for life, with remainder in tail, and other remainders over, and the tenant for life is defirous to fuffer a valid recovery; either he, or the tenant to the *praecipe* by him made,
muft *vouch* the remainder-man in tail, otherwife the recovery is
void : but if he does vouch fuch remainder-man, and he appears
and vouches the common vouchee, it is then good ; for if a man
be vouched and appears, and fuffers the recovery to be had, it is
as effectual to bar the eftate-tail as if he himfelf were the recoveree [c].

I N all recoveries it is neceffary that the recoveree, or tenant
to the *praecipe*, as he is ufually called, be actually feifed of the
freehold, elfe the recovery is void [d]. For all actions, to recover
the feifin of lands, muft be brought againft the actual tenant of
the freehold, elfe the fuit will lofe it's effect ; fince the freehold
cannot be recovered of him who has it not. And, though thefe
recoveries are in themfelves fabulous and fictitious, yet it is neceffary that there be *actores fabulae*, properly qualified. But the
nicety thought by fome modern practitioners to be requifite in
conveying the legal freehold, in order to make a good tenant to the
praecipe, is removed by the provifions of the ftatute 14 Geo. II.
c. 20. which enacts, with a retrofpect and conformity to the antient rule of law [e], that, though the legal freehold be vefted in
leffees, yet thofe who are intitled to the next freehold eftate in
remainder or reverfion may make a good tenant to the *praecipe* :
and that, though the deed or fine which creates fuch tenant be
fubfequent to the judgment of recovery, yet, if it be in the fame
term, the recovery fhall be valid in law: and that, though the recovery itfelf do not appear to be entered, or be not regularly entered, on record, yet the deed to make a tenant to the *praecipe*,
and declare the ufes of the recovery, fhall after a poffeffion of

[c] Salk. 571,
[d] Pigott. 28,

[e] Pigott. 41, &c. 4 Burr. I. 115.

twenty

twenty years be fufficient evidence, on behalf of a purchafor for valuable confideration, that fuch recovery was duly fuffered. And this may fuffice to give the ftudent a general idea of common recoveries, the laft fpecies of affurances by matter of record.

BEFORE I conclude this head, I muft add a word concerning deeds to *lead,* or to *declare,* the *ufes* of fines, and of recoveries. For if they be levied or fuffered without any good confideration, and without any ufes declared, they, like other conveyances, enure only to the ufe of him who levies or fuffers them [f]. And if a confideration appears, yet as the moft ufual fine, " *fur cog-* " *nizance de droit come ceo, &c,*" conveys an abfolute eftate, without any limitations, to the cognizee ; and as common recoveries do the fame to the recoveror ; thefe affurances could not be made to anfwer the purpofe of family fettlements, (wherein a variety of ufes and defignations is very often expedient) unlefs their force and effect were fubjected to the direction of other more complicated deeds, wherein particular ufes can be more particularly expreffed. The fine or recovery itfelf, like a power once gained in mechanics, may be applied and directed to give efficacy to an infinite variety of movements, in the vaft and intricate machine of a voluminous family fettlement. And, if thefe deeds are made previous to the fine or recovery, they are called deeds to *lead* the ufes ; if fubfequent, deeds to *declare* them. As, if A tenant in tail, with remainder to himfelf in fee, would fettle his eftate on B for life, remainder to C in tail, remainder to D in fee ; this is what by law he has no power of doing effectually, while his own eftate-tail is in being. He therefore ufually covenants to levy a fine (or, if there be any remainders over, to fuffer a recovery) to E, and that the fame fhall enure to the ufes in fuch fettlement mentioned. This is now a deed to *lead* the ufes of the fine or recovery ; and the fine when levied, or recovery when fuffered, fhall enure to the ufes fo fpecified and no other. For though E, the conufee or recoveree, hath a fee-fimple vefted in himfelf by the fine or recovery ; yet, by the operation of this deed, he be-

[f] Dyer. 18.

comes

comes a mere inftrument or conduit-pipe, feifed only *to the ufe* of B, C, and D, in fucceffive order : which ufe is executed immediately, by force of the ftatute of ufes[g]. Or, if a fine or recovery be had without any previous fettlement, and a deed be *afterwards* made between the parties, *declaring* the ufes to which the fame fhall be applied, this will be equally good, as if it had been exprefsly levied or fuffered, in confequence of a deed directing it's operation to thofe particular ufes. For by ftatute 4 & 5 Ann. c. 16. indentures to *declare* the ufes of fines and recoveries, made *after* the fines and recoveries had and fuffered, fhall be good and effectual in law, and the fine and recovery fhall enure to fuch ufes, and be efteemed to be only in truft, notwithftanding the ftatute of frauds 29 Car. II. c. 3. enacts, that all trufts fhall be declared in writing, *at* (and not *after*) the time when fuch trufts are created.

[g] This doctrine may perhaps be more clearly illuftrated by example. In the deed or marriage fettlement in the appendix, N°. II. §. 2. we may fuppofe the lands to have been originally fettled on Abraham and Cecilia Barker for life, remainder to John Barker in tail, with divers other remainders over, reverfion to Cecilia Barker in fee ; and now intended to be fettled to the feveral ufes therein exprefled, viz of Abraham and Cecilia Barker till the marriage ; remainder to John Barker for life ; remainder to truftees to preferve the contingent remainders ; remainder to his widow for life, for her jointure ; remainder to other truftees, for a term of five hundred years ; remainder to their firft and other fons in tail ; remainder to their daughters in tail ; remainder to John Barker in tail ; remainder to Cecilia Barker in fee. Now it is neceffary, in order to bar the eftate-tail of John Barker, and the remainders expectant thereon, that a recovery be fuffered of the premifes ; and it is thought proper (for though ufual, it is by no means neceffary : fee Forrefter. 167.) that in order to make a good tenant of the freehold, or tenant to the *praecipe*, during the coverture, a fine fhould be levied by Abraham, Cecilia, and John Barker ; and it is agreed that the recovery itfelf be fuffered againft this tenant to the *praecipe*, who fhall vouch John Barker, and thereby bar his eftate-tail ; and become tenant of the fee-fimple by virtue of fuch recovery : the ufes of which eftate, fo acquired, are declared to be thofe exprefled in this deed. Accordingly the parties covenant to do thefe feveral acts, (fee pag. viii.) And in confequence thereof the fine and recovery are had and fuffered (N°. IV. and N°. V.) of which this conveyance is a deed to *lead* the ufes.

CHAPTER THE TWENTY SECOND.

OF ALIENATION BY SPECIAL CUSTOM.

WE are next to confider affurances by fpecial cuftom, obtaining only in particular places, and relative only to a
particular fpecies of real property. This therefore is a very narrow title; being confined to copyhold lands, and fuch cuftomary
eftates, as are holden in antient demefne, or in manors of a fimilar nature: which, being of a very peculiar kind, and originally no more than tenancies in pure or privileged villenage, were
never alienable by deed; for, as that might tend to defeat the
lord of his figniory, it is therefore a forfeiture of a copyhold[a].
Nor are they transferrable by matter of record, even in the king's
courts, but only in the court baron of the lord. The method
of doing this is generally by *furrender*; though in fome manors,
by fpecial cuftom, recoveries may be fuffered of copyholds[b]: but
thefe differing in nothing material from recoveries of free land,
fave only that they are not fuffered in the king's courts, but in
the court baron of the manor, I fhall confine myfelf to conveyances by furrender, and their confequences.

SURRENDER, *furfumredditio*, is the yielding up of the eftate
by the tenant into the hands of the lord, for fuch purpofes as in
the furrender are expreffed. As, it may be, to the ufe and behoof of A and his heirs; to the ufe of his own will; and the
like. The procefs, in moft manors, is, that the tenant comes to

---

[a] Litt. §. 74.   [b] Moor. 637.

the

the fteward, either in court, (or, if the cuftom permits, out of
court) or elfe to two cuftomary tenants of the fame manor, provided that alfo have a cuftom to warrant it; and there by delivering up a rod, a glove, or other fymbol, as the cuftom directs,
refigns into the hands of the lord, by the hands and acceptance
of his faid fteward, or of the faid two tenants, all his intereft and
title to the eftate; in truft to be again granted out by the lord,
to fuch perfons and for fuch ufes as are named in the furrender,
and the cuftom of the manor will warrant. If the furrender be
made out of court, then, at the next or fome fubfequent court,
the jury or homage muft prefent and find it upon their oaths;
which prefentment is an information to the lord or his fteward of
what has been tranfacted out of court. Immediately upon fuch
furrender in court, or upon prefentment of a furrender made out
of court, the lord by his fteward grants the fame land again to
ceftuy que ufe, (who is fometimes, though rather improperly, called
the furrenderee) to hold by the antient rents and cuftomary fervices; and thereupon admits him tenant to the copyhold, according to the form and effect of the furrender, which muft be
exactly purfued. And this is done by delivering up to the new
tenant the rod, or glove, or the like, in the name, and as the
fymbol, of corporal feifin of the lands and tenements. Upon
which admiffion he pays a fine to the lord, according to the cuftom of the manor, and takes the oath of fealty.

IN this brief abftract, of the manner of transferring copyhold
eftates, we may plainly trace the vifible footfteps of the feodal
inftitutions. The fief, being of a bafe nature and tenure, is un-
alienable without the knowlege and confent of the lord. For this
purpofe it is refigned up, or furrendered into his hands. Cuftom,
and the indulgence of the law, which favours liberty, has now
given the tenant a right to name his fucceffor; but formerly it was
far otherwife. And I am apt to fufpect that this right is of much
the fame antiquity with the introduction of ufes with refpect to
freehold lands: for the alienee of a copyhold had merely *jus fiduciarium*, for which there was no remedy at law, but only by *fubpoena*

in

in chancery[c]. When therefore the lord had accepted a furrender of his tenant's intereft, upon confidence to re-grant the eftate to another perfon, either then exprefly named or to be afterwards named in the tenant's will, the chancery inforced this truft as a matter of confcience; which jurifdiction, though feemingly new in the time of Edward IV[d], was generally acquiefced in, as it opened the way for the alienation of copyholds, as well as of freehold eftates, and as it rendered the *ufe* of them both equally devifable by teftament. Yet, even to this day, the new tenant cannot be admitted but by compofition with the lord, and paying him a fine by way of acknowlegement for the licence of alienation. Add to this the plain feodal inveftiture, by delivering the fymbol of feifin in prefence of the other tenants in open court; " *quando hafta vel aliud corporeum quidlibet porrigitur a domino fe in-* " *veftituram facere dicente; quae faltem coram duobus vafallis fo-* " *lenniter fieri debet*[e] :" and, to crown the whole, the oath of fealty annexed, the very bond of feodal fubjection. From all which we may fairly conclude, that, had there been no other evidence of the fact in the reft of our tenures and eftates, the very exiftence of copyholds, and the manner in which they are transferred, would inconteftably prove the very univerfal reception, which this northern fyftem of property for a long time obtained in this ifland; and which communicated itfelf, or at leaft it's fimilitude, even to our very villeins and bondmen.

THIS method of conveyance is fo effential to the nature of a copyhold eftate, that it cannot poffibly be transferred by any other affurance. No feoffment, fine, or recovery (in the king's courts) has any operation thereupon. If I would exchange a copyhold eftate with another, I cannot do it by an ordinary deed of exchange at the common law; but we muft furrender to each other's ufe, and the lord will admit us accordingly. If I would devife a copyhold, I muft furrender it to the ufe of my laft will

[c] Cro. Jac. 568.
[d] Bro. *Abr. tit. Tenant per copie.* 10.
[e] *Feud. l. 2. t. 2.*

and

and teftament; and in my will I muft declare my intentions, and name a devifee, who will then be entitled to admiffion f.

In order the more clearly to apprehend the nature of this peculiar affurance, let us take a feparate view of it's feveral parts; the furrender, the prefentment, and the admittance.

1. A surrender, by an admittance fubfequent whereto the conveyance is to receive it's perfection and confirmation, is rather a manifeftation of the alienor's intention, than a transfer of any intereft in poffeffion. For, till admittance of *ceftuy que ufe*, the lord taketh notice of the furrenderor as his tenant; and he fhall receive the profits of the land to his own ufe, and fhall difcharge all fervices due to the lord. Yet the intereft remains in him not abfolutely, but *fub modo*; for he cannot pafs away the land to any other, or make it fubject to any other incumbrance than it was fubject to at the time of the furrender. But no manner of legal intereft is vefted in the nominee before admittance. If he enters, he is a trefpaffer and punifhable in an action of trefpafs: and if he furrenders to the ufe of another, fuch furrender is merely void, and by no matter *ex poft facto* can be confirmed. For though he be admitted in purfuance of the original furrender, and thereby acquires afterwards a fufficient and plenary intereft as abfolute owner, yet his fecond furrender previous to his own admittance is abfolutely void *ab initio*; becaufe at the time of fuch furrender he had but a poffibility of an intereft, and could therefore transfer nothing: and no fubfequent admittance can make an act good, which was *ab initio* void. Yet, though upon the original furrender the nominee hath but a poffibility, it is however fuch a poffibility, as may whenever he pleafes be reduced to a certainty: for he cannot either by force or fraud be deprived or deluded of the effect and fruits of the furrender; but if the lord refufe to admit him, he is compellable to do it by a bill in chancery or a *mandamus* g: and the furrenderor can in no wife defeat his grant; his hands being for ever bound from difpofing of the land

f Co. Copyh. §. 36.   g 2 Roll. Rep. 107.

in

in any other way, and his mouth for ever ſtopped from revoking or countermanding his own deliberate act [h]; except in the caſe of a ſurrender to the uſe of his will, which is always revocable [j].

2. As to the *preſentment*: that, by the *general* cuſtom of manors, is to be made at the next court baron immediately after the ſurrender; but by *ſpecial* cuſtom in ſome places it will be good, though made at the ſecond or other ſubſequent court. And it is to be brought into court by the *ſame* perſons that took the ſurrender, and then preſented by the homage; and in all points material muſt correſpond with the true tenor of the ſurrender itſelf. And therefore, if the ſurrender be conditional, and the preſentment be abſolute, both the ſurrender, preſentment, and admittance thereupon are wholly void [i]: the ſurrender, as being never truly preſented; the preſentment, as being falſe; and the admittance, as being founded on ſuch untrue preſentment. If a man ſurrenders out of court, and dies before preſentment, and preſentment be made after his death, according to the cuſtom, this is ſufficient [k]. So too, if *ceſtuy que uſe* dies before preſentment, yet, upon preſentment made after his death, his heir according to the cuſtom ſhall be admitted. The ſame law is, if thoſe, into whoſe hands the ſurrender is made, die before preſentment; for, upon ſufficient proof in court that ſuch a ſurrender was made, the lord ſhall be compelled to admit accordingly. And if the ſteward, the tenants, or others into whoſe hands ſuch ſurrender is made, do refuſe or neglect to bring it in to be preſented, upon a petition preferred to the lord in his court baron the party grieved ſhall find remedy. But if the lord will not do him right and juſtice, he may ſue both the lord, and them that took the ſurrender, in chancery, and ſhall there find relief [l].

[h] Co. Copyh. §. 39.
[j] 4 Rep. 23.
[i] Co. Copyh. 40.

[k] Co. Litt. 62.
[l] Co. Copyh. §. 40.

3. ADMITTANCE is the laft ftage, or perfection, of copyhold affurances. And this is of three forts: firft, an admittance
upon a voluntary grant from the lord; fecondly, an admittance
upon furrender by the former tenant; and thirdly, an admittance
upon a defcent from the anceftor.

IN admittances, even upon a *voluntary grant* from the lord,
when copyhold lands have efcheated or reverted to him, the lord
is confidered as an inftrument. For, though it is in his power to
keep the lands in his own hands, or to difpofe of them at his
pleafure, by granting an abfolute fee-fimple, a freehold, or a
chattel intereft therein; and quite to change their nature from
copyhold to focage tenure, fo that he may well be reputed their
abfolute owner and lord; yet, if he will ftill continue to difpofe
of them as copyhold, he is bound to obferve the antient cuftom
precifely in every point, and can neither in tenure nor eftate introduce any kind of alteration; for that were to create a new
copyhold: wherefore in this refpect the law accounts him cuftom's inftrument. For if a copyhold for life falls into the lord's
hands, by the tenant's death, though the lord may deftroy the
tenure and enfranchife the land, yet if he grants it out again by
copy, he can neither add to nor diminifh the antient rent, nor
make any the minuteft variation in other refpects [m]: nor is the
tenant's eftate, fo granted, fubject to any charges or incumbrances by the lord [n].

IN admittances upon *furrender* of another, the lord is to no
intent reputed as owner, but wholly as an inftrument: and the
tenant admitted fhall likewife be fubject to no charges or incumbrances of the lord; for his claim to the eftate is folely under
him that made the furrender.

[m] Co. Cop. §. 41.   [n] 4 Rep. 27. Co. Litt. 59.
[n] 8 Rep. 63.

AND,

AND, as in admittances upon furrenders, fo in admittances *upon defcents* by the death of the anceftor, the lord is ufed as a mere inftrument; and, as no manner of intereft paffes into him by the furrender or the death of his tenant, fo no intereft paffes out of him by the act of admittance. And therefore neither in the one cafe, nor the other, is any refpect had to the quantity or quality of the lord's eftate in the manor. For whether he be tenant in fee or for years, whether he be in poffeffion by right or by wrong, it is not material; fince the admittances made by him fhall not be impeached on account of his title, becaufe they are judicial, or rather minifterial, acts, which every lord in poffeffion is bound to perform [p].

ADMITTANCES, however, upon furrender differ from admittances upon defcent in this; that by furrender nothing is vefted in *ceftuy que ufe* before admittance, no more than in voluntary admittances; but upon defcent the heir is tenant by copy immediately upon the death of his anceftor : not indeed to all intents and purpofes, for he cannot be fworn on the homage nor maintain an action in the lord's court as tenant; but to moft intents the law taketh notice of him as of a perfect tenant of the land inftantly upon the death of his anceftor, efpecially where he is concerned with any ftranger. He may enter into the land before admittance; may take the profits; may punifh any trefpafs done upon the ground [q]; nay, upon fatisfying the lord for his fine due upon the defcent, may furrender into the hands of the lord to whatever ufe he pleafes. For which reafons we may conclude, that the admittance of an heir is principally for the benefit of the lord, to intitle him to his fine, and not fo much neceffary for the ftrengthening and compleating the heir's title. Hence indeed an obfervation might arife, that if the benefit, which the heir is to receive by the admittance, is not equal to the charges of the fine, he will never come in and be admitted

[p] 4 Rep. 27. 1 Rep. 140.   [q] 4 Rep. 23.

to

to his copyhold in court; and fo the lord may be defrauded of his fine. But to this we may reply in the words of fir Edward Coke[r], " I affure myfelf, if it were in the election of " the heir to be admitted or not to be admitted, he would be " beft contented without admittance; but the cuftom in every " manor is in this point compulfory. For, either upon pain of " forfeiture of their copyhold, or of incurring fome great pe-" nalty, the heirs of copyholders are inforced, in every manor, " to come into court and be admitted according to the cuftom, " within a fhort time after notice given of their anceftor's de-" ceafe."

[r] Copyh. §. 41.

CHAPTER THE TWENTY THIRD.

OF ALIENATION BY DEVISE.

THE laſt method of conveying real property, is by *deviſe*,
or diſpoſition contained in a man's laſt will and teſtament.
And, in conſidering this ſubject, I ſhall not at preſent enquire
into the nature of wills and teſtaments, which are more properly
the inſtruments to convey perſonal eſtates ; but only into the original and antiquity of deviſing real eſtates by will, and the conſtruction of the ſeveral ſtatutes upon which that power is now
founded.

IT ſeems ſufficiently clear, that, before the conqueſt, lands
were deviſable by will [a]. But, upon the introduction of the military tenures, the reſtraint of deviſing lands naturally took place,
as a branch of the feodal doctrine of non-alienation without the
conſent of the lord [b]. And ſome have queſtioned, whether this
reſtraint (which we may trace even from the antient Germans [c])
was not founded upon truer principles of policy, than the power
of wantonly diſinheriting the heir by will, and transferring the
eſtate, through the dotage or caprice of the anceſtor, from thoſe
of his blood to utter ſtrangers. For this, it is alleged, maintained
the ballance of property, and prevented one man from growing
too big or powerful for his neighbours ; ſince it rarely happens,

[a] Wright of tenures. 172.   [c] *Tacit. de mcr. Germ. c.* 21.
[b] See pag. 57.

that

that the fame man is heir to many others, though by art and management he may frequently become their devifee. Thus the antient law of the Athenians directed that the eftate of the deceafed fhould always defcend to his children; or, on failure of lineal defcendants, fhould go to the collateral relations: which had an admirable effect in keeping up equality and preventing the accumulation of eftates. But when Solon [d] made a flight alteration, by permitting them (though only on failure of iffue) to difpofe of their lands by teftament, and devife away eftates from the collateral heir, this foon produced an excefs of wealth in fome, and of poverty in others: which, by a natural progreffion, firft produced popular tumults and diffentions; and thefe at length ended in tyranny, and the utter extinction of liberty; which was quickly followed by a total fubverfion of their ftate and nation. On the other hand, it would now feem hard, on account of fome abufes, (which are the natural confequence of free agency, when coupled with human infirmity) to debar the owner of lands from diftributing them after his death, as the exigence of his family affairs, or the juftice due to his creditors, may perhaps require. And this power, if prudently managed, has with us a peculiar propriety; by preventing the very evil which refulted from Solon's inftitution, the too great accumulation of property: which is the natural confequence of our doctrine of fucceffion by primogeniture, to which the Athenians were ftrangers. Of this accumulation the ill effects were feverely felt even in the feodal times; but it fhould always be ftrongly difcouraged in a commercial country, whofe welfare depends on the number of moderate fortunes engaged in the extenfion of trade.

HOWEVER this be, we find that, by the common law of England fince the conqueft, no eftate, greater than for term of years, could be difpofed of by teftament [e]; except only in Kent, and in fome antient burghs, and a few particular manors, where their Saxon immunities by fpecial indulgence fubfifted [f]. And

---

[d] Plutarch. *in vita Solon.*   [f] Litt. §. 167. 1 Inft. 111.
[e] 2 Inft. 7.

though

though the feodal reftraint on alienations by deed vanifhed very early, yet this on wills continued for fome centuries after; from an apprehenfion of infirmity and impofition on the teftator *in extremis,* which made fuch devifes fufpicious. Befides, in devifes there was wanting that general notoriety, and public defignation of the fucceffor, which in defcents is apparent to the neighbourhood, and which the fimplicity of the common law always required in every transfer and new acquifition of property.

BUT when ecclefiaftical ingenuity had invented the doctrine of ufes, as a thing diftinct from the land, ufes began to be devifed very frequently[g], and the devifee of the ufe could in chancery compel it's execution. For it is obferved by Gilbert[h], that, as the popifh clergy then generally fate in the court of chancery, they confidered that men are moft liberal when they can enjoy their poffeffions no longer; and therefore at their death would choofe to difpofe of them to thofe, who, according to the fuperftition of the times, could intercede for their happinefs in another world. But, when the ftatute of ufes[i] had annexed the poffeffion to the ufe, thefe ufes, being now the very land itfelf, became no longer devifable: which might have occafioned a great revolution in the law of devifes, had not the ftatute of wills been made about five years after, viz. 32 Hen.VIII. c. i. explained by 34 Hen.VIII. c.5. which enacted, that all perfons being feifed in fee-fimple (except feme-coverts, infants, idiots, and perfons of nonfane memory) might by will and teftament in writing devife to any other perfon, but not to bodies corporate, two thirds of their lands, tenements, and hereditaments, held in chivalry, and the whole of thofe held in focage: which now, through the alteration of tenures by the ftatute of Charles the fecond, amounts to the whole of their landed property, except their copyhold tenements.

CORPORATIONS were excepted in thefe ftatutes, to prevent the extenfion of gifts in mortmain; but now, by conftruc-

g Plowd. 414.   i 27 Hen.VIII. c. 10.
h on devifes. 7.

tion of the ſtatute 43 Eliz. c. 4. it is held, that a deviſe to a corporation for a charitable uſe is valid, as operating in the nature
of an *appointment*, rather than of a *bequeſt*. And indeed the piety
of the judges hath formerly carried them great lengths in ſup-
porting ſuch charitable uſes [k] ; it being held that the ſtatute of
Elizabeth, which favours appointments to charities, ſuperſedes
and repeals all former ſtatutes [l], and ſupplies all defects of aſſurances [m] : and therefore not only a deviſe to a corporation, but a
deviſe by a copyhold tenant without ſurrendering to the uſe of
his will [n], and a deviſe (nay even a ſettlement) by tenant in tail
without either fine or recovery, if made to a charitable uſe, are
good by way of appointment [o].

WITH regard to deviſes in general, experience ſoon ſhewed
how difficult and hazardous a thing it is, even in matters of public utility, to depart from the rules of the common law; which
are ſo nicely conſtructed and ſo artificially connected together,
that the leaſt breach in any one of them diſorders for a time the
texture of the whole. Innumerable frauds and perjuries were
quickly introduced by this parliamentary method of inheritance:
for ſo looſe was the conſtruction made upon this act by the courts
of law, that bare notes in the hand writing of another perſon
were allowed to be good wills within the ſtatute [p]. To remedy
which, the ſtatute of frauds and perjuries, 29 Car. II. c. 3. directs, that all deviſes of lands and tenements ſhall not only be in
writing, but ſigned by the teſtator, or ſome other perſon in his
preſence, and by his expreſs direction; and be ſubſcribed, in
his preſence, by three or four credible witneſſes. And a ſimilar
ſolemnity is requiſite for revoking a deviſe.

IN the conſtruction of this laſt ſtatute, it has been adjudged
that the teſtator's name, written with his own hand, at the beginning of his will, as, " I John Mills do make this my laſt will

[k] Ch. Prec. 272.
[l] Gilb. Rep. 45. 1 P. Wms. 248.
[m] Duke's charit. uſes. 84.

[n] Moor. 890.
[o] 2 Vern. 453. Ch. Prec. 16.
[p] Dyer. 72. Cro. Eliz. 100.

" and

" and teſtament," is a ſufficient ſigning, without any name at the bottom [q]; though the other is the ſafer way. It has alſo been determined, that though the witneſſes muſt all ſee the teſtator ſign, or at leaſt acknowlege the ſigning, yet they may do it at different times [r]. But they muſt all ſubſcribe their names as witneſſes *in his preſence*, left by any poſſibility they ſhould miſtake the inſtrument [s]. And, in a caſe determined about twenty years ago [t], the judges were extremely ſtrict in regard to the credibility, or rather the competency, of the witneſſes : for they would not allow any legatee, nor by conſequence a creditor, where the legacies and debts were charged on the real eſtate, to be a competent witneſs to the deviſe, as being too deeply concerned in intereſt not to wiſh the eſtabliſhment of the will; for, if it were eſtabliſhed, he gained a ſecurity for his legacy or debt from the real eſtate, whereas otherwiſe he had no claim but on the perſonal aſſets. This determination however alarmed many purchaſors and creditors, and threatened to ſhake moſt of the titles in the kingdom, that depended on deviſes by will. For, if the will was atteſted by a ſervant to whom wages were due, by the apothecary or attorney whoſe very attendance made them creditors, or by the miniſter of the pariſh who had any demand for tithes or eccleſiaſtical dues, (and theſe are the perſons moſt likely to be preſent in the teſtator's laſt illneſs) and if in ſuch caſe the teſtator had charged his real eſtate with the payment of his debts, the whole will, and every diſpoſition therein, ſo far as related to real property, were held to be utterly void. This occaſioned the ſtatute 25 Geo. II. c. 6. which reſtored both the competency and the credit of ſuch *legatees*, by declaring void all legacies given to witneſſes, and thereby removing all poſſibility of their intereſt affecting their teſtimony. The ſame ſtatute likewiſe eſtabliſhed the competency of *creditors*, by directing the teſtimony of all ſuch creditors to be admitted, but leaving their credit (as well as that of all other witneſſes) to be conſidered, on a view of all the circumſtances, by the court and

[q] 3 Lev. 1.   [s] 1 P. W[ms]. 740.
[r] Freem. 486. 2Ch. Caſ. 109. Pr. Ch. 185.   [t] St a. 1253.

jury before whom fuch will fhall be contefted. And in a much later cafe [u] the teftimony of three witneffes, who were creditors, was held to be fufficiently credible, though the land was charged with the payment of debts; and the reafons of the former determination were adjudged to be infufficient.

ANOTHER inconvenience was found to attend this new method of conveyance by devife; in that creditors by bond and other fpecialties, which affected the heir provided he had affets by defcent, were now defrauded of their fecurities, not having the fame remedy againft the devifee of their debtor. To obviate which, the ftatute 3 & 4 W. & M. c. 14. hath provided, that all wills, and teftaments, limitations, difpofitions, and appointments of real eftates, by tenants in fee-fimple or having power to difpofe by will, fhall (as againft fuch creditors only) be deemed to be fraudulent and void: and that fuch creditors may maintain their actions jointly againft both the heir and the devifee.

A WILL of lands, made by the permiffion and under the controll of thefe ftatutes, is confidered by the courts of law not fo much in the nature of a teftament, as of a conveyance declaring the ufes to which the land fhall be fubject: with this difference, that in other conveyances the actual *fubfcription* of the witneffes is not required by law [w], though it is prudent for them fo to do, in order to affift their memory when living and to fupply their evidence when dead; but in devifes of lands fuch fubfcription is now abfolutely neceffary by ftatute, in order to identify a conveyance, which in it's nature can never be fet up till after the death of the devifor. And upon this notion, that a devife affecting lands is merely a fpecies of conveyance, is founded this diftinction between fuch devifes and teftaments of perfonal chattels; that the latter will operate upon whatever the teftator dies poffeffed of, the former only upon fuch real eftates as were his at the time of executing and publifhing his will [x]. Wherefore no after-

[u] M. 31 Geo. II. 4 Burr. I. 430.   [x] 1 P. W[ms]. 575.
[w] See pag. 307.

purchafed

purchafed lands will pafs under fuch devife[y], unlefs, fubfequent
to the purchafe or contract[z], the devifor re-publifhes his will[a].

WE have now confidered the feveral fpecies of common affurances, whereby a title to lands and tenements may be tranf-
ferred and conveyed from one man to another. But, before we
conclude this head, it may not be improper to take notice of a
few general rules and maxims, which have been laid down by
courts of juftice, for the conftruction and expofition of them all.
Thefe are

1. THAT the conftruction be *favourable*, and as near the
minds and apparent intents of the parties, as the rules of law
will admit[b]. For the maxims of law are, that " *verba inten-*
" *tioni debent infervire ;*" and, " *benigne interpretamur chartas*
" *propter fimplicitatem laicorum.*" And therefore the conftruction muft alfo be *reafonable*, and agreeable to common underftanding[c].

2. THAT *quoties in verbis nulla eft ambiguitas, ibi nulla expo-
fitio contra verba fienda eft*[d]: but that, where the *intention* is clear,
too minute a ftrefs be not laid on the ftrict and precife fignification
of *words* ; *nam qui haeret in litera, haeret in cortice.* Therefore,
by a grant of a remainder a reverfion may well pafs, and *e converfo*[e]. And another maxim of law is, that " *mala grammatica*
" *non vitiat chartam ;*" neither falfe Englifh nor bad Latin will
deftroy a deed[f]. Which perhaps a claffical critic may think to
be no unneceffary caution.

3. THAT the conftruction be made upon the entire deed, and
not merely upon disjointed parts of it. " *Nam ex antecedentibus*

[y] Moor. 255. 11 Mod. 127.
[z] 1 Ch. Caf. 39. 2 Ch. Caf. 144.
[a] Salk. 238.
[b] And. 60.
[c] 1 Bulftr. 175. Hob. 304.
[d] 2 Saund. 157.
[e] Hob. 27.
[f] 10 Rep. 133. Co. Litt. 223. 2 Show. 334.

" *et*

"*et confequentibus fit optima interpretatio* [g]." And therefore that every part of it, be (if poffible) made to take effect; and no word but what may operate in fome fhape or other [h]. " *Nam* " *verba debent intelligi cum effectu, ut res magis valeat quem pe-* " *reat* [i]."

4. THAT the deed be taken moft ftrongly againft him that is the agent or contractor, and in favour of the other party. " *Verba* " *fortius accipiuntur contra proferentem.*" For the principle of felf-prefervation will make men fufficiently careful, not to prejudice their own intereft by the too extenfive meaning of their words: and hereby all manner of deceit in any grant is avoided; for men would always affect ambiguous and intricate expreffions, provided they were afterwards at liberty to put their own conftruction upon them. But here a diftinction muft be taken between an indenture and a deed poll: for the words of an indenture, executed by both parties, are to be confidered as the words of them both; for, though delivered as the words of one party, yet they are not his words only, but the other party hath given his confent to every one of them. But in a deed poll, executed only by the grantor, they are the words of the grantor only, and fhall be taken moft ftrongly againft him [k]. However, this, being a rule of fome ftrictnefs and rigor, is the laft to be reforted to, and is never to be relied upon, but where all other rules of expofition fail [l].

5. THAT, if the words will bear two fenfes, one agreeable to, and another againft, law; that fenfe be preferred, which is moft agreeable thereto [m]. As if tenant in tail lets a leafe for life generally, it fhall be conftrued for his own life only, for that ftands with the law; and not for the life of the leffee, which is beyond his power to grant.

[g] 1 Bulftr. 101.
[h] 1 P. W[ms]. 457.
[i] Plowd. 156.

[k] Plowd. 134.
[l] Bacon's Elem. c. 3.
[m] Co. Litt. 42.

6. THAT

6. THAT, in a deed, if there be two clauſes ſo totally repugnant to each other, that they cannot ſtand together, the firſt ſhall be received and the latter rejected [n]: wherein it differs from a will; for there, of two ſuch repugnant clauſes the latter ſhall ſtand [o]. Which is owing to the different natures of the two inſtruments; for the firſt deed, and the laſt will are always moſt available in law. Yet in both caſes we ſhould rather attempt to reconcile them [p].

7. THAT a deviſe be moſt favourably expounded, to purſue if poſſible the will of the deviſor, who for want of advice or learning may have omitted the legal and proper phraſes. And therefore many times the law diſpenſes with the want of words in deviſes, that are abſolutely requiſite in all other inſtruments. Thus a fee may be conveyed without words of inheritance [q]; and an eſtate-tail without words of procreation [r]. By a will alſo an eſtate may paſs by mere implication, without any expreſs words to direct it's courſe. As, where A deviſes lands to his heir at law, after the death of his wife: here, though no eſtate is given to the wife in expreſs terms, yet ſhe ſhall have an eſtate for life by implication [s]; for the intent of the teſtator is clearly to poſtpone the heir till after her death; and, if ſhe does not take it, nobody elſe can. So alſo, where a deviſe is of black-acre to A and of white-acre to B in tail, and if they both die without iſſue, then to C in fee: here A and B have *croſs remainders* by implication, and on the failure of either's iſſue, the other or his iſſue ſhall take the whole; and C's remainder over ſhall be poſtponed till the iſſue of both ſhall fail [t]. But, to avoid confuſion, no croſs remainders are allowed between more than two deviſees [u]: and, in general, where any implications are allowed, they muſt be ſuch as are *neceſſary* (or at leaſt highly *probable*) and not merely

[n] Hardr. 94.
[o] Co. Litt. 112.
[p] Cro. Eliz. 420. 1 Vern. 30.
[q] See pag. 108.
[r] See pag. 115.
[s] 1 Ventr. 376.
[t] Freem. 484.
[u] Cro. Jac. 655. 1 Ventr. 224. 2 Show. 139.

poſſible

poſſible implications ^w. And herein there is no diſtinction between the rules of law and of equity ; for the will, being conſidered in both courts in the light of a limitation to uſes ^x, is conſtrued in each with equal favour and benignity, and expounded rather on it's own particular circumſtances, than by any general rules of poſitive law.

AND thus we have taken a tranſient view, in this and the three preceding chapters, of a very large and diffuſive ſubject, the doctrine of common aſſurances : which concludes our obſervations on the *title* to things real, or the means by which they may be reciprocally loſt and acquired. We have before conſidered the *eſtates* which may be had in them, with regard to their duration or quantity of intereſt, the time of their enjoyment, and the number and connexions of the perſons entitled to hold them : we have examined the *tenures,* both antient and modern, whereby thoſe eſtates have been, and are now, holden : and have diſtinguiſhed the object of all theſe enquiries, namely, things real, into the corporeal or ſubſtantial, and incorporeal or ideal *kind ;* and have thus conſidered the rights of real property in every light wherein they are contemplated by the laws of England. A ſyſtem of laws, that differs much from every other ſyſtem, except thoſe of the ſame feodal origin, in it's notions and regulations of landed eſtates ; and which therefore could in this particular be very ſeldom compared with any other.

THE ſubject, which has thus employed our attention, is of very extenſive uſe, and of as extenſive variety. And yet, I am afraid, it has afforded the ſtudent leſs amuſement and pleaſure in the purſuit, than the matters diſcuſſed in the preceding volume. To ſay the truth, the vaſt alterations which the doctrine of real property has undergone from the conqueſt to the preſent time ; the infinite determinations upon points that continually ariſe, and which have been heaped one upon another for a courſe

---

^w Vaugh. 262.　　　　　　　^x Fitzg. 236. 11 Mod. 153.

of feven centuries, without any order or method ; and the multiplicity of acts of parliament which have amended, or fometimes only altered, the common law ; thefe cafes have made
the ftudy of this branch of our national jurifprudence a little
perplexed and intricate. It hath been my endeavour principally
to felect fuch parts of it, as were of the moft general ufe, where
the principles were the moft fimple, the reafons of them the
moft obvious, and the practice the leaft embarraffed. Yet I cannot prefume that I have always been thoroughly intelligible to
fuch of my readers, as were before ftrangers even to the very
terms of art, which I have been obliged to make ufe of : though,
whenever thofe have firft occurred, I have generally attempted a
fhort explication of their meaning. Thefe are indeed the more
numerous, on account of the different languages which our law
has at different periods been taught to fpeak ; the difficulty arifing from which will infenfibly diminifh by ufe and familiar acquaintance. And therefore I fhall clofe this branch of our enquiries with the words of fir Edward Coke[y]: "albeit the ftu-
"dent fhall not at any one day, do what he can, reach to the
"full meaning of all that is here laid down, yet let him no way
"difcourage himfelf, but proceed ; for on fome other day, in
"fome other place," (or perhaps upon a fecond perufal of the
fame) "his doubts will be probably removed."

[y] Proeme to 1 Inft.

CHAPTER THE TWENTY FOURTH.

Of THINGS PERSONAL.

UNDER the name of things *personal* are included all sorts of things *moveable*, which may attend a man's person wherever he goes ; and therefore, being only the objects of the law while they remain within the limits of it's jurisdiction, and being also of a perishable quality, are not esteemed of so high a nature, nor paid so much regard to by the law, as things that are in their nature more permanent and *immoveable*, as lands, and houses, and the profits issuing thereout. These being constantly within the reach, and under the protection of the law, were the principal favourites of our first legislators : who took all imaginable care in ascertaining the rights, and directing the disposition, of such property as they imagined to be lasting, and which would answer to posterity the trouble and pains that their ancestors employed about them ; but at the same time entertained a very low and contemptuous opinion of all personal estate, which they regarded only as a transient commodity. The amount of it indeed was, comparatively, very trifling, during the scarcity of money and the ignorance of luxurious refinements, which prevailed in the feodal ages. Hence it was, that a tax of the *fifteenth, tenth,* or sometimes a much larger proportion, of all the moveables of the subject, was frequently laid without scruple, and is mentioned with much unconcern by our antient historians, though now it would justly alarm our opulent merchants and stockholders. And hence likewise may be derived the frequent forfeitures inflicted

by

by the common law, of all a man's goods and chattels, for mif-
behaviours and inadvertencies that at prefent hardly feem to deferve fo fevere a punifhment. Our antient law-books, which are
founded upon the feodal provifions, do not therefore often con-
defcend to regulate this fpecies of property. There is not a chapter in Britton or the mirroir, that can fairly be referred to this
head ; and the little that is to be found in Glanvil, Bracton, and
Fleta, feems principally borrowed from the civilians. But of
later years, fince the introduction and extenfion of trade and commerce, which are entirely occupied in this fpecies of property,
and have greatly augmented it's quantity and of courfe it's value,
we have learned to conceive different ideas of it. Our courts
now regard a man's perfonalty in a light nearly, if not quite,
equal to his realty : and have adopted a more enlarged and lefs
technical mode of confidering the one than the other ; frequently drawn from the rules which they found already eftablifhed by
the Roman law, wherever thofe rules appeared to be well-grounded and appofite to the cafe in queftion, but principally from reafon and convenience, adapted to the circumftances of the times ;
preferving withal a due regard to antient ufages, and a certain
feodal tincture, which is ftill to be found in fome branches of
perfonal property.

B u t things perfonal, by our law, do not only include things
moveable, but alfo fomething more. The whole of which is comprehended under the general name of *chattels*, *catalla* ; which,
fir Edward Coke fays [a], is a French word fignifying goods. And
this is true, if underftood of the Norman dialect ; for in the
grand couftumier [b], we find the word *chattels* ufed and fet in oppofition to a fief or feud : fo that not only goods, but whatever
was not a feud, were accounted chattels. And it is, I apprehend, in the fame large, extended, negative fenfe, that our law
adopts it ; the idea of goods, or moveables only, being not fufficiently comprehenfive to take in every thing that our law con-

---

[a] 1 Inft. 118.   [b] c. 87.

fiders as a chattel intereft. For fince, as the commentator on the *couftumier* obferves, there are two requifites to make a fief or heritage, duration as to time, and immobility with regard to place; whatever wants either of thefe qualities is not, according to the Normans, an heritage or fief [c]; or, according to us, is not a *real* eftate: the confequence of which in both laws is, that it muft be a perfonal eftate, or chattel.

Chattels therefore are diftributed by the law into two kinds; chattels *real*, and chattels *perfonal*.

1. Chattels *real*, faith fir Edward Coke [d], are fuch as concern, or favour of, the realty; as terms for years of land, wardfhips in chivalry (while the military tenures fubfifted) the next prefentation to a church, eftates by ftatute-merchant, ftatute-ftaple, *elegit*, or the like; of all which we have already fpoken. And thefe are called real chattels, as being interefts iffuing out of, or annexed to real eftates: of which they have one quality, viz. immobility, which denominates them *real*; but want the other, viz. a fufficient, legal, indeterminate duration: and this want it is, that conftitutes them *chattels*. The utmoft period for which they can laft is fixed and determinate, either for fuch a fpace of time certain, or till fuch a particular fum of money be raifed out of fuch a particular income; fo that they are not equal in the eye of the law to the loweft eftate of freehold, a leafe for another's life: their tenants were confidered, upon feodal principles, as merely bailiffs or farmers; and the tenant of the freehold might at any time have deftroyed their intereft, till the reign of Henry VIII [e]. A freehold, which alone is a real eftate, and feems (as has been faid) to anfwer to the fief in Normandy, is conveyed by corporal inveftiture and livery of feifin; which gives the tenant fo ftrong a hold of the land, that it never after can

[c] *Cateux font meubles et immeubles: ficomme vrais meubles font qui tranfporter fe peuvent, et enfuivir le corps; immeubies font chofes qui ne peuvent enfuivir le corps, nieftre tranfportees,* et tout ce qui n'*eft point en heritage.* LL. Will. Nothi, c 4. afud Eu refne. II. 409.
[d] 1 Inft. 118.
[e] See pag. 141, 142.

be

be wrefted from him during his life, but by his own act, of voluntary transfer or of forfeiture; or elfe by the happening of fome
future contingency, as in eftates *pur auter vie,* and the determinable freeholds mentioned in a former chapter [f]. And even thefe,
being of an uncertain duration, may by poffibility laft for the
owner's life; for the law will not prefuppofe the contingency to
happen before it actually does, and till then the eftate is to all
intents and purpofes a life eftate, and therefore a freehold intereft. On the other hand, a chattel intereft in lands, which the
Normans put in oppofition to fief, and we to freehold, is conveyed by no feifin or corporal inveftiture, but the poffeffion is
gained by the mere entry of the tenant himfelf; and it is fure
to expire at a time prefixed and determined, if not fooner. Thus
a leafe for years muft neceffarily fail at the end and completion of
the term; the next prefentation to a church is fatisfied and gone
the inftant it comes into poffeffion, that is, by the firft avoidance
and prefentation to the living; the conditional eftates by ftatutes
and *elegit* are determined as foon as the debt is paid; and fo
guardianfhips in chivalry were fure to expire the moment that
the heir came of age. And if there be any other chattel real, it
will be found to correfpond with the reft in this effential quality,
that it's duration is limited to a time certain, beyond which it
cannot fubfift.

2. CHATTELS perfonal are, properly and ftrictly fpeaking,
things *moveable*; which may be annexed to or attendant on the
perfon of the owner, and carried about with him from one part
of the world to another. Such are animals, houfehold-ftuft,
money, jewels, corn, garments, and every thing elfe that can
properly be put in motion, and transferred from place to place.
And of this kind of chattels it is, that we are principally to fpeak
in the remainder of this book; having been unavoidably led to
confider the nature of chattels real, and their incidents, in the
former chapters which were employed upon real eftates: that

[f] pag. 121.

kind of property being of a mongrel amphibious nature, originally endowed with one only of the characteristics of each species of things; the immobility of things real, and the precarious duration of things personal.

CHATTEL interests being thus distinguished and distributed, it will be proper to confider, first, the nature of that *property*, or dominion, to which they are liable; which must be principally, nay solely, referred to personal chattels: and, secondly, the *title* to that property, or how it may be lost and acquired. Of each of these in it's order.

CHAPTER THE TWENTY FIFTH.

OF PROPERTY IN THINGS PERSONAL.

PROPERTY, in chattels perfonal, may be either in *poffef-fion*; which is where a man hath not only the right to enjoy, but hath the actual enjoyment of, the thing: or elfe it is in *action*; where a man hath only a bare right, without any occupation or enjoyment. And of thefe the former, or property in *poffeffion*, is divided into two forts, an *abfolute* and a *qualified* property.

I. FIRST then of property in *poffeffion abfolute*; which is where a man hath, folely and exclufively, the right, and alfo the occupation, of any moveable chattels; fo that they cannot be transferred from him, or ceafe to be his, without his own act or default. Such may be all *inanimate* things, as goods, plate, money, jewels, implements of war, garments, and the like: fuch alfo may be all *vegetable* productions, as the fruit or other parts, when fevered from the plant, or the whole plant itfelf, when fevered from the ground; none of which can be moved out of the owner's poffeffion without his own act or confent, or at leaft without doing him an injury, which it is the bufinefs of the law to prevent or remedy. Of thefe therefore there remains little to be faid.

BUT with regard to *animals*, which have in themfelves a principle and power of motion, and (unlefs particularly confined) can convey themfelves from one part of the world to another, there

there is a great difference made with refpect to their feveral claffes, not only in our law, but in the law of nature and of all civilized nations. They are diftinguifhed into fuch as are *domitae*,
and fuch as are *ferae naturae*; fome being of a *tame*, and others
of a *wild* difpofition. In fuch as are of a nature tame and domeftic, (as horfes, kine, fheep, poultry, and the like) a man
may have as abfolute a property as in any inanimate beings; becaufe thefe continue perpetually in his occupation, and will not
ftray from his houfe or perfon, unlefs by accident or fraudulent
enticement, in either of which cafes the owner does not lofe
his property[a]: in which our law agrees with the laws of France
and Holland[b]. The ftealing, or forcible abduction, of fuch property as this, is alfo felony; for thefe are things of intrinfic value, ferving for the food of man, or elfe for the ufes of hufbandry[c]. But in animals *ferae naturae* a man can have no abfolute
property.

OF all tame and domeftic animals, the brood belongs to the
owner of the dam or mother; the Englifh law agreeing with the
civil, that "*partus fequitur ventrem*" in the brute creation, though
for the moft part in the human fpecies it difallows that maxim.
And therefore in the laws of England[d], as well as Rome[e], "*fi*
"*equam meam equus tuus praegnantem fecerit, non eft tuum fed*
"*meum quod natum eft.*" And, for this, Puffendorf[f] gives a fenfible reafon: not only becaufe the male is frequently unknown;
but alfo becaufe the dam, during the time of her pregnancy, is
almoft ufelefs to the proprietor, and muft be maintained with
greater expence and care: wherefore as her owner is the lofer by
her pregnancy, he ought to be the gainer by her brood. An exception to this rule is in the cafe of young cygnets; which belong equally to the owner of the cock and hen, and fhall be divided between them[g]. But here the reafons of the general rule

[a] 2 Mod. 319.
[b] *Vinn. in Inft. l.* 2. *tit.* 1. §. 15.
[c] 1 Hal. P. C. 511, 512.
[d] Bro. *Abr. tit. Propertie.* 29.

[e] *Ff.* 6. 1. 5.
[f] L. of N. l. 4. c. 7.
[g] 7 Rep. 17.

ceafe,

ceafe, and " *ceffante ratione ceffat et ipfa lex:*" for the male is well known, by his conftant affociation with the female ; and for the fame reafon the owner of the one doth not fuffer more difadvantage, during the time of pregnancy and nurture, than the owner of the other.

II. OTHER animals, that are not of a tame and domeftic nature, are either not the objects of property at all, or elfe fall under our other divifion, namely, that of *qualified, limited,* or *fpecial* property : which is fuch as is not in it's nature permanent, but may fometimes fubfift, and at other times not fubfift. In difcuffing which fubject, I fhall in the firft place fhew, how this fpecies of property may fubfift in fuch animals, as are *ferae naturae,* or of a wild nature ; and then, how it may fubfift in any other things, when under particular circumftances.

FIRST then, a man may be invefted with a qualified, but not an abfolute, property in all creatures that are *ferae naturae,* either *per induftriam, propter impotentiam,* or *propter privilegium.*

1. A QUALIFIED property may fubfift in animals *ferae naturae, per induftriam hominis :* by a man's *reclaiming* and making them tame by art, induftry, and education ; or by fo confining them within his own immediate power, that they cannot efcape and ufe their natural liberty. And under this head fome writers have ranked all the former fpecies of animals we have mentioned, apprehending none to be originally and naturally tame, but only made fo by art and cuftom : as, horfes, fwine, and other cattle ; which, if originally left to themfelves, would have chofen to rove up and down, feeking their food at large, and are only made domeftic by ufe and familiarity, and are therefore, fay they, called *manfueta, quafi manui affueta.* But however well this notion may be founded, abftractedly confidered, our law apprehends the moft obvious diftinction to be, between fuch animals as we generally fee tame, and are therefore feldom, if ever, found wandering at large, which it calls *domitae naturae ;* and fuch crea-

tures

tures as are ufually found at liberty, which are therefore fuppofed
to be more emphatically *ferae naturae,* though it may happen
that the latter fhall be fometimes tamed and confined by the art
and induftry of man. Such as are deer in a park, hares or rabbets
in an enclofed warren, doves in a dovehoufe, pheafants or partridges in a mew, hawks that are fed and commanded by their owner,
and fifh in a private pond or in trunks. Thefe are no longer the
property of a man, than while they continue in his keeping or
actual poffeffion : but, if at any time they regain their natural
liberty, his property inftantly ceafes ; unlefs they have *animum
revertendi,* which is only to be known by their ufual cuftom of
returning [h]. A maxim which is borrowed from the civil law [i];
" *revertendi animum videntur definere habere tunc, cum revertendi*
" *confuetudinem deferuerint."* The law therefore extends this
poffeffion farther than the mere manual occupation; for my
tame hawk that is purfuing his quarry in my prefence, though
he is at liberty to go where he pleafes, is neverthelefs my property ; for he hath *animum revertendi.* So are my pigeons,
that are flying at a diftance from their home (efpecially thofe of
the carrier kind) and likewife the deer that is chafed out of my
park or foreft, and is inftantly purfued by the keeper or fo-
refter : all which remain ftill in my poffeffion, and I ftill preferve
my qualified property in them. But if they ftray without my
knowlege, and do not return in the ufual manner, it is then lawful for any ftranger to take them [k]. But if a deer, or any wild
animal reclaimed, hath a collar or other mark put upon him, and
goes and returns at his pleafure ; or if a wild fwan is taken, and
marked and turned loofe in the river, the owner's property in him
ftill continues, and it is not lawful for any one elfe to take him [l]:
but otherwife, if the deer has been long abfent without returning,
or the fwan leaves the neighbourhood. Bees alfo are *ferae naturae;* but, when hived and reclaimed, a man may have a qualified property in them, by the law of nature, as well as by the
civil law [m]. And to the fame purpofe, not to fay in the fame

[h] Bracton. *l.* 2. *c.* 1. 7 Rep. 17.
[i] *Inft.* 2. 1. 15.
[k] Finch. L. 177.

[l] Crompt. of courts. 167. 7 Rep. 16.
[m] Puff. *l.* 4. *c.* 6. §. 5. *Inft.* 2. 1. 14.

words,

words, with the civil law, fpeaks Bracton [n] : occupation, that is, hiving or including them, gives the property in bees; for, though a fwarm lights upon my tree, I have no more property in them till I have hived them, than I have in the birds which make their nefts thereon; and therefore if another hives them, he fhall be their proprietor : but a fwarm, which flie from and out of my hive, are mine fo long as I can keep them in fight, and have power to purfue them; and in thefe circumftances no one elfe is intitled to take them. But it hath been alfo faid [o], that with us the only ownerfhip in bees is *ratione foli*; and the charter of the foreft [p], which allows every freeman to be entitled to the honey found within his own woods, affords great countenance to this doctrine, that a qualified property may be had in bees, in confideration of the property of the foil whereon they are found.

I N all thefe creatures, reclaimed from the wildnefs of their nature, the property is not abfolute, but defeafible : a property, that may be deftroyed if they refume their antient wildnefs, and are found at large. For if the pheafants efcape from the mew, or the fifhes from the trunk, and are feen wandering at large in their proper element, they become *ferae naturae* again; and are free and open to the firft occupant that has ability to feife them. But while they thus continue my qualified or defeafible property, they are as much under the protection of the law, as if they were abfolutely and indefeafibly mine : and an action will lie againft any man that detains them from me, or unlawfully de-ftroys them. It is alfo as much felony by common law to fteal fuch of them as are fit for food, as it is to fteal tame animals [q] : but not fo, if they are only kept for pleafure, curiofity, or whim, as dogs, bears, cats, apes, parrots, and finging birds [r]; becaufe their value is not intrinfic, but depending only on the caprice of the owner [s] : though it is fuch an invafion of property as may

[n] *l.* 2. *c.* 1. §. 3.
[o] Bro. *Abr. tit. Propertie.* 37. cites 43 Edw. III. 24.
[p] 9 Hen. III. c. 13.

[q] 1 Hal. P. C. 512.
[r] Lamb. Eiren. 275.
[s] 7 Rep. 18. 3 Inft. 109.

amount to a civil injury, and be redreſſed by a civil action [t]. Yet to ſteal a reclaimed hawk is felony both by common law and ſtatute [u]; which ſeems to be a relick of the tyranny of our antient ſportſmen. And, among our elder anceſtors the antient Britons, another ſpecies of reclaimed animals, *viz.* cats, were looked upon as creatures of intrinſic value; and the killing or ſtealing one was a grievous crime, and ſubjected the offender to a fine; eſpecially if it belonged to the king's houſhold, and were the *cuſtos horrei regii,* for which there was a very peculiar forfeiture [w]. And thus much of qualified property in wild animals, reclaimed *per induſtriam.*

2. A QUALIFIED property may alſo ſubſiſt with relation to animals *ferae naturae, ratione impotentiae,* on account of their own inability. As when hawks, herons, or other birds build in my trees, or coneys or other creatures make their neſts or burrows in my land, and have young ones there; I have a qualified property in thoſe young ones, till ſuch time as they can fly, or run away, and then my property expires [x]: but, till then, it is in ſome caſes treſpaſs, and in others felony, for a ſtranger to take them away [y]. For here, as the owner of the land has it in his power to do what he pleaſes with them, the law therefore veſts a property in him of the young ones, in the ſame manner as it does of the old ones if reclaimed and confined: for theſe cannot through weakneſs, any more than the others through reſtraint, uſe their natural liberty and forſake him.

3. A MAN may, laſtly, have a qualified property in animals *ferae naturae, propter privilegium :* that is, he may have the privilege of hunting, taking, and killing them, in excluſion of other

---

[t] Bro. *Abr. tit. Treſpaſs.* 407.

[u] 1 Hal. P. C. 512. 1 Hawk. P. C. c. 33.

[w] " *Si quis felem, horrei regii cuſtodem, oc-*" *ciderit vel furto abſtulerit, felis ſumma cau-*" *da ſuſpendatur, capite aream attingente, et in*" *eam grana tritici effundantur, uſquedum ſum-*" *mitas caudae tritico co-operiatur.*" Wotton.

LL. Wall. l. 3. c. 5. §. 5. An amercement ſimilar to which, ſir Edward Coke tells us (7 Rep. 18.) there antiently was for ſtealing ſwans; only ſuſpending them by the beak, inſtead of the tail.

[x] *Carta de foreſt.* 9 Hen. III. c. 13.

[y] 7 Rep. 17. Lamb. Eiren. 274.

perſons.

perſons. Here he has a tranſient property in theſe animals, uſually called game, ſo long as they continue within his liberty[z];
and may reſtrain any ſtranger from taking them therein : but the
inſtant they depart into another liberty, this qualified property
ceaſes. The manner, in which this privilege is acquired, will be
ſhewn in a ſubſequent chapter.

THE qualified property which we have hitherto conſidered, extends only to animals *ferae naturae,* when either reclaimed, im-
potent, or privileged. Many other things may alſo be the objects
of qualified property. It may ſubſiſt in the very elements, of fire
or light, of air, and of water. A man can have no abſolute permanent property in theſe, as he may in the earth or land ; ſince
theſe are of a vague and fugitive nature, and therefore can admit only of a precarious and qualified ownerſhip, which laſts ſo
long as they are in actual uſe and occupation, but no longer. If
a man diſturbs another, and deprives him of the lawful enjoyment of theſe ; if one obſtructs another's antient windows[a], cor-
rupts the air of his houſe or gardens[b], fouls his water[c], or un-
pens and lets it out, or if he diverts an antient watercourſe that
uſed to run to the other's mill or meadow[d]; the law will animad-
vert hereon as an injury, and protect the party injured in his poſſeſſion. But the property in them ceaſes the inſtant they are out
of poſſeſſion : for, when no man is engaged in their actual occupation, they become again common, and every man has an equal
right to appropriate them to his own uſe.

THESE kinds of qualification in property depend upon the
peculiar circumſtances of the ſubject matter, which is not capable of being under the abſolute dominion of any proprietor. But
property may alſo be of a qualified or ſpecial nature, on account
of the peculiar circumſtances of the owner, when the thing itſelf is very capable of abſolute ownerſhip. As in caſe of *bail-*

[z] Cro. Car. 554. Mar. 48. 5 Mod. 376.
12 Mod. 144.
  [a] 9 Rep. 58.
        [b] *Ibid.* 59 Lutw. 92.
        [c] 9 Rep. 59.
        [d] 1 Leon. 273. Skinn. 389.

ment,

ment, or delivery, of goods to another perſon for a particular uſe; as to a carrier to convey to London, to an innkeeper to ſecure in his inn, or the like. Here there is no abſolute property in either the bailor or the bailee, the perſon delivering, or him to whom it is delivered : for the bailor hath only the right, and not the immediate poſſeſſion; the bailee hath the poſſeſſion, and only a temporary right. But it is a qualified property in them both; and each of them is entitled to an action, in caſe the goods be damaged or taken away : the bailee on account of his immediate poſſeſſion; the bailor, becauſe the poſſeſſion of the bailee is, mediately, his poſſeſſion alſo[e]. So alſo in caſe of goods pledged or pawned upon condition, either to repay money or otherwiſe; both the pledgor and pledgee have a qualified, but neither of them an abſolute, property therein: the pledgor's property is con-ditional, and depends upon the performance of the condition of re-payment, *&c*; and ſo too is that of the pledgee, which de-pends upon it's non-performance[f]. The ſame may be ſaid of goods diſtreined for rent, or other cauſe of diſtreſs : which are in the nature of a pledge, and are not, at the firſt taking, the abſolute property of either the diſtreinor, or party diſtreined; but may be redeemed, or elſe forfeited, by the ſubſequent con-duct of the latter. But a ſervant, who hath the care of his maſ-ter's goods or chattels, as a butler of plate, a ſhepherd of ſheep, and the like, hath not any property or poſſeſſion either abſolute or qualified, but only a mere charge or overſight[g].

H A V I N G thus conſidered the ſeveral diviſions of property in *poſſeſſion*, which ſubſiſts there only, where a man hath both the right and alſo the occupation of the thing; we will proceed next to take a ſhort view of the nature of property in *action*, or ſuch where a man hath not the occupation, but merely a bare right to occupy the thing in queſtion; the poſſeſſion whereof may however be recovered by a ſuit or action at law : from whence

[e] 1 Roll. Abr. 607.　　　　　[g] 3 Inſt. 108.
[f] Cro. Jac. 245.

the

the thing so recoverable is called a thing or *chose, in action* [h]. Thus money due on a bond is a *chose* in action; for a property in the debt vests at the time of forfeiture mentioned in the obligation, but there is no possession till recovered by course of law. If a man promises, or covenants with me, to do any act, and fails in it, whereby I suffer damage; the recompense for this damage is a *chose* in action : for though a right to some recompense vests in me, at the time of the damage done, yet what and how large such recompense shall be, can only be ascertained by verdict; and the possession can only be given me by legal judgment and execution. In the former of these cases the student will observe, that the property, or right of action, depends upon an *express* contract or obligation to pay a stated sum : and in the latter it depends upon an *implied* contract, that if the covenantor does not perform the act he engaged to do, he shall pay me the damages I sustain by his breach of covenant. And hence it may be collected, that all property in action depends entirely upon contracts, either express or implied; which are the only regular means of acquiring a *chose* in action, and of the nature of which we shall discourse at large in a subsequent chapter.

AT present we have only to remark, that upon all contracts or promises, either express or implied, and the infinite variety of cases into which they are and may be spun out, the law gives an action of some sort or other to the party injured in case of nonperformance; to compel the wrongdoer to do justice to the party with whom he has contracted, and, on failure of performing the identical thing he engaged to do, to render a satisfaction equivalent to the damage sustained. But while the thing, or it's equivalent, remains in suspense, and the injured party has only the right and not the occupation, it is called a *chose* in action; being a thing rather *in potentia* than *in esse :* though the owner may

---

[h] The same idea, and the same denomination, of property prevailed in the civil law. "*Rem in bon.: nostris habere intelligimur,* "*quotiens ad reciperandam eam actionem habe-* "*amus.*" (*Ff.* 41.1.52.) And again; "*ae-* "*que bonis adnumerabitur etiam, si quid est in-* "*actionibus, petitionibus, persecutionibus. Nam.* "*et haec in bonis esse videntur.*" (*Ff.* 50.16.49.)

have

have as abfolute a property of fuch things in action, as of things in poffeffion.

AND, having thus diftinguifhed the different *degree* or *quantity* of *dominion* or *property* to which things perfonal are fubject, we may add a word or two concerning the *time* of their *enjoyment*, and the *number* of their *owners*; in conformity to the method before obferved in treating of the property of things real.

FIRST, as to the *time* of *enjoyment*. By the rules of the antient common law, there could be no future property, to take place in expectancy, created in perfonal goods and chattels; becaufe, being things tranfitory, and by many accidents fubject to be loft, deftroyed, or otherwife impaired, and the exigencies of trade requiring alfo a frequent circulation thereof, it would occafion perpetual fuits and quarrels, and put a ftop to the freedom of commerce, if fuch limitations in remainder were *generally* tolerated and allowed. But yet in laft wills and teftaments fuch limitations of perfonal goods and chattels, in remainder after a bequeft for life, were permitted [i]: though originally that indulgence was only fhewn, when merely the *ufe* of the goods, and not the goods themfelves, was given to the firft legatee [k]; the property being fuppofed to continue all the time in the executor of the devifor. But now that diftinction is difregarded: and therefore if a man either by deed or will limits his books or furniture to A for life, with remainder over to B, this remainder is good. But, where an eftate-tail in things perfonal is given to the firft or any fubfequent poffeffor, it vefts in him the total property, and no remainder over fhall be permitted on fuch a limitation [m]. For this, if allowed, would tend to a perpetuity, as the devifee or grantee in tail of a chattel has no method of barring the entail; and therefore the law vefts in him at once the entire dominion of the goods, being analogous to the fee-fimple which a tenant in tail may acquire in a real eftate.

[i] 1 Equ. Caf. abr. 360.
[k] Mar. 106.

[l] 2 Freem. 206.
[m] 1 P. W^{ms}. 290.

NEXT,

N e x t, as to the *number* of *owners*. Things perfonal may belong to their owners, not only in feveralty, but alfo in joint-tenancy, and in common, as well as real eftates. They cannot indeed be vefted in coparcenary; becaufe they do not defcend from the anceftor to the heir, which is neceffary to conftitute co-parceners. But if a horfe, or other perfonal chattel, be given to two or more, abfolutely, they are joint-tenants hereof; and, un-lefs the jointure be fevered, the fame doctrine of furvivorfhip fhall take place as in eftates of lands and tenements [n]. And, in like manner, if the jointure be fevered, as by either of them fell-ing his fhare, the vendee and the remaining part-owner fhall be tenants in common, without any *jus accrefcendi* or furvivorfhip [o]. So alfo if 100 *l.* be given by will to two or more, *equally to be divided* between them, this makes them tenants in common [p]; as, we have formerly feen [p], the fame words would have done, in regard to real eftates. But, for the encouragement of hufbandry and trade, it is held that a ftock on a farm, though occupied jointly, and alfo a ftock ufed in a joint undertaking, by way of partnerfhip in trade, fhall always be confidered as common and not as joint property; and there fhall be no furvivorfhip therein [r].

[n] Litt. §. 282. 1 Vern. 482.
[o] Litt. §. 321.
[p] 1 Equ. Caf. abr. 292.

[q] pag. 193.
[r] 1 Vern. 217. Co. Litt. 182.

CHAPTER THE TWENTY SIXTH.

OF TITLE TO THINGS PERSONAL
BY OCCUPANCY.

WE are next to confider the *title* to things perfonal, or the various means of *acquiring*, and of *lofing*, fuch property as may be had therein : both which confiderations of gain and lofs fhall be blended together in one and the fame view, as was done in our obfervations upon real property ; fince it is for the moft part impoffible to contemplate the one, without contemplating the other alfo. And thefe methods of acquifition or lofs are principally twelve : 1. By occupancy. 2. By prerogative. 3. By forfeiture. 4. By cuftom. 5. By fucceffion. 6. By marriage. 7. By judgment. 8. By gift. 9. By contract. 10. By bankruptcy. 11. By teftament. 12. By adminiftration.

AND, firft, a property in goods and chattels may be acquired by *occupancy :* which, we have more than once [a] remarked, was the original and only primitive method of acquiring any property at all ; but which has fince been reftrained and abridged, by the pofitive laws of fociety, in order to maintain peace and harmony among mankind. For this purpofe, by the laws of England, gifts, and contracts, teftaments, legacies, and adminiftrations have been introduced and countenanced, in order to transfer and continue that property and poffeffion in things perfonal, which

[a] See pag. 3. 8. 258.

has

has once been acquired by the owner. And, where fuch things are found without any other owner, they for the moft part belong to the king by virtue of his prerogative; except in fome few inftances, wherein the original and natural right of occupancy is ftill permitted to fubfift, and which we are now to confider.

1. THUS, in the firft place, it hath been faid, that any body may feife to his own ufe fuch goods as belong to an alien enemy[b]. For fuch enemies, not being looked upon as members of our fociety, are not entitled during their ftate of enmity to the benefit or protection of the laws; and therefore every man that has opportunity is permitted to feife upon their chattels, without being compelled as in other cafes to make reftitution or fatisfaction to the owner. But this, however generally laid down by fome of our writers, muft in reafon and juftice be reftrained to fuch captors as are authorized by the public authority of the ftate, refiding in the crown[c]; and to fuch goods as are brought into this country by an alien enemy, after a declaration of war, without a fafe-conduct or paffport. And therefore it hath been held[d], that where a foreigner is refident in England, and afterwards a war breaks out between his country and ours, his goods are not liable to be feifed. It hath alfo been adjudged, that if an enemy take the goods of an Englifhman, which are afterwards retaken by another fubject of this kingdom, the former owner fhall lofe his property therein, and it fhall be indefeafibly vefted in the fecond taker; unlefs they were retaken the fame day, and the owner before fun-fet puts in his claim of property[e]. Which is agreeable to the law of nations, as underftood in the time of Grotius[f], even with regard to captures made at fea; which were held to be the property of the captors after a poffeffion of twenty four hours: though the modern authorities[g] require, that before the property can be changed, the goods muft have been brought into

[b] Finch. L. 178.
[c] Freem. 40.
[d] Bro. *Abr. tit. propertie.* 38. *forfeiture.* 57.
[e] *Ibid.*

[f] *de j. b. & p. l.* 3. *c.* 6. § 3.
[g] Bynkerfh. *quaeft. jur. publ. I.* 4. Rccc. de. *Affecur. not.* 66.

VOL. II.   C c c   port,

port, and have continued a night *intra praefidia*, in a place of fafe cuftody, fo that all hope of recovering them is loft.

AND, as in the *goods* of an enemy, fo alfo in his *perfon*, a man may acquire a fort of qualified property, by taking him a prifoner in war[h]; at leaft till his ranfom be paid[j]. And this doctrine feems to have been extended to negro-fervants[i], who are purchafed, when captives, of the nations with whom they are at war, and continue therefore in fome degree the property of their mafters who buy them : though, accurately fpeaking, that property confifts rather in the perpetual *fervice*, than in the *body* or *perfon*, of the captive[k].

2. THUS again, whatever moveables are found upon the furface of the earth, or in the fea, and are unclaimed by any owner, are fuppofed to be abandoned by the laft proprietor ; and, as fuch, are returned into the common ftock and mafs of things : and therefore they belong, as in a ftate of nature, to the firft occupant or fortunate finder, unlefs they fall within the defcription of waifs, or eftrays, or wreck, or hidden treafure ; for thefe, we have formerly feen[l], are vefted by law in the king, and form a part of the ordinary revenue of the crown.

3. THUS too the benefit of the elements, the light, the air, and the water, can only be *appropriated* by occupancy. If I have an antient window overlooking my neighbour's ground, he may not erect any blind to obftruct the light: but if I build my houfe clofe to his wall, which darkens it, I cannot compel him to demolifh his wall ; for there the firft occupancy is rather in him, than in me. If my neighbour makes a tan-yard, fo as to annoy

---

[h] Bro. *Abr. tit. propertie.* 18.
[i] We meet with a curious writ of trefpafs in the regifter (102.) for breaking a man's houfe, and fetting fuch a prifoner at large. "*Quare domum ipfius A. apud W. (in* "*qua idem A. quendam H. Scotum per ipfum* "*A. de guerra captum tanquam prifonem fuum,* "*quoufque fibi de centum libris, per quas idem*

"*H. redemptionem fuam cum praefato A. pro* "*vita fua falvanda fecerat, fatisfactum foret,* "*detinuit) fregit, et ipfum H. cepit et abduxit,* "*vel quo voluit abire permifit, &c.*"
[l] 2 Lev. 201.
[k] Carth. 396. Lᵈ Raym. 147. Salk. 667.
[l] Book I. ch. 8.

                                                                    and

and render lefs falubrious the air of my houfe or gardens, the law will furnifh me with a remedy; but if he is firft in poffeffion of the air, and I fix my habitation near him, the nufance is of my own feeking, and muft continue. If a ftream be unoccupied, I may erect a mill thereon, and detain the water; yet not fo as to injure my neighbour's prior mill, or his meadow : for he hath by the firft occupancy acquired a property in the current.

4. WITH regard likewife to animals *ferae naturae*, all mankind had by the original grant of the creator a right to purfue and take any fowl or infect of the air, any fifh or inhabitant of the waters, and any beaft or reptile of the field : and this natural right ftill continues in every individual, unlefs where it is reftrained by the civil laws of the country. And when a man has once fo feifed them, they become while living his *qualified* property, or, if dead, are *abfolutely* his own : fo that to fteal them, or otherwife invade this property, is, according to the refpective values, fometimes a criminal offence, fometimes only a civil injury. The reftrictions which are laid upon this right, by the laws of England, relate principally to royal fifh, as whale and fturgeon, and fuch terreftrial, aërial, or aquatic animals as go under the denomination of *game*; the taking of which is made the exclufive right of the prince, and fuch of his fubjects to whom he has granted the fame royal privilege. But thofe animals, which are not expreffly fo referved, are ftill liable to be taken and appropriated by any of the king's fubjects, upon their own territories; in the fame manner as they might have taken even game itfelf, till thefe civil prohibitions were iffued : there being in nature no diftinction between one fpecies of wild animals and another, between the right of acquiring property in a hare or a fquirrel, in a partridge or a butterfly; but the difference, at prefent made, arifes merely from the pofitive municipal law.

5. To this principle of occupancy alfo muft be referred the method of acquiring a fpecial perfonal property in corn growing on the ground, or other *emblements*, by any *poffeffor* of the land

who hath fown or planted it, whether he be owner of the inheritance in fee or in tail, or be tenant for life, for years, or at will :
which emblements are diftinct from the real eftate in the land,
and fubject to many, though not all, the incidents attending perfonal
chattels. They were devifable by teftament before the ftatute of
wills [m], and at the death of the owner fhall veft in his executor
and not his heir : they are forfeitable by outlawry in a perfonal
action [n]: and by the ftatute 11 Geo. II. c. 19. though not by the
common law [o], they may be diftreined for rent arrere. The reafon for admitting the acquifition of this fpecial property, by tenants who have temporary interefts, was formerly given [p]; and
it was extended to tenants in fee, principally for the benefit of
their creditors : and therefore, though the emblements are affets
in the hands of the executor, are forfeitable upon outlawry, and
diftreinable for rent, they are not in other refpects confidered as
perfonal chattels; and, particularly, they are not the object of
larciny, before they are fevered from the ground [q].

6. THE doctrine of property arifing from *acceffion* is alfo
grounded on the right of occupancy. By the Roman law, if any
given corporeal fubftance received afterwards an acceffion by natural or by artificial means, as by the growth of vegetables, the
pregnancy of animals, the embroidering of cloth, or the converfion of wood or metal into veffels and utenfils, the original
owner of the thing was intitled by his right of poffeffion to the
property of it under fuch it's ftate of improvement [r]: but if the
thing itfelf, by fuch operation, was changed into a different fpecies, as by making wine, oil, or bread, out of another's grapes,
olives, or wheat, it belonged to the new operator; who was only
to make a fatisfaction to the former proprietor for the materials,
which he had fo converted [s]. And thefe doctrines are implicitly
copied and adopted by our Bracton [t], in the reign of king Henry III; and have fince been confirmed by many refolutions of the

[m] Perk. §. 512.

[n] Bro. *Abr. tit. emblements*.21. 5Rep.116.

[o] 1 Roll. Abr. 666.

[p] pag. 122. 146.

[q] 3 Inft. 109.

[r] *Inft.* 2. 1. 25, 26, 31. *Ff.* 6. 1. 5.

[s] *Inft.* 2. 1. 25, 34.

[t] *l.* 2. *c.* 2 & 3.

courts [u].

courts[u]. It hath even been held, that if one takes away another's wife or son, and cloaths them, and afterwards the husband or father retakes them back, the garments shall cease to be the property of him who provided them, being now annexed to the person of the child or woman[w].

7. BUT in the case of *confusion* of goods, where those of two persons are so intermixed, that the several portions can be no longer distinguished, the English law partly agrees with, and partly differs from, the civil. If the intermixture be by consent, I apprehend that in both laws the proprietors have an interest in common, in proportion to their respective shares[x]. But, if one wilfully intermixes his money, corn, or hay, with that of another man, without his approbation or knowlege, or casts gold in like manner into another's melting-pot or crucible, the civil law, though it gives the sole property of the whole to him who has not interfered in the mixture, yet allows a satisfaction to the other for what he has so improvidently lost[y]. But our law, to guard against fraud, allows no remedy in such a case; but gives the intire property, without any account, to him, whose original dominion is invaded, and endeavoured to be rendered uncertain, without his own consent[z].

8. THERE is still another species of property, which, being grounded on labour and invention, is more properly reducible to the head of occupancy than any other; since the right of occupancy itself is supposed by Mr Locke[a], and many others[b], to be founded on the personal labour of the occupant. And this is the right, which an author may be supposed to have in his own original literary compositions: so that no other person without his leave may publish or make profit of the copies. When a man by the exertion of his rational powers has produced an original work, he has clearly a right to dispose of that identical work as

---

[u] Bro. *Abr. tit. propertie.* 23.   Moor. 20.
Poph. 38.

[w] Moor. 214.

[x] *Inst.* 2. 1. 27, 28.   1 Vern. 217.

[y] *Inst.* 2. 1. 28.

[z] Poph. 38.   2 Bulstr. 325.   2 Vern. 516.

[a] on Gov. part 2. ch. 5.

[b] See pag. 8.

he

he pleaſes, and any attempt to take it from him, or vary the diſ-poſition he has made of it, is an invaſion of his right of property. Now the identity of a literary compoſition conſiſts intirely in the *ſentiment* and the *language*; the ſame conceptions, cloathed in the ſame words, muſt neceſſarily be the ſame compoſition : and what-ever method be taken of conveying that compoſition to the ear or the eye of another, by recital, by writing, or by printing, in any number of copies or at any period of time, it is always the identical work of the author which is ſo conveyed; and no other man can have a right to convey or transfer it without his conſent, either tacitly or expreſſly given. This conſent may perhaps be tacitly given, when an author permits his work to be publiſhed, without any reſerve of right, and without ſtamping on it any marks of ownerſhip : it is then a preſent to the public, like the building of a church, or the laying out a new highway : but, in caſe of a bargain for a ſingle impreſſion, or a ſale or gift of the copyright, the reverſion is plainly continued in the original pro-prietor, or the whole property transferred to another.

THE Roman law adjudged, that if one man wrote any thing, though never ſo elegantly, on the paper or parchment of an-other, the writing ſhould belong to the original owner of the materials on which it was written [c] : meaning certainly nothing more thereby, than the mere mechanical operation of writing, for which it directed the ſcribe to receive a ſatisfaction ; eſpecial-ly as, in works of genius and invention, ſuch as a picture paint-ed on another man's canvas, the ſame law [d] gave the canvas to the painter. We find no other mention in the civil law of any property in the works of the underſtanding, though the ſale of literary copies, for the purpoſes of recital or multiplication, is certainly as antient as the times of Terence [e], Martial [f], and Statius [g]. Neither with us in England hath there been any direct determination upon the right of authors at the common law.

[c] *Si in chartis membraniſve tuis carmen vel biſtoriam vel orationem Titius ſcripſerit, hujus corporis non Titius ſed tu dominus eſſe videris. Inſt.* 2. 1. 33.

[d] *Ibid.* §. 34.
[e] *Prol. in Eunuch.* 20.
[f] *Epigr.* i. 67. iv. 72. xiii. 3. xiv. 194.
[g] *Juv.* vii. 83.

But

But much may be gathered from the frequent injunctions of the court of chancery, prohibiting the invasion of this property: especially where either the injunctions have been *perpetual*[h], or have related to unpublished manuscripts[i], or to such antient books, as were not within the provisions of the statute of queen Anne[k]. Much may also be collected from the several legislative recognitions of copyrights[l]; and from those adjudged cases at common law, wherein the crown hath been considered as invested with certain prerogative copyrights[m]; for, if the crown is capable of an exclusive right in any one book, the subject seems also capable of having the same right in another.

But, exclusive of such copyright as may subsist by the rules of the common law, the statute 8 Ann. c. 19. hath protected by additional penalties the property of authors and their assigns for the term of fourteen years; and hath directed that if, at the end of that term, the author himself be living, the right shall then return to him for another term of the same duration: and a similar privilege is extended to the inventors of prints and engravings, for the term of fourteen years, by the statute 8 Geo. II. c. 13. Both which appear to have been copied from the exception in the statute of monopolies, 21 Jac. I. c. 3. which allows a royal patent of privilege to be granted for fourteen years to any inventor of a new manufacture, for the sole working or making of the same; by virtue whereof a temporary property becomes vested in the patentee[n].

[h] Knaplock v. Curl. 9 Nov. 1722. Viner Abr. *tit. Books.* pl. 3. — Baller v. Watson. 6 Dec. 1737.

[i] Webb v. Rose. 24 May 1732. — Pope v. Curl. 5 Jun. 1741.—Forrester v. Waller. 13 Jun 1741. — Duke of Queensberry v. Shebbeare. 31 July 1758.

[k] Knaplock v. Curl. before cited.—Eyre v. Walker. 9 Jun. 1735.— Motte v. Faulk-ner. 28 Nov. 1735. —Walthoe v. Walker. 27 Jan. 1736.—Tonson v. Walker. 12 May 1739. and 30 Apr. 1752.

[l] *A. D.* 1649. c. 60. Scobell. 92. 13 & 14 Car. II. c. 33. 10 Ann. c. 19. §. 112. 5 Geo. III. c. 12. §. 26.

[m] Cart. 89. 1 Mod. 257. 4 Burr. 661.

[n] 1 Vern. 62.

C H A P T E R T H E T W E N T Y S E V E N T H.

O F TITLE B Y PREROGATIVE, A N D
FORFEITURE.

A SECOND method of acquiring property in perfonal
chattels is by the *king's prerogative:* whereby a right
may accrue either to the crown itfelf, or to fuch as claim under
the title of the crown, as by grant or by prefcription.

SUCH in the firft place are all *tributes, taxes,* and *cuftoms;*
whether conftitutionally inherent in the crown, as flowers of the
prerogative and branches of the *cenfus regalis* or antient royal
revenue, or whether they be occafionally created by authority of
parliament ; of both which fpecies of revenue we treated largely
in the former volume. In thefe the king acquires and the fubject lofes a property the inftant they become due : if paid, they
are a *chofe* in poffeffion ; if unpaid, a *chofe* in action. Hither alfo
may be referred all forfeitures, fines, and amercements due to
the king, which accrue by virtue of his antient prerogative, or
by particular modern ftatutes : which revenues created by ftatute do always affimilate, or take the fame nature, with the antient revenues ; and may therefore be looked upon as arifing from
a kind of artificial or fecondary prerogative. And, in either
cafe, the owner of the thing forfeited, and the perfon fined or
amerced, do lofe and part with the property of the forfeiture,
fine, or amercement, the inftant the king or his grantee acquires it.

I N

IN thefe feveral methods of acquiring property by prerogative there is alfo this peculiar quality, that the king cannot have a *joint* property with any perfon in one entire chattel, or fuch a one as is not capable of divifion or feparation; but where the titles of the king and a fubject concur, the king fhall have the whole: in like manner as the king can, neither by grant nor contract, become a joint-tenant of a chattel real with another perfon[a]; but by fuch grant or contract fhall become intitled to the whole in feveralty. Thus, if a horfe be given to the king and a private perfon, the king fhall have the fole property: if a bond be made to the king and a fubject, the king fhall have the whole penalty; the debt or duty being one fingle chattel[b]: and fo, if two perfons have the property of a horfe between them, or have a joint debt owing them on bond, and one of them affigns his part to the king, or is attainted, whereby his moiety is forfeited to the crown; the king fhall have the entire horfe, and entire debt[c]. For, as it is not confiftent with the dignity of the crown to be partner with a fubject, fo neither does the king ever lofe his right in any inftance; but, where they interfere, his is always preferred to that of another perfon[d]: from which two principles it is a neceffary confequence, that the innocent, though unfortunate, partner muft lofe his fhare in both the debt and the horfe, or in any other chattel in the fame circumftances.

THIS doctrine has no opportunity to take place in certain other inftances of title by prerogative, that remain to be mentioned; as the chattels thereby vefted are originally and folely vefted in the crown, without any transfer or derivative affignment either by deed or law from any former proprietor. Such is the acquifition of property in wreck, in treafure-trove, in waifs, in eftrays, in royal fifh, in fwans, and the like; which are not *transferred* to the fovereign from any former owner, but are ori-

[a] See pag. 184.
[b] Fitzh. *Abr. t. dette.* 38. Plowd. 243.

[c] Cro. Eliz. 263. Plowd. 323. Finch. Law. 178. 10 Mod. 245.
[d] Co. Litt. 30.

ginally *inherent* in him by the rules of law, and are derived to particular fubjects, as royal franchifes, by his bounty. Thefe are afcribed to him, partly upon the particular reafons mentioned in the eighth chapter of the former book; and partly upon the general principle of their being *bona vacantia*, and therefore vefted in the king, as well to preferve the peace of the public, as in truft to employ them for the fafety and ornament of the commonwealth.

WITH regard to the prerogative *copyrights*, which were mentioned in the preceding chapter, they are held to be vefted in the crown upon different reafons. Thus, 1. The king, as the executive magiftrate, has the right of promulging to the people all acts of ftate and government. This gives him the exclufive privilege of printing, at his own prefs, or that of his grantees, all *acts of parliament, proclamations,* and *orders of council.* 2. As fupreme head of the church, he hath a right to the publication of all *liturgies* and books of *divine fervice.* 3. He hath a right by purchafe to the copies of fuch *lawbooks, grammars,* and other compofitions, as were compiled or tranflated at the expenfe of the crown. And upon thefe two laft principles the exclufive right of printing the tranflation of the *bible* is founded. 4. *Almanacks* have been faid to be prerogative-copies, either as things derelict, or elfe as being fubftantially nothing more than the calendar prefixed to our liturgy[e]. And indeed the regulation of time has been often confidered as a matter of ftate. The Roman *fafti* were under the care of the pontifical college: and Romulus, Numa, and Julius Caefar, fucceffively regulated the Roman calendar.

THERE ftill remains another fpecies of prerogative property, founded upon a very different principle from any that have been mentioned before; the property of fuch animals *ferae naturae,* as are known by the denomination of *game,* with the right of purfuing, taking, and deftroying them: which is vefted in the king alone, and from him derived to fuch of his fubjects as have

[e] 1 Mod. 257.

received

received the grants of a chafe, a park, a free warren, or free fifhery. This may lead us into an enquiry concerning the original of
thefe franchifes, or royalties, on which we touched a little in a
former chapter[f]; the right itfelf being an incorporeal hereditament, though the fruits and profits of it are of a perfonal nature.

IN the firft place then we have already fhewn, and indeed it
cannot be denied, that by the law of nature every man, from
the prince to the peafant, has an equal right of purfuing, and
taking to his own ufe, all fuch creatures as are *ferae naturae,*
and therefore the property of nobody, but liable to be feifed by
the firft occupant. And fo it was held by the imperial law, even
fo late as Juftinian's time : " *ferae igitur beftiae, et volucres, et*
" *omnia animalia quae mari, coelo, et terra nafcuntur, fimul atque*
" *ab aliquo capta fuerint, jure gentium ftatim illius effe incipiunt.*
" *Quod enim nullius eft, id naturali ratione occupanti conceditur*[g]."
But it follows from the very end and conftitution of fociety,
that this natural right, as well as many others belonging to man
as an individual, may be reftrained by pofitive laws enacted for
reafons of ftate, or for the fuppofed benefit of the community.
This reftriction may be either with refpect to the *place* in which
this right may, or may not, be exercifed ; with refpect to the
animals that are the fubject of this right ; or with refpect to the
perfons allowed or forbidden to exercife it. And, in confequence
of this authority, we find that the municipal laws of many nations have exerted fuch power of reftraint ; have in general forbidden the entering on another man's grounds, for any caufe,
without the owner's leave ; have extended their protection to
fuch particular animals as are ufually the objects of purfuit ; and
have invefted the prerogative of hunting and taking fuch animals
in the fovereign of the ftate only, and fuch as he fhall authorize[h]. Many reafons have concurred for making thefe conftitutions : as, 1. For the encouragement of agriculture and improvement of lands, by giving every man an exclufive dominion over

[f] pag. 38, 39.   [h] Puff. L. N. l. 4. c. 6. §. 5.
[g] *Inft.* 2. 1. 12.

Ddd 2   his

his own foil. 2. For prefervation of the feveral fpecies of thefe animals, which would foon be extirpated by a general liberty. 3. For prevention of idlenefs and diffipation in hufbandmen, artificers, and others of lower rank; which would be the unavoidable confequence of univerfal licence. 4. For preventing of popular infurrections and refiftance to the government, by difarming the bulk of the people[i] : which laft is a reafon oftener meant, than avowed, by the makers of foreft or game laws. Nor, certainly, in thefe prohibitions is there any *natural* injuftice, as fome have weakly enough fuppofed : fince, as Puffendorf obferves, the law does not hereby take from any man his prefent property, or what was already his own, but barely abridges him of one means of acquiring a future property, that of occupancy; which indeed the law of nature would allow him, but of which the laws of fociety have in moft inftances very juftly and reafonably deprived him.

YET, however defenfible thefe provifions in general may be, on the footing of reafon, or juftice, or civil policy, we muft notwithftanding acknowlege that, in their prefent fhape, they owe their immediate original to flavery. It is not till after the irruption of the northern nations into the Roman empire, that we read of any other prohibitions, than that natural one of not fporting on any private grounds without the owner's leave; and another of a more fpiritual nature, which was rather a rule of ecclefiaftical difcipline, than a branch of municipal law. The Roman or civil law, though it knew no reftriction as to *perfons* or *animals*, fo far regarded the article of *place*, that it allowed no man to hunt or fport upon another's ground, but by confent of the owner of the foil. " *Qui alienum fundum ingreditur, venandi aut aucu-* " *pandi gratia, poteft a domino prohiberi ne ingrediatur*[k]." For if there can, by the law of nature, be any inchoate imperfect property fuppofed in wild animals before they are taken, it feems moft reafonable to fix it in him upon whofe land they are found. And as to the other reftriction, which relates to *perfons* and not

---

[i] Warburton's alliance. 324.   [k] *Inft.* 2. 1. §. 12.

to *place*, the pontificial or canon law[1] interdicts "*venationes, et "sylvaticas vagationes cum canibus, et accipitribus*" to all *clergymen* without diftinction; grounded on a faying of St. Jerom [m], that it never is recorded that thefe diverfions were ufed by the faints, or primitive fathers. And the canons of our Saxon church, pub-lifhed in the reign of king Edgar [n], concur in the fame pro-hibition: though our fecular laws, at leaft after the conqueft, did even in the times of popery difpenfe with this canonical im-pediment; and fpiritual perfons were allowed by the common law to hunt for their recreation, in order to render them fitter for the performance of their duty: as a confirmation whereof we may obferve, that it is to this day a branch of the king's prerogative, at the death of every bifhop, to have his kennel of hounds, or a compofition in lieu thereof [o].

BUT, with regard to the rife and original of our prefent civil prohibitions, it will be found that all foreft and game laws were introduced into Europe at the fame time, and by the fame po-licy, as gave birth to the feodal fyftem; when thofe fwarms of barbarians iffued from their northern hive, and laid the founda-tion of moft of the prefent kingdoms of Europe, on the ruins of the weftern empire. For when a conquering general came to fettle the oeconomy of a vanquifhed country, and to part it out among his foldiers or feudatories, who were to render him mili-tary fervice for fuch donations; it behoved him, in order to fe-cure his new acquifitions, to keep the *ruftici* or natives of the country, and all who were not his military tenants, in as low a condition as poffible, and efpecially to prohibit them the ufe of arms. Nothing could do this more effectually than a prohibition of hunting and fporting: and therefore it was the policy of the conqueror to referve this right to himfelf, and fuch on whom he fhould beftow it; which were only his capital feudatories, or greater barons. And accordingly we find, in the feudal conftitu-tions [p], one and the fame law prohibiting the *ruftici* in general

[1] *Decretal. l. 5. tit. 24. c. 2.*
[m] *Decret. part. 1. dift. 34. l. 1.*
[n] *cap. 64.*

[o] 4 Inft. 309.
[p] *Feud. l. 2. tit. 27. §. 5.*

from

from carrying arms, and also proscribing the use of nets, snares, or other engines for destroying the game. This exclusive privilege well suited the martial genius of the conquering troops, who delighted in a sport[q] which in it's pursuit and slaughter bore some resemblance to war. *Vita omnis,* (says Caesar, speaking of the antient Germans) *in venationibus atque in studiis rei militaris consistit*[r]. And Tacitus in like manner observes, that *quotiens bella non ineunt, multum venatibus, plus per otium transigunt*[s]. And indeed, like some of their modern successors, they had no other amusement to entertain their vacant hours; they despising all arts as effeminate, and having no other learning, than was couched in such rude ditties, as were sung at the solemn carousals which succeeded these antient huntings. And it is remarkable that, in those nations where the feodal policy remains the most uncorrupted, the forest or game laws continue in their highest rigor. In France all game is properly the king's; and in some parts of Germany it is death for a peasant to be found hunting in the woods of the nobility[t].

WITH us in England also, hunting has ever been esteemed a most princely diversion and exercise. The whole island was replenished with all sorts of game in the times of the Britons; who lived in a wild and pastoral manner, without inclosing or improving their grounds, and derived much of their subsistence from the chase, which they all enjoyed in common. But when husbandry took place under the Saxon government, and lands began to be cultivated, improved, and enclosed, the beasts naturally fled into the woody and desart tracts; which were called the forests, and, having never been disposed of in the first distribution of lands, were therefore held to belong to the crown. These were filled with great plenty of game, which our royal sports-

---

[q] In the laws of Jenghiz Khan, founder of the Mogul and Tartarian empire, published *A. D.* 1205. there is one which prohibits the killing of all game from March to October; that the court and soldiery might find plenty enough in the winter, during their recess from war. (Mod. Univ. Hist. iv. 468.)

[r] *De bell. Gall. l.* 6. *c.* 20.

[s] *c.* 15.

[t] Mattheus *de Crimin. c.*3. *tit.*1. Carpzov. *Practic. Saxonic. p.* 2. *c.* 84.

men referved for their own diverfion, on pain of a pecuniary for-feiture for fuch as interfered wtih their fovereign. But every freeholder had the full liberty of fporting upon his own territo-ries, provided he abftained from the king's forefts : as is fully expreffed in the laws of Canute[v], and of Edward the confeffor[u]; "*fit quilibet homo dignus venatione fua, in fylva, et in agris, fibi* "*propriis, et in dominio fuo : et abftineat omnis homo a venariis re-* "*gis, ubicunque pacem eis habere voluerit :*" which indeed was the antient law of the Scandinavian continent, from whence Canute probably derived it. "*Cuique enim in proprio fundo quamlibet fe-* "*ram quoquo modo venari permiffum[w].*"

HOWEVER, upon the Norman conqueft, a new doctrine took place; and the right of purfuing and taking all beafts of chafe or *venary*, and fuch other animals as were accounted *game*, was then held to belong to the king, or to fuch only as were autho-rized under him. And this, as well upon the principles of the feodal law, that the king is the ultimate proprietor of all the lands in the kingdom, they being all held of him as the chief lord, or lord paramount of the fee; and that therefore he has the right of the univerfal foil, to enter thereon, and to chafe and take fuch creatures at his pleafure : as alfo upon another maxim of the common law, which we have frequently cited and illuftrated, that thefe animals are *bona vacantia*, and, having no other owner, belong to the king by his prerogative. As there-fore the former reafon was held to veft in the king a *right* to purfue and take them any where; the latter was fuppofed to give the king, and fuch as he fhould authorize, a *fole* and *ex-clufive* right.

THIS right, thus newly vefted in the crown, was exerted with the utmoft rigor, at and after the time of the Norman ef-tablifhment; not only in the antient forefts, but in the new ones which the conqueror made, by laying together vaft tracts of

[v] *c.* 77.
[u] *c.* 36.

[w] Stiernhook. *de jure Sueon. l.* 2. *c.* 8.

country, depopulated for that purpofe, and referved folely for the king's royal diverfion ; in which were exercifed the moft horrid tyrannies and oppreffions, under colour of foreft law, for the fake of preferving the beafts of chafe; to kill any of which, within the limits of the foreft, was as penal as the death of a man. And, in purfuance of the fame principle, king John laid a total interdict upon the *winged* as well as the *fourfooted* creation : " *capturam avium per totam Angliam interdixit*[x]." The cruel and infupportable hardfhips, which thefe foreft laws created to the fubject, occafioned our anceftors to be as zealous for their refor- mation, as for the relaxation of the feodal rigors and the other exactions introduced by the Norman family ; and accordingly we find the immunities of *carta de forefta* as warmly contended for, and extorted from the king with as much difficulty, as thofe of *magna carta* itfelf. By this charter, confirmed in parliament[y], many forefts were difafforefted, or ftripped of their oppreffive privileges, and regulations were made in the regimen of fuch as remained ; particularly[z] killing the king's deer was made no lon- ger a capital offence, but only punifhed by fine, imprifonment, or abjuration of the realm. And by a variety of fubfequent fta- tutes, together with the long acquiefcence of the crown without exerting the foreft laws, this prerogative is now become no lon- ger a grievance to the fubject.

But, as the king referved to himfelf the *forefts* for his own exclufive diverfion, fo he granted out from time to time other tracts of land to his fubjects under the names of *chafes* or *parks*[a]; or gave them licence to make fuch in their own grounds ; which indeed are fmaller forefts, in the hands of a fubject, but not go- verned by the foreft laws : and by the common law no perfon is at liberty to take or kill any beafts of chafe, but fuch as hath an antient chafe or park ; unlefs they be alfo beafts of prey.

[x] M. Paris. 303.
[y] 9 *Hen. III.*
[z] *cap.* 10.
[a] See pag. 38.

As

As to all inferior species of game, called beasts and fowls of warren, the liberty of taking or killing them is another franchise or royalty, derived likewise from the crown, and called *free warren*; a word, which signifies preservation or custody: as the exclusive liberty of taking and killing fish in a public stream or river is called a *free fishery*; of which however no new franchise can at present be granted, by the express provision of *magna carta, c.* 16 [b]. The principal intention of granting a man these franchises or liberties was in order to protect the game, by giving him a sole and exclusive power of killing it himself, provided he prevented other persons. And no man, but he who has a chase or free warren, by grant from the crown, or prescription which supposes one, can justify hunting or sporting upon another man's soil; nor indeed, in thorough strictness of common law, either hunting or sporting at all.

HOWEVER novel this doctrine may seem, it is a regular consequence from what has been before delivered; that the sole right of taking and destroying game belongs exclusively to the king. This appears, as well from the historical deduction here made, as because he may grant to his subjects an exclusive right of taking them; which he could not do, unless such a right was first inherent in himself. And hence it will follow, that no person whatever, but he who has such derivative right from the crown, is by common law entitled to take or kill any beasts of chase, or other game whatsover. It is true, that by the acquiescence of the crown, the frequent grants of free warren in antient times, and the introduction of new penalties of late by certain statutes for preserving the game, this exclusive prerogative of the king is little known or considered; every man, that is exempted from these modern penalties, looking upon himself as at liberty to do what he pleases with the game: whereas the contrary is strictly true, that no man, however well *qualified* he may vulgarly be esteemed, has a right to encroach on the royal

[b] Mirr. c. 5. §. 2. See pag. 39.

prerogative by the killing of game, unlefs he can fhew a particular grant of free warren; or a prefcription, which prefumes a grant; or fome authority under an act of parliament. As for the latter, I know but of two inftances wherein an exprefs permiffion to kill game was ever given by ftatute; the one by 1 Jac. I. c. 27. altered by 7 Jac. I. c. 11. and virtually repealed by 22 & 23 Car. II. c. 25. which gave authority, fo long as they remained in force, to the owners of free warren, to lords of manors, and to all freeholders having 40 *l. per annum* in lands of inheritance, or 80 *l.* for life or lives, or 400 *l.* perfonal eftate, (and their fervants) to take partridges and pheafants upon their own, or their mafter's, free warren, inheritance, or freehold: the other by 5 Ann. c. 14. which empowers lords and ladies of manors to appoint gamekeepers to kill game for the ufe of fuch lord or lady; which with fome alterations ftill fubfifts, and plainly fuppofes fuch power not to have been in them before. The truth of the matter is, that thefe game laws (of which we fhall have occafion to fpeak again in the fourth book of thefe commentaries) do indeed *qualify* nobody, except in the inftance of a gamekeeper, to kill game: but only, to fave the trouble and formal procefs of an action by the perfon injured, who perhaps too might remit the offence, thefe ftatutes inflict *additional* penalties, to be recovered either in a regular or fummary way, by any of the king's fubjects, from certain perfons of inferior rank who may be found offending in this particular. But it does not follow that perfons, excufed from thefe additional penalties, are therefore *authorifed* to kill game. The circumftances, of having 100 *l. per annum*, and the reft, are not properly qualifications, but exemptions. And thefe perfons, fo exempted from the penalties of the game ftatutes, are not only liable to actions of trefpafs by the owners of the land; but alfo, if they kill game within the limits of any royal franchife, they are liable to the actions of fuch who may have the right of chafe or free warren therein.

UPON

UPON the whole it appears, that the king, by his prerogative, and such persons as have, under his authority, the royal franchises of chase, park, free warren, or free fishery, are the *only* persons, who may acquire any property, however fugitive and transitory, in these animals *ferae naturae*, while living; which is said to be vested in them, as was observed in a former chapter, *propter privilegium*. And it must also be remembered, that such persons as may thus lawfully hunt, fish, or fowl, *ratione privilegii*, have (as has been said) only a qualified property in these animals; it not being absolute or permanent, but lasting only so long as the creatures remain within the limits of such respective franchise or liberty, and ceasing the instant they voluntarily pass out of it. It is held indeed, that if a man starts any game within his own grounds, and follows it into another's, and kills it there, the property remains in himself[c]. And this is grounded on reason and natural justice[d]: for the property consists in the possession; which possession commences by the finding it in his own liberty, and is continued by the immediate pursuit. And so, if a stranger starts game in one man's chase or free warren, and hunts it into another liberty, the property continues in the owner of the chase or warren; this property arising from privilege[e], and not being changed by the act of a mere stranger. Or if a man starts game on another's private grounds and kills it there, the property belongs to him in whose ground it was killed, because it was also started there[f]; this property arising *ratione soli*. Whereas if, after being started there, it is killed in the grounds of a third person, the property belongs not to the owner of the first ground, because the property is local; nor yet to the owner of the second, because it was not started in his soil; but it vests in the person who started and killed it[g], though guilty of a trespass against both the owners.

[c] 11 Mod. 75.
[d] Puff. L. N. l. 4. c. 6.
[e] Lord Raym. 251.
[f] *Ibid.*
[g] Farr. 18. Lord Raym. *ibid.*

III. I PROCEED now to a third method, whereby a title to goods and chattels may be acquired and loft, *viz.* by *forfeiture*; as a punifhment for fome crime or mifdemefnor in the party forfeiting, and as a compenfation for the offence and injury committed againft him to whom they are forfeited. Of forfeitures, confidered as the means whereby *real* property might be loft and acquired, we treated in a former chapter [h]. It remains therefore in this place only to mention, by what means or for what offences goods and chattels become liable to forfeiture.

IN the variety of penal laws with which the fubject is at prefent incumbered, it were a tedious and impracticable tafk to reckon up the various forfeitures, inflicted by fpecial ftatutes, for particular crimes and mifdemefnors : fome of which are *mala in fe*, or offences againft the divine law, either natural or revealed; but by far the greateft part are *mala prohibita*, or fuch as derive their guilt merely from their prohibition by the laws of the land: fuch as is the forfeiture of 40 s. *per* month by the ftatute 5 Eliz. c. 4. for exercifing a trade without having ferved feven years as an apprentice thereto; and the forfeiture of 10 l. by 9 Ann. c. 23. for printing an almanac without a ftamp. I fhall therefore confine myfelf to thofe offences only, by which *all* the goods and chattels of the offender are forfeited : referring the ftudent for fuch, where pecuniary mulcts of different quantities are inflicted, to their feveral proper heads, under which very many of them have been or will be mentioned; or elfe to the collections of Hawkins and Burn, and other laborious compilers. Indeed, as moft of thefe forfeitures belong to the crown, they may feem as if they ought to have been referred to the preceding method of acquiring perfonal property, namely, by prerogative. But as, in the inftance of partial forfeitures, a moiety often goes to the informer, the poor, or fometimes to other perfons; and as one total forfeiture, namely that by a bankrupt who is guilty of felony by

[h] See pag. 267.

concealing

concealing his effects, accrues entirely to his creditors, I have therefore made it a diftinct head of transferring property.

GOODS and chattels then are totally forfeited by conviction of *high treafon*, or *mifprifion* of treafon; of *petit treafon*; of *felony* in general, and particularly of *felony de fe*, and of *manflaughter*; nay even by conviction of *excufable homicide*[1]; by *outlawry* for treafon or felony; by conviction of *petit larceny*; by *flight* in treafon or felony, even though the party be acquitted of the fact; by *ftanding mute*, when arraigned of felony; by *drawing a weapon on a judge*, or *ftriking* any one *in the prefence of the king's courts*; by *praemunire*; by *pretended prophecies*, upon a fecond conviction; by *owling*; by the *refiding abroad* of artificers; and by *challenging to fight* on account of money won at gaming. All thefe offences, as will more fully appear in the fourth book of thefe commentaries, induce a total forfeiture of goods and chattels.

AND this forfeiture commences from the time of *conviction*, not the time of committing the fact, as in forfeitures of real property. For chattels are of fo vague and fluctuating a nature, that to affect them, by any relation back, would be attended with more inconvenience than in the cafe of landed eftates: and part, if not the whole of them, muft be expended in maintaining the delinquent, between the time of committing the fact and his conviction. Yet a fraudulent conveyance of them, to defeat the intereft of the crown, is made void by ftatute 13 Eliz. c. 5.

[1] Co. Litt. 391   2 Inft. 316.   3 Inft. 320.

CHAPTER THE TWENTY EIGHTH.

Of TITLE by CUSTOM.

A FOURTH method of acquiring property in things
perfonal, or chattels, is by *cuftom:* whereby a right vefts
in fome particular perfons, either by the local ufage of fome particular place, or by the almoft general and univerfal ufage of the
kingdom. It were endlefs, fhould I attempt to enumerate all the
feveral kinds of fpecial cuftoms, which may entitle a man to a
chattel intereft in different parts of the kingdom : I fhall therefore content myfelf with making fome obfervations on three forts
of cuftomary interefts, which obtain pretty generally throughout
moft parts of the nation, and are therefore of more univerfal
concern; viz. *heriots, mortuaries,* and *heir-looms.*

1. HERIOTS, which were flightly touched upon in a former
chapter [a], are ufually divided into two forts, heriot-*fervice,* and
heriot-*cuftom.* The former are fuch as are due upon a fpecial refervation in a grant or leafe of lands, and therefore amount to
little more than a mere rent [b]: the latter arife upon no fpecial
refervation whatfoever, but depend merely upon immemorial ufage
and cuftom [c]. Of thefe therefore we are here principally to
fpeak : and they are defined to be a cuftomary tribute of goods
and chattels, payable to the lord of the fee on the deceafe of the
owner of the land.

[a] pag. 97.
[b] 2 Saund. 166.
[c] Co. Cop. §. 24.

THE

THE firft eftablifhment, if not introduction, of compulfory heriots into England, was by the Danes : and we find in the laws of king Canute[d] the feveral *heregeates* or heriots fpecified, which were then exacted by the king on the death of divers of his fub-jects, according to their refpective dignities ; from the higheft *eorle* down to the moft inferior *thegne* or landholder. Thefe, for the moft part, confifted in arms, horfes, and habiliments of war ; which the word itfelf, according to fir Henry Spelman[e], fignifies. Thefe were delivered up to the fovereign on the death of the va-fal, who could no longer ufe them, to be put into other hands for the fervice and defence of the country. And upon the plan of this Danifh eftablifhment did William the conqueror fafhion his law of reliefs, as was formerly obferved[f] ; when he afcertained the precife relief to be taken of every tenant in chivalry, and, contrary to the feodal cuftom and the ufage of his own duchy of Normany, required arms and implements of war to be paid in-ftead of money[g].

THE Danifh compulfive heriots, being thus tranfmuted into reliefs, underwent the fame feveral viciffitudes as the feodal te-nures, and in focage eftates do frequently remain to this day, in the fhape of a double rent payable at the death of the tenant : the heriots which now continue among us, and preferve that name, feeming rather to be of Saxon parentage, and at firft to have been merely difcretionary[h]. Thefe are now for the moft part confined to copyhold tenures, and are due by cuftom only, which is the life of all eftates by copy ; and perhaps are the only inftance where cuftom has favoured the lord. For this payment was originally a voluntary donation, or gratuitous legacy of the tenant ; perhaps in acknowlegement of his having been raifed a degree above villenage, when all his goods and chattels were quite at the mercy of the lord : and cuftom, which has on the

[d] c. 69.
[e] of feuds. c. 18.
[f] pag. 65.

[g] *LL. Guil. Conqu.* c 22, 23, 24.
[h] Lambard. Peramb. of Kent. 492.

one

one hand confirmed the tenant's intereft in exclufion of the lord's will, has on the other hand eftablifhed this difcretional piece of gratitude into a permanent duty. An heriot may alfo appertain to free land, that is held by fervice and fuit of court; in which cafe it is moft commonly a copyhold enfranchifed, whereupon the heriot is ftill due by cuftom. Bracton[i] fpeaks of heriots as frequently due on the death of both fpecies of tenants: " *eft* " *quidem alia praeftatio quae nominatur heriettum*; *ubi tenens, liber* " *vel fervus, in morte fua dominum fuum, de quo tenuerit, refpicit* " *de meliori averio fuo, vel de fecundo meliori, fecundum diverfam lo-* " *corum confuetudinem.*" And this, he adds, " *magis fit de gratia* " *quam de jure*;" in which Fleta[k] and Britton[l] agree: thereby plainly intimating the original of this cuftom to have been merely voluntary, as a legacy from the tenant; though now the immemorial ufage has eftablifhed it as of right in the lord.

THIS heriot is fometimes the beft live beaft, or *averium*, which the tenant dies poffeffed of, (which is particularly denominated the villein's relief in the twenty ninth law of king William the conqueror) fometimes the beft inanimate good, under which a jewel or piece of plate may be included: but it is always a *perfonal* chattel, which, immediately on the death of the tenant who was the owner of it, being afcertained by the option of the lord[m], becomes vefted in him as his property; and is no charge upon the lands, but merely on the goods and chattels. The tenant muft be the owner of it, elfe it cannot be due; and therefore on the death of a feme-covert no heriot can be taken; for fhe can have no ownerfhip in things perfonal[n]. In fome places there is a cuftomary compofition in money, as ten or twenty fhillings in lieu of a heriot, by which the lord and tenant are both bound, if it be an indifputably antient cuftom: but a new compofition of this fort will not bind the reprefentatives of either party; for that amounts to the creation of a new cuftom, which is now impoffible[o].

[i] *l. 2. c. 36. §. 9.*
[k] *l 3. c. 18.*
[l] *c. 69.*

[m] Hob. 60.
[n] Keilw. 84. 4 Leon. 239.
[o] Co. Cop. §. 31.

2. MOR-

2. Mortuaries are a fort of ecclefiaftical heriots, being a cuftomary gift claimed by and due to the minifter in very many parifhes on the death of his parifhioners. They feem originally to have been, like lay heriots, only a voluntary bequeft to the church ; being intended, as Lyndewode informs us from a conftitution of archbifhop Langham, as a kind of expiation and amends to the clergy for the perfonal tithes, and other ecclefiaftical duties, which the laity in their life-time might have negleted or forgotten to pay. For this purpofe, *after* [p] the lord's heriot or beft good was taken out, the fecond beft chattel was referved to the church as a mortuary : " *fi decedens plura habuerit* " *animalia, optimo cui de jure fuerit debitum refervato, ecclefiae fuae* " *fine dolo, fraude, feu contradictione qualibet, pro recompenfatione* " *fubtractionis decimarum perfonalium, necnon et oblationum, fecun-* " *dum melius animal refervetur, poft obitum, pro falute animae fuae* [q]." And therefore in the laws of king Canute [r] this mortuary is called foul-fcot (ꞃaplꞃceaꞇ) or *fymbolum animae*. And, in purfuance of the fame principle, by the laws of Venice, where no perfonal tithes have been paid during the life of the party, they are paid at his death out of his merchandize, jewels, and other moveables [s]. So alfo, by a fimilar policy, in France, every man that died without bequeathing a part of his eftate to the church, which was called *dying without confeffion*, was formerly deprived of chriftian burial : or, if he died inteftate, the relations of the deceafed, jointly with the bifhop, named proper arbitrators to determine what he ought to have given to the church, in cafe he had made a will. But the parliament, in 1409, redreffed this grievance [t].

It was antiently ufual in this kingdom to bring the mortuary to church along with the corpfe when it came to be buried; and thence [u] it is fometimes called a *corfe-prefent :* a term, which

p Co. Litt. 185.
q *Provinc. l* 1. *tit.* 3.
r c. 13.

s Panormitan. *ad Decretal. l.* 3. *t.* 20. *c.* 32.
t Sp. L. b. 28. c. 41.
u Selden. hift. of tithes. c. 10.

befpeaks it to have been once a voluntary donation. However in Bracton's time, fo early as Henry III, we find it rivetted into an eftablifhed cuftom : infomuch that the bequefts of heriots and mortuaries were held to be neceffary ingredients in every teftament of chattels. " *Imprimis autem debet quilibet, qui teftamentum* "*fecerit, dominum fuum de meliori re quam habuerit recognofcere ;* " *et poftea ecclefiam de alia meliori :*" the lord muft have the beft good left him as an heriot ; and the church the fecond beft as a mortuary. But yet this cuftom was different in different places : " *in quibufdam locis habet ecclefia melius animal de confuetudine ; in* " *quibufdam fecundum, vel tertium melius ; et in quibufdam nihil :* " *et ideo confideranda eft confuetudo loci* [w]." This cuftom ftill varies in different places, not only as to the mortuary to be paid, but the perfon to whom it is payable. In Wales, a mortuary or corfeprefent was due upon the death of every clergyman to the bifhop of the diocefe ; till abolifhed, upon a recompenfe given to the bifhop, by the ftatute 12 Ann. ft. 2. c. 6. And in the archdeaconry of Chefter a cuftom alfo prevailed, that the bifhop, who is alfo archdeacon, fhould have at the death of every clergyman dying therein, his beft horfe or mare, bridle, faddle, and fpurs, his beft gown or cloak, hat, upper garment under his gown, and tippet, and alfo his beft fignet or ring [x]. But by ftatute 28 Geo. II. c. 6. this mortuary is directed to ceafe, and the act has fettled upon the bifhop an equivalent in it's room. The king's claim to many goods, on the death of all prelates in England, feems to be of the fame nature ; though fir Edward Coke [y] apprehends, that this is a *duty due upon death* and not a *mortuary :* a diftinction which feems to be without a difference. For not only the king's ecclefiaftical character, as fupreme ordinary, but alfo the fpecies of the goods claimed, which bear fo near a refemblance to thofe in the archdeaconry of Chefter, which was an acknowleged mortuary, puts the matter out of difpute. The king, according to the record vouched by fir Edward Coke, is entitled to fix things ; the bifhop's beft horfe or palfrey, with his furniture : his cloak,

[w] Bracton. *l.* 2. *c.* 26. Flet. *l.* 2. *c.* 57.　　　[y] 2 Inft. 491.
[x] Cro. Car. 237.

or gown, and tippet : his cup, and cover : his bafon, and ewer :
his gold ring : and, laftly, his *muta canum*, his mew or kennel
of hounds ; as was mentioned in the preceding chapter [z].

THIS variety of cuftoms, with regard to mortuaries, giving
frequently a handle to exactions on the one fide, and frauds or
expenfive litigations on the other ; it was thought proper by ftatute 21 Hen. VIII. c. 6. to reduce them to fome kind of certainty.
For this purpofe it is enacted, that all mortuaries, or corfe-prefents
to parfons of any parifh, fhall be taken in the following manner ;
unlefs where by cuftom lefs or none at all is due : viz. for every
perfon who does not leave goods to the value of ten marks, nothing : for every perfon who leaves goods to the value of ten
marks, and under thirty pounds, 3*s*. 4*d*. if above thirty pounds,
and under forty pounds, 6*s*. 8*d*. if above forty pounds, of what
value foever they may be, 10*s*. and no more. And no mortuary
fhall throughout the kingdom be paid for the death of any feme-
covert ; nor any child ; nor for any one of full age, that is not
a houfekeeper ; nor for any wayfaring man ; but fuch wayfaring
man's mortuary fhall be paid in the parifh to which he belongs.
And upon this ftatute ftands the law of mortuaries to this day.

3. HEIR-LOOMS are fuch goods and perfonal chattels, as, contrary to the nature of chattels, fhall go by fpecial cuftom to the
heir along with the inheritance, and not to the executor of the
laft proprietor. The termination, *loom*, is of Saxon original ; in
which language it fignifies a limb or member [a] ; fo that an heir-
loom is nothing elfe, but a limb or member of the inheritance.
They are generally fuch things as cannot be taken away without
damaging or difmembering the freehold ; otherwife the general
rule is, that no chattel intereft whatfoever fhall go to the heir,
notwithftanding it be exprefsly limited to a man and his heirs,
but fhall veft in the executor [b]. But deer in a real authorized
park, fifhes in a pond, doves in a dove-houfe, &*c*, though in

[z] pag. 413.   [b] Co. Litt. 388.
[a] Spelm. *Gloff.* 277.

themſelves perſonal chattels, yet they are ſo annexed to and ſo neceſſary to the well-being of the inheritance, that they ſhall accompany the land wherever it veſts, by either deſcent or pur-chaſe ᶜ. For this reaſon alſo I apprehend it is, that the antient jewels of the crown are held to be heir-looms ᵈ: for they are neceſſary to maintain the ſtate, and ſupport the dignity, of the ſovereign for the time being. Charters likewiſe, and deeds, court-rolls, and other evidences of the land, together with the cheſts in which they are contained, ſhall paſs together with the land to the heir, in the nature of heir-looms, and ſhall not go to the executor ᵉ. By ſpecial cuſtom alſo, in ſome places, carriages, utenſils, and other houſehold implements may be heir-looms ᶠ; but ſuch cuſtom muſt be ſtrictly proved. On the other hand, by almoſt general cuſtom, whatever is ſtrongly affixed to the free-hold or inheritance, and cannot be ſevered from thence without violence or damage, "*quod ab aedibus non facile revellitur* ᵍ," is become a member of the inheritance, and ſhall thereupon paſs to the heir; as marble chimney-pieces, pumps, old fixed or dor-mant tables, benches, and the like ʰ. A very ſimilar notion to which prevails in the duchy of Brabant; where they rank cer-tain things moveable among thoſe of the immoveable kind, call-ing them, by a very peculiar appellation, *praedia volantia,* or vo-latile eſtates: ſuch as beds, tables, and other heavy implements of furniture, which (as an author of their own obſerves) "*dig-*
"*nitatem iſtam nacta ſunt, ut villis, ſylvis, et aedibus, aliiſque prae-*
"*diis, comparentur; quod ſolidiora mobilia ipſis aedibus ex deſtina-*
"*tione patrisfamilias cohaerere videantur, et pro parte ipſarum ae-*
"*dium aeſtimentur* ⁱ."

OTHER perſonal chattels there are, which alſo deſcend to the heir in the nature of heir-looms, as a monument or tombſtone in a church, or the coat-armor of his anceſtor there hung up,

ᶜ Co Litt. 8.
ᵈ *Ibid.* 18.
ᵉ Bro. *Abr. tit. chatteles.* 18.
ᶠ Co. Litt. 18. 185.

ᵍ Spelm. *Gloſſ.* 277.
ʰ 12 Mod. 520.
ⁱ Stockmans *de jure devolutionis. c.* 3.
§. 16.

with

with the pennons and other enfigns of honor, fuited to his degree.   In this cafe, albeit the freehold of the church is in the
parfon, and thefe are annexed to that freehold, yet cannot the
parfon or any other take them away or deface them, but is liable
to an action from the heir [k].   Pews in the church are fomewhat
of the fame nature, which may defcend by cuftom immemorial
(without any ecclefiaftical concurrence) from the anceftor to the
heir [l].   But though the heir has a property in the monuments
and efcutcheons of his anceftors, yet he has none in their bodies
or afhes ; nor can he bring any civil action againft fuch as inde-
cently at leaft, if not impioufly, violate and difturb their remains,
when dead and buried.   The parfon indeed, who has the freehold of the foil, may bring an action of trefpafs againft fuch as
dig and difturb it : and, if any one in taking up a dead body
fteals the fhrowd or other apparel, it will be felony [m] ; for the
property thereof remains in the executor, or whoever was at the
charge of the funeral.

BUT to return to heir-looms : thefe, though they be mere
chattels, yet cannot be devifed away from the heir by will ; but
fuch a devife is void [n], even by a tenant in fee-fimple.   For, though
the owner might during his life have fold or difpofed of them, as
he might of the timber of the eftate, fince as the inheritance
was his own, he might mangle or difmember it as he pleafed ;
yet, they being at his death inftantly vefted in the heir, the devife (which is fubfequent, and not to take effect till *after* his
death) fhall be poftponed to the cuftom, whereby they have already defcended.

---

[k] 12 Rep. 105. Co. Litt. 18.   [m] 3 Inft. 110. 12 Rep. 113. 1 Hal. P. C.
[l] 3 Inft. 202. 12 Rep. 105.   515.
                                          [n] Co. Litt. 185.

CHAPTER THE TWENTY NINTH.

OF TITLE BY SUCCESSION, MARRIAGE, AND JUDGMENT.

IN the prefent chapter we fhall take into confideration three other fpecies of title to goods and chattels.

V. THE fifth method therefore of gaining a property in chattels, either perfonal or real, is by *fucceffion:* which is, in ftrict-nefs of law, only applicable to corporations aggregate of many, as dean and chapter, mayor and commonalty, mafter and fellows, and the like ; in which one fet of men may, by fucceeding an-other fet, acquire a property in all the goods, moveables, and other chattels of the corporation. The true reafon whereof is, becaufe in judgment of law a corporation never dies ; and therefore the predeceffors, who lived a century ago, and their fucceffors now in being, are one and the fame body corporate [a]. Which identity is a property fo inherent in the nature of a body politic, that, even when it is meant to give any thing to be taken in fucceffion by fuch a body, that fucceffion need not be expreff-ed ; but the law will of itfelf imply it. So that a gift to fuch a corporation, either of lands or of chattels, without naming their fucceffors, vefts an abfolute property in them fo long as the cor-poration fubfifts [b]. And thus a leafe for years, an obligation, a

[a] 4 Rep. 65.   [b] Bro. *Abr. t. eftates.* 90. Cro. Eliz. 464.

jewel,

jewel, a flock of sheep, or other chattel interest, will vest in the
succeffors, by succeffion, as well as in the identical members, to
whom it was originally given.

BUT, with regard to sole corporations, a confiderable diftinction muft be made. For if fuch fole corporation be the reprefentative of a number of perfons; as the mafter of an hofpital,
who is a corporation for the benefit of the poor brethren; an
abbot, or prior, by the old law before the reformation, who reprefented the whole convent; or the dean of fome antient cathedrals, who ftands in the place of, and reprefents in his corporate
capacity, the chapter; fuch fole corporations as thefe have in
this refpect the fame powers, as corporations aggregate have, to
take perfonal property or chattels in fucceffion. And therefore a
bond to fuch a mafter, abbot, or dean, and his fucceffors, is good
in law; and the fucceffor fhall have the advantage of it, for the
benefit of the aggregate fociety, of which he is in law the reprefentative[c]. Whereas in the cafe of fole corporations, which reprefent no others but themfelves, as bifhops, parfons, and the like,
no chattel intereft can regularly go in fucceffion : and therefore, if
a leafe for years be made to the bifhop of Oxford and his fucceffors, in fuch cafe his executors or adminiftrators, and not his
fucceffors, fhall have it[d]. For the word *fucceffors*, when applied to
a perfon in his politic capacity, is equivalent to the word *heirs* in
his natural : and as fuch a leafe for years, if made to John and
his heirs, would not veft in his heirs, but his executors ; fo, if it
be made to John bifhop of Oxford and his fucceffors, who are
the heirs of his body politic, it fhall ftill veft in his executors and
not in fuch his fucceffors. The reafon of this is obvious : for,
befides that the law looks upon goods and chattels as of too low
and perifhable a nature to be limited either to heirs, or fuch fucceffors as are equivalent to heirs ; it would alfo follow, that if
any fuch chattel intereft (granted to a fole corporation and his
fucceffors) were allowed to defcend to fuch fucceffor, the property
thereof muft be in abeyance from the death of the prefent owner

[c] Dyer. 48. Cro. Eliz. 464.   [d] Co. Litt. 46.

until

until the fucceffor be appointed : and this is contrary to the nature of a chattel intereft, which can never be in abeyance or
without an owner[e]; but a man's right therein, when once fufpended, is gone for ever. This is not the cafe in corporations aggregate, where the right is never in fufpence; nor in the other
fole corporations before-mentioned, who are rather to be confidered as heads of an aggregate body, than fubfifting merely in
their own right: the chattel intereft therefore, in fuch a cafe,
is really and fubftantially vefted in the hofpital, convent, chapter, or other aggregate body; though the head is the vifible perfon in whofe name every act is carried on, and in whom every
intereft is therefore faid (in point of form) to veft. But the general rule, with regard to corporations merely fole, is this, that
no chattel can go or be acquired by right of fucceffion[f].

YET to this rule there are two exceptions. One in the cafe
of the king, in whom a chattel may veft by a grant of it formerly made to a preceding king and his fucceffors[g]. The other
exception is, where, by a *particular* cuftom, fome *particular* corporations fole have acquired a power of taking *particular* chattel
interefts in fucceffion. And this cuftom, being againft the general tenor of the common law, muft be ftrictly interpreted, and
not extended to any other chattel interefts than fuch immemorial
ufage will ftrictly warrant. Thus the chamberlain of London,
who is a corporation fole, may by the cuftom of London take
bonds and *recognizances* to himfelf and his fucceffors, for the benefit of the orphan's fund[h]: but it will not follow from thence,
that he has a capacity to take a *leafe for years* to himfelf and his
fucceffors for the fame purpofe; for the cuftom extends not to
that : nor that he may take a *bond* to himfelf and his fucceffors,
for any other purpofe than the benefit of the orphan's fund; for
that alfo is not warranted by the cuftom. Wherefore, upon the
whole, we may clofe this head with laying down this general
rule; that fuch right of fucceffion to chattels is univerfally inhe-

[e] Brownl. 132.
[f] Co. Litt. 46.

[g] *Ibid.* 90.
[h] 4 Rep. 65. Cro. Eliz. 682.

rent

rent by the common law in all aggregate corporations, in the king, and in such single corporations as represent a number of persons; and may, by special custom, belong to certain other sole corporations for some particular purposes: although, generally, in sole corporations no such right can exist.

VI. A SIXTH method of acquiring property in goods and and chattels is by *marriage*; whereby those chattels, which belonged formerly to the wife, are by act of law vested in the husband, with the same degree of property and with the same powers, as the wife, when sole, had over them.

THIS depends entirely on the notion of an unity of person between the husband and wife; it being held that they are one person in law [i], so that the very being and existence of the woman is suspended during the coverture, or entirely merged and incorporated in that of the husband. And hence it follows, that whatever personal property belonged to the wife, before marriage, is by marriage absolutely vested in the husband. In a real estate he only gains a title to the rents and profits during coverture: for that, depending upon feodal principles, remains entire to the wife after the death of her husband, or to her heirs, if she dies before him; unless, by the birth of a child, he becomes tenant for life by the curtesy. But, in chattel interests, the sole and absolute property vests in the husband, to be disposed of at his pleasure, if he chuses to take possession of them: for, unless he reduces them to possession, by exercising some act of ownership upon them, no property vests in him, but they shall remain to the wife, or to her representatives, after the coverture is determined.

THERE is therefore a very considerable difference in the acquisition of this species of property by the husband, according to the subject-matter; viz. whether it be a chattel *real*, or a

i See Book I. c. 15.

chattel *perfonal*; and, of chattels perfonal, whether it be in *poffeffion*, or in *action* only. A *chattel real* vefts in the hufband, not abfolutely, but *fub modo*. As, in cafe of a leafe for years; the hufband fhall receive all the rents and profits of it, and may, if he pleafes, fell, furrender, or difpofe of it during the cover-ture [k] : if he be outlawed or attainted, it fhall be forfeited to the king [l] : it is liable to execution for his debts [m] : and, if he furvives his wife, it is to all intents and purpofes his own [n]. Yet if he has made no difpofition thereof in his lifetime, and dies before his wife, he cannot difpofe of it by will [o] : for, the huf-band having made no alteration in the property during his life, it never was transferred from the wife; but after his death fhe fhall remain in her antient poffeffion, and it fhall not go to his executors. So it is alfo of chattels perfonal (or *chofes*) in *action*; as debts upon bond, contracts, and the like : thefe the hufband may have if he pleafes; that is, if he reduces them into poffeffion by receiving or recovering them at law. And, upon fuch receipt or recovery, they are abfolutely and entirely his own; and fhall go to his executors or adminiftrators, or as he fhall bequeath them by will, and fhall not reveft in the wife. But, if he dies before he has recovered or reduced them into poffeffion, fo that at his death they ftill continue *chofes in action*, they fhall furvive to the wife; for the hufband never exerted the power he had of obtaining an exclufive property in them [p]. And fo, if an eftray comes into he wife's franchife, and the hufband feifes it, it is abfolutely his property : but, if he dies without feifing it, his executors are not now at liberty to feife it, but the wife or her heirs [q]; for the hufband never exerted the right he had, which right determined with the coverture. Thus in both thefe fpecies of property the law is the fame, in cafe the wife furvives the hufband; but, in cafe the hufband furvives the wife, the law is very different with refpect to *chattels real* and *chofes in action* :

[k] Co. Litt. 46.
[l] Plowd. 263.
[m] Co. Litt. 351.
[n] *Ibid.* 300.

[o] Poph. 5. Co. Litt. 351.
[p] Co. Litt. 351.
[q] *Ibid.*

for

for he shall have the *chattel real* by survivorship, but not the *chose in action*[r]; except in the case of arrears of rent, due to the wife before her coverture, which in case of her death are given to the husband by statute 32 Hen. VIII. c. 37. And the reason for the general law is this : that the husband is in absolute possession of the *chattel real* during the coverture, by a kind of joint-tenancy with his wife; wherefore the law will not wrest it out of his hands, and give it to her representatives : though in case he had died first, it would have survived to the wife, unless he thought proper in his lifetime to alter the possession. But a *chose in action* shall not survive to him, because he never was in possession of it at all, during the coverture; and the only method he had to gain possession of it, was by suing in his wife's right : but as, after her death, he cannot (as husband) bring an action in her right, because they are no longer one and the same person in law, therefore he can never (as such) recover the possession. But he still will be intitled to be her administrator; and may, in that capacity, recover such things in action as became due to her before or during the coverture.

THUS, and upon these reasons, stands the law between husband and wife, with regard to *chattels real,* and *choses in action:* but, as to *chattels personal* (or *choses*) *in possession,* which the wife hath in her own right, as ready money, jewels, household goods, and the like, the husband hath therein an immediate and absolute property, devolved to him by the marriage, not only potentially but in fact, which never can again revest in the wife or her representative[s].

AND, as the husband may thus, generally, acquire a property in all the personal substance of the wife, so in one particular instance the wife may acquire a property in some of her husband's goods; which shall remain to her after his death, and shall not go to his executors. These are called her *paraphernalia;* which is a term borrowed from the civil law [t], and is derived from the Greek language, fignifying fomething over and above her dower. Our law ufes it to fignify the apparel and ornaments of the wife, fuitable to her rank and degree; which fhe becomes entitled to at the death of her hufband over and above her jointure or dower, and preferably to all other reprefentatives : and the jewels of a peerefs, ufually worn by her, have been held to be *parapherna-lia* [w]. Neither can the hufband devife by his will fuch ornaments and jewels of his wife; though during his life perhaps he hath the power (if unkindly inclined to exert it) to fell them or give them away [x]. But if fhe continues in the ufe of them till his death, fhe fhall afterwards retain them againft his executors and adminiftrators, and all other perfons, except creditors where there is a deficiency of affets [y]. And her neceffary apparel is protected even againft the claim of creditors [z].

VII. A JUDGMENT, in confequence of fome fuit or action in a court of juftice, is frequently the means of vefting the right and property of chattel interefts in the prevailing party. And here we muft be careful to diftinguifh between property, the *right* of which is before vefted in the party, and of which only *poffef-fion* is recovered by fuit or action; and property, to which a man before had no determinate title or certain claim, but he gains as well the right as the poffeffion by the procefs and judgment of the law. Of the former fort are all debts and *chofes in action*; as if a man gives bond for 20 *l*, or agrees to buy a horfe at a ftated fum, or takes up goods of a tradefman upon an implied contract to pay as much as they are reafonably worth : in all thefe cafes the right accrues to the creditor, and is completely vefted in him at the time of the bond being fealed, and the contract or agreement made; and the law only gives him a remedy to reco-

---

[t] *Ff.* 23. 3. 9. §. 3.
[u] Cro. Car. 343.   1 Roll. Abr. 911.
2 Leon. 166.
[w] Moor. 213.

[x] Noy's Max. c. 49. — Grahme v. Lord Londonderry. 24 Nov. 1746. Canc.
[y] 1 P. W[ms]. 730.
[z] Noy. *ibid.*

ver

ver the poffeffion of that right, which already in juftice belongs to him. But there is alfo a fpecies of property to which a man has not any claim or title whatfoever, till after fuit commenced and judgment obtained in a court of law : where the right and the remedy do not follow each other, as in common cafes, but accrue at one and the fame time ; and where, before judgment had, no man can fay that he has any abfolute property, either in poffeffion or in action. Of this nature are,

1. SUCH penalties as are given by particular ftatutes, to be recovered on an action *popular* ; or, in other words, to be recovered by him or them that will fue for the fame. Such as the penalty of 500 *l*, which thofe perfons are by feveral acts of parliament made liable to forfeit, that, being in particular offices or fituations in life, neglect to take the oaths to the government ; which penalty is given to him or them that will fue for the fame. Now here it is clear that no particular perfon, A or B, has any right, claim, or demand, in or upon this penal fum, till after action brought[a] ; for he that brings his action and can *bona fide* obtain judgment firft, will undoubtedly fecure a title to it, in exclufion of every body elfe. He obtains an inchoate imperfect degree of property, by commencing his fuit ; but it is not confummated till judgment, for if any collufion appears, he lofes the priority he had gained[b]. But, otherwife, the right fo attaches in the firft informer, that the king (who before action brought may grant a pardon which fhall be a bar to all the world) cannot after fuit commenced remit any thing but his own part of the penalty[c]. For by commencing the fuit the informer has made the popular action his own private action, and it is not in the power of the crown, or of any thing but parliament, to releafe the informer's intereft. This therefore is one inftance, where a fuit and judgment at law are not only the means of re-

[a] 2 Lev. 141. Stra. 1169. Combe v. Pitt. B. R. T. 3 Geo. III.

[b] Stat. 4 Hen. VII. c. 20.

[c] Cro. Eliz. 138. 11 Rep. 65.

covering,

covering, but alfo of acquiring, property. And what is faid of this one penalty is equally true of all others, that are given thus at large to a common informer, or to any perfon that will fue for the fame. They are placed as it were in a ftate of nature, acceffible by all the king's fubjects,. but the acquired right of none of them : open therefore to the firft occupant, who declares his intention to poffefs them by bringing his action ; and who carries that intention into execution, by obtaining judgment to recover them.

2. ANOTHER fpecies of property, that is acquired and loft by fuit and judgment at law, is that of *damages* given to a man by a jury, as a compenfation and fatisfaction for fome injury fuftained ; as for a battery, for imprifonment, for flander, or for trefpafs. Here the plaintiff has no certain demand till after verdict ; but, when the jury has affeffed his damages, and judgment is given thereupon, whether they amount to twenty pounds or twenty fhillings, he inftantly acquires, and the defendant lofes at the fame time, a right to that fpecific fum. It is true, that this is not an acquifition fo perfectly original as in the former inftance : for here the injured party has unqueftionably a vague and indeterminate right to fome damages or other, the inftant he receives the injury ; and the verdict of the jurors, and judgment of the court thereupon, do not in this cafe fo properly veft a *new* title in him, as fix and afcertain the *old* one ; they do not *give*, but *define*, the right. But however, though ftrictly fpeaking the primary right to a fatisfaction for injuries is given by the law of nature, and the fuit is only the means of afcertaining and recovering that fatisfaction ; yet, as the legal proceedings are the only vifible means of this acquifition of property, we may fairly enough rank fuch damages, or fatisfaction affeffed, under the head of property acquired by fuit and judgment at law.

3. HITHER

3. HITHER alfo may be referred, upon the fame principle, all title to cofts and expenfes of fuit; which are often arbitrary, and reft entirely in the determination of the court, upon weighing all circumftances, both as to the *quantum*, and alfo (in the courts of equity efpecially, and upon motions in the courts of law) whether there fhall be any cofts at all. Thefe cofts therefore, when given by the court to either party, may be looked upon as an acquifition made by the judgment of law.

CHAPTER THE THIRTIETH.

OF TITLE BY GIFT, GRANT, AND CONTRACT.

W E are now to proceed, according to the order marked out, to the difcuffion of two of the remaining methods of acquiring a title to property in things perfonal, which are much connected together, and anfwer in fome meafure to the conveyances of real eftates; being thofe by *gift* or *grant*, and by *contract*: whereof the former vefts a property in *poffeffion*, the latter a property in *action*.

VIII. GIFTS then, or *grants*, which are the eighth method of transferring perfonal property, are thus to be diftinguifhed from each other, that *gifts* are always gratuitous, *grants* are upon fome confideration or equivalent: and they may be divided, with regard to their fubject-matter, into gifts or grants of chattels *real*, and gifts or grants of chattels *perfonal*. Under the head of gifts or grants of chattels *real* may be included all leafes for years of land, affignments, and furrenders of thofe leafes; and all the other methods of conveying an eftate lefs than freehold, which were confidered in the twentieth chapter of the prefent book, and therefore need not be here again repeated: though thefe very feldom carry the outward appearance of a gift, however freely beftowed; being ufually expreffed to be made in confideration of blood, or natural affection, or of five or ten fhillings nominally paid to the grantor; and, in cafe of leafes, always referving a rent, though it be but a peppercorn: any of which confiderations will, in the eye of the law, convert the gift, if executed, into a grant; if not executed, into a contract.

GRANTS

GRANTS or gifts, of chattels *perfonal*, are the act of tranf-
ferring the right and the poffeffion of them; whereby one man
renounces, and another man immediately acquires, all title and
intereft therein: which may be done either in writing, or by
word of mouth [a] attefted by fufficient evidence, of which the
delivery of poffeffion is the ftrongeft and moft effential. But this
conveyance, when merely voluntary, is fomewhat fufpicious: and
is ufually conftrued to be fraudulent, if creditors or others become
fufferers thereby. And, particularly, by ftatute 3 Hen. VII. c. 4.
all deeds of gift of goods, made in truft to the ufe of the donor,
fhall be void; becaufe otherwife perfons might be tempted to
commit treafon or felony, without danger of forfeiture; and the
creditors of the donor might alfo be defrauded of their rights.
And by ftatute 13 Eliz. c. 5. every grant or gift of chattels, as
well as lands, with intent to defraud creditors or others [b], fhall
be void as againft fuch perfons to whom fuch fraud would be prejudicial; but, as againft the grantor himfelf, fhall ftand good and
effectual: and all perfons partakers in, or privy to, fuch fraudulent grants, fhall forfeit the whole value of the goods, one moiety
to the king, and another moiety to the party grieved; and alfo on
conviction fhall fuffer imprifonment for half a year.

A TRUE and proper gift or grant is always accompanied with
delivery of poffeffion, and takes effect immediately; as if A gives
to B 100*l*, or a flock of fheep, and puts him in poffeffion of them
directly, it is then a gift executed in the donee; and it is not in
the donor's power to retract it; though he did it without any
confideration or recompenfe [c]: unlefs it be prejudicial to creditors; or the donor were under any legal incapacity, as infancy,
coverture, durefs, or the like; or if he were drawn in, circum-
vented, or impofed upon, by falfe pretences, ebriety, or furprize.
But if the gift does not take effect, by delivery of immediate
poffeffion, it is then not properly a gift, but a contract: and this

[a] Perk. §. 57.						[c] Jenk. 109.
[b] See 3 Rep. 82.
VOL. II.				H h h				a man

a man cannot be compelled to perform, but upon good and fufficient confideration; as we fhall fee under our next divifion.

IX. A CONTRACT, which ufually conveys an intereft merely in action, is thus defined : " an agreement, upon fufficient con-"fideration, to do or not to do a particular thing." From which definition there arife three points to be contemplated in all contracts; 1. The *agreement:* 2. The *confideration:* and 3. The *thing* to be done or omitted, or the different fpecies of contracts.

FIRST then it is an *agreement,* a mutual bargain or convention; and therefore there muft at leaft be two contracting parties, of fufficient ability to make a contract : as where A contracts with B to pay him 100 *l.* and thereby transfers a property in fuch fum to B. Which property is however not in poffeffion, but in action merely, and recoverable by fuit at law ; wherefore it could not be transferred to another perfon by the ftrict rules of the antient common law : for no *chofe* in action could be affigned or granted over[d], becaufe it was thought to be a great encouragement to litigioufnefs, if a man were allowed to make over to a ftranger his right of going to law. But this nicety is now difregarded : though, in compliance with the antient principle, the form of affigning a *chofe* in action is in the nature of a declaration of truft, and an agreement to permit the affignee to make ufe of the name of the affignor, in order to recover the poffeffion. And therefore, when in common acceptation a debt or bond is faid to be affigned over, it muft ftill be fued in the original creditor's name ; the perfon, to whom it is transferred, being rather an attorney than an affignee. But the king is an exception to this general rule; for he might always either grant or receive a *chofe* in action by affignment[e] : and our courts of equity, confidering that in a commercial country almoft all perfonal property muft neceffarily lie in contract, will protect the affignment of a *chofe* in action, as much as the law will that of a *chofe* in poffeffion[f].

[d] Co. Litt. 214.
[e] Dyer. 30. Bro. *Abr. tit. chofe in action.*
1 & 4.
[f] 3 P. W^{ms}. 199.

THIS

THIS contract or agreement may be either exprefs or implied. *Exprefs* contracts are where the terms of the agreement are openly uttered and avowed at the time of the making, as to deliver an ox, or ten load of timber, or to pay a ftated price for certain goods. *Implied* are fuch as reafon and juftice dictate, and which therefore the law prefumes that every man undertakes to perform. As, if I employ a perfon to do any bufinefs for me, or perform any work; the law implies that I undertook, or contracted, to pay him as much as his labour deferves. If I take up wares from a tradefman, without any agreement of price, the law concludes that I contracted to pay their real value. And there is alfo one fpecies of implied contracts, which runs through and is annexed to all other contracts, conditions, and covenants; *viz.* that if I fail in my part of the agreement, I fhall pay the other party fuch damages as he has fuftained by fuch my neglect or refufal. In fhort, almoft all the rights of perfonal property (when not in actual poffeffion) do in great meafure depend upon contracts of one kind or other, or at leaft might be reduced under fome of them: which indeed is the method taken by the civil law; it having referred the greateft part of the duties and rights, which it treats of, to the head of obligations *ex contractu* and *quafi ex contractu*[s].

A CONTRACT may alfo be either *executed,* as if A agrees to change horfes with B, and they do it immediately; in which cafe the poffeffion and the right are transferred together: or it may be *executory,* as if they agree to change next week; here the right only vefts, and their reciprocal property in each other's horfe is not in poffeffion but in action: for a contract *executed* (which differs nothing from a grant) conveys a *chofe in poffeffion;* a contract *executory* conveys only a *chofe in action.*

HAVING thus fhewn the general nature of a contract, we are, *fecondly,* to proceed to the *confideration* upon which it is founded; or the reafon which moves the party contracting to enter into

[s] *Inft.* 3. 14. 2.

the

the contract. "It is an agreement, upon *fufficient confideration.*" The civilians hold, that in all contracts, either exprefs or implied, there muft be fomething given in exchange, fomething that is mutual or reciprocal [h]. This thing, which is the price or motive of the contract, we call the confideration: and it muft be a thing lawful in itfelf, or elfe the contract is void. A *good* confideration, we have before feen [i], is that of blood or natural affection between near relations; the fatisfaction accruing from which the law efteems an equivalent for whatever benefit may move from one relation to another [j]. This confideration may fometimes however be fet afide, and the contract become void, when it tends in it's confequences to defraud creditors or other third perfons of their juft rights. But a contract for *any valuable* confideration, as for marriage, for money, for work done, or for other reciprocal contracts, can never be impeached at law; and, if it be of a fufficient adequate value, is never fet afide in equity: for the perfon contracted with has then given an equivalent in recompenfe, and is therefore as much an owner, or a creditor, as any other perfon.

THESE valuable confiderations are divided by the civilians [k] into four fpecies. 1. *Do, ut des:* as when I give money or goods, on a contract that I fhall be repaid money or goods for them again. Of this kind are all loans of money upon bond, or promife of repayment; and all fales of goods, in which there is either an exprefs contract to pay fo much for them, or elfe the law implies a contract to pay fo much as they are worth. 2. The fecond fpecies is, *facio, ut facias:* as when I agree with a man to do his work for him, if he will do mine for me; or if two perfons agree to marry together; or to do any other pofitive acts on both fides. Or, it may be to forbear on one fide in confideration of fomething done on the other; as, that in confideration A, the tenant, will repair his houfe, B, the landlord, will not fue him for wafte. Or, it may be for mutual forbearance on both

---

[h] *In omnibus contractibus, five nominatis five innominatis, permutatio continetur.* Gravin. *l.* 2. §. 12.

[i] pag. 297.
[j] 3 Rep. 83.
[k] *Ff.* 19. 5. 5.

fides;

fides; as, that in confideration that A will not trade to Lifbon, B will not trade to Marfeilles; fo as to avoid interfering with each other. 3. The third fpecies of confiderations is, *facio, ut des:* when a man agrees to perform any thing for a price, either fpecifically mentioned, or left to the determination of the law to fet a value on it. As when a fervant hires himfelf to his mafter, for certain wages or an agreed fum of money: here the fervant contracts to do his mafter's fervice, in order to earn that fpecific fum. Otherwife, if he be hired generally; for then he is under an implied contract to perform this fervice for what it fhall be reafonably worth. 4. The fourth fpecies is, *do, ut facias:* which is the direct counterpart of the other. As when I agree with a fervant to give him fuch wages upon his performing fuch work: which, we fee, is nothing elfe but the laft fpecies inverted; for *fervus facit, ut herus det,* and *herus dat, ut fervus faciat.*

A CONSIDERATION of fome fort or other is fo abfolutely neceffary to the forming of a contract, that a *nudum pactum* or agreement to do or pay any thing on one fide, without any compenfation on the other, is totally void in law; and a man cannot be compelled to perform it[l]. As if one man promifes to give another 100 *l.* here there is nothing contracted for or given on the one fide, and therefore there is nothing binding on the other. And, however a man may or may not be bound to perform it, in honor or confcience, which the municipal laws do not take upon them to decide; certainly thofe municipal laws will not compel the execution of what he had no vifible inducement to engage for: and therefore our law has adopted [m] the maxim of the civil law [n], that *ex nudo pacto non oritur actio.* But any degree of reciprocity will prevent the pact from being nude: nay, even if the thing be founded on a prior moral obligation, (as a promife to pay a juft debt, though barred by the ftatute of limitations) it is no longer *nudum pactum.* And as this rule was principally eftablifhed, to avoid the inconvenience that would arife from fetting up mere verbal promifes, for which no good reafon could

[l] D. & t. d. 2 c. 24.   [n] *Cod.* 2. 3. 10. & 5. 14. 1.
[m] Bro. *Abr. tit. nette.* 79. Salk. 129.

be affigned °, it therefore does not hold in fome cafes, where fuch promife is authentically proved by written documents. For if a man enters into a voluntary bond, or gives a promiffory note, he fhall not be allowed to aver the want of a confideration in order to evade the payment : for every bond from the folemnity of the inftrument ᵖ, and every note from the fubfcription of the drawer ᑫ, carries with it an internal evidence of a good confideration. Courts of juftice will therefore fupport them both, as againft the contractor himfelf; but not to the prejudice of creditors, or ftrangers to the contract.

WE are next to confider, *thirdly*, the thing agreed to be done or omitted. " A contract is an agreement, upon fufficient confi-" deration, *to do or not to do a particular thing*." The moft ufual contracts, whereby the right of chattels perfonal may be acquired in the laws of England, are, 1. That of *fale* or *exchange*. 2. That of *bailment*. 3. That of *hiring* and *borrowing*. 4. That of *debt*.

1. SALE or *exchange* is a tranfmutation of property from one man to another, in confideration of fome recompenfe in value : for there is no fale without a recompenfe; there muft be *quid pro quo* ʳ. If it be a commutation of goods for goods, it is more properly an *exchange*; but, if it be a transferring of goods for money, it is called a *fale :* which is a method of exchange introduced for the convenience of mankind, by eftablifhing an univerfal medium, which may be exchanged for all forts of other property; whereas if goods were only to be exchanged for goods, by way of barter, it would be difficult to adjuft the refpective values, and the carriage would be intolerably cumberfome. All civilized nations adopted therefore very early the ufe of money; for we find Abraham giving " four hundred fhekels of filver, cur-" rent money with the merchant," for the field of Machpelah ˢ; though the practice of exchanges ftill fubfifts among feveral of the favage nations. But with regard to the *law* of fales and exchanges,

---

° Plowd. 308, 309.
ᵖ Hardr 200. 1 Ch. Rep. 157.
ᑫ Lord Raym. 760.

ʳ Noy's Max. c. 42.
ˢ Gen. c. 23. v. 16.

there is no difference. I fhall therefore treat of them both under the denomination of fales only; and fhall confider their force and effect, in the firft place where the vendor *hath* in himfelf, and fecondly where he *hath not*, the property of the thing fold.

WHERE the vendor *hath* in himfelf the property of the goods fold, he hath the liberty of difpofing of them to whomever he pleafes, at any time, and in any manner : unlefs judgment has been obtained againft him for a debt or damages, and the writ of execution is actually delivered to the fheriff. For then, by the ftatute of frauds [f], the fale fhall be looked upon as fraudulent, and the property of the goods fhall be bound to anfwer the debt, from the time of delivering the writ. Formerly it was bound from the *tefte*, or iffuing, of the writ [t], and any fubfequent fale was fraudulent; but the law was thus altered in favour of *pur-chafors*, though it ftill remains the fame between the *parties :* and therefore, if a defendant dies after the awarding and before the delivery of the writ, his goods are bound by it in the hands of his executors [v].

IF a man agrees with another for goods at a certain price, he may not carry them away before he hath paid for them ; for it is no fale without payment, unlefs the contrary be exprefsly agreed. And therefore, if the vendor fays, the price of a beaft is four pounds, and the vendee fays he will give four pounds, the bar-gain is ftruck ; and they neither of them are at liberty to be off, provided immediate poffeffion be tendered by the other fide. But if neither the money be paid, nor the goods delivered, nor ten-der made, nor any fubfequent agreement be entered into, it is no contract, and the owner may difpofe of the goods as he pleafes [u]. But if any part of the price is paid down, if it be but a penny, or any portion of the goods delivered by way of *earneft* (which the civil law calls *arrha,* and interprets to be " *emptionis-vendi-*

29 Car. II. c. 3.
[t] 8 Rep. 171. 1 Mod. 188.

[v] Comb. 33. 12 Mod. 5. 7 Mod. 95.
[u] Hob 41. Noy's Max. c. 42.

" *tionis*

"*tionis contractae argumentum* [w]," the property of the goods is abſolutely bound by it: and the vendee may recover the goods by action, as well as the vendor may the price of them [x]. And ſuch regard does the law pay to earneſt as an evidence of a contract, that, by the ſame ſtatute 29 Car. II. c.3. no contract for the ſale of goods, to the value of 10 *l.* or more, ſhall be valid, unleſs the buyer actually receives part of the goods ſold, by way of earneſt on his part; or unleſs he gives part of the price to the vendor by way of earneſt to bind the bargain, or in part of payment; or unleſs ſome note in writting be made and ſigned by the party, or his agent, who is to be charged with the contract. And, with regard to goods under the value of 10 *l*, no contract or agreement for the ſale of them ſhall be valid, unleſs the goods are to be delivered within one year, or unleſs the contract be made in writing, and ſigned by the party who is to be charged therewith. Antiently, among all the northern nations, ſhaking of hands was held neceſſary to bind the bargain; a cuſtom which we ſtill retain in many verbal contracts. A ſale thus made was called *handſale*, "*venditio per mutuam manuum complexionem* [y];" till in proceſs of time the ſame word was uſed to ſignify the price or earneſt, which was given immediately after the ſhaking of hands, or inſtead thereof.

A s ſoon as the bargain is ſtruck, the property of the goods is transferred to the vendee, and that of the price to the vendor; but the vendee cannot take the goods, until he renders the price agreed on [z]. But if he tenders the money to the vendor, and he refuſes it, the vendee may ſeiſe the goods, or have an action againſt the vendor for detaining them. And by a regular ſale, without delivery, the property is ſo abſolutely veſted in the vendee; that if A ſells a horſe to B for 10 *l*, and B pays him earneſt, or ſigns a note in writing of the bargain; and afterwards, before the delivery of the horſe or money paid, the horſe dies in the vendor's cuſtody; ſtill he is entitled to the money, becauſe by

[w] *Inſt.* 3. *tit.* 24.
[x] Noy, *ibid.*

[y] Stiernhook *de jure Goth. l.* 2. *c.* 5.
[z] Hob. 41.

the

the contract, the property was in the vendee[a]. Thus may property in goods be transferred by sale, where the vendor *hath* such property in himself.

BUT property may also in some cases be transferred by sale, though the vendor *hath none at all* in the goods: for it is expedient that the buyer, by taking proper precautions, may at all events be secure of his purchase; otherwise all commerce between man and man must soon be at an end. And therefore the general rule of law is[b], that all sales and contracts of any thing vendible, in fairs or markets *overt*, (that is, open) shall not only be good between the parties, but also be binding on all those that have any right or property therein. And for this purpose, the mirroir informs us[c], were tolls established in markets, viz. to testify the making of contracts; for every private contract was discountenanced by law. Wherefore our Saxon ancestors prohibited the sale of any thing above the value of twenty pence, unless in open market, and directed every bargain and sale to be contracted in the presence of credible witnesses[d]. Market overt in the country is only held on the special days, provided for particular towns by charter or prescription; but in London every day, except Sunday, is market day[e]. The market place, or spot of ground set apart by custom for the sale of particular goods, is also in the country the only market overt[f]; but in London every shop in which goods are exposed publicly to sale, is market overt, for such things only as the owner professes to trade in[g]. But if my goods are stolen from me, and sold, out of market overt, my property is not altered, and I may take them wherever I find them. And it is expressly provided by statute 1 Jac. I. c. 21. that the sale of any goods wrongfully taken, to any pawnbroker in London or within two miles thereof, shall not alter the property. For this, being usually a clandestine trade, is therefore made an

[a] Noy, c. 42.
[b] 2 Inst. 713.
[c] c. 1. §. 3.
[d] *LL. Ethel.* 10, 12. *LL. Eadg.* Wilk. 80.

[e] Cro. Jac. 68.
[f] Godb. 131.
[g] 5 Rep. 83. 12 Mod. 521.

exception to the general rule. And, even in market overt, if the
goods be the property of the king, such sale (though regular in
all other respects) will in no case bind him; though it binds infants, feme coverts, ideots or lunatics, and men beyond sea or in
prison : or if the goods be stolen from a common person, and
then taken by the king's officer from the felon, and sold in open
market; still, if the owner has used due diligence in prosecuting
the thief to conviction, he loses not his property in the goods [h].
So likewise, if the buyer knoweth the property not to be in the
seller ; or there be any other fraud in the transaction ; if he
knoweth the seller to be an infant, or feme covert, not usually
trading for herself; if the sale be not originally and wholly made
in the fair or market, or not at the usual hours ; the owner's
property is not bound thereby [i]. If a man buys his own goods in
a fair or market, the contract of sale shall not bind him so as that
he shall render the price, unless the property had been previously
altered by a former sale [k]. And, notwithstanding any number of
intervening sales, if the original vendor, who sold without having
the property, comes again into possession of the goods, the original owner may take them, when found in his hands who was
guilty of the first breach of justice [l]. By which wise regulations
the common law has secured the right of the proprietor in personal chattels from being devested, so far as was consistent with
that other necessary policy, that purchasors, *bona fide*, in a fair,
open, and regular manner, should not be afterwards put to difficulties by reason of the previous knavery of the seller.

BUT there is one species of personal chattels, in which the
property is not easily altered by sale, without the express consent
of the owner, and those are horses; the sale of which, even in
fairs or markets overt, is void in many instances, where that of
other property is valid : because a horse is so fleet an animal,
that the stealers of them may flee far off in a short space [m], and

---

[h] Bacon's use of the law. 158.   [l] 2 Inst. 713.
[i] 2 Inst. 713, 714.   [m] *Ibid.* 714.
[k] Perk. §. 93.

be out of the reach of the moft induftrious owner. All perfons therefore that have occafion to deal in horfes, and are therefore liable fometimes to buy ftolen ones, would do well to obferve, that whatever price they may give, or how long foever they may keep poffeffion before it be claimed, they gain no property in a horfe that has been ftolen, unlefs it be bought in a fair or market overt : nor even then, unlefs the directions be purfued that are laid down in the ftatutes 2 P. & M. c. 7. and 31 Eliz. c. 12. By which it is enacted, that every horfe, fo to be fold, fhall be openly expofed, in the time of fuch fair or market, for one whole hour together, between ten in the morning and funfet, in the open and public place ufed for fuch fales, and not in any private yard or ftable : that the horfe fhall be brought by both the vendor and vendee to the tollgatherer or bookkeeper of fuch fair or market : that toll be paid, if any be due; and if not, one penny to the bookkeeper, who fhall enter down the price, colour, and marks of the horfe, with the names, additions, and abode of the vendee and the vendor; the latter either upon his own knowlege, or the teftimony of fome credible witnefs. And, even if all thefe points be fully complied with, yet fuch fale fhall not take away the property of the owner, if within fix months after the horfe is ftolen he puts in his claim before the mayor, or fome juftice, of the diftrict in which the horfe fhall be found; and within forty days after that, proves fuch his property by the oath of two witneffes before fuch mayor or juftice; and alfo tenders to the perfon in poffeffion fuch price as he *bona fide* paid for him in market overt. But in cafe any one of the points beforementioned be omitted, or not obferved in the fale, fuch fale is utterly void; and the owner fhall not lofe his property, but at any diftance of time may feife or bring an action for his horfe, wherever he happens to find him. Wherefore fir Edward Coke obferves [n], that, both by the common law and thefe two ftatutes, the property of horfes is fo well preferved, that if the owner be of capacity to underftand them, and be vigilant and induftrious to purfue the fame, it is almoft impoffible that the property of any horfe, either

[n] 2 Inft. 719.

ftolen

ſtolen or not ſtolen, ſhould be altered by any ſale in market overt by him that is *malae fidei poſſeſſor*.

BY the civil law [o] an implied warranty was annexed to every ſale, in reſpect to the title of the vendor: and ſo too, in our law, a purchaſor of goods and chattels may have a ſatisfaction from the ſeller, if he ſells them as his own, and the title proves deficient, without any expreſs warranty for that purpoſe [p]. But, with regard to the goodneſs of the wares ſo purchaſed, the vendor is not bound to anſwer; unleſs he expreſſly warrants them to be ſound and good [q], or unleſs he knew them to be otherwiſe and hath uſed any art to diſguiſe them [r], or unleſs they turn out to be different from what he repreſented to the buyer.

2. BAILMENT, from the French *bailler*, to deliver, is a delivery of goods in truſt, upon a contract expreſſed or implied, that the truſt ſhall be faithfully executed on the part of the bailee. As if cloth be delivered, or (in our legal dialect) bailed, to a taylor to make a ſuit of cloaths, he has it upon an implied contract to render it again when made, and that in a workmanly manner [s]. If money or goods be delivered to a common carrier, to convey from Oxford to London, he is under a contract in law to pay, or carry, them to the perſon appointed [t]. If a horſe, or other goods, be delivered to an inn-keeper or his ſervants, he is bound to keep them ſafely, and reſtore them when his gueſt leaves the houſe [u]. If a man takes in a horſe, or other cattle, to graze and depaſture in his grounds, which the law calls *agiſtment*, he takes them upon an implied contract to return them ſafe to the owner [w]. If a pawnbroker receives plate or jewels as a pledge, or ſecurity, for the repayment of money lent thereon at a day certain, he has them upon an expreſs contract or condition to reſtore them, if the pledgor performs his part by redeeming them in due time [x]: for the due execution of which

[o] *Ff.* 21. 2. 1.

[p] Cro. Jac. 474. 1 Roll. Abr. 90.

[q] F. N. B. 94.

[r] 2 Roll. Rep. 5.

[s] 1 Vern. 268.

[t] 12 Mod. 482.

[u] Cro. Eliz. 622.

[w] Cro. Car. 271.

[x] Cro. Jac. 245. Yelv. 178.

contract

contract many useful regulations are made by statute 30 Geo. II. c. 24. And so if a landlord distreins goods for rent, or a parish officer for taxes, these for a time are only a pledge in the hands of the distreinors, and they are bound by an implied contract in law to restore them on payment of the debt, duty, and expenses, before the time of sale; or, when sold, to render back the overplus. If a friend delivers any thing to his friend to keep for him, the receiver is bound to restore it on demand: and it was formerly held that in the mean time he was answerable for any damage or loss it might sustain, whether by accident or otherwise[y]; unless he expressly undertook[z] to keep it only with the same care as his own goods, and then he should not be answerable for theft or other accidents. But now the law seems to be settled upon a much more rational footing[a]; that such a general bailment will not charge the bailee with any loss, unless it happens by gross neglect, which is construed to be an evidence of fraud: but, if the bailee undertakes specially to keep the goods safely and securely, he is bound to answer all perils and damages, that may befal them for want of the same care with which a prudent man would keep his own[b].

In all these instances there is a special qualified property transferred from the bailor to the bailee, together with the possession. It is not an absolute property in the bailee, because of his contract for restitution; and the bailor hath nothing left in him but the right to a *chose* in action, grounded upon such contract, the possession being delivered to the bailee. And, on account of this qualified property of the bailee, he may (as well as the bailor) maintain an action against such as injure or take away these chattels. The taylor, the carrier, the innkeeper, the agisting farmer, the pawnbroker, the distreinor, and the general bailee, may all

[y] Co. Litt. 89.
[z] 4 Rep. 84.
[a] Lord Raym. 909. 12 Mod. 487.
[b] By the laws of Sweden, the depositary or bailee of goods is not bound to restitu-

tion, in case of accident by fire or theft: provided his own goods perished in the same manner: "*jura enim nostra*, says Stiernhook, "*dolum praesumunt, si una non pereant.*" (*De jure Sueon. l. 2. c. 5.*)

of

of them vindicate, in their own right, this their poffeffory intereft, againft any ftranger or third perfon[c]. For, as fuch bailee
is refponfible to the bailor, if the goods are loft or damaged by
his wilful default or grofs negligence, or if he do not deliver up
the chattels on lawful demand, it is therefore reafonable that he
fhould have a right to recover either the fpecific goods, or elfe a
fatisfaction in damages, againft all other perfons, who may have
purloined or injured them; that he may always be ready to anfwer the call of the bailor.

3. H I R I N G and *borrowing* are alfo contracts by which a
qualified property may be transferred to the hirer or borrower:
in which there is only this difference, that hiring is always for
a price, a ftipend, or additional recompenfe; borrowing is
merely gratuitous. But the law in both cafes is the fame.
They are both contracts, whereby the poffeffion and a tranfient
property is transferred for a particular time or ufe, on condition and agreement to reftore the goods fo hired or borrowed,
as foon as the time is expired or ufe performed; together with
the price or ftipend (in cafe of hiring) either expreffly agreed
on by the parties, or left to be implied by law according to the
value of the fervice. By this mutual contract, the hirer or borrower gains a temporary property in the thing hired, accompanied with an implied condition to ufe it with moderation and
not abufe it; and the owner or lender retains a reverfionary intereft in the fame, and acquires a new property in the price or
reward. Thus if a man hires or borrows a horfe for a month,
he has the poffeffion and a qualified property therein during that
period; on the expiration of which his qualified property determines, and the owner becomes (in cafe of hiring) intitled to
the premium or price, for which the horfe was hired[d].

T H E R E is one fpecies of this price or reward, the moft ufual
of any, but concerning which many good and learned men have

[c] 13 Rep. 69.   [d] Yelv. 172. Cro. Jac. 236.

in

in former times very much perplexed themfelves and other people, by raifing doubts about it's legality *in foro confcientiae*. That
is, when money is lent on a contract to receive not only the
principal fum again, but alfo an increafe by way of compenfation
for the ufe; which is generally called *intereft* by thofe who think
it lawful, and *ufury* by thofe who do not fo. It may not be
amifs therefore to enter into a fhort enquiry, upon what footing this matter of intereft or ufury does really ftand.

THE enemies to intereft in general make no diftinction between that and ufury, holding any increafe of money to be in-
defenfibly ufurious. And this they ground as well on the prohibition of it by the law of Mofes among the Jews, as alfo upon
what is laid down by Ariftotle [e], that money is naturally barren,
and to make it breed money is prepofterous, and a perverfion of
the end of it's inftitution, which was only to ferve the purpofes of exchange, and not of increafe. Hence the fchool di-
vines have branded the practice of taking intereft, as being contrary to the divine law both natural and revealed; and the canon
law [f], has profcribed the taking any, the leaft, increafe for the
loan of money as a mortal fin.

BUT, in anfwer to this, it may be obferved, that the mofai-
cal precept was clearly a political, and not a moral precept. It
only prohibited the Jews from taking ufury from their brethren
the Jews; but in exprefs words permitted them to take it of a
ftranger [g]: which proves that the taking of moderate ufury, or
a reward for the ufe, for fo the word fignifies, is not *malum in
fe*, fince it was allowed where any but an Ifraelite was concerned.
And as to Ariftotle's reafon, deduced from the natural barrennefs
of money, the fame may with equal force be alleged of houfes,
which never breed houfes; and twenty other things, which nobody doubts it is lawful to make profit of, by letting them to

[e] *Polit. l.* 1. *c.* 10.
[f] *Decretal. l.* 5. *tit.* 19.

[g] "Unto a ftranger thou mayeft lend up-
"on ufury, but unto thy brother thou fhalt
"not lend upon ufury." Deut. xxiii. 20.

hire.

hire. And though money was originally ufed only for the purpofes of exchange, yet the laws of any ftate may be well juftified in permitting it to be turned to the purpofes of profit, if the
convenience of fociety (the great end for which money was invented) fhall require it. And that the allowance of moderate intereft tends greatly to the benefit of the public, efpecially in a
trading country, will appear from that generally acknowleged
principle, that commerce cannot fubfift without mutual and extenfive credit. Unlefs money therefore can be borrowed, trade
cannot be carried on : and if no premium were allowed for the
hire of money, few perfons would care to lend it ; or at leaft the
eafe of borrowing at a fhort warning (which is the life of commerce) would be entirely at an end. Thus, in the dark ages of
monkifh fuperftition and civil tyranny, when intereft was laid under a total interdict, commerce was alfo at it's loweft ebb, and
fell entirely into the hands of the Jews and Lombards : but when
men's minds began to be more enlarged, when true religion and
real liberty revived, commerce grew again into credit ; and again
introduced with itfelf it's infeparable companion, the doctrine of
loans upon intereft.

AND, really, confidered abftractedly from this it's ufe, fince
all other conveniences of life may either be bought or hired, but
money can only be hired, there feems no greater impropriety in
taking a recompenfe or price for the hire of this, than of any
other convenience. If I borrow 100 *l.* to employ in a beneficial
trade, it is but equitable that the lender fhould have a proportion
of my gains. To demand an exorbitant price is equally contrary to confcience, for the loan of a horfe, or the loan of a fum
of money : but a reafonable equivalent for the temporary inconvenience the owner may feel by the want of it, and for the hazard
of his lofing it entirely, is not more immoral in one cafe than it
is in the other. And indeed the abfolute prohibition of lending
upon any, even moderate intereft, introduces the very inconvenience
which it feems meant to remedy. The neceffity of individuals
will make borrowing unavoidable. Without fome profit allowed

by

by law there will be but few lenders : and thofe principally bad men, who will break through the law, and take a profit; and then will endeavour to indemnify themfelves from the danger of the penalty, by making that profit exorbitant. Thus, while all degrees of profit were difcountenanced, we find more complaints of ufury, and more flagrant inftances of oppreffion, than in modern times, when money may be eafily had at a low intereft. A capital diftinction muft therefore be made between a moderate and exorbitant profit; to the former of which we ufually give the name of intereft, to the latter the truly odious appellation of ufury : the former is neceffary in every civil ftate, if it were but to exclude the latter, which ought never to be tolerated in any well-regulated fociety. For, as the whole of this matter is well fummed up by Grotius[h], " if the compenfation allowed by law does " not exceed the proportion of the hazard run, or the want felt, " by the loan, it's allowance is neither repugnant to the revealed " nor the natural law : but if it exceeds thofe bounds, it is then " oppreffive ufury; and though the municipal laws may give it " impunity, they never can make it juft."

WE fee, that the exorbitance or moderation of intereft, for money lent, depends upon two circumftances; the inconvenience of parting with it for the prefent, and the hazard of lofing it entirely. The inconvenience to individual lenders can never be eftimated by laws ; the rate therefore of general intereft muft depend upon the ufual or general inconvenience. This refults entirely from the quantity of fpecie or current money in the kingdom : for, the more fpecie there is circulating in any nation, the greater fuperfluity there will be, beyond what is neceffary to carry on the bufinefs of exchange and the common concerns of life. In every nation or public community there is a certain quantity of money thus neceffary; which a perfon well fkilled in political arithmetic might perhaps calculate as exactly, as a private banker can the demand for running cafh in his own fhop : all above this necef-

<hr>

[h] *de j. b. & p. l.* 2. *c.* 12. §. 22.

fary quantity may be fpared, or lent, without much inconvenience to the refpective lenders; and the greater this national fuperfluity is, the more numerous will be the lenders, and the lower ought the rate of the national intereft to be: but where there is not enough, or barely enough, circulating cafh, to anfwer the ordinary ufes of the public, intereft will be proportionably high; for lenders will be but few, as few can fubmit to the inconvenience of lending.

So alfo the hazard of an entire lofs has it's weight in the regulation of intereft: hence, the better the fecurity, the lower will the intereft be; the rate of intereft being generally in a compound *ratio*, formed out of the inconvenience and the hazard. And as, if there were no inconvenience, there fhould be no intereft, but what is equivalent to the hazard; fo, if there were no hazard, there ought to be no intereft, fave only what arifes from the mere inconvenience of lending. Thus, if the quantity of fpecie in a nation be fuch, that the general inconvenience of lending for a year is computed to amount to *three per cent* : a man that has money by him will perhaps lend it upon good perfonal fecurity at *five per cent*, allowing two for the hazard run; he will lend it upon landed fecurity, or mortgage, at *four per cent*, the hazard being proportionably lefs; but he will lend it to the ftate, on the maintenance of which all his property depends, at *three per cent*, the hazard being none at all.

But fometimes the hazard may be greater, than the rate of intereft allowed by law will compenfate. And this gives rife to the practice, 1. Of bottomry, or *refpondentia*. 2. Of policies of infurance.

And firft, *bottomry* (which originally arofe from permitting the mafter of a fhip, in a foreign country, to hypothecate the fhip in order to raife money to refit) is in the nature of a mortgage of a fhip; when the owner takes up money to enable him to carry on his voyage, and pledges the keel or *bottom* of the fhip

(pars

(*pars pro toto*) as a fecurity for the repayment. In which cafe it is underftood, that, if the fhip be loft, the lender lofes alfo his whole money; but, if it returns in fafety, then he fhall receive back his principal, and alfo the premium or intereft agreed upon, however it may exceed the legal rate of intereft. And this is allowed to be a valid contract in all trading nations, for the benefit of commerce, and by reafon of the extraordinary hazard run by the lender[i]. And in this cafe the fhip and tackle, if brought home, are anfwerable (as well as the perfon of the borrower) for the money lent. But if the loan is not upon the veffel, but upon the goods and merchandize, which muft neceffarily be fold or exchanged in the courfe of the voyage, then only the borrower, perfonally, is bound to anfwer the contract; who therefore in this cafe is faid to take up money at *refpondentia*. Thefe terms are alfo applied to contracts for the repayment of money borrowed, not on the fhip and goods only, but on the mere hazard of the voyage itfelf; when a man lends a merchant 1000*l.* to be employed in a beneficial trade, with condition to be repaid with extraordinary intereft, in cafe fuch a voyage be fafely performed[k]: which kind of agreement is fometimes called *foenus nauticum*, and fometimes *ufura maritima*[l]. But, as this gave an opening for ufurious and gaming contracts, efpecially upon long voyages, it was enacted by the ftatute 19 Geo. II. c. 37. that all monies lent on bottomry or at *refpondentia*, on veffels bound to or from the Eaft Indies, fhall be expreffly lent only upon the fhip or upon the merchandize; that the lender fhall have the benefit of falvage; and that, if the borrower has not on board effects to the value of the fum borrowed, he fhall be refponfible to the lender for fo much of the principal as hath not been laid out, with legal intereft and all other charges, though the fhip and merchandize be totally loft.

---

[i] Moll. *de jur. mar.* 361. Malyne *lex mercat.* b. 1. c. 31. Cro. Jac. 208. Bynkerfh. *quaeft. jur. privat. l.* 3. *c.* 16.

[k] 1 Sid. 27.
[l] Molloy *ibid.* Malyne *ibid.*

SECONDLY, a policy of *infurance* is a contract between A and B, that, upon A's paying a premium equivalent to the hazard run, B will indemnify or infure him againft a particular event. This is founded upon one of the fame principles as the doctrine of intereft upon loans, that of hazard; but not that of inconvenience. For if I infure a fhip to the levant, and back again, at *five per cent*; here I calculate the chance that fhe performs her voyage to be twenty to one againft her being loft : and, if fhe be loft, I lofe 100 *l.* and get 5 *l.* Now this is much the fame as if I lend the merchant, whofe whole fortunes are embarked in this veffel, 100 *l.* at the rate of *eight per cent.* For by a loan I fhould be immediately out of my money, the inconvenience of which we have computed equal to *three per cent :* if therefore I had actually lent him 100 *l,* I muft have added 3 *l.* on the fcore of inconvenience, to the 5 *l.* allowed for the hazard ; which together would have made 8 *l.* But as, upon an infurance, I am never out of my money till the lofs actually happens, nothing is therein allowed upon the principle of inconvenience, but all upon the principle of hazard. Thus too, in a loan, if the chance of repayment depends upon the borrower's life, it is frequent (befides the ufual rate of intereft) for the borrower to have his life infured till the time of repayment ; for which he is loaded with an additional premium, fuited to his age and conftitution. Thus, if Sempronius has only an annuity for his life, and would borrow 100 *l.* of Titius for a year ; the inconvenience and general hazard of this loan, we have feen, are equivalent to 5 *l.* which is therefore the legal intereft : but there is alfo a fpecial hazard in this cafe ; for, if Sempronius dies within the year, Titius muft lofe the whole of his 100 *l.* Suppofe this chance to be as one to ten : it will follow that the extraordinary hazard is worth 10 *l.* more ; and therefore that the reafonable rate of intereft in this cafe would be *fifteen per cent.* But this the law, to avoid abufes, will not permit to be taken : Sempronius therefore gives Titius the lender only 5 *l,* the legal intereft ; but applies to Gaius an infurer, and gives him the other 10 *l.* to indemnify Titius againft the

the extraordinary hazard. And in this manner may any extraordinary or particular hazard be provided againſt, which the eſtabliſhed rate of intereſt will not reach; that being calculated by the ſtate to anſwer only the ordinary and general hazard, together with the lender's inconvenience in parting with his ſpecie for the time.

THE learning relating to marine inſurances hath of late years been greatly improved by a ſeries of judicial deciſions, which have now eſtabliſhed the law in ſuch a variety of caſes, that (if well and judiciouſly collected) they would form a very complete title in a code of commercial juriſprudence. But, being founded on equitable principles, which chiefly reſult from the ſpecial circumſtances of the caſe, it is not eaſy to reduce them to any general heads in mere elementary inſtitutes. Thus much may however be ſaid; that, being contracts, the very eſſence of which conſiſts in obſerving the pureſt good faith and integrity, they are vacated by any the leaſt ſhadow of fraud or undue concealment: and, on the other hand, being much for the benefit and extenſion of trade, by diſtributing the loſs or gain among a number of adventurers, they are greatly encouraged and protected both by common law and acts of parliament. But, as a practice had obtained of inſuring large ſums without having any property on board, which were called inſurances, *intereſt or no intereſt*; and alſo of inſuring the ſame goods ſeveral times over; both of which were a ſpecies of gaming, without any advantage to commerce, and were denominated *wagering* policies: it is therefore enacted by the ſtatute 19 Geo. II. c. 37. that all inſurances, intereſt or no intereſt, or without farther proof of intereſt than the policy itſelf, or by way of gaming or wagering, or without benefit of ſalvage to the inſurer, (all which had the ſame pernicious tendency) ſhall be totally null and void, except upon privateers, or ſhips in the Spaniſh and Portugueſe trade, for reaſons ſufficiently obvious; and that no re-aſſurance ſhall be lawful, except the former inſurer ſhall be inſolvent, a bankrupt, or dead; and laſtly that, in the Eaſt India trade, the lender of money on bottomry, or at *reſpondentia*, ſhall alone.

alone have a right to be infured for the money lent, and the borrower fhall (in cafe of a lofs) recover no more upon any infurance than the furplus of his property, above the value of his bottomry or *refpondentia* bond. But, to return to the doctrine of common intereft on loans:

UPON the two principles of inconvenience and hazard, compared together, different nations have at different times eftablifhed different rates of intereft. The Romans at one time allowed *centefimae,* or *twelve per cent,* to be taken for common loans; but Juftinian[m] reduced it to *trientes,* or one third of the *as* or *centefimae,* that is, *four per cent;* but allowed higher intereft to be taken of merchants, becaufe there the hazard was greater[n]. So too Gro-

---

[m] *Cod.* 4. 32. 26. *Nov.* 33, 34, 35.

[n] A fhort explication of thefe terms, and of the divifion of the Roman *as,* will be ufeful to the ftudent, not only for underftanding the civilians, but alfo the more claffical writers, who perpetually refer to this diftribution. Thus Horace, *ad Pifones.* 325.

> *Romani pueri longis rationibus* affem
> *Difcunt in partes* centum *diducere. Dicat*
> *Filius Albini, fi de* quincunce *remota eft*
> Uncia, *quid fuperet?* poterat dixiffe, triens: *eu,*
> *Rem poteris fervare tuam!* redit uncia, *quid fit?*
> Semis. ──────

It is therefore to be obferved, that, in calculating the rate of intereft, the Romans divided the principal fum into an *hundred* parts; one of which they allowed to be taken monthly: and this, which was the higheft rate of intereft permitted, they called *ufurae centefimae,* amounting yearly to twelve *per cent.* Now as the *as,* or Roman pound, was commonly ufed to exprefs any integral fum, and was divifible into twelve parts or *unciae,* therefore thefe twelve monthly payments or *unciae* were held to amount annually to one pound, or *as ufurarius;* and fo the *ufurae affes* were fynonymous to the *ufurae centefimae.* And all lower rates of intereft were denominated according to the relation they bore to this centefimal ufury, or *ufurae affes:* for the feveral multiples of the *unciae,* or duodecimal parts of the *as,* were known by different names according to their different combinations; *fextans, quadrans, triens, quincunx, femis, feptunx, bes, dodrans, dextrans, deunx,* containing refpectively 2, 3, 4, 5, 6, 7, 8, 9, 10, 11 *unciae* or duodecimal parts of an *as.* (*Ff.* 28. 5. 50. §. 2. Gravin. *orig. jur. civ. l.* 2. §. 47.) This being premifed, the following table will clearly exhibit at once the fubdivifions of the *as,* and the denominations of the rate of intereft.

USURAE

tius informs us °, that in Holland the rate of intereſt was then eight *per cent* in common loans, but twelve to merchants. Our law eſtabliſhes one ſtandard for all alike, where the pledge or ſecurity itſelf is not put in jeopardy; leſt, under the general pretence of vague and indeterminate hazards, a door ſhould be opened to fraud and uſury: leaving ſpecific hazards to be provided againſt by ſpecific inſurances, or by loans upon *reſpondentia*, or bottomry. But as to the rate of legal intereſt, it has varied and decreaſed for two hundred years paſt, according as the quantity of ſpecie in the kingdom has encreaſed by acceſſions of trade, the introduction of paper credit, and other circumſtances. The ſtatute 37 Hen.VIII. c.9. confined intereſt to ten *per cent*, and ſo did the ſtatute 13 Eliz. c. 8. But as, through the encouragements given in her reign to commerce, the nation grew more wealthy, ſo under her ſucceſſor the ſtatute 21 Jac.I. c. 17. reduced it to eight *per cent*; as did the ſtatute 12 Car. II. c. 13. to ſix: and laſtly by the ſtatute 12 Ann. ſt. 2. c. 16. it was brought down to five *per cent* yearly, which is now the extremity of legal intereſt that can be taken. But yet, if a contract, which carries intereſt, be made in a foreign country, our courts will direct the payment of intereſt according to the law of that country in which the contract was made ᴾ. Thus Iriſh, American,

USURAE.	PARTES ASSIS.	PER ANNUM.
Aſſes, ſive centeſimae	*integer*	12 *per cent.*
Deunces	$\frac{11}{12}$	11
Dextances, vel decunces	$\frac{5}{6}$	10
Dodrantes	$\frac{3}{4}$	9
Beſſes	$\frac{2}{3}$	8
Septunces	$\frac{7}{12}$	7
Semiſſes	$\frac{1}{2}$	6
Quincunces	$\frac{5}{12}$	5
Trientes	$\frac{1}{3}$	4
Quadrantes	$\frac{1}{4}$	3
Sextances	$\frac{1}{6}$	2
Unciae	$\frac{1}{12}$	1

° *de jur. b. & p.* 2. 12. 22.   ᴾ 1 Equ. Caſ. abr. 289. 1 P. Wᵐˢ. 395.

Turkiſh,

Turkifh, and Indian intereft, have been allowed in our courts, to the amount of even twelve *per cent*. For the moderation or exorbitance of intereft depends upon local circumftances ; and the refufal to inforce fuch contracts would put a ftop to all foreign trade.

4. THE laft general fpecies of contracts, which I have to mention, is that of *debt* ; whereby a *chofe* in action, or right to a certain fum of money, is mutually acquired and loft [q]. This may be the counterpart of, and arife from, any of the other fpecies of contracts. As, in cafe of a fale, where the price is not paid in ready money, the vendee becomes indebted to the vendor for the fum agreed on ; and the vendor has a property in this price, as a *chofe* in action, by means of this contract of debt. In bailment, if the bailee lofes or detains a fum of money bailed to him for any fpecial purpofe, he becomes indebted to the bailor in the fame numerical fum, upon his implied contract, that he fhall execute the truft repofed in him, or repay the money to the bailor. Upon hiring or borrowing, the hirer or borrower, at the fame time that he acquires a property in the thing lent, may alfo become indebted to the lender, upon his contract to reftore the money borrowed, to pay the price or premium of the loan, the hire of the horfe, or the like. Any contract in fhort whereby a determinate fum of money becomes due to any perfon, and is not paid but remains in action merely, is a contract of debt. And, taken in this light, it comprehends a great variety of acquifition ; being ufually divided into debts of *record*, debts by *fpecial*, and debts by *fimple* contract.

A DEBT of *record* is a fum of money, which appears to be due by the evidence of a court of record. Thus, when any fpecific fum is adjudged to be due from the defendant to the plaintiff, on an action or fuit at law ; this is a contract of the higheft nature, being eftablifhed by the fentence of a court of judicature. Recognizances alfo are a fum of money, recognized or acknowleged to be due to the

[q] F. N. B. 119.

crown

crown or a fubject, in the prefence of fome court or magiftrate, with a condition that fuch acknowlegement fhall be void upon the appearance of the party, his good behaviour, or the like : and thefe, together with ftatutes merchant and ftatutes ftaple, &c, if forfeited by non-performance of the condition, are alfo ranked among this firft and principal clafs of debts, *viz.* debts of record ; fince the contract, on which they are founded, is witneffed by the higheft kind of evidence, *viz.* by matter of record.

DEBTS by *fpecialty*, or fpecial contract, are fuch whereby a fum of money becomes, or is acknowleged to be, due by deed or inftrument under feal. Such as by deed of covenant, by deed of fale, by leafe referving rent, or by bond or obligation : which laft we took occafion to explain in the twentieth lecture of the prefent book ; and then fhewed that it is an acknowlegement or creation of a debt from the obligor to the obligee, unlefs the obligor performs a condition thereunto ufually annexed, as the payment of rent or money borrowed, the obfervance of a covenant, and the like ; on failure of which the bond becomes forfeited and the debt becomes due in law. Thefe are looked upon as the next clafs of debts after thofe of record, being confirmed by fpecial evidence, under feal.

DEBTS by *fimple contract* are fuch, where the contract upon which the obligation arifes is neither afcertained by matter of record, nor yet by deed or fpecial inftrument, but by mere oral evidence, the moft fimple of any ; or by notes unfealed, which are capable of a more eafy proof, and (therefore only) better, than a verbal promife. It is eafy to fee into what a vaft variety of obligations this laft clafs may be branched out, through the numerous contracts for money, which are not only expreffed by the parties, but virtually implied in law. Some of thefe we have already occafionally hinted at ; and the reft, to avoid repetition, muft be referred to thofe particular heads in the third book of thefe commentaries, where the breach of fuch contracts will be

confidered.

confidered. I fhall only obferve at prefent, that by the ftatute 29 Car. II. c. 3. no executor or adminiftrator fhall be charged upon any fpecial promife to anfwer damages out of his own eftate, and no perfon fhall be charged upon any promife to anfwer for the debt or default of another, or upon any agreement in confideration of marriage, or upon any contract or fale of any real eftate, or upon any agreement that is not to be performed within one year from the making, unlefs the agreement or fome memorandum thereof be in writing, and figned by the party himfelf or by his authority.

BUT there is one fpecies of debts upon fimple contract, which, being a tranfaction now introduced into all forts of civil life, under the name of *paper credit,* deferves a more particular regard. Thefe are debts by *bills of exchange,* and *promiffory notes.*

A BILL *of exchange* is a fecurity, originally invented among merchants in different countries, for the more eafy remittance of money from the one to the other, which has fince fpread itfelf into almoft all pecuniary tranfactions. It is an open letter of requeft from one man to another, defiring him to pay a fum named therein to a third perfon on his account; by which means a man at the moft diftant part of the world may have money remitted to him from any trading country. If A lives in Jamaica, and owes B who lives in England 1000 *l,* now if C be going from England to Jamaica, he may pay B this 1000 *l,* and take a bill of exchange drawn by B in England upon A in Jamaica, and receive it when he comes thither. Thus does B receive his debt, at any diftance of place, by transferring it to C; who carries over his money in paper credit, without danger of robbery or lofs. This method is faid to have been brought into general ufe by the Jews and Lombards, when banifhed for their ufury and other vices; in order the more eafily to draw their effects out of France and England, into thofe countries in which they had chofen to refide. The invention of them was a little earlier: for the Jews were banifhed out of Guienne in 1287, and out of of England in 1290ʳ; and in 1236 the uſe of paper credit was introduced into the Mogul empire in China˙. In common ſpeech ſuch a bill is frequently called a *draught*, but a *bill of exchange* is the more legal as well as mercantile expreſſion. The perſon however, who writes this letter, is called in law the *drawer*, and he to whom it is written the *drawee*; and the third perſon, or negotiator, to whom it is payable (whether ſpecially named, or the *bearer* generally) is called the *payee*.

T H E S E bills are either *foreign*, or *inland: foreign*, when drawn by a merchant reſiding abroad upon his correſpondent in England, or *vice verſa*; and *inland*, when both the drawer and the drawee reſide within the kingdom. Formerly foreign bills of exchange were much more regarded in the eye of the law than inland ones, as being thought of more public concern in the advancement of trade and commerce. But now by two ſtatutes, the one 9 & 10 W. III. c. 17. the other 3 & 4 Ann. c. 9. inland bills of exchange are put upon the ſame footing as foreign ones; what was the law and cuſtom of merchants with regard to the one, and taken notice of merely as ſuchᵗ, being by thoſe ſtatutes expreſsly enaⅽted with regard to the other. So that there is now in law no manner of difference between them.

P R O M I S S O R Y notes, or notes of hand, are a plain and direⅽt engagement in writing, to pay a ſum ſpecified at the time therein limited to a perſon therein named, or ſometimes to his order, or often to the bearer at large. Theſe alſo by the ſame ſtatute 3 & 4 Ann. c. 9. are made aſſignable and indorſable in like manner as bills of exchange.

T H E payee, we may obſerve, either of a bill of exchange or promiſſory note, has clearly a property veſted in him (not indeed in poſſeſſion but in aⅽtion) by the *expreſs* contraⅽt of the drawer in the caſe of a promiſſory note, and, in the caſe of a bill of exchange, by his *implied* contraⅽt; *viz.* that, provided the drawee

ʳ 2 Carte. 203. 206.   ᵗ 1 Roll. Abr. 6.
ˢ Mod. Un. Hiſt. iv. 499.   L l l 2   does

does not pay the bill, the drawer will : for which reafon it is ufual, in bills of exchange, to exprefs that the *value* thereof hath been *received* by the drawer [u]; in order to fhew the confideration, upon which the implied contract of repayment arifes. And this property, fo vefted, may be transferred and affigned from the payee to any other man; contrary to the general rule of the common law, that no *chofe* in action is affignable : which affignment is the life of paper credit. It may therefore be of fome ufe, to mention a few of the principal incidents attending this transfer or affignment, in order to make it regular, and thereby to charge the drawer with the payment of the debt to other perfons, than thofe with whom he originally contracted.

In the firft place then the payee, or perfon to whom or whofe *order* fuch bill of exchange or promiffory note is payable, may by indorfement, or writing his name *in dorfo* or on the back of it, affign over his whole property to the bearer, or elfe to another perfon by name, either of whom is then called the indorfee; and he may affign the fame to another, and fo on *in infinitum*. And a promiffory note, payable to A or *bearer*, is negotiable without any indorfement, and payment thereof may be demanded by any bearer of it [v]. But, in cafe of a bill of exchange, the payee, or the indorfee, (whether it be a general or particular indorfement) is to go to the drawee, and offer his bill for acceptance; which acceptance (fo as to charge the drawer with cofts) muft be in writing, under or on the back of the bill. If the drawee accepts the bill, either verbally or in writing [w], he then makes himfelf liable to pay it; this being now a contract on his fide, grounded on an acknowlegement that the drawer has effects in his hands, or at leaft credit fufficient to warrant the payment. If the drawee refufes to accept the bill, and it be of the value of 20 *l.* or upwards, and expreffed to be for value received, the payee or indorfee may proteft it for *non-acceptance* : which proteft muft be made in writing, under a copy of fuch bill

[u] Stra. 1212.   4 Geo. III. B. R.
[v] 2 Show. 235.—Grant v. Vaughan. T. [w] Stra. 1000.

of

of exchange, by some notary public; or, if no such notary be resident in the place, then by any other substantial inhabitant in the presence of two credible witnesses; and notice of such protest must, within fourteen days after, be given to the drawer.

B u t, in case such bill be accepted by the drawee, and after acceptance he fails or refuses to pay it within three days after it becomes due (which three days are called days of grace) the payee or indorsee is then to get it protested for *non-payment*, in the same manner and by the same persons who are to protest it in case of non-acceptance: and such protest must also be notified, within fourteen days after, to the drawer. And he, on producing such protest, either of non-acceptance or non-payment, is bound to make good to the payee, or indorsee, not only the amount of the said bills, (which he is bound to do within a reasonable time after non-payment, without any protest, by the rules of the common law *) but also interest and all charges, to be computed from the time of making such protest. But if no protest be made or notified to the drawer, and any damage accrues by such neglect, it shall fall on the holder of the bill. The bill, when refused, must be demanded of the drawer as soon as conveniently may be: for though, when one draws a bill of exchange, he subjects himself to the payment, if the person on whom it is drawn refuses either to accept or pay, yet that is with this limitation, that if the bill be not paid, when due, the person to whom it is payable shall in convenient time give the drawer notice thereof; for otherwise the law will imply it paid: since it would be prejudicial to commerce, if a bill might rise up to charge the drawer at any distance of time; when in the mean time all reckonings and accounts may be adjusted between the drawer and the drawee [y].

I f the bill be an indorsed bill, and the indorsee cannot get the drawee to discharge it, he may call upon either the drawer or the indorsor, or if the bill has been negotiated through many

[x] Lord Raym. 993.   [y] Salk. 127.

hands,

hands, upon any of the indorfors; for each indorfor is a warrantor for the payment of the bill, which is frequently taken in payment as much (or more) upon the credit of the indorfor, as of the drawer. And if fuch indorfor, fo called upon, has the names of one or more indorfors prior to his own, to each of whom he is properly an indorfee, he is alfo at liberty to call upon any of them to make him fatisfaction; and fo upwards. But the firft indorfor has nobody to refort to, but the drawer only.

WHAT has been faid of bills of exchange is applicable alfo to promiffory notes, that are indorfed over, and negotiated from one hand to another: only that, in this cafe, as there is no drawee, there can be no proteft for non-acceptance; or rather, the law confiders a promiffory note in the light of a bill drawn by a man upon himfelf, and accepted at the time of drawing. And, in cafe of non-payment by the drawer, the feveral indorfees of a promiffory note have the fame remedy, as upon bills of exchange, againft the prior indorfors.

CHAPTER THE THIRTY FIRST.

OF TITLE BY BANKRUPTCY.

THE preceding chapter having treated pretty largely of the acquisition of personal property by several commercial methods, we from thence shall be easily led to take into our present consideration a tenth method of transferring property, which is that of

X. BANKRUPTCY; a title which we before lightly touched upon [a], so far as it related to the transfer of the real estate of the bankrupt. At present we are to treat of it more minutely, as it principally relates to the disposition of chattels, in which the property of persons concerned in trade more usually consists, than in lands or tenements. Let us therefore first of all consider, 1. *Who* may become a bankrupt: 2. What *acts* make a bankrupt: 3. The *proceedings* on a commission of bankrupt: and, 4. In what manner an estate in goods and chattels may be *transferred* by bankruptcy.

1. WHO may become a bankrupt. A bankrupt was before [b] defined to be " a trader, who secretes himself, or does certain " other acts, tending to defraud his creditors." He was formerly considered merely in the light of a criminal or offender [c]; and in this spirit we are told by sir Edward Coke [d], that we have fetched as well the name, as the wickedness, of bankrupts from foreign

[a] See pag. 285.
[b] *Ibid.*

[c] Stat. 1 Jac. I. c. 15. §. 17.
[d] 4 Inst. 277.

nations [e]

nations[e]. But at prefent the laws of bankruptcy are confidered as laws calculated for the benefit of trade, and founded on the principles of humanity as well as juftice; and to that end they confer fome privileges, not only on the creditors, but alfo on the bankrupt or debtor himfelf. On the creditors; by compelling the bankrupt to give up all his effects to their ufe, without any fraudulent concealment: on the debtor; by exempting him from the rigor of the general law, whereby his perfon might be confined at the difcretion of his creditor, though in reality he has nothing to fatisfy the debt; whereas the law of bankrupts, taking into confideration the fudden and unavoidable accidents to which men in trade are liable, has given them the liberty of their perfons, and fome pecuniary emoluments, upon condition they furrender up their whole eftate to be divided among their creditors.

IN this refpect our legiflature feems to have attended to the example of the Roman law. I mean not the terrible law of the twelve tables; whereby the creditors might cut the debtor's body into pieces, and each of them take his proportionable fhare: if indeed that law, *de debitore in partes fecando,* is to be underftood in fo very butcherly a light; which many learned men have with reafon doubted[f]. Nor do I mean thofe lefs inhuman laws (if they may be called fo, as *their* meaning is indifputably certain) of imprifoning the debtor's perfon in chains; fubjecting him to ftripes and hard labour, at the mercy of his rigid creditor; and fometimes felling him, his wife, and children, to perpetual foreign flavery *trans Tiberim*[g]: an oppreffion, which produced fo

[e] The word itfelf is derived from the word *bancus* or *banque*, which fignifies the table or counter of a tradefman (Dufrefne. I. 969.) and *ruptus*, broken; denoting thereby one whofe fhop or place of trade is broken and gone; though others rather chufe to adopt the word *route*, which in French fignifies a trace or track, and tell us that a bankrupt is one who hath removed his banque, leaving but a trace behind. (4 Inft. 277.) And it is obfervable that the title of the firft Englifh ftatute concerning this offence, 34 Hen. VIII. c. 4. " againft "fuch perfons as do make bankrupt," is a literal tranflation of the French idiom, *qui font banque route.*

[f] Taylor. *Comment. in L. decemviral.* Bynkerfh. *Obferv. Jur. I.* 1. Heinecc. *Antiqu. III.* 30. 4.

[g] In Pegu, and the adjacent countries in Eaft India, the creditor is entitled to difpofe of the debtor himfelf, and likewife of

his

many popular infurrections, and fecessions to the *mons sacer*. But I mean the law of *cession*, introduced by the christian emperors; whereby if a debtor ceded, or yielded up, all his fortune to his creditors, he was fecured from being dragged to a goal, " *omni* " *quoque corporali cruciatu femoto* [h]." For, as the emperor justly obferves [i], " *inhumanum erat fpoliatum fortunis fuis in folidum* " *damnari.*" Thus far was just and reafonable : but, as the departing from one extreme is apt to produce it's oppofite, we find it afterwards enacted [k], that if the debtor by any unforefeen accident was reduced to low circumftances, and would *fwear* that he had not fufficient left to pay his debts, he should not be compelled to cede or give up even that which he had in his poffeffion : a law, which under a falfe notion of humanity, feems to be fertile of perjury, injuftice, and abfurdity.

THE laws of England, more wifely, have fteered in the middle between both extremes : providing at once against the inhumanity of the creditor, who is not fuffered to confine an honeft bankrupt after his effects are delivered up; and at the fame time taking care that all his juft debts shall be paid, fo far as the effects will extend. But ftill they are cautious of encouraging prodigality and extravagance by this indulgence to debtors; and therefore they allow the benefit of the laws of bankruptcy to none but actual *traders*; fince that fet of men are, generally fpeaking, the only perfons liable to accidental loffes, and to an inability of paying their debts, without any fault of their own. If perfons in other fituations of life run in debt without the power of payment, they muft take the confequences of their own indifcretion, even though they meet with fudden accidents that may reduce their fortunes : for the law holds it to be an unjuftifiable practice, for any perfon but a tradefman to encumber himfelf with debts of any confiderable value. If a gentleman, or one in a

his wife and children ; infomuch that he may even violate with impunity the chaftity of the debtor's wife : but then, by fo doing, the debt is underftood to be dif-

charged. (Mod. Un. Hift. vii. 128)
[h] *Cod.* 7. 71. *per tot.*
[i] *Inft.* 4. 6. 40.
[k] *Nov.* 135. *c.* 1.

liberal profeſſion, at the time of contracting his debts, has a ſufficient fund to pay them, the delay of payment is a ſpecies of
diſhoneſty, and a temporary injuſtice to his creditor : and if, at
ſuch time, he has no ſufficient fund, the diſhoneſty and injuſtice
is the greater. He cannot therefore murmur, if he ſuffers the
puniſhment which he has voluntarily drawn upon himſelf. But
in mercantile tranſactions the caſe is far otherwiſe. Trade cannot
be carried on without mutual credit on both ſides : the contracting of debts is therefore here not only juſtifiable, but neceſſary.
And if by accidental calamities, as by the loſs of a ſhip in a
tempeſt, the failure of brother traders, or by the non-payment
of perſons out of trade, a merchant or tradeſman becomes incapable of diſcharging his own debts, it is his misfortune and not
his fault. To the misfortunes therefore of debtors the law has
given a compaſſionate remedy, but denied it to their faults : ſince,
at the ſame time that it provides for the ſecurity of commerce,
by enacting that every conſiderable trader may be declared a bankrupt, for the benefit of his creditors as well as himſelf, it has
alſo to diſcourage extravagance declared, that no one ſhall be capable of being made a bankrupt, but only a *trader ;* nor capable
of receiving the full benefit of the ſtatutes, but only an *induſtrious* trader.

THE firſt ſtatute made concerning any Engliſh bankrupts, was
34 Hen. VIII. c. 4. when trade began firſt to be properly cultivated in England : which has been almoſt totally altered by ſtatute
13 Eliz. c. 7. whereby bankruptcy is confined to ſuch perſons
only as have *uſed the trade of merchandize,* in groſs or by retail,
by way of bargaining, exchange, rechange, bartering, chevi-
ſance[1], or otherwiſe ; or have *ſought their living by buying and
ſelling.* And by ſtatute 21 Jac. I. c. 19. perſons uſing the trade
or profeſſion of a *ſcrivener,* receiving other mens monies and e-
ſtates into their truſt and cuſtody, are alſo made liable to the ſtatutes of bankruptcy : and the benefits, as well as the penal parts
of the law, are extended as well to *aliens* and *denizens* as to na-

[1] that is, making contracts. (Dufreſne. II. 569.)

tural

tural born subjects ; being intended entirely for the protection of
trade, in which aliens are often as deeply concerned as natives.
By many subsequent statutes, but lastly by statute 5 Geo. II. c. 30.[m]
bankers, brokers, and *factors,* are declared liable to the statutes
of bankruptcy; and this upon the same reason that scriveners are
included by the statute of James I. *viz.* for the relief of their
creditors; whom they have otherwise more opportunities of defrauding than any other set of dealers : and they are properly to be
looked upon as traders, since they make merchandize of money,
in the same manner as other merchants do of goods and other
moveable chattels. But by the same act[n], no *farmer, grazier,* or
drover, shall (as such) be liable to be deemed a bankrupt : for,
though they buy and sell corn, and hay, and beasts, in the course
of husbandry, yet trade is not their principal, but only a collateral, object ; their chief concern being to manure and till the
ground, and make the best advantage of it's produce. And, besides, the subjecting them to the laws of bankruptcy might be a
means of defeating their landlords of the security which the law
has given them above all others, for the payment of their reserved rents : wherefore also, upon a similar reason, a *receiver of
the king's taxes* is not capable[o], as such, of being a bankrupt ;
lest the king should be defeated of those extensive remedies against
his debtors, which are put into his hands by the prerogative.
By the same statute[p], no person shall have a commission of bankrupt awarded against him, unless at the petition of some *one* creditor, to whom he owes 100*l*; or of *two*, to whom he is indebted 150*l*; or of *more*, to whom all together he is indebted
200 *l.* For the law does not look upon persons, whose debts a-
mount to less, to be traders considerable enough, either to enjoy
the benefit of the statutes, themselves, or to entitle the creditors, for the benefit of public commerce, to demand the distribution of their effects.

[m] §. 39.
[n] §. 40.
[o] §. eod.
[p] §. 23.

IN

IN the interpretation of thefe feveral ftatutes, it hath been held, that buying only, or felling only, will not qualify a man to be a bankrupt; but it muft be both buying and felling, and alfo getting a livelyhood by it. As, by exercifing the calling of a merchant, a grocer, a mercer, or, in one general word, a *chapman*, who is one that buys and fells any thing. But no handicraft occupation (where nothing is bought and fold, and therefore an extenfive credit, for the ftock in trade, is not neceffary to be had) will make a man a regular bankrupt; as that of a hufbandman, a gardener, and the like, who are paid for their work and labour[q]. Alfo an inn-keeper cannot, as fuch, be a bankrupt[r]: for his gain or livelyhood does not arife from buying and felling in the way of merchandize, but greatly from the ufe of his rooms and furniture, his attendance, and the like: and though he may buy corn and victuals, to fell again at a profit, yet that no more makes him a trader, than a fchoolmafter or other perfon is, that keeps a boarding houfe, and makes confiderable gains by buying and felling what he fpends in the houfe, and fuch a one is clearly not within the ftatutes[s]. But where perfons buy goods, and make them up into faleable commodities, as fhoe-makers, fmiths, and the like; here, though part of the gain is by bodily labour, and not by buying and felling, yet they are within the ftatutes of bankrupts[t]; for the labour is only in melioration of the commodity, and rendering it more fit for fale.

ONE fingle act of buying and felling will not make a man a trader; but a repeated practice, and profit by it. Buying and felling bank-ftock, or other government fecurities, will not make a man a bankrupt; they not being goods, wares, or merchandize, within the intent of the ftatute, by which a profit may be fairly made[u]. Neither will buying and felling under particular reftraints, or for particular purpofes; as if a commiffioner of the

[q] Cro. Car. 31.
[r] Cro. Car. 549. Skinn. 291.
[s] Skinn. 292. 3 Mod. 330.
[t] Cro. Car. 31. Skinn. 292.
[u] 2 P. W[ms]. 308.

navy

navy uſes to buy victuals for the fleet, and diſpoſe of the ſurplus and refuſe, he is not thereby made a trader within the ſtatutes ʷ. An infant, though a trader, cannot be made a bankrupt : for an infant can owe nothing but for neceſſaries ; and the ſtatutes of bankruptcy create no new debts, but only give a ſpeedier and more effectual remedy for recovering ſuch as were before due : and no perſon can be made a bankrupt for debts, which he is not liable at law to pay ˣ. But a feme-covert in London, being a ſole trader according to the cuſtom, is liable to a commiſſion of bankrupt ʸ.

2. HAVING thus conſidered, who may, and who may not, be made a bankrupt, we are to inquire, ſecondly, by what *acts* a man may become a bankrupt. A bankrupt is " a trader, who " ſecretes himſelf, or does certain other acts, tending to defraud " his creditors." We have hitherto been employed in explaining the former part of this deſcription, " a trader :" let us now at-tend to the latter, " who ſecretes himſelf, or does certain other " acts, tending to defraud his creditors." And, in general, when-ever ſuch a trader, as is before deſcribed, hath endeavoured to avoid his creditors or evade their juſt demands, this hath been declared by the legiſlature to be an act of bankruptcy, upon which a commiſſion may be ſued out. For in this extrajudicial method of proceeding, which is allowed merely for the benefit of commerce, the law is extremely watchful to detect a man, whoſe circumſtances are declining, in the firſt inſtance, or at leaſt as early as poſſible : that the creditors may receive as large a pro-portion of their debts as may be ; and that a man may not go on wantonly waſting his ſubſtance, and then claim the benefit of the ſtatutes, when he has nothing left to diſtribute.

To learn what the particular acts of bankruptcy are, which render a man a bankrupt, we muſt conſult the ſeveral ſtatutes, and the reſolutions formed by the courts thereon. Among theſe

---

ʷ 1 Salk. 110. Skin. 292.   ʸ *La Vie* v. *Philips.* M. 6 Geo. III. B. R.
ˣ Lord Raym. 443.

may therefore be reckoned, 1. Departing from the realm, whereby a man withdraws himſelf from the juriſdiction and coërcion of the law, with intent to defraud his creditors ᶻ. 2. Departing from his own houſe, with intent to ſecrete himſelf, and avoid his creditors ᵃ. 3. Keeping in his own houſe, privately, ſo as not to be ſeen or ſpoken with by his creditors, except for juſt and neceſſary cauſe; which is likewiſe conſtrued to be an intention to defraud his creditors, by avoiding the proceſs of the law ᵇ. 4. Procuring or ſuffering himſelf willingly to be arreſted, or outlawed, or impriſoned, without juſt and lawful cauſe; which is likewiſe deemed an attempt to defraud his creditors ᶜ. 5. Procuring his money, goods, chattels, and effects to be attached or ſequeſtered by any legal proceſs; which is another plain and direct endeavour to diſappoint his creditors of their ſecurity ᵈ. 6. Making any fraudulent conveyance to a friend, or ſecret truſtee, of his lands, tenements, goods, or chattels; which is an act of the ſame ſuſpicious nature with the laſt ᵉ. 7. Procuring any protection, not being himſelf privileged by parliament, in order to ſcreen his perſon from arreſts; which alſo is an endeavour to elude the juſtice of the law ᶠ. 8. Endeavouring or deſiring, by any petition to the king, or bill exhibited in any of the king's courts againſt any creditors, to compel them to take leſs than their juſt debts; or to procraſtinate the time of payment, originally contracted for; which are an acknowlegement of either his poverty or his knavery ᵍ. 9. Lying in priſon for two months, or more, upon arreſt or other detention for debt, without finding bail, in order to obtain his liberty ʰ. For the inability to procure bail argues a ſtrong deficiency in his credit, owing either to his ſuſpected poverty, or ill character; and his neglect to do it, if able, can ariſe only from a fraudulent intention: in either of which caſes it is high time for his creditors to look to

ᶻ Stat. 13 Eliz. c. 7.
ᵃ *Ibid.* 1 Jac. I. c. 15.
ᵇ Stat. 13 Eliz. c. 7.
ᶜ *Ibid.* 1 Jac. I. c. 15.
ᵈ Stat. 1 Jac. I. c. 15.
ᵉ *Ibid.*
ᶠ Stat. 21 Jac. I. c. 19.
ᵍ *Ibid.*
ʰ *Ibid.*

themſelves,

themselves, and compel a diſtribution of his effects. 10. Eſca-
ping from priſon after an arreſt for a juſt debt of 100*l.* or upwards[i]. For no man would break priſon, that was able and de-
ſirous to procure bail; which brings it within the reaſon of the
laſt caſe. 11. Neglecting to make ſatisfaction for any juſt debt
to the amount of 100*l.* within two months after ſervice of legal
proceſs, for ſuch debt, upon any trader having privilege of parliament[k].

THESE are the ſeveral acts of bankruptcy, expreſſly defined
by the ſtatutes relating to this title : which being ſo numerous,
and the whole law of bankrupts being an innovation on the common law, our courts of juſtice have been tender of extending or
multiplying acts of bankruptcy by any conſtruction, or implication. And therefore ſir John Holt held[l], that a man's removing
his goods privately, to prevent their being ſeiſed in execution,
was no act of bankruptcy. For the ſtatutes mention only fraudulent gifts to third perſons, and procuring them to be ſeiſed by
ſham proceſs, in order to defraud creditors : but this, though a
palpable fraud, yet falling within neither of thoſe caſes, cannot
be adjudged an act of bankruptcy. So alſo it has been determined expreſſly, that a banker's ſtopping or refuſing payment is no
act of bankruptcy; for it is not within the deſcription of any of
the ſtatutes, and there may be good reaſons for his ſo doing, as,
ſuſpicion of forgery, and the like : and if, in conſequence of ſuch
refuſal, he is arreſted, and puts in bail, ſtill it is no act of bankruptcy[m] : but if he goes to priſon, and lies there two months,
then, and not before, is he become a bankrupt.

WE have ſeen *who* may be a bankrupt, and what *acts* will
make him ſo : let us next conſider,

3. THE *proceedings* on a commiſſion of bankrupt; ſo far as
they affect the bankrupt himſelf. And theſe depend entirely on

[i] Stat. 21 Jac. I. c. 19.
[k] Stat. 4 Geo. III. c. 33.

[l] Lord Raym. 725.
[m] 7 Mod. 139.

the feveral ftatutes of bankruptcy [n]; all which I fhall endeavour
to blend together, and digeft into a concife methodical order.

A N D, firft, there muft be a *petition* to the lord chancellor by
one creditor to the amount of 100*l*, or by two to the amount of
150 *l*, or by three or more to the amount of 200 *l*; upon which
he grants a *commiffion* to fuch difcreet perfons as to him fhall
feem good, who are then ftiled commiffioners of bankrupt. The
petitioners, to prevent malicious applications, muft be bound in
a fecurity of 200 *l*, to make the party amends in cafe they do
not prove him a bankrupt. And, if on the other hand they receive any money or effects from the bankrupt, as a recompenfe
for fuing out the commiffion, fo as to receive more than their ratable dividends of the bankrupt's eftate, they forfeit not only
what they fhall have fo received, but their whole debt. Thefe
provifions are made, as well to fecure perfons in good credit from
being damnified by malicious petitions, as to prevent knavifh
combinations between the creditors and bankrupt, in order to
obtain the benefit of a commiffion. When the commiffion is a-
warded and iffued, the commiffioners are to meet, at their own
expenfe, and to take an oath for the due execution of their commiffion, and to be allowed a fum not exceeding 20 *s*. *per diem*
each, at every fitting. And no commiffion of bankrupt fhall
abate, or be void, upon any demife of the crown.

W H E N the commiffioners have received their commiffion,
they are firft to receive proof of the perfon's being a trader, and
having committed fome act of bankruptcy; and then to declare
him a bankrupt, if proved fo; and to give notice thereof in the
gazette, and at the fame time to appoint three meetings. At the
firft of thefe meetings an election muft be made of affignees, or
perfons to whom the bankrupt's eftate fhall be affigned, and in
whom it fhall be vefted for the benefit of the creditors; which
affignees are to be firft named by the commiffioners, and after-

[n] 13Eliz. c 7. 1Jac.I. c.15. 21Jac.I. c.19. 7Geo.I. c.31. 5Geo.II. c.30. 19Geo.II.
c.32. & 24Geo.II. c.57.

wards to be approved or rejected at the said meeting by the major part, in value, of the creditors who shall then prove their debts : but no creditor shall be admitted to vote in the choice of assignees, whose debt on the ballance of accounts does not amount to 10*l.* At the second meeting any farther business relating to the commission may be proceeded on. And at the third meeting, at fartheft, which muft be on the forty second day after the advertisement in the gazette, the bankrupt, upon notice also perfonally ferved upon him or left at his ufual place of abode, muft furrender himself perfonally to the commiffioners, and muft thenceforth in all refpects conform to the directions of the ftatutes of bankruptcy; or, in default thereof, fhall be guilty of felony without benefit of clergy, and fhall fuffer death, and his goods and eftate fhall be diftributed among his creditors.

In cafe the bankrupt abfconds, or is likely to run away, between the time of the commiffion iffued, and the laft day of furrender, he may by warrant from any judge or juftice of the peace be committed to the county goal, in order to be forthcoming to the commiffioners; who are also empowered immediately to grant a warrant for feifing his goods and papers.

When the bankrupt appears, the commiffioners are to examine him touching all matters relating to his trade and effects. They may also fummon before them, and examine, the bankrupt's wife and any other perfon whatfoever, as to all matters relating to the bankrupt's affairs. And in cafe any of them fhall refufe to anfwer, or fhall not anfwer fully, to any lawful queftion, or fhall refufe to fubfcribe fuch their examination, the commiffioners may commit them to prifon without bail, till they make and fign a full anfwer; the commiffioners fpecifying in their warrant of commitment the queftion fo refufed to be anfwered. And any goaler, permitting fuch perfons to efcape, or go out of prifon, fhall forfeit 500 *l.* to the creditors.

THE brankrupt, upon this examination, is bound upon pain of death to make a full difcovery of all his eftate and effects, as well in expectancy as poffeffion, and how he has difpofed of the fame; together with all books and writings relating thereto: and is to deliver up all in his own power to the commiffioners; (except the neceffary apparel of himfelf, his wife, and his children) or, in cafe he conceals or imbezzles any effects to the amount of 20 *l*, or withholds any books or writings, with intent to defraud his creditors, he fhall be guilty of felony without benefit of clergy °.

AFTER the time allowed to the bankrupt for fuch difcovery is expired, any other perfon voluntarily difcovering any part of his eftate, before unknown to the affignees, fhall be entitled to *five per cent.* out of the effects fo difcovered, and fuch farther reward as the affignees and commiffioners fhall think proper. And any truftee wilfully concealing the eftate of any bankrupt, after the expiration of the two and forty days, fhall forfeit 100 *l*, and double the value of the eftate concealed, to the creditors.

HITHERTO every thing is in favour of the creditors; and the law feems to be pretty rigid and fevere againft the bankrupt: but, in cafe he proves honeft, it makes him full amends for all this rigor and feverity. For if the bankrupt hath made an ingenuous difcovery, hath conformed to the directions of the law, and hath acted in all points to the fatisfaction of his creditors; and if they, or four parts in five of them in number and value, (but none of them creditors for lefs than 20 *l*.) will fign a certificate to that purport; the commiffioners are then to authenticate fuch certificate under their hands and feals, and to tranfmit it to the lord chancellor: and he, or two judges whom he fhall ap-

---

° By the laws of Naples all fraudulent bankrupts, particularly fuch as do not furrender themfelves within four days, are punifhed with death: alfo all who conceal the effects of a bankrupt, or fet up a pretended debt to defraud his creditors. (Mod. Un. Hift. xxviii. 320.)

point,

point, on oath made by the bankrupt that such certificate was obtained without fraud, may allow the same; or disallow it, upon cause shewn by any of the creditors of the bankrupt.

IF no cause be shewn to the contrary, the certificate is allowed of course; and then the bankrupt is entitled to a decent and reasonable allowance out of his effects, for his future support and maintenance, and to put him in a way of honest industry. This allowance is also in proportion to his former good behaviour, in the early discovery of the decline of his affairs, and thereby giving his creditors a larger dividend. For, if his effects will not pay one half of his debts, or ten shillings in the pound, he is left to the discretion of the commissioners and assignees, to have a competent sum allowed him, not exceeding *three per cent:* but if they pay ten shillings in the pound, he is to be allowed *five per cent*; if twelve shillings and sixpence, then *seven and a half per cent*; and if fifteen shillings in the pound, then the bankrupt shall be allowed *ten per cent:* provided, that such allowance do not in the first case exceed 200*l*, in the second 250*l*, and in the third 300*l*. ᴾ

BESIDES this allowance, he has also an indemnity granted him, of being free and discharged for ever from all debts owing by him at the time he became a bankrupt; even though judgment shall have been obtained against him, and he lies in prison upon execution for such debts; and, for that among other purposes, all proceedings on commissions of bankrupt are, on petition, to be entered of record, as a perpetual bar against actions to be commenced on this account : though, in general, the production of the certificate properly allowed shall be sufficient evidence of all previ-

---

ᴾ By the Roman law of cession, if the debtor acquired any considerable property subsequent to the giving up of his all, it was liable to the demands of his creditors. (*Ff.* 42. 3. 4.) But this did not extend to such allowance as was left to him on the score of compassion, for the maintenance of himself and family. *Si quid misericordiae causa ei fuerit relictum, puta menstruum vel annuum, alimentorum nomine, non oportet propter hoc bona ejus iterato venundari: nec enim fraudandus est alimentis quotidianis.* (*Ibid l.6.*)

ous proceedings. Thus the bankrupt becomes a clear man again; and, by the affiftance of his allowance and his own induftry, may become a ufeful member of the commonwealth : which is the rather to be expected, as he cannot be entitled to thefe benefits, but by the teftimony of his creditors themfelves of his honeft and ingenuous difpofition ; and unlefs his failures have been owing to misfortunes, rather than to mifconduct and extravagance.

F o r no allowance or indemnity fhall be given to a bankrupt, unlefs his certificate be figned and allowed, as before-mentioned; and alfo, if any creditor produces a fictitious debt, and the bankrupt does not make difcovery of it, but fuffers the fair creditors to be impofed upon, he lofes all title to thefe advantages. Neither can he claim them, if he has given with any of his children above 100 *l.* for a marriage portion, unlefs he had at that time fufficient left to pay all his debts ; or if he has loft at any one time 5 *l,* or in the whole 100 *l,* within a twelvemonth before he became bankrupt, by any manner of gaming or wagering whatfoever ; or, within the fame time, has loft to the value of 100 *l.* by ftockjobbing. Alfo, to prevent the too common practice of frequent and fraudulent or carelefs breaking, a mark is fet upon fuch as have been once cleared by a commiffion of bankrupt, or have compounded with their creditors, or have been delivered by an act of infolvency : which is an occafional act, frequently paffed 9 by the legiflature ; whereby all perfons whatfoever, who are either in too low a way of dealing to become bankrupts, or not being in a mercantile ftate of life are not included within the laws of bankruptcy, are difcharged from all fuits and imprifonment, upon delivering up all their eftate and effects to their creditors upon oath, at the feffions or affifes ; in which cafe their perjury or fraud is ufually, as in cafe of bankrupts, punifhed with death. Perfons who have been once cleared by this, or either of the other methods, (of compofition with their creditors, or bankruptcy) and afterwards become bankrupts

9 Stat. 28 Geo. II. c 13. 32 Geo. II. c. 28. 1 Geo. III. c. 17. 5 Geo. III. c. 41.

again,

again, unless they pay full fifteen shillings in the pound, are only thereby indemnified as to the confinement of their bodies; but any future estate they shall acquire remains liable to their creditors, excepting their necessary apparel, household goods, and the tools and implements of their trades.

THUS much for the proceedings on a commission of bankrupt, so far as they affect the bankrupt himself personally. Let us next consider,

4. HOW such proceedings affect or transfer the *estate* and *property* of the bankrupt. The method whereby a *real* estate, in lands, tenements, and hereditaments, may be transferred by bankruptcy, was shewn under it's proper head, in a former chapter[r]. At present therefore we are only to consider the transfer of things *personal* by this operation of law.

BY virtue of the statutes before-mentioned all the personal estate and effects of the bankrupt are considered as vested, by the act of bankruptcy, in the future assignees of his commissioners, whether they be goods in actual *possession*, or debts, contracts, and other choses in *action*; and the commissioners by their warrant may cause any house or tenement of the bankrupt to be broken open, in order to enter upon and seize the same. And, when the assignees are chosen or approved by the creditors, the commissioners are to assign every thing over to them; and the property of every part of the estate is thereby as fully vested in them, as it was in the bankrupt himself, and they have the same remedies to recover it[s].

THE property vested in the assignees is the whole that the bankrupt had in himself, at the time he committed the first act of bankruptcy, or that has been vested in him since, before his debts are satisfied or agreed for. Therefore it is usually said, that once a bankrupt, and always a bankrupt: by which is meant,

[r] pag. 285.   [s] 12 Mod. 324.

that

that a plain direct act of bankruptcy once committed cannot be purged, or explained away, by any subsequent conduct, as a dubious equivocal act may be [u]; but that, if a commission is afterwards awarded, the commission and the property of the assignees shall have a relation, or reference, back to the first and original act of bankruptcy [u]. Insomuch that all transactions of the bankrupt are from that time absolutely null and void, either with regard to the alienation of his property, or the receipt of his debts from such as are privy to his bankruptcy; for they are no longer his property, or his debts, but those of the future assignees. And, if an execution be sued out, but not served and executed on the bankrupt's effects till after the act of bankruptcy, it is void as against the assignees. But the king is not bound by this fictitious relation, nor is within the statutes of bankrupts [w]; for if, after the act of bankruptcy committed and before the assignment of his effects, an extent issues for the debt of the crown, the goods are bound thereby [x]. In France this doctrine of relation is carried to a very great length; for there every act of a merchant, for ten days *precedent* to the act of bankruptcy, is presumed to be fraudulent, and is therefore void [y]. But with us the law stands upon a more reasonable footing: for, as these acts of bankruptcy may sometimes be secret to all but a few, and it would be prejudicial to trade to carry this notion to it's utmost length, it is provided by statute 19 Geo. II. c. 32. that no money paid by a bankrupt to a *bona fide* or real creditor, in a course of trade, even after an act of bankruptcy done, shall be liable to be refunded. Nor, by statute 1 Jac. I. c. 15. shall any debtor of a bankrupt, that pays him his debt, without knowing of his bankruptcy, be liable to account for it again. The intention of this relative power being only to reach fraudulent transactions, and not to distress the fair trader.

THE assignees may pursue any *legal* method of recovering this property so vested in them, by their own authority; but cannot

[t] Salk. 110.
[u] 4 Burr. 32.
[w] Atk. 262.
[x] Viner. Abr. t. creditor and bankr. 104.
[y] Sp. L. b. 29. c. 16.

commence

commence a fuit in *equity*, nor compound any debts owing to the bankrupt, nor refer any matters to arbitration, without the confent of the creditors, or the major part of them in value, at a meeting to be held in purfuance of notice in the gazette.

WHEN they have got in all the effects they can reafonably hope for, and reduced them to ready money, the affignees muft, within twelve months after the commiffion iffued, give one and twenty days notice to the creditors of a meeting for a dividend or diftribution ; at which time they muft produce their accounts, and verify them upon oath, if required. And then the commiffioners fhall direct a dividend to be made, at fo much in the pound, to all creditors who have before proved, or fhall then prove, their debts. This dividend muft be made equally, and in a ratable proportion, to all the creditors, according to the *quantity* of their debts ; no regard being had to the *quality* of them. Mortgages indeed, for which the creditor has a real fecurity in his own hands, are entirely fafe ; for the commiffion of bankrupt reaches only the equity of redemption[z]. So are alfo perfonal debts, where the creditor has a chattel in his hands, as a pledge or pawn for the payment, or has taken the debtor's lands or goods in execution. And, upon the equity of the ftatute 8 Ann. c. 14. (which directs, that, upon all executions of goods being on any premifes demifed to a tenant, one year's rent and no more fhall, if due, be paid to the landlord) it hath alfo been held, that under a commiffion of bankrupt, which is in the nature of a ftatute-execution, the landlord fhall be allowed his arrears of rent to the fame amount, in preference to other creditors, even though he hath neglected to diftrein, while the goods remained on the premifes ; which he is otherwife intitled to do for his intire rent, be the *quantum* what it may[a]. But, otherwife, judgments and recognizances, (both which are debts of record, and therefore at other times have a priority) and alfo bonds and obligations by deed or fpecial inftrument (which are called debts by fpecialty, and are ufually the next in order) thefe are all put

[z] Finch. Rep. 466.   [a] Atk. 103, 104.

on a level with debts by mere fimple contract, and all paid *pari paffu*. Nay, fo far is this matter carried, that, by the exprefs provifion of the ftatutes, debts not due at the time of the dividend made, as bonds or notes of hand payable at a future day, fhall be paid equally with the reft[b], allowing a difcount or drawback in proportion. And infurances, and obligations upon bottomry or *refpondentia*, *bona fide* made by the bankrupt, though forfeited after the commiffion is awarded, fhall be looked upon in the fame light as debts contracted before any act of bankruptcy.

WITHIN eighteen months after the commiffion iffued, a fecond and final dividend fhall be made, unlefs all the effects were exhaufted by the firft. And if any furplus remains, after paying every creditor his full debt, it fhall be reftored to the bankrupt. This is a cafe which fometimes happens to men in trade, who involuntarily, or at leaft unwarily, commit acts of bankruptcy, by abfconding and the like, while their effects are more than fufficient to pay their creditors. And, if any fufpicious or malevolent creditor will take the advantage of fuch acts, and fue out a commiffion, the bankrupt has no remedy, but muft quietly fubmit to the effects of his own imprudence; except that, upon fatisfaction made to all the creditors, the commiffion may be *fuperfeded*[c]. This cafe may alfo happen, when a knave is defirous of defrauding his creditors, and is compelled by a commiffion to do them that juftice, which otherwife he wanted to evade. And therefore, though the ufual rule is, that all intereft on debts carrying intereft fhall ceafe from the time of iffuing the commiffion, yet, in cafe of a furplus left after payment of every debt, fuch intereft fhall again revive, and be chargeable on the bankrupt[d], or his reprefentatives.

[b] Lord Raym. 1549.			[d] Atk. 244.
[c] 2 Ch. Caf. 144.

CHAPTER THE THIRTY SECOND.

OF TITLE BY TESTAMENT, AND ADMINISTRATION.

THERE yet remain to be examined, in the prefent chapter, two other methods of acquiring perfonal eftates, *viz.* by *teftament* and *adminiftration*. And thefe I propofe to confider in one and the fame view; they being in their nature fo connected and blended together, as makes it impoffible to treat of them diftinctly, without manifeft tautology and repetition.

XI. XII. IN the purfuit then of this joint fubject, I fhall, firft, enquire into the original and antiquity of teftaments and adminiftrations; fhall, fecondly, fhew who is capable of making a laft will and teftament; fhall, thirdly, confider the nature of a teftament and it's incidents; fhall, fourthly, fhew what an executor and adminiftrator are, and how they are to be appointed; and, laftly, fhall felect fome few of the general heads of the office and duty of executors and adminiftrators.

FIRST, as to the *original* of teftaments and adminiftrations. We have more than once obferved, that, when property came to be vefted in individuals by the right of occupancy, it became neceffary for the peace of fociety, that this occupancy fhould be continued, not only in the prefent poffeffor, but in thofe perfons to whom he fhould think proper to transfer it; which introduced the doctrine and practice of alienations, gifts, and contracts. But these precautions would be very short and imperfect, if they were confined to the life only of the occupier; for then upon his death all his goods would again become common, and create an infinite variety of strife and confusion. The law of very many societies has therefore given to the proprietor a right of continuing his property after his death, in such persons as he shall name; and, in defect of such appointment or nomination, the law of every society has directed the goods to be vested in certain particular individuals, exclusive of all other persons [a]. The former method of acquiring personal property, according to the express directions of the deceased, we call a *testament :* the latter, which is also according to the will of the deceased, not expressed indeed but presumed by the law [b], we call in England an *administration ;* being the same which the civil lawyers term a succession *ab inteflato,* and which answers to the descent or inheritance of real estates.

TESTAMENTS are of very high antiquity. We find them in use among the antient Hebrews; though I hardly think the example usually given [c], of Abraham's complaining [d] that, unless he had some children of his body, his steward Eliezer of Damascus would be his heir, is quite conclusive to shew that he had made him so by *will.* And indeed a learned writer [e] has adduced this very passage to prove, that in the patriarchal age, on failure of children or kindred, the servants born under their master's roof succeeded to the inheritance as heirs at law [f]. But, (to omit what Eusebius and others have related of Noah's testament, made in *writing* and witnessed under his *seal,* whereby he disposed of the whole world [g]) I apprehend that a much more authentic instance of the early use of testaments may be found in the sacred writings [h], wherein Jacob bequeaths to his son Jo-

[a] Puff. L. of N. b. 4. c. 10.
[b] *Ibid.* b 4. c. 11.
[c] Barbeyr. Puff. 4. 10. 4. Godolph. Orph. Leg. 1. 1.
[d] Gen. c. 15.
[e] Taylor's elem. civ. law. 517.
[f] See pag. 12.
[g] Selden. *de succ. Ebr. c.* 24.
[h] Gen. c. 48.

feph

feph a portion of his inheritance double to that of his brethren:
which will we find carried into execution many hundred years
afterwards, when the posterity of Joseph were divided into two
distinct tribes, those of Ephraim and Manasseh, and had two
several inheritances assigned them; whereas the descendents of
each of the other patriarchs formed only one single tribe, and
had only one lot of inheritance. Solon was the first legislator
that introduced wills into Athens[i]; but in many other parts of
Greece they were totally discountenanced[k]. In Rome they were
unknown, till the laws of the twelve tables were compiled, which
first gave the right of bequeathing[l]: and, among the northern
nations, particularly among the Germans[m], testaments were not
received into use. And this variety may serve to evince, that
the right of making wills, and disposing of property after death,
is merely a creature of the civil state[n]; which has permitted it
in some countries, and denied it in others: and, even where it
is permitted by law, it is subjected to different formalities and
restrictions in almost every nation under heaven[o].

WITH us in England this power of bequeathing is co-eval
with the first rudiments of the law: for we have no traces or
memorials of any time when it did not exist. Mention is made
of intestacy, in the old law before the conquest, as being merely
accidental; and the distribution of the intestate's estate, after
payment of the lord's heriot, is then directed to go according to
the established law. "*Sive quis incuria, sive morte repentina, fuerit
intestatus mortuus, dominus tamen nullam rerum suarum partem
(praeter eam quae jure debetur hereoti nomine) sibi assumito. Verum
possessiones uxori, liberis, et cognatione proximis, pro suo cuique
jure, distribuantur*[p]." But we are not to imagine, that the
power of bequeathing extended originally to *all* a man's personal
estate. On the contrary, Glanvil will inform us[q], that by the

[i] Plutarch. *in vita Solon.*
[k] Pott. Antiq. l. 4. c. 15.
[l] *Inst.* 2. 22. 1.
[m] Tacit. *de mor. Germ.* 21.
[n] See pag. 13.

[o] Sp. L. b. 27. c. 1. Vinnius *in Inst. l.2.
tit.* 10.
[p] LL. *Canut.* c. 68.
[q] *l.* 2. *c.* 5.

common law, as it ſtood in the reign of Henry the ſecond, a
man's goods were to be divided into three equal parts; of which
one went to his heirs or lineal deſcendants, another to his wife,
and the third was at his own diſpoſal: or if he died without a
wife, he might then diſpoſe of one moiety, and the other went
to his children; and ſo *e converſo*, if he had no children, the
wife was entitled to one moiety, and he might bequeath the o-
ther: but, if he died without either wife or iſſue, the whole was
at his own diſpoſal[r]. The ſhares of the wife and children was
called their *reaſonable* part; and the writ *de rationabili parte bo-*
norum was given to recover it[s].

THIS continued to be the law of the land at the time of *magna*
carta, which provides, that the king's debts ſhall firſt of all be
levied, and then the reſidue of the goods ſhall go to the executor to perform the will of the deceaſed: and, if nothing be owing
to the crown, " *omnia catalla cedant defuncto; ſalvis uxori ipſius*
" *et pueris ſuis rationabilibus partibus ſuis*[t]." In the reign of king
Edward the third this right of the wife and children was ſtill
held to be the univerſal or common law[u]; though frequently
pleaded as the local cuſtom of Berks, Devon, and other counties[w]: and ſir Henry Finch lays it down expreſſly[x], in the reign
of Charles the firſt, to be the general law of the land. But this
law is at preſent altered by imperceptible degrees, and the deceaſed may now by will bequeath the whole of his goods and
chattels; though we cannot trace out when firſt this alteration

[r] Bracton. *l. 2. c. 26.* Flet. *l. 2. c. 57.*
[s] F. N. B. 122.
[t] 9 Hen. III. c. 18.
[u] A widow brought an action of detinue
againſt her huſband's executors, *quod cum*
per conſuetudinem totius regni Angliae hactenus
uſitatam et approbatam, uxores debent et ſolent
a tempore &c, habere ſuam rationabilem par-
tem bonorum maritorum ſuorum: ita videlicet,
quod ſi nullos habuerint liberos, tunc medieta-
tem; et, ſi habuerint, tunc tertiam partem, &c;
and that her huſband died worth 200,000

marks, without iſſue had between them;
and thereupon ſhe claimed the moiety.
Some exceptions were taken to the pleadings, and the fact of the huſband's dying
without iſſue was denied; but the rule of
law, as ſtated in the writ, ſeems to have
been univerſally allowed. *(M. 30 Edw.*
III. 25.) And a ſimilar caſe occurs in
H. 17 *Edw. III. 9.*
[w] *Reg. Brev.* 142. Co. Litt. 176.
[x] Law. 175.

began. Indeed fir Edward Coke [y] is of opinion, that this never was the general law, but only obtained in particular places by fpecial cuftom : and to eftablifh that doctrine he relies on a paffage in Bracton, which in truth, when compared with the context, makes directly againft his opinion. For Bracton [z] lays down the doctrine of the *reafonable part* to be the common law ; but mentions that as a particular exception, which fir Edward Coke has haftily cited for the general rule. And Glanvil, *magna carta*, Fleta, the year-books, Fitzherbert, and Finch, do all agree with Bracton, that this right to the *pars rationabilis* was by the common law : which alfo continues to this day to be the general law of our fifter kingdom of Scotland [a]. To which we may add, that, whatever may have been the cuftom of later years in many parts of the kingdom, or however it was introduced in derogation of the old common law, the antient method continued in ufe in the province of York, the principality of Wales, and the city of London, till very modern times : when, in order to favour the power of bequeathing, and to reduce the whole kingdom to the fame ftandard, three ftatutes have been provided ; the one 4 & 5 W. & M. c. 2. explained by 2 & 3 Ann. c. 5. for the province of York ; another 7 & 8 W. III. c. 38. for Wales ; and a third, 11 Geo. I. c.18. for London : whereby it is enacted, that perfons within thofe diftricts, and liable to thofe cuftoms, may (if they think proper) difpofe of *all* their perfonal eftates by will ; and the claims of the widow, children, and other relations, to the contrary, are totally barred. Thus is the old common law now utterly abolifhed throughout all the kingdom of England, and a man may devife the whole of his chattels as freely, as he formerly could his third part or moiety. In difpofing of which, he was bound by the cuftom of many places (as was ftated in a former chapter [b]) to remember his lord and the church, by leaving them his two beft chattels, which was the original of heriots and mortuaries ; and afterwards he was left at his own liberty, to bequeath the remainder as he pleafed.

[y] 2 Inft. 33.
[z] *l.* 2. *c.* 26. §. 2.

[a] Dalrymp. of feud. property. 145.
[b] pag. 426.

I N

IN case a person made no disposition of such of his goods as were testable, whether that were only part or the whole of them, he was, and is, said to die intestate; and in such cases it is said, that by the old law the king was entitled to seise upon his goods, as the *parens patriae*, and general trustee of the kingdom[c]. This prerogative the king continued to exercise for some time by his own ministers of justice; and probably in the county court, where matters of all kinds were determined: and it was granted as a franchise to many lords of manors, and others, who have to this day a prescriptive right to grant administration to their intestate tenants and suitors, in their own courts baron and other courts, or to have their wills there proved, in case they made any disposition[d]. Afterwards the crown, in favour of the church, invested the prelates with this branch of the prerogative; which was done, saith Perkins[e], because it was intended by the law, that spiritual men are of better conscience than laymen, and that they had more knowlege what things would conduce to the benefit of the soul of the deceased. The goods therefore of intestates were given to the ordinary by the crown; and he might seise them, and keep them without wasting, and also might give, alien, or sell them at his will, and dispose of the money *in pios usus*: and, if he did otherwise, he broke the confidence which the law reposed in him[f]. So that properly the whole interest and power, which were granted to the ordinary, were only those of being the king's almoner within his diocese; in trust to distribute the intestate's goods in charity to the poor, or in such superstitious uses as the mistaken zeal of the times had denominated pious[g]. And, as he had thus the disposition of intestates effects, the probate of wills of course followed: for it was thought just and natural, that the will of the deceased should be proved to the satisfaction of the prelate, whose right of distributing his chattels for the good of his soul was effectually superseded thereby.

[c] 9 Rep. 38.
[d] *Ibid.* 37.
[e] §. 486.
[f] Finch, Law. 173, 174.
[g] Plowd. 277.

THE

THE goods of the inteſtate being thus veſted in the ordinary upon the moſt ſolemn and conſcientious truſt, the reverend prelates were therefore not accountable to any, but to God and themſelves, for their conduct [h]. But even in Fleta's time it was complained [i], "*quod ordinarii, hujuſmodi bona nomine eccleſiae occu-*"*pantes, nullam vel ſaltem indebitam faciunt diſtributionem.*" And to what a length of iniquity this abuſe was carried, moſt evidently appears from a gloſs of pope Innocent IV [k], written about the year 1250; wherein he lays it down for eſtabliſhed canon law, that "*in Britannia tertia pars bonorum decedentium ab inteſtato in* "*opus eccleſiae et pauperum diſpenſanda eſt.*" Thus the popiſh clergy took to themſelves [l] (under the name of the church and poor) the whole reſidue of the deceaſed's eſtate, after the *partes rationabiles*, or two thirds, of the wife and children were deducted; without paying even his lawful debts, or other charges thereon. For which reaſon it was enacted by the ſtatute of Weſtm. 2. [m] that the ordinary ſhall be bound to pay the debts of the inteſtate ſo far as his goods will extend, in the ſame manner that executors were bound in caſe the deceaſed had left a will : a uſe more truly pious, than any *requiem*, or maſs for his ſoul. This was the firſt check given to that exorbitant power, which the law had entruſted with ordinaries. But, though they were now made liable to the creditors of the inteſtate for their juſt and lawful demands, yet the *reſiduum*, after payment of debts, remained ſtill in their hands, to be applied to whatever purpoſes the conſcience of the ordinary ſhould approve. The flagrant abuſes of which power occaſioned the legiſlature again to interpoſe, in order to prevent the ordinaries from keeping any longer the adminiſtration in their own hands, or thoſe of their immediate de-

[h] Plowd. 277.
[i] *l.* 2. *c.* 57. §. 10.
[k] *in Decretal. l.* 5. *t.* 3. c. 42.
[l] The proportion given to the prieſt, and to other pious uſes, was different in different countries. In the archdeaconry of Rich-

mond in York ſhire, this proportion was ſettled by a papal bulle *A. D.* 1254. (*Regiſt. honoris de Richm.* 101.) and was obſerved till aboliſhed by the ſtatute 26 Hen. VIII. c. 15.
[m] 13 Edw. I. c. 19.

pendents : and therefore the ftatute 31 Edw. III. c. 11. provides, that, in cafe of inteftacy, the ordinary fhall depute the neareft
and moft lawful friends of the deceafed to adminifter his goods ;
which adminiftrators are put upon the fame footing, with regard
to fuits and to accounting, as executors appointed by will. This
is the original of adminiftrators, as they at prefent ftand ; who
are only the officers of the ordinary, appointed by him in purfuance of this ftatute, which fingles out the *next and moft lawful
friend* of the inteftate ; who is interpreted [n] to be the *next of
blood* that is under no legal difabilities. The ftatute 21 Hen. VIII.
c. 5. enlarges a little more the power of the ecclefiaftical judge ;
and permits him to grant adminiftration *either* to the widow, *or*
the next of kin, *or* to both of them, at his own difcretion ; and,
where two or more perfons are in the fame degree of kindred,
gives the ordinary his election to accept whichever he pleafes.

UPON this footing ftands the general law of adminiftrations
at this day. I fhall, in the farther progrefs of this chapter, mention a few more particulars, with regard to who may, and who
may not, be adminiftrator ; and what he is bound to do when
he has taken this charge upon him : what has been hitherto remarked only ferving to fhew the original and gradual progrefs of
teftaments and adminiftrations ; in what manner the latter was
firft of all vefted in the bifhops by the royal indulgence ; and
how it was afterwards, by authority of parliament, taken from
them in effect, by obliging them to commit all their power to
particular perfons nominated exprefsly by the law.

I PROCEED now, *fecondly*, to enquire who may, or may not,
make a teftament ; or what perfons are abfolutely obliged by law
to die inteftate. And this law [o] is entirely prohibitory ; for, regularly, every perfon hath full power and liberty to make a will,
that is not under fome fpecial prohibition by law or cuftom :
which prohibitions are principally upon three accounts ; for want

---

[n] 9 Rep. 39.   [o] Godolph. Orph. Leg. *p.* 1. *c.* 7.

of

of fufficient difcretion; for want of fufficient liberty and free
will; and on account of their criminal conduct.

1. IN the firft fpecies are to be reckoned infants under the age
of fourteen if males, and twelve if females; which is the rule of
the civil law [p]. For, though fome of our common lawyers have
held that an infant of any age (even four years old) might make
a teftament [q], and others have denied that under eighteen he is
capable [r], yet as the ecclefiaftical court is the judge of every teftator's capacity, this cafe muft be governed by the rules of the
ecclefiaftical law. So that no objection can be admitted to the
will of an infant of fourteen, merely for want of age : but, if the
teftator was not of fufficient difcretion, whether at the age of fourteen or four and twenty, that will overthrow his teftament. Mad-
men, or otherwife *non compotes*, idiots or natural fools, perfons
grown childifh by reafon of old age or diftemper, fuch as have
their fenfes befotted with drunkennefs, --- all thefe are incapable,
by reafon of mental difability, to make any will fo long as fuch
difability lafts. To this clafs alfo may be referred fuch perfons as
are *born* deaf, blind, and dumb; who, as they want the common
inlets of underftanding, are incapable of having *animum teftandi*,
and their teftaments are therefore void.

2. SUCH perfons, as are inteftable for want of liberty or freedom of will, are by the civil law of various kinds; as prifoners,
captives, and the like [s]. But the law of England does not make
fuch perfons abfolutely inteftable ; but only leaves it to the difcretion of the court to judge, upon the confideration of the particular circumftances of durefs, whether or no fuch perfons could
be fuppofed to have *liberum animum teftandi*. And, with regard
to feme-coverts, our laws differ ftill more materially from the
civil. Among the Romans there was no diftinction; a married woman was as capable of bequeathing as a feme-fole [t]. But with us

[p] Godolph. p. 1. c. 8. Wentw. 212.
2 Vern. 104. 469. Gilb. Rep. 74.
[q] Perkins. §. 503.
[r] Co. Litt. 89.
[s] Godolph. p. 1. c. 9.
[t] *Ff.* 31. 1. 77.

a married woman is not only utterly incapable of devifing *lands*, being excepted out of the ftatute of wills, 34 & 35 Hen. VIII. c. 5. but alfo fhe is incapable of making a teftament of *chattels*, without the licence of her hufband. For all her perfonal chattels are abfolutely his own; and he may difpofe of her chattels real, or fhall have them to himfelf if he furvives her: it would be therefore extremely inconfiftent, to give her a power of defeating that provifion of the law, by bequeathing thofe chattels to another [v]. Yet by her hufband's licence fhe may make a teftament [u]; and the hufband, upon marriage, frequently covenants with her friends to allow her that licence: but fuch licence is more properly his affent; for, unlefs it be given to the particular will in queftion, it will not be a complete teftament, even though the hufband beforehand hath given her permiffion to make a will [w]. Yet it fhall be fufficient to repel the hufband from his general right of adminiftring his wife's effects; and adminiftration fhall be granted to her appointee, with fuch teftamentary paper annexed [x]. So that in reality the woman makes no will at all, but only fomething like a will [y]; operating in the nature of an appointment, the execution of which the hufband by his bond, agreement, or covenant, is bound to allow. A diftinction fimilar to which, we meet with in the civil law. For, though a fon who was *in poteftate parentis* could not by any means make a formal and legal teftament, even though his father permitted it [z], yet he might, with the like permiffion of his father, make what was called a *donatio mortis caufa* [a]. The queen confort is an exception to this general rule, for fhe may difpofe of her chattels by will, without the confent of her lord [b]: and any feme-covert may make her will of goods, which are in her poffeffion *in auter droit*, as executrix or adminiftratix; for thefe can never be the property of the hufband [c]: and, if fhe has any pinmoney or feparate maintenance, it is faid fhe may difpofe of her favings thereout by teftament, without the control of

[v] 4 Rep. 51.
[u] Dr & St. d. 1. c. 7.
[w] Bro. *Abr. tit devife.* 34. Stra. 891.
[x] *The king v. di Pettefworth.* T. 13 Geo. II. B. R.
[y] Cro. Car. 376. 1 Mod. 211.
[z] *Ff.* 28. 1. 6.
[a] *Ff.* 39. 6. 25.
[b] Co. Litt. 133.
[c] Godolph. 1. 10.

her

her hufband[d]. But, if a feme-fole makes her will, and afterwards marries, fuch fubfequent marriage is efteemed a revocation in law, and intirely vacates the will[e].

3. PERSONS incapable of making teftaments, on account of their criminal conduct, are in the firft place all traitors and felons, from the time of conviction; for then their goods and chattels are no longer at their own difpofal, but forfeited to the king. Neither can a *felo de fe* make a will of goods and chattels, for they are forfeited by the act and manner of his death; but he may make a devife of his lands, for they are not fubjected to any forfeiture[f]. Outlaws alfo, though it be but for debt, are incapable of making a will, fo long as the outlawry fubfifts, for their goods and chattels are forfeited during that time[g]. As for perfons guilty of other crimes, fhort of felony, who are by the civil law precluded from making teftaments, (as ufurers, libellers, and others of a worfe ftamp) at the common law their teftaments may be good[h]. And in general the rule is, and has been fo at leaft ever fince Glanvil's time[j], *quod libera fit cujufcunque ultima voluntas.*

LET us next, *thirdly*, confider what this laft will and teftament is, which almoft every one is thus at liberty to make; or the nature and incidents of a teftament. Teftaments both Juftinian[i] and fir Edward Coke[k] agree to be fo called, becaufe they are *teftatio mentis*; an etymon, which feems to favour too much of the conceit; it being plainly a fubftantive derived from the verb *teftari*, in like manner as *juramentum, incrementum,* and others, from other verbs. The definition of the old Roman lawyers is much better than their etymology; " *voluntatis nof-* " *trae jufta fententia de eo, quod quis poft mortem fuam fieri velit* [l]:" which may be thus rendered into Englifh, " the legal declara- " tion of a man's intentions, which he wills to be performed af-

[d] Prec. Chan. 44.

[e] 4 Rep. 60. 2 P. W[ms]. 624.

[f] Plowd. 261.

[g] Fitzh. *Abr. t. defcent.* 16.

[h] Godolph. p. 1. c. 12.

[j] *l.* 7. *c.* 5.

[i] *Inft.* 2. 10.

[k] 1 Inft. 111. 322.

[l] *Ff.* 28. 1. 1.

" ter his death." It is called *sententia* to denote the circumspection and prudence with which it is supposed to be made : it is *voluntatis nostrae sententia*, because it's efficacy depends on it's declaring the testator's intention, whence in England it is emphatically stiled his *will:* it is *justa sententia* ; that is, drawn, attested, and published with all due solemnities and forms of law : It is *de eo, quod quis post mortem suam fieri velit*, because a testament is of no force till after the death of the testator.

THESE testaments are divided into two sorts; *written*, and *verbal* or *nuncupative* ; of which the former is committed to writing, the latter depends merely upon oral evidence, being declared by the testator *in extremis* before a sufficient number of witnesses, and afterwards reduced to writing. A *codicil, codicillus*, a little book or writing, is a supplement to a will ; or an addition made by the testator, and annexed to, and to be taken as part of, a testament : being for it's explanation, or alteration, or to make some addition to, or else some subtraction from, the former dispositions of the testator[m]. This may also be either written or nuncupative.

BUT, as *nuncupative* wills and codicils, (which were formerly more in use than at present, when the art of writing is become more universal) are liable to great impositions, and may occasion many perjuries, the statute of frauds, 29 Car. II. c. 3. enacts; 1. That no written will shall be revoked or altered by a subsequent nuncupative one, except the same be in the lifetime of the testator reduced to writing, and read over to him, and approved ; and unless the same be proved to have been so done by the oaths of three witnesses at the least ; who, by statute 4 & 5 Ann. c.16. must be such as are admissible upon trials at common law. 2. That no nuncupative will shall in any wife be good, where the estate bequeathed exceeds 30*l*, unless proved by three such witnesses, present at the making thereof (the Roman law requiring seven[n]) and unless they or some of them were specially required to bear

[m] Godolph. p. 1. c. 1. §. 3.   [n] *Inst.* 2. 10. 14.

witness

witnefs thereto by the teftator himfelf, and unlefs it was made in his laft ficknefs, in his own habitation or dwelling-houfe, or where he had been previoufly refident ten days at the leaft, except he be furprized with ficknefs on a journey, or from home, and dies without returning to his dwelling. 3. That no nuncupative will fhall be proved by the witneffes after fix months from the making, unlefs it were put in writing within fix days. Nor fhall it be proved till fourteen days after the death of the teftator, nor till procefs hath firft iffued to call in the widow, or next of kin, to conteft it if they think proper. Thus has the legiflature provided againft any frauds in fetting up nuncupative wills, by fo numerous a train of requifites, that the thing itfelf is fallen into difufe; and hardly ever heard of, but in the only inftance where favour ought to be fhewn to it, when the teftator is furprized by fudden and violent ficknefs. The teftamentary words muft be fpoken with an intent to bequeath, not any loofe idle difcourfe in his illnefs; for he muft require the by-ftanders to bear witnefs of fuch his intention : the will muft be made at home, or among his family or friends, unlefs by unavoidable accident; to prevent impofitions from ftrangers : it muft be in his *laft* ficknefs; for, if he recovers, he may alter his difpofitions, and has time to make a written will : it muft not be proved at too long a diftance from the teftator's death, left the words fhould efcape the memory of the witneffes; nor yet too haftily and without notice, left the family of the teftator fhould be put to inconvenience, or furprized.

As to *written* wills, they need not any witnefs of their publication. I fpeak not here of devifes of lands, which are entirely another thing, a conveyance by ftatute, unknown to the feodal or common law, and not under the fame jurifdiction as perfonal teftaments. But a teftament of chattels, written in the teftator's own hand, though it has neither his name nor feal to it, nor witneffes prefent at it's publication, is good; provided fufficient proof can be had that it is his hand-writing°. And though written in another man's hand, and never figned by the teftator, yet

° Godolph. p. r. c. 21. Gilb. Rep. 260.

if

if proved to be according to his inftructions and approved by him, it hath been held a good teftament of the perfonal eftate [p]. Yet it is the fafer, and more prudent way, and leaves lefs in the breaft of the ecclefiaftical judge, if it be figned or fealed by the teftator, and publifhed in the prefence of witneffes ; which laft was always required in the time of Bracton [q] ; or, rather, he in this refpect has implicitly copied the rule of the civil law.

N o teftament is of any effect till after the death of the teftator. " *Nam omne teftamentum morte confummatum eft ; et voluntas* " *teftatoris eft ambulatoria ufque ad mortem* [r]." And therefore, if there be many teftaments, the laft overthrows all the former [s]: but the republication of a former will revokes one of a later date, and eftablifhes the firft again [t].

H E N C E it follows, that teftaments may be avoided three ways : 1. If made by a perfon labouring under any of the incapacities before-mentioned : 2. By making another teftament of a later date: and, 3. By cancelling or revoking it. For, though I make a laft will and teftament irrevocable in the ftrongeft words, yet I am at liberty to revoke it : becaufe my own act or words cannot alter the difpofition of law, fo as to make that irrevocable, which is in it's own nature revocable [u]. For this, faith lord Bacon [w], would be for a man to deprive himfelf of that, which of all other things is moft incident to human condition ; and that is, alteration or repentance. It hath alfo been held, that, without an exprefs revocation, if a man, who hath made his will, afterwards marries and hath a child, this is a prefumptive or implied revocation of his former will, which he made in his ftate of celibacy [x]. The Romans were alfo wont to fet afide teftaments as being *inofficiofa*, deficient in natural duty, if they difinherited or totally paffed by (without affigning a true and

[p] Comyns. 452, 3, 4.
[q] *l*. 2. *c*. 26.
[r] Co. Litt. 112.
[s] Litt. §. 168. Perk. 478.

[t] Perk. 479.
[u] 8 Rep. 82.
[w] Elem. c. 19.
[x] Lord Raym. 441. 1 P. W[ms]. 304.

　　　　　　　　　　　　　　　　　　　　　　　　fufficient

fufficient reafon[y]) any of the children of the teftator[z]. But if the child had any legacy, though ever fo fmall, it was a proof that the teftator had not loft his memory or his reafon, which otherwife the law prefumed; but was then fuppofed to have acted thus for fome fubftantial caufe: and in fuch cafe no *querela inofficiofi teftamenti* was allowed. Hence probably has arifen that groundlefs vulgar error, of the neceffity of leaving the heir a fhilling or fome other exprefs legacy, in order to difinherit him effectually: whereas the law of England makes no fuch wild fuppofitions of forgetfulnefs or infanity; and therefore, though the heir or next of kin be totally omitted, it admits no *querela inofficiofi*, to fet afide fuch a teftament.

WE are next to confider, *fourthly*, what is an executor, and what is an adminiftrator; and how they are both to be appointed.

AN executor is he to whom another man commits by will the execution of that his laft will and teftament. And all perfons are capable of being executors, that are capable of making wills, and many others befides; as feme-coverts, and infants: nay, even infants unborn, or *in ventre fa mere*, may be made executors[a]. But no infant can act as fuch till the age of feventeen years; till which time adminiftration muft be granted to fome other, *durante minore aetate*[b]. In like manner as it may be granted *durante abfentia*, or *pendente lite*; when the executor is out of the realm[c], or when a fuit is commenced in the ecclefiaftical court touching the validity of the will[d]. This appointment of an executor is effential to the making of a will[e]: and it may be performed either by exprefs words, or fuch as ftrongly imply the fame. But if the teftator makes his will, without naming any executors, or if he names incapable perfons, or if the executors named refufe to act; in any of thefe cafes, the ordinary muft

[y] See Book I. ch. 16.
[z] *Inft.* 2. 18. 1.
[a] Weft. Symb. p. 1. §. 635.
[b] Went. Off. Ex. c. 18.

[c] 1 Lutw. 342.
[d] 2 P. W[ms]. 589, 590.
[e] Wentw. c. 1. Plowd. 281.

grant adminiſtration *cum teſtamento annexo*[f] to ſome other perſon; and then the duty of the adminiſtrator, as alſo when he is conſtituted only *durante minore aetate, &c,* of another, is very little different from that of an executor. And this was law ſo early as the reign of Henry II, when Glanvil[g] informs us, that "*teſta-* "*menti executores eſſe debent ii, quos teſtator ad hoc elegerit, et cu-* "*ram ipſe commiſerit: ſi vero teſtator nullos ad hoc nominaverit,* "*poſſunt propinqui et conſanguinei ipſius defuncti ad id faciendum ſe* "*ingerere.*"

BUT if the deceaſed died totally inteſtate, without making either will or executors, then general letters of adminiſtration muſt be granted by the ordinary to ſuch adminiſtrator as the ſtatutes of Edward the third, and Henry the eighth, before-mentioned, direct. In conſequence of which we may obſerve; 1. That the ordinary is compellable to grant adminiſtration of the goods and chattels of the wife, to the huſband, or his repreſentatives[h]: and, of the huſband's effects, to the widow, or next of kin; but he may grant it to either, or both, at his diſcretion[i]. 2. That, among the kindred, thoſe are to be preferred that are the neareſt in degree to the inteſtate; but, of perſons in equal degree, the ordinary may take which he pleaſes[k] 3. That this *nearneſs* or propinquity of degree ſhall be reckoned according to the computation of the civilians[l]; and not of the canoniſts, which the law of England adopts in the deſcent of real eſtates[m]: becauſe in the civil computation the inteſtate himſelf is the *terminus, a quo* the ſeveral degrees are numbered; and not the common anceſtor, according to the rule of the canoniſts. And therefore in the firſt place the children, or (on failure of children) the parents of the deceaſed, are intitled to the adminiſtration: both which are indeed in the firſt degree; but with us[n] the children

[f] 1 Roll. Abr. 907. Comb. 20.
[g] *l.* 7. *c.* 6.
[h] Cro. Car. 106. Stat. 29 Car. II. c. 3.
[i] P. Wms. 381.
[j] Salk. 36. Stra. 532.

[k] Stat. 28 Hen. VIII. c. 5. See pag. 496.
[l] Prec. Chanc. 593.
[m] See pag. 203. 207. 224.
[n] Godolph. p. 2. c. 34. §. 1. 2 Vern. 125.

are

are allowed the preference [o]. Then follow brothers [p], grandfathers [q], uncles or nephews [r], (and the females of each claſs reſpectively) and laſtly couſins. 4. The half blood is admitted to the adminiſtration as well as the whole: for they are of the kindred of the inteſtate, and only excluded from inheritances of land upon feodal reaſons. Therefore the brother of the half blood ſhall exclude the uncle of the whole blood [s]: and the ordinary may grant adminiſtration to the ſiſter of the half, or the brother of the whole blood, at his own diſcretion [t]. 5. If none of the kindred will take out adminiſtration, a creditor may, by cuſtom, do it [u]. 6. If the executor refuſes, or dies inteſtate, the adminiſtration may be granted to the reſiduary legatee, in excluſion of the next of kin [w]. And, laſtly, the ordinary may, in defect of all theſe, commit adminiſtration (as he might have done [x] before the ſtatute Edw. III.) to ſuch diſcreet perſon as he approves of: or may grant him letters *ad colligendum bona defuncti*, which neither make him executor nor adminiſtrator; his only buſineſs being to keep the goods in his ſafe cuſtody [y], and to do other acts for the benefit of ſuch as are entitled to the property of the deceaſed [z]. If a baſtard, who has no kindred, being *nullius filius*, or any one elſe that has no kindred, dies inteſtate and without wife or child, it hath formerly been held [a] that the ordinary might ſeiſe his goods, and diſpoſe of them *in pios uſus*. But the

[o] In Germany there was long a diſpute, whether a man's children ſhould inherit his effects during the life of their grandfather; which depends (as we ſhall ſee hereaſter) on the ſame principles as the granting of adminiſtrations. At laſt it was agreed at the diet of Arenſberg, about the middle of the tenth century, that the point ſhould be decided by combat. Accordingly, an equal number of champions being choſen on both ſides, thoſe of the children obtained the victory; and ſo the law was eſtabliſhed in their favour, that the iſſue of a perſon deceaſed ſhall be intitled to his goods and chattels in preference to his parents. (Mod. Un. Hiſt. xxix. 28.)

[p] Harris *in Nov.* 118. *c.* 2.

[q] Prec. Chanc. 527. 1 P. Wms. 41.

[r] Atk. 455.

[s] 1 Ventr. 425.

[t] Aleyn. 36. Styl. 74.

[u] Salk. 38.

[w] 1 Sid. 281. 1 Ventr. 219.

[x] Plowd. 278.

[y] Went. ch. 14.

[z] 2 Inſt. 398.

[a] Salk. 37.

ufual courfe now is for fome one to procure letters patent, or other authority, from the king; and then the ordinary of courfe grants adminiftration to fuch appointee of the crown [b].

THE intereft, vefted in an executor by the will of the deceafed, may be continued and kept alive by the will of the fame executor: fo that the executor of A's executor is to all intents and purpofes the executor and reprefentative of A himfelf [c]: but the executor of A's adminiftrator, or the adminiftrator of A's executor, is not the reprefentative of A [d]. For the power of an executor is founded upon the fpecial confidence and actual appointment of the deceafed; and fuch executor is therefore allowed to tranfmit that power to another, in whom he has equal confidence: but the adminiftrator of A is merely the officer of the ordinary, prefcribed to him by act of parliament, in whom the deceafed has repofed no truft at all; and therefore, on the death of that officer, it refults back to the ordinary to appoint another. And, with regard to the adminiftrator of A's executor, he has clearly no privity or relation to A; being only commiffioned to adminifter the effects of the inteftate executor, and not of the original teftator. Wherefore, in both thefe cafes, and whenever the courfe of reprefentation from executor to executor is interrupted by any one adminiftration, it is neceffary for the ordinary to commit adminiftration afrefh, *of the goods* of the deceafed *not* adminiftred by the former executor or adminiftrator. And this adminiftrator, *de bonis non*, is the only legal reprefentative of the deceafed in matters of perfonal property [e]. But he may, as well as an original adminiftrator, have only a *limited* or *fpecial* adminiftration committed to his care, viz. of certain fpecific effects, fuch as a term of years and the like; the reft being committed to others [f].

[b] 3 P. W^{ms}. 33.
[c] Stat. 25 Edw. III. ft. 5. c. 5. 1 Leon. 275.
[d] Bro. *Abr. tit. adminiftrator.* 7.

[e] Styl. 225.
[f] 1 Roll. Abr. 908. Godolph. p. 2. c. 30. Salk. 36.

HAVING

HAVING thus fhewn what is, and who may be, an execu-
tor or adminiftrator, I proceed now, *fifthly* and laftly, to enquire
into fome few of the principal points of their office and duty.
Thefe in general are very much the fame in both executors and
adminiftrators; excepting, firft, that the executor is bound to
perform a will, which an adminiftrator is not, unlefs where a
teftament is annexed to his adminiftration, and then he differs
ftill lefs from an executor : and, fecondly, that an executor may
do many acts before he proves the will.[g], but an adminiftrator
may do nothing till letters of adminiftration are iffued; for the
former derives his power from the will and not from the probate[h],
the latter owes his entirely to the appointment of the ordinary.
If a ftranger takes upon him to act as executor, without any juft
authority (as by intermeddling with the goods of the deceafed[i],
and many other tranfactions[k]) he is called in law an executor of
his own wrong, *de fon tort*, and is liable to all the trouble of an
executorfhip, without any of the profits or advantages : but
merely doing acts of neceffity or humanity, as locking up the
goods, or burying the corpfe of the deceafed, will not amount
to fuch an intermeddling, as will charge a man as executor of his
own wrong[l]. Such a one cannot bring an action himfelf in right
of the deceafed[m], but actions may be brought againft him. And, in
all actions by creditors againft fuch an officious intruder, he fhall
be named an executor, generally[n]; for the moft obvious conclufion, which ftrangers can form from his conduct, is that he
hath a will of the deceafed, wherein he is named executor, but
hath not yet taken probate thereof[o]. He is chargeable with the
debts of the deceafed, fo far as affets come to his hands[p] : and,
as againft creditors in general, fhall be allowed all payments made
to any other creditor in the fame or a fuperior degree[q], himfelf

[g] Wentw. ch. 3.
[h] Comyns. 151.
[i] 5 Rep. 33, 34.
[k] Wentw. ch. 14. Stat. 43 Eliz. c. 8.
[l] Dyer. 166.

[m] Bro. *Abr. t. adminiftrator.* 8.
[n] 5 Rep. 31.
[o] 12 Mod. 471.
[p] Dyer. 166.
[q] 1 Chan Caf. 33.

only excepted [r]. And though, as againſt the rightful executor or adminiſtrator, he cannot plead ſuch payment, yet it ſhall be allowed him in mitigation of damages [s]; unleſs perhaps upon a deficiency of aſſets, whereby the rightful executor may be prevented from ſatisfying his own debt [t]. But let us now ſee what are the power and duty of a rightful executor or adminiſtrator.

1. HE muſt *bury* the deceaſed in a manner ſuitable to the eſtate which he leaves behind him. Neceſſary funeral expences are allowed, previous to all other debts and charges; but if the executor or adminiſtrator be extravagant, it is a ſpecies of *devaſtation* or waſte of the ſubſtance of the deceaſed, and ſhall only be prejudicial to himſelf, and not to the creditors or legatees of the deceaſed [u].

2. THE executor, or the adminiſtrator *durante minore aetate*, or *durante abſentia*, or *cum teſtamento annexo*, muſt *prove the will* of the deceaſed : which is done either in *common form*, which is only upon his own oath before the ordinary, or his ſurrogate; or *per teſtes*, in more ſolemn form of law, in caſe the validity of the will be diſputed [w]. When the will is ſo proved, the original muſt be depoſited in the regiſtry of the ordinary; and a copy thereof in parchment is made out under the ſeal of the ordinary, and delivered to the executor or adminiſtrator, together with a certificate of it's having been proved before him : all which together is uſually ſtiled the *probate*. In defect of any will, the perſon entitled to be adminiſtrator muſt alſo at this period take out letters of adminiſtration under the ſeal of the ordinary; whereby an executorial power to collect and adminiſter, that is, diſpoſe of the goods of the deceaſed, is veſted in him : and he muſt, by ſtatute 22 & 23 Car. II. c. 10. enter into a bond with ſureties, faithfully to execute his truſt. If all the goods of the deceaſed lie within the ſame juriſdiction, a probate before the

[r] 5 Rep. 30. Moor. 527.
[s] 12 Mod. 441. 471.
[t] Wentw. ch. 14.

[u] Salk. 196. Godolph. p. 2. c. 26. §. 2.
[w] Godolph. p. 1. c. 20. §. 4.

ordinary

ordinary, or an adminiſtration granted by him, are the only proper ones: but if the deceaſed had *bona notabilia*, or chattels to
the value of a *hundred ſhillings*, in two diſtinct dioceſes or juriſ-
dictions, then the will muſt be proved, or adminiſtration taken
out, before the metropolitan of the province, by way of ſpecial
prerogative[x]; whence the court where the validity of ſuch wills
is tried, and the office where they are regiſtered, are called the
prerogative court, and the prerogative office, of the provinces of
Canterbury and York. Lyndewode, who flouriſhed in the beginning of the fifteenth century, and was official to arch-biſhop
Chichele, interprets theſe hundred ſhillings to ſignify *ſolidos le-
gales*; of which he tells us ſeventy two amounted to a pound of
gold, which in his time was valued at fifty nobles or 16 *l.* 13 *s.* 4 *d.*
He therefore computes[y] that the hundred ſhillings, which conſtituted *bona notabilia*, were then equal in current money to 23 *l.*
3 *s.* 0¼ *d.* This will account for what is ſaid in our antient
books, that *bona notabilia* in the dioceſe of London[z], and indeed
every where elſe[a], were of the value of ten pounds by *compoſition:*
for, if we purſue the calculations of Lyndewode to their full extent, and conſider that a pound of gold is now almoſt equal in value
to an hundred and fifty nobles, we ſhall extend the preſent amount
of *bona notabilia* to nearly 70 *l.* But the makers of the canons of
1603 underſtood this antient rule to be meant of the ſhillings
current in the reign of James I, and have therefore directed[b] that
five pounds ſhall for the future be the ſtandard of *bona notabilia,*
ſo as to make the probate fall within the archiepiſcopal prerogative. Which prerogative (properly underſtood) is grounded
upon this reaſonable foundation: that, as the biſhops were
themſelves originally the adminiſtrators to all inteſtates in their
own dioceſe, and as the preſent adminiſtrators are in effect no
other than their officers or ſubſtitutes, it was impoſſible for
the biſhops, or thoſe who acted under them, to collect any
goods of the deceaſed, other than ſuch as lay within their own

---

[x] 4 Inſt. 335.
[y] *Provinc. l.* 3. *t.* 13. *c. item. v. centum. &
c. ſtatutum. v. laicis.*

[z] 4 Inſt. 335. Godolph. p. 2. c. 22.
[a] Plowd. 281.
[b] can. 92.

diocefes,

diocefes, beyond which their epifcopal authority extends not. But it would be extremely troublefome, if as many adminiftrations were to be granted, as there are diocefes within which the deceafed had *bona notabilia*; befides the uncertainty which creditors and legatees would be at, in cafe different adminiftrators were appointed, to afcertain the fund out of which their demands are to be paid. A prerogative is therefore very prudently vefted in the metropolitan of each province, to make in fuch cafes one adminiftration ferve for all. This accounts very fatisfactorily for the reafon of taking out adminiftration to inteftates, that have large and diffufive property, in the prerogative court: and the probate of wills naturally follows, as was before obferved, the power of granting adminiftrations; in order to fatisfy the ordinary that the deceafed has, in a legal manner, by appointing his own executor, excluded him and his officers from the privilege of adminiftring the effects.

3. THE executor or adminiftrator is to make an *inventory* [c] of all the goods and chattels, whether in poffeffion or action, of the deceafed; which he is to deliver in to the ordinary upon oath, if thereunto lawfully required.

4. HE is to *collect* all the goods and chattels fo inventoried; and to that end he has very large powers and interefts conferred on him by law; being the reprefentative of the deceafed [d], and having the fame property in his goods as the principal had when living, and the fame remedies to recover them. And, if there be two or more executors, a fale or releafe by one of them fhall be good againft all the reft [e]; but in cafe of adminiftrators it is otherwife [f]. Whatever is fo recovered, that is of a faleable nature and may be converted into ready money, is called *affets* in the hands of the executor or adminiftrator [g]; that is, fufficient or enough (from the French *affez*) to make him chargeable to a creditor or legatee, fo far as fuch goods and chattels extend.

[c] Stat. 21 Hen. VIII. c. 5.
[d] Co. Litt. 209.
[e] Dyer. 23.

[f] Atk. 460.
[g] See pag. 244.

What-

Whatever affets fo come to his hands he may convert into ready
money, to anfwer the demands that may be made upon him:
which are the next thing to be confidered; for,

5. THE executor or adminiftrator muft *pay* the *debts* of the
deceafed. In payment of debts he muft obferve the rules of priority; otherwife, on deficiency of affets, if he pays thofe of a
lower degree firft, he muft anfwer thofe of a higher out of his
own eftate. And, firft, he may pay all funeral charges, and the
expenfe of proving the will, and the like. Secondly, debts due
to the king on record or fpecialty [h]. Thirdly, fuch debts as are
by particular ftatutes to be preferred to all others; as the forfeitures for not burying in woollen [i], money due on poors rates [k],
for letters to the poft-office [l], and fome others. Fourthly, debts
of record; as judgments (docketted according to the ftatute
4 & 5 W. & M. c. 20.) ftatutes, and recognizances [m]. Fifthly,
debts due on fpecial contracts; as for rent, (for which the
leffor has often a better remedy in his own hands, by diftrain-
ing) or upon bonds, covenants, and the like, under feal [n].
Laftly, debts on fimple contracts, viz. upon notes unfealed,
and verbal promifes. Among thefe fimple contracts, fervants
wages are by fome [o] with reafon preferred to any other: and fo
ftood the antient law, according to Bracton [p] and Fleta [q], who
reckon, among the firft debts to be paid, *fervitia fervientium et
ftipendia famulorum.* Among debts of equal degree, the executor
or adminiftrator is allowed to pay himfelf firft; by retaining in
his hands fo much as his debt amounts to [r]. But an executor of
his own wrong is not allowed to retain: for that would tend to
encourage creditors to ftrive who fhould firft take poffeffion of the
goods of the deceafed; and would befides be taking advantage of
their own wrong, which is contrary to the rule of law [s]. If a

[h] 1 And. 129.
[i] Stat. 30 Car. II. c. 3.
[k] Stat. 17 Geo. II. c. 38.
[l] Stat. 9 Ann. c. 10.
[m] 4 Rep. 60. Cro. Car. 363.
[n] Wentw. ch. 12.

[o] 1 Roll. Abr 927.
[p] *l.* 2. *c.* 26.
[q] *l.* 2. *c.* 57. §. 10.
[r] 10 Mod. 496.
[s] 5 Rep. 30.

creditor

creditor conftitutes his debtor his executor, this is a releafe or difcharge of the debt, whether the executor acts or no [t]; provided there be affets fufficient to pay the teftator's debts: for, though this difcharge of the debt fhall take place of all legacies, yet it were unfair to defraud the teftator's creditors of their juft debts by a releafe which is abfolutely voluntary [u]. Alfo, if no fuit is commenced againft him, the executor may pay any one creditor in equal degree his whole debt, though he has nothing left for the reft : for, without a fuit commenced, the executor has no legal notice of the debt [w].

6. WHEN the debts are all difcharged, the *legacies* claim the next regard; which are to be paid by the executor fo far as his affets will extend : but he may not give himfelf the preference herein, as in the cafe of debts [x].

A LEGACY is a bequeft, or gift, of goods and chattels by teftament; and the perfon to whom it is given is ftiled the legatee : which every perfon is capable of being, unlefs particularly difabled by the common law or ftatutes, as traitors, papifts, and fome others. This bequeft transfers an inchoate property to the legatee ; but the legacy is not perfect without the affent of the executor : for if I have a *general* or *pecuniary* legacy of 100 *l*, or a *fpecific* one of a piece of plate, I cannot in either cafe take it without the confent of the executor [y]. For in him all the chattels are vefted; and it is his bufinefs firft of all to fee whether there is a fufficient fund left to pay the debts of the teftator: the rule of equity being, that a man muft be juft, before he is permitted to be generous; or, as Bracton expreffes the fenfe of our antient law [z], " *de bonis defuncti primo deducenda funt ea quae funt* " *neceffitatis, et poftea quae funt utilitatis, et ultimo quae funt vo-* " *luntatis.*" And in cafe of a deficiency of affets, all the *general* legacies muft abate proportionably, in order to pay the debts ;

[t] Plowd. 184. Salk. 299.
[u] Salk. 303. 1 Roll. Abr. 921.
[w] Dyer. 32. 2 Leon. 60.

[x] 2 Vern 434. 2 P. W[ms]. 25.
[y] Co. Litt. 111. Aleyn. 39.
[z] *l.* 2. *c.* 26.

but

but a *specific* legacy (of a piece of plate, a horse, or the like) is not to abate at all, or allow any thing by way of abatement, unless there be not sufficient without it[a]. Upon the same principle, if the legatees have been paid their legacies, they are afterwards bound to refund a ratable part, in case debts come in, more than sufficient to exhaust the *residuum* after the legacies paid[b]. And this law is as old as Bracton and Fleta, who tell us[c], "*si plura* "*sint debita, vel plus legatum fuerit, ad quae catalla defuncti non* "*sufficiant, fiat ubique defalcatio, excepto regis privilegio.*"

IF the legatee dies before the testator, the legacy is a lost or *lapsed* legacy, and shall sink into the *residuum*. And if a *contingent* legacy be left to any one; as, *when* he attains, or *if* he attains, the age of twenty one; and he dies before that time; it is a lapsed legacy[d]. But a legacy to one, *to be paid* when he attains the age of twenty one years, is a *vested* legacy; an interest which commences *in praesenti*, although it be *solvendum in futuro*: and, if the legatee dies before that age, his representatives shall receive it out of the testator's personal estate, at the same time that it would have become payable, in case the legatee had lived. This distinction is borrowed from the civil law[e]; and it's adoption in our courts is not so much owing to it's intrinsic equity, as to it's having been before adopted by the ecclesiastical courts. For, since the chancery has a concurrent jurisdiction with them, in regard to the recovery of legacies, it was reasonable that there should be a conformity in their determinations; and that the subject should have the same measure of justice in whatever court he sued[f]. But if such legacies be charged upon a real estate, in both cases they shall lapse for the benefit of the heir[g]; for, with regard to devises affecting lands, the ecclesiastical court hath no concurrent jurisdiction. And, in case of a vested legacy, due immediately, and charged on land or money in the funds, which yield an im-

[a] 2 Vern. 111.
[b] *Ibid.* 205.
[c] Bract. *l.* 2. *c.* 26. Flet. *l.* 2. *c.* 57. §.: 1.
[d] Dyer. 59. 1 Equ. Caf. abr. 295.
[e] *Ff.* 35. 1. 1 & 2.
[f] 1 Equ. Caf. abr. 295.
[g] 2 P. W^{ms}. 601.

mediate profit, intereſt ſhall be payable thereon from the teſtator's death ; but if charged only on the perſonal eſtate, which
cannot be immediately got in, it ſhall carry intereſt only from
the end of the year after the death of the teſtator [h].

BESIDES theſe formal legacies, contained in a man's will
and teſtament, there is alſo permitted another death-bed diſpoſition of property; which is called a donation *cauſa mortis*. And
that is, when a perſon in his laſt ſickneſs, apprehending his diſſolution near, delivers or cauſes to be delivered to another the
poſſeſſion of any perſonal goods, (under which have been included bonds, and bills drawn by the deceaſed upon his banker) to
keep in caſe of his deceaſe. This gift, if the donor dies, needs
not the aſſent of his executor : yet it ſhall not prevail againſt
creditors; and is accompanied with this implied truſt, that, if
the donor lives, the property thereof ſhall revert to himſelf, being
only given in contemplation of death, or *mortis cauſa* [i]. This
method of donation might have ſubſiſted in a ſtate of nature, being
always accompanied with delivery of actual poſſeſſion [k]; and ſo
far differs from a teſtamentary diſpoſition : but ſeems to have been
handed to us from the civil lawyers [l], who themſelves borrowed it
from the Greeks [m].

7. WHEN all the debts and particular legacies are diſcharged,
the ſurplus or *reſiduum* muſt be paid to the reſiduary legatee, if
any be appointed by the will; and, if there be none, it was long a
ſettled notion that it devolved to the executor's own uſe, by virtue
of his executorſhip [n]. But, whatever ground there might have
been formerly for this opinion, it ſeems now to be underſtood [o]
with this reſtriction; that, although where the executor has no
legacy at all the *reſiduum* ſhall in general be his own, yet where-

[h] 2 P. Wms. 26, 27.

[i] Prec. Chan. 269. 1 P. Wms. 406. 441.
3 P. Wms. 357.

[k] Law of forfeit. 16.

[l] *Inſt.* 2. 7. 1. *Ff. l.* 39. *t.* 6.

[m] There is a very complete *donatio mortis
cauſa*, in the Odyſſey b.17. v.78, made by

Telemachus to his friend Piraeus; and another by Hercules, in the Alceſtes of Euri-
pides, v. 1020.

[n] Perkins. 525.

[o] Prec. Chanc. 323. 1 P. Wms. 7. 544.
2 P. Wms. 338. 3 P. Wms. 43. 194. Stra. 559.

ever there is sufficient on the face of a will, (by means of a competent legacy or otherwise) to imply that the testator intended his executor should *not* have the residue, the undevised surplus of the estate shall go to the next of kin, the executor then standing upon exactly the same footing as an administrator: concerning whom indeed there formerly was much debate[p], whether or no he could be compelled to make any distribution of the intestate's estate. For, though (after the administration was taken in effect from the ordinary, and transferred to the relations of the deceased) the spiritual court endeavoured to compel a distribution, and took bonds of the administrator for that purpose, they were prohibited by the temporal courts, and the bonds declared void at law[q]. And the right of the husband not only to administer, but also to enjoy exclusively, the effects of his deceased wife, depends still on this doctrine of the common law: the statute 29 Car. II. declaring only that the statute of distributions does not extend to this case. But now these controversies are quite at an end; for by the statute 22 & 23 Car. II. c.10. it is enacted, that the surplusage of intestates' estates, except of femes covert[r], shall (after the expiration of one full year from the death of the intestate) be distributed in the following manner. One third shall go to the widow of the intestate, and the residue in equal proportions to his children, or, if dead, to their representatives; that is, their lineal descendants: if there are no children or legal representatives subsisting, then a moiety shall go to the widow, and a moiety to the next of kindred in equal degree and their representatives: if no widow, the whole shall go to the children: if neither widow nor children, the whole shall be distributed among the next of kin in equal degree, and their representatives: but no representatives are admitted, among collaterals, farther than the children of the intestate's brothers and sisters[s]. The next of kindred, here referred to, are to be investigated by the same rules of consanguinity, as those who are intitled to letters of administration; of whom we have sufficiently spoken[t]. And therefore by this statute

<hr>

[p] Godolph. p. 2. c. 32.
[q] 1 Lev. 233. Cart. 125. 2 P. Wms. 447.
[r] Stat. 29 Car. II. c. 3. §. 25.

[s] Raym. 496. Lord Raym. 571.
[t] pag. 504.

the

the mother, as well as the father, fucceeded to all the perfonal effects of their children, who died inteftate and without wife or iffue : in exclufion of the other fons and daughters, the brothers and fifters of the deceafed. And fo the law ftill remains with refpect to the father; but by ftatute 1 Jac. II. c. 17. if the father be dead, and any of the children die inteftate without wife or iffue, in the lifetime of the mother, fhe and each of the remaining children, or their reprefentatives, fhall divide his effects in equal portions.

I t is obvious to obferve, how near a refemblance this ftatute of diftributions bears to our antient Englifh law, *de rationabili parte bonorum,* fpoken of at the beginning of this chapter [u]; and which fir Edward Coke [w] himfelf, though he doubted the generality of it's reftraint on the power of devifing by will, held to be univerfally binding upon the adminiftrator or executor, in the cafe of either a total or partial inteftacy. It alfo bears fome refemblance to the Roman law of fucceffions *ab inteftato* [x] : which, and becaufe the act was alfo penned by an eminent civilian [y], has occafioned a notion that the parliament of England copied it from the Roman praetor : though indeed it is little more than a reftoration, with fome refinements and regulations, of our old conftitutional law ; which prevailed as an eftablifhed right and cuftom from the time of king Canute downwards, many centuries before Juftinian's laws were known or heard of in the weftern parts of Europe. So likewife there is another part of the ftatute of diftributions, where directions are given, that no child of the inteftate, (except his heir at law) on whom he fettled in his lifetime any eftate in lands, or pecuniary portion, equal to the diftributive fhares of the other children, fhall have any part of the furplufage with their brothers and fifters ; but if the eftates fo

[u] pag. 492.

[w] 2 Inft. 33.

[x] The general rule of fuch fucceffions was this : 1. The children or lineal defcendants in equal portions. 2. On failure of thefe, the parents cr lineal afcendants, and with them the brethren or fifters of the whole blood ; or, if the parents were dead,

all the brethren and fifters, together with the reprefentatives of a brother or fifter deceafed. 3. The next collateral relations in equal degree. 4. The hufband or wife of the deceafed. (*Ff.* 38. 15. 1. *Nov.* 118. *c.* 1, 2, 3. 127. *c.* 1.)

[y] Sir Walter Walker. Lord Raym. 574.

given

given them, by way of advancement, are not quite equivalent to the other shares, the children so advanced shall now have so much as will make them equal. This just and equitable provision hath been also said to be derived from the *collatio bonorum* of the imperial law [z]: which it certainly resembles in some points, though it differs widely in others. But it may not be amiss to observe, that, with regard to goods and chattels, this is part of the antient custom of London, of the province of York, and of our sister kingdom of Scotland: and, with regard to lands descending in coparcenary, that it hath always been, and still is, the common law of England, under the name of *hotchpot* [a].

BEFORE I quit this subject, I must however acknowlege, that the doctrine and limits of representation, laid down in the statute of distributions, seem to have been principally borrowed from the civil law: whereby it will sometimes happen, that personal estates are divided *per capita*, and sometimes *per stirpes*; whereas the common law knows no other rule of succession but that *per stirpes* only [b]. They are divided *per capita*, to every man an equal share, when all the claimants claim in their own rights, as in equal degree of kindred, and not *jure repraesentationis*, in the right of another person. As if the next of kin be the intestate's three brothers, A, B, and C; here his estate is divided into three equal portions, and distributed *per capita*, one to each: but if one of these brothers, A, had been dead leaving three children, and another, B, leaving two; then the distribution must have been *per stirpes*; viz. one third to A's three children, another third to B's two children, and the remaining third to C the surviving brother: yet if C had also been dead, without issue, then A's and B's five children, being all in equal degree to the intestate, would take in their own rights *per capita*, viz. each of them one fifth part [c].

THE statute of distributions expressly excepts and reserves the customs of the city of London, of the province of York, and

[z] *Ff*. 37. 6. 1.
[a] See ch. 12. pag. 191.
[b] See ch. 14. pag. 217.
[c] Prec. Chanc. 54.

of all other places having peculiar cuftoms of diftributing inteftates' effects. So that, though in thofe places the reftraint of devifing is removed by the ftatutes formerly mentioned [d], their antient cuftoms remain in full force, with refpect to the eftates of
inteftates. I fhall therefore conclude this chapter, and with it
the prefent book, with a few remarks on thofe cuftoms.

IN the firft place we may obferve, that in the city of London [e], and province of York [f], as well as in the kingdom of Scotland [g], and therefore probably alfo in Wales, (concerning which
there is little to be gathered, but from the ftatute 7 & 8 W. III.
c. 38.) the effects of the inteftate, after payment of his debts,
are in general divided according to the antient univerfal doctrine
of the *pars rationabilis*. If the deceafed leaves a widow and children, his fubftance (deducting the widow's apparel and furniture
of her bed-chamber, which in London is called the *widow's
chamber*) is divided into three parts; one of which belongs to the
widow, another to the children, and the third to the adminiftrator : if only a widow, or only children, they fhall refpectively,
in either cafe, take one moiety, and the adminiftrator the other [h]:
if neither widow nor child, the adminiftrator fhall have the
whole [i]. And this portion, or *dead man*'s part, the adminiftrator
was wont to apply to his own ufe [k], till the ftatute 1 Jac. II. c.17.
declared that the fame fhould be fubject to the ftatutes of diftribution. So that if a man dies worth 1800*l.* leaving a widow and
two children, the eftate fhall be divided into eighteen parts;
whereof the widow fhall have eight, fix by the cuftom and two
by the ftatute ; and each of the children five, three by the cuftom
and two by the ftatute : if he leaves a widow and one child, they
fhall each have a moiety of the whole, or nine fuch eighteenth
parts, fix by the cuftom and three by the ftatute : if he leaves
a widow and no child, the widow fhall have three fourths of
the whole, two by the cuftom and one by the ftatute ; and the

[d] pag. 493.
[e] Lord Raym. 1329.
[f] 2 Burn. eccl. law. 746.
[g] *Ibid.* 782.

[h] 1 P. W^ms. 341. Salk. 246.
[i] 2 Show. 175.
[k] 2 Freem. 85. 1 Vern. 133.

remaining fourth fhall go by the ftatute to the next of kin. It is alfo to be obferved, that if the wife be provided for by a join-ture before marriage, in bar of her cuftomary part, it puts her in a ftate of non-entity, with regard to the cuftom only[1]; but fhe fhall be intitled to her fhare of the dead man's part under the ftatute of diftributions, unlefs barred by fpecial agreement[m]. And if any of the children are advanced by the father in his life-time with any fum of money (not amounting to their full pro-portionable part) they fhall bring that portion into hotchpot with the reft of the brothers and fifters, but not with the widow, before they are intitled to any benefit under the cuftom[n]: but, if they are fully advanced, the cuftom intitles them to no farther dividend[o].

THUS far in the main the cuftoms of London and of York agree: but, befides certain other lefs material variations, there are two principal points in which they confiderably differ. One is, that in London the fhare of the children (or orphanage part) is not fully vefted in them till the age of twenty one, before which they cannot difpofe of it by teftament[p]: and, if they die under that age, whether fole or married, their fhare fhall furvive to the other children; but, after the age of twenty one, it is free from any orphanage cuftom, and, in cafe of inteftacy, fhall fall under the ftatute of diftributions[q]. The other, that in the province of York, the heir at common law, who inherits any lands either in fee or in tail, is excluded from any filial portion or reafonable part[r]. But, notwithftanding thefe provincial varia-tions, the cuftoms appear to be fubftantially one and the fame. And, as a fimilar policy formerly prevailed in every part of the ifland, we may fairly conclude the whole to be of Britifh origi-nal; or, if derived from the Roman law of fucceffions, to have been drawn from that fountain much earlier than the time of

[1] 2 Vern. 665.　3 P. Wms. 16.

[m] 1 Vern. 15.　2 Chan. Rep. 252.

[n] 2 Freem. 279.　1 Equ. caf. abr. 155. 2 P. Wms. 526.

[o] 2 P. Wms. 527.

[p] 2 Vern. 558.

[q] Prec. Chan. 537.

[r] 2 Burn. 754.

Juftinian,

Juftinian, from whofe conftitutions in many points (particularly in the advantages given to the widow) it very confiderably differs: though it is not improbable that the refemblances which yet remain may be owing to the Roman ufages; introduced in the time of Claudius Caefar, (who eftablifhed a colony in Britain to inftruct the natives in legal knowlege[s]) inculcated and diffufed by Papinian (who prefided at York as *praefectus praetorio* under the emperors Severus and Caracalla[t]) and continued by his fucceffors till the final departure of the Romans in the beginning of the fifth century after Chrift.

[s] Tacit. *Annal. l.* 12. *c.* 32. [t] Selden *in Fletam. cap.* 4. §. 3.

THE END OF THE SECOND BOOK.

APPENDIX.

N°. I.

Vetus Carta FEOFFAMENTI.

SCIANT prefentes et futuri, quod ego Willielmus, filius Wil- *Premifes.*
lielmi de Segenho, dedi, conceffi, et hac prefenti carta mea con-
firmavi, Johanni quondam filio Johannis de Saleford, pro qua-
dam fumma pecunie quam michi dedit pre manibus, unam acram terre
mee arabilis, jacentem in campo de Saleford, juxta terram quondam Ri-
chardi de la Mare : **Habendam et Tenendam** totam predictam acram *Habendum, and*
terre, cum omnibus ejus pertinentiis, prefato Johanni, et heredibus fuis, *Tenendum.*
et fuis affignatis, de capitalibus dominis feodi : **Reddendo** et faciendo *Reddendum.*
annuatim eifdem dominis capitalibus fervitia inde debita et confueta : **Et** *Warranty.*
ego predictus Willielmus, et heredes mei, et mei affignati, totam predictam acram terre, cum omnibus fuis pertinentiis, predicto Johanni de
Saleford, et heredibus fuis, et fuis affignatis, contra omnes gentes war-
rantizabimus in perpetuum. **In cujus** rei teftimonium huic prefenti car- *Conclufion.*
te figillum meum appofui : **Hiis** teftibus, Nigello de Saleford, Johanne
de Seybroke, Radulpho clerico de Saleford, Johanne molendario de eadem villa, et aliis. **Data** apud Saleford die Veneris proximo ante fef-
tum fancte Margarete virginis, anno regni regis EDWARDI filii regis
EDWARDI fexto.

(L. S.)

Memorandum, quod die et anno infrafcriptis *Livery of feifin*
plena et pacifica feifina acre infrafpecificate, cum *endorfed.*
pertinentiis, data et deliberata fuit per infranomi-
natum Willielmum de Segenho infranominato Johanni de Saleford, in propriis perfonis fuis, fecundum tenorem et effectum carte infrafcripte, in
prefentia Nigelli de Saleford, Johannis de Seybroke, et aliorum.

Nº. II.

A modern Conveyance by L E A S E *and* R E L E A S E.

§. I. L E A S E, *or* B A R G A I N *and* S A L E, *for a year.*

Premises.

𝕿 𝕳 𝕴 𝕾 𝕴𝖓𝖉𝖊𝖓𝖙𝖚𝖗𝖊, made the third day of September, in the twenty
firſt year of the reign of our ſovereign lord G E O R G E the ſecond
by the grace of God king of Great Britain, France, and Ireland, defender of the faith, and ſo forth, and in the year of our Lord one thou-
Parties. ſand, ſeven hundred, and forty ſeven, between Abraham Barker of Dale
Hall in the county of Norfolk, eſquire, and Cecilia his wife, of the one
part, and David Edwards of Lincoln's Inn in the county of Middleſex,
eſquire, and Francis Golding of the city of Norwich, clerk, of the
other part, witneſſeth ; that the ſaid Abraham Barker and Cecilia his
Conſideration. wife, in conſideration of five ſhillings of lawful money of Great Britain
to them in hand paid by the ſaid David Edwards and Francis Golding
at or before the enſealing and delivery of theſe preſents, (the receipt
whereof is hereby acknowleged,) and for other good cauſes and conſiderations them the ſaid Abraham Barker and Cecilia his wife hereunto
Bargain and ſpecially moving, 𝕳𝖆𝖛𝖊 bargained and ſold, and by theſe preſents do,
ſale. and each of them doth, bargain and ſell, unto the ſaid David Edwards
Parcels. and Francis Golding, their executors, adminiſtrators, and aſſigns, 𝕬𝖑𝖑
that the capital meſſuage, called Dale Hall in the pariſh of Dale in the
ſaid county of Norfolk, wherein the ſaid Abraham Barker and Cecilia
his wife now dwell, and all thoſe their lands in the ſaid pariſh of Dale
called or known by the name of Wilſon's farm, containing by eſtimation five hundred and forty acres, be the ſame more or leſs, together
with all and ſingular houſes, dovehouſes, barns, buildings, ſtables, yards,
gardens, orchards, lands, tenements, meadows, paſtures, feedings, commons, woods, underwoods, ways, waters, watercourſes, fiſhings, privileges, profits, eaſements, commodities, advantages, emoluments, hereditaments, and appurtenances whatſoever to the ſaid capital meſſuage
and farm belonging or appertaining, or with the ſame uſed or enjoyed,
or accepted, reputed, taken, or known, as part, parcel, or member
thereof, or as belonging to the ſame or any part thereof ; and the reverſion and reverſions, remainder and remainders, yearly and other rents,
Habendum. iſſues, and profits thereof, and of every part and parcel thereof: 𝕿𝖔
𝖍𝖆𝖛𝖊 𝖆𝖓𝖉 𝖙𝖔 𝖍𝖔𝖑𝖉 the ſaid capital meſſuage, lands, tenements, hereditaments, and all and ſingular other the premiſes herein before mentioned
or

or intended to be bargained and fold, and every part and parcel thereof,
with their and every of their rights, members, and appurtenances, unto
the faid David Edwards and Francis Golding, their executors, adminiftrators, and affigns, from the day next before the day of the date of
thefe prefents, for and during, and unto the full end and term of, one
whole year from thence next enfuing and fully to be complete and ended:
𝔜𝔦𝔢𝔩𝔡𝔦𝔫𝔤 and paying therefore unto the faid Abraham Barker, and Ce- *Reddendum.*
cilia his wife, and their heirs or affigns, the yearly rent of one peppercorn at the expiration of the faid term, if the fame fhall be lawfully demanded: 𝔗𝔬 𝔱𝔥𝔢 𝔦𝔫𝔱𝔢𝔫𝔱 and purpofe, that by virtue of thefe prefents, *Intent.*
and of the ftatute for transferring ufes into poffeffion, the faid David Edwards and Francis Golding may be in the actual poffeffion of the premifes,
and be thereby enabled to take and accept a grant and releafe of the freehold, reverfion, and inheritance of the fame premifes, and of every part
and parcel thereof, to them, their heirs, and affigns; to the ufes, and
upon the trufts, thereof to be declared by another indenture, intended
to bear date the day next after the day of the date hereof. 𝔍𝔫 𝔴𝔦𝔱𝔫𝔢𝔰𝔰 *Conclufion.*
whereof the parties to thefe prefents their hands and feals have fubfcribed
and fet, the day and year firft abovewritten.

Sealed, and delivered, being
  firft duly ftamped, in the   Abraham Barker. (L. S.)
    prefence of   Cecilia Barker. (L. S.)
      George Carter.   David Edwards. (L. S.)
      William Browne.   Francis Golding. (L. S.)

§. 2. *Deed of* RELEASE.

𝔗𝔥𝔦𝔰 𝔍𝔫𝔡𝔢𝔫𝔱𝔲𝔯𝔢 of five parts, made the fourth day of September, *Premifes.*
in the twenty-firft year of the reign of our fovereign lord GEORGE the
fecond by the grace of God king of Great Britain, France, and Ireland, defender of the faith, and fo forth, and in the year of our Lord
one thoufand, feven hundred, and forty-feven, between Abraham *Parties.*
Barker, of Dale Hall in the county of Norfolk, efquire, and Cecilia
his wife, of the firft part; David Edwards of Lincoln's Inn in the
county of Middlefex, efquire, executor of the laft will and teftament
of Lewis Edwards, of Cowbridge in the county of Glamorgan, gentleman, his late father, deceafed, and Francis Golding of the city of
Norwich, clerk, of the fecond part; Charles Browne of Enftone in
the county of Oxford, gentleman, and Richard More of the city of
Briftol, merchant, of the third part; John Barker, efquire, fon and
heir apparent of the faid Abraham Barker, of the fourth part; and
Katherine Edwards, fpinfter, one of the fifters of the faid David Ed-

wards,

wards, of the fifth part. *Whereas* a marriage is intended, by the per-
miſſion of God, to be ſhortly had and ſolemnized between the ſaid
John Barker and Katherine Edwards : *Now this Indenture witneſſeth*,
that in conſideration of the ſaid intended marriage, and of the ſum
of five thouſand pounds, of good and lawful money of Great Britain, to
the ſaid Abraham Barker, (by and with the conſent and agreement of
the ſaid John Barker, and Katherine Edwards, teſtified by their being
parties to, and their ſealing and delivery of, theſe preſents,) by the ſaid
David Edwards in hand paid at or before the enſealing and delivery hereof, being the marriage portion of the ſaid Katherine Edwards, bequeathed to her by the laſt will and teſtament of the ſaid Lewis Edwards, her
late father, deceaſed ; the receipt and payment whereof the ſaid Abraham Barker doth hereby acknowlege, and thereof, and of every part and
parcel thereof, they the ſaid Abraham Barker, John Barker, and Katherine Edwards, do, and each of them doth, releaſe, acquit, and diſcharge
the ſaid David Edwards, his executors, and adminiſtrators, for ever
by theſe preſents : and for providing a competent jointure and proviſion of maintenance for the ſaid Katherine Edwards, in caſe ſhe ſhall,
after the ſaid intended marriage had, ſurvive and overlive the ſaid
John Barker her intended huſband : and for ſettling and aſſuring the
capital meſſuage, lands, tenements, and hereditaments, hereinafter
mentioned, unto ſuch uſes, and upon ſuch truſts, as are hereinafter
expreſſed and declared : and for and in conſideration of the ſum of
five ſhillings of lawful money of Great Britain to the ſaid Abraham
Barker and Cecilia his wife in hand paid by the ſaid David Edwards
and Francis Golding, and of ten ſhillings of like lawful money to them
alſo in hand paid by the ſaid Charles Browne and Richard More, at or
before the enſealing and delivery hereof, (the ſeveral receipts whereof are
hereby reſpectively acknowleged,) they the ſaid Abraham Barker and

Cecilia his Wife, *Have*, and each of them hath, granted, bargained,
ſold, releaſed, and confirmed, and by theſe preſents do, and each of
them doth, grant, bargain, ſell, releaſe, and confirm unto the ſaid David

Edwards and Francis Golding, their heirs and aſſigns, *All* that the capital meſſuage called Dale Hall, in the pariſh of Dale in the ſaid county
of Norfolk, wherein the ſaid Abraham Barker and Cecilia his wife
now dwell, and all thoſe their lands in the ſaid pariſh of Dale called
or known by the name of Wilſon's farm, containing by eſtimation
five hundred and forty acres, be the ſame more or leſs, together with
all and ſingular houſes, dovehouſes, barns, buildings, ſtables, yards,
gardens, orchards, lands, tenements, meadows, paſtures, feedings,
commons, woods, underwoods, ways, waters, water-courſes, fiſhings,
privileges, profits, eaſements, commodities, advantages, emoluments,
hereditaments, and appurtenances whatſoever to the ſaid capital meſſuage and farm belonging or appertaining, or with the ſame uſed or
enjoyed,

enjoyed, or accepted, reputed, taken, or known, as part, parcel, or member thereof, or as belonging to the same or any part thereof ; (all which said premises are now in the actual poffeffion of the said David Edwards and Francis Golding, by virtue of a bargain and sale to them thereof made by the said Abraham Barker and Cecilia his wife for one whole year, in confideration of five fhillings to them paid by the said David Edwards and Francis Golding, in and by one indenture bearing date the day next before the day of the date hereof, and by force of the ftatute for transferring ufes into poffeffion ;) and the reverfion and reverfions, remainder and remainders, yearly and other rents, iffues, and profits thereof, and every part and parcel thereof, and alfo all the eftate, right, title, intereft, truft, property, claim, and demand whatfoever, both at law and in equity, of them the said Abraham Barker and Cecilia his wife, in, to, or out of, the said capital meffuage, lands, tenements, hereditaments, and premifes : **To have and to hold** the said capital meffuage, lands, tenements, hereditaments, and all and fingular other the premifes herein before mentioned to be hereby granted and releafed, with their and every of their appurtenances, unto the said David Edwards and Francis Golding, their heirs and affigns, to fuch ufes, upon fuch trufts, and to and for fuch intents and purpofes as are hereinafter mentioned, expreffed, and declared, of and concerning the fame : that is to fay, to the ufe and behoof of the said Abraham Barker, and Cecilia his wife, according to their feveral and refpective eftates and interefts therein, at the time of, or immediately before, the execution of thefe prefents, until the folemnization of the said intended marriage : and from and after the folemnization thereof, to the ufe and behoof of the said John Barker, for and during the term of his natural life ; without impeachment of or for any manner of wafte : and from and after the determination of that eftate, then to the ufe of the said David Edwards and Francis Golding, and their heirs, during the life of the said John Barker, upon truft to fupport and preferve the contingent ufes and eftates hereinafter limited from being defeated and deftroyed, and for that purpofe to make entries, or bring actions, as the cafe fhall require ; but neverthelefs to permit and fuffer the said John Barker, and his affigns, during his life, to receive and take the rents and profits thereof, and of every part thereof, to and for his and their own ufe and benefit : and from and after the deceafe of the said John Barker, then to the ufe and behoof of the said Katherine Edwards, his intended wife, for and during the term of her natural life, for her jointure, and in lieu, bar, and fatisfaction of her dower and thirds at common law, which fhe can or may have or claim, of, in, to, or out of, all, and every, or any, of the lands, tenements, and hereditaments, whereof or wherein the said John Barker now is, or at any time or times hereafter during the coverture between them fhall be, feifed of any eftate of freehold

N°. II.

Mention of bargain and fale.

Habendum,

To the ufe of the grantors till marriage :

Then of the hufband for life, fans wafte :

Remainder to truftees to preferve contingent remainders :

Remainder to the wife for life, for her jointure, in bar of dower :

N°. II.

Remainder to other truftees for a term, upon trufts after mentioned :

Remainder to the firft and other fons of the marriage in tail :

Remainder to the daughters,

as tenants in common, in tail :

Remainder to the hufband in tail :

Remainder to the hufband's mother in fee.

The truft of the term declared ;

freehold or inheritance : and from and after the deceafe of the faid Katherine Edwards, or other fooner determination of the faid eftate, then to the ufe and behoof of the faid Charles Browne and Richard More, their executors, adminiftrators, and affigns, for and during, and unto the full end and term of, five hundred years from thence next enfuing and fully to be complete and ended, without impeachment of wafte : upon fuch trufts neverthelefs, and to and for fuch intents and purpofes, and under and fubject to fuch provifoes and agreements, as are hereinafter mentioned, expreffed, and declared of and concerning the fame : and from and after the end, expiration, or other fooner determination of the faid term of five hundred years, and fubject thereunto, to the ufe and behoof of the firft fon of the faid John Barker on the body of the faid Katherine Edwards his intended wife to be begotten, and of the heirs of the body of fuch firft fon lawfully iffuing; and for default of fuch iffue, then to the ufe and behoof of the fecond, third, fourth, fifth, fixth, feventh, eighth, ninth, tenth, and of all and every other the fon and fons of the faid John Barker on the body of the faid Katherine Edwards his intended wife to be begotten, feverally, fucceffively, and in remainder, one after another, as they and every of them fhall be in feniority of age and priority of birth, and of the feveral and refpective heirs of the body and bodies of all and every fuch fon and fons lawfully iffuing; the elder of fuch fons, and the heirs of his body iffuing, being always to be preferred and to take before the younger of fuch fons, and the heirs of his or their body or bodies iffuing : and for default of fuch iffue, then to the ufe and behoof of all and every the daughter and daughters of the faid John Barker on the body of the faid Katherine Edwards his intended wife to be begotten, to be equally divided between them, (if more than one,) fhare and fhare alike, as tenants in common and not as jointenants, and of the feveral and refpective heirs of the body and bodies of all and every fuch daughter and daughters lawfully iffuing : and for default of fuch iffue, then to the ufe and behoof of the heirs of the body of him the faid John Barker lawfully iffuing : and for default of fuch heirs, then to the ufe and behoof of the faid Cecilia, the wife of the faid Abraham Barker, and of her heirs and affigns for ever. And as to, for, and concerning the term of five hundred years herein before limited to the faid Charles Browne and Richard More, their executors, adminiftrators and affigns, as aforefaid, it is hereby declared and agreed by and between all the faid parties to thefe prefents, that the fame is fo limited to them upon the trufts, and to and for the intents and purpofes, and under and fubject to the provifoes and agreements, hereinafter mentioned, expreffed, and declared, of and concerning the fame : that is to fay, in cafe there fhall be an eldeft or only fon and one more or other child or children of the faid John Barker,

ker, on the body of the said Katherine, his intended wife to be begotten, then upon trust that they the said Charles Browne and Richard More, their executors, administrators, and assigns, by sale or mortgage of the said term of five hundred years, or by such other ways and means as they or the survivor of them, or the executors or administrators of such survivor shall think fit, shall and do raise and levy, or borrow and take up at interest, the sum of four thousand pounds of lawful money of Great Britain, for the portion or portions of such other child and children (besides the eldest or only son) as aforesaid, to be equally divided between them (if more than one) share and share alike; the portion or portions of such of them as shall be a son or sons to be paid at his or their respective age or ages of twenty-one years; and the portion or portions of such of them as shall be a daughter or daughters to be paid at her or their respective age or ages of twenty one years, or day or days of marriage, which shall first happen. And upon this further trust, that in the mean time and until the same portions shall become payable as aforesaid, the said Charles Browne and Richard More, their executors, administrators, and assigns, shall and do, by and out of the rents, issues, and profits of the premises aforesaid, raise and levy such competent yearly sum and sums of money for the maintenance and education of such child or children, as shall not exceed in the whole the interest of their respective portions after the rate of four pounds in the hundred yearly. **Provided** always, that in case any of the same children shall happen to die before his, her, or their portions shall become payable as aforesaid, then the portion or portions of such of them so dying shall go and be paid unto and be equally divided among the survivor or survivors of them, when and at such time as the original portion or portions of such surviving child or children shall become payable as aforesaid. **Provided** also, that in case there shall be no such child or children of the said John Barker on the body of the said Katherine his intended wife begotten, besides an eldest or only son; or in case all and every such child or children shall happen to die before all or any of their said portions shall become due and payable as aforesaid; or in case the said portions, and also such maintenance as aforesaid, shall by the said Charles Browne and Richard More, their executors, administrators, or assigns, be raised and levied by any of the ways and means in that behalf aforementioned; or in case the same by such person or persons as shall for the time being be next in reversion or remainder of the same premises expectant upon the said term of five hundred years, shall be paid, or well and duly secured to be paid, according to the true intent and meaning of these presents; then and in any of the said cases, and at all times thenceforth, the said term of five hundred years, or so much thereof as shall remain unsold or undisposed of for the purposes aforesaid, shall cease, determine, and be utterly void to all intents and purposes,

N°. II.

to raise portions for younger children,

payable at certain times,

with maintenance at the rate of 4 per cent.

and benefit of survivorship.

If no such child,

or if all die,

or if the portions be raised,

or paid,

or secured by the person next in remainder; the residue of the term to cease.

purposes, any thing herein contained to the contrary thereof in any wise notwithstanding. **Provided** also, and it is hereby further declared and agreed by and between all the said parties to these presents, that that in case the said Abraham Barker or Cecilia his wife, at any time during their lives, or the life of the survivor of them, with the approbation of the said David Edwards and Francis Golding, or the survivor of them, or the executors and administrators of such survivor, shall settle, convey, and assure other lands and tenements of an estate of inheritance in fee simple, in possession, in some convenient place or places within the realm of England, of equal or better value than the said capital messuage, lands, tenements, hereditaments and premises, hereby granted and released, and in lieu, and recompense thereof, unto and for such and the like uses, intents, and purposes, and upon such and the like trusts, as the said capital messuage, lands, tenements, hereditaments, and premises are hereby settled and assured unto and upon, then and in such case, and at all times from thenceforth, all and every the use and uses, trust and trusts, estate and estates herein before limited, expressed, and declared of or concerning the same, shall cease, determine, and be utterly void to all intents and purposes; and the same capital messuage, lands, tenements, hereditaments, and premises, shall from thenceforth remain and be to and for the only proper use and behoof of the said Abraham Barker or Cecilia his wife, or the survivor of them, so settling, conveying, and assuring such other lands and tenements as aforesaid, and of his or her heirs and assigns for ever: and to and for no other use, intent, or purpose whatsoever; any thing herein contained to the contrary thereof in any wise notwithstanding. **And,** for the considerations aforesaid, and for barring all estates tail, and all remainders or reversions thereupon expectant and depending, if any be now subsisting and unbarred or otherwise undetermined, of and in the said capital messuage, lands, tenements, hereditaments, and premises, hereby granted and released, or mentioned to be hereby granted and released, or any of them, or any part thereof, the said Abraham Barker for himself and the said Cecilia his wife, his and her heirs, executors, and administrators, and the said John Barker for himself, his heirs, executors, and administrators, do, and each of them doth, respectively covenant, promise, and grant, to and with the said David Edwards and Francis Golding, their heirs, executors, and administrators, by these presents, that they the said Abraham Barker and Cecilia his wife, and John Barker, shall and will, at the costs and charges of of the said Abraham Barker, before the end of Michaelmas term next ensuing the date hereof, acknowlege and levy, before his Majesty's justices of the court of common pleas at Westminster, one or more fine or fines, *sur cognizance de droit, come ceo, &c.* with proclamations according

APPENDIX.

according to the form of the ſtatutes in that caſe made and provided, and the uſual courſe of fines in ſuch caſes accuſtomed, unto the ſaid David Edwards, and his heirs, of the ſaid capital meſſuage, lands, tenements, hereditaments, and premiſes, by ſuch apt and convenient names, quantities, qualities, number of acres, and other deſcriptions to aſcertain the ſame, as ſhall be thought meet: which ſaid fine or fines, ſo as aforeſaid or in any other manner levied and acknowleged, or to be levied and acknowleged, ſhall be and enure, and ſhall be adjudged, deemed, conſtrued, and taken, and ſo are and were meant and intended, to be and enure, and are hereby declared by all the ſaid parties to theſe preſents to be and enure, to the uſe and behoof of the ſaid David Edwards, and his heirs and aſſigns; to the intent and purpoſe that the ſaid David Edwards may, by virtue of the ſaid fine or fines ſo covenanted and agreed to be levied as aforeſaid, be and become perfect tenant of the freehold of the ſaid capital meſſuage, lands, tenements, hereditaments, and all other the premiſes, to the end that one or more good and perfect common recovery or recoveries may be thereof had and ſuffered, in ſuch manner as is hereinafter for that purpoſe mentioned. And it is hereby declared and agreed by and between all the ſaid parties to theſe preſents, that it ſhall and may be lawful to and for the ſaid Francis Golding, at the coſts and charges of the ſaid Abraham Barker, before the end of Michaelmas term next enſuing the date hereof, to ſue forth and proſecute out of his majeſty's high court of chancery one more writ or writs of entry *ſur diſſeiſin en le poſt*, returnable before his majeſty's juſtices of the court of common pleas at Weſtminſter, thereby demanding by apt and convenient names, quantities, qualities, number of acres, and other deſcriptions, the ſaid capital meſſuage, lands, tenements, hereditaments, and premiſes, againſt the ſaid David Edwards; to which ſaid writ, or writs, of entry he the ſaid David Edwards ſhall appear *gratis*, either in his own proper perſon, or by his attorney thereto lawfully authorized, and vouch over to warranty the ſaid Abraham Barker, and Cecilia his wife, and John Barker; who ſhall alſo *gratis* appear in their proper perſons, or by their attorney, or attorneys, thereto lawfully authorized, and enter into the warranty, and vouch over to warranty the common vouchee of the ſame court; who ſhall alſo appear, and after imparlance ſhall make default; ſo as judgment ſhall and may be thereupon had and given for the ſaid Francis Golding, to recover the ſaid capital meſſuage, lands, tenements, hereditaments, and premiſes, againſt the ſaid David Edwards, and for him to recover in value againſt the ſaid Abraham Barker, and Cecilia his wife, and John Barker, and for them to recover in value againſt the ſaid common vouchee, and that execution ſhall and may be thereupon awarded and had accordingly, and all and every other act and thing be done and executed, needful and requiſite for the ſuffering and

in order to make a tenant to the praccipe, that a recovery may be ſuffered;

to enure

perfecting of fuch common recovery or recoveries, with vouchers as aforefaid. And it is hereby further declared and agreed by and between all the faid parties to thefe prefents, that immediately from and after the fuffering and perfecting of the faid recovery or recoveries, fo as aforefaid, or in any other manner, or at any other time or times, fuffered or to be fuffered, as well thefe prefents and the affurance hereby made, and the faid fine or fines fo covenanted to be levied as aforefaid, as alfo the faid recovery or recoveries, and alfo all and every other fine and fines, recovery and recoveries, conveyances, and affurances in the law whatfoever heretofore had, made, levied, fuffered, or executed, or hereafter to be had, made, levied, fuffered, or executed, of the faid capital meffuage, lands, tenements, hereditaments, and premifes, or any of them, or any part thereof, by and between the faid parties to thefe prefents or any of them, or whereunto they or any of them are or fhall be parties or privies, fhall be and enure, and fhall be adjudged, deemed, conftrued, and taken, and fo are and were meant and intended, to be and enure, and the recoveror or recoverors in the faid recovery or recoveries named or to be named, and his or their heirs, fhall ftand and be feifed of the faid capital meffuage, lands, tenements, hereditaments, and premifes, and of every part and parcel

to the preceding ufes in this deed.

thereof, to the ufes, upon the trufts, and to and for the intents and purpofes, and under and fubject to the provifoes, limitations, and agreements, herein before mentioned, expreffed, and declared, of and

Other covenants;

concerning the fame. And the faid Abraham Barker, party hereunto, doth hereby for himfelf, his heirs, executors, and adminiftrators, further covenant, promife, grant, and agree, to and with the faid David Edwards and Francis Golding, their heirs, executors, and adminiftra-

for quiet enjoyment,

tors, in manner and form following; that is to fay, that the faid capital meffuage, lands, tenements, hereditaments, and premifes, fhall and may at all times hereafter remain, continue, and be, to and for the ufes and purpofes, upon the trufts, and under and fubject to the provifoes, limitations, and agreements, hereinbefore mentioned, expreffed, and declared, of and concerning the fame; and fhall and may be peaceably and quietly had, held, and enjoyed accordingly, without any lawful let or interruption of or by the faid Abraham Barker or Cecilia his wife, parties hereunto, his or her heirs or affigns, or of or by any other perfon or perfons lawfully claiming or to claim from, by, or under, or in truft for him, her, them, or any of them, or from, by, or under

free from incumbrances;

his or her anceftors, or any of them; and fhall fo remain, continue, and be, free and clear, and freely and clearly acquitted, exonerated, and difcharged, or otherwife by the faid Abraham Barker, or Cecilia his wife, parties hereunto, his or her heirs, executors, or adminiftrators, well and fufficiently faved, defended, kept harmlefs, and indemnified of, from, and againft all former and other gifts, grants, bargains, fales,

leafes,

leafes, mortgages, eftates, titles, troubles, charges, and incumbrances whatfoever, had, made, done, committed, occafioned, or fuffered, or to be had, made, done, committed, occafioned, or fuffered, by the faid Abraham Barker, or Cecilia his wife, or by his or her anceftors, or any of them, or by his, her, their, or any of their act, means, affent, confent, or procurement: **And moreover** that he the faid Abraham Barker, and Cecilia his wife, parties hereunto, and his and her heirs, and all other perfons having or lawfully claiming, or which fhall or may have or lawfully claim, any eftate, right, title, truft, or intereft, at law or in equity, of, in, to, or out of, the faid capital meffuage, lands, tenements, hereditaments, and premifes, or any of them, or any part thereof, by or under or in truft for him, her, them, or any of them, or by or under his or her anceftors or any of them, fhall and will from time to time, and at all times hereafter, upon every reafonable requeft, and at the cofts and charges, of the faid David Edwards and Francis Golding, or either of them, their or either of their heirs, executors, or adminiftrators, make, do, and execute, or caufe to be made, done, and executed, all fuch further and other lawful and reafonable acts, deeds, conveyances, and affurances in the law whatfoever, for the further, better, more perfect, and abfolute granting, conveying, fettling, and affuring of the fame capital meffuage, lands, tenements, hereditaments, and premifes, to and for the ufes and purpofes, upon the trufts, and under and fubject to the provifoes, limitations, and agreements, herein before mentioned, expreffed, and declared, of and concerning the fame, as by the faid David Edwards and Francis Golding or either of them, their or either of their heirs, executors, or adminiftrators, or their or any of their counfel learned in the law fhall be reafonably advifed, devifed, or required: fo as fuch further affurances contain in them no further or other warranty or covenants than againft the perfon or perfons, his, her, or their heirs, who fhall make or do the fame ; and fo as the party or parties, who fhall be requefted to make fuch further affurances, be not compelled or compellable, for making or doing thereof, to go and travel above five miles from his, her, or their then refpective dwellings, or places of abode. **Provided laftly**, and it is hereby further declared and agreed by and between all the parties to thefe prefents, that it fhall and may be lawful to and for the faid Abraham Barker and Cecilia his wife, John Barker and Katherine his intended wife, and David Edwards, at any time or times hereafter, during their joint lives, by any writing or writings under their refpective hands and feals and attefted by two or more credible witneffes, to revoke, make void, alter, or change all and every or any the ufe and ufes, eftate and eftates, herein and hereby before limited and declared, or mentioned or intended to be limited and declared, of and in the capital meffuage, lands, tenements, hereditaments, and

** 2   premifes

Margin notes:

No. II.

and for further affurance.

Power of revocation.

N°. II.

Conclufion.

premifes aforefaid, or of and in any part or parcel thereof, and to declare new and other ufes of the fame, or of any part or parcel thereof,
any thing herein contained to the contrary thereof in any wife notwithftanding. 𝔍𝔫 𝔴𝔦𝔱𝔫𝔢𝔰𝔰 𝔴𝔥𝔢𝔯𝔢𝔬𝔣 the parties to thefe prefents their hands
and feals have fubfcribed and fet, the day and year firft above written.

Sealed, and delivered, being
firft duly ftamped, in the
prefence of
   George Carter.
   William Browne.

Abraham Barker. (L. S.)
Cecilia Barker. (L. S.)
David Edwards. (L. S.)
Francis Golding. (L. S.)
Charles Browne. (L. S.)
Richard More. (L. S.)
John Barker. (L. S.)
Katherine Edwards. (L. S.)

N°. III.

N°. III.

An OBLIGATION, *or* BOND, *with* CONDITION *for the Payment of Money.*

𝕶𝕹𝕺𝖂 all men by thefe prefents, that I David Edwards, of Lincoln's Inn in the county of Middlefex, efquire, am held and firmly bound to Abraham Barker of Dale-Hall in the county of Norfolk, efquire, in ten thoufand pounds of lawful money of Great Britain, to be paid to the faid Abraham Barker, or his certain attorney, executors, adminiftrators, or affigns; for which payment well and truly to be made, I bind myfelf, my heirs, executors, and adminiftrators, firmly by thefe prefents, fealed with my feal. Dated the fourth day of September in the twenty firft year of the reign of our fovereign lord GEORGE the fecond by the grace of God king of Great Britain, France, and Ireland, defender of the faith, and fo forth, and in the year of our Lord one thoufand, feven hundred, and forty feven.

𝕿𝖍𝖊 𝖈𝖔𝖓𝖉𝖎𝖙𝖎𝖔𝖓 of this obligation is fuch, that if the above bounden David Edwards, his heirs, executors, or adminiftrators, do and fhall well and truly pay, or caufe to be paid, unto the above named Abraham Barker, his executors, adminiftrators, or affigns, the full fum of five thoufand pounds of lawful Britifh money, with lawful intereft for the fame, on the fourth day of March next enfuing the date of the above written obligation, then this obligation fhall be void and of none effect, or elfe fhall be and remain in full force and virtue.

Sealed, and delivered, being firft duly ftamped, in the prefence of
  George Carter.
  William Browne.

David Edwards. (L. S.)

N°. IV.

N°. IV.

A FINE *of Lands,* fur Cognizance de Droit, come ceo, &c.

§. 1. *Writ of Covenant*; *or* PRAECIPE.

𝕲𝕰𝕺𝕽𝕲𝕰 the fecond by the grace of God of Great Britain, France, and Ireland king, defender of the faith, and fo forth; to the fheriff of Norfolk, greeting. **Command** Abraham Barker, efquire, and Cecilia his wife, and John Barker, efquire, that juftly and without delay they perform to David Edwards, efquire, the covenant made between them of two meffuages, two gardens, three hundred acres of land, one hundred acres of meadow, two hundred acres of pafture, and fifty acres of wood, with the appurtenances, in Dale; and unlefs they fhall fo do, and if the faid David fhall give you fecurity of profecuting his claim, then fummon by good fummoners the faid Abraham, Cecilia, and John, that they appear before our juftices, at Weftminfter, from the day of faint Michael in one month, to fhew wherefore they have not done it: and have you there the fummoners, and this writ. **Witnefs** ourfelf at Weftminfter, the ninth day of October, in the twenty firft year of our reign.

Sheriff's return. Pledges of { John Doe. profecution, { Richard Roe.   Summoners of the within named Abraham, Cecilia, and John. { John Den. { Richard Fen.

§. 2. *The Licence to agree.*

Norfolk, } **David Edwards**, efquire, gives to the lord the king ten to wit. } marks, for licence to agree with Abraham Barker, efquire, of a plea of covenant of two meffuages, two gardens, three hundred acres of land, one hundred acres of meadow, two hundred acres of pafture, and fifty acres of wood, with the appurtenances, in Dale.

§. 3. *The Concord.*

And the agreement is fuch, to wit, that the aforefaid Abraham, Cecilia, and John, have acknowleged the aforefaid tenements, with
the

the appurtenances, to be the right of him the said David, as those which the said David hath of the gift of the aforesaid Abraham, Cecilia, and John; and those they have remised and quitted claim, from them and their heirs, to the aforesaid David and his heirs for ever. And further, the same Abraham, Cecilia, and John, have granted, for themselves and their heirs, that they will warrant to the aforesaid David, and his heirs, the aforesaid tenements, with the appurtenances, against all men for ever. And for this recognition, remise, quit-claim, warranty, fine, and agreement, the said David hath given to the said Abraham, Cecilia, and John, two hundred pounds sterling.

§. 4. *The Note, or Abstract.*

Norfolk, ⎰ **Between** David Edwards, esquire, complainant, and A-
to wit. ⎱ braham Barker, esquire, and Cecilia his wife, and John Barker, esquire, deforciants, of two messuages, two gardens, three hundred acres of land, one hundred acres of meadow, two hundred acres of pasture, and fifty acres of wood, with the appurtenances, in Dale, whereupon a plea of covenant was summoned between them; to wit, that the said Abraham, Cecilia, and John, have acknowleged the aforesaid tenements, with the appurtenances, to be the right of him the said David, as those which the said David hath of the gift of the aforesaid Abraham, Cecilia, and John; and those they have remised and quitted claim, from them and their heirs, to the aforesaid David and his heirs for ever. And further, the same Abraham, Cecilia, and John, have granted for themselves, and their heirs, that they will warrant to the aforesaid David, and his heirs, the aforesaid tenements, with the appurtenances, against all men for ever. And for this recognition, remise, quit-claim, warranty, fine, and agreement, the said David hath given to the said Abraham, Cecilia, and John, two hundred pounds sterling.

§. 5. *The Foot, Chirograph, or Indentures, of the* FINE.

Norfolk, ⎰ **This is the final agreement**, made in the court of the lord
to wit. ⎱ the king at Westminster, from the day of saint Michael in one month, in the twenty first year of the reign of the lord GEORGE the second by the grace of God of Great Britain, France, and Ireland king, defender of the faith, and so forth, before John Willes, Thomas Abney, Thomas Burnet, and Thomas Birch, justices, and other faithful subjects of the lord the king then there present, between David Edwards, esquire, complainant, and Abraham Barker, esquire, and Cecilia

cilia his wife, and John Barker, efquire, deforciants, of two meffuages, two gardens, three hundred acres of land, one hundred acres of meadow, two hundred acres of pafture, and fifty acres of wood, with the appurtenances, in Dale, whereupon a plea of covenant was fummoned between them in the fame court; to wit, that the aforefaid Abraham, Cecilia, and John, have acknowleged the aforefaid tenements, with the appurtenances, to be the right of him the faid David, as thofe which the faid David hath of the gift of the aforefaid Abraham, Cecilia, and John; and thofe they have remifed and quitted claim, from them and their heirs, to the aforefaid David and his heirs for ever. And further, the fame Abraham, Cecilia, and John, have granted for themfelves and their heirs, that they will warrant to the aforefaid David and his heirs, the aforefaid tenements, with the appurtenances, againft all men for ever. And for this recognition, remife, quit-claim, warranty, fine, and agreement, the faid David hath given to the faid Abraham, Cecilia, and John, two hundred pounds fterling.

§. 6. *Proclamations, endorfed upon the* F I N E, *according to the Statutes.*

The firſt proclamation was made the fixteenth day of November, in the term of faint Michael, in the twenty firſt year of the king withinwritten.

The fecond proclamation was made the fourth day of February, in the term of faint Hilary, in the twenty firſt year of the king withinwritten.

The third proclamation was made the thirteenth day of May, in the term of Eafter, in the twenty firſt year of the king withinwritten.

The fourth proclamation was made the twenty eighth day of June, in the term of the holy Trinity, in the twenty fecond year of the king withinwritten.

N°. V.

A common RECOVERY *of Lands, with * double Voucher.*

§. 1. *Writ of Entry* fur Diffeifin *in the* Poſt; *or,* PRAECIPE.

𝕲𝕰𝕺𝕽𝕲𝕰 the ſecond by the grace of God of Great Britain, France, and Ireland king, defender of the faith, and ſo forth; to the ſheriff of Norfolk, greeting. **Command** David Edwards, eſquire, that juſtly and without delay he render to Francis Golding, clerk, two meſſuages, two gardens, three hundred acres of land, one hundred acres of meadow, two hundred acres of paſture, and fifty acres of wood, with the appurtenances, in Dale, which he claims to be his right and inheritance, and into which the ſaid David hath not entry, unleſs after the diffeifin, which Hugh Hunt thereof unjuſtly, and without judgment, hath made to the aforeſaid Francis, within thirty years now laſt paſt, as he ſaith, and whereupon he complains that the aforeſaid David deforceth him. And unleſs he ſhall ſo do, and if the ſaid Francis ſhall give you ſecurity of proſecuting his claim, then ſummon by good ſummoners the ſaid David, that he appear before our juſtices at Weſtminſter, on the octave of ſaint Martin, to ſhew wherefore he hath not done it : and have you there the ſummoners, and this writ. **Witneſs** ourſelf at Weſtminſter, the twenty ninth day of October, in the twenty firſt year of our reign.

Pledges of { John Doe.   Summoners of the { John Den.   Sheriff's return.
proſecution, { Richard Roe.   withinnamed David, { Richard Fen.

§. 2. *Exemplification of the* RECOVERY *Roll.*

𝕲𝕰𝕺𝕽𝕲𝕰 the ſecond by the grace of God of Great Britain, France, and Ireland king, defender of the faith, and ſo forth; to all to whom theſe our preſent letters ſhall come, greeting. **Know ye,** that among the pleas of land, enrolled at Weſtminſter, before Sir John Willes, knight, and his fellows, our juſtices of the bench, of the term of ſaint Michael, in the twenty firſt year of our reign, upon the fifty ſecond roll it is thus contained. **Entry** returnable on the oc- Return.

---

* Note, that if the recovery be had with ſingle voucher, the parts marked "thus" in §. 2. are omitted.

tave of faint Martin. **Norfolk**, to wit: Francis Golding, clerk, in his proper perfon demandeth againft David Edwards, efquire, two meffuages, two gardens, three hundred acres of land, one hundred acres of meadow, two hundred acres of pafture, and fifty acres of wood, with the appurtenances, in Dale, as his right and inheritance, and into which the faid David hath not entry, unlefs after the diffeifin, which Hugh Hunt thereof unjuftly, and without judgment, hath made to the aforefaid Francis, within thirty years now laft paft. And whereupon he faith, that he himfelf was feifed of the tenements aforefaid, with the appurtenances, in his demefne as of fee and right, in time of peace, in the time of the lord the king that now is, by taking the profits thereof to the value [*of fix fhillings and eight pence, and more, in rents, corn, and grafs :] and into which [the faid David hath not entry, unlefs as aforefaid :] and thereupon he bringeth fuit, [and good proof.] **And** the faid David in his proper perfon comes and defendeth his right, when [and where the court fhall award,] and thereupon voucheth to warranty "John Barker, efquire; " who is prefent here in court in his proper perfon, and the tenements " aforefaid with the appurtenances to him freely warranteth, [and " prays that the faid Francis may count againft him.] **And** hereupon " the faid Francis demandeth againft the faid John, tenant by his own " warranty, the tenements aforefaid with the appurtenances, in form " aforefaid, &c. And whereupon he faith, that he himfelf was feifed " of the tenements aforefaid, with the appurtenances, in his demefne " as of fee and right, in time of peace, in the time of the lord the king " that now is, by taking the profits thereof to the value, &c. And into " which, &c. And thereupon he bringeth fuit, &c. **And** the aforefaid " John, tenant by his own warranty, defends his right, when, &c. and " thereupon he further voucheth to warranty" Jacob Morland; who is prefent here in court in his proper perfon, and the tenements aforefaid, with the appurtenances, to him freely warranteth, &c. **And** hereupon the faid Francis demandeth againft the faid Jacob, tenant by his own warranty, the tenements aforefaid, with the appurtenances, in form aforefaid, &c. And whereupon he faith, that he himfelf was feifed of the tenements aforefaid, with the appurtenances, in his demefne as of fee and right, in time of peace, in the time of the lord the king that now is, by taking the profits thereof to the value, &c. And into which, &c. And thereupon he bringeth fuit, &c. **And** the aforefaid Jacob, tenant by his own warranty, defends his right, when, &c. And faith that the aforefaid Hugh did not diffeife the aforefaid Francis of the tenements aforefaid, as the aforefaid Francis by his writ and count afore-

Side notes (left margin):

N°. V.
Demand againft the tenant.

Count.

Efplees.

Defence of the tenant.

Voucher.
"Warranty.

"Demand againft "the vouchee.

"Count.

"Defence of the "vouchee.

"Second voucher.
Warranty.
Demand againft the common vouchee.

Count.

Defence of the common vouchee.

Plea, nui diffeifin.

---

* The claufes, between hooks, are no otherwife expreffed in the record than by an &c.

said

said above doth suppose : and of this he puts himself upon the country. And the aforesaid Francis thereupon craveth leave to imparl ; and he hath it. And afterwards the aforesaid Francis cometh again here into court in this same term in his proper person, and the aforesaid Jacob, though solemnly called, cometh not again, but hath departed in contempt of the court, and maketh default. **Therefore it is considered,** that the aforesaid Francis do recover his seisin against the aforesaid David of the tenements aforesaid, with the appurtenances ; and that the said David have of the land of the aforesaid " John, to the value " [of the tenements aforesaid;] and further, that the said John, have of " the land of the said" Jacob to the value [of the tenements aforesaid.] And the said Jacob in mercy. **And** hereupon the said Francis prays a writ of the lord the king, to be directed to the sheriff of the county aforesaid, to cause him to have full seisin of the tenements aforesaid with the appurtenances : and it is granted unto him, returnable here without delay. Afterwards, that is to say, the twenty eighth day of November in this same term, here cometh the said Francis in his proper person ; and the sheriff, namely sir Charles Thompson, knight, now sendeth, that he by virtue of the writ aforesaid to him directed, on the twenty fourth day of the same month, did cause the said Francis to have full seisin of the tenements aforesaid with the appurtenances, as he was commanded. **All and singular** which premises, at the request of the said Francis, by the tenor of these presents we have held good to be exemplified. In testimony whereof we have caused our seal, appointed for sealing writs in the bench aforesaid, to be affixed to these presents. **Witness** sir John Willes, knight, at Westminster, the twenty eighth day of November, in the twenty first year of our reign.

No. V.

Imparlance.

Default of the common vouchee.

Judgment for the demandant.

Recovery in value.

Amercement.

Award of the writ of seisin, and return.

Exemplification continued.

T.ſt.

Cooke.

THE END